Schola Illustris

For

ALBERT HAMILTON GORDON '19

Life Trustee and Benefactor

with gratitude

Si monumentum requiris, circumspice

JOHN ELIOT · THE FOUNDER

𝕾𝖈𝖍𝖔𝖑𝖆 𝕴𝖑𝖑𝖚𝖘𝖙𝖗𝖎𝖘

The Roxbury Latin School
1645-1995

F. Washington Jarvis

DAVID R. GODINE · PUBLISHER · BOSTON

First published in 1995 by
David R. Godine, Publisher, Inc.
P.O. Box 9103
Lincoln, Massachusetts 01773

ISBN: 1-56792-066-7

First edition
Printed in the United States of America

Preface

The things which we have heard with our ears and which our ancestors have made known unto us, we shall not hide from our children. . . . He commanded our ancestors that they should make them known to their children, that the generation to come might know them. — PSALM 78

THIS 350TH ANNIVERSARY HISTORY of The Roxbury Latin School has four principal objectives. There is, first, the narrower objective: to provide for the Roxbury Latin family a fully-documented *institutional* history of the School. In that sense, this book may be considered a "house history." I have spent many hours attempting to trace and document assertions made by Richard W. Hale, Jr., (in his 1946 unfootnoted history) and others in their accounts of the School's story. To spare future historians this labor, I have documented what I have written; I hope that my lengthy endnotes will enable future historians to find the sources for what I have written. As regards interpretation, I have tried to steer between the Scylla of hagiography (a tendency of eighteenth and nineteenth century historians of colonial America) and the Charybdis of cynical iconoclasm (which seems to be the fashion of the late twentieth century). I have been given complete freedom in writing this book and have painted the picture as I saw it, warts and all. No historian is objective; each brings to his analysis his own biases and interests. I do not claim that I have produced an objective account, but I ask the reader to believe that I have *tried* to write one. I also ask the reader to remember that this book attempts only to be an institutional history. It does not, for instance, record the successes of famous alumni (some of whom are mentioned in the Quinquennial that appeared last May). Nor does it explore in depth the many fascinating masters who have taught here over the years.

Second, I have written with a broader purpose. Here Frederick S. Allis's 1979 history of Phillips Academy, Andover, has in some ways been my model. I believe that Roxbury Latin's story has considerable interest and importance for anyone interested in American education. That it is one of very few American institutions to survive for 350 years is alone noteworthy. But also remarkable, in comparison to other enduring ancient academies (such as Harvard and Boston Latin), is its remarkably close adherence to its original mission and form. That fidelity to its past may, in fact, be the leading cause of its modern flowering. Bernard Bailyn and others have noted that American writers on education have tended to focus almost exclusively on the nation's so-called "public" schools. A strong case can be made, however, that Roxbury Latin has both survived and prospered *because* it is independent—free of government control and interference. As British historian Jonathan Gathorne-Hardy notes in his brilliant work, *The Public School Phenomenon* (p. 28): "We [the independent schools] go to the wall if we don't produce results. If we start getting deplorable results, we soon empty. A state school goes on *however* inefficient." Roxbury Latin has very nearly "emptied" at several points in its 350-year existence. Yet, at each such crisis, it has somehow dug deep and found the inner strength to renew itself—to enjoy yet another renaissance. Arguably, that self-renewing capacity also springs from its most precious attribute: its constant and bracing exposure to the risks of independence.

Third, I believe the Roxbury Latin story has a certain "inspirational" quality. Some professional historians reading the word "inspirational" will recoil in horror and dismay. Let me explain. On the one hand, there is a kind of negative inspiration: the School's history is by no means a record of perpetual success; it does not go "from glory to glory advancing," *excelsior.* The record is replete with quarrels, legal wrangles, wrong turns, disastrous decisions, and equally disastrous indecisions. Roxbury Latin, at numerous junctures, provides a model of how a school should *not* be run. On the other hand, the record is also filled with shining moments and heroic individuals, and, in these instances, the School presents an inspiring model of how a school should be run. In the darker hours of my own time here, I have always been lifted up by the great and good individuals, the "cloud of witnesses" who have labored so abundantly in this vineyard over the past 350 years. I therefore share some of the *pietas* of Cotton Mather, who, in his preface to *The Life of the Renowned John Eliot* (1702), quotes the words of Theodorit: "For I believed it an act of impiety to see the renown of shining actions and useful sentiments stifled by oblivion."

Though there have been dark and painful moments, my years at Roxbury Latin have been for me a time of the greatest possible happiness and fulfillment. If it is a bias, then I "confess" that I love the School and regard it as worth a life. Finally, then, this book is an attempt to express my gratitude to a community that has given me so much. When you are on the inside of an institution—and I have been inside Roxbury Latin for twenty-two years—you know far better than anyone else its weaknesses and inadequacies; I cannot therefore paint it as a perfect place—in the past or in the present. That does not prevent me from loving it wholeheartedly. I am grateful beyond expression that, because of Roxbury Latin, mine has been the most rewarding of lives. *Et ego in Arcadia vixi.*

Contents

Acknowledgements

· ⟨~~~~~~~~~~~~~~~~~~~~~~~~~~~⟩ ·

M ANY PEOPLE HAVE HELPED with this book. All or portions of Parts I and II were read by the Reverend Deryck Collingwood, Professor Charles L. Glenn, Professor Philip H. Hansen, Dr. Richard I. Melvoin, and Dr. John Tyler.

Part III grew out of the discovery of the correspondence of William Coe Collar, as edited by his daughter Sibyl Collar Holbrook. Her son, Professor William Collar Holbrook '16, gave the School his grandfather's European diary and endured lengthy interviews regarding his family and the School.

All or portions of Parts IV and V were read by Stanley J. Bernstein, William E. Chauncey, Professor John A. Davey, Richard B. Fowler, Professor Philip H. Hansen, Mary Kay Guy Hubbard, Robert S. Jorgensen, William B. O'Keeffe, Cary Potter, and Gerhard Rehder. More than thirty other people were interviewed in connection with Part V.

I have enjoyed working with David Mittell on his concluding memoir. The reader will find it more entertaining and more accessible than the rest of the book, because the author has been free to paint his own impressions of what he has seen and experienced.

Several people have been with me every step of the way. The above-mentioned Professor Holbrook has proofread the entire text with meticulous devotion. Professor Harry R. Lewis '65, David A. Mittell '35, and John J. Regan, Esq., have, with heroic self-sacrifice and true friendship, slogged their way through every part (sometimes more than once). Professor John A. Davey has been most helpful in securing photographs.

Each of the people mentioned above has helped save me from blunders and offered useful suggestions for improving the manuscript. Words cannot adequately express the gratitude I bear toward them. For errors and misjudgments that remain, I am alone responsible.

My profound thanks are due also to David R. Godine, alumnus of Roxbury Latin and distinguished publisher, for taking the book from the typescript to the handsome finished product with patience and generosity. He arranged for Scott-Martin Kosofsky to design the book and for Marlowe Bergendoff to copyedit it. Both are geniuses in their field and working with them has been delightful and inspiring.

To no one, however, am I more grateful than to my assistant Joanna Buxton Gormley. Deciphering my handwriting with fortitude and patience and correcting my eccentric spelling, she has typed and retyped the chapters, and worst of all—the attendant endnotes—on top of all her normal onerous duties. A golden crown awaits her in Heaven!

Part One

John Eliot, Apostle to the Indians. Born in Widford 1604, his first years seasoned with the fear of God, the Word, and prayer. Educated at Jesus College, Cambridge. Came to the New World 1631, pre-engaged to the Church in Roxbury....1645 founded the Roxbury Latin School.... One of the authors of the Bay Psalm Book. 1646 began his marvelous work among the native tribes of New England. 1660 founded at Natick the first Indian church in the Massachusetts Colony. 1663 completed his translation of the Bible. In zeal equal to St. Paul, in charity to St. Francis. He traversed the land for forty years, in perils of the wilderness, in perils of the heathen, in fearlessness to bear the Gospel to the children of the woods who were to him the children of God. Died May 21, 1690. First among Puritan saints.

— MEMORIAL PLAQUE IN THE FIRST CHURCH, ROXBURY

Part One
The Founder

THIS BOOK IS THE BIOGRAPHY OF A SCHOOL. Like most biographies it begins with a consideration of the subject's parentage. John Eliot is The Roxbury Latin School's spiritual father. It was he who inspired the farmers of Roxbury to give it birth. Not only did he imprint it with his genes, he nourished and guided it through childhood and adolescence and came to its rescue when it got into trouble. It has ever since, and to a remarkable degree, reflected his personality and values.

Eliot's life encompasses the seventeenth century: he was born in England in 1604 and buried in New England in 1690. His parents were in a position to provide him with a secure and comfortable home and with the finest education late Renaissance England had to offer. Both at home and university, he was influenced by Puritanism, a contemporary expression of reformed Christianity. Under this influence, Eliot eventually left his native land for Massachusetts where he and his fellow settlers hoped and labored to establish the City of God on earth.

Though he founded The Roxbury Latin School, and though that "little nursery" (as Cotton Mather called it) today flourishes as his most enduring monument, Eliot was not famous to his contemporaries as the School's founder. From the time Eliot arrived in the New World in his late twenties until his death nearly sixty years later, he devoted most of his remarkable energy to serving the people of Roxbury as pastor of their church. But fame came neither from his devoted pastoral work nor from founding and nourishing a school. What made Eliot a celebrity in both the Old and New Worlds was his work among and for the natives of his new country, a population decimated by the European invasion. To his contemporaries he was always "the Apostle to the Indians." Eliot founded Roxbury Latin, raised money for it, defended it legally, and saved its life at a critical juncture. His devotion to it is all the more remarkable, considering that the School ranked in his concern, time, and effort far below his parish and the Indians. To his contemporaries, the School was one of Eliot's *minor* achievements.

Today—more than three hundred years after his death—Eliot is still the subject of intense historical interest. Controversial in life, he remains controversial in death. Many of his New England contemporaries despised him as a "do-gooder" for his work among the Indians. Several present-day historians despise him as a cultural imperialist for that very work. No discussion of Eliot would be complete without considering Eliot's Indian and pastoral work, and we shall do so. But our principal focus will be Eliot the *educator*—of whites, Indians, and blacks. Here, as elsewhere in his life, there is controversy aplenty.

1. *The English Years*

The founders of New England were making history; their focus lay far more on the future than on the past. Even Cotton Mather, the exception to the rule, writes that "The Atlantick ocean, like the river of Lethe, may easily cause us to forget many of the things which happened on the other side." Mather himself makes several errors regarding Eliot's English years; but modern research has uncovered a significant amount of information about Eliot's twenty-seven years in his native land.

The register of the Parish of St. John the Baptist at Widford in Hertfordshire records that "John Elliott the sonne of Bennett Elliott was baptised the fifte daye of August in the year of our Lord 1604." Since baptism normally occurred within a few days of birth, we may assume that Eliot was born in early August 1604. Queen Elizabeth I had died the year before, and Shakespeare was writing *Othello*.

Eliot's father was an affluent yeoman who owned considerable properties in Hertfordshire and Essex counties, and Eliot grew up with every advantage. While he was still a child his family moved from Widford, twenty-five miles north of London, to nearby Nazeing in Essex

FIG. 1, *top.* The Parish Church of St. John the Baptist in Widford, Hertfordshire, England, where John Eliot was baptized August 5, 1604.

FIG. 2, *above.* The baptismal record of John Eliot from the Widford Parish Register.

FIG. 3, *right.* Memorial window at Widford Church, placed by Eliot's descendants in 1894.

FIG. 4. Eliot's family moved to Nazeing in Essex County while Eliot was a child. All Saints', Nazeing was a stronghold of Puritanism.

County. Both these villages remain today the rural backwaters they were in Eliot's time. His father was easily able to pay the fees for him to attend Cambridge, and when Bennett Eliot died in 1621 he provided in his will a handsome eight-year stipend so that seventeen-year-old John could earn his bachelor or arts degree and undertake the necessary courses thereafter in theology.[1]

Though Eliot's mother died in childbirth eight months before his father's death, when John was only sixteen,[2] the family appears to have been close-knit. Eliot was the third of seven children — six of whom survived to adulthood and emigrated to New England. Eliot testifies to the strength of the religious training he received as a boy at home and at his parish, All Saints', Nazeing: "I do see that it was a great favour of God unto me, to season my first times with the fear of God, the word, and prayer."[3]

That religious training was influenced by a reform movement in the Church of England known as Puritanism. The part of England in which Eliot was raised was a stronghold of Puritanism, and since 1541 the clergy at All Saints' had been sympathetic to church reform and Puritan tenets. In contrast to most of the population of England, the Puritans had a very high literacy rate: probably 85 percent could sign their names and even more could read. Many of the Puritan leaders were Renaissance men of learning who had read the Bible, often in the original Hebrew and Greek.[4] Since the Bible was, in their view, the Word of God, it was the standard by which everything should be measured, as well as the blueprint for one's personal life and for the government of the church and nation. Unlike the separatist Pilgrims who founded Plymouth, the Puritans had no desire to leave the Church of England. They wanted to rid it of what they regarded as corruptions and accretions. Their goal was to reform the church "from within," to restore it to the purity it had enjoyed in the earliest times under Jesus' apostles. They considered themselves loyal to both the Church and Crown of England, even when they opposed the sovereign and the bishops on certain issues.

By the mid-1500s, the Puritans had emerged as a powerful and self-confident force in English society.[5] Just as the Bible, in their view, had liberated them from the "corruptions" of medieval religion, so it freed them from outdated customs and procedures in business and commerce. Combining this innovative outlook with a biblically-inspired capacity for hard work, Bennett Eliot and Puritan yeomen like him tended to be very successful at accumulating earthly treasure. Because they believed that personal ethics should be biblically based, the Puritans' code of behavior was stricter than that of their contemporaries. To their opponents they could appear smug and self-righteous; they saw themselves as an elite, as "the elect" (to use the term of their theological hero John Calvin).

King James I (1603–1625) had been hostile to the Puritans, and they had hoped for a more sympathetic monarch in his son. Charles I (1625–1649), however, turned out to be every bit as set against them as his father. His wife was Catholic, and he himself regretted some of the changes the Protestant Reformation had brought to the Church of England. American historians have tended to paint him as a reactionary in religious matters. But, in fairness, it should be noted that Charles was trying to bring the Church of England back to the center of the Christian spectrum by restoring some elements of the church's ancient Catholic practices after a century of Protestant ascendancy. The greatest patron of the arts ever to sit upon the English throne, Charles sought, for example, to stop further vandalism of sculpture, stained glass, and art in churches.

As Charles's reign progressed, the Puritans realized that the king was opposed to their desire for further reform of church and society. Their hopes dashed, they reacted in one of two ways.

On the one hand, many of them emigrated to the New World in the Great Migration of 1630–1650. Half the prosperous yeomen of Eliot's village of Nazeing, including the entire Eliot clan, left the old country with the intention of establishing a purified church and state in New England. They did not intend to split from the church. In their departing statement as they sailed for New England on April 7, 1630, John Winthrop and Thomas Dudley, speaking for the whole contingent—all Puritan—aboard four ships, asked for the prayers of "the rest of our Brethren in and of the Church of England," and called "the Church of England, from whence we rise, our dear mother." Their hope was that their new "City of God" would provide a model and beacon by which the English church and nation would reform themselves. Francis Higginson, who had sailed a year earlier, expressed this same sentiment more eloquently as he and all on board his departing ship took their final look at England:

> We will not say, as the separatists are wont to say at their leaving England, "Farewel Babylon! farewel Rome!" but we will say, "farewel, dear England! Farewel, the Church of God in England, and all the Christian friends there! We do not go to New England as separatists from the Church of England; though we cannot but separate from the corruptions in it: but we go to practice the posi-

tive part of church reformation, and propagate the gospel in America.[6]

On the other hand, a larger number of Puritans remained in England. They not only sent support to their fellow Puritans who were establishing the City of God in the New World, but soon took up arms at home against the king and bishops in the Civil War of 1642–49.

Eliot's youth and young adulthood—his English years—took place in the context of these turmoils. Both his home and his parish at Nazeing strongly reflected Puritan values. But Eliot's enrollment in Jesus College at Cambridge University indicates that his parents were by no means fanatical Puritans. A number of Cambridge colleges— most notably the recently-founded Emmanuel—were strongly Puritan in orientation. At the time of Eliot's matriculation—March 20, 1618/19— Jesus was *not* among the colleges in which Puritanism predominated. Since the mid-sixteenth century, some of the fellows (i.e., faculty) of the college had been Puritans, and they seem to have peacefully co-existed with a larger number of colleagues who were not of that persuasion. Not until after Eliot's time—when the political and religious controversies of the 1630s and 1640s forced people and institutions to "take sides"—did the college lose its tolerant tranquility, eschewing Puritanism and siding with King Charles.[7]

What made a college friendly or hostile to Puritanism was not its curriculum, but rather its atmosphere outside the classroom. The curriculum in every college was rigidly "scholastic." For five hundred years the universities of Europe and England had adhered to scholasticism as their philosophy of education. It was unchallenged at Cambridge in Eliot's time and, because many of New England's founders were Cambridge graduates, it became the educational philosophy of Harvard College at its founding.

Scholasticism, as Morison has noted, was essentially "a course on the works of Aristotle, in Latin translation."[8] To oversimplify, there were three *arts* which dealt with method: logic (how to think), rhetoric (how to speak), and ethics (how to act). There were, additionally, four *sciences* which dealt with knowledge: metaphysics (the philosophical truths—such as the good, the true, and the beautiful—beyond those things which can be seen, felt, etc.), physics (the truth about how visible things work), mathematics, and cosmography (i.e., geography). The Cambridge Eliot attended placed extremely little emphasis on these latter two sciences. Most of the then-modern discoveries of the past two hundred years were simply not discussed at Cambridge.[9] We therefore find Eliot later explaining to the Indians that the sun revolved around the earth, a long-outdated concept.

The average age of admission to Cambridge was slightly below seventeen. Eliot was admitted as a pensioner (i.e., as a fee-paying undergraduate) of Jesus College four months before his fifteenth birthday,[10] indicating either that he was unusually able or unusually well prepared—or, probably, both. Unfortunately we know nothing of his early schooling. A typical boy of Eliot's socio-economic status would have learned the alphabet and simple reading at home or at a dame school in his village. There were at least seventeen grammar schools in the County of Essex at the time and we may conjecture that Eliot was enrolled in one when he was six or seven,[11] though he could have been tutored privately by Nazeing's vicar.

Cambridge University was a collection of colleges, such as Eliot's Jesus College. A student lived throughout his time at Cambridge in a single college where he was guided by a college tutor who supervised both his life and studies. A typical day was encompassed by the hours of the sun: At 5 A.M. there was chapel, followed by a bread-and-beer breakfast. From 6 to 11 A.M. the student either attended lectures suggested by his tutor or studied the notes he had taken from his tutor or a lecturer. (Books were scarce and most learning was oral.) At eleven he had his main meal of the day: dinner in the college hall, after which he had an hour's recreation. From 1 to 3 P.M. he was either attending "disputations" or studying. At three he had more bread and beer and he was then free (except for supper at five) until bedtime, following prayers with his tutor, at 7 P.M. Once it was dark, his schoolday was over.[12]

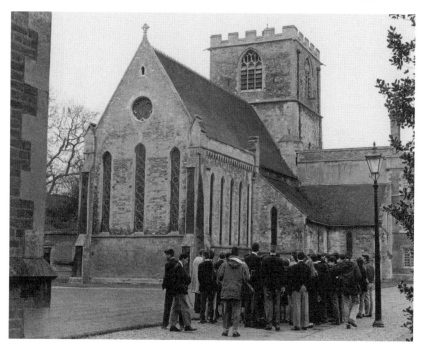

FIG. 5. The Glee Club visited Jesus College, Cambridge University, in March 1992. The ancient chapel is in the background.

Cambridge students studied mostly the Greek and Roman classics and the Bible. They were required to state and defend theses in the frequent public disputations and to submit to rigorous oral examinations. One can feel distinct echoes of his Cambridge experience in Eliot's unvarying question-and-answer approach to explaining Christianity to the Indians and in his *Indian Dialogues* and *Logic Primer*. Although the scholastic method was by then on the way out at Cambridge University, Eliot was still using it in the 1670s to train Indians to become teachers. One can scarcely imagine what the Indians made of it!

Eliot seems to have loved his time at Jesus College. To this day his Indian Bible is the treasured possession of the college library. It was Eliot's gift to his alma mater, and he inscribed it: "Pro Collegio Jesu: Accipias mater quod alumnus humillimus offert filius, oro preces sem-

Pro Collegio Jesu :

Accipe, mater quod alumnus humillimus ffert

filius, oxo precibus semper habere tuas

Johannes Eliot :

FIG. 6. Eliot gave his alma mater, Jesus College, a copy of his Indian Bible inscribed in his own handwriting.

per habens tuas. Johannes Eliot." ("Accept, Mother, I pray, what a most humble alumnus offers, a son ever having thy prayers.")

Eliot received his bachelor's degree from Cambridge University on June 24, 1622, not long before his eighteenth birthday. We know little about his activities between this date and 1629 when he went to live with Thomas Hooker at Little Baddow. Bennett Eliot's large eight-year legacy (at his death in 1621) would have enabled Eliot to do postgraduate study in theology in preparation for ordination in the Church of England.

One reason we may safely surmise that Eliot studied theology after receiving his B.A. is his oft-expressed love of Hebrew, which was not part of the undergraduate curriculum at Cambridge.[13] Mather says Eliot was an "acute grammarian and understood well the language God first wrote the Bible in [i.e., Hebrew]." He quotes from Eliot's now-lost book of reflections in old age:

> Oh that the Lord would put it into the heart of his religious and
> learned servants, to take such pains about the Hebrew language as
> to fit it for universal use! Considering that, above all languages
> spoken by the lip of man, it is most capable to be enlarged and

fitted to express all things . . .—considering that it is the invention of God himself—and what one is fitter to be the universal language?[14]

Eliot received his master of arts degree from the university in January 1624/25. Even though the Great Plague of 1625–26 caused the university to be largely evacuated, the Jesus College register records that testimonials of the sort required by those seeking a bishop's ordination in the Church of England were sent on Eliot's behalf on July 8, 1625. The granting of such testimonials recurs throughout the register, and never is their destination specified. It would seem likely that in Eliot's case they were sent to the Bishop of Ely. Cambridge was located in his diocese and the bishop was "visitor" to Jesus College. Unfortunately, the Ely records of this period have been lost for hundreds of years, so Eliot's ordination cannot be proven.[15]

The case for Eliot's ordination in the Church of England is therefore based on the Jesus College testimonials and on three other pieces of circumstantial evidence. First, in his journal John Winthrop records the arrival of his wife and children on the same voyage as Eliot and speaks of only one other passenger: "Mr. Eliot, a minister."[16] Second, Mather lists Eliot in the First Classis of New England clergy: "such as were in actual exercise of their ministry when they left England."[17] Records exist to prove the ordination of almost all seventy-seven of these clerics by bishops in England. Third, immediately upon his arrival in Boston Eliot was asked to be minister of the First Church in Boston—whose pastor John Wilson, a priest of the Church of England, had temporarily returned to England. Roger Williams had previously refused the parish's request to fill in for Wilson on the grounds that the parish was "unseparated" from the Church of England. It is very unlikely that someone without episcopal ordination would have been invited to become pastor of the First Church as early as 1631.[18]

But to return to Eliot's "hidden years": we know only that they were concluded about 1629 when he went to live with Thomas Hooker and his family. Hooker would later (1633) follow Eliot to Massachusetts and serve as minister at Newtown (renamed Cambridge) before leading a large contingent to Hartford in 1636. His "Fundamental Orders," asserting that "the foundation of all authority is laid . . . in the free consent of the people," served as Connecticut's constitution, and he has been called, with some justification, the "founder of American democracy." When Eliot came to him in 1629, however, Hooker was still living in England at Little Baddow outside of Chelmsford in Essex.

Hooker had grown up in Leicestershire, far from Eliot's part of England. The fact that he held one of the two Dixie Fellowships at Cambridge enhances the likelihood that he attended Sir Wolstan Dixie's grammar school at Market Bosworth in Leicestershire, twenty-five miles from his hometown. After a miserable year as a sizar (poor scholarship boy) at Queens' College, Cambridge, he moved to Emmanuel College. Emmanuel had only recently been founded—in 1584—as a deliberately modern and reformed college, by the Puritan Sir Walter Mildmay of Chelmsford. (John Harvard, after whom New England's college was named, and many of the early settlers of Massachusetts were members of Emmanuel.) Hooker rose to considerable eminence at Cambridge, was ordained to the priesthood, and won the Dixie Fellowship on his way to becoming dean of Emmanuel and proctor in the university. The watershed experience of Hooker's life was his conversion experience while teaching at Cambridge. Cotton Mather describes its effects:

> [T]he more effectual grace of God gave him the experience of a true regeneration. It pleased the spirit of God very powerfully to break into the soul of this person with such a sense of . . . the just wrath of Heaven, as filled him with the most unusual degrees of horror and anguish which broke not only his rest but his heart also. . . . He afterwards gave this account of himself, "That in the time of his agonies, he could . . . conclude that there was no way but submission to God, and lying at the foot of his mercy in Christ Jesus, and waiting humbly there . . . : nevertheless, when he came to apply this rule unto himself in his own condition, his reasoning would fail him, he was able to do nothing. Having been a consid-

FIG. 7. The Dixie Grammar School at Market Bosworth in Leicestershire, in all likelihood Thomas Hooker's boyhood school.

> erable while thus troubled . . . [in this] "spirit of bondage," . . . [finally] he received "the spirit of adoption" [as a son of God] in the new covenant.[19]

Sometime after this experience—about the time Eliot was arriving at Cambridge—Hooker left the university. He returned to his native Leicestershire briefly, but soon accepted the position of rector of the parish of Esher in Surrey, near London. Here he lived with an eminent Puritan, Francis Drake, whose wife he healed of spiritual distress and whose "waiting gentlewoman," Susannah Garbrand, he married. His considerable fame as a preacher led Chelmsford, the county town of Essex, to invite him in 1626 to come and serve as their "lecturer." This whole area of England, north and northeast of London (including Cambridge, Widford and Nazeing, Chelmsford and Little Baddow), was "Puritan country," and "lectureships" sprang up as the means by which wealthy Puritans could sponsor clergymen of their own persuasion. Lecturers were expected only to give two weekly public lectures, one on Market Day during the week and the other on Sunday afternoon.[20]

Hooker's appointment as lecturer in Chelmsford came only a year or so after Charles I became king. By placing Hooker and other clergy of their persuasion in parishes as lecturers, the Puritans were trying to free them from the "Catholic" pressures which the bishops—at the king's urging—were placing on the regular parish clergy. And for a time at Chelmsford, Hooker was able to speak without interference. Mather writes:

> Here his lecture was exceedingly frequented . . . ; and the light of his ministry shown through the whole county of Essex . . . ; and his hearers felt those penetrating impressions . . . upon their souls which caused them to reverence him as 'a teacher sent from God.' . . . Hereby there was a great reformation wrought, not only in the town, but in the adjacent country from all parts whereof they came to [hear him].

Chelmsford's rector appears to have delighted in Hooker's popularity, and Hooker happily assisted him with the Sunday services. However, Hooker's conscientious refusal to adopt certain customs and apparel the bishops now required of parish clergy would eventually make it "necessary for him to lay down his ministry in Chelmsford, when he had been about four years there employed in it."[21]

Since Hooker's presence in Chelmsford was needed only twice a week, he and his family lived at Little Baddow, a village of about two hundred, four miles outside of Chelmsford, an easy "commute" on horseback.[22] Here in nearby Great Graces Manor lived Sir Henry Mildmay—from a branch of the famous Puritan family that had founded Emmanuel College, Cambridge. At the request of several leading and wealthy Puritan families of the region, Hooker established at Little Baddow a boarding school in which boys could receive their pre-university education in a Puritan context. This he did "in his own hired house, having one Mr. John Eliot as his usher."[23] That house—Cuckoos Farm—still stands today. The school established there was defiantly free of government and church control: it was not chartered, and neither Hooker nor Eliot had a license from the vicar-general to teach.[24]

From his own probable boyhood experience as a student at the Dixie Grammar School, Hooker had some concept of what a grammar school should be. Mather says

> he managed his charge with such discretion, with such authority, and such efficacy, that, able to do more with a word or a look than most men could have by a severer discipline, he did a very great service . . . in the education of such as afterwards proved themselves not a little serviceable.[25]

If Mather's description is accurate, Hooker would have been the ideal role model for the novice teacher living under his roof.

It is unclear how or when Eliot came to know Hooker, who was some eighteen years older than he. By 1629, when Eliot arrived to live with Hooker at Little Baddow, he would have been twenty-five. His eight-year legacy from his father would have expired, and he would have had time to finish his education and to receive ordination.[26] Eliot may have been attracted to Hooker simply because of Hooker's fame as a Puritan preacher. But we may also speculate that Eliot—coming as he did to Cambridge from a Puritan family and parish—would have been told at age fourteen (when he came to Jesus College as a student) to attend Hooker's preaching. Eliot's college may not have been Puritan, but Puritan ideals were swirling around the university, which numbered only fifteen hundred to two thousand students.[27] If, as seems likely, Hooker was still there when Eliot arrived, it is probable that Eliot heard him preach and possible that he came to know him personally.

At any rate, in 1629 Eliot found himself living—right along with the boys—in the midst of Hooker's family at Cuckoos Farm. In a document quoted by Cotton Mather but now sadly lost, Eliot attests to the profound impact (described in the language of "conversion") which this experience had on him:

> To this place I was called, through the infinite riches of God's mercy in Christ Jesus to my poor soul: for here the Lord said unto my dead soul, *live,* and through the grace of Christ, I do live, and I shall live for ever! When I came to this blessed family I then saw,

FIG. 8. Cuckoos Farm at Little Baddow, near Chelmsford in Essex County, England. Here Eliot lived with Thomas Hooker and his family and served as "usher" in the grammar school Hooker conducted in his home.

FIG. 9. The Glee Club at Cuckoos Farm in March 1992.

and never before, the power of godliness in its lively vigour and efficacy.[28]

Hooker also used Cuckoos Farm as a Puritan conference center. Here he gathered each month—for mutual support, prayer, and discussion—those clergy of the region who had Puritan inclinations. William Laud—the anti-Puritan Bishop of London appointed by King Charles in 1628—regarded these sessions as seditious. Yet such was Hooker's esteem that forty-seven "conformable ministers," parish clergy of the region, put themselves at risk by petitioning Laud to allow Hooker to continue his ministry at Chelmsford. They testified "that they esteem and know the said Mr. Thomas Hooker to be for doctrine, orthodox; for life and conversation, honest; for disposition, peaceable, and in no wise turbulent or factious."[29] Their petition was denied.

The Arcady that was Little Baddow appears to have lasted for Eliot not much more than a single shining year. By 1630 Hooker was in serious trouble with the ecclesiastical authorities, summoned to court and threatened with fines or worse. As Mather remarks, "As [Saint] Paul was advised by his friends that he [should] not venture into the theatre at Ephesus, thus Mr. Hooker's friends advised him to forfeit his bonds, rather than to throw him self any further into the hands of his enemies."[30] He therefore went the way of many other Puritans in trouble and fled in 1631 by ship to the Netherlands where he remained until he returned secretly to England to sail with Essex friends to the New World in 1633. If Eliot had had any remaining illusions about a future in England they were certainly shattered by the persecution of Hooker. By 1630–31 he had set his heart and mind on establishing a new life in an unsullied New England across the sea.

2. Roxbury—The Early Years

Disillusioned about their prospects under Charles, many leading Puritans now came to regard emigration as their last best hope. Without revealing their true motives, a group of Puritan merchants and men of property—joined by a number of respectable non-Puritans—

pressed the King to grant them a royal charter to establish a settlement north of Plymouth in New England. They were successful, and in March 1629, Charles granted lands to "the Governor and Company of the Massachusetts Bay in New England." The charter provided for the shareholders (called "freemen") of the joint-stock company—which controlled the colony—to elect each year a governor and a council of eighteen "assistants." Immediately after the king granted the charter, the Puritan shareholders bought out the non-Puritans. The charter had neglected to specify a place for the annual meeting (which Charles and most others would have assumed would be London, under the immediate scrutiny of the king). These shrewd Puritans, however, took the charter with them: all annual meetings (after the first in London) would be held in Boston. The settlers would govern themselves with as little reference to distant England as possible.[31]

The first attempt to settle the area north of Plymouth Colony was the Dorchester merchants' effort to establish a settlement at Cape Ann in 1626. The effort failed, though a few settlers moved to Naumkeag (Salem). Even before receiving their charter, the Company in 1628 sent out John Endecott and a contingent of two hundred settlers to take over the Salem settlement from the miserable stragglers who survived.

The Company's second wave of two hundred (planters plus hired farm laborers) left in April 1629, a month after the charter was granted. It was led by Francis Higginson, an ordained priest of the Church of England who had been influenced by Hooker and others to join the Puritan party. Unable to endure the terrible hardships, he died in August 1630, a little more than a year after arriving. The colony barely clung to life.

In England, 1629 and 1630 brought disastrous harvests to East Anglia where Eliot and many of the Puritans lived. The resulting destitution brought a great outburst of crime—a further indication, as the Puritans saw it, that England was irrevocably sliding into immorality. This perception added further impetus to the emigration movement.[32] As a result, in 1630 some seventeen ships were commissioned to carry a third

FIG. 10. The Charter of March 1629 by which King Charles I granted land to "the Governor and Company of the Massachusetts Bay in New England."

wave of Puritan families to New England under the 1629 charter. The most prominent of these were John Winthrop, wealthy squire of his family's manor at Groton, Suffolk, and Thomas Dudley, the eminently capable high steward (i.e., estate administrator) to the Earl of Lincoln. At the first and only meeting of the company in London, John Winthrop had been elected governor and Thomas Dudley deputy governor. Years later, as governor, Dudley would be the first person to sign the Agreement of 1645 that established The Roxbury Latin School.

When these 1630 immigrants arrived at Salem, they found it unappealing, and the main fleet headed south to unsettled locations on the coast which they soon named Boston and Charlestown. Here they settled. In his exalted statement of purpose, Winthrop had eloquently stated the ideals that had motivated the Puritan emigration:

> For wee must consider that wee shall be as a citty upon a hill. The eies of all people are uppon us. Soe that if wee shall not deal falsely with our God in this worke wee have undertaken, and soe cause him to withdrawe his present help from us, wee shall be made a story and a by-word through the world.[33]

That was the ideal. Apologizing for writing "rudely, having yet no table, nor other room to write in, than by the fireside upon my knee, in this sharp winter," Thomas Dudley drew a vivid picture of the reality in his letter to the Countess of Lincoln of March 12, 1630/31. He spoke first of what they discovered when they arrived at Salem: "Wee found the Colony in a sadd and unexpected condition, above 80 of them beeing dead the winter before, and many of those alive weake and sicke; all the corne and bread amongst them all, hardly sufficient to feed upon a fortnight."

Dudley then described the trials associated with establishing the Boston settlement. Each person who paid his passage to New England was entitled to fifty acres of land, each investor of £50 in the company's stock was entitled to two hundred acres (or proportionally more or less, according to the size of the investment), and each settler was entitled to an additional fifty acres for each farm worker he brought with him at his own expense. Many of the 1630 settlers had brought such farm workers with them, but the terrible conditions they encountered upon arrival forced many of them to release these workers to fend for themselves. More than a hundred of the settlers—whether out of fear, laziness, or discontent with their fellow settlers— returned to England: "And glad were wee so to bee ridd of them," wrote Dudley. Those

> who had health to labour fell to building, wherein many were interrupted with sicknes and many dyed weekely, yea almost dayley. . . . And of the people who came with us [from April–December 1630] there dyed by estimacon about 200 at the least—Soe lowe hath the Lord brought us!
>
> I should alsoe have remembered how the halfe of our cowes and almost all our mares and goats, sent us out of England, dyed at sea in their passage hither. . . . In a word, we yett enjoy little to be envyed, but endure much to be pittyed in the sicknes and mortallitye of our people.

Dudley then declared in emphatic terms that only people of faith and affluence should come to New England: "If any come hither to plant for worldly ends that cannot live well at home, he committs an errour, of which he will soone repent him." Those who decide to come need to have money to fall back on for at least eighteen months.

> If any godly men, out of religious ends, will come over to helpe us in the goode worke we are about, I think they cannot dispose of themselves nor of their estates more to God's glory, and the furtherance of their owne reckoninge; but *they must not bee of the poorer sort* yett, for diverse years. . . . If there be any endued with grace and furnished with meanes to feed themselves and theirs for 18 months, and to build and plant, lett them come over into our Macedonia and helpe us. . . . [Emphasis added.]

Dudley concluded his letter by asserting the colonists' loyalty to the Crown of England, in order to quash "malicious aspersions" circulating in England to the contrary:

> Wee doe continue to pray dayly for our Soveraigne lord the King, the Queene, the Prince, the royal blood, the counsaile and whole state, as duty bindes us to doe, and reason perswades others to believe, for how ungodly and unthankful should wee bee if wee did not thus doe, who came hither by his Majties letters patent, and under his gracious protection.[34]

John Eliot was part of 1631's small fourth wave of about seventy mostly affluent immigrants, in numbers hardly enough to balance those who were already returning in disillusionment. He arrived at Boston—following a ten-week voyage on the *Lyon*—on November 2, 1631, three months after his twenty-seventh birthday. In addition to its sixty passengers (including Governor John Winthrop's wife and family), the *Lyon* brought a "great store of provisions, as fat hogs, kids, venison, poultry, geese, partridges, etc., so as the like joy and manifestations of love, had never been seen in New England."[35] As the colonists faced their third winter, such provisions were welcome indeed.

Since March the people of Boston had been without a minister; John Wilson had returned to England in March to try to persuade his wife to come to New England. Eliot was forthwith drafted to take his place and was so popular and respected that, when Wilson returned (without wife) in May 1632, the congregation asked Eliot to remain as "teacher." The founders of New England thought parishes should have both a "minister" and a "teacher"—who would preach in alternation and undertake other work in concert[36]—so they were not "making work" for Eliot. "Boston laboured all they could, both with the congregation of Roxbury and with Mr. Eliot himself" to persuade him to stay.[37]

Fond as he was of his Boston parishioners, Eliot went instead to "Rocksbury." It would be many years before the modern-day "Back Bay" was filled in; in Eliot's time Boston was connected to the mainland only by a narrow "neck" of land, and Roxbury was the shoulders to which that neck was attached. The first contingent of immigrants from Eliot's hometown, Nazeing, had arrived and settled at Roxbury the year before. In their East Anglian accent, which would be the dominant influence on the development of a distinctive New England accent, they would have pronounced his name *Eli't*.[38] Back in England he had promised to be their pastor; now he would serve as "teacher" of the parish established by Thomas Weld a few months earlier. Weld had graduated from Trinity College, Cambridge, about a decade before Eliot finished at Jesus and had been ordained to the priesthood of the Church of England by the Bishop of Peterborough. He had known both Eliot and Hooker when he was vicar of Terling, an Essex town adjoining Little Baddow. Weld and Eliot worked happily together at Roxbury until Weld returned to England in 1641. In England, Weld sought support for the new colony and its college, especially by means of his propaganda piece, *New Englands First Fruits*, published in London in 1643.[39]

At Roxbury, a 20x30-foot log meetinghouse with a thatched roof had already been erected when Eliot arrived. Inside its unplastered walls, men and women sat on separate sides on backless benches. Though there was a table at the front, the room was really a lecture hall. The pulpit was the dominant fixture since the preaching of the Word was the main feature of the two lengthy Sunday services held in the late morning and early afternoon with a brief interval between.[40] Though additions and modest improvements were made to this structure from time to time, it remained the church's home for more than forty years.

Writing in 1654, Captain Edward Johnson noted the ugliness of the meetinghouse in his otherwise rather favorable description of Roxbury:

> The fift [5th] Church of Christ was gathered at Roxbury . . . being well watered with coole and pleasant Springs issuing forth the Rocky-hills, and with small Freshets, watering the Vallies of this fertill Towne . . . filled with a very laborious people whose labours the Lord hath so blessed, that in the roome of dismall Swampes and tearing Bushes, they have very goodly Fruit-trees, fruitfull Fields and Gardens, their Hearde of Cowes, Oxen and other young Cattell of the kind about 350, and dwelling-houses neare upon 120. Their streets are large and some fayre Houses, yet have they built their House for Church-assembly, destitute and

unbeautiful with other buildings. The Church of Christ here is increased to about 120 persons, their first Teaching Elder called to office is Mr. Eliot a young man, at his comming thither of a cheerfull spirit, apt to teach, as by his indefatigable paines both with his own flock, and the poor Indians doth appeare.[41]

This building was called a "meetinghouse" rather than a "church," because all the town's business—not just worship—was conducted here. The early settlers had fled the state Church of England, but in New England their intention was to found a church-state. Since their goal was nothing less than to establish the City of God on earth, there would be no division between community and church, no "separation of church and state." They also felt they had to protect the newly gathered community of saints from being defiled by non-believers. The charter had established that the Company's shareholders—called "freemen"—were annually to elect a governor and eighteen assistants (the "General Court") who would establish suitable laws. Since less than twenty freemen lived in New England—where the General Court met—power was narrowly concentrated. Winthrop almost immediately widened the definition of "freeman" so that it included the approximately one hundred adult males in the colony who were not servants. In the future, as new immigrants arrived, non-servant adult males could become freemen after they had been examined for their beliefs and admitted to church membership. The Company was thereby transformed into a church-state.[42]

FIG. II. Illustration of Roxbury's 20' x 30' log church from Francis S. Drake's *Town of Roxbury*.

Winthrop was a staunch opponent of democracy. He regarded the servant class as unfit to share in ruling, and though he broadened the definition of freeman so that the numbers rose first to one hundred and then higher, he simultaneously abolished their right to elect a governor. He ruled that the

FIG. 12. Part of "An Exact Draught of Bostone harbour" made in 1711. From an 1883 copy of the original in the British Museum. Note that before the Back Bay was filled in in the nineteenth century, Boston was connected by a "neck" to the mainland at Roxbury.

FIG. 13. The School gathered for the 350th anniversary, Founder's Day, 1994, in the 1803 meeting house, the fifth on the site of the original log church.

assistants would elect the governor as well as enact laws. Winthrop's ab-rogation of the freemen's right to elect the governor and his effectual reduction of their influence was challenged when he and his assistants began to levy taxes. By 1632 the freemen called him to account for vio-lating the charter, and Winthrop had to agree to the freemen's direct election of the governor and to towns sending representatives to advise the General Court (the governor and assistants) each year. By 1634, the freemen turned Winthrop out as governor and elected his deputy Dud-ley (with whom he had long been at odds). However, Winthrop was soon reelected governor—a post which he, like Dudley (notably in the year of the School's founding), held several times off and on.

There was no concept of "freedom of religion" among the founders of New England: orthodoxy in belief and rectitude in character were prerequisites to enfranchisement in this covenant society. The division between the ministers and civil (as we, but not they, would put it) magistrates was largely functional: the ministers (whose wages and housing were provided from civil funds) proclaimed the truth, and the magistrates enforced and guarded it. The City of God was a single undivided city and all aspects of it affirmed all other aspects.[43]

The elders' examination of the adult males who wished to join a church such as the one at Roxbury was by no means perfunctory or superficial. The elders had to be convinced "not only about their perswasion [i.e., their beliefs], but also whether they have attained unto the work of grace upon their souls [i.e., their conduct]." For, as Mather noted, Eliot

> could not comprehend that this church-state can arise from any other formal cause [than] the consent, concurrence, confederation of those concerned in it; [relationship with a church was] a voluntary thing . . . to be entered no otherwise than by an holy covenant, or, as Scripture speaks, by 'giving our selves first unto the Lord, and then one unto another.' . . . For subjects to be admitted by churches unto all the privileges of this fellowship with them, he thought they ought to be . . . *regenerate*.[44]

The adult congregation to which Weld and Eliot ministered at Roxbury was thus a "church of the saints," a body of already-regenerate Christian believers. Together with their children they numbered in the spring of 1632 fewer than fifty. The number soon swelled. Eliot's sister Sarah Curtis, her husband William and four children, as well as Eliot's fiancée Hanna Mumford,[45] arrived that year from England. The town's first marriage was that of John and Hanna in October 1632. A minister's wife was an important figure in the community. She sat on the front bench at Sunday worship, and in addition to bearing children (the Eliots had five sons and a daughter), she was expected to engage in good works for others. Hanna acted as the community's doctor and nurse, having been "trained in physic," and she helped her husband by skillfully managing their farmlands on her own.

Eliot's first decade in Roxbury was consumed in ministering to the immediate needs of his people. (Roxbury Latin would not be founded until 1645, and his work among the Indians did not begin until 1646.) Cotton Mather talks about Eliot's onerous duties as pastor:

> It was no easy thing to feed the souls of such a people, and of the children and the neighbours, which were to be brought into the same sheepfold with them; to bear their manners with all patience, not being by any of their infirmities discouraged from teaching them, and from watching and praying over them; to value them highly, as "the flock which God has purchased with his own blood," notwithstanding all their miscarriages; and in all to examine the rule of Scripture for the warrant of whatever *shall* be done; and to remember the day of judgment, wherein account must be given of all that *has* been done; having in the mean time no expectation of the riches and grandeurs which accompany a *worldly* domination.[46]

Eliot kept the Roxbury church records himself, and we can read them today. The joys of life—births and weddings and recoveries from sickness—are set side by side, day by day, with disease, suffering, discord, and death. Here are recorded acts of theft, deceit, adultery, cruelty, and murder, as well as extraordinary acts of generosity and saintliness. Here we read of controversy, heresy, and schism, repentance and forgiveness, excommunication, and execution. All these events required the involvement and counsel of the minister. Beyond the demands made upon him by one of the leading parishes of New England, Eliot was also required to devote enormous amounts of time and energy to the affairs and controversies of the synod (gathering) of all the parishes that together constituted the reformed church in the Colony.[47]

Two observations are always made about Eliot the person and—indistinguishably—Eliot the minister: He was a man of charity and a man of prayer.

"He that will write of Eliot must write of charity, or say nothing," says Cotton Mather. "Many hundreds of pounds did he bestow upon the poor . . . [who] counted him their father."[48] His response to the needs of others was instantaneous and uninhibited:

> So great was Mr. Eliot's charity, that his salary was often distributed for the relief of his needy neighbours, so [often] his own family was straitened for the comforts of life. One day the parish treasurer on paying the money for salary due, which he put into a handkerchief in order to prevent Mr. Eliot from giving away his money before he got home, tied the ends of the handkerchief in as many hard knots as he could. . . . Eliot immediately went to the house of a sick and necessitous family. On entering he gave them his blessing, and told them God had sent them some relief. The sufferers with tears of gratitude welcomed their pious benefactor who with moistened eye began to untie the knots in his handkerchief. After many efforts to get at his money, and impatient at the perplexity and delay, he gave the handkerchief and all the money to the mother of the family. . . . "Here, my dear, take it. I believe the Lord designs it all for you."[49]

His wife, as we have noted, ran the family farm, since he had no interest in accumulation. He later frustrated the English charitable society that supported his Indian work because he kept little account of how he spent their grants, but they continued their support ever more generously because they knew what they gave went to the Indian work.

His charity counted no person an enemy. Once, says Mather, a townsman reviled and abused Eliot for one of his sermons. When the man was injured, Eliot sent his wife to nurse him and then invited him to supper in his home when he was well.[50] Eliot regarded the Roman Catholic Church as corrupt and unreformed, but the French Canadian Jesuit missionary Father Gabriel Dreuillette wrote in his diary of the affectionate welcome Eliot extended to him at Roxbury on Christmas Eve 1650:

> I arrived at Roxbury where the minister named Master Eliot (who is teaching some savages) invited me to his home because the night had overtaken me and treated me with respect and affection and beseeched me to spend the winter with him.[51]

Since Eliot spoke no French and Dreuillette no English, the two undoubtedly conversed in Latin, the language both had learned in their youth. Eliot's attitude towards Dreuillette is little short of astounding in context: it would be 130 years before Catholic worship would be permitted in Massachusetts and 170 before Catholics could hold public office.

Eliot was preeminently a man of prayer. "His whole breath," writes Mather, "seemed in a sort made up of ejaculatory prayers, many scores of which . . . he dispatched away to Heaven, upon pious errands every day." When something momentous occurred he would say, "Brethren, let us turn all this into prayer." And when he visited his parishioners in their homes, he would suggest, "Come, let us not have a visit without a prayer."[52]

His own family's life was governed by these principles. There were Bible readings and prayers together morning and night. Meals were simple, extravagances frowned upon. Mather calls Eliot's home "a school of piety . . . , a perpetual mixture of a Spartan and a Christian discipline."[53] One evidence of Eliot's success is that, of his four sons who reached adulthood, three became ministers and the fourth was studying for the ministry at his death.

3. *Leader in Education*

As might be expected of a Cambridge University graduate and former grammar school teacher, Eliot placed an extremely high value on education. He regarded learning as the all-important handmaid of religion in the effort to create the City of God in New England. Whether catechizing children, founding schools, or helping to create a college, Eliot was a zealous champion of education.

Church membership in the City of God was not automatic; it required education. Eventually, every adult who wished to join the church had to make a public profession of faith and be examined before the church. Of the varieties of Christianity, in fact, Puritanism is arguably the most essentially intellectual. Nothing was more central to Eliot's efforts in his parish, therefore, than the catechizing of children: they must learn the faith before they could decide to profess it. Mather writes:

He always had a mighty concern upon his mind for young children
. . . he was very solicitous that the lambs . . . be brought . . . under
the "bond of the covenant." . . . But having once baptised the children of his neighbours, he did not, as too many ministers do, think
that he was now done with them. No; another thing wherein he
was very laborious for poor children was the catechising of them
. . . so, if any seducers were let loose to wolve it among the good
people of Roxbury, I am confident they would find as little prey in
that well-instructed place, as in any part of all the country.[54]

His first great educational endeavor beyond the parish was his effort
to obtain financial support from England for the founding of a college
in New England. Professor Franklin M. Wright discovered and published in 1954 a hitherto unknown letter of John Eliot to Sir Simonds
D'Ewes. Harvard's great historian, Samuel Eliot Morison, had stated in
his 1935 history that the first proposal for a college was in 1636.[55] Eliot's
1633 letter to Simonds D'Ewes "possesses historical importance of the
first rank: it provides clear evidence for a detailed plan for the foundation of a college in New England that antedates by nearly three years
the earliest known reference to such a project."[56]

In his letter Eliot thanks D'Ewes for his "remembrance" of him and
his new wife, referring evidently to a wedding present or letter of con-
gratulation. D'Ewes, who attended St. John's College, was a year ahead
of Eliot at Cambridge. D'Ewes's closest friend at the university was
Richard Saltonstall, a member of Jesus College, so D'Ewes and Eliot
may well have known one another. D'Ewes was also a close friend of Sir
Henry Mildmay of Great Graces Hall, Little Baddow, so it is perhaps
here that D'Ewes came to know both Hooker—with whom he corre-
sponded—and Eliot. Fortunately for us, D'Ewes was an antiquarian
scholar who carefully preserved every letter he received, including this
one from Eliot. Eliot knew D'Ewes had inherited a fortune (upon his
father's death in 1631) and hoped he could persuade him to part with
some of it. Wright believes that Eliot's "shrewd insistence upon a commemoration of D'Ewes's 'name and honour' in New England also hints

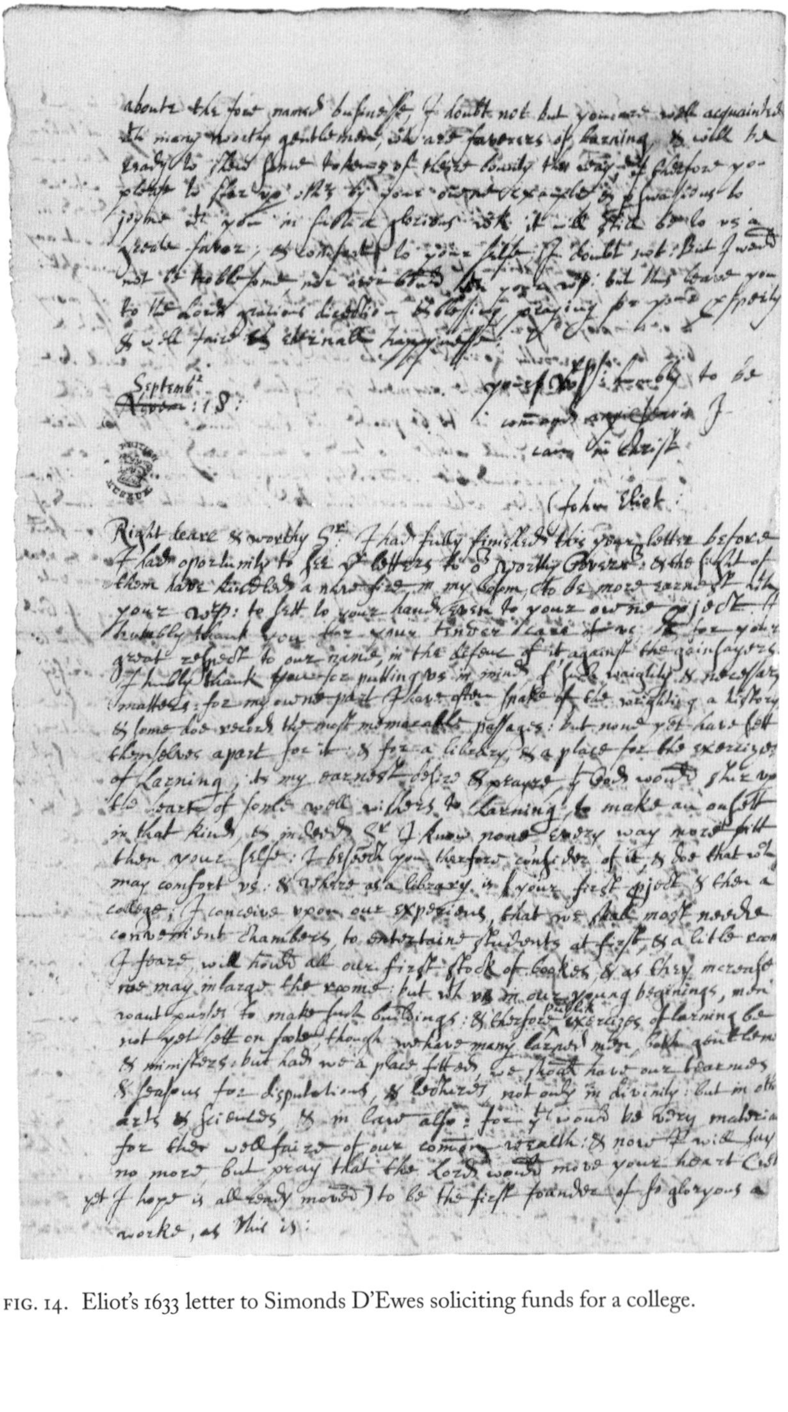

that the writer was familiar with that large self-esteem which at times made D'Ewes a near-comic figure in both public and private life."[57] This is the proposal Eliot sent to D'Ewes:

> Now for your selfe to come, I doe earnestly desire it, if God move your heart, & not only for the common wealth sake; but also for Larnings sake, which I know you love, & will be ready to furder, & indeede we want store of such men, as will furder that, for if we norish not Larning both church & common wealth will sinke; & because I am vpon this poynt I beseech you let me be bould to make one motion, for the furtheranc of larning among vs: God hath bestowed upon you a bounty full blessing; now if you should please, to imploy but one mite, of that greate welth which God hath given, to erect a schoole of larning, a colledg among vs; you should do a most glorious work, acceptable to God & man; & the commemoration of the founder of the means of Larning, would be a perpetuating of your name & honor among vs. . . .
>
> [All that's needed] is the building, of such a place, as may be fitt for such a purpose, & such larned men as be here, & may come, must of theire owne proper charge frequent those places, at fitt seasons, for the exercizing of larning, & such yung men as may be trained vp [m]ust beare theire own charges: only we want a house convenient, now the bare building of a house big enough for our young beginings will be done with litle charge: I doubt not but if you should sett apart but 500 pound for that work, it would be a sufficient begining . . . , nay 400 or 300 would doe pretty well. . . .
>
> Now I beseech you consider what an oportunity God hath put into your hand of doeing good with that rich portion God hath given you; & if you should passe vs by, & misse the oportunity, you may loose what you have, & never have the like oportunity againe: but I will say no more, only pray vnto the Lord, to move your heart vnto it.[58]

Just as Eliot was finishing this solicitation, Governor Winthrop received a letter from D'Ewes expressing interest in a library. So Eliot added a post script, first thanking D'Ewes "for your tender care of vs" and then enjoining him to alter his priorities:

> [F]or a library, & a place for the exercize of Larning, it is my
> earnest desire & prayre that God would stir vp the heart of some
> well wishers to Larning, to make an onsett in that kind, & indeed
> Sir I know none, every way more fitt than your selfe: I beseech you
> therfore consider of it, & doe that which may comfort vs: & where
> as a library is your first project, & then a college; I conceive vpon
> our experiens, that we shall most need convenient chambers . . .
> first, & a litle room I feare, will hould all our first stock of bookes.[59]

This letter also shows that Eliot had no narrow concept of education.
The college he proposed was not to be narrowly theological, but a place
where all branches of learning would be taught. He closes his letter with
this capacious view of the college's curriculum:

> Had we a place fitted, we should have our tearmes & seasons for
> disputations, & lectures, not only in divinity: but in other arts &
> sciences, & in law also: for that would be very material for the well-
> faire of our common wealth: & now I shall say no more, but pray
> that the Lord would move your heart . . . to be the first founder of
> so gloryous a worke as this is.[60]

D'Ewes was a courteous man and undoubtedly responded to Eliot in
a letter now lost. D'Ewes was quite suspicious of the growing
"congregational" tendency in New England church government, and
a year later he wrote urging Winthrop to adhere to the episcopal
governance of the Church of England. (He received back a far from
conciliatory response.)[61] Whatever the reason, D'Ewes chose not to
give the building for a college, and generations have received their
diplomas from "Harvard" rather than from "D'Ewes U."

Since no patron had come forth to found a college, the Court (the
local governing body of Massachusetts Bay) in 1636 gave £400 "towards
a schoale or colledge," leaving it to the next session to "appoint wheare
and what building."[62] But the next session, the court was so embroiled
in the Anne Hutchinson controversy that no attention was paid to
erecting a college. The future course of education in the colony rested
on the outcome of this controversy.

In 1636 Anne Marbury Hutchinson was forty-five; she had arrived in New England two years earlier. Her childhood in England was a turbulent one: her clergyman father's outspoken dissenting views and judgmental pronouncements got him booted out of one parish after another and resulted in at least one term of imprisonment. She was married to a quite successful merchant, William Hutchinson, whom John Winthrop nonetheless described as a man "of a very mild temper and weak parts and wholly guided by his wife." Weak he may have been, but he and Anne had fourteen children by the time they arrived in New England. John Cotton, minister at the monumental St. Botolph's Church in the English Boston, not far from the Lincolnshire town where she lived, was the only clergyman she trusted. When Cotton left for New England's Boston (to assist John Wilson, the minister), she and her entire family followed him in order to remain "under his preaching." She made a favorable first impression on her new neighbors by her skill in nursing.

Along with the nursing, however, went a tendency to "talk religion," and she amazed the people of Boston by her knowledge of Scripture and her eagerness to expound on it. She began teaching classes in her house and was soon correctly perceived as a "rival" to John Wilson, Boston's minister. She often, in fact, took his Sunday sermon as the launching point for her classes and then offered a different interpretation. She first suggested and then stated that Wilson did not rely entirely on the most central Protestant doctrine—salvation by the grace of God received only through faith; rather, she complained, Wilson was preaching salvation by the doing of good works.

The situation was further destabilized by the surprising election of Henry Vane as governor in 1636. Vane had arrived a year earlier and was only twenty-four years old. He came from a family with close connections to the king and his conversion to Puritanism and emigration to the New World had caused a sensation. His charm and charisma enthralled his new countrymen. Alarm spread among the old guard, especially among the clergy. Vane was something of a mystic and his attraction to Hutchinson disturbed and threatened many of the ministers. Well it might. Like father, like daughter: she took the occasion of the new governor's election to denounce all the clergy of New England (except for John Cotton and her newly arrived brother-in-law John Wheelwright). They were not fit to be ministers, she railed, because they had not been "sealed of the Spirit."

Hutchinson insisted that her accusation arose not from any rational process in her mind, but rather from God's direct revelation to her. She was, she claimed, governed by an "inner voice." She further asserted the theory that "sanctification is not evidence of justification." In standard Puritan theology, "sanctification" (a righteous life) was one sign that a person was "justified" (in a right relationship with God). If a person was "justified," that person would show it by the quality of his life: by right-thinking and good deeds ("sanctification"). But Hutchinson denied that good deeds or right-thinking were evidence of justification. The only evidence you could have of being in a right relationship with God was an inner illumination, a rapturous sense of God's presence, the sound of God's voice speaking within you. This was the "sealing of the Spirit" that, in her view, was absent in most of the New England clergy.

The founders of the Massachusetts Bay Colony had crossed the Atlantic to establish a purified church-state. Membership in that church-state was granted only after examination by the ministers of the Gospel. The "City of God" could not be established if people of deviant beliefs were admitted or if they were allowed to remain once their deviance was detected. Since the success of the enterprise was still uncertain, the community's unity was of utmost importance. Hutchinson's attack on almost all the ministry of New England thus struck at the very heart of the City of God less than a decade after it was founded.

In particular, Hutchinson vilified Boston's minister, John Wilson. Wilson was a graduate of Eton and King's College, Cambridge, a man of erudition who had given up his family and a life of certain success and relative ease in order to come to the wilderness of North America. Labelling him a false hireling and a priest of Baal, Hutchinson organized his harassment: her followers would either ostentatiously walk out when he began his sermons or ask him rude and accusatory questions when he finished.

Eliot recognized Hutchinson's theological position as the "antinomian" heresy. That heresy he knew to be, at its very heart, anti-intellectual: all the arts Eliot had recommended to D'Ewes as fit studies for the new college were, in Hutchinson's view, worthless, as was the study of Hebrew and Greek and of the Church fathers. As one of her partisans put it, "I had rather hear such a one that speakes from the meere motion of the spirit, without any study at all, than any of your learned Scollers, although they may be fuller of Scripture."[63] Morison rightly asks, "If learned ministers could be silenced by the 'immediate revelations' of an untrained woman, what was the use of a college to train ministers?"[64] At the Great Synod of New England in August 1637 all the clergy (except Wheelwright, her brother-in-law) "condemned some eighty [of Hutchinson's] 'erroneous opinions,' together with sundry 'unlawful practices' such as evening seances of female prophets, and contemptuous heckling of parsons."[65]

Only a court, however, could convict her of error and discipline her, and such a court was convened on November 2. John Winthrop, once again elected governor, presided, assisted by Thomas Dudley, the deputy governor. The court first banished Wheelwright and disarmed and disenfranchised forty-five of his supporters who refused to recant. Then came Anne Hutchinson. For two days she confounded the court, denying charges, returning questions with questions. But then, as she seemed on the verge of winning, she seized defeat from the jaws of victory by claiming that she could distinguish whether a given clergyman's ministry was valid or invalid: "I bless the Lord, he hath let me see which was the clear [i.e., true] ministry and which was the wrong."

"How do you know that that was the spirit [speaking through your conscience]?" she was asked.

"How did Abraham know that it was God that bid him offer his son . . . ?" she answered, characteristically, with her own question.

"By an immediate voice," said Thomas Dudley.

Yes, she replied fatally. "So to me by an immediate revelation. . . . By the voice of [God's] own spirit to my soul." She then went even further, claiming God had said to her, "I am the same God that delivered Daniel out of the lion's den, I will also deliver thee. . . . But now having seen Him which is invisible, I fear not what man can do unto me."

"Daniel was delivered by miracle. Do you think to be deliver'd so too?" asked Governor Winthrop.

"I do here speak it before the Court. I look that the Lord should deliver me by his providence," she replied.

The governor responded: "Now the mercy of God by a providence hath answered our desires and made her to lay open herself and the ground of all these disturbances to be by revelations . . . and that is the means by which she hath very much abused the country that they shall look for revelations and are not bound to the ministry of the word [the Bible], but God will teach them by immediate revelations and this hath been the ground of all these tumults and troubles . . . the root of all the mischief."

That was all the court needed. "We all consent with you," they said to the governor. "I am fully persuaded that Mrs. Hutchinson is deluded by the devil, because the spirit of God speaks truth in all his servants," said Dudley, and Winthrop concurred: "I am persuaded that the revelation she brings forth is delusion." Again, "all the Court but some two or three ministers" cried out their agreement.[66]

Eliot was one of the three ministers called to testify against her. Under oath he said he had tried to reason with her regarding her assertion that a good life did not reveal a right belief: "We did labour then to convince her that our doctrine was the same with Mr. Cotton's: She said no, for we were not sealed."[67]

Shortly thereafter, Governor Winthrop declared the court's sentence: "Mrs. Hutchinson, the sentence of the court you hear is that you are banished from out of our jurisdiction as being a woman not fit for our society; and are to be imprisoned until the court send you away."[68]

But she could not be banished until she had been tried by the membership of the Boston church. Her "imprisonment" while she awaited this trial was at the Roxbury home of Joseph Weld, brother of Eliot's pastor colleague, Thomas Weld. When the trial finally came, it was a lengthy and muddled affair in which Eliot—among others—accused her of lying. Even John Cotton turned against her at the end. And the congregation excommunicated her. She moved first with nine of her children to Rhode Island, and, after she caused division there, to Rye, New York, where she and twelve members of her family perished in an Indian raid in 1643.

Had Hutchinson prevailed, it seems likely that New England would have been divided into a host of sects—each guided by an inner light, each intolerant of the other—and education would have been reduced to a low priority. But the forces of anti-intellectualism had been defeated. It is no coincidence that, within a few days of convicting Hutchinson, the General Court effectuated Eliot's cherished dream by authorizing the construction of a college at Newtown (which within a year was renamed Cambridge). The college was soon named after John Harvard, who in 1638 left his books and half his estate to it; Eliot served as an overseer of Harvard from 1642 to 1685.

Despite the Hutchinson affair, the clergy were able to devote some of their energy to scholarly endeavor. In their first decade in the New World, they focused their scholarly attentions on providing a new translation of the Biblical psalms for use in worship. One aspect of Puritan worship involved the people singing the psalms in meter (i.e., in a poetic translation). In 1630 they had brought with them a standard English metric psalter known as Sternhold-Hopkins. It was flawed, in their view, because it was too loose a translation of the original Hebrew. They had a fairly high view of the Ainsworth metric psalter, but it was used by the Plymouth pilgrims, and the Puritans did not want to identify with these separatists. As a result, Eliot and a number of other New England ministers who had studied Hebrew (most of them at Cambridge) decided to do their own translation. Judged by the English standards of the day—Shakespeare had recently died and Milton was their contemporary—the results of the labors of Eliot and his colleagues can only be termed appalling, at least from a poetic point of view. But Cotton Mather asserts their virtue:

> Now, though I heartily join with those gentlemen who wish the poetry [of this work] were mended; yet I must confess, that the Psalms has never yet seen a translation, that I know of, nearer the Hebrew original; and I am willing to receive the excuse which our translators themselves do offer us, when they say: "If the verses are not always so elegant as some desire or expect, let them consider that God's altar needs not our polishings; we have respected rather a plain translation, than to smooth our verses with the sweetness of any paraphrase. We have attended conscience rather than elegance, fidelity rather than ingenuity."[69]

Leaving aside the question of the poetic or scholarly quality of their labors, we must admire their effort. They set out to present, "according to our own light and time," a translation of the psalms for singing that was, on the one hand, absolutely faithful to the Word of God, and yet, on the other hand, also spoke to the particular circumstances of a people in the wilderness who believed they were ushering in a whole new era in human history. Appropriately, this effort has always been known as the *Bay Psalm Book*. Coming off the Stephen Daye press in 1640, it was the first book published in English America, a fitting commemoration of the tenth anniversary of the founding of the City of God.[70]

But of all Eliot's intellectual efforts, of all his contributions to education, the most enduring has been The Roxbury Latin School. John and Hanna Eliot gave birth first to a daughter and then five sons between 1633 and 1646. John, the oldest son, was born August 31, 1636. Is it merely a coincidence that on John Jr.'s ninth birthday in 1645 Eliot gathered most of the men of Roxbury to sign the Agreement that brought a grammar school into being in the town? John and Hanna's marriage had been the first in Roxbury and their son's birth among the first. As young John's contemporaries grew up, Eliot and the planters of

Roxbury had to face the problem of educating the first generation of white children born in the New World. The four Eliot sons who reached school age all attended this new school, beginning with young John who was among its first-year pupils. The story of Eliot's founding and nourishing of the School will be considered in Part II.

Important as the School was to him, it was just one of several "extra" duties he undertook on top of his consuming duties as pastor and teacher. He had been called, after all, to minister to people with great needs—who had left behind their native land and families to come to "the uttermost parts of the earth." Such a people in such a place drained their pastor's energy day by day as he taught, preached, counseled, consoled, rebuked, and advised them, all the while feeding them with spiritual manna in the wilderness. Such labors alone were more than enough to justify a life. What is remarkable in these first fourteen years (1631–1645) is how much else Eliot did, and how much of it had to do with education. He was the first to propose a college for the New World. Battling the anti-intellectual Hutchinson movement, he supported the teaching of a broad range of studies at the new college, of which he was an overseer. A Hebrew scholar of some quality, he played a major role in writing the colony's first book. And he was the person principally responsible for founding what is now the oldest school in continuous existence in North America.

There was no stauncher proponent of the efficacy of education in all New England. Cotton Mather recalls:

> I cannot forget the ardour with which I once heard him pray, in a synod . . . which met at Boston to consider "how the miscarriages which were among us might be prevented;" I say, with what fervour he uttered an expression to this purpose: "Lord, for schools every where among us! That our schools may flourish! That every member of this assembly may go home, and procure a good school to be encouraged in the town where he lives! That before we die, we may be so happy as to see a good school encouraged in every plantation of the country!"[71]

4. *Apostle to the Indians*

Eliot came to the New World to establish a church-state purified of the "corruptions" of the English state church. Initially, he seems to have shown little if any interest in the indigenous population. The City upon a Hill was to be a beacon—an example—to the people of England he had left behind, more than to the native Americans he and his fellow settlers encountered when they arrived.[72]

The number of Indians in New England—Maine to Connecticut—before the English invasions has been variously estimated at between 25,000 and 144,000. The present greater Boston area—into which Eliot arrived in 1631—was very lightly inhabited by the Massachuset tribe, part of the Algonquian linguistic group. The Massachuset tribe had arrived in this area only a century or so before the English landed. They may have numbered as many as 24,000 at their peak. With no immunity to the Old World diseases brought to these shores by the early English explorers, they were laid waste. The plague of 1616–18 obliterated 70 to 90 percent of the Massachuset tribe. By the time the Puritans landed in 1630, the tribe numbered only 750 and would soon be further decimated by smallpox.[73] Far from containing quantities of fierce and hostile "savages", as the English had feared, the land was largely uninhabited. Into this land, over the next twenty years of the Great Migration, poured thousands of English settlers. The English population of the Massachusetts Bay Colony doubled and redoubled: 2000 in 1632, 4000 in 1634, 8000 in 1637.

Survival was a full time job for Eliot and his fellow immigrants. They had to protect themselves from the rigors of the New England winter, build houses, find food and fuel, all the while keeping a wary eye on their native neighbors. To Eliot fell the principal role in building and nourishing the new community at Roxbury as well as burdensome responsibilities in the wider affairs of the colony, including Harvard College. And he was, of course, raising his own family. It is hardly surprising that he did not focus on the Indians in his early years.

But to history he is forever "the Apostle to the Indians." Eliot nowhere records exactly what it was that crystallized his concern. But we may surmise a number of factors that conspired to arouse his interest. In his Great Patent (Charter) of 1620, King James I had laid upon English settlers at Plymouth the obligation of the "reducing and Conversion of such Savages as remaine wandering [it is unclear whether he knew about the 1616–18 plague or was speaking figuratively] in Desolacion and Distress to Civil Societie and Christian Religion."[74] In his 1629 charter of the "Governor and Company of the Massachusetts Bay in New England" (as the colony was called), King Charles I stated that "the *principall ende* of this plantation," both by "royall intention and the adventurers' free profession," was that their "good life and orderlie conversations maie wynn and incite the natives of [the] country to the knowledg and obedience of the onlie true God and Savior of mankinde and the Christian faythe."[75] If, as is extremely doubtful, it had ever been the colonists' principal aim to evangelize the Indians, they had been too busy surviving and establishing a new community in the wilderness to do anything about it. But John Eliot was a man of conscience; if others could "forget," he could not, especially as he came increasingly to see the Indians more as pitiful victims of the English invasion than as potentially dangerous predators. Having come to the New World to establish a City upon a Hill that would be an example and beacon to the England he had left behind, Eliot came more and more to feel that the new and purified church had an even greater obligation to be an example and beacon to the Indians.[76]

Eliot's interest in the Indians was enhanced by a (to us) curious anthropological aberration. Like many of his most enlightened contemporaries—Roger Williams, John Davenport, Edward Winslow, and the renowned scholar Rabbi Menasseh ben Israel of Amsterdam—Eliot gradually came to believe that the Indians were Jews, part of the ten lost tribes of Israel.[77] He shared the widely held Puritan belief that the conversion of the Jews would herald the Second Coming of Christ, and so he was predisposed to grasp at the available straws of evidence that the Indians were Jews.[78] He noted, for example, that like the Jews, the Indians spoke in parables, anointed their heads, enjoyed dancing, and disliked the pigs which the English had imported.[79] Writing to London benefactors, he recounted a story told him by Thomas Dudley: "He said that Captaine Cromwell . . . told him that he saw many Indians to the Southward Circumcised. . . ."[80] Bringing the Gospel to the Indians would not only enlighten and comfort them, therefore, it would also hasten the coming of Christ's Kingdom to earth.

Eliot was no racist. To him the Indians were—in our terminology— "*culturally* deprived." They lacked the Gospel and "civilitie" (enlightened education, habits, dress, etc.); but they were not, in his view, *racially* deprived.[81]

The numerical success of the Catholic missionaries in Canada has often been contrasted with the comparatively tiny number of Indians John Eliot and the other Puritan "missionaries" converted. The Jesuits and other Catholic orders were, of course, freed of all other duties in order to evangelize the natives; Eliot and the Puritans were missionaries in addition to being pastors and teachers of their own congregations

FIG. 15. The seal of the Massachusetts Bay Colony pictured an Indian from whose mouth are coming the the words, "Come over and help us." (Acts 16:9)

(who called them to and paid them for their parochial labors). While the Catholics quickly won over large numbers of Indians by beautiful liturgies and music, by distributing medals, and by baptizing in vast numbers, Eliot insisted absolutely that to become a church member each aspiring Indian must first understand the faith profoundly, decide to profess it publicly, and practice it obediently.[82] For Eliot there could be no shortcuts: to become a Christian, each Indian—one by one—would be required to go through a process that would require years of aspiration and effort. No missionary can ever have set more rigorous standards.

Except for the Mayhew family on Martha's Vineyard, Eliot was virtually alone in evangelizing the Indians in New England. There was no established pattern to follow; he had to invent his own methods. Years later, in his book *The Indian Grammar Begun*, Eliot explained how he learned the Algonquian language in his "spare" time from an intelligent Indian household servant:

> And a word or two to satisfie the prudent enquirer how I found out these new wayes of Grammar which no other learned language (so farre as I know) useth. . . . I found out (by God's wise providence) a pregnant witted young man [named Cockenoe], who had been a servant in an English home [in Dorchester], who pretty well understood our language, and hath clear pronunciation; him I made my Interpreter. By his help I translated the Commandments, the Lord's Prayer, and many texts of Scripture; also I compiled both Exhortations and Prayers by his help. I diligently marked the difference in their grammar from ours. When I found the way of them, I would pursue a Word, a Noun, a Verb through all the varietins I could think of. And thus I came at it. We must not sit down and hope for Miracles. Up and be doing, and the Lord will be with thee. Prayer and Pains, through Faith in Christ Jesus, will do anything.[83]

In September 1646, Eliot went to Dorchester Mills to try to communicate the faith to an Indian gathering. The results were disastrous: the Indians were unmoved and derided him.[84] But Eliot was not to be deterred. On October 28 he tried again, at the teepee of an Indian leader named Waban in Nonantum (in modern Newton near Watertown). This time he succeeded. We have Eliot's own account:

> Four of us [Eliot plus Thomas Shepard, Minister in Cambridge; Daniel Gookin, and probably John Wilson, Minister in Boston] (having sought God) went unto the Indians inhabiting within our bounds, with desire to make known the things of their peace to them. A little before we came to their Wigwams, five or six of the chief of them met us with English salutations, bidding us much welcome . . . leading us to the principall Wigwam of Waaubon, we found many more Indians, men, women, children, gathered

together from all quarters about, according to appointment, to meet with us, and learne of us. Waaubon, the chief minister of justice among them exhorting and inviting them . . . [who] since wee first began to deale seriously with him, hath voluntarily offered his eldest son to be educated and trained up in the knowledge of God. . . . [His son], now at school in Dedham . . . we found at this time standing by his father among the rest of his Indian brethren in English clothes.

We began with prayer, which now was in English, being not so farre acquainted with the Indian language as to express our hearts herein before God or them.

It was a glorious affecting spectacle to see a company of perishing, forlorne outcasts, diligently attending to the blessed word of salvation then delivered; professing they understood all that was taught them in their owne tongue. . . . For about an houre and a quarter the sermon continued, wherein [I] ran thorough [*sic*] all the principall matter of religion, beginning . . . with the ten Commandments, and a briefe explication of them, then shewing the . . . dreadfull wrath of God against all those who brake them . . . and so applyed it unto the conditions of the Indians present, with much sweet affection; and then preached Jesus Christ to them the onely meanes of recovery from sinne and wrath and eternall death, and what Christ was . . . and of the blessed estate of all those that by faith beleeve in Christ, and know him feelingly. [I] spoke to them also . . . about the creation and fall of man, about the greatnesse and infinite being of God, the maker of all things, about the joyes of heaven and the terrors . . . of hell, perswading them to repentance for severall sins which they live in . . . not medling with any matters more difficult . . . untill they had tasted and beleeved more plaine and familiar truths.

These things were spoken by [me] . . . borrowing now and then some small help from the Interpreter whom wee brought with us, and who could oftentimes express our minds more distinctly than any of us could; but this we perceived, that a few words from the Preacher were more regarded than many from the Indian Interpreter.

The next thing wee intended was . . . propounding certaine

questions to see what they would say to them, that so wee might skrue by variety of meanes something or other of God into them . . . whereupon several of them propounded . . . questions . . . *viz.* 1. What was the cause of Thunder. 2. The Ebbing and Flowing of the Sea. 3. Of the wind. . . . [But six questions struck us, of which the first was]:

How may wee come to know Jesus Christ?

Our first answer was, That if they were able to read our Bible, the book of God, therin they should see most cleerly what Jesus Christ was: but because they could not do that . . . we wisht them to . . . meditate [on what] had been taught them . . . and to think much and often upon it, both when they did lie downe on their Mats in their Wigwams, and when they rose up, and to goe alone in the fields and woods and muse on it, and so God would teach them, especially if they used a third helpe which was Prayer to God to teach them and reveale Jesus Christ unto them; and we told them that, although they could not make . . . long prayers as the English could, yet if they did but sigh or groane and say . . . Lord make me know Jesus Christ . . . againe and againe with their hearts that God would teach them Jesus Christ, because hee . . . will bee found of them that seeke him with all their hearts, and he is a God hearing the prayers of all men both Indian as well as English.

One Indian told Eliot that a fellow Indian had told him that "hee prayed in vaine, because Jesus Christ understood not what Indians speake in prayer." Eliot replied that God "made all things and makes all men, not onely English but Indian men," and then pointed out that the Indian basket next to the man was made of interwoven black and white straws. God made both the white man and the Indian and "knew all that was within" each one, "all his desires . . . , all his prayer."

Eliot then asked "Whether they did not desire to see God, and were not tempted to think there was no God, because they cannot see him?" Answering his own question, he

asked them if they saw a great Wigwam . . . would they think that Racoones or Foxes built it that had no wisedom? or would they think it made it selfe? or that no wise workman made it? . . . They would beleeve some wise workman made it though they did not see him. . . .

Thus after three hours thus spent with them, wee asked them if they were not weary, and they answered, No. But wee resolved to leave them with an appetite; the chief of them seeing us conclude with prayer, desired to know when wee would come againe, and wee appointed the time, [at the end giving] the children some apples and the men some tobacco and what else we then had at hand.[85]

Eliot strongly opposed the smoking of tobacco, and yet he was not unbending in the face of human weakness: knowing the Indians' love of tobacco, he gave a little to each of the men. Eliot visited Nonantum every few weeks; each visit followed the pattern described above, except that he added instruction of children as well. Eliot seems to have been especially tender towards children. He writes, after his second visit, "that so when wee came againe wee might see their profiting, the better to encourage them hereunto, wee therefore gave something to every childe."[86]

Each visit brought new questions: "How it comes to passe," they asked, for example, "that the Sea water was salt and the Land water fresh?" Eliot was on solid ground in answering, "'Tis so from the wonderfull worke of God, as why are Strawberries sweet and Cranberries soure. . . ." Yet when he ventured into more scientific explanations, it was a case of the blind leading the blind: Answering an Indian's question about why the waters did not overflow the earth, "We tooke an apple and thereby shewed them how the earth and water made one round globe like that apple; and how the sun moved about it. . . ."[87]

Each visit brought tears of joy and repentance from the Indians. Eliot describes one listener who fell "weeping more aboundantly by himselfe, which one of us perceiving, went to him, and spake to him encouraging words; at the hearing of which hee fell a weeping more and more. . . . So we resolved to goe againe both of us to him . . . and he there fell into more abundant renewed weeping . . . which forced us to such bowels of compassion that wee could not forbeare weeping over him also: and so wee parted greatly rejoicing for such sorrowing."[88] (Nonantum means "Rejoicing" in the Algonquian language.)

Eliot wrote to his friends in England that there were two significant differences between the English and the Indians:

> First, we know, serve, and pray unto God, and they doe not: Secondly, we labour and work in building, planting, clothing ourselves, &c. and they doe not: and would they but doe as wee doe in these things, they would be all one with English men.[89]

His strategy, then, was simple: to change their belief and their behavior. Or, as he put it: "I find it absolutely necessary to carry on civility with Religion."[90]

His tactics to achieve this strategy were two-fold, and he expressed them after his second visit to Waban:

> God having begun thus with some few it may bee that they are better soile for the Gospel than wee can thinke: I confesse I think no good will bee done till they bee more civilized, but why may not God begin with some few, to awaken others by degrees?[91]

His first tactic, then, was patience. He refused to be discouraged by small numbers and he was content to go a step at a time, winning the Indians over one by one, wigwam by wigwam. His second tactic was to work with the Indians simultaneously on Christian belief and behavior. (Naturally his concept of Christian behavior was conditioned, as it is for people of every place and time, by the limitations of his own background and culture.)

When Waban told Eliot that his people "desired some more ground to build a town together," Eliot wrote, "We did much like" the request, and he promised "to speak for them to the generall Court that they might possesse all the compasse of that hill, upon which their wigwams then stood." Eliot at once persuaded the General Court that this request was a sign that this particular group of Indians was prepared to become a settled Christian community. The Court in November 1646 granted them the land and appointed a commission to look into their needs.[92]

Eliot meanwhile was helping Waban and his community to establish "lawes," regulations against idleness, fornication, wife-beating, naked breasts, lice-killing with their teeth, etc.[93] These "lawes" encapsulated the "civility"—the standard of *behavior*—which Eliot believed was the necessary outgrowth of their acceptance of Christian *belief*.[94] Eliot was greatly moved to hear Waban and the other Indians praying in their own words (which Eliot had not taught them) for God's help to live up to the "lawes" they had now established:

> Amanaomen, Jehovah, tahassen metagh.
> Take away, Lord, my stony heart.
>
> Chechesom, Jehovah, kekowhogkow.
> Wash, Lord, my soule.[95]

Eliot continued to visit Waban's camp every other week throughout the winter. He and Waban—who, at forty-two, were exactly the same age[96]—obviously "hit it off." Eliot wrote in the parish record that "we never had a bad day to goe preach to the Indians all this winter, praised be the Lord."[97] Word of the Indians' enthusiastic response to Eliot quickly spread throughout the Colony. In May of the new year (1647), just seven months after he had begun his work, Eliot brought some of Waban's community to the synod of all the churches at Cambridge. That "the Lord Jesus [was] so much known and spoken of among such as never heard [of] him before" ... "did marvelously affect all the wise and godly Ministers, Magistrates, and people."[98]

Perhaps the most poignant vignette from Eliot's early Indian work is recounted in a letter of September 1647, in which he describes how, as was his custom, he asked at the end of one of his Indian meetings if there were questions:

> One was Wabbakoxets question, who is a reputed old Powwaw:
> ... seeing the English had been 27 yeers ... in this land, why did
> wee never teach them to know God until now? had you done it
> sooner, said hee, wee might have known much of God by this time,

and much sin might have been prevented, but now some of us are grown old in sin. . . . To whom we answered that we doe repent that wee did not long agoe, as now we do.[99]

This same letter contains Eliot's proposal for the founding of a medical school, in many ways an even more visionary proposal than his earlier one to D'Ewes for a college. The medical school at Harvard would not be founded for another 135 years—in 1782. This is what Eliot proposed to his potential contributors in England in 1647:

> It is a very needfull thing to informe [the Indians] in the use of Physick. . . . Some of the wiser sort I have stirred up to get this skill; I have showed them the anatomy of man's body, and some generall principles of Physick . . . but they are so extremely ignorant . . . that it were a singular good work, if the Lord would stirre up the hearts of some or other of his people in England to give some maintenance toward some schoole or Collegiate exercise this way, wherein there should be Anatomies and other instructions that way. . . . There is also another reason which moves my thought and desires this way, namely that our young [English] Students in Physick may be trained up better than yet they bee, who have only theoreticall knowledge.

Eliot also suggests that Indians who "bring in any vegetable or other thing that is vertuous in the way of Physick" (that is, herbs that might cure disease) should be compensated.[100]

Eliot's accounts of his work among the Indians—along with accounts by his admirers—were, bit by bit, being published in London in order to raise financial support. These accounts described how Waban's Indians were asking for schools to learn to read English, and had offered Eliot their children; how he taught them to use farming tools and ploughs, to keep cows and develop orchards, and to make and sell brooms, baskets, and other handicraft.[101] Schools and tools and animals were all costly.

In 1649—the year that saw the English Civil War concluded with the beheading of King Charles I and the triumph of Parliament—Parlia-

FIG. 16. John Eliot preaching to the Indians. Limestone relief on the facade of Congregational House, 14 Beacon Street, Boston

ment responded to Eliot's appeal by establishing the Society (often referred to as "the Corporation") for the Promoting and Propagating of the Gospel in New England. The Society had a governor and fourteen assistants, mostly affluent London merchants. One of these assistants, Thomas Bell, had been an early planter in Roxbury and a member of Eliot's church. He was a particularly generous supporter of Eliot's Indian work—and, as we shall see in Part II, also a strong supporter of Roxbury's school. Starting with a house-to-house collection throughout England, ordered by Parliament in 1649, the Society raised large sums for Eliot's work from all elements of the English church: established Anglican, as well as Puritan Congregational and Presbyterian. Since virtually no support was forthcoming from his fellow New Englanders, it was these English funds that would sustain Eliot's efforts.

Eliot saw Waban's Indians as the "first fruits," as the grain of mustard seed that would become a great bush. As fellow "sons of Adam" they could aspire to all the responsibilities and privileges of membership in a "gathered" church. As new Indians came to join Waban's, their land at Nonantum (even with that added by the Court in 1646) was too small to support their numbers. After lengthy searchings and discussions, Eliot finally persuaded the Court in 1650 to grant them an unsettled corner of the town of Dedham. This six thousand acres, known as the Natick territory, included much of modern Wellesley, Needham, Sherborn, and Natick. The enraged town of Dedham, after much complaining, was compensated with eight thousand acres in what, a generation later, became Deerfield.[102]

Eliot supervised the Indians in the establishment of their new settlement at Natick. At its center stood a 25x50-foot meetinghouse of two stories, larger than Roxbury's meetinghouse. It included a schoolroom in which Monequassun, a young Indian who had lived in Eliot's own home, taught both children and adults to read English and Algonquian. Above this room was a small bedroom for Eliot to sleep in on his fortnightly visits. The Indians revered Eliot and called upon him to settle disputes. They treated his room as a sacred place—though it had no lock—and stored their furs and other treasures there.[103] Natick was to be a "pattern and Copie . . . , to imitate in all the Countrey." Therefore, Eliot wrote, "great care lyeth upon me to set them straight at first, to lay a sure foundation for such a building, as I foresee will be built upon it. . . ."[104] Natick would be the model church-state: "I intend to direct them . . . to set up the Kingdome of Jesus Christ fully, so that Christ shall reyne both in Church and Commonwealth, both in Civil and Spiritual matters; we will . . . fly to the Scriptures, for every Law, Rule, Direction, Form, or what ever we do."[105]

Eliot and his fellow Puritans "flew to the Scriptures" for just about everything: in Massachusetts even the size of a beer barrel was determined by a regulation in Deuteronomy![106] Naturally, since he regarded the Indians as the descendants of the lost tribes of Israel, Eliot turned to the Hebrew Scripture when he established for them a form of governance: Exodus 18:17–26, where Jethro tells Moses how to govern by delegation of authority. Following this pattern, the Natick Indians had one ruler for every one hundred men, then two sub-rulers of each fifty, then ten subrulers of each ten.[107]

Eliot believed that what had been achieved at Natick was nothing less than the quintessential model Christian government—not only for the Indians, but also for the people of England—who had overthrown the monarchy of Charles I. To describe this biblically-based government, therefore, he dashed off a pamphlet entitled *The Christian Commonwealth*. In it he advised the English to let "the holy Scriptures of God onely . . . be your onley Magna Charta, by which you should be ruled in all things" as was now the case in Natick, and to "set the Crown of England upon the head of Christ, whose only true inheritance it is."[108] Unfortunately, nearly a decade elapsed before the book was published in England in 1659, just as the monarchy was being restored. New Englanders had enjoyed considerable independence under the 1629 charter of Charles I; the accession of Charles II filled them with anxiety. Would the new king annul the charter and restrict their freedom? They feared Eliot's pamphlet would antagonize the new monarch, and in 1661 the colonial governor and council forced Eliot to recant publicly any notions in the pamphlet that seemed to attack earthly monarchy as a legitimate form of government. His recantation was displayed throughout the Colony, and all copies of the pamphlet were confiscated.[109]

Eliot himself wrote the Covenant by which the Natick Indians dedicated their new community to God. Each element of the Covenant had been discussed at length in advance, so the solemn dedication meeting of September 24, 1651, marked the culmination of much arduous planning and effort. As we might expect, Eliot's Covenant articulates the Puritan ideal of the church-state which he hoped would be realized at Natick. The English translation reads as follows:

> We doe give our selves and our Children unto God to be his people, he shall rule us in all our affaires, not onely in our religion, and affaires of the Church (these we desire as soone as we can, if God will) but also in all our works and affaires in this world, God shall

rule over us. Isa. 33,22. The Lord is our Judge; the Lord is our Law giver; the Lord is our King, He will save us; the Wisedome which God hath taught us in his Booke, that shall guide us and direct us in the way. O Jehovah, teach us wisedome to finde out thy wisedome in thy Scriptures, let the Grace of Christ helpe us, because Christ is the wisedome of God, send thy spirit into our hearts, and let it teach us, Lord take us to be thy people, and let us take thee to be our God.[110]

In 1651 Governor John Endecott rode forty miles on horseback to see the Natick settlement and came away amazed.

> The Foundation is laid, and one that I verily beleeve the gates of Hell shall never prevaile against. . . . I could hardly refrain tears from very joy to see their diligent attention to the word first taught by one of the Indians, who before his Exercise prayed . . . with such reverence, zeale, good affection, and distinct utterance, that I could not but admire it.[111]

Eliot was now ready to have his fellow clerics come to Natick to test the Indians and "to discern the Reality of Grace" in them. Leading ministers assembled all day October 13, 1652, to test the Indians' progress in faith. In his tract, "Tears of Repentence," published in England and dedicated to Oliver Cromwell, Eliot describes the occasion in vivid detail.[112] A modern reader is astonished by the level of theological sophistication in these new and mostly illiterate converts. Few modern Congregationalists could give testimonies as profound and affecting as the Indians who spoke that day. Nevertheless, the visiting Puritan divines decided that it would be wrong for the Indians to have a church "on a sudden" and counseled further study and prayer.[113]

In his preface to the Indian testimonies, Eliot again reminded his readers that he was not attracting thousands to the faith, but rather working with one small community that it might be a beacon for all Indians, and an inspiration to all Christians.

> It is a day of small things with us [that God is making] the single beauty of his humbling Grace to shine in them, that are the veriest

> ruines of mankind that are known on earth (as Mr. Hooker was
> wont to describe the forlorn condition of these poor Indians). I see
> evident demonstrations that Gods Spirit by his word hath taught
> them, because their expressions both in Prayer and in the Confes-
> sions which I have now published, are far more, and more full, and
> spiritual . . . than ever I was able to express to them; in that poor
> broken manner of Teaching which I have used among them.[114]

Eliot and his fellow ministers did not condescend: the highest standards would be applied—probably higher than were being applied in
English congregations even in that rigorously pious time. There would
be no instant Christians. The Indians would have to demonstrate—in
further public testimonies in succeeding years—the permanence as well
as the depth of their conversion. It would, in fact, take until 1660, ten
long years after the founding of Natick—fourteen years after Eliot's
first preachments to them at Nonantum—for them to attain their own
church and equal status as Christians with their English mentors.[115]

We can but marvel at the patience of Eliot and his co-workers as they
struggled to help the Natick Indian community win a church of equal
status with that of the English community. Natick—because of its
proximity to Roxbury—was the showcase of Eliot's Indian work, but by
the 1660s there were thirteen other Indian "praying towns" (as they
were commonly known) at various stages of development. Eliot visited
them all. The visits took many hours on horseback and were cold and
wet in winter. He was absent for days at a time each week from his family and parish.

There were times of discouragement—of terrible loneliness—as
Eliot was willing to admit. In 1651, for example, he wrote to friends in
England: "The truth is [the Indian work] is one discouragement to me
. . . that so few looke after what we doe, or so much as ask about it." And
yet he always found strength from God to go on:

> I find recompense enough to my soule in the work it selfe, and the
> joy of the Lord is my strength in this particular, whatever else the
> Lord casteth in . . . is more than I ever expected when I sett upon

this work and I humbly blesse the Lord who caryeth my soule above all discouragement.[116]

As early as 1649 Eliot had begun to express his conviction that the Indians needed a Bible in their own language.[117] In the earlier years, feeling that the Indians could not "possess" the Bible through preaching alone, he instituted the teaching of English among them in order that they might read it. But further experience taught him that learning a new religion was hard enough without also having to learn a new language. By 1653 he determined that the Bible must be translated into their language and that he must do it. When King James I had commissioned the English Bible (published in 1611) he had summoned fifty-four of England's greatest scholars to undertake what was regarded as a stupendous task. Eliot now took upon himself alone the burden of translating—from the original Hebrew and Greek—the entire Bible into a language he had only recently tried to understand and learn.

When one considers the demands placed upon Eliot by his own burgeoning congregation in Roxbury, and, on top of that, the care of the hundreds of "praying Indians" scattered long horseback rides distant from Roxbury, this new undertaking staggers the imagination. And, at times, the burden he had placed upon himself nearly broke him. In the first year (1653) of his decade-long effort, he could, for example, write to his friend Thomas Thorowgood:

> I have had a great lingering desire . . . that our Indian language might be sanctified by the translation of the holy Scriptures into it . . . but I fear it will not be obtained in my dayes. I cannot stick to the work, because of my necessary attendance to my ministrie in Roxbury and among the Indians in sundry places.[118]

But somehow he found the time, the energy, and the courage, cutting his teeth the following year by producing—in Algonquian—a *Catechism* or primer of faith, the first of his many Indian works.

By early 1658 he was able to write to this same man (Thorowgood), with whom he had shared his discouragement, this exultant note: "The whole book of God is translated into their own language; it wanteth nothing but revising, transcribing, and printing. Oh, that the Lord would so move, that by some means or other it may be printed."[119] The Lord did so move, with a good deal of help from Eliot's own forceful fund-raising. Financing came entirely from England: the Society (established, as described, by Parliament in 1649 and re-chartered at the restoration of Charles II) paid the entire cost of printing the Bible by the Cambridge Press at Harvard, and for the twenty-nine-year period from 1660 to 1689 raised an average of £400 a year to support the Indian work of Eliot and others.[120]

In 1661, the same year Eliot recanted the "seditious" antimonarchial views he had expressed in *The Christian Commonwealth*, his Indian New Testament was published—prominently dedicated to the restored monarch Charles II. Two years later, in 1663, 1500 copies of the entire Bible—in 1180 two-column pages—came off the press, the first Bible published in the New World. Its Indian title: *Mamusse Wunneetupanatamwe Up-Biblum God*. Renowned scientist Robert Boyle, governor of the Society, presented a beautifully bound copy to King Charles II.

> I waited this day upon the King with your translation of the Bible, which, I hope I need not tell you, he received according to his custome very gratiously. But though he looked a pretty while upon it, and shewd some things in it to those that had the honour to be about him in his bed-chamber, into which he carryd it. Yet the Unexpected comming in of an Extraordinary Envoye from the Emperour hindred me from receiving that fuller expression of his grace towards the translators and Dedicators that might otherwise have been expected.

In 1989, the Trustees of The Roxbury Latin School purchased, from Christie's sale of the estate of the Countess Doheny, what is believed to be this very copy.[121]

Once Eliot finished the Bible, he turned his attention to translating other literature, including Baxter's *Call to the Unconverted* (1664) and *Godly Living*, an abridged version of Bayly's *Practice of Piety* (1665). At Boyle's request he produced *The Indian Grammar Begun* in 1666, which

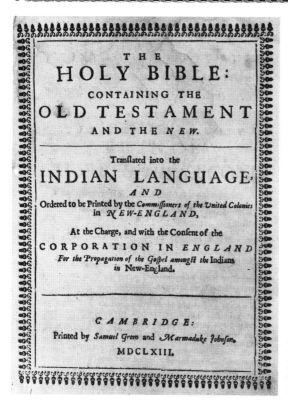

THE
HOLY BIBLE:
CONTAINING THE
OLD TESTAMENT
AND THE *NEW*.

Tranflated into the

INDIAN LANGUAGE
AND
Ordered to be Printed by the *Commiffioners of the United Colonies*
in *NEW-ENGLAND*,

At the Charge, and with the Confent of the

CORPORATION IN *ENGLAND*
For the Propagation of the Gofpel amongft the Indians
in New-England.

CAMBRIDGE:
Printed by *Samuel Green* and *Marmaduke Johnfon*,
MDCLXIII.

FIG. 17. Title page of the School's copy of Eliot's Indian Bible, 1663. It is probably the copy presented by Robert Boyle to King Charles II.

set out, in textbook style, the Algonquian language.[122] Historically the most interesting of these small works is *The Indian Primer* of 1669. With the Royal Arms of King Charles II displayed on the first and last pages, this textbook is essentially an Algonquian translation of the Colony's standard catechism, *The New England Primer*, published in England for North American use.[123]

Eliot founded schools—such as Monequassun's at Natick—in the praying towns, hoping that such schools would produce students capable of attending a grammar school, such as the one he had founded at Roxbury in 1645, and then the College. From 1655 to 1664 the "Commissioners of the United Colonies" (who represented the Society for the Propagation of the Gospel in New England on this side of the

Atlantic) provided sizable annual grants to Roxbury's master, Daniel Weld, "for the diett and teaching of Indian boys" and, on at least one occasion, "one gerle." Much as we would like to picture these young Indians learning side by side in school with their white contemporaries, it is far more probable that Weld was paid by the Commissioners to teach them "on the side."[124] The record (doubtless incomplete) shows that from 1655 to 1664 Weld received at least forty annual "diett and teaching" tuitions from the Commissioners for (sadly, unnamed) Indian students. We have no way of knowing how many of these are repeats (students who studied with him more than a year).[125] Nor do we know what happened next for any of these students, except in one case (in 1662) in which a student went on to the Cambridge grammar school. Of all the Indians placed with English schoolmasters at Roxbury and elsewhere, only a few made it to Harvard and only one graduated.[126]

Eliot's devoted co-worker, Daniel Gookin, explains some of the reasons why these efforts at integrating Indians into the English educational system were such a failure:

> Some of the choice Indian students were put to school with English schoolmasters, to learn both the English, Latin, and Greek Tongues. [The Society supported the cost.] In truth, the design was prudent, noble, and good; but it proved ineffectual to the ends proposed. For several of the said youth died, after they had been sundry years at learning and made a good progress therein. Others were disheartened and left learning after they were almost ready for college. And some returned to live among their countrymen, where some of them are improved for schoolmasters and teachers. . . . Some others have entered other callings. . . . I remember but two of them that lived at the college in Cambridge. . . . Of this disease of consumption, sundry of these Indian youths died, that we bred up in school among the English. . . . A hecktic fever, issuing in a consumption, is a common and mortal disease among them. I know some have apprehended other causes of the mortality of these Indian scholars. Some have attributed it unto the great change upon their bodies, in respect of their diet, lodging, apparel,

studies, so much different to what they were inured to among their own countrymen.[127]

The trauma that resulted from wrenching children from an Indian to a white way of life was often—quite simply—unendurable.

No New England whites, however, were willing to leave their own communities to live permanently among the Indians as teachers or ministers. Eliot was therefore driven to rely on Indians for these purposes. Twenty-four Indians in Eliot's time went through the arduous process of ordination; an unknown but sizable number of others became teachers.

To instruct them in the faith and in the art of teaching, in 1671 Eliot hastily produced (in English) his *Indian Dialogues* "for the instruction in the great service of Christ, in calling home their country-men to the knowledge of God, and of themselves." In 1672 this was followed by *The Logic Primer* "to initiate the Indians in the Knowledge and rule of Reason," a handbook of logic and disputation as he had learned it at Cambridge. From our twentieth century perspective, this work seems utterly irrelevant to Indian life, but, as always, Eliot refused to condescend. Even though these were Indian teachers who would be working among simple folk, they were to be fully clothed with a thorough knowledge of both divine revelation and human reason.

Though his Natick Indian church had been received into full fellowship with the English churches in 1660, the parishes were segregated. Eliot continued to hope that they would not remain so. He expressed this remarkable—anachronistic—aspiration in 1673 in a letter to the Reverend Thomas Shepard, Jr., of Charlestown:

> Onc when I was at the vinyard, I administered the Sacraments in the English church, and they accepted the Indian church to joyne with them. I tould them that Christ did first please to beautyfy this his little Spouse [i.e., the Church], with this Jewel of love to imbrace into their communion the Indian converts, in church order. Another time I administered the Sacraments in the Indian church. and such of the English church as saw meet, joyned with us.

Brother if you know not, you may know how I have moved and argued among the Elders, that it will be an act of honour to Christ, to the churches, and to yourselves, and but a fit, yea necessary incouragement unto the work, to accept them into your communion, whom the Lord so manifestly undenyably accepted.[128]

The following year, 1674, Eliot and his coworker Daniel Gookin decided to undertake their own experiment in integration. There was a tract of land in Marlborough that was quite close both to the English town and to a nearby Indian settlement. They proposed that the Society build here an "Indian free school" taught—at the expense of the Society—by an English schoolmaster who could live in the English town. "Morever," wrote Gookin, "it is very probable that the English people at Marlborough will gladly and readily send their children to the same school"—paying fees. "The English and Indian children, learning together in the same school, will much promote the Indians' learning to speak the English tongue, of which we have had experience when Indian children were taught by English schoolmasters at Roxbury and Cambridge in former years when several Indian children were kept at those schools at the great charge of the Society."[129] A huge additional advantage was that the school's nearness would enable the Indian students to continue to live at home in familiar surroundings and with familiar food.

But it was not to be. Just as this experiment was about to be tried, just as Eliot's Roxbury congregation moved into a new meeting house, just as fourteen praying Indian villages totalling eleven hundred souls[130] began to flourish, just as Eliot had given the Indians their own Bible and a raft of textbooks and other aids, just as he turned seventy, came King Philip's War of 1675, a conflict that would leave his Indian work in ruins.

King Philip was the name by which Metacom, leader of the Wampanoag tribe, was popularly known. The essential cause of this disastrous war was Metacom's realization that the white man was advancing and the Indian retreating. He made up his mind to buck this tide or to die in the process. The result was the most costly war ever fought on this continent—to the Indians and certainly to the English (as they still called themselves): per capita, more lives were lost and more property destroyed than in any future war in North America. It was also the most violent: the Indians "scalped" the English, cut off their heads and put them on poles, ripped open their stomachs, and cut off their fingers and wore them around their necks; and the English responded with equal savagery.[131]

The English population was largely overcome with hysterical paranoia regarding *all* Indians, not unlike the fear of Japanese Americans which gripped the United States in 1941 and led to the internment of these possible "enemies within." Public uproar resulted in Eliot's (almost entirely loyal[132]) praying Indians being suddenly packed off (in no small part to protect them from hotheaded whites) to conditions of utter misery—cold, disease, imprisonment—on Deer Island in Boston Harbor.

Eliot and Gookin, who ministered to the Indians in their miserable dislocation, were called traitors by their fellow whites and threatened with violence.[133] In the Roxbury Church records Eliot describes one visit to the Indians at Deer Island:

> On our way thither, a great boat of about 14 ton, meeting us, turned hard upon us (whether willfully or by negligence, God knoweth) [and rammed] the stern of the boat where we . . . sat, under water. . . . I so sunke that I drank salt water twice, and could not help it. God assisted my two cousins to deliver us all and help us into the great boat. . . . We went ashore, dryed, and refreshed, and then went to the Iland, and performed our work, and returned well home at night, praise the Lord. Some thanked God and some wished we had been drowned.[134]

It is a tribute to Eliot's Roxbury congregation that they remained loyal to their minister, even when he was vilified up and down the colony.

Nothing could dissuade Eliot from taking unpopular stands in the cause of right. When popular sentiment clamored to sell captive

Indians into slavery, Eliot petitioned the governor and council, warning that

> the terror of selling away such Indians . . . for perpetual slaves . . . may produce, we know not what evil consequences, upon all the land. Christ hath saide, blessed are the mercyfull, for they shall obtaine mercy. . . . When we came, we declared to the world . . . the indeavour of the Indians conversion, not their exstirpation. . . . My humble request is that you would follow Christ his designe, in this matter, to promote the free passage of Religion among them, and not to destroy them. . . . To sell soules for money seemeth to me a dangerous merchandise.[135]

By the time the fifteen-month war ended in August 1676 with King Philip's death, all the praying towns had been either severely damaged or destroyed and their former inhabitants devastated by death, disease, disillusionment, and alcohol. Only four praying towns (reduced to three in 1681) were rebuilt and resettled. When the war ended, the English were entirely preoccupied in dealing with their own staggering financial losses and rebuilding their own lives. Only Eliot—his life's work in ruins—seemed to care about the devastated Indians.

Aged though he was, Eliot threw himself wholeheartedly into rebuilding the praying towns. In the Roxbury Church records, Eliot describes how virtually all the first edition Indian Bibles had been lost in the war:

> When the Indians were hurried away to an Iland at half an hours warning, the pore soales in terror left theire goods, books, bibles, only some few carried bibles; the rest were spoyled & lost so that when the wares were finished, & they returned to their places, they were greatly impoverished, but they especially bewailed their want of Bibles, which made me meditate upon a second impression of the Bible.[136]

Eliot now pushed the Society to print a second edition. But the New England mood was anything but supportive of such an effort for the Indians, and many in both England and New England felt that the

Indians should learn English. But Eliot pressed on:

> [I] tooke pains to revise the first edition. I also intreated Mr. John
> Cotton to help in that work, he having obtained some ability so to
> doe. He read over the whole Bible, & whatever doubts he had, he
> writ them down in order, & gave them to me, to try them . . . over
> among the Indians. I obtained the favor of a reprint of the New
> Testament and psalmes, but I met with much obstruction for
> reprinting the Old Testament, yet by prayre to God, Patience &
> intreatye, I at last obtained it also, praised be the Lord.[137]

The following letter to Sir Robert Boyle, the Society's head, is typical of Eliot's relentless importunings. It was written in 1683 while he was
trying to raise funds to publish the Old Testament.

> Your hungry alumns do cry unto your honour for the milk of the
> word in the whole book of God, and . . . are very grateful for what
> they have, and importunately desirous to enjoy the whole book of
> God. It is the greatest charity in the world to provide for their
> souls. . . . My age makes me importunate. I shall depart [life]
> joyfully, may I but leave the bible among them, for it is the word of
> life; and there be some goodly souls among them that live thereby.
> The work is under great incumberments and discouragements. My
> heart hath much ado to hold up my head.[138]

After scraping together what money he could and loading himself
with debt, Eliot authorized the printer to go ahead with the Old Testament. Fortunately for him, the Society eventually came through with
funds to cover the cost. The second edition of the whole Bible finally
appeared in 1685, after nine years of incessant begging by the now
eighty-one-year-old Eliot.

Historians over the centuries have reached widely disparate conclusions in evaluating Eliot's work among the Indians. Some have compared his efforts unfavorably with those of the Catholic missionaries in
the north. Such a comparison, as we noted above, is unfair for at least
two reasons. Unlike the Catholic missionaries who were "full-time,"
Eliot could only work with the Indians "part-time." He continued to

bear the onerous burden of ministering to an ever-increasing white congregation. And Eliot's aim was not to take his converts "unawares" and admit them at once to baptism and the Lord's Supper. To become a Christian, each individual Indian would have to make in informed choice: each would first have to know the faith as revealed in the Bible, and then profess and live it over a sustained period before being admitted to the fellowship. Such exalted standards made it inevitable that "success" could come only to relatively small numbers and only after a protracted period, and that the rate of "failure" would be high.[139] Eliot's task was also harder than that of the (quantitatively more successful) Mayhew family Indian missionaries on Martha's Vineyard. Their environment was more sheltered; Eliot had the tougher task of working with Indians in an area where a dynamic white population was increasing geometrically while the Indians were more and more marginalized.

When historians have judged Eliot on his own terms, they have generally regarded his work up to King Philip's War as a great success. Most, however, have gone on to speak of his ultimate "failure" when they view his work in ruins at the war's end.

Discouraged as Eliot might be, he did not talk of failure. Even if only one soul had been saved as a result of his efforts, he would have regarded his work as worthwhile.[140] But, in actuality, the numbers do not demonstrate a "failure."[141] Eight years after Eliot's death, statistics of the New England Company revealed "some thirty congregations of praying Indians, which were served by thirty-seven full-time native preachers, teachers, and catechists and only seven or eight native-speaking English ministers, usually on a part-time basis." By the outbreak of the American Revolution a century later, "there had been at various times in New England twenty-two Indian churches, ninety-one praying towns or reservations, seventy-two white missionaries, and 133 native preachers and teachers." Most of these latter, like their white colleagues, ministered to a single congregation.[142] As historian James Axtell remarks, "The other colonies fell far short of [Eliot's] standard for both conversion and civilization."[143]

Two issues remain to be considered. Why did these Indians become Christians? And was their conversion a good or bad thing for *them?*

There has been a good deal of Puritan-bashing by historians over the last quarter century, and Eliot has been a particular target. These revisionists paint a picture of the "noble savage" luxuriating in a life of utopian happiness in the woods until the European arrived to destroy his paradise. To these historians, Eliot's Christianity was merely a front for the political and social imperialism that overwhelmed the hapless native; his expression of concern for the Indian nothing other than hypocritical "cant."[144]

This revisionist view has had a stimulating effect on contemporary historians, but has by no means found universal acceptance. James Axtell, for example, addresses the question of why the Indians, in the face of overwhelming difficulties, became Christians. Axtell notes that Eliot's extremely high standards alone erected discouraging barriers, and that strong sociological factors also militated against the conversion of the Indians. The Puritans despised idleness and leisure and constantly harped on the virtues of hard work when they attempted to "civilize" the Indians. The Indian way of life was more "laid back": "Familiar ways were softer [for the Indians], psychically safer, and socially smoother than the new [Christian ways]. . . . The 'fear of what others would say' was a potent factor in the oral intimacy of woodland society [and the converts dreaded the ridicule of their kinsmen if they converted]. . . . Even the missionaries' promise that converts would eventually go to the Christian heaven carried the implicit threat of separation from loved ones and relatives in the traditional land of the dead. 'We are well as we are,' protested a Massachuset woman, 'and desire not to be troubled with these new wise sayings.' The sharp exclusivity of Christianity in all things—ritual, morality, afterlife—was [a problem]. . . . It made little sense to put one's whole trust in such novelties until they could be tested by time." To convert also entailed submitting to new wise men from an alien culture, and giving up many familiar pleasures.[145]

What made these Indians overcome all these obstacles to conversion? Christians might respond, of course, that the Indians—as people of other races and nations before and since—discovered in this new religion something that, though costly and demanding, gave them a far greater sense of the meaning of life than their own religion. But such an answer might not satisfy a non-Christian. The non-Christian would, perhaps, be more moved by James Axtell's thesis that "Christianity provided a better—comparatively better—answer to the urgent social and religious questions that the Indians were facing *at this particular juncture in their cultural history.*"[146] Still others might cite the palpable reality of John Eliot's love for them, an affection that drew the response of affection and led them to open themselves to all he tried to offer them.[147]

No one can answer this second question—was the Indians' conversion a good or bad thing?—in a definitive way that will satisfy all. We can paint romanticized pictures of the pre-invasion "noble savage," and we can lament the arrival of the Europeans. But we cannot turn back the pages of history. The English came, saw, and conquered. Given the new realities of their existence (and here we speak *not* from a Christian viewpoint), adopting Christian religion and civilization was objectively the Indians' best hope for survival. Axtell writes, "So thoroughly were they crippled by the plague of 1616–18, and so thoroughly overrun by the colonial juggernaut in the following two decades, that only John Eliot's program of moral rearmament, social reconstruction, and religious vitalization was capable of saving them from ethnic annihilation."[148]

One benefit—unintended by Eliot, perhaps, at least for the long run—was the preservation of their lives together as Indians. As Axtell points out, "Even though [conversion] entailed wholesale cultural changes from the life they had known before [the English arrived], it preserved their ethnic identity as particular Indian groups on familiar pieces of land that carried their ethnic history. At the cost of a certain amount of material and spiritual continuity with the past, their acceptance of Christianity—however complete or sincere—allowed them not only to survive in the present but gave them a long lease on life when their colonial landlords threatened to foreclose all future options."[149]

5. *As He Taught, He Lived*

In his charter for the Governor and Company of the Massachusetts Bay in New England, King Charles I declared the "the principall ende of this plantation" was for the new colonists, by their "good life and orderlie conversation, [to] wynn and incite the natives of [the] country to . . . the Christian faythe." That was his "royall intention" in granting the charter, and that was "the adventurers free [i.e., voluntary] profession" in going there.[150]

In the colony's early days, not a single settler, even John Eliot, seems to have remembered what Charles I had declared to be the "principall ende" of the settlement. It was, in fact, because of the Catholic direction of the King's reforms in England that most of them left their native land. Their real "principall ende" was to form an uncorrupted apostolic City upon a Hill in the New World. The Indians were far from their minds, except as a potential danger to their survival.

What is remarkable about John Eliot is that, after he had established a flourishing parish, encouraged and overseen the Colony's first college, and founded its most enduring grammar school, he did not sit back to enjoy the fruits and prestige of his labor. Rather, in his fifteenth year in the New World, he turned his energies—as no one else in the Bay Colony had yet done—to the original "principall ende of this plantation," the welfare of its native population. This inconvenient and costly commitment added immense hardship to an already overburdened life. He received scant support—spiritual or financial—from his fellow colonists, and often, in fact, endured their derogation and enmity for his work among the Indians.

All significant actors on the stage of history are "reviewed" and judged by those who follow. The intrinsic merit of Eliot's ideas and plans for the Indians—and the effectiveness of their execution—are

FIG. 18. The Eliot School in Jamaica Plain was established by Eliot's Deed of Gift in 1689 "for the teaching and Instructing of the Children of that end of the Town (together with such Negroes or Indians as may or shall come . . .)." Leo Abdalian Collection, Boston Public Library, 1920.

fair game for future generations to evaluate; critics will draw varying conclusions. Like all men and women in every age, Eliot was subject to the limitations of his own time and place. But his *intention* was entirely noble: he sought to help the natives of America achieve a better and happier life and he selflessly poured out his energies to achieve that goal.

Nor at the end did he rest. Now in his eighties, as African slaves became more and more numerous in Boston, Eliot turned his vestigial energies to their condition. Mather writes that he lamented

> with a bleeding and burning passion, that the English used their negroes [as if they were] their horses or their oxen, and that so little care was taken about their immortal souls; he looked upon it as

FIG. 19. Boys of the School laying a wreath on Eliot's tomb in Dudley Square, Roxbury, on May 17, 1946, a celebration of the school's 300th anniversary, delayed by World War II.

FIG. 20. Timothy Killgoar, president of the Class of 1995, laying a wreath on the Founder's tomb on Founder's Day, November 2, 1994.

a [wonder] that any wearing the name of Christians, should so much have the heart of devils in them, as to prevent and hinder the instruction of the poor blackamores, and confine the souls of their miserable slaves to a destroying ignorance, meerly for fear of thereby losing the benefit of their vassalage; but now he made a motion to the English within two or three miles of him, that at such a time and place they [could] send their negroes once a week unto him: for he would then catecise them, and enlighten them, to the utmost of his power in the things of their everlasting peace.[151]

His concern for the negro was prominent also in his gift to what is now called the Eliot School—then as now located in Jamaica Plain (at that time a section of the town of Roxbury). In 1676 Eliot had helped found a school there for students "who by reason of their remoteness from the School in the said Roxbury towne street [in the eastern part of the town] cannot receive like benefit and advantage from said schoole with others who live nearer to the same." By Deed of Gift in 1689 he gave this new school seventy-five acres of his own land: "for the teaching and Instructing of the Children of that end of the Town (*together [with] such Negroes or Indians as may or shall come* to the said Schoole)."[152] In almost the last act of his life, therefore, Eliot expressed again his long-cherished hope (for Harvard, Roxbury Latin, the ill-fated Anglo-Indian school at Marlborough, and now the Eliot School) of integrated education.

His final days were taken up in this work and in teaching a blind boy the Scripture and Latin. As he lay dying, his own focus remained, as ever, on the things of eternal peace. On May 20, 1690—after he had uttered the words "Welcome Joy"—he urged those at his bedside to "Pray, Pray, Pray!" and died.[153]

His remains have lain ever since in the parish grave—marked with his name—at the burial ground in Roxbury's Dudley Square, and still, from time to time today, the boys of Roxbury Latin place flowers there.

Notes to Part One

1. Henry F. Waters, *Genealogical Gleanings in England* (Boston: New England Historic Genealogical Society, 1901), II: 904–05: "For the space of eight years from the time of my decease quarterly to pay my son John Elliott the sum of eight pounds a year . . . for and towards his maintenance in the University of Cambridge where he is now a scholar."

2. The Nazeing Parish Register (Essex County Records Office, Chelmsford: microfilm) records the dates of the burial of "Lettes Ellyot" as 16 March 1620/21 and that of "Benet Eliot" as 21 November 1621.

3. Cotton Mather, *Magnalia Christi Americana* (Hartford: Silas Andrus, 1855), I: 529. (The River Lethe passage three paragraphs above is also found on this page.) See also Deryck Collingwood, "The Founder's Formative Years, Part I," *The Roxbury Latin School Newsletter* 65, 3 (April 1992) who advances some highly suggestive conjectures as to the influence of historic events and local traditions on Eliot as a boy.

4. See J. and J. A. Venn, *Alumni Cantabrigienses* (Cambridge: Cambridge U. Press, 1922), Part I, ii, 491, on Edward Judd (or, variously, Jude) vicar of Nazeing 1608–1640. Although Judd matriculated at Emmanuel in 1596, he received his bachelor of arts from St. John's in 1600. See also Collingwood, "The Formative Years, Part I," 15. See also F. G. Emmison, *Elizabethan Life: Morals and the Church Courts* (Chelmsford: Essex County Council, 1973), 194, on how John Hopkins was in 1589 deprived as vicar of Nazeing for his Puritan views, a fairly rare occurrence. The term "Puritan" was not much used before the 1560s — when it was invented by their enemies as a description of excessive piety and zeal. On Puritan literacy, see David Hackett Fischer, *Albion's Seed* (New York: Oxford U. Press, 1989), 130–31.

5. See especially the fine short book by William Haller, *Elizabeth I and the Puritans* (Washington, D.C.: Folger Books, 1964). On the "clashing ambiguities" of the Puritan reforms (their desire to lead "ancient lives" of apostolic purity and their freeing themselves from corrupt old ways to be successful), see Roger Thompson, *Mobility and Migration, East Anglian Founders of New England, 1629–1640* (Amherst: U. of Massachusetts Press, 1994), 231–32.

6. For the Winthrop-Dudley statement, see "The Puritans' Farewell to England, Being The Humble Request of the Governor and Company of the Massachusetts-Bay in New England about to depart upon the Great Emigration, April 6, 1630" (1912 reprint, New York: New England Society of New York). For the Higginson statement, see Mather, *Magnalia* I: 362.

7. For the date of Eliot's matriculation, see UA/Matr. 2 in the Cambridge University Library; it was evidently just before the new master of Jesus, Roger Andrewes, started the college register. For a discussion of Jesus College in Eliot's time, see Arthur Gray and Frederick Brittain, *A History of Jesus College Cambridge* (Lon-

don: Heinemann, 1979) especially 61–66, 71. Ola E. Winslow and others err in describing Jesus College as "anti-Puritan" or "high church." It did not become so until well after Eliot was in North America, under the mastership of the Laudian Sterne. In 1642 it gave Charles I its silver plate to support his cause.

8.   Samuel Eliot Morison, *The Founding of Harvard College* (Cambridge: Harvard U. Press, 1935), 26

9.   For most of the information in this paragraph I rely on William T. Costello, *The Scholastic Curriculum of Early Seventeenth Century Cambridge* (Cambridge: Harvard U. Press, 1958). For the final sentence, see especially 149.

10. U.A./Matr. 2 (not paginated), Cambridge University Library. The Old Style calendar was still in effect which meant the year did not change until March 25 (the Feast of the Annunciation). So Eliot was *not*, as Ola Elizabeth Winslow, *John Eliot, "Apostle to the Indians"* (Boston: Houghton Mifflin, 1968), 14, suggests, "several months before his fourteenth birthday." See Morison, *The Founding of Harvard College*, 25, for average age of entry, and 378 for Eliot.

11. See Winslow, *John Eliot*, 13; and J. and J. A. Venn, *Alumni Cantab.*, I, xv: By 1600 "every boy, even in the remotest parts of the country, could find a place of education in his own neighborhood competent at any rate to fit him to enter college." Nicholas Orme, *English Schools in the Middle Ages* (London: Methuen, 1973), 323, says that by the Middle Ages there were seven grammar schools in Essex. Historian Deryck Collingwood noted to me in a letter of 8 February 1994, that the Puritan rectors often founded their own mini-grammar schools. Thomas Boyle instructed village boys at Tilton-on-the-Hill, Leicestershire, in Hooker's time. Robert Challoner, who married Hooker and his wife Susannah, held such a school in his rectory—which grew into the grammar school still in existence today in Amersham. He concludes, "When I first visited Nazeing, I met the retired Town Clerk cum local historian (now deceased) who told me he thought John [Eliot] was first educated at All Saints [Nazeing] by the vicar, and called it an embryo grammar school."

12. This paragraph is based on Morison, *The Founding of Harvard College*, 63–64.

13. Morison, *The Founding of Harvard College*, 74.

14. Mather, *Magnalia* I: 546. The celebrated Dutch philologist Jean Leusden dedicated his 1688 Hebrew-English psalter to John Eliot.

15. Both college and university records agree on the date of the master of arts. See College Register (pages unnumbered) for that date. See also UA/Subscriptiones I, 202, in the Cambridge University Library. The section is headed B.A. but must be M. A. in Eliot's case since his bachelor of arts is given in the same volume (130) as 24 June 1622. See letter of Peter Meadows to me of 31 March 1993, in school vault. The Jesus Register entry of 8 July 1625 records ordination testimonials (though some of the writing is indecipherable) for Do Elyot. Gray and Brittain, *A History of Jesus College Cambridge*, state definitively (66) that Eliot obtained "College testimonials for ordination in 1625." The spelling of the name is no issue; Eliot was

spelled many different ways (even by Eliot himself) in an age indifferent to consistent spelling. There was another Eliot (Thomas) in the college, but he was too young to receive such testimonials. On the Ely diocesan records, see the letter of Peter M. Meadows, Keeper of the Ely Diocesan Archives, to me of 7 April 1992. I confirmed this at the Cambridge University Library in 1993 in person. The particular register has been missing for hundreds of years. Other registers, also now missing, are quoted by eighteenth and nineteenth century historians. Not so this one. Widford (the parish in which Eliot was baptised), Nazeing (where he was confirmed), and Chelmsford and Little Baddow (where he was associated with Hooker) were all in the Diocese of London during this period. As others have before me, I have checked the London Diocesan records at the Guildhall Library and found nothing there to indicate Eliot received ordination in that diocese. I have also seen Melanie Barber at the Lambeth Palace Library: no Canterbury diocesan ordination records exist for this period.

16. John Winthrop, *The History of New England from 1630 to 1649* (Boston: Little, Brown, 1853), I: 76. I believe Deryck Collingwood errs in concluding that W. C. P. Tyack in his unpublished thesis, "Migration from East Anglia to New England before 1660," says that the ship's list for the Lyon called John Eliot "cleric." I believe that "cleric" and the title "Reverend" are both Tyack's conclusions and not original.

17. Mather, *Magnalia* I: 235.

18. "Authorities" disagree on whether Eliot was episcopally ordained. Writing in the *Dictionary of National Biography*, ed. Leslie Stephen (London: Smith, Elder, 1908), VI: 608, H. R. Tedder says Eliot was episcopally ordained. J. and J. A. Venn, *Alumni Cantabrigienses*, Part I, ii, 190, say Eliot was probably ordained. Samuel Eliot Morison, *Builders of the Bay Colony*, 1st Northeastern ed. (Boston: Northeastern U. Press, 1981), 291, says, "As there is no reason to suppose that Eliot took holy orders in England, he was probably the first New England minister who was never 'bishoped,' whose sole ordination was in the Congregational way." Morison's view seems highly dubious. Had Eliot been the first (especially) or even among the first, the later "Congregational" Puritans such as Mather would have certainly "bragged" about it. The Congregationalist scholar, David Chamberlin, *Eliot of Massachusetts* (London: Independent Press, 1928), 22, concludes: "Eliot had probably taken orders [i.e., received episcopal ordination] before leaving England. He must certainly have preached or lectured."

19. Mather, *Magnalia* I: 333–34.

20. For a detailed account of this and other periods of Hooker's life, see Frank Shuffelton, *Thomas Hooker, 1586–1647* (Princeton: Princeton U. Press, 1977). The great Puritan scholar Perry Miller called Hooker "the most impassioned orator in the first generation of [New England] preachers."

21. This quotation and the indented one above come from Mather, *Magnalia* I: 335.

22. Strangely, over the last three hundred plus years, no effort appears to have been

made by anyone at Roxbury Latin to find this house (or most of the other Eliot sites, for that matter, at Widford and Nazeing). I found it—after several attempts—and established contact in 1983 with the Reverend Deryck C. Collingwood, minister of the Little Baddow United Reformed Church, who also had a passionate interest in history. Collingwood arranged the Thomas Hooker-John Eliot celebrations in 1986, the 400th anniversary of Hooker's birth. A commemorative plaque was placed at Cuckoo's Farm, and I preached at a large open-air service. See *The Roxbury Latin School Newsletter* 60, 1 (October 1986). Since that time, "connections" have multiplied, including a visit by the R. L. Glee Club in 1992.

23. Mather, *Magnalia* I: 335. In his unpublished MS "The Intelligent Pilgrim's Guide to Thomas Hooker's England" (153–54), Collingwood writes: "[At Cuckoos Farm] a stern Puritan figure [the ghost of Thomas Hooker], wrapped in a long cloak, stove-pipe hat on head, emerges with unhurried dignity from the hedgerow, crosses the lane towards Cuckoos, and disappears. There is no recorded feeling of fear, only awe, as he strides purposefully past the pond into the house. The last known sighting was some thirty years ago. This [ghost] story is documented, and well vouched for amongst the papers in the [Little Baddow] History Centre, as is the appearance within Cuckoos of none other than, supposedly, the great John Eliot. He is a cheerful, bouncy little ghost seen by the children of the previous occupant. He sits on the end of [their] bed, smiles merrily, and, when last seen, insistently pointed to a section of the bedroom wall where, on investigation, an unsuspected stairway was disclosed which led to the kitchen below. John Eliot was a young man when he lodged at Cuckoos, doubtless with a hearty appetite. . . . He may be been concerned for the children's easier access to food. At any rate, the stairway was uncovered, and the children said to be filled with happiness from this apparition. He was always a favourite with children. Mather says he carried sweetmeats in his pockets, especially for the impoverished Indian children. Sadly the ghostly Eliot stairs are in use no longer."

24. See Deryck C. Collingwood, "The Founder's Formative Years, Part II," *The Roxbury Latin School Newsletter* 66, 1 (October 1992): 12. Emmison, *Elizabethan Life*, 315: "By the Royal Injunctions of 1559, repeated in the Canons of 1571, nobody was allowed to teach children, openly in a school or privately in a house, without a licence [*sic*] from the ordinary."

25. Mather, *Magnalia* I: 335.

26. Collingwood, historian and former minister of the United Reformed Church in Little Baddow, confesses to a prejudice in hoping that Eliot arrived earlier in Little Baddow, and, admittedly, we know nothing of Eliot's activities between 1625 and 1629. "Thomas Hooker's Writings in England and Holland, 1626–1633" in *Harvard Theological Studies* XXVIII, 1975: 20, suggests that Eliot may have joined Hooker at Cockoos Farm as early as 1625.

27. William T. Costello, *The Scholastic Curriculum at Early Seventeenth-Century Cam-

bridge, 6 (see n. also). Relying on what I would regard as an inferior source, Morison (in *The Founding of Harvard College*, 42) says Cambridge in 1623 was "just short of three thousand."

28. Mather, *Magnalia* I: 336.

29. Ibid. Charles would very soon make Laud Archbishop of Canterbury. Laud, incidentally, was a clothier's son whose grammar school education launched him on his eminently successful career, which ended in his martyrdom under Cromwell.

30. Ibid., 338.

31. See *Encyclopedia of the North American Colonies* (New York: Scribners, 1993), I: 158: "The governor and the General Court of the company thus became, respectively, the governor and legislative assembly of the colony." See Fischer, *Albion's Seed*, 14–16. During the years 1629–1640, King Charles's eleven-year rule without Parliament in England, some eighty thousand left England, about twenty-one thousand of whom came to New England. (Others place the figure at thirteen thousand.) See also Richard W. Wilkie and Jack Tager, eds., *Historical Atlas of Massachusetts* (Amherst: U. of Massachusetts Press, 1991), 17, and Richard Emmet Wall, Jr., *Massachusetts Bay: The Crucial Decade, 1640–1650* (New Haven: Yale U. Press, 1972), 4–5.

32. Wall, *Massachusetts Bay: The Crucial Decade*, 1–2, discusses economic motives of the Puritan emigration. Winthrop clearly believed that if they were faithful to their covenant with God, God would bless them (including materially). But that was a possible result of their departure not a major cause of it. And, as we shall see, the blessings were far from abundant in the early years. See especially, Fischer, *Albion's Seed*, 18: "[Religion] was [the settlers'] only motive." On the harvests of 1628, 1629, and 1630, see Thompson, *Mobility and Migration*, 21.

33. John Winthrop, *A Modell of Christian Charity, written on Board the Arbella, on the Atlantic Ocean*, Collections of the Massachusetts Historical Society (hereafter Coll. Mass. Hist. Soc.), Series 3, VII (Boston: Charles C. Little and James Brown, 1838), 47.

34. Thomas Dudley, "Letter to the Countess of Lincoln, March 1631," *Collections of the New Hampshire Historical Society* (Concord: Marsh, Capen, and Lyon, 1834), IV: 224–237. For land rights, see Justin Winsor, *The Memorial History of Boston* (Boston: Ticknor, 1880), I, 407.

35. Winthrop, *The History of New England* I: 80. See Arthur Quinn, *A New World* (New York: Faber and Faber, 1994), 124–26, for a description of Winthrop's brilliant leadership in planting the new colony. He even brought a shipbuilder from England so they could build their own trading vessels.

36. Chamberlin, *Eliot of Massachusetts*, 23.

37. Winthrop, *The History of New England* I: 111.

38. Fischer, *Albion's Seed*, 59. On Eliot's commitment to joining his "friends coming from England" (and who they were), see Thompson, *Mobility and Migration*, 187 (and n. 15).

39. Morison, *The Founding of Harvard College*, 404. Weld left Roxbury in 1641 to return to England as agent of the Massachusetts General Court to raise funds for
the colony and the college. He served in this capacity until about 1646, when he
reentered the parish ministry. He never returned to New England. See *Dictionary
of American Biography* for further particulars on his controversial later life. See
Charles M. Ellis, *The History of Roxbury Town* (Boston: Drake, 1847), 132–33.
There was no clear definition of the difference between the role of pastor and that
of teacher. They were colleagues who divided responsibility. For a contrary view—
which defines the two roles—see Lawrence A. Cremin, *American Education, The
Colonial Experiment 1607–1783* (New York: Harper, 1970), 154–55.

40. Walter Eliot Thwing, *History of the First Church in Roxbury* (Boston: Butterfield,
1908), 3ff. See *Tercentenary Celebration of the First Church in Roxbury, 1630–1930*,
12. It is probably true that Roxbury, like the other New England churches, did not
use the Church of England's *Book of Common Prayer* in its worship (along with
Episcopal ordination and polity, it was dropped immediately—or soon—after
arrival by the settlers). See John Winthrop's letter to Sir Simonds D'Ewes, 21 July
1634, in Everett Emerson, *Letters from New England* (Amherst: U. of Massachusetts Press, 1976), 119ff.

41. Capt. Edward Johnson, "Wonder Working Providence of Sions Saviour in New
England," printed at the Angel in Cornhill, London, 1654, in Nathaniel B. Shurtleff, *A Topographical and Historical Description of Boston* (Boston: City Council,
1871), 44–45. For a further discourse on and description of the New England meetinghouse, see Fischer, *Albion's Seed*, 117–25.

42. After 1662 freemen were no longer required to be church members. King Charles
II agreed to renew the charter only if "all free holders of competent estates, not
vitious [*sic*] in conversation and oxthodox in religion (though of different persua-
sions concerning church government) may have their vote." The General Court
complied by means of the "Half-Way Covenant": free men could vote if a clergyman certified their orthodoxy.

43. Church attendance was made mandatory in 1635 and the financial support of the
ministry by male adult inhabitants made mandatory in 1638. See Charles M. Segal
and David C. Stinebeck, *Puritans, Indians, and Manifest Destiny* (New York: Putnam 1977), 34. Wall, *Massachusetts Bay: The Crucial Decade, 1640–1650* discusses the
battles over this and related issues and "the victory of reaction" by the end of the
decade. This same book discusses how the company became a colony, with
increasing representative government, something Eliot himself describes in his
September 1633 letter to Sir Simonds D'Ewes (see below). See also Wall, 4–5, on
Winthrop's church-state: "It was as arbitrary a government as that of King
Charles." See also Emerson, *Letters from New England*, 189, who sees the church
and state as more separate than most see them.

44. Mather, *Magnalia* I: 553. See also Fischer, *Albion's Seed*, 21.

45. Her name takes many variant forms. *A Report of the Record Commissioners*

containing the Roxbury Land and Church Records [Document 114–1880] (Boston: Rockwell and Churchill, 1881), 76, refers to "Mris Ann Eliot, the wife of Mr. John Eliot." John Langdon Sibley, *Biographical Sketches of Graduates of Harvard University* (Cambridge: Sever 1873), I: 476, refers to her as Anne Mountfort.

46. Mather, *Magnalia* I: 545.

47. *A Report of the Record Commissioners containing the Roxbury Land and Church Records*, [Document 114–1880] (Boston: Rockwell and Churchill, 1881), 73–100, 187–196. Roxbury was the fifth church founded in the colony and so had an eminence of age. The Harvard College Charter of 27 September 1642 provided that the minister (called in the Charter "teaching elder") at Roxbury would be an overseer of the college, and Eliot was. Another reason Roxbury can be called a "leading parish" is the eminence Eliot himself brought to it.

48. Mather, *Magnalia* I: 540.

49. Letter of James May in Coll. Mass. Hist. Soc., X (1809): 186–87.

50. Mather, *Magnalia* I: 541.

51. J. G. Shea, ed., *Recueil de Pièces sur La Négociation entre la Nouvelle France et la Nouvelle Angleterre* (New York: Cramoisy, 1866), 13. Gabriel Dreuillette's diary: "Le 24 [of December] . . . Jarrivay a Rosqbray ou le ministre nomme Maistre heliot qui enseignoit quelcq. sauvages me recust chez lui a cause que la nuict surprenoit et me traita avec respect et affection me pria de passer liver avec luy."

52. Mather, *Magnalia* I: 532. See also 544 on the efficacy of prayer.

53. Ibid., 547.

54. Ibid., 549–51.

55. Morison, *The Founding of Harvard College*, 162. See Franklin M. Wright, "A College First Proposed, 1633," *Harvard Library Bulletin* VIII, 3 (1954): 255 for the letter and Wright's account of its discovery. The MS was discovered in the British Museum: MS Harley, folios., 256–57. It is reprinted in Emerson, *Letters from New England*, 103ff.

56. Wright, "A College First Proposed, 1633," 255.

57. Ibid., 269. See D'Ewes's diary from his undergraduate days in the St. John's College magazine, *The Eagle* IX, 1875: 369–381; and X, 1878: 1–22. He there discusses his close friendship with Richard Saltonstall of Jesus College.

58. Wright, "A College First Proposed, 1633," 273–74.

59. Ibid., 276.

60. Ibid.

61. Ibid., 267–68.

62. Morison, *The Founding of Harvard College*, 168, 172.

63. Perry Miller, *The New England Mind, The Seventeenth Century*, (Boston: Beacon Press, 1939), 74.

64. This quotation and, indeed, my overall view of Hutchinson is drawn from Morison's brilliant chapter "Dux Femina Facti" in *The Founding of Harvard College*. This quotation comes from p. 176. For a very different view of Hutchinson, see

James DeNormandie's "Anne Hutchinson" in Box 1 of his papers in the Boston Athenæum. In *New England Magazine* XXI, 4 (June 1895): 403, he refers to her as "one of the most brilliant and beautiful characters Boston has ever had." It probably reveals more about DeNormandie, minister of Roxbury Church and president of the trustees (1883–1917), than it does about Hutchinson. For a feminist perspective, see Kyle Koehler, "The Case of the American Jezebels," *William and Mary Quarterly* XXXI, 1 (January 1974): 55–78. For still other views (opposed to Morison), see Andrew Delbanco, *The Puritan Ordeal* (Cambridge: Harvard U. Press, 1989), 133–59; and Selma R. Williams, *Divine Rebel* (New York: Holt, Rinehart and Winston, 1981). For an excellent insight into Vane, see James K. Hosmer, *The Life of Young Sir Henry Vane* (Boston: Houghton Mifflin, 1889), especially 32–60.

65. Morison, *The Founding of Harvard College*, 177.

66. David D. Hall, *The Antinomian Controversy, 1636–1638*, 2d ed. (Durham: Duke, 1990), 336–344. See also Charles Francis Adams, ed., *Antinomianism in the Colony of Massachusetts Bay, 1636–1638* (Boston: Prince Society, 1894), 269–275.

67. Hall, *The Antinomian Controversy*, 346; Adams, *Antinomianism*, 282.

68. Hall, *The Antinomian Controversy*, 348; Adams, *Antinomianism*, 284.

69. Mather, *Magnalia* I: 407.

70. The definitive work on the *Bay Psalm Book* is Zoltan Haraszti's *The Enigma of the Bay Psalm Book* (Chicago: U. of Chicago Press, 1956). It demonstrates conclusively that Eliot's role in this book is nothing like as great as has traditionally been thought. The traditional view is well (even stridently) stated in George P. Winship's *The Cambridge Press 1638–1692* (Philadelphia: U. of Pennsylvania Press, 1945).

71. Mather, *Magnalia* I: 551.

72. This view is brilliantly expressed by David M. Scobey, "Revising the Errand: New England's Ways and the Puritan Sense of the Past," *William and Mary Quarterly* XLI, 1 (January 1984): 12: "The Puritan work of reformation took the form of an errand into the wilderness, then, at least partly in response to the vision of history within which the Puritans situated themselves. The only way they could redeem the Old World was to withdraw from it. The wilderness . . . was a place God had held back from cultivation so that his elect might have a New World to come to in the latter days. The Puritan thinkers valued it solely in opposition to the European past, as a space for segregation and mustering. That is why, the efforts of John Eliot notwithstanding, the Puritans generally took such a negligent attitude toward the conversion of the Indians. *What was new in New England was not the making of new Christians but the purifying of the institutions of the old ones.*" [Emphasis added.]

73. See Alden T. Vaughan, *New England Frontier* (Boston: Little, Brown, 1965), 28–29, 94, 97; James Axtell, *The Invasion Within* (New York: Oxford U. Press, 1985), 219–20; Francis Jennings, *The Invasion of America* (Chapel Hill: U. of North

Carolina Press, 1975), 15–31; Neal Salisbury, *Manitou and Providence: Indians, Euro-peans, and the Making of New England, 1500–1643* (New York: Oxford U. Press, 1982), 30. The Puritans, of course, saw the hand of God in all this: God had cleared the land for them.

74. See Axtell, *The Invasion Within*, 135.

75. Nathaniel B. Shurtleff, ed., *Records of the Governor and Company of the Massachu-setts Bay in New England* (hereafter *Mass. Bay Records*) (Boston: William White, 1853), I: 17.

76. See Segal and Stinebeck, *Puritans, Indians*, 34. Even before leaving for the New World, Winthrop had talked of converting the natives, "the work tending to the enlargement of the Kingdom of Jesus Christ." (*Winthrop Papers* 2:145 quoted in Segal and Stinebeck, *Puritans, Indians*, 141).

77. Vaughan, *New England Frontier*, 20; Eliot wrote a brief statement expressing his beliefs in Thomas Thorowgood's *Jewes in America*, 2d ed., (London, 1660). See especially, J. F. Maclear, "New England and the Fifth Monarchy: The Quest for the Millenium in Early American Puritanism," *William and Mary Quarterly*, Series 3, XXXII, 2 (April 1975). See also Segal and Stinebeck, *Puritans, Indians*, 141–143, regarding the contemporary Messianic visions of rabbis, Cromwell's desire for the Jews to return, etc. See also Daniel Gookin, *Historical Collections*, in Coll. Mass. Hist. Soc., I (1806), 144–45; and Mather, *Magnalia* I: 560–61. See Del-banco, *The Puritan Ordeal*, 110–11 on the rise and fall of the theory that the Indi-ans were Jews in Eliot's time. Mormons believe, incidentally, that the Angel Moroni revealed to Joseph Smith in 1830 that ancient Hebrews migrated to North America about 600 B.C. He further revealed that Jesus Christ came later to North America to preach to these lost tribes, who were the ancestors of the American Indians.

78. See William Gouge et al., *Strength out of Weaknesse or a Glorious Manifestation of the Further Progress of the Gospel among the Indians of New England.* Coll. Mass. Hist. Soc., Series 3, IV: 156–57.

79. See Eliot's letter in Thomas Thorowgood, *Jewes in America* (London 1650); and Chamberlin, *Eliot of Massachusetts*, 48.

80. John Eliot, *The Light appearing more and more towards the perfect Day or A farther Discovery . . .* , 128. Coll. Mass. Hist. Soc., Series 3, IV: 128.

81. Here, of course, I use terms in a way that would have been unfamiliar to Eliot and his contemporaries. The distinction is valid, however, even though stated in anachronistic terms. Vaughan, *New England Frontier*, 20f., feels Mather's attitude in the *Magnalia* (1702) shows a shift towards racism. "By 1700 [ten years after Eliot's death] the New Englanders were more inclined than they had been eighty years before to consider the Indians a race apart." Nathaniel Hawthorne (in *Grandfather's Clock*) speculates that John Eliot may have been the only white man of his time to recognize that the Indians were not an inferior race.

82. See Vaughan, *New England Frontier*, 237–38: "It became increasingly evident to

the Puritan that religious conversion must be preceded, or at least accompanied, by social conversion. . . . He must also live in accordance with Scriptural regulations: polygamy must be rejected; fornication, blasphemy, idolatry, and immodesty must be repudiated. . . . The native, in short, must live like the Puritans' image of a true Christian if he was to qualify for the consolation of God's church."

83. John Eliot, *The Indian Grammar Begun*, Coll. Mass. Hist. Soc., Series 2, IX: 312. See also William Wallace Tooker, *John Eliot's First Indian Teacher and Interpreter, Cockenoe-de-Long Island* (New York: Francis P. Harper, 1896), 12. Cockenoe had been taken prisoner in the Pequot War in 1637.

84. See Eliot in *The Clear Sun-shine of the Gospel*, Coll. Mass. Hist. Soc., Series 3, IV: 50.

85. *The Day-Breaking if not The Sun-Rising of the Gospell with the Indians in New England* (London, 1647). Coll. Mass. Hist. Soc., Series 3, IV: 3–8.

86. Ibid., 9.

87. Ibid., 11–12.

88. Ibid., 13–14.

89. *The Cleare Sun-Shine*, 50, (Sept. 24, 1647).

90. John Eliot, *The Glorious Progress of the Gospel amongst the Indians in New England* (London 1649), Coll. Mass. Hist. Soc., Series 3, IV: 88.

91. *The Day-Breaking*, 15.

92. N. B. Shurtleff, ed., *Mass. Bay Records* III: 85. (Nov. 4, 1646).

93. *The Day-Breaking*, 20.

94. For another view, see the various works of Neal Salisbury and Francis Jennings. They view these "lawes" as "cultural imperialism" and as "a cultural holocaust". George E. Tinker holds Eliot "accountable for the cultural genocide" of the Indians, since "to teach the rejection of one's culture, history, and structures of spirituality is to teach self-hate."

95. *The Day-Breaking*, 21.

96. Winthrop, *The History of New England* II: 372, n.

97. *A Report of the Record Commissioners containing the Roxbury Land and Church Records*, 189.

98. See Morison, *The Founding of Harvard College*, 342.

99. *The Cleare Sun-Shine*, 55.

100. Ibid., 56–57. Samuel Eliot Morison, *Harvard College in the Seventeenth Century* (Cambridge: Harvard U. Press, 1936), 281, takes a rather more cynical view of this proposal. See also *The Glorious Progress*, 84; Henry W. Bowden and James P. Ronda, *John Eliot's Indian Dialogues* (Westport: Greenwood, 1980), 88–89; and Axtell, *The Invasion Within*, 228.

101. See *The Day Breaking* and *The Cleare Sun-Shine*; Gookin, *Historical Collections*, 34; Axtell, *The Invasion Within*, 161–64.

102. Massachusetts Archives 30:16. For a lengthier discussion of these transactions and other related matters, see Richard I. Melvoin's excellent book, *New England Out-*

post, *War and Society in Colonial Deerfield* (New York: Norton, 1989), especially 50–51. Deerfield's original name was Pocumtuck.

103. *Strength out of Weaknesse*, Coll. Mass. Hist. Soc., Series 3, IV: 177. See also Harold W. Van Lonkhuyzen, "A Reappraisal of the Praying Indians," *New England Quarterly* LXIII, 3 (September 1990): 415.

104. *Strength out of Weaknesse*, Coll. Mass. Hist. Soc., Series 3, IV: 171.

105. Eliot, *The Light Appearing*, Coll. Mass. Hist. Soc., Series 3, IV: 131.

106. Fischer, *Albion's Seed*, 130.

107. *Strength out of Weaknesse*, Coll. Mass. Hist. Soc., Series 3, IV: 171.

108. John Eliot, *The Christian Commonwealth: or, The Civil Policy of the Rising Kingdom of Jesus Christ* (London: Livewell Chapman, [1659]), Preface (pages unnumbered).

109. Shurtleff, *Massachusetts Bay Records*, IV, Part 2: 6. See also Philip F. Gura, *A Glimpse of Sion's Glory, Puritan Radicalism in New England, 1620–1660* (Middletown: Wesleyan U. Press, 1984), 134–36; and George P. Winship, *The Cambridge Press*, 185. This was not the first time Eliot had had to recant a political view publically expressed. In 1634 he had rashly attacked the leaders who concluded an Indian treaty without consulting the rest of the citizens. His fellow ministers persuaded him to recant his views publically. (See Winthrop, *The History of New England*, I, 179f.)

110. *Strength out of Weaknesse*, Coll. Mass. Hist. Soc., Series 3, IV: 172.

111. Ibid., 190.

112. *Tears of Repentence: Or, A further Narrative of the Progress of the Gospel Amongst the Indians in New-England*, Coll. Mass. Hist. Soc., Series 3, IV: 227f.

113. *Tears of Repentence*, 221. (Richard Mather).

114. Ibid., 215.

115. For Eliot's summary of the years 1646–1655, see *A Late and Further Manifestation of the Gospel amongst the Indians in New England*, Coll. Mass. Hist. Soc., Series 3, IV: 269–76. James Axtell, *After Columbus, Essays on the Ethno-history of North America* (New York: Oxford 1988), 115–16, points out that by the 1650s the requirements for whites to enter the church were becoming less stringent, something the Half-Way Covenant of 1662 acknowledged. Indian churches as late as 1705, however, continued to require new members to demonstrate their faith "according to the manner of the churches in primitive times."

116. *New England Historical and Genealogical Register* XXXVI (1882): 292–93. Letter to Edward Winslow, 20 October 1651.

117. Eliot to Edward Winslow, July 8, 1649: "I do very much desire to translate some parts of the Scriptures into their language, and to print some Primer in their language wherein to initiate and teach them to read." In *The Light Appearing*, Coll. Mass. Hist. Soc., Series 3, IV: 121.

118. Winslow, *John Eliot*, 138.

119. Ibid., 141.

120. For the interesting story of the Bible's financing, and Eliot's finding of funds, see

Winship, *The Cambridge Press*. For a good summary of events, see Cremin, *American Education*, 159ff.

121. James C. Pilling, *Bibliography of the Algonquian Language* (Washington, D.C.: Government Printing Office, 1891), 141, contains the Boyle quotation. The Trustees purchased the Bible for $330,000, the highest price ever paid for a book published in North America.

122. See Winship, *The Cambridge Press*, 276–77: *The Indian Grammar Begun* "was undertaken at the suggestion of Governor Boyle, which Eliot correctly interpreted as a command. He may or may not have suspected, as a critical reader of the correspondence is apt to think, that Boyle had been moved to ask for proof of the Apostle's command of the medium . . . by doubts inspired by a persistent lack of enthusiasm on the part of many who knew the New England natives firsthand."

123. See Winship, *The Cambridge Press*, 299ff. The *New England Primer* went through many editions and was still in use at the end of the nineteenth century. Even the facsimile edition of the *Indian Primer*, issued in 1880 by the Librarian of Edinburgh University, John Small, (Edinburgh: Andrew Eliot, 1880) is today a rare book. The School possesses it.

124. Hale, *Tercentenary History*, 17, states definitively that, "During the early 1650's several payments were made to Daniel Weld, for the education of Indians, nine of them attending the school in 1658, in the fruitless hope of sending them through Harvard." Of the records of payments to Weld (which date from 1655), only one— that of 1658—offers the possibility that the Indians attended the School: "Joane the Indian Mayde now at Mr. Welds is to be with the Governor of the [sic] Massachusetts after her yeare is up untill she bee otherwise disposed hee finding her Clothes for his service The other Indians at Scoole are to be disposed of by the Commissioners of the Massachusetts." (R. W. Hale, Jr., "The First Independent School in America," Publications of the Colonial Society of Massachusetts, XXXV: 246.) Since the School's records give no indication of Indians having attended the School, it seems more likely that the "Scoole" referred to is Master Weld's private ("on the side") preparatory school. However, Gookin (*Historical Collections*, in Coll. Mass. Hist. Soc., I (1806), 219–20) says Indian students "were kept at those schools" (i.e., Roxbury and Cambridge). Since Gookin in this passage is calling for integrated education, it is suspicious that he did not *clearly* assert that that had occurred: being "kept at" by the schoolmaster and "attending" could be quite different experiences. One wishes that one could assert that they were attenders, but the record only partially supports such a view. John Winthrop, *The History of New England*, II: 264, writes: "Divers free schools were erected, as at Roxbury . . . and at Boston." In the parenthesis following Boston, he writes, "and Indians' children were to be taught freely, and the charge to be by yearly contribution." It seems clear that Boston's school was for whites, financed by the town. The Indians were to be taught separately, by implication, since their education is separately financed. See also Part II, n. 51.

125. Hale, *The First Independent School in America*, 245–49.
126. Morison, *Harvard College in the Seventeenth Century*, 354. Morison also details Eliot's placement and support of Harvard's first Indian student, 340, 353. Ten years before Indians were placed with Weld, two were sent in August 1645 (the same month Roxbury Latin was founded) to live with President Dunster of Harvard. After spending £18 on them, Dunster asked to be relieved of responsibility for them on the grounds that they were "incapable of the benefit of such learning as was my desire to impart to them." See Axtell, *The Invasion Within*, 182–83.
127. Gookin, *Historical Collections*, 172–73. For a good summary, see Axtell, *The Invasion Within*, 183.
128. Eliot letter to Thomas Shepard (or, variously, Shepheard), Jr., 22 August 1673, published by Boston University (whose library owns it) in facsimile.
129. Gookin, *Historical Collections*, 219–20. Axtell, *The Invasion Within*, 189, documents the enthusiasm of Indian children in the early eighteenth century attending English schools.
130. In *After Columbus*, 49–50, James Axtell breaks down these figures as follows: of Eliot's fourteen "praying towns," seven were old and seven recent. Their total population was eleven hundred. "Excluding the new towns (because they were founded too recently to bear spiritual fruit), the old towns totalled 500 persons, of whom about 125 were baptised and another 70 or so were in full communion." Cremin, *American Education*, 160, and Vaughan, *New England Frontier*, 303, estimate that in all New England there were about twenty-five hundred Christian Indians, some 20 percent of the Indian population in 1674. See Jennings, *The Invasion of America*, 28–31 who places the New England Indian population even lower.
131. See Sarah S. Jacobs, *The White Oak and Its Neighbors (Nonantum and Natick)*, (Boston: Massachusetts Sabbath School Society, 1858); Winslow, *John Eliot*, 167–177; Michael J. Puglisi, *Puritans Beseiged* (Lanham: University Press of America, 1991), 10ff; Richard I. Melvoin, *New England Outpost*, 93ff.
132. See especially Puglisi, *Puritans Beseiged*, 35, and Sarah S. Jacobs, *Nonantum and Natick*, 256–60.
133. See Puglisi, *Puritans Beseiged*, 36, and in general regarding the whole war.
134. *A Report of the Record Commissioners containing the Roxbury Land and Church Records*, 193. (Spelling and punctuation have been improved.)
135. Puglisi, *Puritans Beseiged*, 44, quoting Massachusetts Archives, 30, 173.
136. *A Report of the Record Commissioners containing the Roxbury Land and Church Records*, 196.
137. Ibid.
138. June 21, 1683, in *Coll. Mass. Hist. Soc.*, III (1794), 182.
139. See especially Vaughan, *New England Frontier*, 239.
140. See William Everett, "Oration," in *Eliot Anniversary, 1646–1896*, City of Newton Memorial Exercises, 11 November 1896, 79.
141. See especially Axtell, *After Columbus*, 50: "These statistics [which are given below

in the text] require explanation, especially in the light of the traditional historian's conclusion that the Christian program [of Eliot] was a failure of the worst sort. Even from the missionary viewpoint, it cannot be said to constitute a failure; the numbers are too impressive." See Frederick L. Weis, *The New England Company of 1649*, P. C. S. M., XXXVIII, 134ff.

142. Axtell, *The Invasion Within*, 225, 273. See also *After Columbus*, 50.

143. Axtell, *The Invasion Within*, 273–75.

144. Jennings, *The Invasion of America*, especially 233–53. See Axtell, *After Columbus*, 101–02: "The Puritans, those favorite whipping boys of the enlightened, predictably fare the worst, particularly 'Apostle' John Eliot of Massachusetts. According to Francis Jennings and Neal Salisbury, Eliot's goals were so tainted by a barely hidden political agenda and his message so 'repressive' that his religious results must be drastically discounted. [Eliot only got] into what Jennings calls the 'missionary racket,' largely for the annuity offered by an English nobleman to encourage American missions. He used an Indian 'slave' . . . as a language teacher, and in 1646 talked the colonial 'oligarchy' into outlawing the practice of native religion under pain of death and into setting aside some land, purloined from the Indians, as bribes to converts seeking 'secure habitation' in the chaos of the Puritan land grab. These reservations or 'praying towns' became the major Puritan institution of 'cold war' against the natives. . . . Moreover, in his published reports abroad, Eliot cooked his results and inflated his own role." Axtell notes, "Neal Salisbury took the indictment one step farther by questioning the quality of Eliot's native conversions as well as their quantity. . . . [He finds] no evidence that the Indian converts 'understood either the [biblical] word . . . or most of the tenets of Puritan theology.' Second, [Salisbury asserts], the [Indian] confessions are also bereft of evidence 'that the missionaries expected their [Indian] saints' conversion experiences to measure up to those of the English.'" See also 115–17 on Salisbury and 26–29 on Jennings.

145. Axtell, *The Invasion Within*, 280–81.

146. Axtell, *After Columbus*, 49.

147. See Vaughan, *New England Frontier*, 246.

148. Axtell, *The Invasion Within*, 285.

149. Axtell, *After Columbus*, 50–51. See also 52: "It would be easy—and foolish—to lament this particular revitalizing break with their pre-Columbian past as a tragic loss of innocence for the Indians. It was indeed a loss for them, but not necessarily a tragic one. *Only if we continue to see the precontact Indian as the only real Indian* [italics added], as the 'noble savage' in other words, can we mourn his loss of innocence. *Only if we persist in equating courage with resistance* [italics added] to the forces of change can we condemn the praying Indians as cultural cop-outs or moral cowards. For life is preferable to death, and those who bend to live are possessed of courage, the courage to change and to live in the face of overwhelming odds as well as the contempt of their brothers who died with stiff necks."

150. Shurtleff, *Mass. Bay Records* I: 17.
151. Mather, *Magnalia* I: 576. Winthrop, *The History of New England*, I: 305 (February 26, 1637/8): "Mr. Peirce, in the Salem ship, the Desire, returned from the West Indies after several months . . . and brought some cotton, and tobacco, and negroes, etc., from thence." The first protest of this trade by the General Court came under Thomas Dudley's governorship in October 1645 (Shurtleff, *Mass. Bay Records* III: 49). Kenneth Silverman, *The Life and Times of Cotton Mather* (New York: Harper & Row, 1984), 281, says that by 1711 "Scarce a house in Boston except the very poor, it was reported, lacked black servants." Every issue of the *News-Letter* carried advertisements offering slaves for sale.
152. From the Suffolk County Registry of Deeds, Lib. 15, folio 44; Boston, 1 August 1689. The Eliot School possesses a 1731 copy of this document, but the following extract comes from the original record:

Mr. John Eliot teacher of the Church of Roxbury in the County of Suffolk in the Massachuset Colony in New England . . . for divers good and weighty causes & Considerations him thereunto moving And more especially for and in Consideration of the great love & affection which he hath and beareth to Learning and for the advancement and propagation thereof among his friends and neighbours at that part of the said town of Roxbury comonly called Jamaica or the Pond Plaine who by reason of their remotenesss from the schoole in the said Roxbury town street cannot receive like benefit & advantage from said Schoole with others who live nearer to the same: . . . Doth . . . Convey & Confirme . . . severall Tracts . . . of Land . . . lying within the Township of said Roxbury [75 acres in three parcels] . . . In Trust only notwithstanding & to & for the Maintenance support & Incouragement of a Schoole and Schoole master at that part of sd. Roxbury commonly called Jamaica or the pond Plaine for the teaching & Instructing of the Children of that End of the town together such Negroes or Indians as may or shall come to the said Schoole and to no other use Intent or purpose under any colour or pretense whatsoever.

153. Mather, *Magnalia* I: 578. John W. Tyler notes that Eliot's death seems to be a classic instance of the "exemplary death" for which the Puritans strove.

Part Two

This School is of very ancient foundation, and its history is rendered highly interesting from its connexion with many eminent individuals, as well as from affording proof of the early solicitude felt for the diffusion of Knowledge, by our wise as well as pious forefathers. The bread which was thus early cast upon the waters has, as it were, been miraculously multiplied, to afford food for thousands; and (if we may be permitted to continue our allusion) the fragments which now remain far exceed in value the few small loaves that fed the multitude in the wilderness.

— R. G. PARKER, MASTER 1825–28

Part Two
"That Little Nursery"
1645-1867

W HAT WE CALL TODAY "The Roxbury Latin School"[1]
came into being in 1645.[2] Inspired by John Eliot, "teacher"
of the church in Roxbury, sixty-four "donors"[3] joined
together to establish the School. Their Agreement of 1645 is the oldest
school charter in America:

> Whereas the Inhabitantes of Roxburie, out of their relligious care
> of posteritie, have taken into consideration how necessarie the
> Education of theire children in Literature will be to fitt them for
> publicke service both in Churche and Commonwealthe, in suc-
> ceeding ages; They therefore unanimously have consented and
> agreed to erect a free schoole in the said towne of Roxburie.[4]

The Charter's date, August 31, 1645, was the ninth birthday of John
Eliot's eldest son John, who enrolled that year in the new school. Eliot's
brother, Philip, was the School's first master. And Edmund Weld, son of
Eliot's pastoral colleague Thomas Weld, was—two years later in 1647—
the School's first graduate.[5]

The founders financed the new school in a peculiar way. The sixty-
four donors who signed the Agreement of 1645 were not making one-
time-only donations. Each of the sixty-four pledged—on behalf of
himself and his heirs—an amount to be paid *annually forever*! Almost
all the landowners of Roxbury pledged something.

The first signature and donation was that of Thomas Dudley. He had
been elected governor that year—for the third of four non-consecutive
one-year terms. A feisty, contentious, strong-minded sixty-nine-year-

old, he had come over in 1630 on the same ship as Winthrop to serve as
the Colony's original deputy governor. He had moved in 1639 to Roxbury, where he built (for the time) an imposing home. He was a hard
man, not known for his philanthropy. Mather's account of Dudley's
childhood gives us a clue, perhaps, as to why he was so uncharacteristi-
cally generous in his support of the new School:

> [After his mother and father died] it pleased God to move the
> heart of one Mrs. Puefroy, a gentlewoman famed in the parts about
> Northampton for wisdom, piety, and works of charity: by her care
> he was trained up in some Latin school, wherein he learned the
> rudiments of grammar, the which he improved afterwards by his
> own industry to considerable advantage, so he was able even in
> [old] age to understand any Latin author.[6]

Dudley pledged £1-4-0 (one pound, four shillings), as did the two
ministers—Thomas Weld and John Eliot—and two others. These were
the five largest donations. When the pledges of the fifty-nine others
were added in, the total came to only slightly more than £22, barely
enough to pay Eliot's brother to be schoolmaster, with nothing left over
to build a schoolhouse.[7] The students were therefore taught in a rented
room. Not until 1652—helped by £6 raised in England by Thomas
Weld, Eliot's former ministerial colleague—was a schoolhouse erected
on Guild Row off the "town street" (in modern-day Dudley Square,
Roxbury). Though the boundaries of Roxbury then included the modern neighborhoods of Jamaica Plain, Roslindale, and West Roxbury,
only the eastern end of the town (what is today called Roxbury) was
settled. It was a rural village gathered by the single "town street" (later
named "Roxbury Street"), with the church's "meeting house" at its center. During its first 280 years the School would be located in six different buildings within a half-mile radius of this meeting house.

1. *"Relligious Care"*

The donors' motive was religious; they founded the School "out of their
relligious care of posteritie." They were English Puritans who came to

Massachusetts in order to establish here a purified church and commonwealth that would be looked upon by those who remained in England as a City upon a Hill—a model to imitate.[8] They could not allow dissidents to undermine or corrupt this purified church and commonwealth. Therefore, although they had been "nonconformists" in England, they insisted on conformity in New England.[9] By 1635 the colony's General Court had made church attendance mandatory; by 1642 it published civil laws and a religious catechism and enjoined the selectmen of each town "to take account from time to time of all parents and masters, and of their children, concerning their calling and implyment of their children, especially of their ability to read & understand the principles of religion & the capitall lawes of this country."[10] The people of Roxbury shared this aspiration. In founding their school they asserted that learning was not an end in itself, but rather a means to an end: "to fit [students] for public service both in Church and Commonwealth."

Unlike many nineteenth and twentieth century immigrants to America who left the "Old World" because of famine or poverty, the Puritans who settled Roxbury were generally people of means and education. As we have seen previously, Thomas Dudley urged that none "of the poorer sort" should come over, but only those affluent enough to support "themselves and theirs for 18 months."[11] Those who came left their comfortable homes in England not for economic but for religious reasons. The first three years of Roxbury's settlement—1629–31—were naturally years of hardship and trial: finding food and shelter, establishing farms. Though there is no trace of any prior Indian settlement at Roxbury, the English newcomers also had to make their peace with the Native Americans in the surrounding territories. The settlers who survived the tough initial years, however, rapidly prospered. By 1634, William Wood, in his *New Englands Prospect*, observed (undoubtedly with hyperbole): "A mile from [Dorchester] lieth Roxberry which is a faire and handsome countrey towne, the inhabitants of it being all very rich."[12]

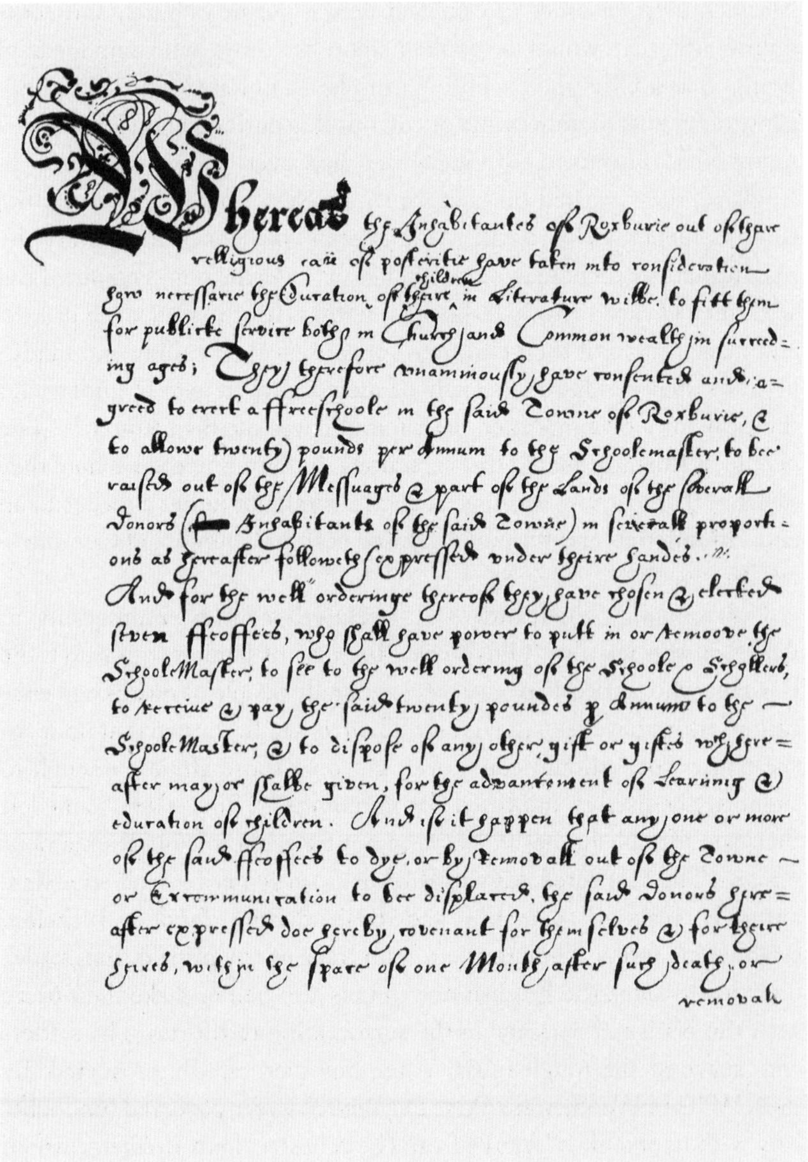

Whereas the Inhabitantes of Roxburie out of their relligious care of posteritie have taken into consideration how necessarie the education of theire children in Literature wilbe, to fitt them for publicke service both in Church and Common wealth in succeeding ages; They therefore unanimously have consented and agreed to erect a ffree schoole in the said Towne of Roxburie, & to allowe twenty pounds per annum to the Schoolemaster, to bee raised out of the Messuages & part of the Lands of the severall donors (Inhabitants of the said Towne) in severall proportions as hereafter followeth expressed under theire handes. &c.

And for the well orderinge thereof they have chosen & elected seven ffeoffees, who shall have power to putt in or remoove the Schoolemaster, to see to the well ordering of the schoole & schollers, to receive & pay the said twenty poundes per annum to the Schoolemaster, & to dispose of any other gift or giftes which here=after may or shalbe given, for the advancement of learning & education of children. And if it happen that any one or more of the said ffeoffees to dye, or by removall out of the Towne or excommunication to bee displaced, the said donors here=after expressed doe hereby covenant for themselves & for theire heires, within the space of one Month after such death, or removall

FIG. 1. The title page of the Agreement of 1645 that established the School.

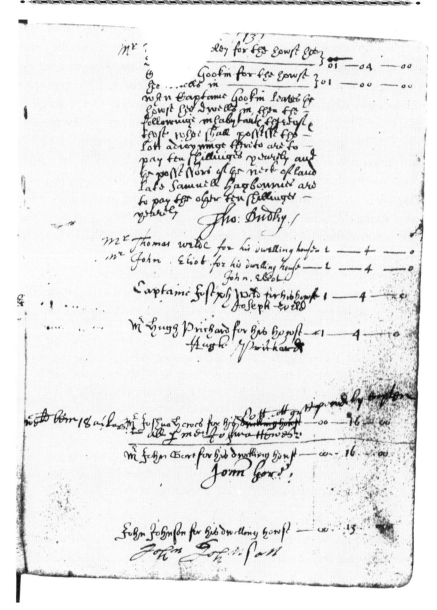

FIG. 2. "Tho: Dudley." The signature of Thomas Dudley appears first on the Agreement of 1645. A resident of Roxbury, he had been elected governor of the colony that year.

The Roxbury planters modelled their new school directly on the English "grammar school" with which they were familiar. Dudley and others attended such a school, and John Eliot had taught in one before coming to America. The fundamental purpose of the English grammar schools was religious. Nothing concerned the trustees of the English grammar schools more than the religious qualifications of the master. For English grammar school boys, every school day began or ended with prayers or with a religious service in the schoolroom or the parish church.[13] Roxbury's new school had the same two-fold purpose as its English model: "giving instruction in the classics and producing Christian citizens."[14] The Agreement of 1645 speaks of "how necessary the Education of their Children in Literature [i.e., Latin] will be to fit them for public service both in Church and Commonwealth."[15] Latin, in other words, was the *means* and godly citizenship the *end*.

The means, of course, was not just Latin literature, but inevitably the example set by the master who taught it. In 1654 the General Court of the Massachusetts Bay Colony decreed:

> Forasmuch as it greatly concernes the welfare of this countrie that the youth thereof be educated, not only in good litterature, but sound doctrine, this Court doth therefore commend it to the serious consideration and speciall care of the overseeres of the colledge and the selectmen of the severall townes, not to admit or suffer any such to be continewed in the office or place of teaching, educating, and instructing of youth or child . . . that have mannifested themselves unsound in the faith or scandalous in theire lives, and not giving due sattisfaction according to the rules of Christ.[16]

John Eliot and his pastoral colleague Samuel Danforth expressed the purposes of Roxbury's School and the obligations of its schoolmaster in their February 1669 contract with the schoolmaster: John Prudden is enjoined to use his "best skill, and endeavour, both by praecept *and example*, to instruct [the children] in all scholasticall, morall, and theologicall discipline."[17] The end of godly citizenship ("public service") is thus to be achieved by three means: *scholasticall* discipline (the "education . . . in [Latin] Literature" referred to in the 1645 Agreement); *morall* discipline (training in character); and *theologicall* discipline (giving students some sense that their lives and the universe have meaning and purpose).[18]

To the School's founders, then, education was a great deal more than mere instruction, a great deal more than conveying of information, a great deal more than teaching young people how to reason. The founders had a far richer definition of education. As John Eliot and Thomas Weld put it a few years later (in 1670), the founders "agreed to lay the foundation of a grammar schoole, for the glory of God, the future good and service of the country, and of the churches of Christ: and for the particular good education of the youth of our church and towne."[19]

2. *A Grammar School*

Roxbury's School was called both a "grammar" and a "free" school. Both terms say something significant about it. We shall begin with "grammar school."

The Agreement of 1645 declares the donors' conviction that children would be fitted for godly citizenship by "education . . . in Literature." The literature they were referring to was Latin; in the English and European world, Latin was the universal language of higher education, of intellectual and scientific discourse, and of international relations. As we have noted, the school Eliot and the donors envisioned was modelled on the English "grammar school." Thomas Hooker had attended such a school,[20] and John Eliot had taught in the grammar school Hooker founded at Little Baddow near Chelmsford before he emigrated to America. When Eliot and Weld petitioned the General Court in 1669 for official sanction, they referred to the School not as a "free school" but as "a Grammar school." The Court, in responding, calls the school "the free school" (and "a free school") but says the duty of the feoffees is the "constant provision of an able Grammar schoole master." And when the School was reorganized by a state charter in 1789, it was

Know all men by these presents, that mr Elliot sen: william parks, thomas welds
John Boles, Robert Williams, Giles payson, at present feoffees in Roxberry, have cove-
nanted, & agreed with John prudden to keep a schoole in ye towne of Roxberry, for ye space
of one full year, begining on ye first of march next ensuing ye date herof: but not longer
except ye said John prudden see cause for to doe; provided he give a quarters warning
to ye aforesaid feoffees & they may other=wise conveniently provide themselves of schoolmaster
where=upon ye said John prudden doth promise & engage to use his best skill, & endeavour, both
by precept, & example, to instruct in all scholasticall, morall, & theologicall, discipline, the children
(for far as they are or shall be capable) of these persons whose names are here under=written
all Abcdarians excepted

			gratie
	Shubal Seavor	widow: peak	John Gorton
po: Dormiter	John Curtice	Samuel Ruggles	John grigs
mr Danforth	william Gary	widow Welos	willis Hopkins
mr Thomas Weld	John Ruggles	John May's sen:	Frizall./
mr Elliot sen:		Raffe Heringway	
mr John purpoint	John Ruggles	Edward Bridge	
John polley	Robert Williams	Abraham How	
ms hemington	phillip Tory	william Cleaves	
John buls	Gibs payson		
Edward morrice	go: waterman	widow Gary	
william parks	Samuel williams	Joseph Bugbee	
widow morral	Joseph wize	Samuel Crafts	
goodman Hally	thomas Gorner	peter Garner	
widow: Danison	Abraham Newel sen:	John stebbin	
Thomas foster	Samuel finch	John Hanchet	
Hue Clarke	Edward payson	thomas Swan	
mash=chraft	Robert Seavor sin:		
Thomas Cheney	Gamblin		
John watson sen:	Richard Sutton		
samuell finck	mr meads		

in consideration wherof ye afore=sayd feoffees (not enjoyning, nor leting ye said John prudden
from teaching any other children; provided ye number therof doe not hinder ye profiting
of ye fore=named youth) doe promise, & engage (for ye due recompence of his labour) to
allow ye said John prudden ye full, & just summe of twenty=five pounds: ye one halfe to be
payed on ye 29 of September next ensuing ye date herof, & ye other halfe on ye 25 of march
next ensuing. i:e: in ye year (70) ye said 25 to be payed by William parks, & Robert
williams, their heirs or administrators, at ye upper=mills in Roxberry, three=quarters
in Indian=corne, or pease, & ye other fourth=part in barley, all good & merchandable, at
price currant in ye countrey rate, at ye days of payment. It is alsoe further added (by
agreement) for ye encouragement of ye said John prudden in ye said employment: yt if any person
or persons in ye towne of Roxberry shall for like ends desire, & upon like grounds with these
above mentioned, see meet to adde their names to this writing; they shall enjoy ye like privi=
ledges with those whose names are above=written, provided yt whatsoever they shall give
in ye way, shall be an addition to ye 25 & to be payd within as afore=sayd. for ye confirmatio
of which covenant, we mutually subscribe our hands herto.

wheras it is above=sayd yt William parks, & robert williams doe engage both for ye
time, place, & manner of ye paying ye afore=said twenty=five pounds: Giles payson
ye Robert Williams their heirs, or administrators doe herby engage for ye payment of
ye one halfe of ye afore=said twentie=five pounds, at ye same place, & in ye manner as above
written, but in ye month commonly called November, next ensuing ye date herof:
& for ye payment of ye other halfe ye fore=said William parks, & John Boles: doe in ye
like manner engage themselves heirs & administrators, to be payed on ye 25 of march
next ensuing that i:i: in ye year (70) or before ye time.

John prudden

this covenant fulfilled to the satisfaction of
the covenanters.   John prudden

John Eliot
William york
thomas weld
John Boles
Robert williams
Giles payson

called, officially, "the Grammar School in the easterly part of the Town of Roxbury."

The term "grammar school" did not, in the seventeenth and eighteenth centuries, mean what it does today. We use the term to describe an "elementary" school for small children. In the seventeenth and eighteenth centuries the term "grammar school" identified a school that taught *Latin* grammar to some or all of its older students.[21] Though the founders referred to "education in . . . Literature" [i.e., Latin] as the school's sole curricular concern, not all students at a grammar school like Roxbury's progressed far enough to study Latin. Some took only the preparatory subjects—reading, writing, arithmetic—and others fell by the wayside (as Benjamin Franklin did at Boston Latin) when they proved incapable of absorbing Latin.

The first sixty years of the seventeenth century were the golden age of grammar schools in England. The donors who signed Roxbury's Agreement of 1645 shared the conviction of their English contemporaries that the founding of a school was a noble endeavor worthy of their charitable generosity. In the period 1560 to 1660, hundreds of such schools were founded and/or endowed in England by landowners and merchants.[22] From our modern perspective it is regrettable to note that, with rare exceptions, the schools founded in this era—in England and New England—were for boys. When the donors of 1645 spoke of "the Education of their children," they were referring only to boys.[23]

Boys entered the English grammar schools when they were about eight years old, having previously received rudimentary instruction in English reading and writing privately or at a "petty school." The New England grammar schools, such as that at Roxbury, followed the English pattern, with one difference. It was more often the case in New England that there was no "petty" or "dame" school in the town to teach the fundamentals. Therefore colonial boys often proceeded to a grammar school without any learning, and the grammar school master had to

---

FIG. 3, *across.* The February 1669 contract between the feoffees and Schoolmaster John Prudden. Note the fourth column of names with the word "gratis" (free) at the top.

devote much of his time and energy to rudimentary instruction of younger boys.[24] At age fourteen to seventeen (depending on their academic aptitude), New England boys left the grammar school (some of them, usually, having had some Latin) either to go to the college or to enter some occupation.[25]

The famous "Old Deluder" Law of 1647 had committed the Massachusetts Bay Colony to educational ambitions far exceeding those of Virginia and other colonial settlements:

> It being one cheife object of that ould deluder, Satan, to keepe men from the knowledge of ye Scriptures, as in former times by keeping them in an unknowne tongue, so in these latter times by perswading from ye use of tongues, that so at least ye true sence and meaning of ye originall might be clouded by false glosses of saint seeming deceivers, that learning may not be buried in ye grave of our fathers.

The law went on to require every town of fifty families to support a schoolmaster and every town of one hundred families to set up a grammar school, "Ye master thereof being able to instruct youth so farr as they may be fited for ye university."[26] So Roxbury in 1645, with only about sixty families (for a population of about 350), had already moved beyond the ambitious requirements of the 1647 law by founding a grammar school.[27]

Like most grammar schools in England and New England, Roxbury's was a one-room building in which a single master taught all the boys, from those who could barely read and spell English to those who were able to translate Latin.[28] It seems likely that, in its early years, Roxbury's School consisted mainly of boys who were studying the preparatory subjects. John Eliot's own son, John, Class of 1652, seems to have spent a year at Cambridge Latin before proceeding to Harvard— perhaps in order to study Latin.

But by the 1660s at the latest the School seems to have realized its principal aim, the teaching of Latin.[29] Samuel Eliot Morison's research shows that by the 1660s Roxbury Latin ranked fourth in Massachusetts among schools preparing boys for Harvard—the Colony's only college—for which Latin was an entrance requirement.[30] It is unlikely that the 1669 Petition referred to above would have called the School (as it did) a "grammar school" if the School was not teaching Latin.[31]

3. A Free School

The Agreement of 1645 describes Roxbury's school as "a free school." Like the term "grammar school," "free school" was a common term with its own distinctive meanings in seventeenth century England and New England. In his definitive study of the English grammar schools, W. A. L. Vincent says that in the seventeenth century the term "free school" could be applied to a school if it met any one or more of three criteria:

1. A school that was *"free from tuition fees,"*
2. A school which was *"subject to no other control* than that of its governors,"
3. A school which was *"open to all* who wish to avail themselves of the education supplied." [Emphasis added.][32]

The "free School at Roxbury" met all three criteria.

Though it was open only to the sons of donors, it was "free from tuition fees." The sixty-four founding donors pledged—for themselves and their heirs—annual donations in perpetuity for the School's maintenance. In return for their donations, the donors were given the right to choose the School's trustees (called, by the medieval term, "feoffees"). If the donors had school-age sons—and many did not—they received an additional privilege: their sons could attend the School at no cost. Whether or not a donor or his heir had school-age sons, his obligation to contribute the originally agreed donation was absolute and perpetual.

The Agreement of 1645 did not establish a school free to all boys who were residents of Roxbury. Rather, it established a school free to the sons of donors. A Roxbury boy whose parents had not made a donation was not allowed to attend the School: "None of the Inhabitants of the said towne of Roxburie that shall not joyne . . . in this act with the rest of the Donors shall have any further benefitt thereby."[33]

There is no reason to think that Eliot or the other founders desired to establish a financially free school for those who could afford to pay. When Eliot asked Sir Simonds D'Ewes to establish a college (see Part I), he requested a *building*. The college, he said, would be financed by charging those who attended it: "Such yong men as may be trained up [m]ust beare their owne charges."[34]

The School records of 1663 show that the School was not limited to Roxbury boys. It was open without distinction to both "inhabitants or neighbors" who made a donation:

> It was unanimously agreed that all the Donors of the schole in Roxbury doe meete together in the schole. . . . And whoever also of the inhabitants *or neighbours* of the said town *that are willinge to joyne in the promotinge the good and benifitt of the said schole* are desired alsoe to be present at the said meetinge. [Emphasis added.][35]

In 1666, the feoffees again sought to enlarge the number of donors (and therefore the number of children eligible to attend the School). Their motive was, of course, to raise new funds with which to pay the schoolmaster. They therefore proposed "that opportunity might be to as many as thought good of the towne to come in and joyne in this worke; *and to help beare the charge, so as to have the priviledg of the schoole.*" [Emphasis added.][36]

In 1669, when they entered into a contract with a new schoolmaster, John Prudden, the feoffees and original donors renewed their invitation to others to join in their endeavor: If others "see meet to adde their names to this writeing; they shall enjoy like priviledges with those whose names are above-written."[37]

The names referred to were those of the fifty-four still-faithful original donors, who are listed in three columns. There is a fourth column, headed by the word "gratis" ("at no cost"), under which four names are listed. In the only place, therefore, where attending the School without any financial charge is mentioned, the word "free" is not used. Though the Agreement of 1645 and the other early documents limited the School to the sons of donors, the early feoffees and donors had decided, of their charity, to admit a few students who were not sons of donors.[38]

Boys admitted *gratis* were not students whose parents *would not* pay, but boys whose parents *could not* pay. Eliot and the feoffees exhibited a stern attitude towards donors (and heirs of donors) who defaulted on their pledges, and they closed the School to boys of parents who would not "do their part" by making donations. But we know that the poor were a matter of deep concern to Eliot, and he appears to have persuaded the feoffees to accept *gratis* a few boys whose parents could not make a donation.

Prudden's contract outlined the conditions under which he might teach the children of parents who were able to make donations, but who chose not to do so. If he wished to teach them, he could do so by charging a fee (what we would call today "tuition"). The School was, thus, open by right only to the sons of donors. A few poor boys attended the School at the discretion of the feoffees, and a few fee-payers at the discretion of the schoolmaster. It was also open by right only to older children. Prudden's contract specifically exempts him from teaching "ABCDarians," children learning their alphabets and numbers:

> Ye said John Prudden doth promise and engage to use his best skill, and endeavour, both by praecept, and example, to instruct in all scholasticall, morall, and theologicall discipline, the children (soe far as they are or shall be capable) of those persons whose names are here under-written. All ABCDarians excepted.[39]

By 1669—twenty-four years after the School's founding—the town had grown and the number of non-donor families had risen to fifteen. By then many of the original donors had died. Their inheritors, some of whom had no children, often resented the burden (sometimes onerous, with changing fortune) inflicted on them by the annual donations. By the 1660s some of the donors were refusing to pay the donations, challenging not only the validity of the obligation, but even the authenticity of the copy of the Agreement of 1645 in the School's possession.

Seeking to escape the perpetual annual donations, these discontented donors clamored for the School to be turned over to the town to be supported by taxes.

This crisis led to John Eliot's direct intervention in school affairs. Though he had inspired the School's founding, he was much preoccupied with his parish duties and Indian work and had been content to leave it in the hands of leading laymen of his parish. At this critical juncture (November 1668), however, he stepped in, accepting election as a feoffee.[40] He first exercised his legendary fund-raising talents by successfully seeking gifts for the School at home and abroad.[41] Then, together with feoffee Thomas Weld, son of his former ministerial colleague, he took on the recalcitrant donors. He petitioned the General Court first, to authenticate the Agreement of 1645 as recorded in the "Old School Book" (still today in the School's possession), and second, to enforce it legally by obligating the donors and their heirs to pay the annual donations:

> 1. That whereas the first inhabitants of Roxbury to the number of more than sixty families, well nigh [but, interestingly, in view of the Agreement's use of the word "unanimously," not] the whole town in those days, have agreed together to lay the foundation of a Grammar School for the glory of God, the future good and service of the Country and of the Church of Christ; and for the particular good education of the youth of our Church and town and for the maintainance thereof, have by a voluntary donation given a small rent forever out of their several habitations and homesteads, as appeareth in the records of our School book, and have settled a company of feoffees in a certain order of their perpetual succession and given unto them full power both to receive, gather and improve the said rents to the end whereunto they are given, as appeareth in the Charter. In which way we have had a school and gone on peaceably for many years, till of late some interruption and opposition hath risen, which hath awakened us to petition the Honored Court, to ratify, confirm, and authorize the said School and the rents due thereunto by voluntary donation, and the feoffees who have power to gather, order and manage the same.

2. Whereas by divine Providence our first book and charter was
burnt . . . , it was again . . . renewed in this form and manner as we
do now present it, yet by reason of the death of sundry of the
donors . . . we are under this defect that some of the hands [i.e., the
signatures] of the donors are not unto this 2nd book personally
which were to the first; nor are they obtainable, being dead; therefore our humble request is . . . that the Honoured Court . . . im-
power the Feoffees to receive and gather the same, as if the names
of the donors were written with their owne hands.[42]

After lengthy hearings and protracted investigations, the Court in 1670
authenticated and confirmed the Agreement of 1645 (as recorded in the
"Old School Book") and validated the donations, as Eliot and Weld had
requested.[43]

Many towns supported their schools by taxation.[44] Roxbury did not.
Its grammar school remained free of government support and control.
It was supported, rather, by the voluntary gifts of private individuals, by
the perpetual annual donations, and by bequests such as that of Isaac
Heath in 1661. When the Court in 1670 gave the Agreement of 1645
enforceable status, it also ruled that if the town should ever decide to
support the School by taxes, the donors — in all fairness — would be
exempt from such taxes.[45]

The new School in Roxbury also meets Vincent's second criterion by
which a school could be called "free": It was a school "subject to no other
control than that of its governors." It was a private corporation:
financed not by public taxation but by the perpetual donations of its
founders and their heirs, and governed not by town meeting or church
officials but by feoffees chosen by the donors. The early financial
receipts often refer to these trustees as "gentlemen enfeoffed with the
care of the School." Roxbury's School was, in short, a "free school" in
that it was independent of outside control by either church or state.[46] By
the Agreement of 1645 the donors

have chosen and elected seven ffeoffees [*sic*] who shall have power
to putt in or remove the Schoole Master, to see to the well order-

ing of the Schoole and schollars, to receive and pay . . . the Schoole
Master, and to dispose of any other gift or giftes which hereafter
may or shall be given for the advancement of Learning and education of children.[47]

The succession of this independent board of feoffees was secured as
follows:

> And if it happen that any one or more of the said ffeoffees to dye,
> or by removall out of the Towne, or excommunication to be dis-
> placed, the said Donors . . . doe hereby covenant for themselves
> and for theire heires, within the space of one month after such
> death or removal . . . to elect and choose other in their room so that
> the Number may be compleate. And if the said Donors . . . doe
> neglect to make election within the tyme forelimited, then shall
> the surviving ffeoffees . . . elect new ffeoffees . . . to fulfill the num-
> ber of seven.[48]

It was the founders' clear intention that the School be completely free
of government control or financing. It was also their clear intention that
the school be free of church control. Even though John Eliot was the
church's pastor, and even though all its feoffees and most of its students
were members of the parish, the School was established as a separate
entity with an independent governing board. The "relligious care of
posteritie" that motivated the School's founding came from individuals
acting on their own behalf as committed Christians, not from a religious organization (such as a parish or denomination)—even though
those individuals were virtually all members of the Roxbury church.
Although the School had a religious *purpose*, it was not an ecclesiastical
institution.[49]

Nothing is more remarkable about the School's founding than the
founders' determination that the School should be independent of government control. As Geraldine Murphy remarks,

> Although for ten years the trend in Massachusetts Bay had been
> definitely toward the initiation and control of schools by town
> meetings, the School established in Roxbury was not in this gen-

eral tradition, nor was it similar to any other previous founding. The people of Roxbury decided to have an independent school. The school was initiated by . . . 'well nigh the whole town at the time,' but these people were not acting as 'town,' but rather as a large private group establishing a school for their own children and those of later donors. They intended to place their school beyond the caprice of town control and support.[50]

The founders' determination to remain free of outside control or financing came at a high price: the School has always had to scramble for adequate resources and to use its treasure carefully. The Puritan simplicity of the original humble schoolhouse, for example, is attested by the furnishings which Daniel Weld,[51] master from 1652 to 1666, was directed to obtain: "convenient Benches and forms with tables for the scholars to sitt on, and to write att, with a convenient seat for the schoolmaster and a desk to put the Dictionarys on and shelves to lay up books."[52]

When Cotton Mather wrote—shortly after Eliot's death in 1690—of this School's success, his underlying intention was to encourage the people of Roxbury to support it generously:

A grammar-school [John Eliot] would always have upon the place, whatever it cost him: and he importuned all other places to have the like. I cannot forget the ardour with which I once heard him pray . . . with what fervour he uttered an expression to this purpose: 'Lord, for schools every where among us! That our schools may flourish!' God so blessed his endeavours, that Roxbury could not live quietly without a free school in the town. . . . From the spring of the school at Roxbury have run a large number of the 'streams which have made glad this whole city of God.' I persuade my self that the good people of Roxbury will for ever scorn to begrutch [*sic*] the cost, or to permit the death of a School which God has made such an honour to them.[53]

Finally, the new school at Roxbury meets Vincent's third criterion by which a school could be called "free": it was "open to all who wish to avail themselves of the education supplied."[54] "All" in Roxbury's case obviously did not include girls, but a coeducational school in the seventeenth century would have been a great oddity. Any boy could apply to the School: it was not limited, as some English grammar schools were, to boys whose parents lived in a certain geographical area or to boys whose fathers were members of a certain guild or profession. Any boy could apply whose parents wanted him to have an education. If parents made a donation, their son was given the "privilege" of the School; if parents were unable to make a donation, they could ask that he be allowed to attend *gratis*. From the start it was an inclusive school, welcoming boys of all backgrounds. Though the School was located in Roxbury (an area that included most of modern day Roxbury, West Roxbury, Jamaica Plain, Roslindale, and parts of Brookline and the Back Bay), the founding documents make clear that sons of the donors—whether "Inhabitants or neighbours"—were welcome to attend the School.

4. *Bell's Bequest, 1671–72*

Thirty years after its founding, Roxbury was one of New England's wealthiest towns. Governor Thomas Dudley—who in 1645 had made a generous donation to the School as one of the founders—lived there, as did many of the Colony's leading citizens.

Yet Roxbury was not without poor families. This was an age in which disease and death struck suddenly and often, leaving wives and children destitute. As we have seen, provision was made for poor boys to attend the School *gratis*. The poor were of great concern to John Eliot, but he also had many other charitable concerns—his own parish, the welfare of the Indians, and the costly publication of his Indian Bible. To sustain these endeavors, he had to devote enormous energy to fund-raising. Although the School was not his first priority, Eliot sought financial backing for it from wealthy persons he had reason to believe might be interested in helping it.

One such man of wealth was Thomas Bell. Bell had lived in Roxbury and had been one of the original donors in 1645. Shortly thereafter he raised his annual donation from thirteen shillings to fifteen shillings. In 1654 he and his wife returned to England, where he was a prominent and successful merchant on Tower Street, London. Nevertheless, he continued his strong charitable support of Eliot's various causes. While still in North America he had become one of the sixteen original members (i.e., trustees) of the Society (often referred to as "the Corporation") for the Propagation of the Gospel in New England. Back in London he was one of only two members of the Society who had been to New England; his close relationship with Eliot from his Roxbury days enabled him to vouch for and lobby for Eliot's projects, such as the printing of the Indian Bible. It was Bell who arranged for Lady Armine's annuity in support of Eliot, and it was Bell who paid for the transatlantic passage of Marmaduke Johnson (who printed Eliot's various works) and for other special Eliot projects.[55] In 1669, shortly before he died, he further raised his donation to Roxbury's School to twenty shillings a year.

The lengthy will of Thomas Bell (dated January 29, 1671, and probated in London on May 22, 1672) made a large number of bequests. One such bequest was the 151 acres he owned in Roxbury. It was made in a peculiar manner: the land was not given directly to the School, but, rather, to three trustees who were to use the income from it to benefit the School at Roxbury. This bequest of his Roxbury lands — referred to ever since as "The Bell Bequest" — reads as follows:

> Unto Mr. John Elliott Minister of ye Church and people of God at Roxbury in New England . . . and Captaine Isack Johnson whom I take to be an officer or overseer of and in ye said Church and to one other like godly person now bearing office in ye said Church and their successors ye Minister and two other such head officers of ye said Church . . . All those my messuages or tenements [etc.] being at Roxbury in New England . . . to ye said Minister and Officers of ye said Church of Roxbury for ye time being and their successors from time to time for ever In trust onely notwithstanding to and *for ye mainteynance of a schoolmaster and free schoole for ye teaching and instructing of poore mens children at Roxbury* aforesaid for ever

and to and for noe other use intent or purpose whatsoever.[56] [Emphasis added.]

Bell's bequest has four interesting characteristics.

First, Bell was not creating a new school. He was establishing a trust for the *"mainteynance"* of an existing school he had helped to found. It was not his purpose to change the School's character. He did not, for example, intend to make the School financially free to all the citizenry. With a schoolhouse provided, the School's only expense (aside from wood for heat in the winter) was the schoolmaster's salary. Hence Bell gave his bequest "for ye mainteynance of a *schoolmaster* and free schoole." But he realized that his legacy was nowhere near sufficient to make the School financially free to all. Even when the income from his trust was added to the continuing donations, the School was still not able to offer the schoolmaster a salary competitive with that offered at Latin schools in other towns.

Second, Bell's special interest was the poor. When he returned to England, Bell had left his Roxbury plantation in the custody of his sister. When she died, he turned it over to Isaac Johnson, who was instructed to use the proceeds from it to benefit the poor.[57] We do not know what was in Bell's will before 1671. But that year, shortly before he died, perhaps in response to Eliot's plea for support, he made the School the beneficiary of his Roxbury holdings. While the bequest was made for the "mainteynance of a schoolmaster" at Roxbury, Bell's principal interest was clearly to provide part of the schoolmaster's salary so that "poore mens children," whose parents could not make donations (and who therefore had no *right* to send their children), could attend the School. Again, Bell was not founding a new school exclusively for "poore mens children." The feoffees were already allowing some boys to attend the School *gratis*. By his bequest Bell was seeking to extend the benefit of attendance to a larger number of "poore mens children."[58]

Though "poore mens children" were clearly Bell's special interest, there is no record of the feoffees ever segregating Bell's income for that or any other special purpose. It was always simply commingled with the

School's general funds "for ye mainteyanance of a schoolmaster and free school."

Third, while Bell identified the location of the "schoolmaster and free schoole" as being "*at* Roxbury," he neither limited the will's benefits to children who were Roxbury residents nor implied that students from outside Roxbury were to be treated differently.

Finally, Bell concluded by stating that his bequest was to be put "to and for noe other use intent or purpose whatsoever" than to support the School. Though the bequest was made to three trustees associated with the church in Roxbury, it was to be used only for the School's benefit, and not the benefit of John Eliot's other charities, such as the parish, the Indians, or the publication of the Indian Bible—all of which Bell had supported during his lifetime.

When the new trustees of Bell's bequest began setting rents on his properties, there was much anger on the part of those who were charged. Some went to Court to complain and to challenge the School's right to receive the income. The "General Court for Election, held at Boston in New England 27th May, 1674" stated that Bell intended to maintain the School at Roxbury already in existence:

> In answer to the petition of the feoffees of the ffree school of Roxbury, setled heretofore by Court order in the toune street, the Generall Court having heard & scene the pleas & evidences in the case, doe, upon mature deliberation, judge that the declared intent of Mr. Thomas Bell, both in his life & at his death, in his will, was the setlement of his estate in Roxbury upon *that ffree school then in being* at his death *in the said toune*. [Emphasis added.] [59]

Under pressure from complaining donors, the School's feoffees—in an effort to improve what we would now call "public relations"— cut the required annual donations in half upon receipt of Bell's bequest. [60]

Unfortunately, Bell's bequest did not significantly improve the School's financial condition. Even when the income from the bequest was added to the now-halved donations, the total was barely enough to cover the schoolmaster's modest salary. Neither did the bequest alter the

School's basic clientele; it continued to be a school largely for the sons of the relatively affluent original and new donors.

In 1674—several years after Bell's bequest—the School's income was only £27, including all donations and rents from Bell's and the School's other lands. The School did not have the resources to hire an experienced schoolmaster. That year Ezekiel Cheever was getting £60 a year as master at Boston Latin, and Benjamin Tompson £30 a year plus a fee for each child at Charlestown.

In desperation, the donors—at a meeting in 1680, eight years after Bell's bequest—were forced to augment their meager funds by charging each student a fee for heating the schoolhouse:

> At a meeting of the donors in Roxbury, March 16, [1680] for the supply of wood for the school. It is ordered that parents, masters, and guardians for the several children comeing to the school, *whether inhabitants or strangers,* shall in the month of October or November pay to the school master four shillings per child coming to school, or bring half a cord of good merchantable wood, *except such as for poverty or otherwise shall be acquitted* by the Feoffees. [Emphasis added.][61]

Though the School was "free" (for the sons of donors and those allowed to attend "gratis"), the donors nevertheless now imposed fees for wood ("wood money") on all the children of the School, in addition to their parents' donations. In doing so, they were following the pattern of the English free grammar schools, most of which—under financial pressure—had been forced to charge fees for one or more services, such as entrance, candles, fires, and cleaning. In other words, the English free schools were really "free" (and often not to all students) only of fees for instruction (the cost of which was covered by endowment). So now, at Roxbury, a fee was charged for wood. Those parents who could not afford this substantial fee were exceptions. Obviously, since the feoffees went out of their way to note that the fee applied to all parents ("whether inhabitants [of Roxbury] or strangers"), they made no distinction between boys who were residents of Roxbury and those who were non-residents. This fee appears to have been collected annually in varying amounts until 1735 when it was raised to eight shillings.[62]

In 1681—nine years after Bell's bequest—Schoolmaster Thomas Barnard described the dismal condition of the schoolhouse, reflective of the School's financial state:

> Of inconveniences I shall instance in no other than that of the school-house, the confused and shattered and nastie posture that it is in, not fitting for to reside in; the glass broken, and thereupon very raw and cold, the floor very much broken and torn up to kindle fires, the hearth spoiled, the seats, some burnt and others out of kilter, [so] that one had as well nigh as good keep school in a hog stie as in it.[63]

Though William Mead (in 1683) and others left legacies to the School upon their deaths,[64] and though Giles Payson (in 1684) and others gave land to the school in exchange for being absolved of their annual donations,[65] the School's financial condition remained precarious. But we must remember to evaluate the School's financial state in the context of the late seventeenth century. King Philip's War of 1675–76 had cost the Colony dearly—not just in lives lost but in towns ruined and financial resources drained. Harvard College barely kept going to the end of the century—its numbers diminished, its presidency often vacant. We would, therefore, hardly expect to discover that the one-room schools of the Colony were flourishing.[66]

In comparative terms, in fact, Roxbury's School was quite successful. After Eliot's death in 1690, Cotton Mather wrote rhapsodically of the School:

> One thing . . . has almost made me put the title *Schola Illustris* upon that little nursery; that is that Roxbury has afforded more scholars first for the college [Harvard], and then for the public, than any town of its bigness, or if I mistake not, of twice its bigness in all New England.[67]

Mather was not exaggerating, according to the statistics of Samuel Eliot Morison: in absolute numbers, Roxbury—from this, its only school—provided thirty boys for Harvard in the seventeenth century, more than any other town except Boston. Boston's sixty-eight came from Boston Latin and several private schools and were far fewer per capita than Roxbury's thirty.[68] Furthermore, many of the School's seventeenth-century graduates went on to noteworthy attainments "in Churche and Commonwealthe." In addition to the array of alumni who held significant pulpits, Caleb Watson '57 became the first master of the Hopkins Grammar School at Hadley, John Bowles '67 became Speaker of the Massachusetts House, John Wise '69 coined the phrase "No taxation without representation" during Massachusetts' 1689 version of Britain's Glorious Revolution, James Pierpont '77 has been called the principal founder of Yale, John Williams '79 was the celebrated "Redeemed Captive" of the Indians, and Paul Dudley '86 served as Chief Justice of Massachusetts, to name but a few.

5. *Joseph Dudley and the Long Leases, 1672–1720*

Such comparative success as the School enjoyed was not the result of financial security. The 117 years between Bell's bequest (1672) and the new charter (1789) were a period of virtually continuous financial crisis for the School. The School itself changed very little: it remained a simple one-room schoolhouse with a single master. The most notable master of the era was Benjamin Tompson, one of the colony's few poets. Something of a rolling stone, he served schools all around the colony for short periods—teaching at Roxbury from about 1700 to 1703. The trustees, however, had difficulty in supporting even a single master, and the turnover for this poorly-paid position was rapid, masters rarely staying more than two or three years.[69]

The dominant figure of the first part of this 117-year era was Governor Thomas Dudley's son Joseph, feoffee for fifty years from 1670 to 1720. Like the Biblical Joseph, he was the child of his father's old age. Born in 1647 when his father was seventy, endowed with every advantage—social position, wealth, education (Harvard '65), opportunity—he cultivated the airs of an English aristocrat. He married at twenty-two and fathered thirteen children by his only wife. After considering the ministry, he chose politics as his career, serving as Roxbury's representative to the General Court and later as a member of the upper house, the Court of Assistants. In 1682 he was selected to go to England to plead the Colony's case when Charles II threatened to revoke the original charter granted by Charles I. His ready acquiescence in the inevitable revocation of the charter and his acceptance of the temporary "presidency" of the Council of New England after the charter was revoked in 1684 earned him the disfavor of many of his fellow New Englanders. When King James II appointed Sir Edmund Andros governor of the new "Dominion of New England" in 1686, Dudley further antagonized the more radical elements in Massachusetts by accepting a position on the Governor's Council, and by holding the positions of censor of the press and chief justice of the Superior Court.

However, having antagonized the various political parties by his pro-Catholic sympathies, James II was overthrown in his third year as king in the "Glorious Revolution" of 1688, and Parliament asserted certain "ancient rights and liberties." When word arrived in Massachusetts in 1689 that James II had been replaced by the joint rule of his daughter Mary and her husband, the Protestant William of Orange (Prince of the Netherlands), there was widespread rejoicing and some revenge on the representatives of the old regime. Having become "in a peculiar manner the object of the people's displeasure," Joseph Dudley was clapped in prison. Although the authorities let him return under guard to his Roxbury home when he became ill, that night several hundred Bostonians broke into his house and "led him back to gaol like a dog." The revolution brought an end to James II's short-lived "Dominion of New England." William and Mary granted a new charter in 1691 for what was now called "The Province of Massachusetts Bay." Though this charter retained a royal governor, it also established an assembly of representatives elected by male property owners within the province.[70]

Hounded out of New England, Joseph Dudley landed on his feet in England: he served for a time as deputy governor of the Isle of Wight

FIG. 4. Governor Joseph Dudley, feof-fee 1670–1720, son of Thomas Dudley.

and as a member of Parliament, and he became quite a prominent figure in English society. Still, he greatly missed his family in Roxbury. Desiring to return, he devoted himself to politicking to gain appointment as governor. On the one hand, he assured the English authorities that he would rule "in strict dependence upon the Crown and Government of England," and on the other hand, he wrote influential figures in the Colony that his "family Estate and Interest is in your Country" and that his time in England had led him to "a New Value of my Country and the Religion and Virtue that dwells in it." His campaign met with success and in 1702 King William, in one of the last deeds of his reign, appointed him governor of the Province of Massachusetts Bay. He ruled with considerable pomp under Queen Anne until 1715, though his stubbornness and Anglophilia resulted in frequent clashes with the elected representatives allowed by the charter.[71]

Although Dudley had joined the Church of England, and although as governor he tried to protect the non-Congregational minorities in Massachusetts from the established, government-financed Congregational Church, he nonetheless often attended the Church in Roxbury—living in the Roxbury home his father had built—and he remained a feoffee of the School. In this latter capacity he was the principal architect of the most catastrophic mistake ever made by those responsible for the School, a mistake that very nearly cost the School its life. Under his leadership, the feoffees persuaded Bell's trustees in 1687 to lease Bell's lands *for five hundred years* for a lump sum of £18 per annum.[72] Then the feoffees leased the School's own lands for the same period for £6.5 per annum. The short-range benefit of these leases was at best modest: even with their income enlarged from the leases, the feoffees were barely able (by adding in the perpetual donations) to pay a salary (£30, a little over half of which came from the Bell leases) that could secure an experienced schoolmaster. But if the short-range effect of these leases was disappointing, the long-range effect was calamitous.

There was criticism of the feoffees' action right from the start: some questioned the wisdom of five-hundred-year leases; others felt that favoritism had been shown in granting the leases. By the start of the eighteenth century, the feoffees' folly was apparent to all. The new century opened with the first great inflation—ironically caused in large part by the costly Indian policy of the new governor, Joseph Dudley. As the value of money decreased and prices increased, the School's fixed income from the five-hundred-year leases quickly became insufficient to support the School. As a result, by the start of the new century (1700), the post of schoolmaster at Roxbury had become a revolving door. It was held by young, usually inexperienced men who were studying for their master of arts degree at Harvard in order to be ordained to the ministry. In 1688 Eliot had ordained Nehemiah Walter as his successor as pastor and teacher at Roxbury's church (where he remained until his death in 1750). Walter was a native of Ireland, and his education there enabled him to converse fluently in Latin by the time he was thirteen. After coming to New England he taught at Cambridge Latin on his way to a pastorate and was therefore able to sympathize with the difficulties these young schoolmasters faced. He often invited them to live in his home. As pastor of one of the Colony's great churches he had considerable influence, and he helped place these schoolmasters (often after only a year in the post) in pastorates throughout New England.[73]

By 1714 the effects of inflation were such that no decent man could be found to accept the mastership at the proffered rate of £32 per annum. In that year, therefore, Joseph Dudley's son William, Class of 1700, moderator of the Roxbury town meeting, proposed at the meeting "to levy ten pounds on the town for the support of a grammar schoolmaster, . . . inasmuch as the rents and donations belonging to the said schoole were not sufficient encouragement for a schoolemaster."[74] Dudley and other supporters of the School were doubtless deeply disappointed when this motion failed. From the perspective of future generations, however, the town's refusal to support the School by taxes can only be regarded with the utmost relief. In towns where similar motions succeeded, the local grammar school lost its independence and fell under government control.[75]

Having failed to obtain relief by public support, the feoffees in 1715 grasped at another straw. One of Governor Dudley's aides found in the file a long-forgotten 1660 General Court grant of land in support of the School: "This Court Judgeth it Meet to Grant the Town of Roxbury Five hundred acres of Land toward the Maintenance of a ffree Schoole."[76] The Feoffees at once petitioned the General Court, arguing

That the said ffree School is one of the ancientest and most famous of Schools in this Province where by the favour of God, more Persons have had their Education, Who have been, and now are worthy Ministers of the everlasting Gospel, than in any, (we may say) many towns of the like Bigness, in the Province, whereby (Your

Petitioners crave leave humbly to suggest) the said Town have deserved well of the Publick. And the Generall Court were Pleased at their Sermon in October anno 1660 So far to Consider the Said School, as to make a Grant of Land . . . , ffive Hundred acres of Land towards the maintenance of a ffreeschool. . . . Your Petitioners therefore now humbly Pray that your Excellency and this Hon'ble Court will Please to Perfect and make effectuall this pious Intention . . . by allowing your Petitioners to Take Up . . . the aforegranted Tract.[77]

After several years of wrangling the Court agreed that, though the lands belonged to the town, they were given for the School's benefit. But no one could be found to purchase them. By 1770, when the lands were finally sold, the proceeds went into the town treasury, and the parish in the "westerly part" of Roxbury successfully lobbied the town for the proceeds. The School was thus—in both the short and long term—deprived by the town of support it had clearly been intended to receive.

All other avenues having been closed off, the feoffees now desperately turned their energies to trying to obtain cancellation of the disastrous five-hundred-year leases which their predecessors had granted thirty years earlier. On the School's behalf, Bell's Trustees petitioned the new governor, "His Excellency Samuel Shute, Esq., General and Commander in Chief in and over his Majesties [*sic*] Province of the Massachusetts Bay,"[78] for relief from the leases. Only one of the School's feoffees from 1687 still remained in office: Joseph Dudley, whose term as governor had just ended. The enraged lessees forced him to make a humiliating public acknowledgment of his signature on their five-hundred-year leases.

On August 3, 1716, the Governor's Council responded in the trustees' favor by ruling:

That the Lands and Tenements of the said Mr. Thomas Bell, &c., . . . being Leased for Five Hundred Years, is contrary to the Law, and Statutes of England . . . , and beyond the Power of the Feoffees [at that time] . . . , and a frustration, in a great Degree of the Pious Intention of the Donor; and that . . . the said Estate, be henceforward restored to the Petitioners.[79]

FIG. 5. Paul Dudley, Class of 1686, justice of the Superior Court, son of Joseph Dudley.

By the terms of the 1691 Massachusetts charter, this motion had to be "sent down" to the House of Representatives for concurrence. The members of the House were not eager to validate the view that the laws of England prevailed in Massachusetts and they despised the School's senior feoffee, Joseph Dudley. They therefore refused to concur.

Blocked in the Legislature, the School now had only one remaining hope—legal action. Money was raised by subscription, and in July 1717 Bell's trustees went to the Inferior Court of Common Pleas and sued their lessee, Ebenezer Gore, for £300. When the jury sided with the trustees, by agreeing that English law prevailed, Gore immediately turned to the Superior Court, filing an appeal in November. In May 1718, the Superior Court's five judges ruled in favor of Gore, overturning the Inferior Court ruling. The trustees appealed this decision, and a year later, in May 1719, the Superior Court—which now included Joseph Dudley's son Paul (Class of 1686) as a justice—reversed itself, ruling that the laws of England, which forbade such long leases by collegiate foundations, "shall be in force here" in Massachusetts. The School had incurred staggering legal fees, but it had—by a hair—escaped from the leases and regained the patrimony that its feoffees had so recklessly squandered in 1687.[80]

Unfortunately, the land leases were not the School's only problem. Simultaneously, schoolmaster Ebenezer Pierpont managed to get the School in trouble with the college. Pierpont had grown up in Roxbury, graduating from the School in 1711. His father dead, he worked his way through Harvard. Finishing college in 1715, he obtained a teaching position in Lancaster, but was unable to take it up because of illness. The following year (1716), having just turned twenty-two, he was appointed (sole) master at his old school in Roxbury. He was a typical appointment for the School of that era: a recent college graduate who would work—briefly, anyway—for a very low wage. Pierpont's most important duty was to prepare the two members of the Class of 1717—Peleg Heath and Benjamin Ruggles—for admission to Harvard College. Harvard, however, had a new president, John Leverett, and that year raised its standards. Both Roxbury boys badly failed their entrance examinations and were rejected. Peleg Heath's father accused Harvard of refusing his son because his family was involved in a lawsuit with Harvard tutor Nicholas Sever's family. (Sever had himself grown up in Roxbury, graduating from the School in 1697.) Pierpont threw gas on the fire by calling Harvard's tutors a set of "Rogues, Dogs & tygars." Harvard retaliated by debarring him from the master's degree he was due to receive at Commencement 1718.

Pierpont was furious and enlisted the support of the Dudley and Mather families, both of which were sulking about their declining influence at Harvard. Together they went to Governor Shute to appeal Harvard's decision. The Harvard officials were barely able to convince the governor that the matter should be decided by a hearing before the Harvard Corporation. Following the hearing, Pierpont was denied his degree by a unanimous vote "for contemning, reproaching and insulting the Government of the College."

But Pierpont was not finished. He now sued Harvard tutor Sever for libel in the Middlesex Court. The Harvard authorities were distraught: Harvard was operating under an improvised charter (arranged by Joseph Dudley) that could become a disputed issue in any court trial. Again, Harvard asked the governor to let the matter be decided by the College—this time by the Overseers. Shute agreed and himself presided. A compromise was struck whereby Pierpont could receive his degree upon signing a very mild apology (written for him by Paul Dudley '86). The truculent Pierpont refused to sign it, however, and the Overseers voted against him. Fortunately for Harvard, the court threw out his case, since it had already been twice heard at Harvard. President Leverett wrote that this "put an End to an affair that was very troublesom, and that which threaten'd the dissolution of the college, and caused many thoughts of heart in those that had the welfare and Safty of that Society . . . at heart."

Pierpont was replaced as master after the School's own 1718 commencement, but he returned for a second round, serving from 1726 to 1731. After he gave up the mastership, he remained in Roxbury, where he was a pillar of the town and church, and devoted his attention to land speculation and milling. He died insolvent in 1755, having failed to expand his milling business into baking. The two Roxbury boys who were rejected by Harvard lived happily ever after: both were admitted to Yale, both later received an A.M. from Harvard, and both became ministers.[81]

There seems to have been no lasting damage from this spat with the College, but the School's financial problems would not go away. The School's tercentennial historian, Richard W. Hale, Jr., makes much of Joseph Dudley's £50 bequest to the School in 1720: by leaving the School money instead of land, "Joseph Dudley bequeathed to it a new policy as to endowment . . . ; he was also ahead of his time in realizing that money invested in land brought in smaller returns than money lent at interest." It is doubtful that Dudley had any such vision; giving money was simply the easiest way to leave his bequest. Regardless of what Dudley had in mind, the amount was a pittance for a man of enormous wealth and made virtually no impact on the School's dismal financial status.[82]

6. *Decay and Chaos, 1720–1789*

Leasing their newly recovered lands for short terms (five to fourteen years), the feoffees secured income sufficient to obtain a respectable master. Even though he was reasonably paid, as Roxbury's only school-master he still had to teach students of all ages. He may have looked with envy at Boston, where the town government, drawing on a larger population—one which was taxed in support of schools—had gradually created three "writing" (elementary) schools (in 1664, 1700, and 1720) and a second grammar (Latin) school (1712). As a result, the Latin schoolmasters of Boston could concentrate on instructing the older pupils in Latin.[83] When, in 1728, Roxbury's master complained that having to teach younger pupils distracted him from his essential calling as a Latin schoolmaster, the feoffees did relieve him from teaching the youngest children of the town:

> For the present until further order the master of the school in Rox-
> bury shall not be obliged to receive any children for his instruction
> at the said school until such time as they can spell common easy
> English words either in the Primer or in the Psalter in some good
> measure.[84]

But within a few years—in the face of renewed inflation—the income from the new short-term leases proved inadequate. Though income from Bell's trustees provided £45 of the School's £72 annual income in 1731, the schoolmaster was poorly paid and the School in trouble. By 1735 expenses were greater than income and the "fire money" charge for all children was doubled from four to eight shillings. The feoffees ordered

> the parents or masters *of each and every child* sent to the said school
> shall either send with each child eight shillings in money or two

feet of good wood, and in case they do neither, the master is hereby ordered to suffer no such children to have the benefit of the fire. Provided always that this order shall not extend to any child or children who shall be *exempted* by the Feoffees *by reason of poverty or low circumstances of the parents or master;* they applying to the Feoffees for the purpose. [Emphasis added.][85]

In 1738 Bell's Trustees sought and received permission of the General Court to sell land: "for the better support of a School Master, it being very difficult to procure one at present, the salary being so low." That year the feoffees personally made up the difference of £14, "the Scool Dues being insufishant."[86]

In 1742 the poor condition of the schoolhouse led the feoffees to raise money by subscription for a new one:

Whereas, the old school House in the Easterly part of Roxbury was gone much to Decay, it was thought proper by the Feoffees to erect a new school house, and, with the help of many well Disposed persons, by way of subscription, they did in the year 1742 erect a new house. . . . The Honourable Paul Dudley Esq. was Pleased to Bestow for the life of the said School a good handsome Bell.[87]

This was the School's second free-standing single-room schoolhouse, and it was erected on the same site in Dudley Square. One of the first students to occupy this new facility was (the later illustrious) Joseph Warren, Class of 1755, who returned to the same building as master in 1760.

Nothing, however, seems to have palliated the ongoing financial crisis. In 1761 Bell's Trustees were forced again to seek legislative permission to sell another piece of Bell's land. Only by depleting the assets of Bell's bequest was the School surviving.

As a sign of the School's quality during this era, Richard W. Hale, Jr., cites five Roxbury schoolmasters between 1752 and 1771 who later became famous. It is noteworthy that they represent the spectrum of political opinion (from revolutionary to loyalist), an indication that

FIG. 6. Samuel Parker, master 1765–66, later Episcopal bishop of Massachusetts.

neither the feoffees nor the townspeople were making politics a test: William Cushing, later justice of the U.S. Supreme Court; Joseph Warren (Class of 1755), Revolutionary general who died at Bunker Hill; Samuel Parker, later Episcopal bishop of Massachusetts; Increase Sumner (Class of 1763), later justice of the Supreme Judicial Court and governor; Ward Chipman, later British deputy mustermaster general in New York, solicitor general in Nova Scotia, and judge of the Supreme Court in New Brunswick. Hale fails to mention that each of these masters served only a single year. The School possesses Joseph Warren's letter to "the Gentlemen entrusted with the Care of the School in Roxbury" requesting the money overdue to him as schoolmaster for the year 1761. Bell's trustees sold more of their land to pay this bill and on the bill's other side, Warren's mother, Mary Warren, notes receipt of payment of the amount due to her son for "keeping the said school."

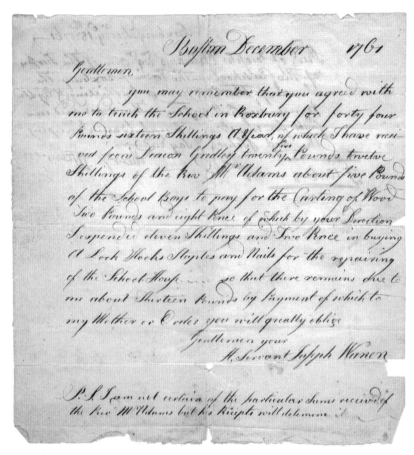

FIG. 7. Joseph Warren's 1761 letter to the feoffees requesting the remainder of his salary.

Short tenures—often "one-year stands"—were, thus, the upshot of the School's financial weakness. Inevitably its academic quality suffered. The School list of 1770—the only such list we have from the School's first 150 years—reveals that in 1770 only nine out of the School's eighty-seven boys were studying Latin. The rest were doing elementary subjects: nineteen were "spellers" (who could write and spell easy words from the Primer or Psalter); ten were reading the Psalter, ten the New Testament; seventeen were "writers," and twenty "cyphers" (studying

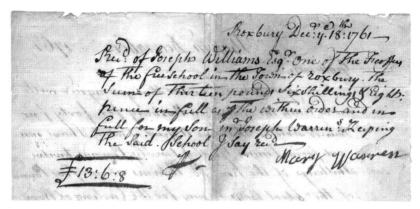

FIG. 8. Mary Warren's 1761 receipt of the money due to her son Joseph "for keeping the said School."

elementary mathematics).[88] All taught by a single master. In 1773 that master was a nineteen-year-old named John Eliot. He was paid in a most peculiar manner:

ROXBURY, APRIL 8, 1773

> Received of Colo. Williams, of the Feoffees of the Grammar School a *Bag of Coppers* weight *thirty-four pounds*, in part of my salary for the year current, the same being by estimation £4-13-4, lawful money, and for which I am to be accountable.

> I say received in part,
> John Eliot[89]

With the mastership a revolving door and with the master's time consumed by the teaching of rudimentary subjects to younger boys, the preparation of students for college—principally by teaching Latin to the older boys—declined in quality. If we assume that one test of a grammar school's quality was its success in preparing boys to attend college, then Roxbury's School was far from successful in this era. No one from Roxbury entered the Colony's college, for example, between 1725 and 1734, between 1740 and 1746,[90] between 1747 and 1752, or between 1757 and 1763.

FIG. 9. The birthplace of Joseph Warren on Warren Street in Roxbury, which is still standing. Photograph from a glass plate by John Murdoch, 1902. (Boston Athenæum Collection)

The people of Roxbury now had their minds on matters of greater import than their school. Since Roxbury closely adjoined Boston, its residents inevitably found themselves drawn into the revolutionary fervor that engulfed the colonial capital.

As we have seen above, one of the principal leaders of the Revolution was Joseph Warren, Class of 1755, whose statue today adorns the School's campus. After graduating from Harvard in 1759, Warren returned for the year 1760–61 to serve as the School's master. He soon proceeded to a career in medicine, but his preoccupation with and involvement in the political controversies of the day all but bankrupted him. He was a fiery revolutionary, authoring the Suffolk Resolves and

FIG. 10. The statue of General Joseph Warren, located on the School's campus since 1970, was executed in Paris by Paul Wayland Bartlett in 1896. It was erected in Warren Square, Roxbury, on June 17, 1904, as pictured above in this John Murdoch photograph. (Society for the Preservation of New England Antiquities Collection)

serving as president of the Provincial Congress, before dying (shortly before receiving his commission as major general) at Bunker Hill leading the forces of rebellion in 1775. Joseph's brother John (Class of 1767) was Harvard's first professor of medicine and ran a hospital for those wounded in the war. General John Greaton, brother of the Reverend James Greaton (probably Class of 1750 and certainly master 1755–58), grew up in Roxbury and also probably attended the School. He pursued the British from Lexington to Concord and fought with Washington in the Battles of Trenton and Princeton. Hale speculates that General William Heath was a graduate as well. Richard Dana, master 1718–22, was the first person publicly to resist the Stamp Tax in 1765 and, leading

FIG. 11. Meeting House Hill in 1790, before the 1803 church (still standing) was erected. From Drake's *Town of Roxbury*, frontispiece. The one-room brick schoolhouse is probably at the far left behind the buildings in the forefront.

a mob, frightened the Province's secretary into agreeing not to handle the stamps.[91]

The schoolmaster's response to the Revolution earned the School its most celebrated title: "oldest school in continuous existence in North America." British troops marched back and forth through Roxbury several times and eventually bombarded the town. Schoolmaster Williams, however, refused to close the School even for a single day. The only two (still existing) schools founded before Roxbury Latin—Boston Latin (1635) and Collegiate (1638)—both closed at length during the Revolution.[92]

The chaos caused by the Revolution brought another wave of inflation to New England, as both the Continental Congress and the government of Massachusetts issued paper money. The School's real income again declined since prices rose faster than the School could raise its rents. During this period, Bell's trustees were without a head from 1775 to 1782: Amos Adams, the church's minister since 1753, leading agitator against the British and chaplain to the Revolutionary army, had died in 1775.[93] The other two trustees, knowledgeable and experienced men who were deacons of the church, died in 1774 and 1779 respectively. Because of these deaths, the First Church was in eclipse. The parish was also affected by the general decline in church influence. Though New England was the most "churched" area of British America, it is estimated that by 1760 fewer than 25 percent of the New England population were church members. The population of the colonies mushroomed from 250,888 in 1700 to 905,563 in 1740 to 2,780,367 in 1780, but church growth did not keep up with the increase.[94] Whereas a century earlier the Puritan parishes had dominated New England, other denominations were now growing at a faster rate. Though the First Church would remain eastern Roxbury's only religious society until denominational parishes began to appear in 1817, and though the First Church in 1803 built the magnificent meeting house which today still dominates John Eliot Square, its influence had begun to wane in the years leading up to the Revolution, and its pastor had ceased to be the community's leading citizen.[95]

In 1783, shortly after Eliphalet Porter became pastor, the feoffees called Bell's trustees to account, describing their bookkeeping as "not Sattisfactory."[96] When the accounting was satisfactorily rendered a few days later, it was clear the feoffees could not afford to pay the schoolmaster his contracted £49, and they had to renege on their agreement.

In 1786 the feoffees again resorted to selling the School's patrimony, seeking and receiving the Legislature's permission to sell "the Great Lots" for two hundred silver pounds. They gained

FIG. 13. Eliphalet Porter, minister of the First Church in Roxbury, 1782–1833. Under him the parish became Unitarian.

immediate relief by this sale, because they could lend the money at thrice the rate they could obtain by leasing the land. But they immediately spent this extra income on annual expenses and lost forever the benefit of the increasing value of the land.

Friction continued between the feoffees and Bell's trustees. Since 1783, the latter had refused to make further accounting of their holdings. They had also ceased to follow the established practice of making payments to the School's treasurer and instead acted capriciously, sometimes making payments directly to the schoolmaster.

Finally, on June 16, 1788, the feoffees determined to force a showdown by closing the School:

> Met at school House [the School's] Feoffees and [Bell's] Trustees and a large number of the Inhabitants to Inquire why the School was Vacant could come to no Settlement with the [Bell] Trustees, therfore would not open the school there being no money in the Treasury and some rents anticipated to pay Mr. Smith [for boarding the master].[97]

Though Bell's trustees blinked and met the feoffees' demand, it was clear that the School could not continue subject to two conflicting boards. Upon a petition from Moses Davis, a prominent citizen, the General Court required that both the feoffees and the trustees appear before it for a hearing on January 7, 1789.

7. The Charter of 1789

At the urging of all elements of the Roxbury community and of Judge (later Governor) Increase Sumner, Class of 1763, and Judge John Lowell, the Great and General Court forthwith combined the two boards and issued a new Charter, signed into law by Governor John Hancock on January 21, 1789.[98]

The Charter made only one change in the School's constitution: the School's feoffees and Bell's trustees were combined into a single governing board known as "The Trustees of the Grammar School in the Easterly Part of the Town of Roxbury." These trustees were to be self-perpetuating: they were to choose their successors, "reputable freeholders of the town," up to thirteen in number, except that three were always to be the minister and the two oldest deacons of the First Church. The members of this board were to be "the true and sole Visitors, Trustees, and Governors of the said school in perpetual succession forever." They were to be in no way subject to the Town of Roxbury, though they were required, if asked, to give yearly a public statement of their accounts to the town meeting. Nine men were appointed, including Sumner and Lowell and members of both previous boards.

The Charter went to great lengths, in all other respects, to affirm that all previous documents—the Agreement of 1645, the Acts of 1670 and 1674, the conditions laid down in the bequests of Bell and of many others—stood with the same full authority they had before, except for this single change in the constituency and succession of the governing board.

The Charter did not require or suggest that the remains of Bell's bequest be segregated in any way from the School's general purpose funds. Neither in 1789 nor ever thereafter did the trustees set aside the Bell funds for any special purposes.

It should also be noted that the Charter says nothing about the perpetual donations (from the Agreement of 1645), and that no further mention of these donations appears in the School records after 1789. The donations had continued to be collected throughout the eighteenth century, and in 1722, when one Samuel Stevens fell five years behind in his payments, he was "Body arrested and bond given" until he agreed, in court, to pay. The "Old School Book" records meetings of the donors in 1763, 1770, 1774, 1779, 1780, and 1787 to elect a feoffee (as was their right until 1789). Roxbury's minister Eliphalet Porter told Richard Parker, the School's first historian, that the new 1789 trustees commuted the annual donations, settling for a once-and-for-all lump sum from each donor which they used to pay off the School's debts.[99]

The schoolhouse was "so much out of Repair and constructed on so small a plan" that it could no longer be used.[100] In the euphoria of the new beginning which the Charter seemed to promise, a subscription of £26 was raised towards the £176 cost of building "a new Brick School-House where the old one now stands, . . . forty feet long and twenty-six feet wide . . ., the walls . . . twelve feet in height . . ., with a hip'd roof." [101]

8. *Uncertainty and Indecision, 1789–1830*

But the euphoria quickly evaporated. Far from ushering in a golden age, the Charter—through no fault of its own—marked the start of fifty-five years in the wilderness during which the School was to reach its nadir.

The Charter did not solve the School's financial problems. While the academic instruction remained free, the trustees continued to charge students a fee to heat the School: the so-called "fire money." Though the School possessed large woodlands and sold wood from them at a profit, we find the trustees in the first year of the Charter voting:

> that the Master be directed to collect of each Schollar who attends the School sixteen pence, except of those poor children, named in a list this day handed to the master by the Trustees—to be appropriated to the use of supplying the School with wood. [102]

The trustee minutes disclose that such a fee was imposed virtually every year. The March 1805 minutes reveal the seriousness with which it was collected:

> [Voted] that the Master be requested to complete the collection of the fire money from all the Scholars, except those who the trustees have excused, and provided there should be any boys who shall refuse or neglect to pay the assessment for fire money aforesaid after a reasonable time which the master shall allow them, then the Master is requested not to instruct such Children. [103]

There is no record that anyone disputed the trustees' right to impose fees on students or to deny an education to those (who were capable of paying) who refused to pay them.

Financially, the trustees were between a rock and a hard place. If they kept their lands and rented them, they would receive an annual return of only about 1.75 percent, and yet they would benefit from the gigantic long-term rise in the value of land. If, on the other hand, they sold their lands, they could lend out the proceeds at an annual rate of 6 percent, but all benefits of the long-term increase in land value would be lost.

By great good fortune, the School had on its board—at this critical hour—someone who could conceive and effectuate a solution to the School's financial plight. Judge John Lowell[104] had been made a charter trustee in 1789. He had belonged to neither board before that and he brought fresh leadership. The trustees did not want to sell their land, but they needed more than the 1.75 percent return they were getting from it. Lowell saw a third option and persuaded the trustees to go for it: the School would not sell its land, but rather sell the *use* of it. The trustees returned, in other words, to the idea of leasing which had caused their predecessors such embarrassment a century earlier, 1687–1713. This time, however, they limited the leases to 120 years, at the end of which the land and everything on it would revert to the School.

Their assumption that people would pay nearly as much for property on a 120-year lease as they would pay for unencumbered property turned out to be correct. Between 1794 and 1796, all the School's lands were leased for lump sums for 120 years, raising a total of $11,000 for the School. By lending out this $11,000, the trustees greatly enhanced their annual income and brought an end to the immediate financial crisis.

Sadly, though, the trustees' decisive wisdom in financial affairs did not extend to educational matters. Roxbury Latin remained the sole secondary school for boys in a town whose population was mushrooming. By 1697 Roxbury's borders had been settled. It was a long narrow wedge extending east-west (to Dedham) almost eight miles, and north-south (from Brookline and Newton to Dorchester) about two miles. The colonial census of 1765 put Roxbury's population at 1,467, most of which was concentrated in the "easterly" part of the town (modern day Roxbury) by the Boston "neck"—where the church and School were located.[105] But the "westerly" parts of the town (modern day Jamaica Plain, Roslindale, and West Roxbury) were now being increasingly settled. Elementary schools had gradually sprung up in various parts of the town, but, as we have seen, by 1770 Roxbury Latin was swamped: eighty-seven boys, only eight of whom were studying Latin, were stuffed into the single schoolroom. The School still continued the practice of admitting boys at an early age, hoping to carry some to preparation for college. Unfortunately, the tail wagged the dog: the master had to devote most of his attention and effort to the many small boys studying elementary subjects, giving short shrift to the few older boys who actually made it to the college preparatory level. The December 11, 1789 trustee minutes record that the trustees tightened only slightly the extremely low admissions standards:

> No schollar shall be admitted under the age of six years, nor under the age of seven, provided there are seventy schollars of that age, and upwards; nor of any age unless they can read tolerably well by spelling words of four syllables — the number is not, however, to be restricted to seventy, if more shall apply for admission, qualified as above mentioned.

The trustees faced in educational matters a trap like the one they faced in financial matters. If they decided to continue to be the sole secondary school serving all interested Roxbury boys, then the trustees would have to build a larger building, hire additional teachers, and offer courses for boys *not* heading to college as well as the traditional Latin school curriculum. Such a decision would require large additional funds. If, on the other hand, the trustees decided to become a more selective college-preparatory Latin school, they would eliminate many boys of the sort they had previously educated.

Several external factors contributed to the trustees' indecision. First, as the nation gained its independence, many questioned the old British-model Latin schools. Debate raged among New Englanders about the value of learning Greek and Latin. The "moderns" in this debate, regarding the ancient languages as useful only to aspiring clergy, wanted to substitute more generally useful subjects. No doubt many of Roxbury's families shared the moderns' viewpoint. Certainly this viewpoint was a major factor behind the Massachusetts Education Act of 1789 which mandated that only towns with two hundred families would now be required to have Latin schools. Freeing 117 towns of the responsibility to maintain Latin schools, this Act appeared to be a big step on the way to abolishing them altogether. And, in fact, though 110 towns were still legally required to maintain such schools, by 1800 only thirty Latin schools remained in the state.[106]

The trustees, therefore, had a worry of the most fundamental sort. Did the people of Roxbury want what the School was founded to teach—Latin "Literature" as a preparation for college? Or did the citizens of the town want something quite different for their children? Economic conditions made the situation even more difficult. The drawn-out War of Independence (in all its phases) had been extremely costly. There was, therefore, a taxpayers' revolt at the end of the eighteenth century. Citizens resisted increases in property taxes to support schools. Roxbury's Latin School was not tax-supported, but the people of Roxbury were nevertheless asking questions about the need for a Latin school and expressing an inimical attitude towards supporting such a school financially.

The demise of the Latin schools created a vacuum that was filled by the new "academies" which sprang up in the thousands all over the country. The era from the Revolution to the Civil War was the heyday of the academies. It is conservatively estimated that by 1855 some 6,185 academies were serving 263,096 pupils in the United States. A good many of these academies were in Massachusetts—including several, such as Phillips Academy at Andover and Lawrence Academy at Groton, which still flourish. By 1855, 13,436 Massachusetts pupils were attending academies.[107]

Three characteristics of the academies are of special interest as we consider Roxbury Latin's situation. First, their governance was much like Roxbury Latin's (and therefore unlike that of the town-controlled Latin Schools). The academies were founded as non-profit charities by public-spirited citizens. These citizens viewed with alarm what had happened to the old New England grammar schools as a result of their being under local political control. The academy founders therefore placed the governance of these new schools in the hands of independent and self-sustaining boards of trustees. Most of the academies went even further to protect themselves from the predations of local political control and harassment: both the Phillips academies (Andover and Exeter) made specific charter provision for moving from their location should that be necessary, and Lawrence Academy's charter provided that a majority of trustees must be non-residents of Groton.[108] Unlike the old New England grammar schools (such as Roxbury's), many of the new academies provided boarding facilities and drew students from a wide geographical area.

The second interesting characteristic of the academies is their financing. While public-spirited donors provided land and buildings—and sometimes more—all the academies counted on tuition payments by parents for a significant proportion of their operating income. They would flourish, in other words, only if they were good enough to woo prospective students.

The third interesting characteristic of the academies is their curriculum. Yale's President Jeremiah Day in 1828 attacked the broadening of the college-preparatory curriculum beyond the narrow classical fare offered by the Latin schools. Soon, however, Day's successor at Yale, as well as Josiah Quincy, Harvard's president from 1829 to 1845, became leading supporters of the academies as college-preparatory schools.[109] In an era of taxpayer stinginess and of antagonism towards Latin and other subjects traditionally regarded as college-preparatory, the academies seemed to the colleges the best hope to uphold some sort of standard of excellence in secondary education.

The academies broadened the scope of education by adding English, mathematics, modern language—and often practical subjects such as agriculture, surveying, and navigation—to the old grammar school staple of Latin, Greek, and arithmetic. But since most of the academies maintained the classical subjects in addition to the newer ones, they were able to offer a rigorous preparation for college to at least some of their students.[110]

The advent of the academies had two important effects. First, the old Latin schools such as Roxbury's suffered by comparison: their curriculum seemed narrow and outdated, out of touch with the "go-ahead" modern attitude of the newly independent nation. (On the other hand, in most Massachusetts towns, non-Latin schools governed by town politicians were offering few or no subjects that led on to college.) Second, towns discovered that the academies provided them with an excuse to abandon their local "grammar school" (i.e., Latin-teaching high school). Local government officials could now assert that parents who wanted their child to go to college could pay for him to go to an academy. Even towns that paid part or all of the tuition for such students at an academy were financially better off since they no longer had to maintain their own grammar school.

It is little wonder that the trustees facing the future after the Charter of 1789 were indecisive. As governors of one of the few remaining Latin schools, they clearly had to have doubts about whether there was any future for such a school. Since they controlled the only boys' high school in the town, they were also more and more pressured to turn control of it over to the town. They were, as well, increasingly aware that new academies, offering a far fuller curriculum than they, were springing up all around them—usually in country towns with more space and fresher air. Taken together, these factors essentially immobilized the trustees as they looked ahead.

The feoffees of the pre-1789 School had failed to decide whether to become a more focused college-preparatory Latin school or to try to be the secondary school for all the boys of Roxbury. The new trustees after 1789 were equally indecisive. Their failure to decide, was, inevitably, a decision for quantity versus quality. Between 1783 and 1794, only three boys from the School went on to college.

On the surface, the School certainly appeared to be a rigorous and demanding place. In his first-hand description of school life at the end of the eighteenth and start of the nineteenth centuries, C. K. Dillaway pictures the torture: boys attended school for seven-and-a-half hours each day, Monday through Friday, and half a day on Saturday. In addition to Sundays, they received only thirteen days of holiday each year: six days in June, two at Thanksgiving, and five single holidays. And yet, as we have seen, quantity of hours did not make for quality of learning.[111]

The mastership after 1789 remained the revolving door it had been before the Charter. In 1793 there were three different masters in succession in a single year. Overcoming their lethargy, the trustees in 1801 made a determined effort to find a permanent qualified master. They advertised an annual salary of $500 a year (as opposed to $12 a month in 1789) and threw in a house and barn to boot; they thereby secured the richly qualified Dr. Nathaniel Sheepard [*sic*] Prentiss.

Nevertheless, for all his learning Prentiss does not seem to have done much to raise standards. Simon Willard, Jr., son of the renowned Roxbury clockmaker Simon Willard, was born at Roxbury on January 13, 1795. He entered the School in 1805. We may assume that his poor preparation was typical:

> Till the age of ten years, I had no regular education, but such rudiments as could be picked up at home, or at primary schools with the aid of the New England Primer. At the age of ten I went to the Public Grammar School of Roxbury, kept by Dr. Prentiss, stayed there four years. The youths of that day were not troubled with over education. Such knowledge as was given them was riveted to their memories by the rod and ferule. Moral suasion was not part of the educator's plan. The only School books used were the Columbian Orator, not the unabridged, but a matter of ten pages, Pike's Arithmetic, and Morse's Geography.

Not one of these elementary texts was used at the more rigorous Boston Latin School.

Like many boys of the time, Simon Willard, Jr., found little of value in school and left before graduating:

Left school at the age of 14 years and entered my father's shop, and worked at clock-making for a time till I was appointed to a watch maker by the name of Pond in Portsmouth, N.H., with whom I stayed till the war of 1812 was declared. Pond failed in 1812 and I came home and stayed with my father till 1813, when I met a fellow townsman named George Blaney who asked me how I should like to go to West Point. The idea meeting favor we both got cadet warrants through General Heath of Roxbury, a General who served in the Revolutionary Army and had some influence in Washington. [He graduated two years later in 1815.] [112]

Like many a teacher of the time, Schoolmaster Prentiss practiced medicine on the side, resulting in his absence from the schoolhouse for hours at a time. He seems also to have been a difficult man in other ways and by 1809, after many a battle, he and the trustees came to a parting of the ways. Following his departure, the trustees lost heart, once again letting the School drift into the former pattern of short tenures by inexperienced masters.

As long as the trustees refused to choose between quantity and quality, the quantity of students—relentlessly increasing—would continue to affect its quality adversely. The trustees made only faint-hearted efforts to deal with the quantity problem. In 1789, as Roxbury's population reached 2,150, the trustees voted that boys under six could no longer attend the School, nor could boys of any age who could not "read tolerably well." In 1803, boys under seven were excluded. Those of any age who could not pass a simple spelling test were also turned away. But these decisions affected the numbers hardly at all. And when the trustees prudently set aside some of their annual income to produce future income to teach the ever-increasing number of children in the town, some of their fellow citizens impugned their motives in an ugly public presentment.

The town's population continued to expand by leaps. By 1808 it had increased some 68 percent over what it had been in 1789. The trustees therefore felt themselves forced in 1808 to place a further—and unprecedented—limitation on the student body:

> Whereas the Inhabitants of the Town of Roxbury have greatly in-
> creased in their numbers, and their children actually residing in the
> Town, and attending the Grammar School have become too
> numerous for one Preceptor to instruct. Therefore voted that no
> Children who do not actually reside in the Town of Roxbury be
> permitted for the future to attend for Instruction in this School.[113]

Three observations about this action are perhaps in order: First and
obviously, there were in the School a number of non-Roxbury students;
otherwise they would not have had to be prohibited from attending.
Second, the right of the trustees to impose a residency requirement
entails perforce the right *not* to impose one. Third, the imposition of
this unprecedented limitation by the trustees was made for reasons of
exigency (numbers) and not for philosophical reasons; that is, neither
the Charter nor any of the founding documents envisioned or enjoined
such a limitation.

Unfortunately, we do not possess the addresses of schoolboys from
this period, but this prohibition does not appear to have been enforced
with much rigor. In 1831, for example, the trustees denied a prize to a
boy in the School when they discovered that he lived in Boston.[114] We
may safely assume that there were other non-Roxbury boys in attendance. As we shall see, by the time this prohibition was officially lifted
in 1868, it was routinely ignored.

In 1819, even with the imposition of both age and geographical limitations, the School still numbered more than eighty boys. The trustees
therefore decided upon a bolder and more costly strategy to deal with
the size problem. They added a second floor to the schoolhouse and
hired a second master to teach younger boys ("Classes IV & III"). They
hoped thereby to free the "upper" master to devote his full attention to
the older boys ("Classes II & I"). There are hints that their hopes were
realized: In 1819 Latin was, for the first time, included in the list of subjects examined by the trustees at their annual visitation; by 1822 prizes
were awarded for Greek and Latin. There was a general "tightening up":
in 1821, for example, boys who came to school without the necessary

books were dismissed, unless their parents were too poor to purchase them.[115]

Still, standards were not high. The two classrooms were badly over-crowded: in 1826, there were sixty boys in the "upper" and another sixty in the "lower" school. Richard G. Parker, "upper" master 1825–28, paints this picture:

> Within a few years past, the number of pupils in classical studies has been but a small proportion of the scholars; and this has prob-ably arisen from the almost fashionable . . . idea of the inutility of the dead languages [i.e., Latin and Greek] as affording proper sub-ject for the attention of the young. . . . It is to be regretted that in this school, little attention has been paid within a few years to the elements of classical literature. The blame . . . cannot however be attached to the Instructers [*sic*]; because it has been optional with the parents of the pupils.[116]

Even in the "upper" school, only a handful of boys were studying Latin. To teach them, Parker introduced a "monitorial system": he left a boy in charge of most of the pupils while he took the Latin boys into a side room for brief periods of instruction.

Parker left in 1828 for two reasons. First, he felt the trustees were not committed to high standards. Not only did the trustees at their visita-tions express their satisfaction with the standards demonstrated each year by the boys, but in 1827 they voted to lower them:

> In future, each scholar who enters the upper School, shall be able to read correctly and readily, and shall have cyphered [i.e., learned arithmetic] through simple Division, their entrance not requiring them to have studied Grammar as was formerly one of the condi-tions.[117]

Parker had grown tired and discouraged teaching elementary subjects to upper school boys. His other reason for leaving was that, with their resources divided between two teachers, the trustees could not afford to pay him the standard salary of a Latin schoolmaster. As a result, in 1829 the trustees ended their experiment with two masters and released the

FIG. 13a, b. George Putnam, minister of the First Church in Roxbury, 1830–1878.

popular lower master. In order to cut down the numbers in the reorganized School, the trustees in 1829 voted

> That no pupil shall hereafter be admitted into the School who is
> not nine years of age. . . . Every candidate for admission shall be
> examined by the Instructor with the assistance of a Trustee. . . . All
> applicants found on examination duly qualified shall be admitted
> provided there shall be any vacant seat or room for their accom-
> modation.[118]

9. *George Putnam*

The year 1830 was a watershed. The church's pastor, Eliphalet Porter,
was seventy-two, and the elders now sought an associate pastor who
could succeed him.[119] Their choice to lead this ancient and prestigious
"religious society" was surprising: a twenty-two-year-old named
George Putnam.

Putnam had grown up on a prosperous farm in Sterling, Massachusetts, the youngest of six children. His childhood was traumatized by
the deaths of his father (before he was two) and four of his five siblings.
These losses, perhaps, gave him the somberness that one of his clerical
contemporaries noted:

> Vivid enjoyment was not his use. Exultation was utterly foreign to
> his nature. Gayety, as we recall him, refuses absolutely to associate
> itself with his idea. The abandonment of a hearty laugh, eyes danc-
> ing with merriment, is what no friend of his manhood, we guess,
> ever witnessed in him. Not that he was discontented or morbid or
> morose, but grave to the verge of sadness.

He had attended two of the new academies—Leicester and Groton
(present day Lawrence Academy)—and entered Harvard at age fifteen
in 1822. After graduating he taught for a year at another new academy,
that at Duxbury. While he was there, Professor Henry Ware, Sr., of the
Harvard Divinity School persuaded him to study for the ministry of the
Unitarian church (though his mother's family was Congregational).
Unitarianism had begun as a liberal movement within the Congregational churches but soon became a separate denomination. During

Porter's pastorate the congregation of the Roxbury church had voted to become Unitarian. Now, in 1830, they chose Putnam as their new pastor, just as he completed divinity school. A year later he married Ware's daughter. (We shall consider in Part IV the ill-effects their son, Henry Ware Putnam, had on the School.) Though he served most of his life as an overseer and fellow of Harvard and was offered the Hollis Professorship there—as well as several enticements from other parishes—he remained pastor at Roxbury for forty-eight years, until his death in 1878.[120] His ministry spanned an era of dramatic change in the nation, the town, the School, and, of course, the parish.

The church elders who elected Putnam were the last vestiges of the farmers who had constituted the rural village of Roxbury.[121] In his funeral sermon for Porter in 1833, Putnam noted not only that Roxbury was changing, but that the First Church was no longer the town's only church: "[Porter] witnessed the growth of what was then a small town and scattered village, into a prosperous and thriving town. He has witnessed the rising of new houses of worship, where till lately there was but one."[122] Dillaway adds:

> The parish at this time, and for some years after, was essentially an agricultural one, a majority of the members being substantial farmers.... Gradually in the course of [Putnam's first] ten years the agricultural element in our [parish] disappeared. The increased value of the land, and the estimates of the assessors, drove our farmers to more profitable fields. The pews they left were soon filled by the commercial class, many of them from the highest mercantile houses in Boston.[123]

Putnam automatically became a trustee of the School upon his arrival, and his forty-eight years in that office were exactly coterminous with his ministry in the parish. He had the dynamism and shrewdness to preside over the complete and successful transformation of his parish. And as a trustee he threw himself into helping the School face the pressures and problems that, as we have seen, were overwhelming it.[124]

FIG. 14. View of the 1803 meeting house (still standing) sometime in the nineteenth century. (Boston Public Library Collection)

He first dedicated himself zealously to improving the School's quality. There was nothing wavering or uncertain about him.[125] He ardently believed in and often reiterated the School's founding motive—education for godly citizenship. His 1844 Phi Beta Kappa Address at Harvard is perhaps his most eloquent statement of the priority of character over scholarship:

> Virtue will not stay in second place. She will serve the intellect, but serve only by reigning. She must have the throne in man, or there is no rule in him but anarchy, and no end for him but defeat. She must have the making of the man, or he is but hollow armor and a whited sepulchre.
>
> Yes, in reason and in fact, character goes before scholarship, invests it, includes it. Genius and learning must walk in the train of virtue and lackey her to her triumphs; so only can they share them with her. The gifts of intellect, the privileges and acquisitions of

scholarship, are worse than lost, unblessed of God and unaccepted of mankind, except as they conspire obediently with their divine teacher, virtue, to furnish forth a man.[126]

The same theme is further developed in his Election Sermon of 1846:

> There is no such thing as education in the true sense of the word, without moral and spiritual culture. To neglect this last, while we stimulate and train the intellect of the child, is to commit an outrage upon that child's natural rights and to do him an irreparable wrong. He is not educated. . . . [The] next great step, which we should look for in the improvement of our schools, is a more distinct recognition of the moral nature of a child, and a more direct and diligent endeavor to develop, guide and train his higher susceptibilities, a more clear recognition that the soul is the chief part of a human being, and that character is the one central object to which all other things, intellect, knowledge, and skill are incidents, great and essential, but subordinate parts of a far greater whole.[127]

Putnam was meddlesome, telling the master how to teach or what textbooks to use, scrutinizing every detail of the School's life and fabric. For all his concern with the minutiae of the School, he never lost this noble vision of the School's great original calling. Whatever his faults, the beginning of the School's renaissance can be dated from his arrival.

Almost immediately he pressed to move the School away from the rapidly developing Dudley Square business district. He persuaded the trustees to purchase part of the Joseph Warren Estate on Mt. Vernon Place (later Kearsarge Avenue) for $800. There was, however, no money to put a schoolhouse on it.

At that moment, the Roxbury Chemical Company, realizing that its land—with all its improvements—would revert to the School in 1916 upon termination of its 120-year lease, offered the School a large sum to purchase ownership of the land. This company was the first of many lessees who would make such offers to the School. The trustees were strongly tempted; the proceeds would pay for the erection of a schoolhouse on the new lot. Among the elders of the church, none had befriended Putnam more than John Lowell, trustee of the School since

1816.[128] Son of the Judge John Lowell who had inspired the successful leases of 1794–96, Lowell argued passionately against the sale of any leased land, and persuaded the trustees not to imitate "the example of the First improvident man in history [Esau], who, in a fit of impatience, sold his birth-right for a mess of pottage."[129] Fortuitously, the sale of the old schoolhouse paid for the erection in 1835 of the $2500 Greek revival, two-room, two-story structure on the new property.

Putnam next turned his prodigious energies to what happened inside the building. And not a moment too soon. In the mastership of F. S. Eastman, 1828–35, only six boys had gone on to college. Kendall Brooks, the only graduate of the Class of 1837, describes his experience:

> You may judge the desperate condition of the School [in 1832] when I say that before I was twelve years of age I heard [i.e., taught] three recitations daily besides attending to my own studies, and from that time had regular classes assigned me [to teach] every day until I had finished preparation for college, when I was not quite sixteen years old.[130]

The 1830s brought an array of Putnam-inspired reforms: standards of admission to the School were established in reading, writing, arithmetic, and geography; the number of boys was limited to sixty; the school day was shortened and vacations slightly lengthened.[131]

Despite Putnam's reforms and the new building, the School's academic quality slipped even further. As long as the trustees refused to choose between quality and quantity, they could not retain a quality master. One master after another came and went, overwhelmed by the huge numbers of boys of vastly diverse ability and academic aspiration, and discouraged by the School's faint-hearted commitment to its grammar school heritage. Between 1836 and 1844 only three boys entered college—one going to Brown and two to Harvard.

The dramatic increase in the population of New England towns in the early nineteenth century placed enormous pressures on the few remaining seventeenth-century endowed "free schools." On the one hand they could choose to narrow their mission, remain relatively small, and cease being schools for the whole town. Hopkins Grammar School in New Haven did this, and so did Collegiate in New York. To preserve their independence such schools would eventually have to support themselves—at least partially—by charging tuition.[132] On the other hand, they could choose to surrender control to the town and become tax-supported "public" schools which served the entire population. The Hopkins schools at Hartford and Hadley and the Ipswich Grammar School chose this course.

Roxbury's population was increasing far more rapidly than that of most towns. Between 1810 and 1870 Roxbury's population would skyrocket from 3,669 to 34,772.[133] In 1840, its population having risen to 9,089, the trustees could no longer avoid making critical choices: serving all the boys of the town or remaining small, surrendering control to the town's politicians in return for tax support or remaining independent and finding the necessary financial resources.

10. *The Experiment of 1839–1860*

Just as the trustees were finally about to face up to this critical decision, a have-your-cake-and-eat-it-too solution appeared to offer itself. Massachusetts' acts of 1835 and 1837 required towns the size of Roxbury—on pain of ruinous fines—to support what was popularly called an "English high school" in which "useful" subjects such as U.S. history, bookkeeping, surveying, algebra, and geometry were taught. (Unlike the Latin schools, such schools did not generally prepare students for college.) The town of Roxbury was in financial straits because of the costly expansion of elementary schools the population boom had forced it to undertake. There were, as we have mentioned, 195 students in the town's five elementary schools in 1790. By 1829, there were eleven town-supported elementary schools with enrollment totaling 770. When these schools were inspected it was found that they were woefully deficient, and large new appropriations were voted for their support.[134] Faced in 1835 and 1837 with the costly prospect of building a new high school and staffing it, the town school committee was only too pleased when the intrepid George Putnam proposed that the School provide the school committee with such a school, at a cost far lower than the town would face if it established its own English high school. The only problem was that the Act of 1835 required that such a high school be managed by the school committee, and the School's trustees had no desire (nor did the Charter authorize them) to give up their positions as sole governors of the School. In 1839 a special Act was therefore passed allowing the Roxbury school committee (which retained control of elementary education) to turn control of high school instruction in the town over to the trustees. For their part, the trustees were granted a subsidy of $300 for the rest of 1839, and $500 a year thereafter, for providing the town with a high school.

With the help of this new income, Putnam went in search of a new master to replace J. H. Purkitt, whose health had been broken by the strenuousness of the job. His first choice was Purkitt's temporary replacement who had held the job for three weeks. But this man declined the offer: "The reasons assigned were the want of discipline and the great number of classes in the school."[135] However, Putnam was not deterred and found an excellent man, an Episcopal clergyman named Daniel Leach, author of several widely used textbooks.

Leach was immediately confronted with an unmanageably large group of students, many of whom were not interested in the Latin school subjects he had been hired to teach. The trustees in December 1840 therefore voted that "after the 1st day of January next, the School shall be a Latin School, and that in the future admissions of Scholars, none shall be received who do not purpose to pursue the course of studies usually taught in a Latin School."[136] In 1841 Leach gave up part of his own salary to hire an assistant, so that he could do true grammar school teaching. By June 1842, the trustees' commitment to their Latin school heritage had cooled and they voted "That the resolve proposed Decr. 8, 1840, declaring this to be exclusively a Latin School, be rescinded."[137] A second master—to teach English subjects—was then officially engaged.

Even with the town's subsidy, the trustees could ill afford to pay for two schoolmasters. They complained to the school committee that the Washington (elementary) School, under the committee's supervision, was not providing entering students with adequate preparation. The committee, however, refused to upgrade the quality of instruction.

The trustees' frustration with the school committee over standards was compounded by their mounting sense that the School was being pulled down by having to teach material that should have been covered in earlier years in the town schools. The trustees' visiting committee—heretofore always positive in its year-by-year inspection of the School—issued a negative report in 1843: "the pupils did not appear as well as usual on the days of examination." [138] In 1844 both Leach and his colleague (who had taught the younger boys) departed.

More perhaps out of exasperation than out of philosophical intro-spection, the trustees now acted decisively, finally making the tough choice between quantity and quality. Announcing the abolition of the costly double mastership, they emphatically restated their 1840 affirma-tion (rescinded in 1842) that the School was a Latin school: "[The] school shall be under the care of one teacher, [and] be considered a Latin School, and that only such classes be formed in English studies as are usual in a Latin school, or are found to be compatible with its inter-ests as a Latin school." [139]

For a few years, the mastership again became, as it had been earlier, a revolving door—with changes almost every year. Under Putnam's watchful eye, however, the masters were, by and large, young men of distinction, such as John Dudley Philbrick (1842–44) who went on to become U.S. Commissioner of Education. Benjamin Apthorp Gould, Jr., came to teach at the School for a year in 1844 right out of Harvard on his way to becoming a world-renowned astronomer. J. E. Greene '50 describes the student rebellion which occurred while he was master:

> Toward the end of Mr. Gould's [one-year] mastership he was ill for
> a week or two and sent one of his [Harvard] classmates as a sub-
> stitute. Then occurred one of the two rebellions which I remember

at the school. The scholars did not actually depose the master, for the older boys were shrewd enough to see that that would bring about a crisis. They simply did as they pleased, allowing the master to remain, but paying no more regard to his authority than was needed to prevent him from abdicating or appealing to the trustees. He tried appealing to force, but was quickly made to understand that, if that was the *ultima ratio,* we were better reasoners than he. . . . The real power lay in the hands of a few big boys.[140]

Henry B. Wheelwright (master 1839–40 and 1845–47) was remembered fondly: "Probably no aggregations of schoolboys ever had a 'chummier' or more congenial teacher, one more respected and obeyed," wrote one of his students. Under Wheelwright's tutelage, all five members of the Class of 1847 went on to college, "probably the largest number ever offered at one time from this school."[141]

Wheelwright's 1847 results were "the exception that proves the rule." Up to this time, "going to college" was still virtually synonymous with "going to Harvard"—the area's only college. In the School's first two hundred years, only five boys attended a college other than Harvard: two went to Yale (both in 1717), two to Dartmouth (1803 and 1809), and one to Brown (1837). The Harvard admissions figures, therefore, are of particular interest. Between 1801 and 1870, Boston Latin sent 750 boys to Harvard, and three academies, Exeter, Andover, and Lawrence, 550, 250, and 50 respectively. Between 1820 and 1870, Cambridge High sent 100, and Salem High 75. Mr. Dixwell's School in Boston sent 75 between 1851 and 1870.[142] Even though it was comparatively a small school, Roxbury Latin's figure of 28 boys to Harvard in the first 47 years of the century reflects the low quality of its academic preparation. (As the School improved in the 1850s and 1860s the count rose: the 1801–1870 Harvard-bound figure for Roxbury Latin was 93.)

In 1847, the trustees raised the entrance age to twelve and hired Charles K. Short. A graduate of Phillips Academy, Andover (1840), and Harvard (1846), he had taught for only two months at Andover before coming to Roxbury at age twenty-six. Because he was given a low-paid

FIG. 15. Charles K. Short, first "headmaster" (1847–1853), later president of Kenyon College and professor of Latin at Columbia. The photograph was probably taken while he was headmaster—or shortly after.

"assistant teacher" (to help with the forty-three boys), he was the first master to be known (during his 1847–53 tenure) as "head master." Like many of the men Putnam chose as master, Short went on to great achievement—first as founder of a school in Philadelphia, then as president of Kenyon College, and later as professor of Latin at Columbia. Professor J. Evarts Greene, Class of 1850, said of him:

> I think the idea of scholarship in the sense of thorough and precise knowledge first came to [Roxbury Latin] through him. He was dissatisfied with the versions of the classics published in this country and insisted upon our using text books of foreign editors imported by him. The revival of learning at this school and the attainment of high standards of proficiency by its scholars . . . seems to me to have begun with him.[143]

This "revival of learning" brought tangible results in terms of college admissions. In the mid-1850s one diarist at Harvard remarked on "the clannish body from the great schools,—Exeter, Andover, Dixwell's, Boston and Roxbury Latin."[144]

Another change Short brought about was the introduction of the School's first summer vacation. The trustees' examination committee, in its September 1848 visitation, excoriated "the bad practice which prevails with some parents of taking their sons from the school four or five weeks before the end of the term in order to extend their vacation."[145] But by June 1849 the trustees capitulated to what was becoming standard American practice and "Voted that the summer vacation commence hereafter on the Monday preceding the third Wednesday in July and continue five weeks."[146]

The tensions underlying the trustees-school committee agreement periodically erupted. Professor Greene writes of his experience as a first year boy in 1844:

> In my time this jealous feeling found expression in a perpetual feud between the town School boys [of the Washington Grammar—i.e., elementary—School, run by the School Committee] and the Latin school boys, with a good deal of fighting, in single combat or in companies somewhat carefully organized and skilfully led. Once, I remember, we were besieged in our own Schoolhouse by a large force of Washington school boys exasperated by some recent occurrence. We were about to make a sortie, armed with ball clubs and other weapons of that character, confidently expecting to defeat and disperse the enemy, who numbered about ten to our one, or to cut our way through and retreat without serious loss, when the higher powers, represented by a selectman and a constable, appeared upon the scene and raised the siege.[147]

These same tensions also existed at the adult level and burst forth in an equally violent—though not physical—form. Distrust bred rumors. The rumor of 1852 was that Roxbury would be fined by the authorities or sued by its citizens if it did not directly run its own English high school. The trustees were tired of such upsets and proposed that the Agreement of 1839 be broken.

Instead, the 1839 arrangements were patched up and a new accommodation reached in June 1852. In addition to providing the now-city (as of 1846) of Roxbury with a Latin school, the trustees would oversee a separate school—variously called "the English department" or "the English high school" or the "High School for Boys"—for the city. While the trustees retained control of faculty appointments and curriculum, the school committee was granted rights of consultation and inspection. The new school met at first in rented quarters. But by 1853 the trustees offered to erect, with their own funds, a $4000 building "of sufficient capacity to accommodate seventy or eighty boys of the English High School," next to the Greek revival Latin schoolhouse.[148] For its part, the city agreed to increase its annual subsidy beyond the current $1000.

At the same time, the trustees increased the Latin School's course from four to five years and hired Augustus Buck as Latin School "principal" to teach its twenty-three boys. Most of the population of Roxbury did not aspire to college and sought the meat-and-potatoes course of the "English Department" which numbered sixty (thirty-six of them new). A year later, Buck had twenty-six Latin students in the old building, while the new one already accommodated seventy-one English students.

Even after the new arrangements of 1853, the trustees continued to express their unhappiness about the inadequate preparation boys were receiving at the school committee's elementary schools. At first the trustees were patient, hoping standards would rise. But by 1857 they had had enough and rejected thirty-six of the thirty-seven applicants for the English School. Parents were predictably outraged and stormed the school committee. The politicians of the school committee would have liked nothing better than to take control of the English High School, but they received all their funds from the Roxbury City Council's committee of public instruction. Headed by the mayor—a trustee of the School—this committee rejected the school committee's takeover attempt:

> After careful examination of the whole subject, it would appear to
> your Committee that the High School for Boys [i.e., the "English
> School"], as at present conducted, is worthy of the confidence of
> the public. It is such a school as is wanted by the people, and the
> repeal of the Act of 1839, already alluded to, would deprive the City
> Government of the means of using a fund [i.e., the School's
> endowment] which, in the present condition of our finances, it is
> desirable to use.[149]

The school committee was thus temporarily checked. And the trustees
noted with pleasure that the boys of the Washington Grammar School
came much better prepared in each of the next three years. By 1858, the
trend, which in 1856 had seen ninety-five boys in the English School
(with twenty-five in the Latin), was reversed: there were fifty in the
Latin "department" and forty-three in the English.[150]

C. K. Dillaway, writing in 1860 just before the breakup that year of
the School-city arrangement, discussed some of the tensions underlying the school committee's relationship with the trustees:

> There have never been wanting men in our community whose hos-
> tility to the Trustees has been incessant and uncompromising. The
> cause of this may be found, not in the mode of administration
> adopted by the Trustees, but in the mode of their election. That
> they are a close corporation, electing their own members indepen-
> dently and without reference to any popular vote, is enough to
> arouse a spirit of jealousy. . . . Within the last twenty years [1840–
> 60] some of our unscrupulous politicians . . . attempted to create a
> popular excitement against the Trustees.[151]

By 1860, the school committee found a way to win over the committee of public instruction: the boys of the English School would be
moved into the girls' school, along with their teachers, and the city
would actually save a little money. The City of Roxbury's subsidy to the
School could then again be reduced to the pre-1852 level of $500 (for the
Latin School alone). Although the reports of the city's visiting committees throughout the decade had been uniformly laudatory, and although

every member of the trustee-appointed English School faculty was hired by the city to teach in its new school, the school committee nonetheless wrote:

> As in 1839, 52, and 57, so now in 1860 do the School Committee find that the rapid growth of our City and the advancement of the age demand a different course and a higher order of instruction for the youth of our city.
>
> [The trustees should] procure, through the legislature, such an alteration of their charter as would enable them to surrender the charge of their School . . . and the control of its funds to the City Authorities.[152]

The trustees' reply is a masterpiece of sarcasm:

> This suggestion is courteously made and is entitled to a respectful consideration both on account of its intrinsic importance and the source from which it comes. We cannot think, however, that it ought to be adopted and acted on by this board. We give three reasons which have brought us to this conclusion:
>
> 1. The founders of the School who endowed it so liberally, appear never to have intended that the School or the property should be confided to the public authorities. They appointed Feoffees and Trustees and made provision for a perpetual succession. And though the present Board is not precisely that which they established or anticipated, yet in the opinion of the Legislature of 1789, it is a Board so constituted as to represent their wishes and interests as nearly as was practicable under the changed circumstances.
>
> 2. We believe it to be proved by long experience everywhere, that Trust funds are generally safer under the guardianship of private and responsible Trustees or Corporations than in the hands of such public bodies or Civic Corporations as Legislatures or Town authorities or City Councils—less liable to peculations and consuming commissions, petty jobbings or high-handed misapplications and the various evils of negligent or corrupt administration.
>
> 3. We think that a body constituted as this Board is, is quite as likely, in general and in the long run, to manage well a school of a high grade, as a body constituted like the School Committee. We

feel quite safe in asserting that in times past, the members of the Board have been, on the average, men of as high and as well recognized qualifications for such service as the Members of the School Committee of the Town or City of Roxbury. The School Committee is a variable body, subject to all the vicissitudes of popular elections. It may not every year and always enjoy the very high character ascribed to the present Board, in the Report of the Committee of Public Institution. And, on the other hand, the time may come, if the care be exercised in filling vacancies as they occur, when this Board of Trustees will also be, in the language applied by the Committee of Public Instruction to the present Board of [the] School Committee, "mostly composed of gentlemen of long experience in school matters and who bring to their duties much knowledge and scientific attainments derived from practical experience and from intimate connection with the best methods of instruction in our public schools and are quick to discern the wants necessary for a full development of the human mind as taught in our institutions of learning."[153]

After reminding the school committee that it was unilaterally breaking the Agreement of 1839, and that the trustees could in law hold the committee to it, the trustees declared their intention not to do so and acknowledged that the Agreement had been ended. In conclusion, they added:

> The best service the Trustees can render to the interest of good education in our City is to devote their attention and their means exclusively to the sustaining and perfecting of their School as a Latin School, organized as it is with a view to fitting boys for college.

Though the city continued for seven years thereafter to make a small annual grant of $500 in support of the School (since it provided the city with its only Latin School), this support ceased in 1868 when Roxbury was annexed to Boston (which already had a Latin School). The City of Boston gave the School a subsidy of $3000 in January 1869, but the School rescinded its requests in 1871 and 1872 and has received nothing since.

Though the trustees had made the tough quality-versus-quantity decision in 1844, the town-school arrangements of 1839 had continued awkwardly and often rancorously for another sixteen years until 1860. Ironically, in the end, it was the town (now a city) that made the break. Once the decision was made, however, the trustees without encumbrance zealously took up the cause of quality.

11. *Augustus H. Buck, 1853–1867*

The School already had the leader it needed. Augustus H. Buck (Amherst '49) was only about twenty-six when he succeeded Short as headmaster in 1853, but he had already served as principal of Hopkins Academy at Hadley.[154] Even before the final split of 1860 he had begun to reestablish the School's academic reputation. In 1857, Buck invited William Coe Collar, then a twenty-three-year-old sophomore at Amherst College, to be his assistant. Collar paints this portrait of Buck:

> He was then a man of imposing presence, being, I should think, six feet high and weighing about two hundred pounds. He was rather heavy in the shoulders and a slight stoop made him seem a little less tall than he actually was. . . . He was already, at about thirty-one, partially bald, with close cut beard and black, thick eyebrows.
> . . .
> His portrait does not, I think, suggest an especially stern character, but such was perhaps the impression he made upon his pupils. This was due in part to a certain Delphic obscurity in his language, when he spoke warningly or threateningly. In the earlier years of his mastership corporal punishment was still very common in schools, and Mr. Buck did not spare the rod altogether. . . . Of the efficiency of his work as a teacher there was no question, and at Harvard the excellence of the preparation at the Roxbury Latin School soon became recognized.
> Forty years ago classical instruction did not concern itself greatly with literary culture and naturally did not, in this school, impart literary enthusiasm.
> [Buck's] teaching was characterized by great thoroughness and exactness, and as a drill master he was unsurpassed. For loose and

slovenly work he had no patience, but he did not fail to recognize merit, and his praise was thought to be worth having. He indulged sometimes in sarcasm, but this was often relieved by a droll and original style of speech. . . .

It was Mr. Buck's habit to make careful preparation of his lessons. He read German readily and had great admiration for German scholarship. I think he had copies of ten or twelve German editions of the classic authors read in schools and on doubtful points all would be consulted. An indefatigable worker himself he believed in the value to a boy of application, and *work or quit* was the unwritten law of the school.

Mr. Buck raised the school from its low state, set it on its feet, and made it self-respecting and respected.[155]

"The rattan [a switch used for beating] for punishing boys was frequently in use," according to Walter Eliot Thwing '68.[156] Perhaps because boys expect their headmaster to be stern, or perhaps because age softens remembrance, David G. Haskins, who was at the School in the years 1859–1862, paints this rather more sympathetic portrait of Buck:

Queer and silly legends were current in Roxbury of Mr. Buck's severity; but experience soon proved their absurdity. He was not a man with whom boys would care to take liberties; he enforced good order; once or twice he even administered the old-fashioned corporal punishment; but, as a rule, his discipline was not severe. . . .

His large muscular frame and the robust strength of his manly character commanded our respect: and his high ideals and contempt for all that was mean and unworthy produced a strong and enduring impression. He was a man of the most original genius; every little remark, every expression of his face, bore the stamp of a strong individuality; his quaint sayings became household words,—like his oft-repeated characterizations of unfortunates as "mentally befogged, morally bewildered and spiritually bedevilled." His comments on our efforts at declamation and composition were sometimes very amusing. One good-natured classmate of my own attempted a tragic speech beginning with the words, "White man, there is eternal war between thee and me." "Pause there," said Mr. Buck, "Your style of declamation is better adapted

FIG. 18. Augustus H. Buck, second headmaster (1853–1867).

to 'Lucy had a little lamb.'" Another boy, after reading aloud his composition, was informed, that, with his views, he was better fitted for Prime Minister of Austria than for an American citizen. . . .

When the great civil war came, he would often spend a good deal of time after the religious services with which the school was opened, giving his views on the news of the day. He always allowed boys to ask questions freely and to express their dissent. . . .

Among my pleasantest memories of these early times are the two field days, which he gave the boys of his division, in place of the usual school exercises. One of these was a long all-day walk over Dorchester Heights, through Boston, Charlestown, Cambridge, Brighton, and Brookline. The historic localities were assigned beforehand to particular boys to investigate and to explain to the rest on the spot. The second of these delightful long walks was to Quincy, where we visited the quarries and the home of the Adamses. . . .

I cannot remember ever to have received an unkind word from Mr. Buck.[157]

Since the "English department" had left the 1853 building, the Latin School moved into it in the fall of 1860. It was to remain the School's home until 1927. Buck (whose salary was $2000) taught thirty-two older boys in one room, while Collar (salary $1000) taught twenty-seven younger boys in another. Newly added that fall was a "preparatory department" for thirty elementary boys under Elizabeth Weston. The School's first woman teacher received a salary of $500.

The school year 1860-61 was, perhaps, the worst of times to revitalize a school. The fall saw a bitter presidential election campaign and the spring brought the outbreak of a civil war that sapped the nation's energies, deranged its finances, and slaughtered its youth. The following year brought required military drill with uniforms, caps, swords, and rifles for the older boys. Walter Eliot Thwing '68 described what it was like:

About 1862 we formed a military company named the 'Warren Cadets' after General Warren. . . . We were given blank cartridges one day, to see what we could do, and were lined up with our guns pointing over the hill on the north side of the school yard. At the command "fire" only three guns went off. . . . [A boy] was ordered to reprime and recharge them which took about an hour. The guns in part were discarded for Springfield muskets, with some lighter ones for small boys, and were kept in racks arranged around the upper school room under the blackboards. The uniform was like [that of] the soldiers in the field. A good sized drum corps preceded us on our marches. . . . We frequently marched up to Miller's field . . . drilled there for an hour and then marched down Warren Street in a double platoon stretching from curb to curb in almost perfect alignment. The boys of the school and those of the high school made up a battalion.[158]

Though the School company was disbanded in 1867, military drill lingered as a not-unpopular aspect of school life until 1885.

The 1860-61 school year was also a trying time because American secondary education was in the initial stages of revolutionary change. Any school that wished to survive the century would have to undergo radical transformation. The simple word "Literature" had described the School's entire curricular aspiration in the Agreement of 1645. To continue to prepare young men for college, the School would have to expand its curriculum greatly in the next thirty years and hire a faculty expert in a variety of newly-required academic fields. The choice facing the trustees was simple: expand or perish. They chose to expand.

The Latin School course (i.e., the curriculum taught by Buck and Collar, as distinct from what was taught in the preparatory department) was extended from five to six years in 1863. In 1865 Buck wrote the trustees

> stating that the amount of work in the Latin School was becoming such that it would be impossible for two teachers to do it longer than the present year. *This he attributed mainly to the ever-increasing exactions of Harvard College in their terms of admission.* [Emphasis added.][159]

Having no new source of funds, the trustees decided reluctantly to drop the preparatory department and use the mistress's salary to hire the required third Latin School teacher. In an arrangement advantageous to all, the preparatory mistress, Miss Weston, then rented a vacant room in the schoolhouse and formed her own preparatory school, charging tuition.

Buck resigned in 1867 to study and travel in Europe;[160] after teaching at Boston Latin for a brief period following his return, he was appointed professor of Greek at Boston University. Collar became headmaster (at a salary of $2500) and immediately hired Moses Grant Daniell as sub-master (at $1500); Daniell had assisted Collar while Buck was in Europe on sabbatical and was delighted to return. The trustees also authorized Collar to appoint the third teacher requested in 1865 by Buck. Miss M. H. Coburn was hired for $800 and served under Collar in his classroom as "assistant teacher."

We shall now pause to consider this newly appointed headmaster — William Coe Collar — whose dramatic transformation of the School was to earn him the title "Second Founder."

Notes to Part Two

1. The School has had many names. The Agreement of 1645 brought into existence "a free schoole in the said towne of Roxburie." In the petition of 1669 the feoffees refer not to a "free schoole" but to a "Grammar School." The Court in 1670 refers both to "a free school" and "the free school at Roxbury," but says the feoffees' duty is to supply a "Grammar school master." The 1674 agreement between Bell's trustees and schoolmaster John Gore refers to the "grammar free school." In 1754 the School's accounts were entered in a book headed "Dr. Joseph Williams, one of the Feoffees of the free Grammar school in Roxbury. Cr." (a phrase repeated in the feoffees' 1788 Petition to the General Court). In 1773 the School is referred to on a receipt as "the Grammar School." In 1789 the School was rechartered by the Commonwealth of Massachusetts as "the Trustees of the Grammar School in the Easterly part of the Town of Roxbury." When it served under contract in the 1840s and 1850s as Roxbury's high school for boys, it was sometimes called the "Latin and English High School" or the "Roxbury Classical High School." Since 1860, when the contract with the town ended, it has usually been called the "Roxbury Latin School," though the trustees' minutes book continues to use the term "Roxbury Grammar School" until 1870. In 1892 (see Trustee Minutes for 14 December 1892)—in preparation for the School's 250th anniversary—its name was Latinized into "Schola Latina Roxburiensis" and placed on the School's new seal. In 1947 the Legislature changed the School's name (Chapter 345—see Trustee Minutes of 12 June 1947) from the "Trustees of the Grammar School in the Easterly Part of the Town of Roxbury" to the "Trustees of the Roxbury Latin School." See also Richard W. Hale, Jr., *Tercentenary History of the Roxbury Latin School* (Cambridge: Riverside Press, 1946), 12–13. The debate over whether to capitalize the T, as in The Roxbury Latin School, will probably continue to the end of time. In most of the legal documents, all letters of the School's name are capitalized.

2. The Agreement of 1645 is dated 31 August 1645. But this Agreement replaces (probably copies) the original Agreement destroyed in a gunpowder explosion on 6 April 1645, probably shortly after it had been signed. John Winthrop's diary entry of 3 July 1645 says that "divers free schools were erected as at Roxbury." A school was envisioned at least as early as 1643. Samuel Hagburne's will, made 19 January 1642/43 and deposed on 8 March 1642/43, reads:

   Further, out of my greate desire to promote learning for God's honor and the good of his Church my will is that when Roxbury shall set up a free schoole in the towne, there shalbe ten shillings per annum out of the house and home lot paid unto it forever.

   (Hagburne's widow, incidentally, married Thomas Dudley, who was the first signer of the Agreement of 1645 and governor that year of the Colony.) In 1644 Lawrence Whittamore left land to the School in a codicil to his will. Those wishing to push back the date of the School's founding have used these two wills as evidence. See Richard Walden Hale, Jr., *First Independent School in America* in Publications of the Colonial Society of Massachusetts (hereafter PCSM) (Boston: By the Society, 1951) XXXV: 225–234, 255.

3.   In their 1669 Petition to the General Court, PCSM XXXV: 252, the feoffees said that sixty-four was "well nigh the whole Towne in those dayes" (i.e., the adult males of the town). Robert Emmett Wall, Jr., *Massachusetts Bay: The Crucial Decade 1640–1650* (New Haven: Yale U. Press, 1972), 39, says there were ninety-four males over twenty-one living in Roxbury in 1647 (two years later), of whom fifty-nine were freemen. So the number sixty-four probably indicates that all or nearly all the adult males contributed.

4.   "Roxbury Latin School Old School Book" (hereafter "RLS Old School Book"), the small, disordered, partly mouse-eaten, handwritten repository of the School's records between 1645 and 1787. Owned by the trustees, it is on permanent loan to the Houghton Library at Harvard (MsAm 1488), 7.

5.   For the date of John Eliot, Jr.'s birth, see *A Report of the Record Commissioners, containing the Roxbury Land and Church Records* [Document 114–1880] (Boston: Rockwell and Churchill, 1881), 76: "John his first borne son, was borne on the 31 day of the 6t month. ano. 1636." The sixth month in the O.S. calendar (when the new year began on March 25) was August. John Langdon Sibley, *Biographical Sketches of Graduates of Harvard University*, (Cambridge: Sever, 1873), I: 476, errs in saying John Jr.'s birthday was August 3. For Philip Eliot's mastership, see Charles M. Ellis, *The History of Roxbury Town* (Boston: Drake, 1847), 57 and 118. See also Hale, *Tercentenary History*, 15. For Edmund Weld, see Sibley, *Biographical Sketches* I: 220.

6.   See Augustine Jones, *The Life and Work of Thomas Dudley* (Boston: Houghton Mifflin, 1899), 11. Dudley's fifty- to sixty-book library was very large for the time. His daughter, Anne Bradstreet, was perhaps the most distinguished female poet of her day. (See Jones, 259–262.)

7.   We do not know what Philip Eliot was paid, but when "Mr. Hanford" was appointed schoolmaster in 1650 he was paid £22 per annum. ("RLS Old School Book," 114). So the annual donations (coming to just over £22) would barely have covered the schoolmaster's salary.

8.   See David Hackett Fischer, *Albion's Seed* (New York: Oxford, 1989), 18: "When most of those immigrants explained their motive for coming to the New World, religion was mentioned not merely as their leading purpose. It was their only purpose." Samuel Eliot Morison, *The Intellectual Life of Colonial New England*, 2d ed. (Ithaca: Cornell U. Press, 1956), 8, defines the Puritans as follows: "They were a party in the Church of England that arose in Elizabeth's reign with the purpose of carrying out the Protestant reformation to its logical conclusion, to base the English Church both in doctrine and discipline on the firm foundation of Sacred Scripture; or in the words of Cartwright, to restore the primitive, apostolic church

'pure and unspotted' by human accretions or inventions. Religion should permeate every phase of living. Man belonged to God alone: his only purpose in life was to enhance God's glory and do God's will, and every variety of human activity, every sort of human conduct, presumably unpleasing to God, must be discouraged if not suppressed." See also James Axtell, *The School Upon a Hill* (New York: Norton, 1974), 2–3, who says the Puritans' City upon a Hill was meant "to beacon the living message of the Reformation to a dying Europe."

9. See Lawrence A. Cremin, *American Education, the Colonial Experience, 1607–1783* (New York: Harper, 1970), 152f.: "Nonconformity quickly allied itself with the civil authority to become a new conformity." See also John G. Brooks, *Memorial Sermons in Recognition of the Two Hundred and Fiftieth Anniversary of the Founding of the First Religious Society of Roxbury* (Boston: G. H. Ellis, 1882), 15: "They neither asked nor allowed anything like perfect freedom in religion. . . . They are often criticized as if they came to found a democracy where all would be equal. They had no such thought. They came to found a theocracy and a government based upon very clearly defined religious ideas that were dearer to them than freedom, or equality or life. . . . The Puritans took for themselves Pym's doctrine in England, which was this: that it is the duty of legislators to establish the true religion and to punish the false."

10. Nathaniel Shurtleff, ed., *Records of the Governor and Company of the Massachusetts Bay in New England* (hereafter *Mass. Bay Records*) (Boston: William White, 1853–54), II: 6–7. See Cremin, *American Education*, 124–25 and Walter Herbert Small, *Early New England Schools* (Boston: Ginn, 1914), 294–304. The Massachusetts Bay Company's charter—which the original settlers agreed to—spoke of their obligation "to teach and catechise the Company's servants and their children, as also the savages and their children." Pauline Holmes, *A Tercentenary History of the Boston Public Latin School* (Cambridge: Harvard U. Press, 1935), 7, says: "This famous law is remarkable in that for the first time in the English-speaking world the state ordered that all children should be taught to read." In discussing the Massachusetts laws of 1642, 1647, and 1648, Holmes calls them the foundation of the present public education system, but admits (9): "It should be emphasized, however, that our present school system is secular, whereas *the aim* of classical education, according to the Colonial legislation of 1647, *was largely religious.*" [Emphasis added.] For a brilliant discussion of the Puritan view of education, see Lorraine Smith Pangle and Thomas L. Pangle, *The Learning of Liberty: The Educational Ideas of the American Founders* (Lawrence: U. of Kansas Press, 1993), especially 21–31.

11. Thomas Dudley, "Letter to the Countess of Lincoln, March 1631," *Collections of the New Hampshire Historical Society* (Concord: Marsh, Capen, and Lyon, 1834), IV: 237.

12. See William Wood, *New Englands Prospect* (1634), ed. Alden T. Vaughan (Amherst: U. of Massachusetts Press, 1977), 58, and Nathaniel B. Shurtleff, *A*

Topographical and Historical Description of Boston (Boston: City Council, 1871), 40. It should be noted, however, that the 1640s were in general (and doubtless to a degree in Roxbury) a period of financial depression. The generosity and commitment of the Roxbury inhabitants—comfortable though they largely were—is therefore the more commendable at this time. Hale, *Tercentenary History*, 11, takes the view that the dividing up of the "Great Lots" at this time put the citizens of Roxbury in a generous mood. Samuel Eliot Morison, *Builders of the Bay Colony* (Boston: Northeastern, 1981), 292, downplays the town's affluence. See also Geraldine Murphy, *"Massachusetts Bay Colony: The Role of Government in Education"* (Ph.D. diss., Radcliffe College, 1960), 74. See also *A Memorial Service in the First Church in Roxbury, November 9, 1913*, (Boston: Ellis, 1914), 14, for William Wallace Fenn's joining of this description with Johnson's of 1654.

13.   John Howard Brown, *Elizabethan Schooldays: An Account of the English Grammar Schools in the Second Half of the Sixteenth Century* (Oxford: Blackwell, 1933), 9, 28–29, 55.

14.   W. A. L. Vincent, *The Grammar Schools* (London: Murray, 1969), 2. Vincent's study begins in 1660 where the monumental study of Foster Watson leaves off. See Foster Watson, *The English Grammar Schools to 1660*, new impression of the 1908 edition (London: Cass, 1968), 9: "Up to the end of the Commonwealth [1660], the Grammar Schools of England may be regarded as exclusively classical in material of instruction, with the exception—a most important exception—as we shall see, that under mediaeval Catholicism, and afterwards under 16th and 17th century Puritanism, they were, in intention and largely in practice, permeated with moral, religious, and pietistic instruction." See also, especially, 25–85.

15.   See Vincent, *The Grammar Schools*, 86–90, on the primacy of the religious aim in the English grammar schools. And recall Cotton Mather's statement (1690): "All the learning that many have serves only as a bag of gold about a drowning man; it sinks them the deeper into the scalding floods of the lake that burns with fiery brimstone. But the knowledge of the Lord Jesus is a saving thing." (Cremin, *American Education*, 289.) Morison, *Intellectual Life of Colonial New England*, 34–35, 57–59, 67, explores the anti-religious bias which has characterized much of the discussion of seventeenth century American education. Extracts from the town of Dorchester's March 1645 regulations reveal the religious nature of contemporary grammar schools: "Seventhly. Every sixth day in the week at two of the clock in the afternoon [the schoolmaster] shall catechise his scholars in the principles of Christian religion. . . . Eighthly . . . it is a chief part of the schoolmaster's religious care to commend his scholars and his labors amongst them unto God by prayer morning and evening, taking care that his scholars do reverently attend during the same." George Emery Littlefield, *Early Schools and School-Books of New England* (1904, reissued New York: Russell and Russell, 1965) 82–84, says the Dorchester School "may be considered as a model of all other grammar schools."

16.   Shurtleff, *Mass. Bay Records* IV, Part 1: 182–83. 3 May 1645.

17. The School possesses the original document. See also Charles Knapp Dillaway, *A History of the Grammar School, etc.* (Roxbury: Crosby, Nichols, Lee, 1860), frontispiece and 30–32.

18. See Charles Leslie Glenn, Jr., *The Myth of the Common School* (Amherst: U. of Massachusetts Press, 1988), especially 255, in which he discusses the effort of well-intentioned people to supplement the areligious experience of public school students with some form of religious instruction outside school. Such efforts accepted the fallacious assumption "that experience and meaning could be compartmentalized." The decline of both educational and moral standards among contemporary youth may be charged to that separation. For the public schools, learning is now an end in itself. See also 10. See also Axtell, *The School Upon a Hill*, 33–36, and Small, *Early New England Schools*, 88, on the church's dominance in New England education.

19. PCSM XXXV: 252. This Thomas Weld is the *son* of Eliot's original pastoral colleague of the same name, and is also the *father* of Thomas Weld, master 1674–79.

20. The Dixie Grammar School at Market Bosworth in Leicestershire, England.

21. See, for example, Brown, *Elizabethan Schooldays*, 1: "[The expression grammar school] is a technical term of very definite meaning and restricted scope."

22. See Vincent, *The Grammar Schools*, 3–5. Edward Eggleston, *The Transit of Civilization from England to America in the Seventeenth Century* (New York: Appleton, 1901), 210–211, writes: "The tide wave of zeal for founding new Latin schools reached its flood about the time that emigration to America began, and the impulse was felt in all the early colonies." See also Godfrey Davies, *The Early Stuarts 1603–1660* (Oxford: Oxford U. Press, 1937), 349, and W. K. Jordan, *The Charities of London 1480–1660* (London: Russell Sage, 1960), 22, 26, 282, 283, 288, 289.

23. See especially Small, *Early New England Schools*, chap. XI, "The Early Education of Girls"; and Robert Middlekauff, *Ancients and Axioms: Secondary Education in Eighteenth-Century New England* (New Haven: Yale U. Press, 1963), chap. 7 and 166–71, on the education of girls in eighteenth century New England. Eggleston, *Transit of Civilization*, 244–45, briefly discusses the education of girls outside of schools. See Vincent, *The Grammar Schools*, 46, on the rarity of grammar schools for girls in England.

24. See Morison, *Intellectual Life of Colonial New England*, 59–60, 89. See 79–82 for an interesting discussion of the hornbooks, primers, and catechisms used for this basic instruction. See also Eggleston, *Transit of Civilization*, 211–14. And Small, *Early New England Schools*, chap. VI, for a discussion of the private neighborhood dame school in New England. For the English pattern, see Vincent, *The Grammar Schools*, 58, 71–72.

25. See Vincent, *The Grammar Schools*, 58, and Cremin, *American Education*, 216: "During Dunster's administration [as president of Harvard], the median age of entering freshmen was about seventeen; during [President] Chauncy's, it dropped to a little over fifteen, and it remained under sixteen for the rest of the century."

26. Nathaniel Shurtleff, *Mass. Bay Records* II: 203.
27. See Cremin, *American Education*, 238. On comparison with Virginia, see Fischer, *Albion's Seed*, 133–34. Within a decade, Roxbury's population had doubled. See Holmes, *A Tercentenary History*, 7–8. Between 1650 (roughly the time of the School's founding) and 1689 (the year before Eliot's death), the population of Massachusetts had soared from 14,037 to 48,529. Churches had increased from forty-three to eighty-eight, schools from eleven to twenty-three. In actual fact, as Murphy demonstrates, the laws of 1647 were not enforced until 1692 after the new charter ("Massachusetts Bay Colony: The Role of Government in Education," 1–2). See *Encyclopedia of the North American Colonies* (New York: Scribners, 1993), III: 462f. for further information on non-enforcement, 1647–1692.
28. See Axtell, *A School Upon a Hill*, 170–72, for a description of the "learning environment" of a typical one-room school. See also Small, *Early New England Schools*.
29. R. G. Parker, *A Sketch of the History of the Grammar School in the Easterly Part of Roxbury* (Boston: Thomas S. Watts, 1826), states on 14–15 that Schoolmaster John How [sic] in 1674 "with an increase of salary had also an increase of duties,—he being required to teach Latin, which had not previously been introduced into the school." Francis S. Drake, *The Town of Roxbury, Its Memorable Persons and Places, Its History, etc.* (Boston: Municipal Printing Office, 1905), 197, probably drawing on Parker, repeats this theory: "Under the mastership of John Howe, the [Roxbury] Grammar School became a Latin School, when, in 1674, the legacy of Mr. Bell became available." For starters, both Parker and Drake get the schoolmaster's name wrong. It was John Gore. Morison, *The Intellectual Life of Colonial New England*, 100, demolishes both Parker and Drake on the key issue: "Roxbury, however, sent more students to Harvard before 1674 than any other town except Boston, Cambridge, and Ipswich; hence it may be inferred that the [Roxbury] Free School prepared for college [by teaching Latin] before that date. See also Cotton Mather, *Magnalia* (1702), book III, 187." See also Hale, *Tercentenary History*, 32: the fact that Prudden's contract of 1669 exempts him from teaching ABC-Darians implies that someone else was doing elementary teaching in the town. On the other hand, the 1674 contract between John Gore and the feoffees (which was ultimately not agreed to—Thomas Weld, Jr., being hired instead) clearly called for him to do more than Latin teaching: "tend the said school and all scholars . . . whether Latin scholars, writers, readers, or spellers." (Dillaway, *History of the Grammar School*, 44). Holmes, *A Tercentenary History*, 255, discusses the evidence for the teaching of Latin at Boston Latin: There are indications in 1653 and 1666 that some Latin was taught, but not until 1699 was it called a "Latine" school in the town records. For information on John Eliot, Class of 1656, see Sibley, *Biographical Sketches*, I: 476f. For an excellent discussion of Latin as the universal language in the seventeenth, eighteenth, and nineteenth centuries, see Hale, *Tercentenary History*, 20–22.
30. Samuel E. Morison, *Harvard College in the Seventeenth Century* (Cambridge: Har-

vard U. Press, 1936), Part I, 79–80. See n. 29 and also Holmes, *A Tercentenary History*, 254–55, on Latin as an entrance requirement for Harvard.

31. In his *Tercentenary History*, Hale, 17, adds further corroboration by showing that in 1668 George Alcock, Class of 1669, possessed Cicero's *Ethics*.

32. Vincent, *Grammar Schools*, 40. Brown, *Elizabethan Schooldays*, 13–18, discusses the fact that even in tuition-free schools there were often many other fees which made their cost "not so widely different from that charged by many schools today." See the useful discussion of the term in Stanley James Curtis, *History of Education in Great Britain*, 6th ed. (London: University Tutorial Press, 1965), 43–48. Curtis adds (44) yet another definition: "a 'free school' was a school in which liberal, *i.e.*, a freeman's education, was provided." See below for another theory he advanced. See Murphy, "Massachusetts Bay Colony: The Role of Government in Education," on one use of the term "free school" with specific reference to Roxbury Latin. See Cremin, *American Education*, 193. See Bernard Newman, *The Bosworth Story* (London: Herbert Jenkins, 1967), 29, on Thomas Hooker's own school: "Bosworth was established as a 'free' school. This did not mean that there were no fees. . . . The word 'free' implied freedom from the control of a superior body. The governors decided the policy." See also Anthony Trott, *No Place For Fop or Idler, The Story of King Edward's School, Birmingham* (London: James & James, 1992), 14, for yet another variation on free school: "Though the education offered at King Edward's School was free to all, the cost to poor families would have been serious because it would have meant a reduction in the family earning power. . . . Moreover, the education offered was not directly relevant to their needs as its logical termination was the university and, as Roger Ascham wrote to Archbishop Cranmer in 1547, the students being admitted to Cambridge were 'for the most part only the sons of rich men.'"

33. "RLS Old School Book," 11.

34. Franklin M. Wright, "A College First Proposed," *Harvard Library Bulletin* VIII, 3 (Autumn 1954): 274.

35. "RLS Old School Book," 21.

36. Rufus Wyman, "Abstract of the Ancient Records and Papers of the Free-Schoole in Roxburie, 1645–1789," a handwritten document in school vault (Roxbury 1841–42), 16. See also Wyman's comment on that page. See also Parker, *A Sketch*, 30.

37. The original document is in the School's vault. It appears in facsimile as the frontispiece of Dillaway, *History of the Grammar School*. It is transcribed in Dillaway on 30–32.

38. It is unclear whether the four names listed under "gratis" are those of fathers or of students. No student bearing the last name of any of the four is known to have been a student in the School in the seventeenth century. The fact that the feoffees admitted some boys "gratis" (without their parents making a donation) technically qualifies Roxbury Latin as a free school even by a narrow financial definition of the

term. Curtis, *History of Education in Great Britain*, 45, defines a "free school" as "a school in which, because of its endowment, all *or some* [emphasis added] of the scholars . . . were freed from fees for teaching." See also Littlefield, *Early Schools and School-Books of New England*, 46: "[The 16th Century English Free Schools] were not public schools in the modern sense. By Free School and Free Grammar School was meant a school for the teaching of Greek and Latin, and in some cases Latin only, and for no other gratuitous teaching. A few of the poor who were unable to pay for their education were to be selected . . . to receive instruction in learned languages." See also 70: "['Free School'] meant a school 'free' to all classes; that is, free to all who paid their tuition and which was supported in part at least by endowments and voluntary contributions." See also Stanley K. Schultz, *The Culture Factory, Boston Public Schools 1789–1860* (New York: Oxford U. Press, 1973), 5: Salem free school was free only to the poor, "in Roxbury free to the subscribers' youth."

39. Original document (transcribed in Dillaway, *History of the Grammar School*, 30–32). See also PCSM XXXV: 251–52.

40. "RLS Old School Book," 23.

41. See Ellis, *The History of Roxbury Town*, 46–49.

42. The Thomas Weld who was Eliot's co-petitioner in 1669 was the son of Thomas Weld (Eliot's former ministerial colleague at Roxbury Church, who died in England on 23 March 1661/2). Co-petitioner Thomas Weld was feoffee of the School from 1658 to 17 January 1682/3 when he died. He was father of Thomas Weld, Class of 1667, who became schoolmaster in 1674. Dillaway, *History of the Grammar School*, 15–17. See also PCSM XXXV: 252–53.

43. Shurtleff, *Mass. Bay Records* IV, ii, 455–56. Hale, *Tercentenary History*, 33, errs, I believe, in saying that this ruling prohibited the charging of fees or tuition. No such prohibition can be found in the 1670 documents (which are printed in full in PCSM XXXV, 254–57). Hale may have extrapolated such a prohibition from the phrase: "to be a free school for all in that towne." The phrase, however, comes from a document enforcing the status quo; it is not intended to change anything. It had always been free—available, open—"to all in that towne" (the "all" being that fraction of the community who were of a certain sex, age, and ability) provided their parents paid donations or provided they were allowed to attend "gratis" (without financial charge). From 1680 to 1725, for example, a "wood money" fee was collected (in wood or money) from all children, except those exempted by reason of poverty.

44. Holmes, *A Tercentenary History*, 27–53, records how Boston Latin was supported first by the voluntary contributions of forty-five "richer inhabitants," then by income from town property (including lands, docks, and ferries), then by land grants of the General Court of Massachusetts, and finally, starting with the town meeting of 11 March 1650, by general town taxation.

45. Murphy, "Massachusetts Bay Colony: The Role of Government in Education,"

127, probably following Hale (and her own pronounced bias), errs in her interpretation of this point. The Court ruled that "*if* [emphasis added], for the necessary & convenient future being of a schoolmaster, there be necessary the future levying of any further summes of money, that the said donors be absolutely & wholly free of any such levy or imposition." (Shurtleff, *Mass. Bay Records* IV, ii, 457). Murphy remains disturbed throughout her account of Roxbury's School by the fact that the School remained free of town control.

46. Curtis, *History of Education in Great Britain*, 43–44, points out that Dr. Kennedy, headmaster of Shrewsbury School, advanced a similar definition to the Public Schools Commission in 1862, pointing out that a school was "free" if it was not subject to external "control by a [cathedral] chapter, a college, or a monastery." Curtis (46–47) goes on to advance a fascinating interpretation of the term "free school": in the thirteenth century wealthy persons succeeded in avoiding the King's taxes by donating lands to the church and receiving it back as tenants. King Edward I got Parliament to enact the Statute of Mortmain, 1279, which allowed the Crown to confiscate land donated to the church. This statute did *not* apply to schools, so people could give schools land—for demonstrably charitable purposes—since they were "free" of the statute. See also Albert William Parry, *Education in England in the Middle Ages* (London: University Tutorial Press, 1920), 67–71. He effectively defends Kennedy against the argument of Leach.

47. "RLS Old School Book," 7; PCSM XXXV: 235.

48. "RLS Old School Book," 7–8; PCSM XXXV: 235.

49. See Glenn's brilliant book *The Myth of the Common School* which makes this distinction on 147. In a letter to me of 7 February 1994, Glenn writes that the School's "founders were following the Calvinist model, what neo-Calvinists call 'sphere sovereignity': the belief that in the creation order, church and state and family and school and other spheres are not arranged hierarchically but each has its own created mission. Thus schools should no more 'belong' to the church than to the state."

50. Murphy, "Massachusetts Bay Colony: The Role of Government in Education," 55. As Murphy goes on to point out: "Twenty-five years passed before they felt obligated to give it a public guarantee by having it 'chartered' as a private corporation by the General Court." See also 60 on the rights of the feoffees.

51. Daniel Weld was paid by the Commissioners of the United Colonies to feed, clothe, house, and teach Indian children during the time he was the School's master. Much as we might like to imagine him teaching whites and Indians together, there is no mention of him doing so in any School record, and it seems unlikely that he taught his Indian charges *within* the School. It seems far more likely he taught them "on the side." (See PCSM XXXV: 245–249.) See also Daniel Weld's 1659 petition for a grant of land from the General Court on the grounds that, because he has been teaching students, he "hath hitherto neglected the lookinge after future supplie in providing land for our selves and our smale Children, our-

selfes having not soe much as one Acre of land. . . . " The Court granted him and his fellow petitioner two hundred acres each. PCSM XVII: 141; XXXV: 246–47. See also Part I, n. 124.

52. "RLS Old School Book," 114. See Littlefield, *Early Schools and School-Books of New England*, 88, for the description of a typical New England schoolroom: the master's desk "loomed like a pulpit," following the English grammar school pattern familiar to the early settlers.

53. Cotton Mather, *Magnalia Christi Americana*, 1702 (Hartford: Silas Andrus, 1855), I: 551.

54. See Parry, *Education in England in the Middle Ages*, 67–71, for the definitive exposition of this definition. Parry argues that "'free' means open to all comers, *i.e.*, that admission to the school was not restricted to any particular social grade or to those who were preparing for any particular profession *or to those who were living in any particular locality*." [Emphasis added.] Parry demonstrates that monastic, almonry, and some cathedral schools were "open only to specified classes of persons." "As the general idea of the period was that each parish was self-sufficing and concerned with its own parishioners only, a *free* school would mean one available to the public generally. Each town regarded every non-burgess of that town as a 'foreigner,' and freedom of trade was allowed only to townsmen. Each in the parish had a responsibility for its own poor; the claim to burial in the churchyard was limited to actual parishioners. The same idea passed on to educational matters. Thus, an entry in the York Episcopal Register of June 1289 states that the schools of Kinoulton were to be open to parishioners only, 'all other clerks and strangers whatsoever being kept out and by no means admitted to the school.' The term 'public' school [used here in the British sense, of course] gradually becomes a substitute for 'free' school. Thus in the 'Acte for the due Execution of the Statutes against Jesuits, Seminaries, Preists [*sic*], Recrusants, etc.,' there is a specific reference to 'publicke or free Grammar School.' The warrant granted in 1446 to Eton College not only provided that it should have a monopoly of teaching grammar within a radius of ten miles, but specifically stated that the school should be open 'to all others whatsoever, whencesoever and *from what parts coming to the said college* [emphasis added] to learn the same science, in the rudiments of grammar, freely.' We may consequently regard the institution of 'free' grammar schools as marking a stage in the policy of breaking down the barriers which separated parish from parish and township from township." Parry then goes on to show that the "Free Grammar School" at Exeter charged fees at its founding; the founders obviously therefore did not intend 'free' to denote 'free of fees.'" See also Curtis, *History of Education in Great Britain*, 44.

55. William Kellaway, *The New England Company* (London: Longmans, 1961), 17, 42–43, 69, 130. See also George P. Winship, *The Cambridge Press 1638–1692* (Philadelphia: U. of Pennsylvania Press, 1945), 204.

56. The School possesses a certified copy of the will. See also "RLS Old School

Book," 40–41.

57. Benjamin Gambling's sworn testimony, 5 November 1717. Superior Court Files 12314. Found in PCSM XXXV: 258–59.

58. One could argue (I am not) that the phrase "poore mens children" does not refer to the financially poor. Even a generation later, in writing the *Magnalia*, Cotton Mather uses the words "poor" and "poor mens" frequently, almost never as a reference to *financial* poverty. Mather was typical in this respect.

59. Shurtleff, *Mass. Bay Records* V: 5–6, 22. See also Dillaway, *History of the Grammar School*, 44. Murphy, "Massachusetts Bay Colony: The Role of Government in Education," 286–87, repeats her error (noted above re the 1670 court decision) when discussing this act.

60. See the comparative columns in PCSM XXXV: 237–243, which show the halving of rents by 1700. Ellis, *The History of Roxbury Town*, 57, speaks of "the reduced rent, which occurs as early as 1674." He also notes the "omission of those who, from their gifts of land, had had their estates freed from rent." Hale, *Tercentenary History*, 36, regards the critical issue of the 27 May 1674 decree as establishing the fact that Bell's trustees had to pay their income to the School.

61. Wyman, "Abstract," 30, from now-lost original. See also Dillaway, *History of the Grammar School*, 45–46.

62. See Brown, *Elizabethan Schooldays, An Account of the English Grammar Schools in the Second Half of the Sixteenth Century*, 15. See also John Lawson and Harold Silver, *A Social History of Education in England* (London: Methuen, 1973), 119–20. For an example of R.L. fees, see "RLS Old Schoolbook," 38, for 1698.

63. Wyman, "Abstract," 31. See also Dillaway, *History of the Grammar School*, 47. Barnard and Bernard are variant spellings.

64. See "RLS Old School Book," 48, for Mead.

65. "RLS Old School Book," 45. See also Wyman, "Abstract," 20–22, 27; Parker, *A Sketch*, 14, 21; Drake, *The Town of Roxbury*, 192–93; Hale, *Tercentenary History*, 30–31.

66. See Eggleston, *Transit of Civilization*, 233–36, and Small, *Early New England Schools*, 32–47.

67. Mather, *Magnalia* I: 551.

68. Morison, *Harvard College in the Seventeenth Century*, Part II, 449.

69. See Peter White, *Benjamin Tompson, Colonial Bard, A Critical Edition* (University Park: Pennsylvania, 1980). (For references to John Eliot in Tompson's poetry, see 114; 118 n. 30; 123; 125 n. 4.) The experience of the English grammar schools in the eighteenth century exactly parallels that of Roxbury Latin. The golden age of grammar school donations had ended. Many schools went under, others were reduced to a handful of students, others charged students tuition, still others took in paying boarders. See Vincent, *Grammar Schools*, 3, 16–22, 40–41, 55–57, 191–219. See also, Lawrence Stone, "The Educational Revolution in England, 1560–1640" in *Past and Present* 28 (July 1964), who speaks (46) of a "prolonged educational

depression which began in the second half of the seventeenth century and lasted
for over one hundred years." But Small, *Early New England Schools*, 32, focuses
more on conditions peculiar to New England: "The intellectual fiber of the English college-bred fathers had largely disappeared. . . . The worth of the grammar
school was not always recognized."

70. Cremin, *American Education*, 251–52. See also Augustine Jones, *Joseph Dudley*
(probably Boston: Dudley Family Association, 1916).

71. For the paragraphs above, see Kenneth Silverman, *The Life and Times of Cotton
Mather* (New York: Harper, 1984), 203ff. Also Everett Kimball, *The Public Life of
Joseph Dudley* (New York: Longmans, Green, 1911); Sibley, *Biographical Sketches*,
II: 166–88; and Robert M. Bliss, *Revolution and Empire, English Politics and the
American Colonies in the Seventeenth Century* (Manchester: Manchester U. Press,
1990), 158, 221f. See also Alison Gilbert Olson, *Making the Empire Work* (Cambridge: Harvard U. Press, 1992), 77–86, on Dudley's conversion to Anglicanism,
and the tightwire act he had to perform as governor. Joseph Dudley's much older
sister was Anne, wife of Governor Simon Bradstreet, whose poems constituted
the first book of poetry published in North America (1650).

72. "RLS Old School Book," 49. Wyman, "Abstract," 32. See Hale's elaborations in
PCSM XXXV: 264.

73. See Walter E. Thwing, *History of the First Church in Roxbury* (Boston: Butterfield,
1908), 84, 86–87; and Sibley, *Biographical Sketches*, III: 294–301. See Drake, *The
Town of Roxbury*, 171–73. See also Small, *Early New England Schools*, 87–88, for the
Dorchester experience. See also Michael G. Hall, *The Last American Puritan*
(Middletown: Wesleyan U. Press, 1988) 339–40. Benjamin Tompson (Schoolmas-
ter 1700–03), poet and physician, was the exception to the rule of young men in
the post: he taught at the School when he was fifty-eight to sixty-one years old.
See Sibley, *Biographical Sketches*, II, 103–111.

74. Roxbury Town Records, MS. I, 276, as recorded in PCSM XXXV: 266.

75. See Hale, *Tercentenary History*, 36, for the experience of Ipswich, which lost its
independent grammar school (eventually) because of a favorable vote by the town
the same year.

76. See School's undated "True Copy" and "RLS Old School Book," 33. See also
Wyman, "Abstract," 41, and Dillaway, *History of the Grammar School*, 55.

77. See Petition in the School's safe and "RLS Old School Book," 33.

78. Dillaway, *History of the Grammar School*, 51. See also PCSM XXXV: 268ff.

79. *Journals of the House of Representatives of Massachusetts, 1715–1748*, as quoted in
PCSM XXXV: 269. See also Dillaway, *History of the Grammar School*, 52.

80. For a detailed account of suit and countersuit, see PCSM XXXV: 270–80, which
lays out the court records. See also M. Halsey Thomas, ed., *The Diary of Samuel
Sewall* (New York: Farrar, Straus and Giroux, 1973), II, 924: "Gave Judgmt for
Roxbury School" [26 May 1719]. On costs, see Dillaway, *History of the Grammar
School*, 53–54. Hale, *Tercentenary History*, says the vote was three to two.

81. Clifford K. Shipton, *Sibley's Harvard Graduates* (Boston: Mass. Hist. Soc., 1942) VI: 98–102. See also Hale,*Tercentenary History*, 60–63. Nicholas Sever was himself a difficult man. See Shipton, *Sibley's Harvard Graduates* V: 90–96 and Morison, *Three Centuries of Harvard* (Cambridge: Harvard U. Press, 1936), 67.

82. Hale, *Tercentenary History*, 64. For the actual bequest from the Suffolk Wills 21, 709, see PCSM XXXV: 281. See also Everett Kimball, *The Public Life of Joseph Dudley*, 201–03. Following the English aristocracy's custom of primogeniture, Joseph Dudley settled most of his estate on his elder surviving son, Paul.

83. Middlekauff, *Ancients and Axioms*, 53–54. See also Holmes, *A Tercentenary History*, 9–10. Holmes also notes (255–56) that Winthrop's *Journal* of 1645 indicates that the Boston schoolmaster had a paid usher who taught the younger children.

84. Wyman, "Abstract," 48. Middlekauff, *Ancients and Axioms*, 16: "Above all, each school had to contend with the village in which it was located. Nurtured on the sanctity of thrift and having lean resources in any case, the village insisted the grammar master should teach children reading, writing, and arithmetic as well as the languages and thereby relieve the public purse of the strain of paying a second master. No independent school—not Ipswich, Hadley, New Haven's Hopkins, or the Roxbury Latin—proved entirely able to resist this demand." See also PCSM XXXV: 282.

85. Wyman, "Abstract," 49–50.

86. "RLS Old School Book," 66.

87. Ibid., 68.

88. MS in School's vault: "Roxbury School-1770." See also Dillaway, *History of the Grammar School*, 66.

89. Dillaway, *History of the Grammar School*, 66 (same lost book). See also Small, *Early New England Schools*, 161, and Samuel A. Eliot, ed., *Heralds of a Liberal Faith* (Boston: Unitarian Universalist Association, 1910), I, 109–121.

90. These poor results occurred despite the presence in 1743-44 of a notable teacher, Job Palmer, a Harvard graduate who wrote a remarkable geometry textbook. (See Middlekauff, *Ancients and Axioms*, 94–97.) See also Shipton, *Sibley's Harvard Graduates* X: 393.

91. For a fuller account of Joseph Warren and speculation regarding General William Heath, see Hale, *Tercentenary History*, 72–76. For the life of James Greaton, see Shipton, *Sibley's Harvard Graduates* XIII: 413–16.

92. See the lengthy discussion of this issue in Hale, *Tercentenary History*, 4–5, 78. See also Parker, *A Sketch* (written in 1826, not long after the Revolution), 19: "The School, however, continued in operation during the whole of that stormy period [of the Revolution]." See also 30: "The School has never at any time been closed since its first establishment, except during the usual vacations." See Holmes, *A Tercentenary History*, 2: "The Boston Latin School was temporarily suspended from April 19, 1775, until June 5, 1776." The only other still-existing school founded before Roxbury Latin is Collegiate School in New York City (which until

recently claimed 1638 as its founding date). It was founded then (or possibly earlier) as an elementary school. It became a secondary school only in 1887. It closed from 1776 until 1783 at the time of the American Revolution. See Jean Parker Waterbury, *A History of Collegiate School 1638–1963* (New York: Potter, 1965), 62–67. See also Massimo Magliore, "The Evidence for the Establishment of Collegiate School in 1628," in *A History of Collegiate School Updated: 1963–1983, with a Study of the Early Origins* (New York: Collegiate School, 1984), 23ff. Hale, *Tercentenary History*, 76, suggests that Roxbury's Master, Joseph Williams, may have given the boys part of a day off to help prepare harassments for the British when they marched back through Roxbury. Hale, 78, also cites the fact that the School made no claims for damages after the war as evidence that the building was intact and used throughout the war years. Harvard College also was suspended during the Revolution. Richard W. Hale's letter to G. N. Northrop of 31 July 1945 states: "In Quincy's History of Harvard [vol. 2, pp.164–66] it is stated that not only did the students at Harvard go home from May 1 to October 4, 1775, and then migrate to Concord, but also that there was no Commencement that year . . . [on p.171] it is stated that on November 19, 1777 the Harvard students were sent home to make room for the prisoners from Burgoyne's army. . . . They stayed away until the first Wednesday in February 1778. . . . In case someone from Dedham writes, and suggests that their school is more continuous by a month or so, the answer is that Dedham was indicted in 1690 for not keeping a school."

93. Shipton, *Sibley's Harvard Graduates* VIII: 178–186. See also Drake, *The Town of Roxbury*, 311–12, and Thwing, *History of the First Church in Roxbury*, 153ff., 175–77.

94. See Edwin Scott Gaustad, *Historical Atlas of Religion in America* (New York: Harper & Row, 1962), 2–3, and Cremin, *American Education*, 493. Cremin notes (496): "The traditional captive audience of the older established churches dissolved, and in their place stood a vast audience of the unchurched virtually crying out to be transformed into congregations through which they might receive some dependable instruction with regard to salvation."

95. See Axtell, *The School Upon a Hill*, 282, 287–88: "On the eve of revolution New England bore little resemblance to John Winthrop's 'Citty upon a Hill.' The church was no longer the physical and emotional center of colonial life, having failed at certain points to fulfill its evangelical potential after the Half-Way Covenant and the Great Awakening. The community, while the ideals of harmony and consensus persisted, was fractured by geographical mobility, economic opportunity, and political cacophony. And the family had forfeited much of its moral and educational importance to other institutions, primarily the school. In the religious culture of New England, the institution most subject to change was the church. And yet both the method and credal content of religious education remained strikingly unchanged throughout the colonial period. This meant that the ideal values of New England continued to be those of the founding fathers; the vision of a 'Citty upon a Hill' was held before each new generation as the norma-

tive standard by which they should measure themselves. Small wonder, then, that successive generations felt themselves to be falling deeper into 'declension' as the gap between their fathers' vision and their own operational values widened. For the churches, once described as silent democracies in the face of speaking aristocracies, changed dramatically by the time of the Great Awakening, often reverting to forms and practices of the English Church they had once been forced to spurn. Congregations no longer remained silent, ministers no longer wielded unchallenged authority, membership requirements were loosened, congregational uniformity gave way to begrudging toleration of other sects, and perhaps most telling of all, economic ambition put intolerable stress upon an ethic that condemned idleness but could not condone worldliness."

96. RLS Account Book, 1783. See also PCSM XXXV: 283–86.

97. RLS Account Book, 1788. See also PCSM XXXV: 286.

98. "Roxbury Grammar School—Secretary's Records 1789–1843," (hereafter RGS-Secretary's Records, 1789–1843), 1–7. References to the 1789 Charter on succeeding pages are not individually footnoted.

99. Parker, *A Sketch*, 12. See also Hale, *Tercentenary History*, 89, for further corroborating conjectures.

100. RGS-Secretary's Records, 1789–1843, 9.

101. Ibid., 9.

102. Ibid., 13. Holmes, *A Tercentenary History*, 387, notes that in 1784 the town of Boston abolished the fire money charge for children in the Boston schools.

103. RGS-Secretary's Records, 1789–1843, 77.

104. Lived 1743–1802, School trustee 1789–1802. Lowell was a member of the Continental Congress, a judge of admiralty, and ultimately chief judge of the First District. He was a staunch opponent of slavery.

105. Drake, *The Town of Roxbury*, 52.

106. Middlekauff, *Ancients and Axioms*, 129–30.

107. Theodore R. Sizer, *The Age of Academies* (New York: Columbia U. Press, 1964), 12. On the academies in general, see Middlekauff, *Ancients and Axioms*, 119–21, 123–24, 136–37, and chap. 10. Middlekauff notes (146) that nineteen of the twenty-one Massachusetts academies received land grants from the state by 1800. See also Harriet Webster Marr, *The Old New England Academies* (New York: Comet, 1959). See also Richard Walden Hale, Jr., *Milton Academy 1798–1948* (Milton: by the Academy, 1948), 3: "The Education Act of 1789 had in effect abolished secondary education in favor of increased primary education, which was the practical result of reducing the number of towns required to keep Latin Grammar Schools."

108. See the brilliant address of Charles Hamilton: "The Foundations of the New England Academies, An Address Delivered at the Dedication of the Lawrence Academy, Groton, June 29, 1871" in *Groton Historical Series*, Groton, Massachusetts, vi, 1885.

109. Sizer, *The Age of Academies*, 18. Hamilton, "The Foundations," 7.

110. Sizer, *The Age of Academies*, 5–9.

111. Dillaway, *History of the Grammar School*, 71.

112. John Ware Willard, *A History of Simon Willard*, new and corrected edition (Mamaroneck: Appel, 1962), 66. Nicholas Pike's *New and Complete System of Arithmetic* had been published in 1788. The Reverend Jedidiah Morse's *Geography Made Easy* was published in New Haven in 1784. See Holmes, *Tercentenary History*, 361–69. For the future life in Roxbury of Prentiss, and another school story, see Drake, *The Town of Roxbury*, 307–08.

113. RGS-Secretary's Records, 1789–1843, 94.

114. Ibid., 265.

115. Ibid., 196. For the Boston experience, see Littlefield, *Early Schools and School-Books of New England*, 81–82: Not until 1818 were there public schools in Boston for children under the age of seven. In 1817 there were 164 private schools educating 4,132 children under seven.

116. Parker, *Sketch*, 22–23. Parker's *Aids to English Composition*, published in 1844, was a widely used textbook.

117. RGS-Secretary's Records, 1789–1843, 250.

118. Ibid., 253.

119. Porter died in 1833 the year in which Putnam officially became the pastor. See Eliot, *Heralds of a Liberal Faith* I: 184.

120. See James DeNormandie, "George Putnam," in Eliot, *Heralds of a Liberal Faith* III: 308–321.

121. Oscar Handlin, *Boston Immigrants*, revised and enlarged edition (Cambridge: Harvard U. Press, 1959), 14, describes Roxbury in 1790 as a "purely agricultural village."

122. George Putnam, "A Sermon Preached at the Funeral of the Rev. Eliphalet Porter" (Boston: Carter, Hendee, 1834), 6. In "An Historical Sketch of the First Church in Roxbury," 1896, 6, an 1820 record is quoted: "The interest in religion had so far declined that, although there are in the first parish in Roxbury, completed and building, three churches within the compass of a few rods, those who prefer to spend their Sabbaths in regular worship to lounging about taverns and pilfering in the fields but half fill a single one." A Baptist church was founded in 1817, St. James's Episcopal Church in 1833, the Eliot Congregational Church in 1834, and St. Joseph's Roman Catholic Church in 1846.

123. Charles Knapp Dillaway, "Biographical Sketch" in *Memorial of The Reverend George Putnam, D.D.* (Boston: for the Society, 1878), 7–9. See also *Tercentenary Celebration of the First Church in Roxbury, 1630–1930* (Roxbury: for the Tercentenary Committee, 1930), 15. See also Thwing, *History of the First Church in Roxbury*, 241–42.

124. Putnam's decisive influence is ironic, because the minister's influence, in general, in New England was fading. Small, *Early New England Schools*, 299, describes what that influence had been before 1828: "The whole school atmosphere was

imbued with the particular religious beliefs of the times; the minister was essentially the parish priest, and the schools were as much parish schools as any we see today. The catechism was taught in all schools until well into the nineteenth century." In his twelfth report, Horace Mann wrote: "It was not until the tenth day of March 1827, that it was made unlawful to use the common schools of the state as the means of proselyting children to the belief in the doctrines of particular sects, whether the parents believed in those doctrines or not." Middlekauff, *Ancients and Axioms*, notes (113–14) that the Congregational Church remained established in Massachusetts after 1789. In 1834 Massachusetts became the last state in New England to disestablish the Church—both in its Trinitarian and Unitarian manifestations.

125. Putnam's political views were equally fervent and got him into trouble with some of his congregation. He was a member of the 1853 constitutional convention, a presidential elector (voting for Abraham Lincoln) in 1864, and an elected representative to the Legislature for a term in 1869. When some in his congregation complained about his expressing political views, Putnam responded that "if he must choose between his parish and his country he should remember that he was a citizen before he became a preacher." See Dillaway, *Memorial of George Putnam*, 11 and 35. In *A Memorial Service in the First Church in Roxbury November 9, 1913*, Dr. Francis Greenwood Peabody, Plummer Professor Emeritus at Harvard, describes vividly Putnam's power as a preacher. He also recalls "that thrilling moment at the service after the death of Lincoln, when there were signs of panic in the overcrowded church, and the little man rose up like a giant in his pulpit, and thundered out, 'Silence, silence in the house of God.'" (18).

126. George Putnam, *An Oration Delivered at Cambridge before the Phi Beta Kappa Society at Harvard University, August 29, 1844* (Boston: Charles C. Little and James Brown, 1844), 36.

127. George Putnam, *A Sermon Delivered before His Excellency George N. Briggs, Governor . . . at the Annual Election* (Boston: Dutton and Wentworth, 1846), 19–20.

128. Dillaway, *Memorial of George Putnam*, 8. Lowell (born in 1769) remained a trustee until 1839 and died in 1840. Lowell was a scientific farmer at Roxbury, as well as a lawyer, overseer of Harvard, and political activist.

129. RGS-Secretary's Records, 1789–1843, Report following 282.

130. Collar in *The Tripod* 11, 7 (March 1899), quoting from a letter written to him in 1895 by Kendall Brooks, who went on to be a college president.

131. RGS-Secretary's Records, 1789–1843, 290–91.

132. See Thomas B. Davis, Jr., *Chronicles of the Hopkins Grammar School* (New Haven: Quinnipiack, 1938), 190: only members of the First Church Society could attend without charge—1719; 228: tuition charged to all students, though fees for those living in town were lower—1746; 279: "Up to this time [1795], the School had ordinarily been free to all resident children. In times of economic crisis the trustees had resorted to tuition fees, or poll taxes, as they called them, in order to help bal-

ance their accounts, but these fees they regarded as purely temporary. Since 1796, however the School has always charged tuition."

133. Drake, *The Town of Roxbury*, 52.

134. See Whitney R. Cross, *The Burned-Over District* (Ithaca: Cornell U. Press, 1950), 274–75, who discusses the effects, also, of the economic depression of 1837–1844. For the 770 elementary enrollment figure, see Drake, *The Town of Roxbury*, 203.

135. RGS-Secretary's Records, 1789–1843, 315.

136. Ibid., 322.

137. Ibid., 327.

138. "Roxbury Grammar School—Secretary's Records, 1843–1870" (hereafter RGS-Secretary's Records, 1843–1870), 24.

139. RGS-Secretary's Records, 1843–1870, 38.

140. J. Evarts Greene, "The Roxbury Latin School—An Outline of Its History" in *Proceedings* of the American Antiquarian Society, 1887, 19.

141. RGS-Secretary's Records, 1843–1870, 78. Benjamin F. Brown '49 wrote a charming piece on the School in 1845–46 in *The Tripod* 21: 8 (May 1909), 5–8, from which the Wheelwright quotation is taken.

142. Ronald Story, "Harvard Students, the Boston Elite, and the New England Preparatory System, 1800–1876," *History of Education Quarterly* XV, 3, Fall 1975.

143. Greene, "The Roxbury Latin School," 19–20. See also Charles Lancaster Short, *Memoir of the Life of Charles Short, M.A., LL.D.* (Privately printed 1892). See also *The Tripod* 23: 2 (November 1910), 7–8, for an article on Short by the same son. Hale, *Tercentenary History*, 119, errs in stating that Short was an Episcopal priest (which Hale takes as a sign of Putnam's lack of sectarianism). Short was a Congregationalist until he became an Episcopalian in 1862. He was never ordained.

144. Mark Sibley Severance, *Hammersmith, His Harvard Days* (Boston: Houghton Osgood, 1878), 44. See also 36.

145. RGS-Secretary's Records, 1843–1870, 91.

146. Ibid., 105.

147. Greene, "The Roxbury Latin School," 18–19.

148. RGS Secretary's Records, 1843–1870, 147.

149. Dillaway, *History of the Grammar School*, 99.

150. RGS-Secretary's Records, 1843–1870, 207. Writing in *The Tripod* in 1899 (11: 8, 6), D. G. Haskins, Jr., '63, describes the scene when he entered Class IV in 1859: "The whole institution then numbered only 54 boys, with two teachers. The four upper classes, (excepting a few of the third class), occupied an old building north of the present [1899] school, having an imposing Doric portico, a broad flight of steps, and a small belfry without, and within, a single school room, with desks for 29 boys.... The rest of the boys, with those of the English High School, occupied the present building until the old school-house was abandoned, and we all moved into the present house in the fall of 1860."

151. Dillaway, *History of the Grammar School*, 79–80.

152. RGS-Secretary's Records, 1843–1870, 225.
153. Ibid., 228f.
154. See Caroline Ober Stone Atherton's recollection of Buck in *The Tripod* 24, 2 (November 1911): 5–7.
155. *The Tripod* 10, 8 (May and June 1899): 5–6. The portrait referred to—by Billings— hangs today in the upper corridor of the schoolhouse.
156. *The Tripod* 24, 5 (February 1912): 7.
157. *The Tripod* 10, 8 (May and June 1899): 6–7. See also *The Tripod* 36, 3 (December 1923) for a touching rehash of earlier memories.
158. *The Tripod* 24, 5 (February 1912): 6–7. See also C. Frank Allen, "The School in the Civil War," in *Forty Years On*, Francis Russell, ed. (West Roxbury: By the School, 1970), 21–22, on military drill.
159. RGS-Secretary's Records, 1843–1870, 287.
160. Buck had already spent two years of his headmastership traveling in Europe. See *The Tripod* 25, 3 (December 1912), 5 with a quotation from the *Norfolk County Journal* account of his intended two-year trip to Europe starting 8 July 1863. Buck left Boston University in 1901 and made his home in Germany until he died there in 1917 at age ninety-two. (See *The Tripod* 29, 8 [May 1917], 9.)

Part Three

In years to come, when we look back upon our school-boy life, one of the pleasantest recollections will be that which will enable us to say, "I was in the Roxbury Latin School when Dr. Collar was there. I remember him, and his inspiring words in the Hall so often, and his kindly manners, and his delightful classes." This will be to us in the future a priceless treasure.

—EDITORIAL IN The Tripod, JUNE 1907

Part Three
The Second Founder

FOR THE FIRST TWO CENTURIES *of its life, Roxbury Latin was essentially a one-room schoolhouse in which a single master taught pupils ranging in age from nine to eighteen. William Coe Collar came to teach at Roxbury Latin in 1857—following his sophomore year at Amherst College—as assistant to the schoolmaster, Augustus Buck. There were forty-two boys in the School; Buck taught the older, Collar the younger. Ten years later, Collar succeeded Buck as headmaster—a position he held for forty years, until 1907.*

Collar is called the "Second Founder" because during his headmastership the School quadrupled in size, adding specialized faculty who could teach the subjects now required for entrance by Harvard and other colleges: physics, chemistry, modern history, and German. His headmastership also witnessed the birth of "extracurricular activities": athletic competition in football, track, baseball, and hockey; the first school theatricals; the newspaper, The Tripod. *Collar's Latin, Greek, and German textbooks were used across the nation, as were those of several of the masters working under him. His right-hand man—and putative successor, until his untimely death—George F. Forbes was the nation's pioneer in teaching science by the experimental method. All these factors combined to make Roxbury Latin one of the nation's most eminent schools. Such was its fame that limits finally had to be placed on the number of educators visiting the campus.*

The oil portraits and photographs of Collar convey the impression that he was physically a giant, and he does figuratively tower over the nineteenth-century history of the School. However, in his diaries and letters below we discover that at the age of thirty-nine Collar stood five feet seven inches and weighed 116 pounds fully clothed. We also learn that this seemingly confident and commanding leader was a man deeply needful of human sympathy and support (even before the tragic death of his son and the loss of his wife), a man constantly burdened by work (both in running a school and writing textbooks), a man much given to hypochondria and depression. In looking "behind" the facade of headmaster, we are in no way diminishing his greatness. Rather, we discover that Collar was an ordinary person with ordinary abilities who somehow managed to achieve extraordinary things.

1. *Husband, Father, and Schoolmaster*

REMINISCENCE OF SIBYL, HIS THIRD DAUGHTER

William Coe Collar was born September 9, 1833, in [Ashford,] a small village of Connecticut, one of a family of four children, evenly divided between boys and girls. His father, Charles Collar, was a shoe-maker, of simple but sterling principles, and without much book-learning except the Bible, most of which he explicitly disbelieved. My grandmother [Mary Ann Coe], a descendant of Priscilla and John Alden through the Coe family, must have been a woman of exceptional refinement and taste for letters, with which she stamped this son early in his life.

By work in the potato-fields and other means, my father managed to get the tuition for Woodstock Academy, from which he was graduated at the head of his class and [after teaching awhile in the district school, he] entered Amherst College [at age twenty-two in 1855, as a member of the Class of 1859], joining the Psi Upsilon Society. But he did not [graduate].

Though he had just turned twenty-four as the 1857–58 school year began, Collar had only completed his sophomore year at Amherst. Nevertheless he accepted the invitation of Roxbury Latin's "Head Master" Augustus H. Buck to become his assistant at the School in September 1857.

There were two buildings on Mount Vernon Place (renamed Kearsarge Avenue after the Civil War): the boys' English High School and the Latin School. By contract with the town of Roxbury, the trustees of the Latin School supervised both schools. The English High School occupied the newer and larger building, erected in 1853. The Latin School's forty-two boys met in the adjoining one-room Greek revival schoolhouse built in 1835.

COLLAR'S REMINISCENCE OF THE SCHOOL IN 1857
The Tripod 18, 7 (April 1906)

When I came to teach in the Roxbury Latin School, early in September 1857, I found the school on the present grounds [Kearsarge Avenue in Roxbury], but not in the present schoolhouse. The Latin schoolhouse stood a few yards to the northwest of our present north wing. The schoolhouse that we now [in 1906] occupy, or rather, the central part of it, minus the rooms in the rear—the laboratories, lecture room and library—stood where it now is, and two rooms of it, that is, the hall and the third class room, were occupied by the Roxbury High School for boys.

Between this building and the Latin School a picket fence ran from the avenue to the back of the school lot. . . . The old Latin schoolhouse . . . was architecturally an odd mixture of the puritanic meeting-house, with a low belfry tower, and the front of a Greek temple—a pediment supported by four Doric columns. The columns themselves were a mixture of the Doric and Ionic orders, that is to say, they were Doric columns with Ionic capitals, and rested, without base, directly on a wooden platform, to which you ascended by several narrow steps.

This building was pulled down after I came to Roxbury. It is a pity that there is no drawing, cut, or photograph of it in existence. One would like to know what became of its bell, a fine one, and no doubt the same that was given to the school by Paul Dudley, while the school was on its original site in Guild Row.

The schoolhouse faced on Kearsarge Avenue. . . . It had but one room, with a raised platform at the back, like a Roman basilica, was well supplied with blackboards, and had inexpensive benches and desks. Not reckoning the entering class, of which I shall speak in a moment, there were in this room twenty-one boys. They were instructed in all the subjects then taught in the school, Latin, Greek, French, mathematics, geography, and ancient history, by the principal, Augustus H. Buck, who, fifteen years or more later, became professor of Greek in Boston University.

Mr. Buck was an exceedingly able disciplinarian and instructor. He was a scholar himself and had high ideals of scholarship. No slovenly, slipshod work passed muster with him, and he impressed the boys with the need and value of thoroughness and exactness. He was exacting with himself and always made most careful preparation of all his lessons. I lived in his family for some months and was acquainted with his habits of study. I remember how he would stretch himself out at full length after supper on a very long sofa, flat on his back, with copies of eight or ten German editions of Caesar's Gallic War ranged on the floor beside him, and not until he had compared readings and annotations in them all, did he consider himself ready for the next day's class. Somehow there seemed to be time then for even a schoolmaster to be a scholar. From him I learned the invaluable lesson, which I have always tried to practice, never to go before a class without adequate preparation. If teachers nowadays would depend less upon methods of instruction, and aim more to make themselves masters of their subjects, they would teach with more enthusiasm and more sense of power.

We used then, the first year in Latin, a book by McClintock and Crook, in which the lessons were diluted to an extraordinary degree. It reminds me of a book widely advertised in England years ago, entitled, *Latin without Tears, or One Word a Day*. Mr. Buck, thinking apparently that I was too much interested in general literature, said, one day, "A man is not fit to teach that book (the Latin book referred to), who does not study every page of it as he would a page of Thucydides."

But to return. Two teachers could not occupy the one schoolroom, something that seems not to have been thought of. But there was a basement under the schoolhouse, and so it was decided to clear out the rubbish and put some benches and desks in there. There I took the new comers, the entering class, and began my work on the munificent salary of $600. But it was all I was worth. How fortunate it is that youth is inclined to be happy and hopeful, and that the struggles of the future, because unknown, cannot cloud the present! I was disappointed, but not depressed. The stairs to the basement were narrower than those in our schoolhouse, but the basement itself was almost as high studded, well ventilated, airy, and cheerful as ours. [*This statement is ironic, a humorous allusion to the low, dark basement of the Kearsarge Avenue schoolhouse.*] It must be confessed it was damp in rainy days, and on dark days it was hard to read ordinary print.

After about three weeks The Rev. Dr. Thomas D. Anderson, who was one of the Trustees, and whose son Robert had just entered the school, paid us a visit. He was evidently not pleased with the school-room, and in a few days we were transferred to a room in our present building, which was not used by the High School, the room that we call the fourth class room. Mr. Samuel M. Weston, Principal of the Boys' High School, had his classes in the hall; Mr. George H. Goreley, his assistant, occupied the third class room. Both schools, by the way, were under the control of the Trustees of the Latin School.

We think we have rather limited playground, and we do; but the two schools, the Latin and the High had only the old Latin School yard. The "campus" was then a graveyard, with row of tombs beginning at Kearsarge Avenue, enclosing the narrow school grounds, running round behind the two schools and across the south end of what is now the "campus."

Corporal punishment was then common and was sometimes administered in the Latin School. I was told that a tall sixteen-year-old boy, whom I remember very well, son of the then mayor of Roxbury, was ferruled because he confused the principal parts of *tego* and *tango*. "Sir," said Dr. Johnson, when complimented on his knowledge of Latin, "my master flogged me excellently."

Lessons really had to be learned in those rude times. The school had a good supply of candles and candlesticks, and boys were often required to return to the school in the evening to make up lessons. I have known

Mr. Buck to stay at the school with delinquents as late as nine o'clock. I cannot remember that boys had to stay in the afternoon of half holidays, Wednesdays and Saturdays.

I wonder how the boys of today would relish a return to the old custom of two sessions daily and a spring term lasting till the last week in July. The summer vacation was just about half its present length, for we began the fall term early in September. School holidays were fewer then. These additions have been made: Washington's birthday, Lincoln's birthday, Good Friday, and the seventeenth of June.

The enlargement of the course of study, the introduction of music, and the practice of athletics, have tended to make school life more varied and interesting than it was in 1857. Besides music and gymnastics, chemistry, modern history, German and physics, were all absent from the curriculum of 1857. There were no athletic meets, no interscholastic contests, no school paper, no school theatricals, no diplomas were given, and no school catalogue was issued.

But though the round of school life was so much narrower than at present, and though the curriculum was limited and rigid, without optional studies, while such a thing as unprepared lessons was unheard of and unthought of, I am not sure that the *education* that the boys got then was inferior to that which they get now. There was less school spirit, perhaps in part because the school was so small. There were forty-two boys, when I came to the school, almost exactly a quarter of the number in attendance last year. But there was more concentration in study and more pride in scholarship. Boys went to college well trained, and early in Mr. Buck's career, before he had an assistant, I think Harvard College had come to expect something of Roxbury Latin School boys.

Collar's daughter gives us some insight as to why Collar came to Roxbury Latin before taking his degree at Amherst College:

REMINISCENCE OF SIBYL, HIS THIRD DAUGHTER

Early in [1857] a position in the Roxbury Latin School as assistant to the Headmaster [Augustus H. Buck] was offered him. Since he had fallen in love with the Deacon's daughter, sweet, demure young Hannah [Caroline] Averill [of Pomfret, Connecticut], also preparing at the Woodstock Academy to be a school-teacher, [he took the Roxbury job,] threw degrees to the wind and married her [on February 24, 1858].

My oldest sister, Alice Averill, was born in December 1858. But the next child, Frederick Averill named for the Deacon, born in January 1861, lived only until May of that year, and Willie, the beloved namesake of his father, born in 1863, was drowned in a flooded excavation close to the house, just before his fourth birthday.

REMINISCENCE OF WILLIAM COLLAR HOLBROOK, '16, HIS GRANDSON, IN 1991

[These children were] probably the reason why [my grandfather] did not serve in the Civil War. He paid a man $200 to take his place.

REMINISCENCE OF SIBYL, HIS THIRD DAUGHTER

Then for some years there were no more babies, and Alice was in her 'teens before the final group of three came along in quick succession: Mildred in April 1872, Mary (later known as Sibyl) in October 1873, and Herbert Coe in June 1875.

Many an inventor, many a scholar, and many mere schoolmasters are notably indifferent to home-life and personal relations. Not so my father. Indeed the depth and sacredness of his emotional life might easily have been the reason of his success with parents, pupils and the teachers under and around him. His sympathy was almost painfully ready, at any call, yet his sense of justice kept him from weak concessions.

When we turn to Collar's letters we discover that his passionate love for Hannah—which led him to break off his college career and to marry her part way through his first year of teaching—never waned during their thirty-four-year marriage. Collar sulks when she doesn't write him as often as he wants her to, and when he doesn't hear from her on his birthday.

Many of his personal characteristics begin to appear in this first set of letters. He is perpetually—we might even say obsessively—concerned with matters of health, diet, and sleep. He is an "absent-minded professor" who forgets to pack necessities and who often leaves things behind. A sense of humor shows itself now and then. After telling his wife that he has been lonely and cold without her at night, he next remarks that the woman in whose house he is boarding "is very good to me (this has nothing to do with the preceding sentence)." We begin to glimpse his love of natural beauty, of flowers in particular. And we can glean that in politics he is a liberal: He favors female suffrage (fifty years before it was enacted), and he complains that women are inadequately remunerated for their labor.

We begin at the end of the summer of 1865, five months after the Civil War's end, four months after Freddie's death. Collar was nearly thirty-two, Alice was seven, and Willie two.

TO HANNAH, HIS WIFE, AT POMFRET, CONNECTICUT

Roxbury

Dearest Wife,   *September 3, 1865*

We arrived yesterday in safety and in good season, having gone from Dayville to Roxbury in less than four hours. We took dinner at a restaurant, Jim [his brother-in-law James B. Averill, studying divinity] dining for thirty cts. and I for thirty-three. We engaged board in the afternoon at Ionic Hall, at a dollar a day each, that being the best we could do.

I have already begun house-hunting but with poor prospect of success. There are fewer houses [in Roxbury] to let now than when we went home [for the summer to Pomfret, Connecticut, his wife's parents' home] and you know there were *none* then.

I should like very much to know how you are and am very sorry that I didn't get a promise from you that you would write tonight. Must I wait till you have received this? I want to see you very much and the dear children. Tell them so, and kiss them for me. It seems odd to be writing to you, *dear* Hannah, but it is the only consolation in being separated from you. How much I want to see you already. Good night dear wife and babies. Your aff. William

TO HANNAH, HIS WIFE, AT POMFRET, CONNECTICUT

Roxbury

My dear Hannah,   *September 12, 1865*

I received your letter today and was very sorry to hear that little Willie [his son, William, aged two] is so much unwell. I shall wait with great anxiety for the next news, and I hope you will not fail to write if he is worse. If he should be much worse, or you should fear his sickness would terminate fatally, do not fail to have me telegraphed-for in season; do not feel alarmed, even if he is worse, at my writing so. I hope and expect he will soon be better, but I do hope you will not have him take any medicine unless there seems to be no other way. I went to see Dr. Bartlett this afternoon, but he suggested nothing but what you would expect. He says, keep him on a very low diet, give as little liquid as possible. He advises brandy and lime-water, and if his bowels continue open, a few drops of laudanum if the sickness continues. The Dr. thinks he will not get very sick if carefully tended, and I know he will not suffer from want of attention. I am sorry, dear wife, I cannot be with you, but

you must have good courage. You ought to have Betsey [the maid], and I would have her, [even] if you are obliged to pay her board. I am almost as much concerned for you as for Willie, and I know it must be very hard for you. Little Alice [aged six] must help you all she can and please tell her from me that I hope she will do so very cheerfully.

Ah! my dear ones, I long to see you all very much. Even the separation for a week or two is bitter, especially when you are not all well. But courage! cooler weather will soon come, and with it, I hope,

FIG. 1. Moses Grant Daniell, master 1867–1884, co-author with Collar of classical texts used across the nation.

health and joy. We shall be together again soon, house or no house. Be sure that I do not remain idle, though I had begun to contemplate the idea of boarding. You wonder at the price I offered for the house in W. place, but I do assure you there is not a house to let at every corner, and if we hire, we shall have to pay an enormous rent or live in [a] mean house.

This afternoon I hired a team and drove through Dorchester with Mr. [Moses Grant] Daniell [master at Roxbury Latin, and co-author with Collar of Greek and Latin textbooks, whose wife had just died]. I took tea with him. Poor man, his home is desolate! And his wife's sister, I should think would not be much of a comforter. Oh! I sincerely hope he will not marry her. She has a face of vinegar. What a wife Ann [the eldest sister of Collar's wife, who was tall] would make for him only she is too long.

I do not see how boarding will be unpracticable, and I was much disappointed at your seeing so many difficulties. The boarders are waited on by the servants just as in a hotel. If we want a pitcher of water or anything else, we ring for a servant, and it is brought. As to the rooms, they are up twenty-six steps only, not much more than one long flight. Mrs. P— [the proprietor] is one of the best of women, and that is a material consideration.

But adieu, dear wife, Alice and Willie, with a kiss for each.

TO HANNAH, HIS WIFE, AT POMFRET, CONNECTICUT

Roxbury

My dear Hannah,   *September 21, 1865*

I opened [your letter] with fear and trembling almost fearing—as it was my turn to write—that the cause of your writing again was Willie's being worse, but I was in a moment relieved and rejoiced to hear that he was better.

My afternoons continue to be spent for the most part in the fruitless task hunting for [a house]. We must not be sanguine. I have thought a number of times already that I was almost sure of a house, and have failed every time. I hardly know what to say about your coming down next week. Our things must be moved from Mr. Buck's [Augustus H. Buck, headmaster of Roxbury Latin, 1853–1867] before the 5th of October, but that I can manage. Don't worry, my dear, in anticipation of the plague and bother and injury to our things; it can't be helped, though it *couldn't* have been much worse for us. Let us face the music and do the best we can.

As for the weather, it is simply *horrible*. I have that old feeling of weakness in my head a great deal, but I attribute it to the weather. My appetite is not good, but that I attribute to the weather. The mosquitoes are thicker than hair on a dog, but I think it is due to the weather. The price of butter is rapidly advancing, unquestionably owing to the weather. But I am in good spirits — so long as the children are well, and you are not sick — in spite of the weather.

I want to see you very much, dear wife, and the children not much less; yes, a good deal less, but still very much. If we can be together, we shall be happy, whether we have one room or twenty. Separation is misery, or rather would be, if we were not *philosophers*.

I wouldn't try to have Alice study till she comes back. Tell her I want to write her a letter but I have to write you so many and such long ones that it is impossible.

My school goes finely and I enjoy teaching more than ever. Mr. Buck finds it almost like living in purgatory; he thinks my boys don't know anything, but I care little for that.

I hope you will wire immediately after making up your mind and James or I will meet you. I wouldn't bring jars of berries, etc. yet. With much love, I am your aff. husband William.

TO HANNAH, HIS WIFE, AT POMFRET, CONNECTICUT

East Cambridge

Dear Hannah, *September 24, 1865*

Abby [Mrs. Joseph Averill, Hannah's sister-in-law] proposes that you bring Betsey [the maid] down, and if we don't go to housekeeping, she would hire her till spring, or till such time as we want her. I think it would be just the thing, if Betsey wants to come and her mother assents. We ought to pay her at least $1.25 a week, for help is extremely scarce, about as much so as the houses, and no decent girl can be hired for less than $2.50.

When shall you come? by Thursday, I hope. You see I am getting impatient. Dear Hannah, adieu for a little time. Your aff. husband

DIARY OF WALTER ELIOT THWING, CLASS OF 1868
The Tripod 35, 6 (March 1927)   *September 2, 1867*
The school opened with Mr. Collar as principal [he had been elected upon Buck's resignation that year] and Moses Grant Daniels [*sic*] as sub-master with Miss Marzette Helen Coburn as the first female assistant teacher.

In this first month of his headmastership, however, tragedy struck.

September 20, 1867.
This was a sad day for us as about 9:45 A.M. a messenger arrived to Mr. Collar and told him the sad news of the death of his only son Willie, by drowning in a puddle at the corner of Honeysuckle Hill.

In spite of this loss—or perhaps because of it—Collar threw himself into the life of the School. C. Frank Allen, Class of 1868, later a professor at Massachusetts Institute of Technology, tells something of the resourcefulness and energy of the young Collar.

REMINISCENCE OF C. FRANK ALLEN, CLASS OF 1868,
IN THE EARLY 1940S
I remember Mr. Collar most fondly not only as a teacher in a general way, but more directly as affecting me personally. In the upper classes we took up mathematics, algebra, and geometry, and I had shown an aptitude in these subjects somewhat greater than was usual in the school. Mr. Collar sensed it and, while his field was Latin and Greek, nevertheless he showed special interest in me and put up a series of geo-

metrical problems for me to solve, taken from *Loomis' Geometry*. I solved them all with some pride.

In these mathematical subjects Mr. Collar did not so much "instruct" me, but developed me by assigning me problems. When I had succeeded in solving every problem put to me, my entire [academic record] improved; not infrequently I stood first in my class, which was unheard of [previously].

REMINISCENCE OF SIBYL, HIS THIRD DAUGHTER

The boarding-house where [Collar and his family lived through the winter of 1865–66] was called Ionic Hall, just out of Eliot Square, recognizable by the Ionian columns that gave it the name. After that, a small house was found in Thornton Street, Roxbury, and there [Willie died in 1867 and] my sister Mildred and I were born [in 1872 and 1873, respectively]. But quite soon we must have overflowed the space available, for my first recollections are of "the Bowditch house," a moderately large house, which we rented not directly on Warren St. but on the estate of one Bowditch's Greenhouses, in the vicinity of Grove Hall.

The minute and affectionate, almost yearning, pre-occupation with his family, which is evident throughout these letters of my father seems not to have blinded him to the value of occasional separations. The following letter was written evidently at the close of a spring vacation trip to New York, where conferences of teachers were held. Mention of train and boat point to the now-extinct Fall River Line.

TO ALICE, AGED TEN, HIS ELDEST—AND NOW ONLY—CHILD, AT POMFRET, CONNECTICUT

Roxbury

Dear Alice,   *April 11, 1869*

It is more lonesome here than you can imagine. It does not seem at all like home without you and mama and it is all the more cheerless on account of the bare floors and the emptiness of the rooms. Then it is so still, and when I step, it seems as though it could be heard all over the house.

When I opened the front door this morning, there stood kitty, and she meowed very dismally and looked up to me as if she would say, "Where is Alice, where is Alice?" I shall let her stay with me in the library when I am at home, and I am going to take a pint of milk a day and give her some of it, so you needn't fear that she will be very hungry. Hattie May has fed her. Hattie has got a new doll, but I forgot to ask its name. She wants to know the name of yours.

I want to hear from you often and know where you are and what you do. I left my night-shirt on the steamboat, but I hope to get it again. I am going to write to the Captain to send it, if he can find it. But it wouldn't surprise me if some one of the negro waiters adorned his body with it. I am sorry on your mother's account, for it is a good deal of work to make such a long one, and I am very much ashamed to be so stupid. Rather an unfortunate trip home, wasn't it? to catch cold, have my pocket picked, leave my night-shirt and miss the train? I think I shan't cross the Sound again without your mother. Write me a letter, and let it be all your own. From the papa

REMINISCENCE OF SIBYL, HIS THIRD DAUGHTER

It was my mother's custom, every summer, to take us children back to her old home in Pomfret, and I do not remember my father's ever going beyond the "depot" with us—that high-perched Mt. Bowdoin station on the "New England" line. To recall that waiting room makes me see linen bags stitched in maroon braid and smell wood car-smoke.

My mother's reluctance to write as often as expected is a puzzle to me. Anybody who knew her will scotch the idea that she did not return my father's intense devotion point for point, but I must admit that his frequent reproaches give an impression of indifference on her part.

TO HANNAH, HIS WIFE, AT WOODSTOCK, CONNECTICUT

Roxbury

My dear Wife,   *May 2, 1869*

Another whole week has gone and more too without a word from you. I hardly know how to explain it, when you urged me repeatedly to write often, before you went away. I have been absent from you more than three weeks, and have received three letters. Well, I am at least glad that you are not plagued with a desire to come back to me before the time.

Tell me what you have read since I left you. I thought of sending you Sumner's great speech on the Alabama claims and earnestly advising you to read it through twice carefully, but upon reflection I thought you would treat it as a joke. But seriously, dear wife, if you want to vote, and you will soon [*here the great man misjudged!*] be allowed to, it isn't too soon to begin to inform yourself, so as to have an intelligent opinion.

I can't help feeling that I shall have a certain feeling of diffidence when I see you again—it will have been so long.

TO HANNAH, HIS WIFE, AT WOODSTOCK, CONNECTICUT

Roxbury
May 4, 1869

How do you get along these cold nights without me? At any rate I don't get along very well without you. I have been cold two or three nights.

Mrs. May is very good to me (this has nothing to do with the preceding sentence) and almost embarrasses me by her expressions of regret that she can't do more for me.

What do you suppose your poor miserable husband has been doing this long dreary day? Reading, and thinking of his dear wife who writes him *once* a week. Write me as soon as you can the day and hour when I shall set eyes on you again. So soon as I know the time, I shall tell the neighbors who inquire, putting it one day later, so that they may make their calls after I have had you exclusively to myself for a time.

Dear Hannah, good night. Think, Hannah, while you are at Lizzie's [the house of her cousin, with whom she boarded while attending Woodstock Academy], of the days when we were there together. How much happiness and oh! what grief we have known since! Let us be thankful for so much happiness as is left us. But, dear wife, there are many hours when an agony of grief makes all my blessings seem nothing. You are my great comfort and blessing, you and Alice. May the Father keep you in safety. Your husband.

P.S. Give my love to Alice. Tell her I was very glad to get her letter. It was a very good one, with better writing and more careful spelling than the other.

TO HANNAH, HIS WIFE, AT GILFORD, NEW HAMPSHIRE

Roxbury

Dear Wife,   *September 1, 1872*

Sarah Coe has got a little one born in May. It is either a boy or girl, but I forget which.

Mr. Daniell and his [new] wife had a great many presents, especially lots of silver. I am pretty well, but shall be better when you and the dear children come. I shall send you a draft for $16 Monday. You will pay Mr. Merrill with that by writing your name on the back. Dear Hannah, I was disappointed not to hear from you again today. Your aff. husband William

TO HANNAH, HIS WIFE, AT GILFORD, NEW HAMPSHIRE

Pomfret

My dear Wife,   *September 2, 1872*

I must take a few minutes, while mother is getting my breakfast, to write a few words. I got to the station, Saturday morning, chilled to the marrow, and much afraid that I had taken a cold; my overcoat, which was in my valise, not seeming to do me the least good. I had the catarrh badly for a few hours, but it passed off, and I have felt no further effects from my chill.

When I got to the station, I put my overcoat on, and didn't take it off till I went to bed. I have been cold most of the time since leaving Gilford, nobody having any fire, except in their kitchens. I went to Abbie's when I got here Saturday night, but staid that night at Louisa's [his elder sister, Mrs. Charles Wagner]. Sunday morning, Louisa and Wagner brought me over home. You will be glad to hear that so far I have only left a book at Abbie's and my tooth-brush at Louisa's. There! all the time that I have been writing what I thought you would want to know, I have been thinking of you and Alice [now thirteen and a half] and the sweet little baby [Mildred, his second daughter, born that April]. Why didn't I have you promise to write me yesterday, so that I could hear from you at Rockville? Don't delay writing and tell me all about yourself and the children. Ah! happy that I can write "children". I will write you as soon as I get to Rockville. Your husband

P.S. Tell Alice to observe that there is a bad repetition of the word "few" in my first sentence, illustrating a point she and I were talking of.

TO HANNAH, HIS WIFE, AT GILFORD, NEW HAMPSHIRE

Rockville, Connecticut

Dear Hannah,   *September 3, 1872*

I got to Rockville yesterday about twelve, and found Hyde at the station. We were weighted yesterday, and I weighed 116, he 112. I have gained four pounds this vacation.

I am eager for a letter and hope I shall not have to wait long. If I hear that you are all well I shall wait patiently till the 12th, but I am already counting the days. I hope baby will know me, when you get home. How about your French? I suppose you will have some questions to ask me. Hyde has a book so that I can look over anything you may want to know. Au revoir, William

TO HANNAH, HIS WIFE, AT GILFORD, NEW HAMPSHIRE

Roxbury

My dear Hannah,   *September 9, 1872*

I sent you a letter this morning with a draft for $16 and, thinking that would not be enough, I put in another dollar. I want you to get seats in a drawing-room car.

Shall you be glad to see me again and to get home? It already seems a long time that I have been away from you. Haven't I written about three [letters] to your one? Well, I have had the most leisure, and I hope it has been pleasant to you to get letters so frequent, though they contain so little. I believe I have not thought of its being my birthday since morning. I hope yours will not pass without our remembering it.

Kiss the dear baby for me, and may you all come home safe to me in a little time. Your affectionate husband

TO HANNAH, HIS WIFE, AT ABINGTON, CONNECTICUT

Congress Hall, Saratoga, New York
Dear Wife,   *July 24, 1873*

I got safely here after a most tedious and hot day's ride. I left home at 7.30 A.M. and got here at 6.30 P.M. Saratoga seems filled with people and all is very brilliant and gay—the most brilliant and gay of all however thus far has been the ball from which I have just returned, though it is now in full blast. Alice will be interested to know that I danced with a Miss Fitzhue of New York, with Mrs. Lascar of Richmond, Virginia, *galloped* with Mademoiselle Fantine of Paris and waltzed with Miss Virginia Schuyler of Saratoga. But stop! Did I? I remember now that it was only in imagination. I should certainly have danced with the "girl with the yaller shawl on" but she took the 7.30 train for New York.

Tomorrow I am going to drink myself full of the waters that abound here. There is a horse race at 12 o'clock which I must attend and at 2.30 I leave for the wilderness. I am writing in an attic room on the fifth story, but the room is a good one. William

REMINISCENCE OF SIBYL, HIS THIRD DAUGHTER

His search for health was instinctive and life-long. It included the finding of health-giving conditions for us all, and he recognized as few did at the time the importance of the best air. He almost worshipped perfection of body and was active in means thereto. We must all learn to swim and to row, to sail, later, and to climb—in all of which he led the way.

TO HANNAH, HIS WIFE, AT ABINGTON, CONNECTICUT

Pottersville, New York
Dear Hannah,   *July 27, 1873*

I enjoyed my stay at Saratoga exceedingly, and would have stayed over Sunday if it had not been so expensive. You can hardly imagine the elegance and splendor at the great hotels there. I was as much delighted with the perfect freedom and ease that prevailed there as with the politeness and brilliancy. At the ball it was the same. People seemed to dance and waltz as much or as little as they liked, stopped when they got warm or tired, and struck in again when the fancy took them. I kept well out of sight in a back seat near the entrance, and had a most excellent chance to scan everyone who came in.

I think the waters must have affected me favorably, for I felt uncommonly well yesterday, though I had but a very short sleep the night before. Alice will be surprised to hear that I exhausted four springs in the space of half an hour, though each sends up thirty-two gallons a minute. After that I felt kind of full and didn't want any more. The water of most of the springs is quite salt[y], and I could not see much difference in the taste, though the properties are very different. There are more than thirty of these springs within a short distance of each other. Congress Spring is not more than twenty yards from Columbian Spring, yet the water of Congress is cathartic, and that of the other a powerful tonic.

At noon I went to see the races. Eight or ten horses were ridden in each race and how they ran! The third race was a steeple-chase and I was very sorry not to see it, but I was obliged to leave to get dinner in time for the train. I came in the cars to Riverside, and from there six miles by stage to Pottersville, where I found Mr. Scott waiting for me. I jumped into his wagon leaving my bag and umbrella in the stage. When I got ready to go to bed last night I missed my bag. Your husband

TO HANNAH, HIS WIFE, AT ABINGTON, CONNECTICUT

Pottersville, New York

My dear Hannah,   *July 30, 1873*

I got your letter telling me of your safe arrival, and that you were all well and glad enough I was to receive the good news. I was sick nearly all day Sunday with diarrhoea and nausea, and was very much afraid I should get to vomiting, but Monday I was all right. It was blueberries and cream that I eat [*sic*] Saturday night that raised the witch with me. Monday forenoon I strolled about in the woods, examining pine and fir cones, and looking for flowers. In the afternoon I went to the P.O. and hotel in hopes to find a letter and my bag. There was no letter and my bag had been carried to Schroon. After I got back I went over to the lake and read for an hour or two, found some more flowers, and so ended the day. Yesterday my bag and umbrella came all right. Honest people they must be here. The key was in my bag but nothing had been disturbed.

As it rained at intervals yesterday all day I spent most of the time reading Taine's "Ideal[s] in Art," read it twice through and enjoyed it very much. I am very well and entirely free from catarrh.

I think Mr. Howison and I shall look for another place right away. I am almost afraid to go far away from a telegraph station, but think I shall probably venture to strike off into the woods for a week. Not however, alone, and not without making arrangements so that a telegram would be brought to me. If only you are all well, I shall be contented. Tell Alice I should like to have her write to me. I suppose you will have something to write to me about the dear baby. The bell has rung for breakfast. Your affectionate husband

TO HANNAH, HIS WIFE, AT ABINGTON, CONNECTICUT

Pottersville, New York

My dear Hannah,   *July 30, 1873*

I have spent the day with Mr. Howison, doing nothing at all. Towards evening we took a sail on the lake, and it was most delightful. Tomorrow I intend to try to hire a boat. I shall probably hardly ever go out alone, and never when there is any danger. I shall not go in swimming, and not even in bathing most likely alone, so you see you will have no occasion for fear. I have had a delightful day, but have exhausted myself talking. The company consists of Mr. and Mrs. Lockwood, Mr. and Mrs. Howison, and Mill Bullard. All are uncommonly pleasant.

Have they a croquet set at Mary's? I hope Alice is well and enjoying herself. I hope she will write to me?

I am extraordinarily well and think I shall get great benefit if I stay in this region long. I want to see you all very very much. I feel almost guilty to be away from you. If you want me to come, write and I'll come. Good night, dear ones. Your loving husband and father

TO HANNAH, HIS WIFE, AT ABINGTON, CONNECTICUT

Pottersville, New York

My dear Hannah, *August 2, 1873*

I felt so little resolution yesterday that I did not write to you, but this morning I take time by the forelock. I got a letter from you night before last, and was very glad to know that little Mildred was better. Your letter made me feel very much troubled, and in the night I resolved to start home at once. I don't feel at all easy, and to know that you are low-spirited takes away all contentment. I am uncertain what to do. The living here is poor, and I don't have any appetite to speak of, and till last night I had slept very poorly indeed. The weather is very bad, as I suppose it is everywhere. I am sorry now that I came away from you and the children, and I would not have done so, but that I felt concerned when I thought how much less strength I had than I had had a year ago, or even six months ago, and I thought I might gain rapidly if I could throw off all care for a little time. Unless I have more appetite and sleep pretty well I shall certainly leave for Abington within a few days.

Since I wrote the last sentence I have eaten a hearty breakfast and I feel quite well. I went a-fishing yesterday and caught a pickerel that weighed two lbs. and a half. I have engaged a boat for a few days, one that I liked very much. I took a row last evening after sunset and enjoyed it very much, but I thought how delightful it would be have you and Alice with me. There is a fine place here to bathe, a long even slope with a sandy bottom. I think we shall all go in today.

Dear Hannah, I hope you and the children will be well and happy. It will not be long before I shall be with you. Your loving husband

TO HANNAH, HIS WIFE, AT ABINGTON, CONNECTICUT

Pottersville, New York

My dear Hannah,   *August 4, 1873*

Mr. and Mrs. Howison think I look a great deal better than when they came back. If I can only sleep, I shall gain fast. I enjoy rowing very much. I only want you and the rest with me. Last night I rowed out a mile or so on the lake to see the mountains as the sun was setting. The sight was very beautiful but I will not describe it now.

Write me about you all. I do hope you are enjoying yourselves. If you have no croquet set, I'll send to Boston and order one. I wish there was a chance to row there. I think of you a great deal. Write me what you are reading. I hope Sarah [the maid] practices writing and reading. I want to know how Alice gets on with her French.

Dear Hannah, adieu for a little time. Your loving husband

TO HANNAH, HIS WIFE, AT ABINGTON, CONNECTICUT

Pottersville, New York

My dear Hannah,   *August 7, 1873*

I hope you will not put up any more huckleberries, it is so hard for you. I wish we could have a few here. I think I can eat blueberries, for I have not refused them for two days, and have felt no ill effects.

Day before yesterday we went up a mountain, and had a very pleasant time. Mr. Lockwood, who was the life of our company, went away Monday. He is absolutely one of the funniest men, if not the funniest that I ever saw. Yesterday I took two good rows, and I have already had one today. After supper, if not before, I shall go again. How I wish you were here with me! The living has improved since we talked of going away, and I enjoy the rowing so much that I would not think of any place for a moment, that did not afford boating. I am getting pretty well tanned, and now that I sleep well, I feel increasing vigor. Why should you feel uneasy? Is it about me? There is not the slightest cause. You did not say in your last letter whether you want me to come home soon. I want to come, but I think I shall get great benefit from rowing. I scarcely read at all.

I hardly know how the days go, except when I play croquet three hours at a time. I am about the worst player of all. You didn't write me whether you have a set there. Don't you think it would be well to try the baby with some other kind of food? I am glad the little dear has got on so far without serious sickness. Tell me what you read, and what you all do. It is two weeks to an hour since I left you all. Don't dream any more of marrying another man, or I shall be jealous. Your loving husband William

TO HANNAH, HIS WIFE, AT ABINGTON, CONNECTICUT

Pottersville, New York

My dear Hannah, *August 13, 1873*

I have engaged a man to bring a telegraphic despatch to me, should any come, but it would take him one day to reach me, and me three days to reach you. It is only a few days, dear wife, and I am not going into any danger. In fact I shall probably be safer than I am here. Only one week and a day, sweet wife, before I expect to be with you again. I want to see you, very much, tho[ugh] on some accounts I should be glad to stay longer. The bell has rung for breakfast, and I must bid you good bye. Your loving husband

REMINISCENCE OF SIBYL, HIS THIRD DAUGHTER

I am proud to say that I did not by a premature appearance shorten my father's camping-trip, for it was not until [October] or, to be exact, on the day that Keats would have been 78 (if one can imagine such a thing) that my father wrote as follows to the family in Connecticut.

TO MRS. T. O. ELLIOTT *Roxbury*

Dear Mary, *October 29, 1873*

Another girl to be provided with a dowry. Truly yours, W. C. Collar

Dear Mary, *October 30, 1873*

I suppose you are waiting to know a few particulars about the advent of our third daughter. Hannah passed a very comfortable night and has had a good day. Her sickness lasted only about two hours, but she suffered a great deal. I went to school at 8.30, and then she was not very sick, but at the end of an hour and a half they sent for me to come home.

The baby is uncommonly large for us—weighed 10 lbs. She seems very healthy and strong and our chief anxiety is likely to be to provide her with food. Hannah hasn't any milk yet and we are afraid won't have.

Heaven seems to refuse me a boy. Truly yours, W. C. Collar

Less than two years later, on June 30, 1875, the hoped-for boy—Herbert Coe Collar—was finally born.

TO ALICE, HIS DAUGHTER, AGED SIXTEEN AND A HALF,
AT SHARON, MASSACHUSETTS *Roxbury*
Dear Alice, *July 2, 1875*

I have seen the boy, but am afraid that he had a bad night. Yesterday your mamma was very well. The boy sucks his fist and sleeps, or did yesterday most of the time. He weighed eleven pounds dressed. He is very fat and solid. I think he is a very fine-looking boy though the Dr. called him homely. He has a well-formed and even handsome head. We shall give him the good old Bible name of Ebenezer, but shall call him Ebby while he is small. Affectionately yours, P

Meanwhile, of course, Collar was in the process of transforming the School. One of his students, a future president of the trustees—who may be credited with saving the School in the years after Collar's retirement—offers this reflection on Collar as schoolmaster:

REMINISCENCE OF ROBERT HALLOWELL GARDINER, '72
The Tripod 35, 3 (December 1922)

I spent [at R.L.] five happy and profitable years under tutelage of Dr. Collar, Mr. Daniell, and Miss Coburn, all admirable teachers with a deep thirst for truth and learning and a great capacity for instilling it in their pupils. . . .

In the fall of 1877, Dr. Collar was good enough to employ me as one of the masters. . . . It gave me . . . a revelation of Dr. Collar's thorough industry and scholarship. Almost the first thing he said to me . . . was that the rule of the School was that each teacher should study harder than every boy in the school and that I must never take a class . . . without studying the lesson myself as if I had never seen it before. . . . [O]ne day when he came into my class [on] Cornelius Nepos he made the class think that they had helped him to discover that day for the first time the meaning and construction of a rather complicated idiom. I remembered his teaching me the same idiom nine or ten years before, with the same enthusiasm.

REMINISCENCE OF SIBYL, HIS THIRD DAUGHTER

A quarter of a mile to the northwest of the first house that I remember as home lay a section bordering on actual fields and woods which were later taken by the city for Franklin Park. As yet, the section was little built-up and here, when I was three, my father set up his nest, buying a half an acre on Maple St. and building a Mansard-roof house, ugly enough by present standards, with perfectly cubical rooms but plenty of them and above all, the luxurious closet and pantry space that my mother yearned for. Though it stood between two lawns, the lot was insignificant compared with the larger estates near by. We children freely roamed and played over these orchards and "grounds" of our neighbors. But our house had one marvel of convenience for the time, which even the rich neighbors didn't possess, namely, a chute from the bathroom to the laundry.

At the left of the front-door, opening by double folding-doors, was my father's Library, with a southwest exposure—and cannily across the hall and diagonally from our headquarters—the Nursery, which never outgrew its name till we girls left home. Both had open fireplaces, in fact the house contained seven in all, but the cosiness of the hard-coal grate in the Nursery has only been appreciated since radiators came in, although always the wood-fire leaping behind shining brass in the

Library was to us the mark of a festive and distinguished occasion. For we were by no means made free of his city. We always knocked on his always-closed doors, except when a crocheted bag for twine was hanging on the knob. That was a sign that he was napping or doing specially concentrated work, and it was religiously respected. When he was not there at all, we might go in and help ourselves to stationery and to the books. Two or three of us would get down MacKnight's *English History* and "choose" in turn the elaborate steel engravings of famous and infamous persons which illustrated the ten or a dozen volumes. On a high shelf stood a row of four-by-three paper novels, published by Harper's and called, I think, the "Half-hour Series" and among these was my first love by Henry James—*Daisy Miller*.

The Library has other and more respectable associations. Here we used to be established to read to my father the English of the Greek and Latin texts that he was teaching, while he followed with the original. In this way, the Butcher and Lang translation of the Odyssey became almost as familiar as Lewis Caroll [*sic*]. I alone used to have Latin lessons with him, rather unsystematically at first in a little conversation-book, but later, when in the Girls' Latin School, I used often to read at sight my entire assignment of Ovid or Virgil to him. Not the help only over hard spots, but the encouragement to express the meaning accurately, neatly and "beautifully"—to use one of his favorite words—was of inestimable value in setting a standard of English for me. Latest of all was our reading French or German aloud to him, so that his ear might get accustomed to the sounds, for he felt deplorably behind the younger generation when confronted with strangers whose tongues were no barrier to us, however fast they moved them. He highly prized [our] accomplishment [in modern languages], as is shown by his taking us all abroad in our 'teens, and his bringing first a young German woman, then a Frenchman to live with us in Maple St. to keep up our practice in speaking these languages. Nothing I can do has given me as deep a tinge of satisfaction all my life.

I do recall definitely my father's failure to interest me in botany, as a science, in spite of his own enthusiasm and his collecting specimens in a tin slung-box every summer on our walks and drives. We were not "made" to read anything as I remember, but we were definitely encouraged. He started me at the age of six by a birthday present of a book of Shakespeare stories, simply told, bound in green and gold, and profusely illustrated in the Oliver Herford linear drawing style. Just as he had in mind the building up of a little dowry for each of us — in my brother's case, it had to be an education fund — so he meant to build up a small library, and within his means he accomplished both intentions. "The readiness is all" — and if I saw parents today *caring* with half his zeal for the future mentality of their offspring, I should not feel that strong need I do to [recall how strongly he influenced us in] "knowing the best that has been thought and said in the world."

TO SIBYL, HIS THIRD DAUGHTER, AGED TEN AND A HALF,
IN BROOKLYN, NEW YORK

Roxbury

My dear Mary, *February 27, 1884*

I was very glad to get your letter and to know that you are having such a pleasant visit. It may be well, when you write without lines, to rule the first line lightly with a pencil, and then it will be much easier to write straight.

I wonder if the morning was as beautiful in Brooklyn as it was here. The trees were loaded almost to breaking with snow, and the sun shone brightly.

I am not sorry that you are to have two weeks, instead of one, of vacation. I think you will learn a great deal, if you keep your eyes wide open. Tell mama that I hope she will show you all she can of New York, for it is likely to be many years before you go again. Wouldn't it be well to take some notes of what is most interesting, for materials for compositions? I suppose New York will be the scene of some of your stories. Write me again when you can. Your loving father

TO SIBYL, HIS THIRD DAUGHTER, ALMOST THIRTEEN,
IN TEMPLE, NEW HAMPSHIRE

Southport
My dear Mary,   *July 16, 1886*

It has stormed here for two days and the South wind has been driving the waves up against the rocks gloriously. The sea is covered with dense fog, and out of it comes the dashing angry sound of the surf beating against Shag Rock, and those that border the shore. I have sat here [a two-room shack with a fireplace, constructed for the family the previous summer, when there was not room for them at the boarding-house] where I am writing, all day, only going over to the house for breakfast and dinner. I was occupied till three o'clock with proofs [of his *Beginners' Latin Book*], and since then have been reading the second volume of the life of Agassiz.

I have read *Old Mortality, A Legend of Montrose, The Black Dwarf,* and *The Bride of Lammermoor,* all by Scott; but I can recommend to you only *A Legend of Montrose.* Perhaps, though, with skipping, you would enjoy *The Bride of Lammermoor.* I am sure one ought not to read too many novels. So few are worth the time. I wasted a day reading *The Wind of Destiny.* For all the good it did me, I might as well have spent the day sniffing the Wind of Newagen [east end of the island of Southport]. I hope you will read a good deal in that Latin book. [Sibyl says this was his *Viri Romae,* "a most readable series of biographies published with a French version on alternate pages."] It will enlarge your vocabulary. It is well not to consciously translate, but read as you do in French.

I suppose you will be sorry to have mama leave you for a week, but I think she needs the change, and you must encourage her to come. I'll try not to forget the chocolate. Is there anything else that you want me to bring? I hope you have your tennis web. Have all the rides you can till mama comes away. I think the ladies here consider me not very attentive; so today, while it was raining great guns, I invited them all to walk to Newagen. Mrs. S. Robbins accepted the invitation, but I told her I couldn't think of going, unless *all* the ladies would accompany me.

Take all pains with what you compose, and I think you'll get something after a while. Your affectionate Papa

TO SIBYL, HIS THIRD DAUGHTER, AGED ALMOST FOURTEEN

Roxbury

My dear Mary: *July 27, 1887*

I am very glad to know that you get along so well with Herbert's Latin, and it is just as well to let *Nepos* go till I come. I know it is hard to do any such work alone. I am glad you found my letter amusing. I didn't think I was writing an amusing letter.

I have no time to read. I envy you all that chance. I am getting on with my work. I hope by the end of August to have it all cleaned up, and then it will await the malediction of critics. [This work was the first edition of his famous *Beginners' Latin Book*.]

Your terms for hearing Herbert's lessons are too moderate. On general principles, because I think female labor is too slightly remunerated, I propose to give you five times as much. Besides, having borrowed a hundred dollars, I feel rich. I hope the horses will be engaged for another month, as I think I shall be able to borrow some more money. How the income will roll in by and by from my books! Whew!!! Your aff. Papa

Clarence W. Gleason, Master 1889–1905 and 1912–1939, recalls Collar's visit to his room in Harvard Yard in 1889 to interview him for an opening at Roxbury Latin.

REMINISCENCE OF CLARENCE W. GLEASON

(unpublished manuscript, 1942)

It was a dismal day in the spring of 1889. The Harvard College yard was dark and dank. In Stoughton 12 a lanky youth [Gleason] was working at the study table, acting as proctor. . . . There was a knock at the door. The lanky youth ran to open it and found a gray-bearded man, with his overcoat collar turned up, rather short and, as it appeared then, somewhat shabby in his general appearance.

Evidently beauty is in the eye of the beholder. Eleven years later, Lewis W. Hill entered the School. His description of his headmaster is dramatically different from Gleason's.

REMINISCENCE OF DR. LEWIS W. HILL '06
The Tripod 66, 2 (January 1954)
Mr. Collar was a beautifully dressed gentleman, always wearing a stiff shirt, stiff collar, and gold studs. He was very dignified; in fact, he looked somewhat like Robert E. Lee.

2. European Interlude, 1889–1890

By 1889 Collar was fifty-five and had been headmaster for twenty-two years. The trustees granted him a fourteen-month sabbatical with full pay, and, following the Closing Exercises, he departed for England on the first leg of the trip. Hannah and the children spent the summer, as usual, in Connecticut, preparing to join him two months later.

One can imagine the excitement with which Collar anticipated this, his first, visit to Europe. For the first time he would be able to see the classical sites he had taught and written about and to hear German spoken by Germans.

Far from lifting his spirits, however, the trip brings out the tendency to depression which dogged him throughout his life. Edward J. Goodwin, principal of Newton High School, touches on this tendency in the normal routine of Collar's life.

MEMORIAL OF WILLIAM COE COLLAR BY EDWARD J. GOODWIN
HEADMASTERS ASSOCIATION ANNUAL MEETING, 1917
Now and then one detected in him a tendency to pessimism; it was not pronounced and, like the storm cloud, had a silver lining. On one occasion I heard him say to his first wife: "I have the most unpromising First Class this year I have ever had." "Oh, William," she rejoined, "you always say that." He drew a little sigh and confessed—"Well, perhaps I do."

Almost from the day of his departure, separation from his family causes him intense loneliness, and he is dispirited throughout much of July and August. Later, in Germany, when he takes short leaves from his family in order to immerse himself in the language, this depression recurs. His diary entry of December 30, 1889—when, alone in Berlin, he calls his whole life into question—reveals the depth of his existential despair. Throughout this period he remains obsessed with his health.

Collar was by now a preeminent figure in American education, his "salary the highest of any schoolmaster in New England." He was also renowned for his Greek and Latin textbooks; his major goal in Germany was to master the language in order to write an introductory German grammar for American schools. Modern psychology reveals to us how difficult it is for anyone aged fifty-six to become fluent in another language. Unaware of this reality, Collar is devastated by his slowness in picking up the language—attributing it to "weak aptitude." Likewise, Collar failed to foresee how complicated family life far from home would be. The anticipated year of refreshment sadly becomes a time of "perpetual straining."

Again, his correspondence and diary tell us much about Collar the man. His early observations of English society bring out his own democratic egalitarianism. He notes that travelling third class on the railway "is good enough for anyone"; the fact that women sit only in the lower part of the bus is "an unmistakable sign that I am not in America." He disparages an Englishman who is impressed by the presence of the titled aristocracy, and he notes repeatedly the contrasts of wealth and poverty in English society.

He visits three English schools—Eton, Harrow, and St. Paul's—and several German gymnasia. We can glean something of his own philosophy of education from his observations. He condemns "dry and solemn" teaching and excessive emphasis on rote learning. He notes with pleasure those teachers who encourage their students.

Collar left for England on June 29, 1889. His first letter is written on board ship.

TO HANNAH, HIS WIFE, IN CONNECTICUT

My dear Wife,   *July 7, 1889*

We are about 500 miles from land, and don't expect to see Queenstown before Tuesday night. Then it will take a day to reach Liverpool.

Our passage, as you see, is very slow indeed. [The journey took eleven days.] Until today we have had head-winds, i.e. winds directly against us, for several days. Then, too, the firemen are said to be green hands, and that, in consequence, the furnace (engine) fires have not been well kept up. There was a long period of fog, with the whistle blowing every minute or two day and night. Wednesday night and the two following nights I scarcely slept at all, but the cause was my imprudence in eating and drinking. Be sure, all of you, however well you feel, not to eat anything but the simplest food, what you are used to, and only moderately of that. The service is excellent, the smells said to be abominable in the extreme. [His daughter Sibyl comments on this statement: "Smells had to be taken on hearsay owing to my father's chronic catarrh."] I advise you to take toilet-water (Cologne) or aromatic vinegar to sprinkle on your pillow or on a handkerchief to lay under your head. I had one very bad night, when I seemed to be threatened with a serious trouble, but with the morning, happily it passed away. You may imagine I thought of you. I thought you would most likely be a widow. How I pitied you, to lose such a husband!

Some of the time I have found it hard to keep warm on deck, where I stay all the time, in sunshine and rain. I wear more clothing than in winter. Be sure to have leggins (is that the way to spell it?) and lots of shawls. I suppose you will have to buy at least two large steamer rugs. I hope Mildred [now seventeen] will not be very seasick, but if she is, or any of you are, I would spend some money [on] Champagne. If only you were with me, I should be altogether happy. Your affectionate husband

TO HANNAH, HIS WIFE, IN CONNECTICUT   *London*
My dear Hannah,   *July 12, 1889*
    Our steamer arrived off Liverpool Wednesday afternoon about 3 P.M. and a tender took us to the city in about two hours. It was too late for the last train to London, and so I staid overnight in Liverpool [at the Adelphi Hotel]. I got here last night, taking the train at Rowsley at 6. I

never rode at such a fearful rate, some of the way 60 miles an hour. The third class was good enough for anyone. Your loving husband William

TO HANNAH, HIS WIFE, IN CONNECTICUT   *London*
My dearest Hannah,   *July 13, 1889*

I count the days now till I shall see you once more, and the day that I see you I believe will be the happiest of my life. You will conclude that I am homesick, but that hardly expresses it. But you will not worry, for I am bodily well, and this feeling of dreadful loneliness will pass away. I left Williamson's [Hotel] this morning because I was almost devoured there by *bed-bugs*. Just as I finished yesterday's letter to you, Mr. E. L. Pierce (The Honorable of Milton, Mass.) called to see me and we spent the whole day together. He was kindness itself. He took me to his tailor's and I engaged a suit of clothes. I rode on the top of an omnibus (everybody says *bus*) through Piccadilly, along Hyde Park. Then we went through some other famous streets, and all the time my thoughts were that I should see it all again with you and the children.

London streets look very different to me from ours. There are no horse-cars in the part of the city where I have been, but the streets are full of *buses* and cabs and hansoms. The name *cab* applies to what we call hacks, though they are drawn by one horse, and to the hansoms, too. The hansoms, as you know, are the two-wheeled carriages, open in front, and with the driver perched up behind, so that he looks and drives over the top of the carriage. Everybody who can rides on the top of the buses, and often there will be as many as sixteen on top and nobody inside. But of women, only shop-women and the like ride on the top. As the best place, it seems to be appropriated to the men, and that is an unmistakable sign that I am not in America. The streets are paved like Columbus Ave. and the vehicles go fast. The result of all is an appearance of far greater bustle and variety than in Boston. The buildings astonish me, many of them are so immense and so splendid. A glass of lager costs twice as much as in Boston, but you get your hair cut for 12 cts. Riding on the buses is astonishingly cheap, especially for not very long distances—*a penny*. Meals cost rather less, clothing just about half. I took a bath today at a *barber's*. That seemed to me dear—a shilling, i.e. 25 cts. With love unutterable I am Your affectionate husband

TO CHARLES COLLAR, HIS FATHER   *London*
My dear father,   *July 14, 1889*
    You will be interested to know a little about prices here. I can get a piece of roast beef and potatoes for about two-thirds the cost in Boston. Beer costs twice as much, clothing about half. Board is about the same. I pay $2 a day in a private boarding house with two meals only. Where there are *bed-bugs* it costs less. I bear about fifty mementos on my body of a place that I left yesterday. Everybody knows that I am an American, the moment that I speak, just as I know Englishmen. Much to my astonishment, I find Englishmen very ready to talk and the policemen are exceedingly courteous and obliging. I sincerely hope you are well and that I shall see you again in a little more than a twelve-month. Yours affectionately, William

DIARY   *London*
                                                     July 14, 1889
    My thoughts are on home and my dear ones. Would to God I had not left them!

DIARY   *London*
                                                     July 15, 1889
    Went to St. Paul's School in West Kensington and was most cordially received by Mr. Carter, to whom I had a letter of introduction. Lunched in the Hall with some of the masters [and] boys. The School [consists] of 600 boys, 150 educated free; the rest pay about $120 tuition. A splendid building with a very large laboratory for chemistry. Science and modern languages rather discouraged. Boys were writing Latin verse at 13. Bright boys taken from time to time into the "Hall" to be partly under the eye of the "High Master", Mr. Walker, then returned to their forms. No fagging, much individual teaching in school hours,

none out; a day school; eight forms. Much pride in honors at universities. There was no objection to my seeing and hearing everything. They were in the thick of examinations. Individual boys were set to construe for me, and to put English into Latin. The masters did not impress me as superior to ours; probably in Latin and Greek scholarship they are.

TO HANNAH, HIS WIFE   *London*
My dearest wife,   *July 16, 1889*

I went to Baring Bros. this morning and was almost overjoyed to get a letter from you. You will never feel quite as I did, when I saw your letter, for I hope you will never be and feel so far away in a strange land.

The chambermaids here [at the hotel] are my ideal of such servants. They also wait on the table in very pretty white caps and white aprons, are silent, modest, quick and handy, and with a deferential air, without being servile. They are paid a pound a month. They can't go to bed before 11 or 12 o'clock, and are up early. Still they seem cheerful. I think of you constantly. Good-night, William

DIARY   *London*
                                                     July 17, 1889

Today [I visited Harrow School at] Harrow-on-the-Hill. [Winston Churchill was a student there at the time.] I was urged by the headmaster [The Rev. J. E. C. Welldon] to stay with him and come again. Heard a recitation of the 5th form in Prometheus; rather poor but not differing from ours. Heard an admirable lesson of 5th form in French. Saw where generations of boys had cut their names—Byron, Peel, Palmerston, Sheridan, etc. Situation unequalled, view most beautiful. Boys in grey trousers and black jackets. Older boys swallow tailed coats. Saw boys' rooms, eat [*sic*] at same table with them.

TO HANNAH, HIS WIFE, IN CONNECTICUT   *London*
My dearest Wife,   *July 18, 1889*

One of the most agreeable of the masters [at Harrow] offered to come up to London and introduce me to his club in Piccadilly. So I met him there this afternoon, and he constituted me a member for a month. It (that is the club-house) is beautifully situated opposite the Green Park. There the members drop in to meet each other, smoke, take tea or coffee, and if they choose, their meals. I got my suit today and was agreeably disappointed with it. They, the clothes, fit me perfectly, and cost $18.75. They would have cost $40 in Boston.

Dr. [Cecil F. P.] Bancroft [Principal of Phillips Academy, 1873–1901] of Andover Academy has been here several days, and is most excellent company. He has just returned from Palestine and Egypt. He has been absent from his family seven months. If I had been absent from you seven months, and were in Palestine or Paradise, I should telegraph for you to come immediately. And you would come, wouldn't you?

When night comes is my lonely hour. Then I would give all to be with you. I have planned several times to go to the theatre, but I am too tired or I get home too late. It is getting late and I must say good-night. I hope you all think of me, Dearest, dear wife, good-night. William

DIARY   *London*
                                                                                     July 18, 1889

It is hard to be separated from my dear wife. When it comes night, I feel as if I could not endure the loneliness.

TO HANNAH, HIS WIFE, IN CONNECTICUT   *London*
My dearest Hannah,   *probably July 21, 1889*

You see my lonesome hour has come again, and so I write a little more. I went to church this morning and this afternoon; in the morning to hear Stopford Brooke, the father of our Stopford [minister at Boston's First Church, Unitarian] and in the afternoon to Westminster Abbey. There couldn't be a greater contrast in the churches—the Unitarian chapel being bare and mean beyond even most of our wooden meeting-houses, and Westminster one of the finest [buildings] in the world. But Stopford Brooke's sermon was as much superior to Canon Somebody's as the Abbey is to the chapel. Really the service of the English Church is beautiful, solemn, awe-inspiring in such a magnificent [building] as Westminster. How the responses of the choir and the solemn organ tones sound through those splendid arches!

You cannot well get off Sundays without fees or contributions, but then I was willing to give sixpence to help on Unitarianism, which is pretty generally despised in London.

I had a sight of my *Latin Composition* a day or two ago, at Ginn's Agency here. It makes a bigger book than I looked for, but it is a very handsome book. How should you like to have me promise you a quarter of the income from it? I will, you shall have it. I am very anxious to know all about the children, how they enjoy themselves, whether Herbert [aged 14] finds anything to do, how they are in health. The gas is so bad in my room that I have to write in the smoking-room, so you must not imagine, if you smell smoke, that I have been smoking. Mr. Bancroft is very interesting about his Eastern travels, but he must have made the money fly. He had leave of absence for a year, and he is going back this week, after an absence as I told you of only seven months. I suppose he has spent in seven months the money he had appropriated for a year. Most affectionately your loving husband

TO MILDRED, HIS DAUGHTER, AGED SEVENTEEN   *London*

My dear Mildred,   *July 25, 1889*

I was very glad indeed to get your letter. I had been grievously disappointed to have only one letter from the mamma in more than twenty days, so that your letter was doubly welcome. Today, at Windsor, I stood in the Chapel of St. George over the spot where [Henry VIII's] accursed bones lie. In the same vault Charles I and one of Henry's numerous wives, Jane Seymour, were laid. In the evening I went to the House of Commons. Yesterday I went into the crypt of St. Paul's, where Wellington and Nelson are buried, then . . . slowly along Fleet St. finding some places where Johnson and Goldsmith used to resort. One place was the *Mitre*, now a Scotch drinking-house. There I sat down and ordered a sausage and a bottle of ale. There was enough for Johnson, Goldsmith and me, and even Bozzy, but I paid for only one.

Yesterday, when I started out, a woman was passing along with some kind of wild flowers for sale, not calling out, or shouting, but singing — a short refrain in a loud but melodious voice. There was a melancholy effect in the notes, or in her voice or both, that went to my heart. The contrasts of wealth and poverty are terrible, as in every great city, but I have felt more and more in these two weeks the hideous cruelty of such a condition of things.

I was most hospitably received [at Eton College] by Dr. Carpenter, one of the masters, shown the school, and invited to dinner. He has thirty boys in his house. His wife served at one end of the table and he at the other. The boys sat on movable benches, not in chairs, and grace was said at the end of the meal instead of at the beginning. The small boys wear jackets and black neckties, and the older ones swallow-tail (or as they say here, tail) coats and white neckties. All wear stove-pipe hats, even the smallest. I saw them play cricket, and on the grounds at play they wear much such a rig as our boys do at play. Only every boy who had won any distinction had a cap or coat with stripes to indicate it. Every distinction, of whatever kind, is made a great deal of, and one sees tables with the names recorded of those who have gained any honors. With much love to all, I am Your affectionate Papa

DIARY   *London*
                                                July 24, 1889

[Additional notes on the visit to Eton College:] Teaching very good, boys not knowing much. Three or four "Fellows" do absolutely nothing whatsoever and get 1000 pounds, a house, their living, and have a very valuable library for their especial delight. Boys breakfast and sup in their rooms, each by himself. Science gets two hours of the six a week ordered by Parliament years ago.

DIARY   *London*
                                                July 25, 1889

Spent all the morning in the British Museum, most of the time in the [room with the "Elgin Marbles," the sculptures brought by Lord Elgin from the Parthenon]. What a barbarous thing to remove those sculptures! It was worse than the bombardment.

TO HANNAH, HIS WIFE, IN CONNECTICUT   *Leamington*
My dearest Wife,   *July 30, 1889*

    I left London yesterday afternoon at 4.30 and arrived here in about two hours and twenty minutes, a distance of 97 $^1/_2$ miles. I am at a private house, Mrs. Enoch's. Funny misunderstandings happen. When I had seen the room, just the size of Herbert's, I said, "I suppose you could board me." "Oh!, no," said she, "I never did that." But it turned out that by "boarding" with her she understood sitting at her table; she hadn't the slightest objection to giving me meals, and cooking for me anything I want. She sets my table in a fine large sitting-room, where I am now writing. Today has been such an one as I don't expect to pass again in England. Stratford-on-Avon, Warwick Castle, and Kenilworth Castle in one day. I staid an hour or so in the house where Shakespeare was born, visited the school where he was educated, drove to the cottage of Anne Hathaway whom he courted and married, visited the church where he and his gentle Anne now lie, and took a boat ride on the Avon. The cottage of Anne Hathaway is said to be almost unchanged from what it was when she received the visits of her William. It looks very ancient, is very low, built of stone and brick and thatched with straw. [Stratford] is a very large village, very quaint, and the neatest place in the world. I didn't see so much as a piece of waste paper in one of the streets, and you would say the stone-paved sidewalks must have been scrubbed the day before. Even the by-streets were watered. All the houses are of brick or stone, low, often differing very much from each other, but neat to the last degree, and many, very many of them with flower gardens outside the windows. In the Shakespearian house I saw his school-desk, and at his school the master pointed out the corner of the room where it used to stand.

    The country is a paradise to me, except that the laborers' cottages are little better than hovels, and even the farmers' houses, few and far between are almost mean. The worst is that I cannot hear from you. I seem more cut off from you than ever. If I could look in upon you to-night! Affectionately, William

TO HANNAH, HIS WIFE   *Glasgow*
My dearest Wife,   *August 2, 1889*
    I had a stage ride today of 21 miles, said to be the finest in the kingdom, from Windermere to Keswick. It was pretty but not to be compared to some of ours in the White Mountains. We passed through the region where Wordsworth and Coleridge and deQuincey lived.
    In two weeks we shall be approaching each other, for by that time, I shall be on my way to the south. How much I shall think of you all in the next three weeks. This will be the last letter I can send to you. It seems hard for you and the children to come without me. In twenty-six days I shall rejoice with all my heart to meet you all, if nothing befalls. Good bye. Affectionately your husband

TO HANNAH, HIS WIFE   *Oban, Scotland*
My dearest Wife,   *August 4, 1889*
    There seems to be a chance that a letter sent tomorrow will reach you before the 20th, and so I write one more last letter. You will be glad to get the latest possible news of me before you start. I have come so far on my travels in safety and good health. One day's journey more to the north and I shall reach my most northerly point, my *apogee* from you, the planet around which I revolve. Tomorrow if it is fair, I go on a sail to Iona and Staffa, the latter Fingal's Cave.
    The best hotels are about as expensive as they are at the White Mts. You would be astonished to see how many order wine at dinner. There must have been forty at dinner, and besides myself only two or three did not order champagne or claret. Is everybody who travels rich? A little while ago I was standing in the hotel doorway when two ladies came along and one looked me full in the face and then asked if it were Mr. Collar. I then recognized Miss Ladd, of Chauncy Hall School. I took a

walk with her and her friend, and though I never fancied her, I could have hugged her, so glad was I to see some one whom I knew.

Don't spare any expense on board the steamer to make yourselves as comfortable as you can. Your affectionate husband

DIARY   *Killair, Scotland*
                                         August 8, 1889

Killair has about half its dwellings thatched cottages, the eaves about six feet from the ground. Often you step down from the street one step in entering them, and I, five feet seven inches in height, had to stoop.

DIARY   *Edinburgh*
                                         August 10, 1889

Yesterday found, as I hoped to, letters from my dear wife. Glad to know that my class [at Roxbury Latin] entered so well at Harvard. Three with honors in English, and only twelve given in all!

Collar's daughter Alice had founded and headed her own elementary school—the Elm Hill School in Roxbury. She was married to Marshall Davis, master at Roxbury Latin 1880–81, 1886–1917.

TO ALICE, HIS DAUGHTER, AGED THIRTY   *Edinburgh*
My dear Alice,   *August 11, 1889*

Riding by stage-coach, I occasionally saw the cabins of farm-laborers, with one door and one window, with an addition for a cow and a pig or goat without a separate entrance. I don't remember ever being told that land belonged to Mr. So and So, but always to Marquis of this, or Duke of that. The Englishman with whom I travelled told me at one hotel, with a good deal of intensity of manner, that he understood that Baron de Worms and Lady Worms were at the hotel, and I said with the same eagerness, "But do his lordship and his lady know that *we* are here?"

At Kenmore, I walked a mile through the park of the Marquis of Breadalbane to his Castle, and was privileged to see the noble lord, a

FIG. 2. Elm Hill School, an elementary school in Roxbury founded and run by Alice Collar Davis.

red-haired, red-whiskered man of thirty-nine with stooping shoulders. I should think the castle would accommodate 200 persons, and it is occupied by himself and his wife. They have no children and the estate will pass to his brother. An hour later, I was riding through his territory (he is the owner of 500,000 acres) and the stage-coach was pursued by beggars with "Please, sir, give me a penny." Bare-legged, bare-footed, bare-headed women stood by the roadside with babies slung upon their backs and hands stretched out for a penny.

Travelling alone is dreary business. I shall stay here four or five days. I am keeping my expenses down quite surprisingly. Goodbye. Affectionately Papa

DIARY   *Lincoln*
                                                                August 18, 1889

I did not feel well and was able to do but very little. The longest and lonesomest day I have spent in England. Is there anything more dismal than to be shut up in the dullest conceivable of English towns on Sunday, in a great hotel, when you don't know a soul, and without the sort of reading that suits your mood?

DIARY   *Southampton*
                                                                    August 22, 1889

I was so sick of sightseeing alone that I didn't go to Westminster [Abbey] which I have hardly seen at all. I had intended all along to stop at Winchester and . . . Salisbury to see the cathedral, but I am sick of the whole business. I am sorry, for Salisbury would have rounded out my studies on architecture.

DIARY   *Ventnor*
                                                                    August 25, 1889

My mind is full of thoughts of wife and children who are now in mid-ocean coming towards me at fifteen or twenty miles an hour. Now, if all is well it will be only four days and a little more. How impossible it is to fortify one's self for a possible catastrophe! If it comes, it is only strength of character than can sustain it, not previous reasoning or any possible preparation.

DIARY   *Ventnor*
                                                                    August 27, 1889

I have got some good from my visit here. My dyspepsia has pretty nearly gone and I feel somewhat less nervous. But one cannot get away from himself and alas, at my age there seems to be no throwing off of chronic ailments, even if they are slight. Well, a new epoch is about to begin in my life. How will the year that I am entering on look to me twelve months hence? I am determined it shall mark a change for the better, but alas, how many times have I so resolved and no resolve ever kept!

DIARY   *Southampton*
                                                                    August 29, 1889

About nine o'clock good news that the Saale [on which his wife and their three younger children were travelling] had been sighted. This morning wore slowly and heavily away, but all things have an end. The tender to take me to the Saale reached the vessel about three, and I had the great joy of meeting wife and children all well. Left my hat on the tender and discovered my loss thirty seconds too late.

DIARY　　　　　　　　　　　　　　　　　　　　　　*Bremen, Germany*
August 30, 1899

Reached Bremerhaven about six o'clock, where we were transferred to a tender. Train from Bremerhaven to Bremen.

REMINISCENCE OF SIBYL, THIRD DAUGHTER

[We all—mother, Mildred, Mary Sibyl, and Herbert—travelled immediately to Weimar where we stayed in] the quaint stone cottage of an officer's widow, Frau Rudolph. From the first morning, when the gate-bell rung by the baker's boy with his glistening loaves called us to our bedroom window, and we looked down on a triangular sloping garden where luncheon and sometimes supper was often served, all was enchantment.

We children were all promptly placed at school, and in a few weeks could answer back in their own lingo the street urchins who made fun of our foreign clothes.

But for my father, there was too much English spoken, and he betook himself to Jena, where he had university introductions, and there tried to concentrate in study.

As he had done in England, he visited schools in Germany.

DIARY　　　　　　　　　　　　　　　　　　　　　　　　　　*Jena*
October 21, 1889

Visited the Gymnasium in Jena and heard three recitations, all in Latin. The Director read himself one of the odes [of Horace] in Latin, in a noble manner and with beautiful elocution, like a man accustomed to public speaking. The first ode was admirably analyzed, much of it repeated by the scholars from memory, and a very few questions asked of a philological sort. The director . . . stood most of the time. The little fellows here . . . were very bright. They did the unprepared work almost as well as the prepared, but not better than my own boys would have done, and I think not so well. The boys in Quarto surpassed any of the same age that I had ever seen. Here the work was Caesar. There was no levity, no inattention in any of the classes. No boy asked a question. Every moment was utilized to the utmost.

The men, as men, seem to me inferior to the same class at home, but they have been highly trained. Heard a lesson on Goethe's *Tasso*. It was too exclusively an analysis of the scenes. There was nothing to inspire a love of literature or help [the student] to good writing.

DIARY *Jena*
October 23, 1889

Spent an hour in the gymnasium hearing Latin in Sexta—most admirable instruction. The most marked features were the impromptu retranslation into Latin of what had been rendered into German, and the frequent demand by the teacher for a repetition of what had been said. The teacher several times had the boys quickly rise and then resume their seats. What seriousness, attention, earnestness! Never have I seen these qualities equalled in any American school in the case of boys of this age. But there is a bit too much strenuousness. The tension is almost painful. The teachers have no police duties to perform. They go to their rooms, give their recitations and depart. The boys are seated when the teacher enters, they rise, and remain standing until he commands them to sit.

REMINISCENCE OF SIBYL, HIS THIRD DAUGHTER

[At Jena, father] was, of course, painfully homesick, and we had to go and pass a day with him before his self-appointed exile was up. [He returned to Weimar on November 17.]

DIARY   *Weimar*

November 24, 1889

Tomorrow we leave Weimar. I have been here two months and in Jena one month. I have given my time faithfully to German but have made much less progress than I hoped to, and am obliged to confess that I must have much less than average aptitude for learning languages. [*He then lists a staggering array of accomplishments in translating.*] But my ear is desperately slow to take in the spoken word. I cannot yet understand a play on the stage, and I don't know whether I ever shall. I can speak tolerably accurately, but only slowly. My enjoyment has been very much marred by my slow progress in understanding. But my freedom has been worth a great deal to me, and I have wasted no time in simple idleness. German remains to me difficult to read even to the present, though it seems as if I had read enough to get great facility. That I shall never have.

REMINISCENCE OF SIBYL, HIS THIRD DAUGHTER

[By way of Leipzig the family was now] transplanted [to Dresden] in early December. [We were] ready now, it seemed, for real opera and perhaps more cosmopolitan comfort than [Weimar] afforded. My own diaries at this point are full of rebellion [she was sixteen] and discouragement at the dreary chill and lack of friends in Dresden, not to mention "la grippe," which made its debut that year—attacking us one after another.

DIARY   *Dresden*

December 19, 1889

Have been twice and spent two hours each time in the Kreuz Schule here in Dresden. This is an immense school of about 600 boys. There was here, as I have noticed always in the [Jena] Gymnasium, the most earnest attention. Every moment of the recitation was well used. I have never yet heard any boy say that he did not know, when asked. The Germans make much greater demands upon the memory than we do. Here, as in Jena, I was struck with the evidence that every boy did his very best. What strenuous attention! What gravity on the part of these little fellows! Then came the exercise in turning German into Latin. As would be supposed the boys were much in advance of boys of the same class with us [in Latin composition]. The boys do as much German into Latin as Latin into German the first three years or more. I have seen better teaching at home, but it was not poor.

Today heard a lesson in religion, and a more mechanical performance one could not well imagine. The boys cared nothing about it, though they decently simulated some interest. [The teacher] seemed to me a dry and very solemn and very empty individual. It was to me an hour miserably wasted. I was glad to see signs that the boys were as badly bored as I was.

[The next class] was an unexceptionally good piece of work on Sophocles' *Antigone*. It was treated as a literary work. The teacher was a very kind man, and helped a fellow through fifteen lines, telling him about everything. He often said *gut, gut.* The class was animated.

DIARY *Dresden*

December 20, 1889

Spent a third morning in the Kreuz Gymnasium. Heard a lesson in German. First [the master] showed me the notebooks in which the boys wrote their dictation and other exercises, all corrected in red pencil. The writing was exceedingly neat and clear. He then read an historical anecdote slowly and very clearly while the boys sat with folded hands, and looked and listened with an almost painful attention. After the reading he called for a suitable title of the piece. The anecdote was so happily chosen that a number of titles seemed almost equally appropriate. Then one and another were called on to relate the anecdote, with various changes to bring out more prominently one or another idea. There was great interest manifested by the boys, but I thought American boys would have been quicker and keener.

REMINISCENCE OF SIBYL, HIS THIRD DAUGHTER

[On December 27, 1889] my father [decided to take another month away from us to immerse himself in German] in Berlin. [But] he actually gave in and had my mother join him, leaving [the three of] us [children] in Dresden.

DIARY   *Berlin*
                                                              December 30, 1889

I sometimes ask myself if I am as happy as at home. I must confess that I am not. If I am with my family, I am perpetually interrupted and cannot be by myself; if I am alone, I am almost always depressed in spirits. Age [he was fifty-six] is rapidly advancing upon me, and I am daily more conscious of my feeble powers. My life has been one of dreary monotony. I have been all my life struggling to get knowledge, and alas how pitiful is the outcome! I shall never know any language well, and what do I know besides? Pitiful is the state of one whose youth and young manhood have passed without getting a good education, and then finds himself launched upon life in a situation where education is by everyone assumed. What then am I to do? I can do nothing but what I have done and am doing. The weary struggle will be over by and by.

But I have many reasons in my outward circumstances to make me contented with my lot. I have all these years, almost a generation, a loving faithful wife. My children are not inclined to evil ways and have fair parts. My position as head of a school has been not too burdensome and my salary the highest of that of any schoolmaster in New England. I have built a house in a healthy spot, a large and convenient house, which has permitted us to live for twelve years in great comfort. I have edited one book, written another, and am joint author of another, and these are bringing in an income that would keep us all from starving. I must first of all maintain my health with more care. While I ought to be industrious, I must give up this perpetual straining.

Berlin surpasses all cities that I have yet seen in beauty in the night. How brilliantly it is lighted. What gas, and how freely it is used. Boston makes a pitiful show in comparison. But why can't the Germans learn to cook! The detestable food is the great and crying drawback. Today I could hardly eat any dinner at all.

TO HANNAH, HIS WIFE, IN DRESDEN *Berlin*

My dear Hannah, *January 10, 1890*

It seems to be of little use for me to write, for I suppose no letter of mine is ever received. In the last three communications that have come to me, there is no word by which I should know that anything has been heard from me since last week.

I feel better today than I have for a week. I should have left for Dresden yesterday, if I had had my washing. I have had feverish, sleepless nights, without energy or spirit days.

The past week I have hardly done anything or gone anywhere. I do not remember to have done so little in a week before. Prof. S.— is a dreary good fellow, but I should be lonesome without him. I hear German at the table but don't understand it, and I have relapsed into silence. I am sick of Deutschland. It is a detestable country. Ever affectionately William

TO HANNAH, HIS WIFE, IN DRESDEN

My dear Hannah, *January 13, 1890*

So you can come! I will gladly postpone my return, if you feel well enough to come. I am not strong myself, but I hope the sleeplessness and fever are over. I slept again without fever last night and without taking anything. I feel the ascent of 100 steps to my room a good deal more than I did.

Dear wife, it will be a great joy to me to see you and I hope will give me better spirits. Perhaps I shall not be strong enough to take you about much, but we shall be together. Write at once. Affectionately your husband

Bring something that we can read together.

REMINISCENCE OF SIBYL, HIS THIRD DAUGHTER

According to my mother's diary, she joined him [in Berlin] on the 16th of January. On the 21st they left for Dresden, and after ten days with us, again departed [for 150 days] for Munich and points south. It was an adventure on both sides, and I have wondered many times at their confidence in us and in the comparatively new friends to whose nominal charge we were confided. But nothing ill came of it, and several life-long friendships developed. My father could read people at sight as well as languages.

TO ALICE DAVIS, HIS ELDEST DAUGHTER, AT ROXBURY

München

My dear Alice: *February 10, 1890*

I hope a better time is in store for me than I have had for two months and a half. The climate and the food of Germany do not agree with me, and except for exemption from bad colds, I have not been so well, by any means, as in America. Before this attack I had grown thin and very sallow, and felt almost all the time an abominable depression of spirits. The monotony of the diet is killing. The mamma happily has gained, since we left Dresden she begins to look more as she used to. The change in her looks was a constant affliction to me. She had grown thinner than I ever saw her, and looked ten years older. She always gains when she is away from the children, and I have hopes that her long stay in Italy will be very good for her. What care she has taken of me the past week!

I am glad to know that Mr. [Marshall] Davis [her husband—and master of French at The Roxbury Latin School] is well again and that he likes his work. His is the best department in the School. Affectionately Papa

TO ALICE DAVIS, HIS ELDEST DAUGHTER, AT ROXBURY

Florence

My dear Alice,   *February 26, 1890*

The mamma and I had a fine walk this morning on the high terraces to the south of the city. The view of Florence, the valley, the Arno, the mountain spurs covered with palaces, the slopes covered with olive and grape vineyards, and back of all the heights of the Apennines, lightly covered with snow and lighted up by the sun shining on them from behind the clouds was a superb sight. I am angry with myself for staying so long in Germany. The last two months I was not happy there. The miserable darkness and drizzle depressed me, and I was not well. I am pushing Italian, almost to the sacrifice of sightseeing, and am getting on fast. My teacher says I could speak well in a month. I love the language. Affectionately, Papa

Leaving his wife in southern Italy, Collar went off on his own to Greece.

TO HANNAH, HIS WIFE, AT NAPLES *Athens*
My dear Wife, *March 18, 1890*
I wish I could see you tonight. I believe I should enjoy the prospect of being with you for two weeks to come much more than I do that of a trip through the Peloponnesus. Our journey is likely to last 16 days. I don't know at all how I shall stand riding on mules or horses. I have not felt so well as I did in Italy, but it is due to poor food and lack of wine. Dearest wife, think of me often and love me as much as you can, not as little as I deserve. You know you are very dear to me . . . Most lovingly your William

TO ALICE DAVIS, HIS ELDEST DAUGHTER, AT ROXBURY *Athens*
My dear Alice, *March 1890*
I am afraid you will find a great change in Mamma. She seems to me to have aged so. I had hoped the year would do a great deal for the health of all, but it is doubtful if it does. I am not so well by a great deal as I was at home.

This morning I ascended Lykabettus, visited the American School, and afterward went to Kolonos, where Sophocles lived and wrote. Terrible is the desolation and neglect. Here, on the Hill of Kolonos, are fine monuments to two great archaeologists, one a Frenchman, the other a German, and the noble Greeks have scratched and written all over them, and used them as targets for shooting, so that they are chipped and broken, and all peppered with shot. I have seen some very handsome men and boys, and a few handsome women. But what poverty and squalor, too! I do not care to stay long in Athens, and I am almost sorry to carry with me the image of the reality in some cases, for imagination will no longer be able to indulge in pleasing illusions.

I hope to hear that you are going to give up your school. [Alice was childless and ran her own private elementary school—the Elm Hill School in Roxbury—which she didn't give up until twenty-five years after this letter was written.] Affectionately Papa

POSTCARD TO HANNAH, HIS WIFE, AT NAPLES   *Nauflia, Greece*
March 20, 1890

We left Athens yesterday morning for Corinth; from there took carriage to Old Corinth and ascended the Acropolis. I knew the ascent would be too hard for me at a rapid pace, and so I rode. It took an hour, and then I had to walk up the steepest part, half an hour more. The mountain is one mighty precipitous rock. Coming down, my horse would kick his heels up into the air, when I struck him to hurry his pace, so I soon left that off. The view of the Bay of Corinth was very beautiful. From Corinth we came on to this place. I was very careful to take everything I wanted, even to a nailbrush, but I didn't take a *nightshirt*! Today we drove all day to Tyryns, then to Argos, then to Mykenae. I picked some beautiful flowers. I have felt very well today. Many of the Greek children look very bright and interesting. Tomorrow we go to Epidaurus and the next day to Sparta. I trust you are well. With great love to you and the children. Wm.

TO SIBYL, HIS THIRD DAUGHTER, AT DRESDEN   *Syracuse*
My dear Sibyl,   *April 7, 1890*

Today has not been a remarkable day, and yet I have seen the Fountain of Arethusa, visited the scenes of the struggles between the Athenians and the Syracusans, about 415 B.C. in the disastrous Sicilian expedition, descended into the vast Catacombs, a little way from the city, seen the wonderful Ear of Dionysius, and lastly walked through the labyrinthine quarries, where the nine thousand Athenian prisoners wore out their lives in dreadful alternations of heat and cold, fever, hunger, thirst, toiling at slavish labor in utter heart-sickness and despair. (That sounds too rhetorical.)

But these were not the only things that interested me. Such an abundance and variety of wildflowers I never saw. It seemed as if the flowers vied with the grass, and for the most part got the larger share of the soil to themselves. Many of the flowers were entirely new to me, but many were familiar, though in more or less modified form. There were sweet peas, marigolds of two colors, mignonette, pinks, and I don't know what else of the prettier familiar flowers, and in the crevices of the rocks, maidenhair fern. Most affectionately Papa

POSTCARD TO HANNAH, HIS WIFE, AT NAPLES

Somewhere in Greece

My dearest dear, *circa April 9, 1890*

I shall be too glad to be with you once more. I wake in the night and think of you and long to have the days pass that still divide us. I am never so happy away from you, and I hope this is the last long separation. Do you still love me? Do you want to see me? Sometimes it seems impossible that you are my wife. Are you in very deed?

TO SIBYL, HIS THIRD DAUGHTER, AT DRESDEN *Naples*

My dear Sibyl, *April 20, 1890*

I wonder if you and the others noticed the amount my books earned last year—$2400. I was very much surprised. Each of you gets $80. I had promised the mamma half on the Latin Composition, and she gets over $500 in all. Ask Mildred to estimate as carefully as she can what the sum total of your expenses will be, provided you don't meet us till June 20, and I will send more money in due season. I should be glad for Herbert to continue his swimming lessons and I suppose he ought to have instruction in German. Affectionately Papa

TO ALICE DAVIS, HIS ELDEST DAUGHTER, AT ROXBURY   *Rome*
My dear Alice,   *May 7, 1890*
   I don't know about parents welcoming my return to the school. Mr.
[George F.] F[orbes, Acting Headmaster] it seems, I judge from his letters, is gloriously successful. He writes me that he has raised the scholarship of the whole school. I think I shall hardly have any place when I
return. There seem to have been not a few innovations.
   I am rejoiced that father is better. But for him, I should not think of
keeping house next year.
   I am astonished at the earnings of my books. I shall have nothing to
pay next year for plate-corrections, and without those, the books have
netted almost $2500 this year.
   We have been in Rome just fourteen days, and have not been prevented an hour from sight-seeing by bad weather. We have had the
cream of Rome in regard to things to be seen, and it is not probable that
we shall remain more than four or five days longer. We shall go to Pisa
for a day, then to Florence for four or five days, take Ravenna for a day
on our way to Venice, and remain there till about the first of June.
   The mamma is supremely happy. The money goes a little too fast. I
want to buy everything, but the mamma will not consent. She has to
pull me out of the mosaic shops, picture shops, etc. Affectionately Papa

TO ALICE DAVIS, HIS DAUGHTER, AT ROXBURY   *Venice*
                                                   May 25, 1890
   The mamma and I went off in a gondola this afternoon and read
Howell's *Venetian Life*. 'Twill be hard to leave Venice. Affectionately Papa

TO ALICE DAVIS, HIS DAUGHTER, AT ROXBURY   *Paris*
                                                   July 23, 1890
   I am often distressed about your mama's appetite. I hope to get her
safely landed in America. The money goes incredibly here, and I am
anxious not to overdraw my account. I enjoy the Louvre—have been
many times, and feel that I have learned not a little. My dull ears are

getting a little used to French. I keep my teacher talking an hour every day, and he is a splendid man. Papa

The family sailed from England for Boston on the Cunard steamship Catalonia, August 28, 1890.

3. National Eminence, 1891–1916

The steady stream of visitors—mostly educators and students in education schools—to the School in the last two decades of the nineteenth century attests to the eminence Roxbury Latin had attained under Collar. He was, by now, a major figure in American education and a prime mover in the creation of what can arguably be called the nation's two most prestigious and enduring educational associations. In 1885, he and his friends John Tetlow of Girls' Latin and Ray G. Huling, principal of Fitchburg High School, enlisted the support of President Eliot of Harvard to form the New England Association of Colleges and Preparatory Schools to address common problems of curriculum and standards. This organization—later renamed the New England Association of Schools and Colleges—continues today to evaluate and accredit all public and private universities, colleges, and schools in New England. Collar served as the association's third president, 1888–1890. In 1893 Collar, with Tetlow (again) and James C. Mackenzie of Lawrenceville School, founded the Headmasters Association—which today remains an eminent organization of school leaders, limited to seventy-five private school and twenty-five public school heads. Collar served as its eighth president in 1902. Harvard awarded him an M.A. honoris causa in 1870, and his own alma mater—Amherst—honored him with an L.H.D. in 1901.

As we shall see in Part IV, however, Collar could not rest on the laurels of his eminence. The final fifteen years of his headmastership were difficult ones as the School grappled with a changing neighborhood, new parental expectations, and financial constraints.

Our look at the final phase of Collar's life begins on a note of personal tragedy. Collar turned fifty-seven upon the family's return from the European sabbatical in September 1890. We take up our story a little over a year later. Collar's father, who lived with them, had contracted pneumonia.

REMINISCENCE OF SIBYL, HIS THIRD DAUGHTER

He recovered, and Miss Lamb [the nurse] left us, but was summoned back within twenty-four hours to attend my mother, who developed the same disease. On New Year's Day [1892], her heart gave out and she did not live through the night. She was fifty-four only. The suddenness of the blow, the weight of his unshared burden of an aged father and three minor children [Mildred, nineteen; Mary Sibyl, eighteen; Herbert, sixteen], beside the privation of his beloved companion, almost drove my father into a decline.

TO SIBYL, HIS THIRD DAUGHTER, AT SMITH COLLEGE   *Roxbury*
My dear Sibyl,   *January 17, 1892*

I was glad to get your letter and to know that you are well and enjoying again your college work.

Your dear mamma wore herself out, in spite of all that I could do to have her spare herself. But I did not do nearly all that I could and ought to have done. Even the spirit of noble self-sacrifice must not be carried too far. I am glad Herbert went back with you and that you were satisfied with him. He enjoyed the time, but found it very pleasant to get home again. I am very glad he had a chance to see Amherst.

Our life goes on just as of old, but oh! the difference to me! It often seems to me too awful to be real. It seems impossible that my heavy-heartedness would ever go, but it must and will. Thanks to the school and [the work I am doing on my textbooks] I get through one day after another. I hope you think of your dear mother often, and that her unspeakable goodness and unselfishness will be to you a constant sacred inspiration.

Let us hear from you at least once a week. Write once in a while to Herbert. Most affectionately, Papa

TO SIBYL, HIS THIRD DAUGHTER, AT SMITH COLLEGE   *Roxbury*
My dear Sibyl,   *February 3, 1892*

I try to fill my days as full of work as I can, but sometimes it seems as if I could not live. I hope you may never know what it is to have all joy

FIG. 3. Collar at his desk at school.

in life and hope of happiness vanish forever. Mildred [his daughter, aged nineteen] is an unspeakable blessing to me, so good, so kind, so affectionate, so capable.

I spend a great deal of time in correspondence in regard to teachers for next year and in interviews. I suppose as many as ten ladies have come to see me, and only one is of any promise. Affectionately, Papa

Despite his desolation, Collar continued to do his duty at school. He believed it was critical for the headmaster to "set the tone" in school life through the spoken word.

FROM *The Tripod* 4, 5 (February 1892)

We are glad to see that Mr. Collar has again begun to read short selections in the morning hall exercises. It makes a pleasant and useful addition to them. It is doubtless a good deal of trouble to find short, interesting, and instructive passages, but Mr. Collar's have always fulfilled these three conditions. More than this, the little hints and suggestions which the selections contain go far toward directing a boy's thoughts and actions, and building up his character.

TO SIBYL, HIS THIRD DAUGHTER, AT SMITH COLLEGE

Roxbury

My dear Sibyl,   *March 10, 1892*

Unfortunately I shall have the benefit of your visit home for only one week. I have decided to go to Washington for our vacation week, for otherwise I should only study and mourn incessantly, and be, I am afraid, in poor condition for the next term's work. Sometimes I can forget myself for a time in study, but then a wave of grief comes over me, and I long to die.

Now, once for all, dear Sibyl, I don't want you to be in the least troubled about your bills. I know that you are not extravagant and wasteful and I have never intimated so. I want you to have more money to spend for unforeseen trifles, and I mean that you shall. I want your college life to be not merely useful, but free and joyous and something to be remembered with pleasure as long as you live. My ship has not come in, but is expected to put into port about the 17th. By the 20th at latest, I hope to send you a cheque. Affectionately, Papa

TO SIBYL, HIS THIRD DAUGHTER, AT SMITH COLLEGE

Roxbury
My dear Sibyl,   *April 8, 1892*

I want to have a picture of the dear mamma framed like Alice's. Do you want one? I want you to be like her in unselfishness, affectionateness, helpfulness, charitableness in judging others and in speaking of them, exquisite neatness, and reserve, and all other good qualities. So I shall find more and more comfort in you in my terrible affliction. Most affectionately, Papa

Collar's first letter to Sibyl following summer vacation contains his first mention by name of the new teacher who—in a few short months—was to become his second wife.

TO SIBYL, HIS THIRD DAUGHTER, AT SMITH COLLEGE

Roxbury
My dear Sibylla,   *September 25, 1892*

Our school opens with 182, about 11 more than ever before. The first class numbers 25 or 26. The schoolhouse [the wooden building on Kearsarge Avenue, recently enlarged and improved] seems very convenient, and the new teachers make a good impression. Miss [Mary Evelyn] Cornwell boards on Waumbeck St. I cannot tell yet how she will succeed, but all signs are favorable. In the two weeks that we have been at home I have done almost nothing but attend to school matters. With so much to occupy my thoughts I suffer less from utter depression of spirits than at So. Yarmouth, yet I cannot overcome in any measure the feeling of the awfulness of my loss and when I am alone and try to study or write, paroxysms of weeping often master me. Joy and hopefulness and ambition seem to have left me. But I didn't mean to write this. I will never again speak of it.

When you come home you must see the schoolhouse. You would hardly think it could have been so improved. Affectionately, Papa

REMINISCENCE OF ROGER ERNST, CLASS OF 1898,
IN THE LATE 1940S

Our Sixth Class [in the fall of 1892] saw probably more of Dr. Collar than most Sixth Classes of that day (perhaps due to the presence of Miss Cornwell), and he gave us instruction in elementary Latin once a week, using a simple reader which he had compiled under the name of "Gradatim". This served the useful purpose of leading us at once above the mere drudgery of grammar into at least a low level of literary appreciation.

Dr. Collar, assisted by Mr. Gleason, had edited our various text books for Latin instruction, and this led Mr. Gleason, at Dr. Collar's suggestion, to follow [Collar's] *Guide to Caesar* with his own *Guide to the Anabasis*, which we used when we began the study of Greek. Of course the celebrated *Collar-Daniell's Latin Grammar* was our standby, although Mr. Daniell had by this time become headmaster of [Chauncy Hall School].

TO SIBYL, HIS THIRD DAUGHTER, AT SMITH COLLEGE *Roxbury*
My dear Sibyl,   *October 17, 1892*

I suppose the coming year will be one of unusual labor for me. I am engaged on a Greek Composition [textbook] with Mr. Daniell, and shall soon be at work on the proof of my [commentary on Vergil's *Aeneid*, Book VII]. Then too, Ginn and Co. are urgent to have a very easy first Latin book prepared to prevent its being done by someone else, so as to cut into our book [Collar and Daniell's] *The Beginners' Latin Book*.

What a blessing it is to have the days of college life before the press of life begins! But I had to teach a part of the little time I was at college, to get money. So I never had leisure, except such as I have taken in summer vacations.

There is an astonishing amount of work done in our school this year, so many boys taking extra work. I am trying to start a movement to improve the penmanship, by getting the boys to write more upright. I believe sloping letters is one principal reason why writing gets bad and deteriorates. Try it. In writing this letter I have been trying to avoid sloping.

I can get almost no time to read. But I look forward to the time when I shall cease making books. Still, there is a degree of fascination about it.

Mr. and Mrs. Atherton [both former teachers at Roxbury Latin] and Miss Cornwell may come to read the history of philosophy once a week in my study. Affectionately, Papa

REMINISCENCE OF SIBYL, HIS THIRD DAUGHTER

During the Christmas holidays [on January 5, 1893], [father] was married to his young assistant, Mary Evelyn Cornwell of Rome, New York, a step which undoubtedly added years to his life and immeasurably to the comfort and happiness of those years. But the suddenness of it was a shock to us daughters, as he evidently foresaw, when he wrote the following:

TO SIBYL, HIS THIRD DAUGHTER, AT SMITH COLLEGE   *Roxbury*
My dear Sibyl,   *January 1, 1893*

I hope you will feel like writing me, but if you don't, I shall understand that it would be painful to you. I am awfully sorry not to see any more of you this vacation. I hope you may find me more companionable, when we see each other again.

Somehow, I seem to think you will not feel it to be so dreadful.

I meant to tell you that I have come to like Pinckney [Holbrook, to whom she had been engaged for a year] very much indeed, and I feel very happy about your choice. Affectionately, Papa

The Tripod *5, 4 (January 1893) notes Miss Cornwell's resignation from the faculty. She was replaced by O. M. Farnham, who became the much-beloved master of Class VI, 1893–1934.*

TO SIBYL, HIS THIRD DAUGHTER, AT SMITH COLLEGE

Roxbury

My dear Sibyl, *January 30, 1893*

Yesterday I sent off the proof of the first half of my book, that had been lying about for many weeks, but on my table is a pile of manuscript of the Greek Composition that Mr. Daniell and I are at work upon.

If we could afford it, Mary [soon called by him and by all "Evelyn"] and I would surprise you with a visit before you come home, but I'm afraid we must economize; however it will be only two months now.

You will be glad to know that I am happier than I thought would ever be possible again. In truth I did not know at all what a treasure I was getting. Mary does everything possible for my health and happiness, and indeed, seems to live almost alone for that. She is most equable, affectionate, and unselfish and I don't see how it would be possible for one to be more gentle, discreet, kind and dignified than she is in a very trying position.

She is most companionable to me, interested in all that interests me, and she greatly enjoys the opportunity to carry on her own education. We read together, whenever I can find leisure and she is going to give English lessons for French to the number of six or eight a week with two French ladies. I feel sure that you and she will be great friends when you come to know her.

My new teacher seems to be an eminent success, and school never went so easily before.

Mildred told me she had received a letter from you and I am glad and relieved to know that you are interested in your studies. I wish for Mildred's sake, that she could find something to do that she would like. [*She became a librarian, married Charles Gardner of Newport, and died childless.*] Affectionately, Papa

TO SIBYL, HIS THIRD DAUGHTER, AT SMITH COLLEGE *Roxbury*
My dear Sibyl, *May 22, 1893*
 Alice comes no more, and from Mildred I have heard but once.
Affectionately, Papa

*Even as Collar was finishing books and coping with the loss of his wife (and
with his daughters' upset about his remarriage), he found time to play a key
role in founding the Headmasters Association—which held its first meeting
at Young's Hotel in Boston on April 6, 1893. A fellow member, Edward J.
Goodwin (sometime principal of Newton High School and later headmaster
of Packer Institute in Brooklyn, N.Y.) describes Collar's leadership at the
meetings:*

MEMORIAL OF WILLIAM COE COLLAR BY EDWARD J. GOODWIN
HEADMASTERS ASSOCIATION ANNUAL MEETING, 1917
 [Collar] was always ready for debate, and generally participated in
the discussion of every important question brought before the meetings. . . . He had a great gift of quiet oratory and was rarely worsted in
an argument, though I have often heard him measure words . . . with the
most skillful. He secured attention by his easy, confident manner, his
musical voice, his careful enunciation, and his perfect pronunciation.
He held attention by his clear and convincing argument, his exquisite
choice of words, and his careful preparation. Though he could speak *ex
tempore* as well as most men, he always shrank from doing so. He preferred, however simple his theme, to come to the discussion after he had
thoroughly threshed out the subject in his own mind.

 *The School's 250th anniversary in 1895 inevitably placed still further
national focus on the man who had virtually refounded an ancient school and
brought it to greatness. In the course of the celebrations he gave, as we might
expect, a clear definition of the particular mission of Roxbury Latin. But he
also went beyond the School to discuss the goals and methods of education in
general.*

 *Collar's own words—"A Small School with Great Ideals"—would be an
appropriate title for the two addresses which he delivered at the School's 250th*

anniversary celebrations on June 19, 1895. Both addresses are forward-looking statements about the School's purposes and goals. The first (to the School) admits that the classics are in decline (how often was their demise to be proclaimed over the next hundred years!) and that the School must offer a range of subjects that prepare boys for modern life. His strong emphasis on art and physical fitness is amazingly consonant with late twentieth century trends. His second address (to the alumni) contains implicit warnings that the School needed to change: to increase the size of its faculty and to move to a new building with a gymnasium and a commodious campus in "the opener part of West Roxbury." To do these things would require enlargement of the trustees' vision and the raising of endowment. Failure to do so would mean the School would no longer be able to compete with its emerging rivals—both public and private. "It would give me infinite pain if the School were to be crippled on account of lack of money . . . ; I had rather give up now than remain at the head of the School to see it in decline."

The following account is taken from The Boston Herald *of June 20, 1895, supplemented by the account in the* Boston Evening Transcript *of the previous day.*

COLLAR'S ADDRESS AT THE SCHOOL'S 250TH
ANNIVERSARY EXERCISES

Mr. William C. Collar, head master of the school, was the next speaker. After paying tribute to the late Augustus H. Buck, he turned to the question of what the School was to stand for in a wider relation. What influence, he asked, shall it exert in secondary education by its course of study, which has not hitherto been without effect, or by its method of instruction, the quality of its work, its purposes and aims?

"I will not predict. Prophesy is unsafe. But some things are clear. There is to be no break with the past. The school has long been known as a classical school. May it long continue to have that name. The trustees, I am glad to say, have great respect for the records of human experience. Not till some more powerful instrument of linguistic and literary training has been found and proven shall we abandon the study of

FIG. 4. The Roxbury Latin faculty in 1895. Seated, from left: Jesse E. Philips, Milford S. Power, William Coe Collar, Clarence Gleason. Standing: O. M. Farnham, D. O. S. Lowell, Marshall Davis (married to Collar's daughter Alice), Frederick Reed.

Latin and Greek. But the school is no longer merely a classical school.

"No school can really prosper, whatever its outward success may be, that does not respond to the demand of the times. Following that law, the school curriculum has been considerably enlarged from the old sacred trinity of Latin, Greek and mathematics. It has added English, modern languages, natural sciences, drawing, and has made a beginning of physical culture. With the single exception of Greek, no one of these subjects is optional, and, as a required course, no expansion is at present practicable.

"I have said that there is no intention of abandoning the study of Latin and Greek. But we cannot be blind to the fact that the tide is setting adversely.

FIG. 5. William Coe Collar, circa 1893.

"We shall by no means suffer ourselves to be swept away by this tide, nor shall we obstinately and hopelessly resist it. If the ancient languages are destined slowly to recede through forces that we cannot control, what subject shall come to the front? I have no hesitation in saying that it will be English. With a literature more varied, copious and rich than the Greeks possessed we are only beginning to find out what they early discovered for themselves, how potent for the best training and culture the native tongue and its literary treasures may be.

"In the meantime why should we altogether neglect that second great agency of education among the Greeks, I mean art, as distinguished from literature. Is it not possible without systematic study and instruction, that by the mere presence and silent influence of objects of art, some appreciation and love of beauty may insensibly steal into the hearts of our boys?

"When some generous benefactor shall build, equip and endow a gymnasium for the school, I think I may promise for the trustees that we shall set ourselves to working out the best scheme and the best methods of physical culture, with as much earnestness as we have applied to the course of study. And we will beat the Greeks, our masters, by pursuing physical culture with an ideal end—the perfection of the body, not the winning of a prize in a competitive contest.

"Our school is small, but a small school may have great ideals. Its ideals, more than its history, its endowment, its buildings, its numbers, its course of study, its alumni, will determine what sort of a school we are to have in the future. I believe I can say with perfect truth that a tone and spirit prevail in the school born of high ideals in the past that we should take pride in maintaining, rather that we should feel it a disgrace not to maintain and transmit in all freshness and vigor. Here again there must be no break with the past, but all the traditions that characterize the school of simplicity, sincerity, courtesy, truthfulness, manliness, and of honest, thorough work, must be passed on to succeeding classes.

"I am hopeful for the future with a board of trustees, always watchful and diligent, always kind and wise, long-suffering and far-seeing; with a body of alumni so loyal and enthusiastic and about to be so helpful; with a corps of teachers, such as my colleagues are, scholarly, earnest, united and so devoted to the school that they prefer to toil here for a most modest stipend rather than work elsewhere for a generous reward, how can we not be hopeful?

"I count those happy whose privilege it will be to labor here for the generations that are to come. But I find the present also a glorious time to serve the school."

The headmaster's address was delivered in an impressive manner, and gave an opportunity for knowledge of Mr. Collar's quiet mannered yet energetic personality that must have been very pleasing to those not previously acquainted with him.

COLLAR'S ADDRESS AT THE 250TH ANNIVERSARY ALUMNI DINNER

Mr. [George Lyman] Kittredge [Class of 1878, Professor of English at Harvard], called for order and introduced the first speaker, Mr. Collar, who said he proposed to look forward, not backward, in what remarks he had to make, pleasant as it would be to recall memories of the past in the presence of so many of his old boys. Continuing, he said:

"I should like to look even into the more distant future, which it is not given me to see—into that great future which lies before our school. Important changes are necessary if we are to make the most of that future. First, the proportion of teachers to pupils should be made larger. We now have eight teachers to 185 pupils, and the number ought to be doubled, if we are to attain that ideal of individual teaching which is possible only [with smaller classes].

"I want again, to see the Roxbury Latin School a national school. I am not ambitious for a great school, but I would have it national. It is important for the Roxbury boys themselves that the school should not be local. They would be better equipped if their classmates came from the West and South and the islands of the sea.

"If we become a national school, we must be able to offer the boys from a distance a home. We must have a dormitory, so that the boys shall not be put off into boarding houses. And the dormitory in its turn means a change of location to the opener part of West Roxbury, from which so many of our best boys already come.

"All these things mean that we must secure a great sum of money, which I do not see why we may not obtain as well as Andover or Exeter or St. Paul's. I want to see the alumni association do something in this matter. It would give me infinite pain if the school were to be crippled on account of a lack of money. True, we are now, as schools go, fairly well manned and equipped, but I had rather give up now than remain at the head of the school to see it decline. That it may not decline I want to see this interest shown here tonight effectively organized."

The Founder John Eliot stated that the purpose of his school was "to fit [students] for public service both in church and commonwealth." Collar's own commitment to character development as the School's principal goal is eloquently stated in his statement, "Advice for New Boys." It is undated, but internal references point to the mid-nineties. "Three qualities, not of intel- lect but of character *are essential to the schoolboy's success: industry ('the willpower to work'), perseverance, and self-restraint," he writes. Yet, with insight into the weakness of human (and especially, boy) nature, he also writes with tender understanding, "How many are the temptations, discouragements, and disappointments that rise up in a boy's school life to thwart and defeat his resolution for steady, hard work!"*

We are also given a glimpse of the School's daily life: class size (about twenty-five to thirty), schedule (with the day ending at 1:30 p.m. with the last class), morning "hall."

COLLAR'S "ADVICE FOR NEW BOYS," MID-1890S

I imagine that a boy coming from a public grammar school, as so many do, to the Roxbury Latin [School], must find the change a very great one. It must be delightful to one who has been accustomed to the restricted areas connected with the grammar schools, paved with stone or brick, to find adjoining the schoolhouse, an open field as a playground for free exercises and games. Then too, a difference that every boy is likely to appreciate, is in the hours of school attendance. Instead of two sessions, the last ending at four o'clock, he now finds himself released from school at half past one, or latest at two, after a single session. This gives him two additional afternoon hours, quite at his own disposal.

Another change which he is likely to think less about, but which is essentially of far greater importance, is to the much smaller numbers in a class. Accustomed hitherto, to being an insignificant unit of a group of forty, fifty, or even sixty, he finds himself on entrance to the Roxbury Latin School, a member of a class of twenty-five or thirty, seldom more. Thus he is in a fair way to receive double the time and personal attention of his teacher.

A difference of minor importance to the new-comer, but one that ought to prove very agreeable, is the custom of the whole school's gathering in the hall mornings for reading from the Scriptures, repeating in concert the Lord's Prayer in Latin, singing, and occasional short addresses by the Head Master. Boys who have gone through the school say that they look back upon these morning exercises as one of the pleasantest memories of their school life.

But the change most vital and far-reaching from a boy's old life lies in the course of study. One may name nine subjects, offered to the pupil successively, and constituting a large part of the Latin School curriculum, all of which are foreign to the grammar school program: French, German, Latin, Greek, Algebra, Geometry, Ancient History, Chemistry, and Physics. This may seem at first sight a pretty stiff program, and a stranger might say "Here is a bow that not every boy can shoot with." True, but only true because not every boy has the ability and the will to work steadily. I think every teacher would say that three qualities not of intellect, but of character must be possessed and practiced by every boy who would succeed in this course. I used to say that it was my practice on looking over the boys' monthly reports to examine first the "Conduct" side, and from that to guess what show the "Studies" side would make, and my guess was seldom wrong.

What are the three qualities to which I have referred that are so essential? They happen to be those which count most for success in life, as well as in school. I put first Industry. If a boy has not the power or will to work, he should set about trying to acquire it, or the Latin School may prove no place for him. Aristotle says, "Virtue is a habit." Accordingly, the best thing any school can do for any boy is to aid him to form good habits. Now by far the commonest cause of failure in school is not lack of intellectual ability, but laziness. Happily for the new-comer, the very requirements of the school tend strongly to induce the habit of industry. Only the co-operation of the boy is needful.

I put the spirit of perseverance second. Industry that is intermittent, I mean that now and then flags, that now and then is subject to lapses or breaks, is hardly industry at all. It will never win your battles. It must be reinforced by the staying power of dogged determination. How many are the temptations, discouragements, and disappointments that rise up in a boy's school life to thwart and defeat his resolutions for steady hard work! There are the calls and beckonings of pleasure always present and alluring. Lessons are sometimes hard and sometimes uninteresting. Problems are often blind and baffling, and in spite of eager search you can find no clue. Faithful effort is not always rewarded with success. You do your best, and confidently expect on your monthly report an "A" or a "B" and lo! you have a miserable "C," or it may be a detestable "D." If you meet all these trials with the spirit of "Never say die," then you have the stuff in you that goes to the making of a man.

Yet possibly not *all* the "stuff." To the spirit of industry and the spirit of perseverance, to which I have scarcely more than alluded, must be added the spirit of self-restraint. This must not be forgotten by the new-comers, and if they desire, as I hope all do, to advance the good name of our School, they can do so in no way more effectually than by the constant and watchful practice of reasonable and becoming self-restraint. Lawlessness is said to be the besetting sin of our American life. It is surely the besetting sin in our schools, and the greatest foe to good order and progress. Some boys are so fortunate as to be born with inclinations which make self-control easy. But most must acquire the habit by persistent practice. I cannot help thinking how fortunate it would be for our old School, and what an enviable reputation, among schools it would win, if a fitting self-restraint in manners, language, and conduct, both in and out of school, should come to be recognized as a characteristic of all Roxbury Latin boys.

One last word to the new boys. It is not enough to do faithfully and well all that the school demands. Throw yourselves whole-heartedly into all the outside interests and activities of the school. There is the *Tripod*, there is the orchestra, there are the school sports and games. You may sometime have the great honor of being Editor of the *Tripod*. If you have musical talents, and can play a musical instrument, join the school orchestra. If you have swiftness of foot or strength of sinew, go in for the field sports. If you have neither the one nor the other, you can still support and encourage those who have, by your presence at games, your voice, and your enthusiasm. Always remember that to get all you can out of the school you must put all you can into the school.

REMINISCENCE OF FREDERIC ALLISON TUPPER '75
The Tripod 29, 5 (February 1917)

[Collar's] sympathies were broad. . . . A lover of the classical music of Handel, Haydn, Beethoven, and Mozart, he learned also to enjoy the works of modern composers. Pictures, too, afforded him life-long enjoyment. Botany, also, added pleasure to his life. If he had been able to shape his life according to his own wishes, he would have been not a teacher but a lawyer, and an actual participant in the public affairs of the nation. He was greatly interested in history, economics, government, and current events.

Tupper was certainly correct in cataloging the breadth of Collar's interests. But the following letter to his daughter demolishes Tupper's assertion that Collar would have preferred "public affairs" to teaching.

Collar's advice to Sibyl as she embarks on a year's teaching in Mississippi in 1895 reveals his love of teaching and his conviction that affection *is the foundation of all good teaching. He urges Sibyl not to expect too much, to be patient: "Be sweet to your children."*

REMINISCENCE OF SIBYL, HIS THIRD DAUGHTER

Smith had been spoiled for me by so many emotional upsets and in September [1893], Virginia [Holbrook, her best friend and fiance's sister] and I transferred to "the Harvard Annex" [Radcliffe College].

There is no question in my mind that my father held me to be the one possible scholar among his children, and that, barring marriage, of which he approved supremely, he would have expected to see me scale the heights in the teaching profession.

A modest enough beginning was my securing a resident position in a southern boarding-school, where Latin and English were my subjects. But my father's interest in my success and his ready help in any difficulty were as hearty and minute as if I had chosen teaching for a life-work. Stanton "College" was a unique place, even among the fragrant old Southern capitals, with their history and beauty.

TO SIBYL, HIS THIRD DAUGHTER, AT STANTON COLLEGE, NATCHEZ, MISSISSIPPI *Roxbury*

My dear Sibyl: *October 2, 1895*

Why *not* say you "love" teaching? It is most delightful work under entirely favorable conditions. You are very fortunate in having no strain of discipline. That is what killeth in teaching.

You must not lose patience with pupils on translations into other languages. Composition is most difficult, and pupils easily get discouraged or timid, and come quickly to dread and hate the work. That ought not to be. And remember that it isn't enough to keep from scolding. If you feel cross your pupils know it.

Be absolutely sure, if your pupils don't like a study, it is your fault. Make a clear distinction in sight work between getting the sense and getting ready a good translation. I encourage my boys to try a passage, as soon as they get hold of the sense, and accept the rudest rendering preparatory to translation. Affectionately, Papa

TO SIBYL, HIS THIRD DAUGHTER, AT STANTON COLLEGE

Roxbury

My dear Sibyl, *November 13, 1895*

You evidently overestimate the mind of the average learner. Your standard is too high and it frets you that your children fall below it. Consider, they probably do as nearly their best as most grown-up people and what you are dissatisfied with is really their natural endowment. It would be just as reasonable to be dissatisfied with the shape of their noses.

Be sweet with your children, make sure that they shall all remember you with affection. Affectionately, Papa

Collar practiced the affection he preached. The following reminiscences all reveal a man who exuded affection—kindness and encouragement—for his boys and colleagues.

REMINISCENCE OF SAMUEL THURBER, CLASS OF 1897, OF 1916

My first meeting with Mr. Collar remains in my mind a clear and pleasant memory. It was a June morning, and with fifty other boys I was taking the entrance examination to The Roxbury Latin School. The test that I feared most of all was the one in oral reading before the headmaster. What was I to say? How should I stand? What if I trembled so that I could not hold the book? And what book would he give me to read? When my turn came I was summoned into the sanctum. I was a very nervous small boy; but in a moment I felt comfortable, and somehow the page from "Two Years Before the Mast" seemed like an old friend. By his genial manner, his few words of encouragement, his kindly voice, Mr. Collar made me feel as though I had always known him, and so it became a pleasant and easy matter to do my best. I left his study—I remember the words he spoke as I went—with a vague sensation of pride that I was to be in his school; for even as a small boy I knew that I had been in the presence of a great and good man.

My experience was not unlike that of many another boy who attended the Latin School in the nineties. Among our most precious memories are those hours when we read the Odyssey in his class, especially when he translated freely the lines of Homer into the clear, rich, forceful English style of which he was a master. By his eloquent and impressive reading of the Old Testament in the morning assemblies he awakened in us an interest in the Psalms, and an appreciation of the English of the Bible, that Sunday School, preachers, and studies had never aroused. We caught the enthusiasm of his voice, the earnestness of his purpose, the wisdom of his large and fruitful mind; and so under him we were stirred to feel, to think, and to strive to do whatever we undertook on a high plane of endeavor.

REMINISCENCE OF MILFORD S. POWER, MASTER 1890–1900, IN 1916

I was impressed with Dr. Collar's genius for summing up in one or two skillfully chosen adjectives, placed at the bottom of the report card, the whole history of the pupil's career during the preceding period. He had that power of estimating a pupil and his work with wonderful precision.

REMINISCENCE OF CLARENCE W. GLEASON, MASTER 1889–1905, 1912–1939, IN 1916

Of his generosity I had many substantial tokens. Beginning with the original "Gate," I assisted in the preparation of a number of his Latin books, always with liberal compensation; and I have reason to believe that the chief cause of his editing one volume was to devise a means to eke out my modest salary. At least I have always thought he paid me more for my part of the work than he himself received from the publishers. In connection with the same book he sent me one graduation day a note, saying that he should be happier that summer if he could think of me as ranging over the hills of Maine, and inclosed a check of $50 towards a bicycle.

Meanwhile, Collar's daughter Sibyl—writing from her school in Mississippi—was planning her large church wedding to Pinckney Holbrook in June. Collar's strongly egalitarian inclinations and his distaste for "society" are manifested in his response to his daughter.

TO SIBYL, HIS THIRD DAUGHTER, AT STANTON COLLEGE

Roxbury

My dear Sibyl,   *November 13, 1895*

I congratulate you now heartily that you are so young (22). Think what it is to be sixty-two! The thing I could most hope for now would

FIG. 6. The First Church in Roxbury at about the time—1896—of Sibyl Collar's marriage there to Pinckney Holbrook. (Boston Public Library Collection)

be two or three years of leisure to read and think. If there were any certainty that my books would yield a good income, I could do that.

I am delighted that you are thinking of a June marriage. I personally dread the public part of the [wedding] vastly. It seems as if it were for richer people, and people of society rather. But I will not say a word more. If you greatly desire it, it ought to be.

TO SIBYL, HIS THIRD DAUGHTER, AT STANTON COLLEGE

Roxbury

My dear Sibyl,   *December 12, 1895*

I have just returned from Miss R—'s wedding at eight o'clock in our church. The bride was not pretty, nor were the bridesmaids. Do not allow your bridesmaids to wear low-neck dresses if they have thin necks and scraggy bosoms. It is painful to see. You and Pinckney will make a much finer-looking couple.

I enjoy your letters very much but I cannot agree to answer them all. You can hardly imagine how proof-sheets of this cursed series that Mr. Tetlow [headmaster of Girls' Latin and close friend] and I are editors-in-chief of consume all my fair leisure, and push, push me. But you will be getting a few dollars yearly many years after I am gone. With much love, Papa

TO SIBYL, HIS THIRD DAUGHTER, AT STANTON COLLEGE

Roxbury

My dear Sibyl,   *December 18, 1895*

You will find, I hope, as I always have, that the dearest happiness is found in home and domestic ties. Affectionately, Papa

REMINISCENCE OF SIBYL, HIS THIRD DAUGHTER

Our wedding came off as planned on the thirtieth of June, 1896, ten days only after my return from the year's teaching in Natchez. This was due not only to my own sentimental desire for a June wedding, and the fear lest my friends would be scattered if we set a later date, but because my father and step-mother were eager to get to Europe and try "wheeling" as we called it then, through the Netherlands. Bicycling for women had come in with a rush during the year that I was in the south.

Incidentally, the "public part" that my father dreaded so, *i.e.*, the march up the long central aisle in the First Church in Roxbury, was performed without a hitch; never did ushers space and pace more accurately; the beautiful old church was not over-decorated but looked bowery and welcoming, and it was nearly full of our friends in festive summer and evening dress.

In a little lull in the receiving-line, [my father] turned to me and said: "My dear, three things are vitally necessary to make marriage a success — patience, and patience, and patience."

TO SIBYL COLLAR HOLBROOK, HIS DAUGHTER, IN DORCHESTER
Amsterdam
July 17, 1899

The telegram has come. Joy to you, dear Sibyl and to Pinckney. To me, double joy because it is a William [William Collar Holbrook '16].

TO SIBYL COLLAR HOLBROOK, HIS DAUGHTER, IN DORCHESTER
Paris
My dear Sibyl,   *August 20, 1899*

I follow the Dreyfus trial with great eagerness, reading oceans of stuff. Sometimes I read the pages of the testimony. I should be sick if he should be sent back to the Ile du Diable. There is absolutely no proof against him. Poor martyr, what he has suffered. Every day some forgery is exposed.

My boys entered Harvard fairly, for so poor a class, but very few took honors. In thirty days, I shall see you and the boy. Affectionately, Papa

REMINISCENCE OF N. HENRY BLACK, MASTER 1900–1924, IN 1916

When I came to the school as a very young teacher [in 1900] I soon felt his *sympathy* and his *openness of mind* in all my work. At my very first teachers' meeting he insisted on getting my impression about the school; and afterwards, whenever I visited another school, he wanted to get any new ideas which I might have picked up for the improvement of our own school. Nevertheless he was not a man who was running after the latest educational fad. Although his own line of study was in the languages, he was always most enthusiastic to improve our scientific equipment.

ALUMNI DINNER *Boston*
The Tripod 14, 7 (April 1902) *March 22, 1902*

If Mr. Collar had any doubts of the sentiment of his old boys toward him, the warmth of their greeting must have dispelled them. When at last he was allowed to go on he spoke of the many changes which have been made. He laid great emphasis on the many things needed to keep the school up to its present standard and to enable it to rank with the other great schools of the country. Among its other needs are an increased endowment and a new school building, both of which would greatly add to the dignity and efficiency of the school. He mentioned in passing the goodly number of fee-payers at present, the income from whom is an important factor, as it pays the salaries of four [of the eight] teachers, without whose services the efficiency of the school would be diminished one-half. This statement was received with some amazement by some present. After an earnest appeal for the long-needed gymnasium, Mr. Collar closed with the assurance that the ideals of the school were still the same — character first, then scholarship.

REMARKS AT HALL-DAY EXERCISES *Roxbury*
The Tripod 14, 7 (April 1902) *April 1, 1902*

Mr. Collar said in substance: The education of the early Greeks is summed up in the phrase from Homer, "A speaker of words and a doer of deeds." The moral side of human nature was entirely disregarded. In the highest period of Greek culture, a boy must, in order to be considered educated, be able to do three things: write well, recite from memory, and sing well. In one thing both Greek and modern education are deficient. Both fail to teach reverence. If we must criticise, let us do so in order to find what is good in things; for what we admire, that we tend to become.

TO SIBYL COLLAR HOLBROOK, HIS DAUGHTER, IN DORCHESTER
South Poland, Maine
My dear Sibyl, *July 26, 1902*

I am afraid I am neglectful about writing, but I am obliged to write many letters and it makes a serious inroad on my leisure time, so I put off those that can wait. I read till one o'clock, ride horseback, drive, botanize or what not in the afternoon, and read again in the evening. My mornings are given up to Greek, my evenings to miscellaneous reading. I have read the *Antigone*, and most of the *Philoctetes* twice over, and if I persevere shall read the *Oedipus Tyrannus* and the *Ajax*. I have carefully re-read four books of the Odyssey. Last night at midnight I finished Kipling's "Light that Failed": a powerful book. It seems like a painting from life, and not a sentence of padding, no analyzing, no moralizing.

I don't know how we could have been more fortunate in situation. We are in a cottage, across the road from the boarding-house that has about twelve or fifteen persons, on high ground, looking down upon a lake that is near, and over to Poland Springs House and hill. It is a very agreeable company at our table, three widows, one spinster, and one elderly pair of married people. The horseback riding is somewhat trying to me, for I am jounced unmercifully; but I persist because it does me so much good. Affectionately, Papa

TO SIBYL COLLAR HOLBROOK, HIS DAUGHTER, IN DORCHESTER
Megansett
My dear Sibyl, *September 11, 1904*
I finished the last lesson [of his new edition of the Eysenbach German textbook] on August 31 at 20 minutes to 6 o'clock, just 17 years and 40 minutes from the time when I put the last touch to the Eysenbach originally. Still a great deal remains to be done and it goes so slowly that it will be February before the book sees the light.

I have been remarkably well and seem to have more vigor than Herbert. Can you believe it, I am seventy-one years old today. Say nothing about it, as I don't want it talked about, though I never made any concealment of my age. Affectionately, Papa

TO SIBYL COLLAR HOLBROOK, HIS DAUGHTER *Roxbury*
My dear Sibyl, *June 5, 1905*
The kind of story that I would tell Willie would be not to make much of the wickedness of stealing or lying, but how a boy not only grieved his

parents, but how other boys, his playmates, wouldn't play with him, and how it was at school. And again of a boy whom everybody liked and trusted. This doesn't seem to me at all crude. Such stories ought to be full of incident, and not have the bare bones of moralizing stick out. Affectionately, Papa

TO WILLIAM COLLAR HOLBROOK, HIS GRANDSON, AGED SIX

Southwest Harbor, Maine

My dear little Grandson, *July 25, 1905*

I was very much pleased to get your nice little letter, and glad to see that you have made such a good beginning in writing. Does Carolyn [Willie's sister] know how to read little words yet? I think you will have to teach her. Most likely you will be a teacher when you grow up and it would be well to begin now. [*Collar was a prophet: William Collar Holbrook '16 later became Chairman of the Romance Language Department at both Northwestern University and Hampden-Sydney College.*]

When you get back to Dorchester perhaps you will write me another letter. I was pleased to see that you spelled all the words of your letter, even the hard ones, without any mistake. Now you are a tall boy, I would write *I* just as I have written it: not *i*, which isn't tall enough. With much love, Grandpapa

TO SIBYL COLLAR HOLBROOK, HIS DAUGHTER, IN DORCHESTER

Roxbury

My dear Sibyl, *April 8, 1907*

We got the word [of the death of Sibyl's third child, Elizabeth, eight months old] with a heavy, heavy heart. I felt strongly drawn to the dear little one and it has always seemed to me she had a stronger tie to your heart than the others did when they were babies. You have grown to be and to look more like your dear mother. How the death of your baby would have wrung her affectionate heart! Poor dear Sibyl, my heart aches for you and Pinckney.

The dear little boy [William, aged seven] has been most sweet-tempered and sweet-mannered. We played backgammon a long while this

FIG. 7. Sibyl Collar Holbrook, circa 1905, aged about thirty-two.

FIG. 8. William Collar Holbrook '16, grandson, professor of modern languages at Hampden-Sydney College.

afternoon and he was delighted to backgammon me. Then we rolled a ball in our long hallway, and he read to me. How eager he is to learn! We talked about his fitting for the Roxbury Latin School, and he said he must work from now on. It is going to be a great incentive to him.

Evelyn sends love and sympathy. Affectionately, Papa

Collar tendered his resignation to the trustees in secret on March 19, 1907, in his fiftieth year of teaching at the School, his fortieth as headmaster. "I take this step, not because I am weary of teaching, but because I think fifty years is as long a time as one should pursue a laborious and absorbing profession." His family and friends also attest that he was plagued by failing eyesight. The Tripod *for June 1907 announced both his resignation and the appointment of his successor (The Reverend Theodore Chickering Williams '72).*

COLLAR'S FAREWELL ADDRESS   *June 20, 1907*

How to bear all these "blushing honors" that have descended so thickly upon my head this morning! I feel somewhat of the awkwardness that Achilles felt, when his goddess mother, Thetis, brought the new suit of armor, forged by Hephaistos, when he had to adjust his limbs to it, before he ventured into battle. And how to give fitting thanks for all the too kind and gracious words that have been spoken, some small part only of which I venture to hope, is, as romancers say in their prefaces, "founded on fact." I suddenly seem to find the English language poor in expressions of thanks. One can say, "I am touched," or "I am grateful," but what else and what more? Well, I *am* touched and I *am* grateful.

I owe a great debt to the Trustees for their forbearance these many years, a debt greater than the world knows; greater, probably, than I myself know. For it must be remembered that I came here a young man, with the impulsiveness, not to say rashness, and the hasty and harsh judgments that characterize youth, altogether too prone also to ultimatums. I recall that once, more than forty years ago, when the Trustees disapproved of some act of mine, I proudly proposed to offer my resignation, though I had a young family dependent upon me, was without a copper, and had no prospect of another place; but the soft answer of dear old Mr. Dillaway turned away wrath. I will not say, for I must speak the truth, that there have not been rare occasions in fifty years when forbearance was called for, or seemed to be called for, on the other side; but I still think I am largely in the Trustees' debt. However, we have planned and worked together for half a century, and we part with feelings of high, mutual esteem.

I must thank the Trustees unreservedly for what I esteem the greatest virtue in the governing Board of a school, I mean the measure of freedom allowed the headmaster in conducting the internal affairs of the school. There has been no disposition shown here, as happens in countless cases, on the part of the legislative power to encroach upon the executive. I hope I do not make the mistake of thinking my work has been of supreme value, though I respect the judgment of President Eliot, but I am sure its value would have been far less, if I had had to struggle with the interference of an omniscient Board of Trustees.

Finally, I want to thank the Trustees for the great honor they have done me on this occasion in bestowing this testimonial of their approbation, expressed in resounding, magniloquent Latin, and for appointing me headmaster *emeritus*. If I am embarrassed and find it impossible to express all I feel, attribute it in part to the fact that I am unused to receive from the Board of Trustees expressions of commendation. They have wisely withheld expressions of approval till this last hour, for two excellent reasons: because if my head is now turned by so much honor, there is no danger that harm will come to the school; and because the Trustees saw that their commendation would be doubly precious at the end of my career. I shall prize this diploma, not less surely than those I have received from my *alma mater*, and not less than that honorary diploma which bears the honored name of the great president of Harvard. One values what has cost one labor, and to win this diploma I have worked longest and hardest. Moreover, it is more than a diploma. It is a benediction.

I must express my grateful obligations to the parents of the boys who have come here, more especially to the mothers. With what patience and assiduity, and self-sacrifice, have many of them followed along with the tasks of their boys, so that not a few must feel that they have themselves gone through the Latin School! How reasonable I have found them! how helpful, how sympathetic, how appreciative! How much they have lightened the task of instruction and discipline!

I must not forget to give praise to the boys for their responsiveness and for the spirit they have shown both here and when they have passed out of the school. If their achievement has not always answered to my desires and the ambitious hopes of parents, they have shown no end of good will. And good will is one of the most precious things of life.

My personal indebtedness is great to the teachers, who have always worked with me so unitedly, and so loyally for the school. But I owe most of all to Mr. Lowell, my near friend and almost brother. For three and twenty years we have worked in the closest intimacy. The school would have continued to exist without Mr. Lowell, but what a different school it would have been! He has enlivened the humdrum of school life for us all by his inimitable humor. How many times, sitting here in my study, in the corner of the building, have I heard peals of laughter from his classroom! But nobody has been so firm in discipline; firm as the hills, or a rock in the sea. Versatile, self-poised, and resourceful, he has been equal to every situation. During my voyage first to Bermuda and again to Jamaica, and twice when accident or sudden illness took me from school and enforced a prolonged absence, he has taken all my burdens in addition to his own, upon his Atlantean shoulders, and borne them lightly. For three and twenty years he has given to the school unremitting, unwearied, and most unselfish labor, and has been to us all a present example of devotion to duty, of justice, of manliness, of large mindedness, and of righteous living.

The school owes much and I owe more to the alumni. Especially during these latter years they have shown active and energetic interest in the school, and largely under the lead and inspiration of Mr. [Robert

Hallowell] Gardiner ['72], once my pupil, then my assistant, and now one of my governors, they have generously contributed to make good a deficiency in the income of the school and to forestall a reduction of salaries. They have outlined a noble scheme for an increased endowment, a better site and better housing of the school, and more ample playgrounds. May success crown their hopes.

Lately it was my good fortune to read a book by Rev. Dr. Dole, which I found to be a golden book, *The Spirit of Democracy*. I read there that the spirit of democracy is the spirit of mutual service, of cooperation, of good will; and as I closed the book I said to myself, "That is the spirit in which we have been working in the Roxbury Latin School—not all the time, nor always consciously and with determined purpose, but partly drifting, carried on by the currents of the time." But in that spirit we must always henceforth work. In that spirit must every school work that aims at the best achievement. In that spirit, I am sure, my successor will work. He has by nature, study, and experience all the advantages requisite for carrying the school forward to greater excellence. You will not wonder that I have high, enthusiastic hopes for the future of the school, for it is my privilege to pass on the scepter to one of the brightest, ablest, and dearest of my old boys, who was trained in the discipline of the school, and is familiar with its spirit and its traditions. A man of rich and varied endowments; an interesting, persuasive, impressive, eloquent preacher; a gifted poet; an elegant and accomplished classical scholar, soaked in the best literature of Greece and Rome; versed in modern languages and literatures; and above all, a man sympathetic and inspiring. I see in Mr. Williams all that I ever hoped and aspired to be, and far more; for I never had any ecclesiastical ambitions and never dreamed of writing poetry.

The Trustees, with Mr. Williams's approval, have provided that my official connection with the school shall not be entirely broken off. It is true this relation is outwardly only nominal or honorary. It implies, at my express desire, neither authority, nor specific duties, nor stipend. But inwardly the tie will be a very real one, binding me to the school till the end comes. I shall please myself with the thought that I shall have a right to share in the prosperity and fame that await the school under its new head. I will not then say to boys and teachers, parents and Trustees "farewell"—much too solemn a word—but rather a cheerful *auf weider-sehen!*

Now my last official act and word shall be to welcome heartily my dear friend as my successor; and if a thing so unprecedented and para-doxical may be permitted, layman as I am, to bestow my blessing on his reverence. *Serus in cielum redeat reverendissimus Theodorus Chickering Williams.*

FIG. 9. William Coe Collar near the end of his career with the Class of 1904 at the closing exercises.

TO SIBYL COLLAR HOLBROOK, HIS DAUGHTER, IN DORCHESTER

Clinton, New York

My dear Sibyl,   *July 10, 1907*

We arrived here in a rain at eight o'clock, I in my usual mood of depression when arriving at a new place that is to be home for weeks or months. But the clouds within, as without, soon broke. We had undervalued everything—situation, hostess, rooms, food.

Sorry you weren't there the last day [the School's Closing Exercises] to see me crowned and hear my *last* speech. Affectionately, Papa

TO CAROLYN HOLBROOK, HIS GRANDDAUGHTER, AGED SIX

Utica, New York

My dear little Carolyn,   *August 7, 1907*

I thank you for your letter, the first I believe, that you have written to me. Now you have done so well, I hope you will write again and again. Why not begin a little diary and put down every day, without ever missing a day, something, even if it is no more than, "Today put my doll to bed before dinner, because she was naughty"? Your aunt wants me to write the story of my life for your mama and aunts Mildred and Alice and your uncle Herbert to read, and I would do it, if I had only kept such a diary as I want you and Willie to keep. Now alas! I am old, old, and cannot remember, and the story of my life will never be written. With much love to you all, your affectionate Grandpapa

Collar and his wife spent the summer in Utica where he was under the care of a famous oculist. His eyesight, however, steadily declined till his death. In the final eight years he employed someone to read to him every day. Upon leaving the School, Collar and his wife had moved their permanent residence to Windsor Road in Waban. Here he died peacefully on February 27, 1916.

D. O. S. Lowell's epitaph is a masterful summary of the Second Founder's life.

"WILLIAM COE COLLAR: AN APPRECIATION"
The Tripod 28, 6 (March 1916)
from the *Boston Evening Transcript*

By the death of Dr. William Coe Collar, in his eighty-third year, the teaching profession has lost one who for many decades wielded a quiet, yet potent influence. In the middle of the nineteenth century he entered a small school as master; after ten years he became its head; and for forty years thereafter he guided its destinies, until the school doubled, trebled, more than quadrupled in size and teaching staff, and became as famous for its scholarship as for its antiquity. Himself an ardent scholar, he was a most inspiring teacher. Many men of mark now living bear loving testimony to the molding influence of his master hand.

His sense of justice was most keen. He could be severe, if occasion demanded, but he was never unjust; if he ever seemed to be, it was because the one to whom he so appeared saw the question at issue from quite another angle. He would not for a moment hesitate to decide a case against his own interest, if he felt such to be a righteous decision.

He never fell into routine—the temptation of all those who teach for many years. Although he passionately loved the classics, he did not hide his head in the dust of ages and imagine that Latin and Greek were the only subjects worth knowing. He welcomed scientific research, provided generously for the sciences in his school, and was a great friend of the modern languages.

Among his peers he was an acknowledged master of English style. His fluency was in part a natural gift; but he cultivated it throughout his life with patience and care. He read broadly and deeply, and derived felicities of expression by direct contact with the philosophers, poets, and historians. He loved to converse with those of keen intelligence and nimble wit; and with them his own words welled forth as fresh and sparkling as waters from a mountain spring.

He was a great advocate for preparedness, and he carried his theory into daily practice. Though he was an unexcelled teacher of Greek, he never went before his class, even in the Anabasis, without a careful preparation of his lesson; the result was a perennial freshness of presentation.

He was unselfish to the last degree. Even a specious plea for help rarely failed to arouse his sympathy, and he often dispensed his charity to the undeserving. The quality of his mercy was never strained, and a penitent wrong-doer was sure to win a dispensation from a penalty, though it were richly deserved.

He was intensely human, with the common frailties of mankind, yet with no vices of any sort. To know him intimately was of itself an education; to be admitted to the privileges of his friendship was a cause for enduring gratitude.

He poured his life freely into the great school founded by John Eliot in 1645, of which he has been justly styled the "second founder." It is given to few men to spend fifty years of active teaching in one institution. Yet he did this, and retired full of years and honors to pass in meditation and study the peaceful twilight of advancing age. Nine years since he became the beloved head master emeritus of Roxbury Latin, and now has joined the ranks of the immortals. His work is ended, but his memory abides. His name is worthy to be enrolled with those of Alcuin, Roger Ascham, Arnold of Rugby, and Horace Mann.

Part Four

This quiet elevation, overlooking Boston and its gilded dome, is a happy location. As the scholars come up the hill they may recall what Eliot once said, as he went up the thorny hill to the First Church: "The path of life is like this hill." Boys from Boston and its brick blocks find in the old school grounds, surrounded by small wooden houses with gardens and by an old cemetery, a pleasant touch of the country; they can look far off from the hillside and breathe fresher air. In the warm, spring days, I remember that I used to see through an open school-room window the flashing gold of an oriole's flight across the yard from elm to elm, and I have never forgotten the May fragrance of neighboring hedges of lilacs and syringas, or the arbors of wisteria which became thereby in after years annual messengers to me of my boyhood, able deliciously to recall ". . . the dewy prime of youth and buried time."

—PERCY STICKNEY GRANT '79, ADDRESS, 1895

Part Four

Kearsarge Avenue
The 1860s to the 1920s

━━━━━━━━━━━━━━━━━━━━━━━━━━━━

INTO THE 1990s, older alumni continue to reminisce about attending the "Kearsarge Avenue" school. Kearsarge Avenue got its name after the Civil War: on this street—previously named Mount Vernon Place—lived John Ancrum Winslow, whose ship, the "Kearsarge," sank the Confederate cruiser "Alabama" in the English Channel in 1864. When now-Admiral Winslow returned to Roxbury at the war's end, the city renamed the street in honor of his ship.[1]

In 1860, Buck and Collar transferred the Latin School boys from their small "Greek temple" to the larger frame building on this street. The trustees had built this larger building, consisting of two ground floor classrooms and an upstairs assembly "hall," for the English School boys in 1853. When the city broke its relationship with the School, however, the English School boys departed for the Girls' High School, and the Latin School boys took over the building. It would serve as the School's home until 1927.

1. *Expanding the School*

Taking the helm at Kearsarge Avenue in 1868, Collar immediately pressed the trustees for several curricular changes. Trustee minutes of the following year record:

> The following changes have been made in courses of instruction during the past year. The introduction of French earlier, and the postponement of Greek later in the course. Requiring Drawing in the three lower classes. Requiring reading and the study of English in all the classes. The study of Botany by familiar illustrations with specimens.[2]

FIG. 1. The original Kearsarge Avenue schoolhouse is on the right. Kearsarge Avenue came almost up to the doorway that has two windows on either side. The tower in the background is that of the Methodist church. The photograph was taken after the addition of 1883 (the left part of the schoolhouse), probably in the late 1880s.

By 1870, "vocal music has been introduced as part of the regular exercises," and $400 was allotted to purchase a piano. In 1871 teachers of music and drawing were authorized "at an expense not exceeding $800" and a teacher of French "at an expense not exceeding $200."

These changes had great appeal to parents, who perceived that the School was enriching and broadening its formerly rather narrow classical curriculum. Applications soared. Though the School could now be more selective, the pressure of increased applications inevitably pushed the School's overall numbers up: sixty-three in 1867 (Collar's first year as headmaster), eighty in 1869, 108 in 1873. Perhaps that is why the trustees took only the briefest look at the Examining Committee's 1872 suggestion that the School admit girls.[3] To accommodate the increased numbers, the trustees in June 1873 authorized the employment of "an

FIG. 2. George F. Forbes, the School's first science master, was hired in 1875. He constructed a physics laboratory during the mid-1880s.

assistant male teacher with a salary not exceeding $2000 per annum" and, at Collar's request, the construction of a two-room addition to the rear of the schoolhouse (costing $5400).[4] That same year the trustees "Voted that the number of scholars be limited to 110." But by 1875 there were 120.

The year 1875 witnessed yet another innovation. Collar hired a twenty-six-year-old fellow Amherst man, George F. Forbes, to be the School's first science master. Harvard had that very year added physics as an entrance requirement. At first, Forbes taught physics by using a textbook, but over the next decade, he came to believe that students learned best by doing experiments. When Harvard—in the mid-80s— allowed boys to fulfill its physics requirement by doing a certain number of experiments, Forbes turned to "the laboratory method" exclusively. Obtaining money from the trustees, he transformed a classroom into a laboratory and, with the help of the janitor, built the necessary equipment himself. As a result of his pioneering work, Roxbury Latin apparently became the first school in the nation to teach science by the experimental method, an innovation that made the School a place of pilgrimage for educators from across the country.[5]

Embarrassed at almost every step by a lack of funds, from his own brain, as often by his own hands, Mr. Forbes constructed [a laboratory] surpassed by [that of] no similar institution. Using as a basis the crude and meagre pamphlet issued by the college [Harvard], he devised a brilliant physical method, which not only fitted the boys for college, but also gave them a working knowledge of physical laws and scientific apparatus. There was not an experiment which he did not rewrite and make more practicable; no piece of apparatus he did not improve or replace by some ingenious device of his own. Necessity compelled him, after planning an experiment, to be his own mechanic and carpenter in preparing it for use. Nature had well fitted him for such work; he had a wonderful mechanical genius and skill as an inventor, a fact evidenced by his automatic railroad gate, for which he secured a patent. The fame of his work spread to other schools, so that hardly a week passed without one or more visitors to see Mr. Forbes and his laboratory.[6]

Clarence Gleason, who loathed science, gives us a glimpse of Forbes's intensity. Gleason had been hired right out of Harvard in 1889 to teach classics. But one of his obligations as a new master was to assist Forbes, whose round-the-clock commitment was legendary:

In spite of the inexperience and lack of self-confidence the work of teaching was interesting and pleasant, but the dreary afternoons in the laboratory, when everybody but Mr. Forbes and his young shadow [Gleason] had gone home, made the days long. Mr. Forbes was compiling a very scholarly new laboratory method [for Advanced Physics] and one of my tasks—besides assisting him in the manufacture of necessary material for the work—was to write out the experiments on the school typewriter and hectograph them, to be pasted in scrapbooks and filled in by the students. That program was followed almost every afternoon until nearly suppertime, unless there was a school game to be attended, and many a Saturday forenoon as well.[7]

Less than a year later (in 1890), Forbes was dead—probably from exhaustion. When Collar went on his sabbatical, Forbes had run the

School and D.O.S. Lowell commented that "everyone expected that Mr. Forbes, then in the morning of life, would succeed" Collar as head-master.[8]

Even the teaching of Latin was revolutionized. The trustee minutes of June 1878 record that

> Mr. Collar has introduced a new feature in his mode of instruc-
> tion. He conducts in Latin the recitations of the youngest class.
> This adds to their vocabulary and familiarizes them with Latin
> constructions. Mr. Collar intends this to be the mode of instruc-
> tion in all the classes after this present term.[9]

Collar's Latin, Greek, and later German textbooks, usually written in conjunction with sub-master Moses Grant Daniell (master 1863–1884),[10] reformed the teaching of languages and became standard texts across the nation, remaining in print for more than fifty years in succes-sive editions.

Breadth of curriculum and quality of academic instruction, however, do not by themselves make a school great. Charles H. Grandgent '79, later professor at Harvard and president of the trustees, conveys the special and distinctive "tone" of the School in the 1870s:

> Long before I came here, I had looked forward to the time when I
> might, with fortune's favor, [come to R.L.]. After my arrival [in
> 1876], my good opinion was corroborated by the contrast between
> the behaviour of these Academicians and that of the motley mob
> with whom I had sat and suffered and fought in the numerous
> public schools of my acquaintance, for I am willing to wager that
> I have attended more Boston schools than anyone else now living.
> . . . Here was a school in which no enforced discipline seemed to be
> needed; a school in which teachers spoke to pupils, and pupils
> spoke to teachers, as if both were human beings, without fear and
> without reproach; a school whose inmates appeared to come from
> the haunts of civilization, where books were read for pleasure and
> boys wrote verse.[11]

The School had become "the place to be." In September 1879, Collar

FIG. 3. The first picture of a Roxbury Latin football team, taken in 1882. Note the football and the motley "uniforms."

wrote that "68 candidates were presented for admission to the School and of these 38 were accepted. The School has now 138 boys."[12]

The only stress and pressure in students' lives came from academics. There were virtually no organized extracurricular activities. Sports were entirely boy-originated, informal, and unsupervised. We know that Roxbury boys were playing football in the eighteenth century, because in 1768 the town refused to prohibit football being played in Roxbury Street ("the town street") where the School was located.[13] The football referred to was undoubtedly English football (i.e., soccer). Walter Eliot Thwing '68 speaks of the first annual football (i.e., soccer) "match between the Latin and High School boys of Roxbury that took place on

September 29, 1859, resulting in a victory of the former, and these matches continued for many years."[14] Such matches were entirely unofficial and unsupervised, for, as C. Frank Allen '68 noted, "In the way of sports and games we were on our own." In 1868 a friendly clergyman named Calthrop organized a cricket team and played on it himself. "Snowballing was lively in winter, one party defending the line of tombs at the northerly end of the [school] yard and the other attacking."[15]

"American" football came into vogue in the late 1870s. Charles Hamlin '79 recalled "the introduction of the Rugby game of football. Up to that time we used to play the old game where you kicked the ball but could not run with it." Roger Ernst '98 said that even in his time at school no forward or lateral passing was allowed in football, and that the team was required only to gain five yards in three "rushes" (i.e., downs). But to return to Hamlin's description of athletics in the 1870s:

> I shall never forget the baseball games on Miller's field some two miles beyond the school. We used to have memorable games with the boys of Roxbury High School. How we hated those boys!— probably because they generally defeated us.

The military drill which lingered from the Civil War days appears to have been far from rigorous:

> We used to go down to Bacon Hill where we were trained by Brigadier-General Hobart Moore. . . . I think it was most valuable training. It taught us discipline and order. . . . When we went down from the school to Bacon Hill, we usually stopped at a bakery on the way, where we bought enormous segments of so-called Washington pie. The pie was certainly delicious, but it laid the foundation for an immutable, eternal dyspepsia.[16]

The 1880s brought further expansion of the academic program. By September 1883 the school numbers had soared to 160, a sixth master had been appointed, and a further addition was authorized to the north side of the school: two new classrooms (so that the hall was no longer needed as a classroom), a small library, and an office for the headmaster. The physics laboratory was also improved:

> The requirements for admission to Harvard having been changed, our boys hereafter must be fitted on the subjects of heat, electricity, etc. This will render necessary the addition of gas into the laboratory with some extra fittings and apparatus.[17]

In 1886, the faculty increased to seven as German was added to the curriculum, and a committee appointed "to examine what would be the expense for furnishing facilities for instruction in elementary chemistry."[18] The introduction of chemistry, long sought by Forbes, was implemented by his successor in 1892.[19]

2. *Financing the Expanded School*

In order to survive, in order to offer the courses now required for college admission, the School had expanded. Its expansion was financed, without public tax support, by selling the 1794–96 120-year leases of the School's lands. These properties were due to return to the School — with all their improvements (and immense increase in value) — in 1914–16 when the leases expired.

In 1834 John Lowell, Jr., had prevailed upon his fellow trustees not to sell the School's birthright when the Roxbury Chemical Company tried to purchase its land forty years into its lease. Lowell died in 1840, and by 1847 the trustees had been forced by the City of Boston — by eminent domain — to sell one small parcel of leased land. Profiting handsomely, they overcame their past scruples. George Putnam was designated to make sure they were legally allowed to sell their land. On his recommendation, the trustees voted in 1848 "to apply to the Legislature for an act empowering the Trustees to alienate the [lease] of their lands and also confirming their past doings in the premises." Approval was duly given in 1848.[20]

Trustee records show that between 1845 and 1866 the trustees sold 3,667,861 square feet of their leased lands in twenty-nine parcels.[21] By

1879 only ten quite small parcels (one of them the schoolhouse lot) remained under the School's ownership.

The proceeds of the lease sales were utilized in two ways: First, for the immediate financing of the additional masters hired to teach the subjects now required by Harvard for entrance, and for the expansion of the building to house a student body now much larger than that of 1861. Second, what remained was invested in mortgages, stocks, bonds, and similar instruments. By 1886 the School's holdings were worth $258,234, of which only $40,891 was invested in real estate (and that figure includes the schoolhouse and lot). Such holdings were obviously not going to be adequate to provide the annual income necessary to sustain a much enlarged school with a specialized faculty.

Collar had brought the School national acclaim for its academic program. Unfortunately, the financial resources that supported the ancient one-room school with a single schoolmaster were not sufficient to sustain the expanded faculty and program that Collar had now put in place.

Alumni concerned about the School's financial situation joined together in 1881 to form the Alumni Association.[22] Their first act was to present a portrait of Collar to the School. Responding to this generous gesture, Collar spoke of the School's poverty at the association's first meeting:

> We are trying still, as in the past, to do good, honest work under the old difficulties. Without room, without a library, without apparatus, without a sufficient staff of teachers, and without money to supply these wants, if we are not precisely making bricks without straw, we are doing the next thing to it. These things I mention not as discouragements, still less as complaints; but to show you what an opportunity there is for the graduates. . . .
>
> One of the blessings and compensations of poverty is the sense of mutual dependence that it creates. . . .
>
> Do not imagine that I am ambitious for the School of outward magnificence. I take a certain pride, I think we all do, in the very homeliness of our surroundings. I do not want a palace.

But in one thing the school feels the pinch of poverty. . . . High scholarship and first rate talents [in a faculty] cannot be commanded at a low salary. Just now I am searching for some most promising young man whom I must try to inveigle to enter the service of the school at the magnificent sum of $900 per annum. I may find such a one. I may succeed. But the mischief is, he is sure not to stay inveigled. I can tell of the venerable antiquity of the school, and of its great expectations. These things appeal to the imagination. Then I can truly say that the privilege of serving under the kindest, wisest and best of trustees instead of a capricious, or meddlesome, or narrow-minded school committee is equivalent of some hundreds of dollars. [But when it becomes time for this man to marry, he cannot afford to remain at Roxbury Latin.]

But that the future of the school may be worthy of what we hope will be its opportunities and resources, we must take care of the present. If men sometimes wake up and find themselves famous, institutions never do.[23]

Roxbury's grammar school was now an anomaly. Virtually all of New England's ancient free grammar schools had either folded—unable to sustain themselves—or had lost their independence by being subsumed into tax-supported public school systems. The same was true of the English grammar schools, virtually all of which had turned to other methods of finance when their ancient endowments proved inadequate to sustain them in the nineteenth century. British historian John Roach writes:

Over and over again the reports of the first Charity Commission (1818–37) make it clear that a successful [grammar] school was one in which the master had succeeded in attracting boarders and paying day pupils as well as boys [attending free on the ancient] foundations. . . . [A grammar school could be successfully maintained] only by attracting private pupils who bought their education from a grammar school as they might have bought it from a private school. In other words, all grammar schools were private schools as well, and those which flourished did so because they had been able to develop the private side. . . . Sir William Grant in his Harrow judgment . . . made two very important points. The first is that a man of education could not, in most cases, live on his basic salary as master of a grammar school. Therefore he needed to take private pupils. The second is that, if the master was able to live on his salary, he would have no stimulus to exert himself. There was a strong belief at the time that dependence on endowments was enervating. . . . [The grammar schools] had adapted themselves to changing circumstances as best they could.[24]

In the 1860s and 1870s new public high schools sprouted everywhere, and historian Oscar Handlin notes that "the academies of an earlier period declined precipitously in number and influence. Few survived unless they were able to transform themselves into select college preparatory schools, specializing in the training of the sons of elite men of wealth."[25]

The School's good fortune in holding vast tracts of appreciating lands had enabled it to postpone making the adaptations forced upon the surviving English grammar schools and American academies. Now, finally, with most of its land sold, the School had to come to grips with the reality that its ancient endowments were no longer adequate to support it.

Various "solutions" were advanced—most of which had already been tried or implemented at the surviving English grammar schools and American academies. One involved the School boys not living in Roxbury. In 1808, you will recall, the trustees, for the first time in the School's history, had prohibited the attendance of non-Roxbury boys as a way of dealing with overcrowding. This prohibition had been honored mostly in the breech. But Collar was a man who played by the rules. Upon becoming headmaster, he requested and received trustee sanction for admitting two Dorchester boys; and the following year the trustees dropped the prohibition against Boston boys. That same year, 1868, Roxbury ceased to exist as a separate entity and was subsumed into the City of Boston. In view of the later efforts made by trustee Henry

Ware Putnam to recreate "Old Roxbury," it is interesting to note that in 1877, when the trustees considered limiting the School to boys of a circumscribed geographical area, they made no reference to "Roxbury" at all. They voted in September 1877 that "hereafter no pupil shall be admitted to the School who does not live within the limits of *Boston*, except by special vote of the trustees."[26] But at the very next meeting, in December, they changed their mind and revoked this prohibition.[27] In fact, as finances grew tighter and as the School's traditional clientele began to move out of Roxbury, the trustees looked upon these non-Boston boys in an increasingly favorable light—as a possible source of revenue. In 1878 they voted "that boys admitted to the School from other towns be required to furnish their own desks."[28] Parents of non-Boston boys were also solicited for voluntary contributions: the treasurer reported in 1878 that "he had received donations amounting to $445 from parents of our boys not living in Roxbury, the object of the donations being to constitute a fund for the purchase of books."[29]

Two other solutions to the School's financial problem were also put forward. One advocated by several trustees was that since the School had been founded (and later endowed) to teach only "Literature" (i.e., Latin), the now-expanded school should be allowed to charge all parents for teaching the new subjects that had recently been added. This was a common practice in England; the Grammar Schools Act of 1840 inferred "that an endowed school could refuse to teach anything but Greek and Latin, or that, even if it had been founded as a free school, the headmaster could exact his own private terms for the teaching of other subjects."[30]

Other trustees believed that the expanded school ought to finance itself in the same way virtually all other privately-funded schools financed themselves: by straightforwardly charging parents the tuition necessary to balance its budget, using endowment income to provide relief for those who could not pay full tuition.

3. *The Putnam Reports*

Henry Ware Putnam offered to make a legal study of the question of charging fees, and his fellow trustees were only too happy to have him do it. Putnam was the son of the deceased trustee president and First Church pastor George Putnam. He had attended the School, and immediately following his graduation in 1863 had left on a tour of Europe (accompanied by Headmaster Buck). The tour was extended for two years, and he avoided military service by returning just as the Civil War ended. While his father was still president, Putnam was elected a trustee in 1872 at the age of twenty-seven. He remained in office forty years until his death in 1912. We need to consider this man and his views at inordinate length because his *Report of 1882* and his later *Report of 1902* not only inflicted nearly fatal damage on the School at that time but continued to threaten its well-being a century later.

Putnam's motive was to preserve the Roxbury of his boyhood—a small school in a small town, both controlled by Yankees. Putnam's attitude is well summarized in a published *Oration*: he celebrates the greatness and inevitable triumph of "the English-speaking race," which he terms "the foremost movement in human history," and rails against the danger posed by the immigration of "alien races" who are undermining "the mission of the Anglo-Saxon race."[31]

Inheritor and standard-bearer of the old Yankee hegemony in Roxbury, Putnam in his *1882 Report* sought to preserve the School as both *private* (controlled by a few people like himself) and *free* to him and his still largely affluent and "Anglo-Saxon" (Yankee and respectable German) neighbors of Roxbury. Coming fourteen years after Roxbury had ceased to exist as an independent entity (following its merger into Boston in 1868), Putnam's *Report* idiosyncratically and unilaterally defines "Roxbury" by its boundaries in 1671 (at the time of Bell's bequest). Upset by eastern Roxbury's rapid urbanization, "West Roxbury" (modern day West Roxbury, Jamaica Plain, and Roslindale) had seceded from the town of Roxbury in 1851 in order to form a separate

FIG. 5. Anna Cabot Lowell, who endowed deturs in Latin and English, with two friends. By the mid-nineteenth century Roxbury had many elegant houses of the sort pictured here.

slow-growth suburban/country town. As West Roxbury's Jamaica Plain neighborhood mushroomed, however, its new Boston-spillover residents outvoted the more affluent but less numerous residents in the outlying Roslindale and West Roxbury neighborhoods and as a result the town of West Roxbury was annexed to Boston in 1874.[32] Though both Roxbury and West Roxbury were now part of the City of Boston, Putnam's "Old Roxbury District" included only the original towns and excluded other Boston neighborhoods such as Dorchester and South Boston.

Putnam's goal was to limit the "privileges" of the School (i.e., the right to attend without paying fees) to boys who lived in the "Old Roxbury District." None of the School's early documents, from the Agreement of 1645 on, supports such a limitation. By his own admission, Putnam bases his entire case on one early document—Bell's bequest of 1671—which he interprets to endorse his position. In a key passage in

FIG. 4. Henry Ware Putnam, trustee 1872–1912, son of George Putnam. *Above:* as a senior at Harvard. *Right:* midlife. (Harvard University Archives Collection)

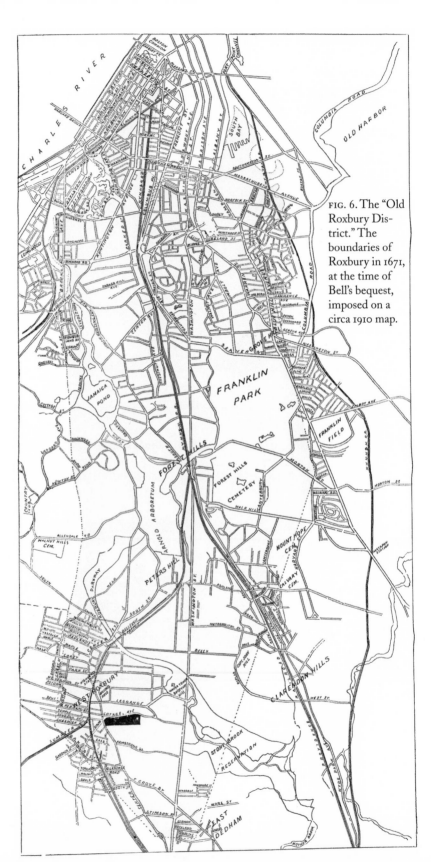

FIG. 6. The "Old Roxbury District." The boundaries of Roxbury in 1671, at the time of Bell's bequest, imposed on a circa 1910 map.

his *1882 Report*, Putnam summarizes his case:

> Whether we have a legal right to charge a tuition fee to any of our
> scholars, and if so to whom, depends for its answer principally on
> the true construction to be given to a clause in the will of Thomas
> Bell, which is recited in full in our Charter [of 1789] as defining the
> terms of our trust.

Putnam's whole case rests on his attempted sleight-of-hand in this
paragraph of his *Report*. He tries to slip in, as if it were an obvious *fact*,
his own *interpretation*: that Bell's bequest, subsumed under the Charter
of 1789, has a determining effect on "our trust" (i.e., on all the trusts and
donations held by the trustees).

Putnam's interpretation cannot be justified. Since the 1789 Charter is
concerned with combining Bell's trustees with the School's feoffees, it
naturally gives a certain prominence to Bell's bequest. But it *always* sets
Bell's bequest in context with other bequests and seeks only to be clear
that *all* previous bequests and donations are to be used for the purposes
given. The charter does not elevate Bell's bequest above the others or
give it a determining effect on all others:

> Whereas several *other persons* [besides Bell] have heretofore be-
> queathed certain other lands and monies, to be applied to and for
> the purposes aforesaid, to be under the direction of certain
> Feoffees . . . all which devises and donations have been ratified and
> confirmed by several Acts of the Legislature. . . .
>
> And whereas . . . a number of the inhabitants of the said Town
> of Roxbury have petitioned the Court, that an Act of Incorpora-
> tion may be passed, to incorporate a competent number of persons
> for the purpose of carrying into effect the benevolent designs of
> the said Thomas Bell *and others.*
>
> . . . the Trustees . . . are hereby required in conducting the
> concerns of said School . . . to regulate themselves conformably
> to the true design and intention of the said Thomas Bell *and
> others.*
>
> . . . neither the said Trustees nor their successors, shall ever
> hereafter receive any grant or donation, the condition of which

shall require them, or any others concerned, to act in any respect contrary to the design expressed in the last will and testament of the said Thomas Bell, *or any donation heretofore made.* [Emphasis added.]

In sum, the charter confirms not just Bell's trust (to be used for *its* stated purpose), but *all other* antecedent trusts and donations to be used for *their* purposes. Nothing in the charter can be found to support Putnam's view that Bell's trust somehow controls all other trusts.

Therefore, before we can even begin to discuss what Putnam regards as the key phrase in Bell's bequest, we must challenge Putnam on two points. First, as we have just shown, a single trust given to a charity cannot exercise a determining effect on all other trusts given to it. Second, the legal doctrine of *cy pres* confirms instinctive common sense in asserting that a bequest (in this case, depleted)—which provided little over half the income needed to finance a spartan one-room school—could not be expected to sustain or control a multi-room school, with a specialized faculty and many more students, more than two hundred years later.

Let us, however, lay aside these fundamental objections to Putnam's case and argue *as if* the phrase he cites from the Bell bequest were all-determining. All would agree that the phrase Putnam selects from the Bell bequest is the key one, namely that Bell gave his lands: "for ye mainteynance of a schoolmaster and free schoole for ye teaching and instructing of poore mens children at Roxbury." In order to argue his position that the School is forever a financially free one whose "privileges and advantages" are limited exclusively to Roxbury residents, Putnam has to make much out of the words "at Roxbury." He does.

Both a plain modern reading and a study of Bell's own usage indicate that Bell used the words "at Roxbury" only to define the location of the school. The general reader will not perhaps be interested in reading the detailed and scholarly study of the language of Bell's bequest made in 1984 by Louis Hamel, Esq., renowned trusts expert, but it reposes for scholars in the School's archives. Hamel categorizes every use of the word "at" in Bell's lengthy bequest. While Bell uses the word frequently for other purposes, "by contrast, one finds no instance in which [Bell] uses 'at' to denote a generic class or source from which individuals are to be selected." In such cases Bell always uses "of": "Ministers and Officers of ye said Church"; "of poor mens children"; "survivors of them"; "monie of England"; "a great part of my estate consisteth."

Twice in his will, Hamel points out, Bell defines a beneficial class that does have geographical specificity. In both cases he uses the words *"of"* and *"unto and amongst"*:

> I doe hereby give and bequest unto and amongst the poor people of ye parrish of Allhallowes Barkeing in London where I now dwell The summe of fifteene pounds. . . .
>
> I doe hereby give and bequeath ye summe of one hundred poundes unto and amongst divers poor necessitous men late Ministers of ye Gospell [*sic*] of wich number I will yt Mr. Knowles and Mr. John Collings both late of New England.

As Hamel comments, "The lesson of these two examples is that the testator is clear and circumspect in defining a beneficial class. In the phrase 'for ye teaching . . . *at* Roxbury' [as opposed to '*of* Roxbury'] there is nothing clear and circumspect to indicate a desire to limit the benefited pupils to those from Roxbury. . . . This conclusion is strongly confirmed by the main uses of 'at' elsewhere in the will."[33]

There is no justification, then, for Putnam's assertion, in his 1902 *Report*, that "We cannot receive any property whatever, whether capital or income, and whether of one kind or another, from any source, for any purpose than to educate Roxbury boys, the sole beneficiaries of the trust."

Bell left his lands for two beneficial classes: first, "to and for ye mainteynance of a School Master and free schoole"; and second, "for ye teaching and instructing of poore mens children." Both the maintenance of schools and the relief of the poor were common charitable concerns of wealthy men of the seventeenth century. Bell meant to combine them—to provide schooling coupled with relief for the children of the poor.

But Putnam was determined to prove that Bell's beneficial class was *not* the poor but rather *Roxbury* boys. He argues that, since the School is free to Roxbury boys—rich or poor, "poore mens children" are thereby served. Never mind that the affluent boys of Roxbury can attend the school free, while "poore mens children"—perhaps the newly immigrant Irish and Jews (neither of whom appear to have been attending the School in 1882)—are denied its benefits because they live in other parts of the city such as Dorchester or East Boston. Bell's money was financing a school mainly for the affluent boys of Roxbury; most of it was not being used to benefit "poore mens children."

Putnam also rejects the other "solution" to the School's financial problems. It had been suggested that the School could charge tuition for all subjects other than Latin, since these were added two hundred years after the School's founding and therefore could not possibly be financed by endowments given long before the addition of these newer subjects. To suppress this solution Putnam advances a fallacy: he asserts that no distinction of subjects can be made since "we simply prepare boys for college as we have done from the earliest times." As Hamel points out, Putnam's response is "a variation of a primitive sophistry which suggests that an identity of predicates warrants a fusion of subjects: 'Socrates is a man; Aristotle is a man; therefore Socrates and Aristotle are one.' Putnam's version is that the 1645 curriculum prepared boys for college; the 1882 curriculum prepares boys for college; therefore the 1645 curriculum and the 1882 curriculum are one."

Putnam is therefore wrong on both counts. He wrongly argues that Bell's bequest is all-determining, and then he wrongly asserts that Bell's bequest restricts the "privileges and advantages" of the School to Roxbury residents. Even if Putnam had been right in his interpretation, one might well question whether such restrictions could be made to stand hundreds of years later. For instance, one could just as well argue (though no one has) that, since Bell's bequest benefits "a [single] schoolmaster," the School can have only one teacher and he must be male.

Putnam's *1882 Report* purports to be an expert study of English schools. In fact, Putnam relies on a single source, the 1877 edition of Howard Staunton's *The Great Schools of England*. Staunton was neither an historian nor an educator. He was a popularizer whose most successful work was a handbook on chess. Far from being a history of English schools, his book is a handbook on contemporary schools—their characteristics and facilities—with a very short synopsis of their histories.

Putnam nowhere mentions the conclusive study of such schools, "The Schools Inquiry Commission" of 1864–68, a Royal Commission appointed by Parliament to investigate the 782 endowed grammar schools of England. Headed by Lord Taunton, it is usually referred to as the Taunton Commission. The commission studied English schools, which were facing the same sort of financial difficulties Roxbury Latin was facing. It reached a conclusion that exactly contradicts Putnam's:

> The truth is that, considering the altered condition of modern society, the *free* grammar school is an anachronism. If a school be free, it is filled with a class of children who do not learn grammar; and if classics are sedulously taught, the school soon ceases to be free. There is not an endowed school . . . which deserves the name of a free grammar school. Everyone of the great schools in which boys are prepared for the universities has ceased to be a free school. And everyone which retains a free character has sunk . . . to the level of a national school [in which classics and university preparation are unknown] or greatly below it. . . .
>
>   . . . The endowment which once sufficed to meet the whole cost of a good education can now only do so in part. It should supplement, not supersede, the payments of parents.[34]

The commission called for the abolition of "gratuitous" (i.e., financially free) schools based on neighborhood residency. It recommended that laws be enacted so that endowments, which had previously been used to provide a free education to boys based on their geographical residence, could be used for "exhibitions" (i.e., scholarships) for boys admitted on the basis of merit. Parliament enacted the commission's recommendations and established by law that merit and not geographical location would be the basis of admission and tuition assistance.

Putnam nowhere mentions the Taunton Commission's definitive study, even though his *Reports* were written fourteen and thirty-four years *after* the commission reached conclusions diametrically opposed to his own. Either Putnam did not know of the commission's existence (an ignorance tantamount to gross incompetence) or, as seems more likely, he suppressed it.

But what will most astonish any lawyer reviewing this case is Putnam's failure to recommend to the trustees that they seek (or consider seeking) judicial instruction—that is, that they ask for a court ruling on the matter. It seems likely that Putnam realized his study could not withstand judicial scrutiny. He therefore adopted the tactic of posing as an expert, hoping to fool his fellow trustees. His tactic worked. His fellow trustees meekly submitted to his bogus expertise, and abandoned the idea of charging fees of any sort for any services to the Roxbury boys, who constituted the overwhelming majority of the student body.

However, since Putnam conceded that fees *could* be charged for non-Roxbury boys, the trustees voted in June 1882 to charge boys "from towns outside the limits of Boston" $100 a year. In the trustee minutes the word "Boston" has been struck out and "Old Roxbury" written in above.[35] In 1883, twenty-one of the 146 boys in the School were non-residents of "Old Roxbury."

The trustees' submission to Putnam ushered in a quarter-century of financial drift. Having ruled out the charging of fees to the vast majority of its students, the trustees failed to come up with an alternative long- or short-range plan to solve the financial crisis entailed by the School's expansion. When a solution finally appeared in the new century, it had to be implemented literally and figuratively over the dead bodies of the trustees.

4. *A School in Decline*

Reading the newspaper accounts of the 250th anniversary celebrations in 1895, one senses few hints of trouble. The underlying public assumption still seemed to be that an institution of such antiquity (at least by American standards) was indestructible. Listening to the effusive speeches, outsiders would have assumed that a golden future lay ahead.

Insiders, however, realized that the future was heavily clouded. Money was not the School's only serious problem. As the century reached its final decade, the School's neighborhood changed quickly and dramatically. In the 1830s and 1840s, Roxbury had been one of greater Boston's two most affluent neighborhoods. Although hourly horse-drawn coaches connected Roxbury and Boston starting in 1826, Roxbury remained the rather distant and isolated dwelling place of the wealthy and fashionable.[36] By mid-century, some 40 percent of Roxbury's population were immigrants or children of immigrants, but they were mostly prosperous German families. Roxbury became a less exclusive enclave in 1856 when Boston's horse-drawn railway was expanded through the "neck" to Roxbury. The country village of 1810—with 3,669

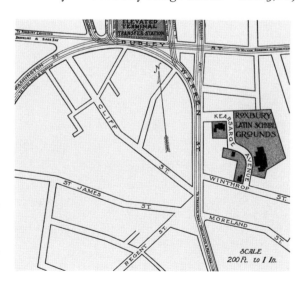

FIG. 7. Plan of the school grounds (from the 1899–1900 catalogue) showing nearby streets in Roxbury. The houses across the street were acquired in the 1890s.

FIG. 8. The School in 1904. Note the entrance has been moved from the original building (before which the boys stand) to the right, where an addition has been made.

FIG. 9. There was also an entrance on the left of the original schoolhouse, at the original addition to the building. (Boston Athenæum Collection)

people—had grown by 1860 into one of the nation's forty largest cities with 25,137 people. By 1868 Roxbury had voted to annex itself to Boston. Its ever-increasing connectedness to Boston was consummated in 1897 when the electric trolley line was extended from Boston to Franklin Park along Warren Street, one minute's walk from the School. By then, Roxbury was no longer a separate suburb or a fashionable address. Within a generation most of Roxbury's old families and affluent newcomers had moved either to the newly developed and posh Back Bay in Boston or to the new suburbs (including West Roxbury), leaving Roxbury to a very different social and economic stratum of society.[37]

The Reverend James DeNormandie was pastor of the First Church and president of the School's trustees from 1883 to 1917, years virtually coincident with Roxbury's transformation. The church's tercentenary history describes the effects:

> [Dr. DeNormandie] spoke once with much feeling of the sadness of a minister who sees his old parishioners melting away as the old people die and the young people remove to other parts of the city. So noticeable was the change that on one occasion he was referred to as a minister having parishioners in every town in Massachusetts except Roxbury.[38]

DeNormandie's youthful vitality had briefly reinvigorated the parish upon his arrival in 1883, but "change and decay" characterized the church's life at century's end. DeNormandie wrote:

> If anyone ought to be utterly discouraged, perhaps I should be. . . . [I]n a carefully prepared list of the parish in 1889, there are 309 families. While here and there one had begun to leave 30 years ago [in 1872], it was not until 15 years ago that the tide of fashion began sweeping our old families into [Boston], or much farther away, so that within the past six or eight years [1894–96], of those 309 families 264 have gone away.[39]

By the 1890s the School looked on with dismay as its traditional constituency melted away. Roger Ernst '98, later president of the

FIG. 10. The Reverend James DeNormandie, minister of the First Church in Roxbury, 1883–1917.

trustees, reflected in later years on this clientele. Writing to Arthur Perry '02, himself later trustee president, Ernst commented:

> Our school, at the time you and I went to it and prior to that, was composed very much of the private school type; that is, the boys came from old New England families, in most cases of moderate means, but who could have perfectly well paid the tuition at a private day school. . . . [40] We did not represent a real cross-section of democratic society.[41]

Roxbury also now had public schools—in large, modern brick buildings—that provided an education which Roxbury's new inhabitants preferred to the traditional classical education offered by Roxbury Latin.

Just as the First Church endeavored to hold onto its parishioners even after they moved away, Roxbury Latin tried to lure back its traditional clientele. But the School faced formidable competition: Roxbury's affluent families were not only moving away; increasing numbers were being attracted to the recently founded country boarding schools, such as St. Mark's (1865), Groton (1884), and soon Middlesex (founded by R.L. alumnus Frederick Winsor in 1901). Excellent private day schools such as Noble's, Volkmann's, and Hopkinson's had also been established in more fashionable parts of the city and were attracting former Roxbury families. Under the leadership of Harrison O. Apthorp, who had taught at Roxbury Latin (1884–86) under Collar, Milton Academy had been reborn on spacious grounds in the attractive and easily accessible town of Milton.

For its first 225 years, Roxbury Latin had been the sole "Latin" school in Roxbury and its environs. Unless a bright and ambitious boy was sent to board at one of the New England academies, there was virtually no other option for him than the School. Now—in the face of strong competition from attractive public and private alternatives—the School, with its ramshackle wooden building on a tiny sloping lot, overshadowed by new multi-story tenements, was increasingly a "hard

FIG. 11. The First Church in the late 1880s.

FIG. 12. Note the dilapidation of the schoolhouse and the barren campus surrounding it.

sell." Enrollment had averaged 165 in the fifteen years leading up to the turn of the century, peaking at 185 in the 250th year (1894–95). But it steadily declined thereafter.[42]

Among the boys, there was a crisis of morale resulting from their sense that the School was in decline. Increasingly, the building was an embarrassment, as this defensive column from *The Tripod* in 1889 indicates:

> The Observer has once or twice of late had his attention called to the impression made upon the barbarian mind [the minds of those not belonging to Roxbury Latin!] by our Latin School building. One exoteric journal [another school's magazine], for instance, has even ventured to suggest that a more elegant building would be more befitting the reputation of the school. Many a visitor, no doubt, on entering the yard, has been disappointed with the general appearance of the school-house. Instead of an imposing brick building, with perhaps some ivy twining on the outside walls, he sees a plain wooden building with no adornment.[43]

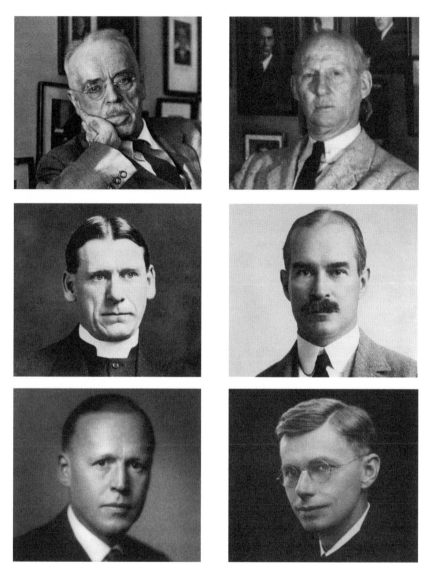

FIG. 13. Six alumni in education: *Top left:* Paul Dudley White '03 professor of medicine at Harvard and physician to President Eisenhower; *top right:* Curtis Wolsey Cate '03, founder of the Cate School in California; *middle left:* the Reverend Samuel S. Drury '97, rector of St. Paul's School; *middle right:* Frederick Winsor '88, founder and headmaster of Middlesex School; *lower left:* Remsen B. Ogilby '98, president of Trinity College; *lower right:* James Bryant Conant '10, president of Harvard. (Harvard University Archives Collection)

A year later, this note is struck again: "As our school can boast of her age, and belongs to the same aristocratic family as Harvard, it is rather a pity that her building should not correspond in age and dignity."[44] Even the locals looked down their nose:

> [The] boys of our school and those of Roxbury High School have a little difficulty as regards the right of way on the sidewalk when they happen to meet each other. . . . The High-School boys are doubtless a little proud and overbearing because of their new school-house.[45]

When it became clear in 1891 that, with the expanded curriculum and numbers, additional space was required, the trustees agreed to consider building a "wholly new school-house of brick and stone, which should furnish accommodations equal to those provided by the present structure with its proposed addition."[46] Trustee Henry Ware Putnam (author of the *Reports* of 1892 and 1902) vigorously opposed this idea. As he watched the old Yankee dominance diminish in Massachusetts and witnessed the decline of the community in which he had lived his entire life, he became ever more reactionary—seeking at all costs to preserve the school of his boyhood without change. Since most of the trustees were older men who shared his outlook, he prevailed in the discussions.[47] So, rather than face up to the School's long-range building needs, the trustees settled in 1892 for temporary relief in the form of a two-classroom addition, equipping a room as a chemistry laboratory and fixing up the basement to provide a small area for gymnastics and lunch. *The Tripod* describes the grandeur of the new luncheon quarters:

> Our present banquet hall consists of an oblong room in the basement (we are almost tempted to say cellar), with floor and ceiling of cement, and walls of stone; at one end is a clean, though scarcely attractive, lunch counter; at the other, a distance of some feet, is an infant gymnasium, usually in a state of sympathetic dejectedness along with the rest of the place; on one flank is a row of windows which admit just about enough light to feel companionable with

FIG. 14. The chemistry laboratory, equipped in 1892.

their surroundings, while, to crown the whole, a furnace and dim perspective of coal bins and ash barrels stare us out of countenance, on the other flank.[48]

Though there were small improvements, such as electric bells replacing the gong in 1890 and the 1893 gift of a stereopticon (used for showing slides in hall), the boys of Roxbury realized that their school was standing still while others advanced:

> Hardly a week passes that we do not read of magnificent donations to other schools. A graduate gives a lecture hall, a trustee offers a gymnasium, a "friend of the school" presents a laboratory or scientific building. . . . In many cases the school is far better off already than we, in spite of our great history and widespread reputation. What is the matter? Have we no rich graduates? Have we no trustees, no "friends of the school", no "well-wishers"?[49]
>
> We need some Teddy Roosevelt to take us out of our sleep.[50]

FIG. 15. The sloping "playground" of the school. The schoolhouse can be seen on the far right. The photograph dates from before 1889 when the graveyard was removed. The Methodist church is the background. (Society for the Preservation of New England Antiquities Collection)

The School had almost no "grounds" except a tiny play yard. F. C. Woodman '84 described it this way:

> Our school yard consisted of an inclined piece of gravel, bordered on one side by a low wall with a graveyard below. Every new boy was initiated by being set on the wall, turned over backwards, and dropped into one of the empty tombs. That miserable schoolyard with no grass, all gravel, stones, and dust, was the happy hunting grounds for all sorts of games.[51]

The graveyard described above was owned by the City of Boston; in 1889 the trustees went to the city to obtain the right to use it. The city allowed them to add fill above the level of the graves if they first bore the expense of clearing away the remains and preserving the tombstones. The trustees also had to open the new field to any school child in the Boston public schools who wished to use it. The city retained title to the land and control of it: "Nothing . . . shall prevent the city from appropriating said land to other public purposes."[52] This agreement, of course, was highly unfavorable to the School in the long run and was at best a temporary palliative.

The first issue of *The Tripod* in March 1889 had referred wistfully to "our long-promised gymnasium."[53] This refrain continued in almost every issue until well into the twentieth century. The new field stimulated old hopes:

> The playground that we have used for the past year [1890–91] has been a great pleasure and convenience to all the pupils of the School. . . . It is a good foundation on which to build castles in the air in the shape of gymnasiums; and the lower end, extending out to Kearsarge Avenue, is certainly a practicable location for tennis courts.[54]

But the same article reveals the problem in neighborhood relations caused by the new playground:

> The grounds bring us into direct contact with several neighboring yards, a state of affairs that will probably cause the neighbors a great deal of annoyance, and this cannot entirely be obviated by wire netting. So we must be as careful of their rights as we possible can, and not break down vines or plants unless it is entirely unavoidable [*sic!*], and above all we must remember never to swear, until we take the oath of allegiance to the United States.

Fences and nettings did little to correct the problem. By the spring of 1892, angry neighbors charged that the use of the graveyard as a playground was "conceived with entire disregard of the living or dead" and was "a disgrace to the fair fame of the Roxbury Grammar (Latin) School." They claimed the playground had "become a common nuisance" and sought an injunction against its further use, it having been "illegally obtained by the City of Boston." Though much of the aggravation came from non-R.L. boys using the field when the School was not in session, *The Tripod* exhorted students to "be more careful not to

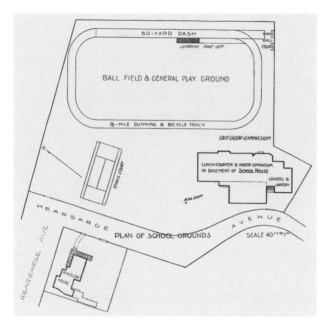

FIG. 16. Plan of the schoolyard after the graveyard was removed in 1889. Note the 1/8-mile "track" and tennis court. From the 1899–1900 catalogue.

disturb these people needlessly, or else the grounds will be taken from us, and we be returned to the small school-yard."[55] Nevertheless, the neighbors filed a petition with the City Council to prohibit use of the grounds.[56] By the following spring, *The Tripod* was complaining that "It seems strange that a fellow must get a note from the head master in order to get a ball from a neighboring yard."[57]

All this trouble arose over what was, in fact, a highly unsatisfactory schoolyard. A decade later, after numerous efforts had been made to re-grade and improve this play area, *The Tripod* still complained: "The campus is still stony and uneven as ever. . . . We might see more fellows on the field, practicing baseball and football and taking excellent exercise in the open air, if our campus was level and grassy, instead of hilly and stony."[58]

Each year brought further deterioration of the neighborhood. The spring of 1896 witnessed:

FIG. 17. View of the School from Kearsarge Avenue. From the 1894–95 catalogue.

FIG. 18. View of the back of the schoolhouse from the "improved" field in the 1894–95 catalogue. Note the Winslow House on the right.

FIG. 19. View of the "improved" campus after the graveyard was removed. From the 1899–1900 catalogue.

the rapid demolition of the old house on Kearsarge Avenue, next to the school; this was quickly followed by the noisy erection of two apartment houses, which now occupy the same lot of land. The general hubbub and fearful dust caused by these operations were extremely irritating to the nerves, deafening to the senses and wearying to the heads of the unfortunate masters and students who occupied the three upper class-rooms. It was a case where we were obliged to choose between uproar and suffocation.[59]

In December 1898, "in order to screen the schoolrooms from the view of the adjoining tenements," a five-foot high lattice was placed on top of the existing fence.[60]

It seems we are to be protected from the temptation of watching the varied colored signals [drying laundry] which have heretofore flaunted in our faces from the neighboring houses; for the trustees have had a lattice built on top of the fence. . . . Now if some inventive Yankee mind could only think of a way to prevent the loud rat-

FIG. 20. Side view of the Hall in 1899—decorated for graduation.

FIG. 21. Front view of the Hall in 1899—decorated for graduation.

tling of pots and kettles (which begins about twelve o'clock each day) from ringing in the ears of the diligent pupils of the first and second classes, he would truly be conferring a great favor upon them. . . . [D]uring the spring term it gets to be almost unbearable.[61]

The neighborhood's degeneration and the school's inadequate and depressing building and grounds, then, contributed to the general aura of decline that clouded the School. The School's perpetual athletic losses were the principal cause of poor "school spirit." In students' minds, at least, poor records were directly related to poor facilities: no gymnasium and no playing field. And, of course, it did wonders for school morale to have boys play every game "away"—often at schools such as St. Mark's and Groton, where they saw lavish campuses.

These new boarding schools modelled themselves after the English "public schools," and regarded athletics as an integral part of their programs. That had never been Roxbury Latin's philosophy. The School existed purely to provide academic instruction. Roger Ernst '98 notes that boys in his time were free every day after their classes ended at 2:00 P.M.[62] As late as the mid-1930s, a boy could leave the minute his last class ended. Francis Russell '28 writes of his after-school escapades while in Class V:

> [M]y friend Carl Johnson and I . . . would spend our afternoons exploring the city. At two o'clock, when the cracked last bell rang in the Fifth Class Room and Mr. Sasserno, the diminutive French Master, dismissed us for the day, we two would be out of the mildewed old building as if it were a cage with the door suddenly sprung, on our way with our 5¢ car [trolley] checks in our hands, down to the Dudley Street Elevated Terminal. Between the two of us—and with the passport of the brown-printed car-check—we knew we had the world at our feet, under our feet.[63]

Through most of the nineteenth century, as we have seen, sport had no official standing in the School's life. When classes were over, boys were free to do as they wished. More and more often, some of them—on their own—got together to play football. The school year 1883–84 appears to mark a transition: the boys who played football had themselves photographed and elegantly framed as a "team." But sports were still not officially sponsored or sanctioned or supervised by the School's trustees or faculty, and the boys themselves did all the arranging of games. All over the nation—and inevitably at Roxbury Latin—a new era was beginning in which school-sponsored athletics would become the vogue.

In the early years of teams, boys had to provide their own uniforms and even their own balls. Writing in 1889, a boy in the First Class describes an event of his Sixth Class year:

> The School foot-ball was purchased by subscription.... [W]hen cold weather began, our class was visited by eloquent members of the first, who called upon us to subscribe to the foot-ball which was to be used in the yard at recess. They informed us that any one who paid 15 cents would be entitled to the privilege of kicking the aforesaid ball. As most of us were eager to enjoy this privilege, it is, I think, probable that we were about the only ones who furnished funds, while the members of the first class got most of the kicks.[64]

For the first time, teams began practicing before games—though these practices were organized by the boys themselves and were voluntary. The captain of the 1889 football team expressed what was to become a perennial lament:

> Out of a school of 160 [actually there were 164] boys, it seems as if there ought to be a good many ready to turn out and practice, but it is with greatest difficulty that twenty-two men can be induced to appear; and very often some of the men whom we most want fail to show up. . . . There should be more of a feeling in the school which makes men play simply for the good of the team.[65]

Not only did few boys turn out for the teams, but they received little support from their schoolmates. In October 1892, a boy wrote:

> It is a most noticeable fact that the cheering at our base-ball and foot-ball games is far below the standard. What cheering there is, is light and produces no effect. . . . This is surely a sample of "Roxbury Indifference" of which so much is said. . . . [C]ertainly with one hundred and ninety [there were actually only 182] boys our school ought to be able to muster one hundred or more to yell for victory.[66]

In May 1893 *The Tripod* gave this analysis of the athletic situation and its effect on the students, following an R.L. team's first-ever loss to Hopkinson's School:

Athletics in our school have been rather on a toboggan slide for several years past, and we seem to gain downward emphasis as the years roll by. This is due in large measure to the fact that so many enter Harvard from the second class, but the main cause of this backsliding epoch is the lack of "backbone" and spirit, or, as it is oftener spoken of, the dreadful "Roxbury Indifference." Our bad luck, which inevitably attends all our sports, is due entirely to this indifference.[67]

The masters made no attempt to exert any control over athletics until June 1891, when the trustees "voted to endorse Mr. Collar's proposition to control the dates of interscholastic match games of ball and upheld him in his attempts to exercise such control."[68] Two years later, faculty influence was further extended:

All school athletics will hereafter be managed by a board of directors consisting of three teachers, the captains of the foot-ball, baseball, tennis, and athletics [i.e., track] teams, and the President of the Athletic Association. By this new arrangement it is hoped that school athletics will receive a new impetus, and that there will be a cordial co-operation between boys and teachers.[69]

By June 1894 the trustees placed full advisory supervision of all school athletics in the hands of "three teachers to be selected by the school Athletic Association during the first fortnight of the school year."[70] By 1897, the trustees added that these three teachers were to work "in conference with and under the authority of the headmaster" to determine what schools would be played and which students would be eligible.[71]

Ice hockey—called "shinny" or "ice polo" at the time and played with a round ball rather than a flat puck—was first mentioned in 1892. By the winter of 1894, the School played its first game: "We played our first polo game against Hoppy [Hopkinson's School, which seems to have been R.L.'s arch rival in all sports in this era], January 8, at Jamaica [Pond], defeating them by a score of 2 to 1."[72] A year later, however, *The Tripod* records that "It has been decided to form no Ice Polo Team this

FIG. 22. The 1893 track team. W. Welles Hoyt '94 won the pole vault in the 1896 Olympics. He is at the center of the back row.

FIG. 23. The 1900 baseball team. Malcolm Farmer '01, the renowned director of athletics at Yale, is seated second from left.

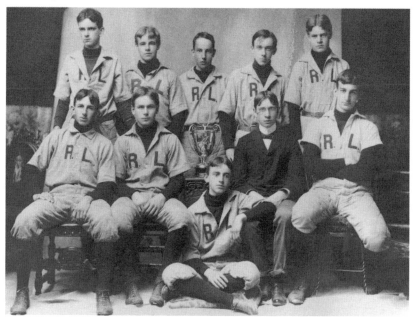

winter as it would conflict with the training of the athletic [track] team."[73]

In 1893, a "physical training" instructor was appointed, the first time in its history that the School had officially committed itself to a concern for boys' physical well-being. Mr. Whitehouse was engaged to work with the lower three classes three hours each Tuesday and Friday. Boys were to be measured, then taught "movements" (i.e., exercises) and how to use some simple apparatus in the basement.[74] Soon "the First Class asked in vain to be allowed to have an hour or so a week of physical training under Mr. Whitehouse."[75] And *The Tripod* editorialized: "Let us hope that the physical training the lower classes are now receiving will create in them a love of athletics which will display itself in a few years in the size of different teams.[76] By the following year, interested boys in the upper three classes were "given opportunity to take such gymnastic instruction as they desire."[77]

Roxbury Latin's efforts were very modest in comparison to the major improvements most other schools were making to enhance their athletic programs. The official tone of the 250th anniversary was celebratory, but *The Tripod* revealed student despondency. Athletic practices were a "joke," attendance and support terrible, the results humiliating:

> Anyone who has been a pupil here for any length of time cannot fail to have noticed the atmosphere of indifference that pervades the School. There seems to be an absolute lack of School spirit, which is lamentable to see. . . . [78]

> For the last several years Roxbury has drunk deeply of her degradation, but certainly this year she had drained the very dregs, or the cup is even deeper than we had supposed. . . . Let us pray that our humiliation has reached its limit this year.[79]

This refrain is repeated to the end of the century. In the 1895–96 school year Roxbury won not a single point in the interscholastic track meet.[80] When some sort of shower/changing room was requested, the trustees provided one cold water "shower bath" and a few lockers in the

FIG. 24. The 1904–05 hockey team. Standing, far left, is Percy Langdon Wendell '09, football All-American and later football coach at Williams and Lehigh.

basement.[81] In 1898 *The Tripod* contrasted R.L.'s pathetic fan support with Milton Academy's enthusiastic support of its teams.[82] Hockey died in 1899 because the School would not and the boys could not support it financially.[83] There was a spill-over effect on other aspects of school life. In 1899 the orchestra died and no play was produced. *The Tripod* commented: "This very lack of energy reflects discredit on the School as a whole."[84]

FIG. 25. The 1898 Interscholastic Rowing Champions. Samuel Huntington Wolcott '99, trustee 1933–1961, is standing second from the right.

Dr. Lewis Webb Hill '06 describes the state of athletics in Dr. Collar's penultimate year as headmaster:

> At the time I was in the school, the teams were not of particular brilliance [though] we occasionally won a game. . . . We had in the basement of the old school building what was called a gymnasium, and it consisted of one of those leather horses which you jump around on and some chestweights and Indian clubs. . . . We had no regular coaches of any teams—we just got together and played. . . . Occasionally some of the [R.L. alumni at] Harvard would come over and coach the football team, but as far as any regular coaching went, there was simply none at all.[85]

Boys continued to be embarrassed by the School's small, unlevel field which necessitated that all games be played on the opponents' fields.

Despite the lack of facilities and of official support, the School produced some remarkable athletes in this period. W. Welles Hoyt '94 was granted a leave of absence from Harvard—in recognition of his high grades—to participate in the first modern Olympics at Athens in 1896. There he won the first place medal in the pole vault. Using a bamboo pole, like others in an era before fiberglass, he cleared 10 feet, 9 inches, a record he himself bested by vaulting 11 feet, 4 inches in the Intercollegiates while still at Harvard.[86] Malcolm D. Whitman '95, went on to become U.S. singles champion in tennis. Malcolm Farmer '01, served for many years as Director of Athletics at Yale. Andrew Marshall '97, George F. Kennedy '06, and Percy Langdon Wendell '09 (later the highly successful football coach at Williams and Lehigh) were football All-Americans.

The first school play occurred in 1894—conceived as a fund-raiser for the School's athletic teams:

FIG. 26. The School's first play, *The Cool Collegians*, was presented at Palladio Hall in Dudley Square, Roxbury, in 1894. Photograph by John Murdoch, April 10, 1909. (Boston Athenæum Collection)

Every winter for the last few years there has been talk of giving an entertainment for the benefit for the Athletic Association; but it has remained to the Class of '94 to really go ahead with any idea of this sort. They have gone ahead and the comedy, "The Cool Collegians," will be given on Wednesday, April 4, at Palladio Hall, by members of the First and Second classes. The School orchestra will play and there will be dancing after the performance. The tickets have sold very rapidly.[87]

So successful was this event—culturally, socially, and financially—that a second performance was given at Winthrop Hall in Dorchester a month later.[88] Although Headmaster Collar canceled the play in 1896 as taking up too much time, it resumed the following year and has been a feature (now, as the "senior play") every year since then except in 1899, 1943, and 1944.[89]

5. The Alumni Uprising

To face these problems—of declining neighborhood, inadequate and decaying facilities, and plummeting student morale—the School needed dynamic and visionary leadership. Unfortunately what it had was a board of trustees capable only of applying a band-aid here and there to the hemorrhaging wound.

The trustees' president from 1884 to 1917, the Reverend Dr. James DeNormandie, had watched his parishioners move away, but had determined that, under no circumstances, would the First Church move. In 1902, he noted that

within 50 years we have seen almost all the old churches of Boston abandon the places made dear by many generations of worshipping men and women . . . , and only last week our old church in Charlestown . . . which had dwindled down to a congregation of from seven to 30, went out of existence. . . .

I want to take this early opportunity to beg that none of us shall ever seriously harbor [any thought of moving]. . . . Only last week I had a letter saying that persons stood ready to take this whole square enclosed by our church if it were for sale. I replied that five times the amount offered for St. Paul's a fortnight since, and this whole area covered with American eagles besides, would not be the least inducement to give it up. . . . I still believe we can live, and that the day may come when renewed prosperity shall be ours, right amidst all these sacred memories.[90]

Viewing the School as an anchor for his parish, DeNormandie was negatively disposed towards any vision of Roxbury Latin that involved its moving from the neighborhood. By the 1789 Charter, DeNormandie and the church's two longest-serving deacons were trustees of the School. And by the same charter, all the trustees had to be Roxbury residents. Inevitably, therefore, the trustees were conservative older men who were too settled to join the ever-growing exodus of their own children to the Back Bay and the new suburbs.[91] They dug in their heels to resist change. Their vision for the School was limited to "sticking it out"; they had little understanding of what "modern" parents and boys were looking for in a school.

The School's inadequate building and lack of playing fields, as well as the ugliness of its now badly deteriorated neighborhood, were obvious to prospective parents and boys. Physically the School could not provide the environment the modern parent and boy were seeking (and could easily find elsewhere). Parents and alumni also became increasingly aware of the low morale of boys in the School.

But the issue that most galvanized concerned alumni and parents was the School's financial condition. By the 250th anniversary year, the School was running gigantic annual deficits. Henry Ware Putnam's *1882 Report* had permitted the trustees to charge tuition to boys who lived outside what Putnam defined as the "Old Roxbury District," and they began doing so in 1883. This outsiders' fee was raised to $125 in 1888 and to $150 in 1892. Since students from outside were not being attracted in large numbers, for reasons we have already discussed, only about 20 percent of the student body (e.g., twenty-seven out of 141 in 1889) were fee-paying "outsiders." Collar would later assert that their fees paid the salaries of four teachers.[92] But even with these fees (total-

FIG. 27. The First Church at the turn of the century, April 5, 1905. John Murdoch, photographer. (Boston Athenæum Collection)

FIG. 28. Admiral Winslow's house directly across from the School on Kearsarge Avenue was renovated to become a dormitory for the School in 1899. The street was renamed Kearsarge Avenue after Winslow's ship, the "Kearsarge," sank the Confederate cruiser "Alabama" in 1864. (Society for the Preservation of New England Antiquities Collection)

ing $4,150) added to the School's endowment income ($11,293.18), total income in 1895 came to only $15,443.18, while expenses totaled $19,421.72.[93] If this trend continued, the School would soon devour its remaining endowment principal.

The problem, of course, was Putnam's *1882 Report* that prohibited any sort of charge to Roxbury boys for any part of their education.

John Tetlow, headmaster of Girls Latin and co-founder with Collar of the Headmasters Association, became a trustee—ex officio as deacon of the First Church—in 1895. The following year, with Collar's support, he proposed an ingenious end run around Putnam's prohibition. The faculty had recently voted to begin the teaching of French in Class VI, postponing Latin until Class V. Tetlow proposed that, since Latin, the subject which the School was endowed to teach, was no longer being taught in Class VI, the School should drop Class VI: "a preparatory class, corresponding to the present sixth class, should be organized and . . . boys admitted to it [no matter where they lived] would be required to pay a fee of $100 a year."[94] The only alternative was to reduce the teaching staff, which would undermine the School's quality and further scare off fee-payers from outside the "Old Roxbury District," whose tuitions were a major source of income. The trustees, however, rejected Tetlow's proposal. A few months later, with a reduction in the number of teachers now certain, Collar proposed that the School could only maintain its quality by becoming a five-year school. His proposal was also rejected.[95]

Though Collar had begged for new endowments throughout the 250th anniversary celebrations, the trustees lacked the vision and energy to plan any sort of campaign for new funds. Pathetically, they turned to cutting costs. In 1896 they lowered Collar's salary from $4500 to $4000 and warned that they were "unable to give assurance at the present time whether they will be able to retain the services of Mr. Farnham and Mr. Dodge [two of the eight faculty] next year."[96] While the number of masters was, in fact, not reduced in 1898, the faculty were naturally nervous about their long-range prospects. In 1900 *The Tripod* reported that

"All graduates and friends of the school . . . will be surprised to learn that Mr. Power [the science master] has left the school. He has gone to accept a position at the Dorchester High School where a larger salary is offered."[97]

The trustees' only constructive effort was to establish a dormitory which they hoped would attract paying students from outside the "Old Roxbury District." In 1899 they purchased the old Winslow house across from the School, converted it to a dormitory, and entered into a complicated financial arrangement with Mr. Farnham, who agreed to manage it.[98] The headmaster, meanwhile, was "authorized to spend a sum not exceeding $100 in advertising the School [with its new dormitory] in the leading papers of the country."[99] With both the School's reputation and the neighborhood in decline, the effort attracted only five boys and was soon abandoned.[100]

Tuition payers from outside Roxbury, whether from greater Boston or from out of state, were now an essential source of income. At an alumni dinner in April 1902, Collar noted "the goodly number of fee payers at present, the income from whom is an important factor, as it pays the salaries of four of the teachers."[101] As the financial crisis worsened, several trustees proposed that the School build up the number of tuition payers as a means of escaping from Putnam's trap. If Roxbury boys had to be taught free (as Putnam insisted), then why not limit their number so that they would be of *"such a number as can be instructed by means of the actual income of the invested funds of the School?"*[102] The proposal was referred to Putnam, who—again, as in 1882—did not advise the trustees to seek judicial instruction. His response was his *Report* of 1902, already discussed extensively above, which stated that "the limitation of Roxbury boys to such a number as could be educated by the income of the invested funds alone, would be illegal."[103]

Roxbury Latin's only remaining strength was its faculty. Its science masters brought the School national renown. Milford S. Power had become the School's second science master following the untimely

FIG. 29. N. Henry Black, science master 1900–1924. James Bryant Conant '10 enticed him to teach chemistry at Harvard in 1924.

death of George F. Forbes in 1890. By 1892 he had created a chemistry laboratory and introduced the study of chemistry, and by 1899 he persuaded the faculty to include elementary science twice a week in the Class V course of study. This innovation attracted national attention and led quickly to the wide acceptance of "General Science" as a junior high school subject across the country.

Upon Power's departure in 1900, Collar appointed an even more distinguished and innovative scientist: N. Henry Black, who remained at the School for twenty-four years. Black had doubts about the Class V science course when he arrived, but he soon realized that "it was in this class that I could detect the boys who had a real aptitude for science, such as James Bryant Conant,"[104] Class of 1910, who went on to become professor of chemistry and then president at Harvard. Collar gave Black the teachers' room to equip as a lecture-demonstration area, and Black went to Switzerland and Germany in 1904 to study European equipment and techniques—both of which were far in advance of their American counterparts. Joining with a colleague at Newton High School, Black persuaded two instrument makers from Holland to come to Boston in order to make all the necessary equipment for his new approach. After a year's study in Germany in 1909, Black worked with colleagues at Harvard and M.I.T. to produce half a dozen texts in physics, chemistry, and electricity (notably Black and Conant's *Practical Chemistry*) which became widely used nationally. The alumni rolls of this era reveal an amazing number of men who went on to careers in science—particularly chemistry. One such, of course, was Conant, who stole Black away from R.L. in 1924 to be teacher of chemistry at the college. After Black returned to visit R.L. in the fall of 1924, *The Tripod* remarked, "We have reason to be proud of our labs. Mr. Black on a recent visit said they were better equipped than most of the Harvard labs."[105]

Science was not the only field in which the School distinguished itself. Marshall W. Davis taught French and German. Like Lowell, he was a Bowdoin man from Maine. When Davis returned briefly to his hometown of Bethel after college, Lowell was serving there as principal of Gould's Academy. Davis then taught for Lowell briefly before going off to Europe for several years. Upon returning he was "usher" for a year (1880–81) at R.L. before going to Thayer to teach. Collar and Lowell lured him back in 1886 and he taught primarily French and German until his death in 1917. He married Collar's eldest daughter Alice, who herself ran the private Elm Hill elementary school in Roxbury. Robert Withington '02 recalled "his stern look before which we quailed."[106] J. B. Sumner '06, who went on to win the Nobel Prize in Chemistry, recorded this vignette:

> Mr. Davis taught us French in a strict military manner. He would come into the classroom, mount the platform, turn to the class and say: 'Smith: read the first sentence.' If Smith faltered, Mr. Davis

would walk down to Smith's desk, pound on it and shout: 'Don't you know me yet? This must not happen again.' We learned French thoroughly and indelibly.[107]

Even though he lived three minutes' walk from the School, he locked his classroom door at 1:30 on the dot and departed. "Tall and thin, a cold fish to boys, he was very unsociable," is the way his nephew described him. The jewel in the faculty crown, however, was D. O. S. Lowell, master of history, English, and music from 1884. Having served as Collar's right-hand man, he inherited the headmastership in 1909. Two other memorable masters of this era must be mentioned: Clarence W. Gleason, master of Greek 1889–1905 and 1912–1939, and O. M. Farnham, Sixth Class master 1893–1934, whom we shall consider at greater length in Part V.

Putnam's reports had closed the door on virtually all sources of financial support to pay these distinguished men an adequate salary. Only one recourse remained: further cutting of costs. Since faculty salaries constituted nearly 90 percent of the School's annual expenses, that

FIG. 30. Clarence W. Gleason, master of Greek 1889–1905 and 1912–1939, and author of the words to "The Founder's Song," here pictured in his first year at Roxbury Latin.

meant reducing the masters' remuneration. In 1903, Mr. Lowell was warned that his salary might be cut, and the physical education instructor was let go "on the grounds of expense."[108] In 1904, Collar proposed a further $500 reduction in his own salary "and the Board so voted with an expression of regret that the financial condition of the School made such a reduction necessary." D. O. S. Lowell's salary was also lowered from $3000 to $2500.[109] In 1905, sixteen-year veteran master Clarence Gleason departed for Volkmann's School when Roxbury could not come close to matching Mr. Volkmann's salary offer. Gleason later reflected: "The problem of living and bringing up a family was serious. Besides I was in need of some new clothes."[110] In 1906, George Fiske, earning $1500 per year at R.L., accepted Mr. Volkmann's offer of $1800 to follow Gleason to Volkmann's School.[111] In 1908, Charles H. Smith "resigned his place in the School to accept a more remunerative position at the University School, Cleveland, O."[112]

Addressing the alumni dinner between these two departures, Collar spoke with unusual vehemence about the trustees' need to raise new endowment:

> He outlined the recent changes, the loss to the School of Prof. Gleason, who has been compelled to resign because the School could no longer pay him a living wage, and another school could; another teacher, he said, had received within a few months, three offers to more lucrative positions. . . . The Trustees cannot expect that the ablest teachers will always be willing to work for about half pay.[113]

A number of prominent alumni had for several years been expressing their increasing concern as they watched the trustees drift and the School's reputation decline. Chief among these was Robert Hallowell Gardiner '72. In June 1903, the boys of the School had sent him nearly $1100 in gifts and pledges towards a new gymnasium. He wrote his fellow concerned alumnus, William A. Gaston: "Do you not think we might as well force the issue by my writing to Putnam telling him about this and announcing our purpose of going ahead and asking for further subscriptions?"[114]

When Gardiner did so, Putnam's reply was, as Gardiner put it, "more unreasonable and extreme even than I had expected."[115] Putnam condemned the raising of money by the boys as "wholly Mr. Collar's doing, entirely disapproved by me for the present. As my convictions on this subject as trustee are perfectly decided as the result of long study and experience on this question and with Mr. Collar, I shall oppose any action."[116] Gaston commented to Gardiner: "I should suppose after reading the copy of Putnam's letter which you sent me that Putnam was the whole committee, the whole Board of Trustees and the only alumnus of the school!"[117]

After the trustees shot down several such individual initiatives, the alumni finally organized themselves. In 1904, fifteen "prominent graduates of the School" petitioned the trustees:

> The undersigned, graduates of the Roxbury Latin School, deeply interested in its welfare, and representing, as we believe, a general desire among the graduates to do what lies in their power to promote the prosperity and efficiency of the School, respectfully request you to call a special meeting of the Board of Trustees to confer with us as to what, if anything, can be done by the graduates to help the School.[118]

Nine graduates made their case to the board at the ensuing meeting. When Gardiner, the real (though unofficial) leader of the group, inquired "as to the financial state of the School, [he] was informed there had been a deficit for a number of years averaging some $2000."[119]

Responding to the news that faculty salaries for the coming year would be cut again, Gardiner offered personally to pay "all or any part of the $2000 to be used to restore the decreases already made, to take effect at the beginning of the next school year, in the salaries of Mr. Collar and Mr. Lowell for that year, and then at the discretion of the Trustees . . . either to increase salaries of those or other teachers or to meet any future deficit in the income of the school."[120]

If the trustees would not take the initiative to raise new funds, obviously some of the alumni were prepared to do so. The trustees "Voted to accept most heartily and thankfully the gift of the graduates in accordance with the terms of the proposition which they have made." It is fascinating to note that "Mr. Putnam desired his vote to be recorded in the negative upon this vote."[121]

With trustee approval, the concerned alumni at once undertook a drive for new endowment. When they asked the trustees for a "Declaration from the board to strengthen their appeal," the trustees issued the following memorandum:

> For several years the expenses of the Roxbury Latin School have exceeded the income by $2000 to $3000 a year. The Trustees feel it would not be proper for them to allow this deficit to continue and unless an endowment fund can be raised which will increase the income, the expenses must be diminished. This can only be done by reducing the salaries of the teachers, with the risk of losing their services, or else by discharging teachers, to the serious injury of the efficiency of the school. The Trustees are extremely reluctant to adopt either of these courses. They learn with great pleasure of the effort being made by the graduates to increase the endowment of the school.[122]

At an alumni dinner shortly thereafter Gardiner proposed that the alumni raise $250,000 for a new school. He suggested Pond Hill in Jamaica Plain "or some other place away from the present unsightly and uninspiring surroundings." He then pledged $6000, in the name of the alumni, towards the deficit. When Trustee H. W. Putnam was called upon to speak, "He declared the trustees would welcome any move towards increasing the endowment, but felt sure that the present site and present equipment were 'better than a brick palace in the wilderness,' like Middlesex and St. Mark's."[123]

When Gardiner repeated his offer regarding the deficit in a letter to the trustees, he also expressed the feeling that the School's charter should be changed so that the alumni could be represented on the board.[124] The alumni were prepared to be generous, but they perceived that without revitalized trustee leadership their money would be squandered.

In June 1905, the trustees agreed to propose to the General Court an amendment to the 1789 Charter providing for alumni representation. The charter had established a board of not less than nine or more than thirteen trustees (of whom three were the pastor and two oldest deacons of the First Church). The proposed amendment provided for thirteen trustees in three classes: "five being elected from nominations by the graduates," another five "from among the residents [not, as formerly, freeholders] of the territory formerly constituting the town of Roxbury" (hereafter the only trustees who had to be residents of Old Roxbury), plus the pastor and two longest-serving deacons of the church.[125] The Legislature passed the enabling Act in March 1906. When the Act was returned to the trustees for their approval, the only negative vote was Henry Ware Putnam's.[126]

Rescue was coming none too soon. Public confidence in the School continued to deteriorate. The opening of the new school year—September 1905—witnessed a drop in numbers from 166 to 140. The number of fee payers, an important source of revenue, had been declining steadily and was now only twenty-two. As for the Roxbury boys, they were less and less well prepared to enter the School, and the trustees had to decree that "Roxbury boys who are obliged to repeat a portion of the year's work in order to be promoted, shall hereafter pay a proportionate tuition fee."[127] Collar's report to the trustees that fall—always given by letter since he was rarely invited to their meetings—noted that "the character of the School, as estimated from the social standing of the families represented, is undergoing a change; and that it is becoming increasingly difficult to maintain the preeminence of the classics in the course of study."[128] The following spring (1906), Collar had to announce another faculty defection to Mr. Volkmann's School: Reginald Foster left for a higher salary. In 1906 numbers had risen to 153, but forty-three of the fifty-two applicants had been accepted, of whom six "failed to appear" at the start of school. Among the entering class in 1907 there was not a single fee-payer.[129]

The School's buildings and grounds were an ever-increasing deterrent to attracting students. Collar himself favored moving the School to the Fenway area, but when he suggested at a March 1906 alumni dinner that, if necessary, the present campus might be workable with the purchase of adjacent property, Robert H. Gardiner '72 "disagreed absolutely with the School staying where it is; he said either there must be a change in the character of the School, on the same location, or a change in location if the School is to retain its present character." At the same dinner, J. H. Sears '84 put the alumni case succinctly: "The very life of the School is at stake in this present juncture."[130]

When, therefore, the City of Boston approached the trustees in November 1906 with an offer to purchase the School's building and land for $30,000 (125 percent of its assessed value), the offer seemed too good to be true. (The city intended to combine Roxbury Latin's property with that of the Winthrop Street School and erect a new High School of Commerce, catering to the desires and needs of the area's new population.)[131] The alumni were ecstatic and at a special meeting urged the trustees to sell and promised "such aid as they might be able to give toward paying for a new location, the site favored by them being the so-called Burrage lot at the corner of Jamaica-Way and Perkins St. [in Jamaica Plain]."[132]

The trustees' land committee, headed by none other then Henry Ware Putnam, vetoed this proposal, recommending that

> no proposition to sell the Schoolhouse and grounds be entertained and considered unless and until the School is provided, without expense to itself, with a satisfactory building and grounds elsewhere with accommodations enough better than our present ones to make it an object to move, and with sufficient additional endowment to maintain the School in its new location. . . . They think that this could not be done at a cost of less than $500,000.[133]

In a letter to Philip Cabot the next day, Putnam poured salt on the wound. He began by asserting that the School's present location was

> exceptionally good and better than any other that we know of. It is perfectly clear therefore that the alumni can look for no encouragement.... I cannot say, of course, that, if we were presented with half a million dollars and the Burrage layout with ample endowment, it might not counterbalance even the decisive reasons against [moving the school], but I do not think it would have any effect.[134]

He then went on to urge the alumni to give the trustees the $40,000 they had raised for a new building, so that it could be used as endowment. Putnam, obviously, was dead opposed to moving the School and the old trustees — as yet unleavened by the addition of any alumni trustees — followed his lead, laying out impossible conditions for the alumni.

The graduates were, naturally, both enraged and discouraged by the trustees' rejection of this — to them, essential — move to save the School. Ten prominent alumni demanded an immediate hearing, telling the board that they had

> reached the limit of their power to raise money under present conditions either for annual contribution or for endowment. [They therefore requested] first the resignation of five Trustees in order to give effect to the alumni representation granted by the amendment to the Charter, and [to] further some expression of general lines of policy by the School on which the endeavor to raise funds might be based.[135]

By early 1907 Gorham Rogers's resignation caused a vacancy on the board and the alumni met for the first time to nominate a candidate in accordance with the 1906 Act.[136] Dissatisfaction was rampant, and the gathered alumni offered resolutions asking the trustees for a full disclosure of the School's finances, and pressing them again to move the School.[137]

FIG. 31. Robert
Hallowell Gardiner
'72, here pictured in
his Harvard graduation
photograph. (Harvard Uni-
versity Archives Collection)

Robert Hallowell Gardiner '72 was the alumni's first choice, and the
trustees duly elected him. He had taken the lead, as we have seen, in
trying to save the School, and his generous donations had propped up
faculty salaries for several years. For the next seventeen years, whether
in office (he ultimately became president in 1917) or out (he resigned in
outrage in 1908), Gardiner was to be the principal architect of the
School's future.

He was uniquely positioned for that role. Scion of the Gardiner family of Gardiner, Maine, he was actually born in California in 1855. He
entered Roxbury Latin at age eleven, leaving after Class III to attend
and graduate from high school in Montreal. Returning in 1871 he graduated also from Roxbury Latin with the Class of 1872. He was not only
a Roxbury boy, but also a classicist:

> At the time of Mr. Gardiner's graduation, honors at Harvard were
> obtainable only in three subjects—Latin, Greek, and Mathe-
> matics. On entering Harvard he secured honors in Greek, took the

highest second year honors in Classics in his Sophomore year, was awarded the only Latin part at Commencement, and was second in the list of Phi Beta Kappa.

Following his graduation in 1876, he taught school for two years: the first at DeVeaux College in Niagara Falls and the second at his alma mater in Roxbury. He then studied law, gaining admission to both the Massachusetts and Maine bars. His principal work was the management of trust property, and he served as director of an array of companies and banks. He was elected to eminent lay leadership positions in the Episcopal church and was a prominent pioneer in the worldwide ecumenical movement. Gardiner, then, was not only extraordinarily conversant with all aspects of the School (as student, alumnus, teacher, parent of an alumnus, donor, and now trustee), but he was a man of unusually wide and significant experience in the world beyond school and beyond Roxbury.[138]

His vision and leadership were at once evident in the councils of the trustees. By the June 1907 meeting he had prepared a statement of the School's finances for publication to the alumni and had obtained trustee approval for a five-fold capital appeal "for an additional endowment; for a new school location; for a new school house; for a gymnasium; and for an athletic field."[139]

A committee of alumni forthwith issued a campaign appeal to raise money for the purposes the trustees had just approved:

> The city of Boston has absorbed Roxbury. The growth of the city has increased the density of population in the district around the School. The locality is tending to become a tenement-house district. Within six hundred yards of the present location is a large public high school, which serves the purpose of educating the children of present residents, for the people who are moving into that part of Roxbury do not require for their sons the kind of education which the Roxbury Latin School provides. They do not send their children to college. They do not want a classical education for them.

It is evident that in a very short time parents looking for the best preparatory education for their children will not send them from a distance to attend a school in such a district. . . .

The present standard cannot be maintained in the present situation of the school. Parents who want their boys to be prepared at a day school for university life will not continue to send their children to a school midst a deteriorating district. If the School is moved to a more suitable and promising part of the old Town, it will remain free to the residents of the old Town of Roxbury who can pass a reasonable examination for admission and maintain a fair standard of scholarship. Any boy in Roxbury therefore who *desires* and *deserves* the best education will receive it here free."[140]

While the alumni brochure noted that "We are not committed to any particular site or locality," it contained plans drawn up by Frederick Law Olmsted, Jr., '90 for A. C. Burrage's land overlooking Jamaica Pond in Jamaica Plain (which had, of course, been part of Old Roxbury). This lot was for sale for $160,000, and Mr. Burrage offered to contribute $35,000 of that amount himself. The cost of a new schoolhouse, gymnasium, field, and tennis court was estimated at $225,000.

But the School needed more than a new location and building. The brochure also details the staggering deficits the School was continuing to incur despite stringent economics. The School's investments of $237,000, plus small rents from a few houses, brought it only $13,962.80. When the tuition of all the non-Roxbury boys was added in ($3,612.50), the total income was $2,786.69 less than the total annual expenses ($20,361.99). To increase the School's annual income, then, at least $150,000 in new endowments had to be raised. The brochure therefore concluded with an urgent appeal for a minimum of $500,000 to relocate and reendow the School.

Putnam not only voted against having such an appeal, but a few days after it was launched wrote *The Evening Transcript* a letter stating his opposition to moving the school.[141]

June 1907 was momentous for another reason. It marked the end of William Coe Collar's fifty years at Roxbury Latin. The trustees met in

FIG. 32. The Reverend Theodore Chickering Williams '72, headmaster 1907–09.

May to choose between two candidates for the headmastership—the senior master, Collar's right-hand man Daniel O. S. Lowell, who had taught at the School since 1884, and the Reverend Theodore Chickering Williams '72. Williams was chosen.

Williams grew up in Brookline and was a member of the same class at Roxbury Latin as Robert Hallowell Gardiner, 1872. Like Gardiner, Williams won glittering prizes at Harvard, being elected to Phi Beta Kappa and chosen as Orator at graduation. Also, like Gardiner, he taught high school before entering his chosen profession, the Unitarian ministry. At his graduation from Harvard Divinity School in 1882 he was again Orator of his class. After obtaining his divinity degree he married and was called to All Souls' Church in New York City, where he ministered for thirteen years.

A slightly built man of medium height, he resigned from the church in 1895 because of ill health and went to Europe for a year's rest. Ill health also forced his resignation from both positions he undertook thereafter. In 1899 he was appointed founding headmaster of a boys school in Tarrytown, New York.

> In five years he built Hackley School from its foundations, constructing its beautiful quadrangle, filling it with students, and establishing such traditions of scholarship, manliness and simplicity as have not been surpassed by the oldest schools in the country. Pupils, teachers and parents joined in admiration and affection for him. But such work cannot be done without friction and fatigue. In 1905 he laid down his work and took two years of recuperation in Europe.[142]

His real love was the classics and English poetry. He published English verse translations of Tibullus (1905) and Vergil (1907, 1908, and 1915). He also authored two books of poetry, a volume of sermons, and at least twenty hymns. He was the School's unofficial poet laureate, producing paeans on occasions like the 250th anniversary and Collar's retirement. Frail of body and sensitive of soul, Williams unfortunately lacked the fortitude to face up to recalcitrant trustees and to address the intractable problems that threatened the School's existence.

From the start, Putnam made trouble for the new headmaster. N. Henry Black has described the toll that Putnam had taken on Collar: "In a very brusque manner and with irritating letters [Putnam] was continually trying to meddle with the school. . . . [H]is misguided efforts were most exasperating to a sensitive nature like that of Dr. Collar."[143] Almost before Williams arrived, Putnam showed himself equally officious toward the new headmaster. On June 27, 1907, Collar wrote Lowell, "The antagonism of Mr. Putnam to Mr. Williams has begun before Mr. Williams enters on his office. I am afraid he will do much to harm him before he has a chance." In the spring of his first year, Williams—with the consent of the trustees' president—fired the janitor. At the next meeting "Mr. Putnam moved that the janitor . . . discharged by the head master, be reinstated."[144]

Though there were now three alumni trustees, the old guard still dominated and controlled the board. When Putnam was elected treasurer in December 1908, the young trustees' hopes seemed to be dashed. Gardiner "desired his protest recorded against Mr. Putnam being chosen to this position" and resigned.[145] Urged to reconsider, Gardiner wrote the trustees:

> My resignation last night was no hasty act and was final. It is evident that I differ very widely from the majority of the Board in my ideas as to the needs and management of the School, and although I think I fairly represent the desires of the majority of the Alumni, yet I have failed to bring the majority [of the trustees] to my way of thinking. I see no further use in wasting my time in a hopeless undertaking.[146]

Gardiner's resignation, and the lack of alumni confidence in the board of trustees it manifested, made further fund-raising impossible, and the opportunity to purchase the Burrage lot was lost. There were small gains, however. When, three months later, William H. Slocum '82 was chosen to finish Gardiner's five-year alumnus trustee term, he was immediately elected treasurer in place of Putnam.[147]

6. *Holding Operation, 1909–1921*

Everything seemed to conspire against the School. Already bearing the double burden of its unattractive campus and public knowledge of its financial woes, the School's reputation received a further blow with the abrupt resignation and departure of the new headmaster. By January of his second year, Williams' doctors ordered him to take an "enforced vacation" for reasons of health. Shortly thereafter he tendered his resignation, effective April 1, 1909.[148] The departure of both Williams and Gardiner—the two younger men whom many saw as the hope of the future—devastated an already reeling School.

This time, the trustees chose D. O. S. Lowell. Neither young nor visionary, he would provide what the trustees were looking for in a headmaster—reassurance and stability. The fifty-eight-year-old

Lowell, a master since 1884, had been a valued aide to both Collar and Williams. Tributes in *The Tripod* give us some insight into "who he was":

> Mr. Lowell was born in Denmark, Maine, April 13, 1851, son of a small farmer, on one of those upland farms beautiful for situation, but with a soil which, as Sydney Smith once said, refuses to laugh when tickled with a hoe. He received his early education in the district school, and at fifteen he moved under the careful tuition of Mr. John G. Wight, then Principal of the Academy at North Bridgton. [He attended] the spring and fall sessions, working on the farm summers, and teaching school himself winters. It was not an uncommon thing to see [him], as a boy, after hoeing across a field of corn and back again, drop down at the end of the row to read a few pages before starting across the field. This love of books persisted.
>
> Mr. Lowell received excellent preparation for Bowdoin College which he entered in the fall of 1870, graduating with the class of 1874, and distinguishing himself equally in all branches of the curriculum. Every winter and one fall term while in college he taught school to aid in paying his college expenses. His chief competition and friendly rival for scholastic honors received a final mark of 96.8; Mr. Lowell's mark was 96.5.
>
> After his graduation he was appointed principal of Gould's Academy in Bethel, Maine, where he taught for a year, and with the facility of a genuine New Englander carried on the study of medicine at the same time. The next year (1876) he went to Europe with his medical preceptor, spending four months visiting hospitals in London and Paris, and in general travel. In 1877 he was graduated from the Medical School of Maine, receiving the highest mark ever given in that institution up to that time.
>
> There can be little doubt that a brilliant future was before Mr. Lowell in his chosen profession. His solid acquirements, combined with his ready wit, would have made him, with a little experience, equal to any emergency; while his genial presence in the sick room would have been more valuable than all the drugs recorded in the pharmacopaeia. These flattering prospects Mr. Lowell cheerfully resigned at the call of duty, and in 1878, after

FIG. 33. D. O. S. Lowell, headmaster 1909–1921.

practicing for a few months, he accepted an appointment as Principal of the Ellsworth High School. . . .

In 1882 he spent a year in New York, where he assisted Frank A. Munsey, a former Maine pupil, in editorial work. But once more his deep regard for others caused him to change his plans, and in the fall of 1883 he became principal of the Edward Little High School in Auburn, Maine, from which in 1884 Dr. Collar invited him to the Latin School.

He is an active and consistent church member, always practicing what he preaches. He is an ardent believer in the future of Esperanto, and in 1907 made his third trip abroad for the special purpose of attending the World Congress of Esperantists in Cambridge, England.

He is the author of *Jason's Quest,* has edited the *Roger de Coverley Papers,* and contributed a great number of articles to such periodicals as the *Educational Review, Munsey's, The Youth's Companion,* and *The New York Independent.*

Dr. Grandgent summed up his virtues this way:

> He took it for granted that people should love one another. His heart overflowing with good will, he expected that others would be as cordial to him as he to them. And so they were.
>
> With kind heart and imperturbable cheerfulness went an insatiable hunger for knowledge. He never neglected a chance to gain information from the men he met. If he happened, at dinner, to sit beside an admiral, he would draw from that officer the most interesting data concerning great guns, their range, their sights, their charges; and these he remembered. When, in 1896 and 1897, he was granted a year's leave of absence, he surely traveled farther and profited more than any tourist before or since.

His former students remembered him as stern but kindly:

> I remember the long, long gaze, silent and portentous, leveled at the mischievous lad, while the class sat hushed and no boy moved except the one who squirmed. Dosl was perhaps the most strenuous disciplinarian in the School. We used to hear about his red hair and his fiery temper. Some of us who had been told those tales had occasion in his office, after the monthly reports, to know the truth of them. . . . The sessions in his office, his cluttered, dingy office, where themes were piled to the ceiling, taught us to learn that here was one of the earth's most kindly men, one of its most patient and thoughtful. We never called him Dr. Lowell, except to his face; to teachers and to fellow-students he was Dosl.[149]

Dosl took the reins at the most difficult of times. Not only was the quantity of the student body diminishing, but also now the quality. In 1911 the trustees appointed a committee to investigate why "few or no honors are now obtained in Latin, Greek and English by the boys [of R.L.] taking the Harvard examinations."[150]

Lowell could do nothing himself about the School's ramshackle building, the rapid decline of the neighborhood, or the falling away of the School's traditional clientele. But the one thing he could do—fill faculty vacancies with sound appointments—he did superbly. Drawing from Earl Taylor's reminiscences, a *Tripod* editor years later wrote this charming account of Mr. Taylor's appointment:

> The late winter afternoon of 1910 had plunged the long upper cor-
> ridor of the old Roxbury Latin School into a chilly gloom. As the
> headmaster, Dr. Lowell, returned the length of the hallway from
> answering the School's one telephone, a pay station, he paused to
> turn up the gas in the jet before his office [to add more light].
> Entering, he left the door open to admit some light, for the old
> school boasted no artificial illumination in any room. At his roll-
> top desk, the portly devotee of Esperanto . . . sat down to write a
> letter. There was no school secretary to take his dictation or to
> make a copy for the files. . . . He wanted a new master, a Latin
> teacher who might take a class or two in English or math, a healthy
> chap who could supervise gym periods and had the musical train-
> ing to lead hymns in hall and to organize a School orchestra. . . .
> Mr. Earl W. Taylor . . . came as the answer to Dr. Lowell's
> prayer.[151]

Taylor was to remain at these very tasks, with utmost fidelity, until his retirement in 1952. In 1912 Lowell lured Clarence Gleason back from Volkmann's School. *The Tripod* commented, "Mr. Gleason . . . shows his loyalty to the School by foregoing a part of his present salary to return after an absence of several years."[152] That same year he appointed William P. Dickey, whom Francis Russell has immortalized as "Mutter Dickey" in *Forty Years On*. We need only note that in addition to being a teacher of German and history—notable for "his sense of humor and warm human qualities"—he was an avid ornithologist and outdoors man who developed a corps of woodchoppers among the boys of the School and who led many a snowshoeing expedition in winter. William Plumer Fowler '17 remarks of Dickey:

> Starting life as a poor Mississippi farm boy, he attended schools
> and colleges in the South; and, after pursuing graduate studies at
> Harvard, entered upon his duties as a master at Roxbury Latin
> School in the fall of 1912, and thereafter [for twenty-seven years

until his retirement in 1939] made the school, its students, and its alumni the ruling passion of his life.[153]

In 1918, Lowell appointed Joseph H. Sasserno to teach French. He was, like Dickey, a bachelor, and R.L. was also the ruling passion of his life. He had grown up in the North End, selling newspapers on the street as a boy. After graduating from English High School, he went on to Harvard and then to teach at Norwich University and to serve in the Great War. Sasserno taught at R.L. for thirty-nine years until he retired in 1957, living by his oft-repeated motto: "No matter what others say about a boy, I can always see good in him."[154]

Lowell's achievement as the builder of a great faculty is all the more remarkable in view of the School's ever-worsening situation. Speaking in the winter of 1912, Trustee W. Dudley Cotton, Jr., '93 revealed the School's dire financial straits. According to *The Tripod*,

> [Cotton] said the finances of the School were so low that the trustees could barely meet the expenses, and of the total expenditure for this year, 89% went for teachers' salaries; he compared the salaries paid at our school with those paid in those schools which are our nearest rivals and said that one-half the present faculty were teaching for salaries less than they had been offered to go elsewhere.[155]

A few months later—on May 18, 1912—the principal obstacle to the School's survival was removed by the death of Henry Ware Putnam. Over a decade later, Charles W. Eliot, president emeritus of Harvard, wrote an alumnus (who was engaged in raising money to build the new school) this epitaph for Putnam:

> Henry W. Putnam held back the proper development of the Roxbury Latin School for many years. Are there any descendants of the brothers George Putnam and Henry W. Putnam who recognize that and would like to make amends by giving a sizeable contribution to the new endowment you are preparing to raise?[156]

FIGS. 34–35. Two pictures of the Class of 1913. *Above:* as sixies in June 1908. Note, in the back row, far left, Headmaster T. C. Williams, standing next to D. O. S. Lowell. On the right, in the back row, from left are three masters: Marshall Davis, O. M. Farnham, and Islay McCormick. Note the new tenement on the right. *Below:* as members of Class I in 1913. In the back row, from left are O. M. Farnham, Howard A. Wiggin, Marshall Davis, William P. Dickey, Earl Taylor, Headmaster D. O. S. Lowell, Leighton S. Thompson, and Clarence Gleason.

FIG. 36. The School Orchestra 1911, organized by O. M. Farnham (standing, far right), and conducted for many years thereafter by Earl W. Taylor, master 1911–1952.

FIG. 37. The annual play, begun in 1894, became a fixture of the school year. The cast of the 1913 play, "Daddy," is pictured here with Clarence Gleason (standing, far right), whom D. O. S. Lowell had brought back as master in 1912.

Putnam's demise effectively marked the passing away of the old board. A new board with vision and energy could now set about trying to save the School. A month after his death the trustees issued an appeal for $100,000 for a "Teachers' Salary Fund." "This money is not asked for bricks and mortar, nor for luxuries and frills. It is for the living human forces that make the School." Four months after Putnam's death, an alumni meeting called for changes in the process of selecting trustees.[157] By December the trustees had unanimously requested the Legislature 1) to allow the orderly election every year of an alumnus [no longer necessarily a "graduate"] trustee, with the five-year term of office as in 1906; 2) to allow the alumni the right to nominate life trustees; 3) to permit the First Church to nominate any two deacons, not necessarily the two longest-serving; and 4) to abolish the Roxbury residence requirement. The Act of 1913 resulted.[158]

With Putnam gone, Robert Hallowell Gardiner accepted election as the first alumnus trustee chosen under the 1913 Act. Four years later, upon the retirement of Dr. DeNormandie as minister of the First Church, he became the first lay president of the trustees since the 1789 Charter. His leadership saved the School.

By Collar's final years, loyal alumni and concerned parents had realized that the School would have to move in order to survive. If the School wished to continue to serve its traditional constituency—families aspiring to send their sons on to university for a liberal arts education—it would have to meet the demands of a new generation of parents who wanted their sons educated in attractive surroundings and who desired an all-day program that included afternoon hours playing sports in healthy fresh air. Suburban public high schools with handsome buildings and capacious campuses were springing up all over greater Boston. The area's affluent families were more and more drawn to the many private day and boarding schools established in proximity to the city. The country day school movement was sweeping the nation, and Boston's private day schools were moving out to spacious country campuses. "The Country Day School for Boys of Boston" had been established in 1906 on Nonantum Hill in Newton. R.L.'s rival, Noble and Greenough, combined with Volkmann's and moved to Dedham in 1922.[159] Belmont Hill was founded on spacious grounds in Belmont in 1923. Milton Academy was adorning its extensive country campus with magnificent buildings.[160]

Within eight months of Putnam's death, the trustees secured an option to buy—for $62,000—118,767 square feet (less than three acres) of land on Seaver Street (between Humboldt and Elm Hill Avenues) in Roxbury, across from Franklin Park. Here, they proposed "that a system be adopted by which the boys are kept all day at school and the day divided into periods for recitation, study and bodily exercise."[161] The architect R. Clipston Sturgis was retained to design a schoolhouse and lay out the grounds. His proposal "provided for the erection of a schoolhouse of brick, two stories with a basement, constructed, finished, and equipped like the Winsor School, and fulfiling [*sic*] the requirements as stated by Dr. Lowell after conference with the other teachers."[162]

Included were a dining room with 160 seats and a long-cherished gymnasium with two hundred lockers.[163] The building's cost was estimated at between $97,500 and $124,500. Frederick Law Olmsted, Jr., '90 was called upon—as he had been in 1906—to lay out the surrounding campus. The trustees agreed to exercise their option at once to purchase the property and to launch an appeal for funds.[164] When Trustee W. Dudley Cotton '93 consulted the now-retired headmaster William Coe Collar, Collar advised that the building be constructed of Roxbury pudding stone like that used in the Walnut Street Church.[165]

Work on the campaign began in the summer of 1913 with committees of trustees, alumni, and faculty. By the time of the official launching in January 1914, $35,000 had already been raised.[166] March and April brought additions, but the campaign was then abruptly aborted. Clarence Gleason, writing in 1920, explains why:

> During the winter months [i.e., early 1914] a vast amount of work was done in preparation, and success seemed assured; but alas! owing to the extreme caution of some members of the committee

FIG. 38. Wash drawing of the proposed new schoolhouse (1913) on Seaver Street in Roxbury, across from Franklin Park. R. Clipston Sturgis was the architect.

..., before the fund was half raised the campaign to build the Roxbury Boys' Club was launched. In spite of the critical point we had reached in our scheme, the Roxbury committee refused absolutely to change their plans; and our committee chose to withdraw gracefully rather than endanger the success of both movements. They hoped, however, to take up their plan again in October, and by increased efforts reach a successful completion by spring. Then in August, 1914, came the war and plans were indefinitely postponed. The committee did not feel like asking for further contributions when there were so many urgent calls for help.[167]

The onset of the Great War of 1914–18, which occurred simultaneously with the death of Lowell's wife, brought the School many additional trials.[168] The infantile paralysis epidemic of 1916 and the catastrophic national influenza epidemic of 1918–19 added further woes. Regarding the latter, Lowell wrote the trustees on December 18, 1918:

The term about to close has been greatly broken up by the influenza; for though there were few if any cases among the pupils and teachers, we suspended all work for about three weeks in September-October. We have made up about one half of the time lost by teaching on Saturdays; and by February 8th, if all goes well, the whole time will be made up.

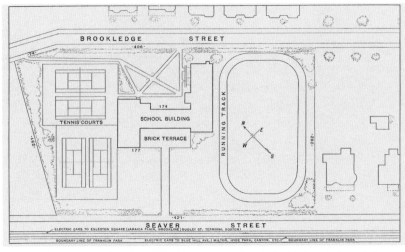

FIG. 39. Plan of the proposed Seaver Street campus by Frederick Law Olmsted, Jr. '90.

It is a wonder that the School suffered so little sickness in the epidemic: there was no drinking fountain and boys drank water from a common cup filled at the tap; they also shared common towels.[169] *The Tripod's* wry comments in 1918 show that there was no weakening in the School's Puritan rigor as regards the weather: "Sept. 1916. Public schools closed on account of heat. R.L.S. stayed open. January 1918. Public schools closed on account of cold. R.L.S. stayed open. Some school!"[170]

Meanwhile, the School's enrollment continued to drop: by the fall of 1918 numbers had fallen to 129 from a high of 185 in 1895. In 1916 Lowell launched a modest initiative to reach out to the new inhabitants of Roxbury. The School announced that it would try to accommodate public school children who wished to finish at their elementary school before transferring to Roxbury Latin: local boys were encouraged to enter Class IV and special adjustments were promised.[171] A special Committee on Reaching Roxbury Citizens was formed[172] and a circular with a "free district" map was sent out to prospective applicants regarding the new four-year program.[173] But this effort bore little fruit, with a mere four boys entering the new program in 1917 and only one in 1918.[174]

Meanwhile, applicants to Class VI continued to fall precipitously: from eighty-three in 1904, to sixty-three in 1911, to thirty-four in 1918.[175]

Quality was as great a problem as quantity. The committee appointed to investigate the decline in academic achievement in the School finally reported in 1915 that "the scholarship at the School . . . was in their opinion below the standard which should be maintained."[176] In 1916, the trustees voted "to employ an educational expert to examine and report on the condition of the School." In the end, they consulted five.[177] Three were R.L. alumni (Professors Kittredge '78 and Grandgent '79 of Harvard and Professor Samuel M. Waxman '04 of Boston University). Two were "outsiders," Professor Inglis of Harvard and Dr. Adam Leroy Jones of Columbia. The three alumni were laudatory in their appraisal, suggesting only minor curricular changes. Inglis's response is lost. Dr. Jones' report is the most interesting, coming as it does from someone with no investment in the place. Though he obviously had his own biases (he was no lover of the classics, for example), his view has a certain objectivity lacking in the others:

> In some cases the instructor was handicapped by having too many in a class. Thirty is pretty generally recognized as a maximum. For ideal teaching a class distinctly smaller, not more than half that size, would be desirable.
>
> Practically without exception the pupils were interested and eager. It should, however, be a matter of some concern that a good school which has a long and honorable history of the Roxbury Latin School should be more fully appreciated by the community in which it is situated. It should have a waiting list for every class, and be able to select the best and most promising. . . .
>
> Why does the School not appeal to a greater number? The fact that the building is old and that the surroundings are not especially attractive may explain the fact at least in part. . . . A course primarily classical makes a somewhat limited appeal. . . . New doctrines are being preached and new experiments are being tried all over the country. Which, if any of these, might have something of value for the Roxbury Latin School?

FIGS. 40–44. The Schoolhouse in the final decade, 1916–1926: *above,* the Hall; *below,.* the Library; *opposite top,* Class I Room; *opposite middle,* Class IV Room; *opposite bottom,* Class V Room

. . . The growing size and heterogeneity of the community and its changing character . . . have in all probability choked out [community] interest to a very great extent. . . . The problem is to re-establish the School in something like its old place in the community. . . . The complete accomplishment of such a program would involve a new site and new buildings. The new site already secured seems to me admirably suited for the purpose. . . .

The first step would seem to me to be a development of the common life of the school, a development which has been admirably carried out in the Country Day school. A longer day, preparation for the next day made for the most part at the school, more work together, more play together, less time for the streets and for the moving picture show, a hundred and one devices for making school life the one great interest of the boy,—these seem to me necessary if the school is to count as it should count. The social life, as well as the intellectual life, of the boys should be centered in the school. . . .

There are many boys of first-rate mental ability [in the community] whom [Roxbury Latin's classical] curriculum would not suit well, but in a school which does not attempt to be all things to all men that is not a matter of serious concern, provided that the school is doing what is worth doing, and provided that it has a sufficient number of applicants of first-rate ability.[178]

The trustees forthwith endorsed the "country day" concept, asking the faculty "to prepare . . . a plan for further developing the School curriculum along the lines of an 'all day' school with prescribed periods for recitation, for study and for physical exercise."[179] Athletics were still not an integral part of school life: there was no "athletic director"; coaches, if any, were brought in to help out for a few hours each day. By 1918, Roxbury Latin's perennial losing records against schools with better facilities and coaching had aroused much concern among the alumni. The Alumni Council petitioned the trustees regarding "the low estate of athletic interest and achievement at the School" and strongly recommended the appointment of an athletic director, the amount of whose salary they offered to raise by subscription."[180] The trustees agreed at once. Not until 1920 was this new position filled. However, the man who filled it—J. Leo Foley, Harvard graduate with five years of coaching experience—was eminently worth waiting for. He almost single-handedly turned around the School's sports fortunes. Serving the School for forty-one years until his retirement in 1961, "Foxy" Foley was famous (to Nobles's headmaster Eliot Putnam, infamous) for his bizarre football plays which often enabled smart but inferior R.L. teams to triumph. Though his real love was track, he also coached varsity baseball.[181]

Meanwhile the old schoolhouse continued to deteriorate. The shortage of coal due to the war and the collapsing heating system combined to create disastrous conditions. In March 1918 Lowell wrote to the trustees:

> The coal shortage affected us, but did not compel us to close the school. We shut off afternoon activities, banked the fires about noon, and tried with indifferent success to keep warm from 9 till 2. But the furnace in the north end of the building behaved wretchedly, and Mr. Farnham reports that on half the days since December his room has not reached the 60° mark during the day. On one day I dismissed the Sixth Class, since the thermometer failed to reach 50°. . . . The furnace on the south end has on several occasions proved inefficient also. Class rooms 3 and 4 have at times been the only ones we could keep comfortable.

Because of new city codes, the trustees could not correct the heating situation without triggering the city's requirement of an extensive ventilating system—which would have necessitated the costly restructuring of the entire building.[182] Naturally, they were reluctant to make major repairs since they intended to move the school. When the war ended, a committee was reappointed in June 1919 "for raising a fund for a new school building and adding to the endowment of the school."[183] Meanwhile, conditions continued to worsen in the old building.[184]

But the trustees could not act immediately. They faced a triple quandary.

First, they needed a headmaster who could lead the School into the future. Lowell was nearing seventy and was tired from the trials of war. Theodore D. Hersey '20 wrote Roger Ernst from his freshman dormitory at Harvard:

> I have heard graduates express dissatisfaction with the 'spirit' of boys at school. . . . Much of the *inertia* at School is because of the general opinion 'oh nothing can happen here while "Dos!" is headmaster.' In other words, *he does not inspire*. I firmly believe that the only kind of man who can put the school on its feet is the kind that boys will 'fall for'; the man whose personality will urge them on. . . . At present, I do not believe there is any wonderful loyalty among the undergrads, for the simple reason they cannot think of the school on any higher level than the head—Dr. Lowell. . . . I believe it of the utmost importance that a new man of ginger and *enthusiasm* be our next headmaster.[185]

Second, the trustees had also begun to worry that the Seaver Street lot—where the new school was to be located—was an unhappy halfway house: the neighborhood adjoining this lot was now itself rapidly declining, and the tiny 2.73–acre lot was by no means large enough for the School to implement a true "country day" program.[186] By the war's end, the School's traditional clientele had almost completely deserted the "easterly part of Roxbury" where both the Kearsarge Avenue and Seaver Street parcels were located. By 1918, the only master still living in Roxbury was O. M. Farnham.

Finally, to the nation at large, war had brought a staggering increase in the cost of living: 79.9 percent from 1915 to 1919. Masters' salaries had fallen considerably in real terms, and the rampant inflation showed no signs of abating.[187] Lowell assessed the situation in his report to the trustees of March 1920:

> Another financial year has rolled around, and I believe the Roxbury Latin School has reached the greatest crisis in its 275 years of existence. With this view I have reason to believe that the Trustees and Alumni Advisory Council concur; that they feel without an immediate increase of our endowment, an evitable decay of our

efficiency must soon begin, and that the Old School that has stood among the leaders in the past will gradually lose its standing and its influence.

But the financial uncertainties of the time in the nation and in New England hardly created a climate conducive to raising the money necessary to relocate and reendow the School. Even for a revitalized board of trustees, the challenge of the future was harrowing indeed.

Notes to Part Four

1. Francis S. Drake, *The Town of Roxbury* (Boston: Municipal Printing Office, 1905), 211–12. Winslow (1811–1873) is buried in Forest Hills Cemetery.
2. Roxbury Grammar School-Secretary's Records (Hereafter RGS-Secretary's Records), 1843–1870, 337 (9 June 1869).
3. See Trustee Minutes 1870–1896 (hereafter TM) 12 (8 March 1871), 35 (25 March 1872), and 38 (12 June 1872). At this third meeting the Examining Committee "recommended the adoption of the following order: Ordered, that hereafter girls as well as boys be allowed the privileges of the Latin School under such regulations as the Examining committee may deem expedient." The report "was accepted and consideration of the order referred to the next meeting of the Board." TM 43 (11 September 1872): "After a full discussion of the subject the passage of the order [admitting girls] was indefinitely postponed." There were two other considerations of coeducation. See RGS-Secretary's Records, 1789–1843, 151 (9 December 1816): when the trustees considered (and later rejected) adding "another storey [to the schoolhouse] for accommodation of females." And see RGS-Secretary's Records, 1843–1870, 213 (21 June 1859) when it was "Voted that Messrs. Sleeper and Anderson be a committee to ascertain what has been the experience of teachers in regard to mixt schools, so called, and report the advantages and disadvantages of such a system, with any information they may be able to obtain on the best mode of High School instruction." In September, their report was "accepted"; it was presumably negative. The investigation was undertaken in the midst of the final stage of the School-City controversy and probably resulted from city pressures. A year later, the relationship had ended.
4. TM 58–61 (11 June 1873).
5. TM 90 (10 March 1875), 95 (13 April 1875), 97 (4 June 1875). See also N. Henry Black, "Science Teaching at the Roxbury Latin School," undated, unpublished MS.
6. *The Tripod* 3, 1 (October 1890): 4–6.
7. Clarence Gleason, unpublished and untitled MS 1942.
8. *The Tripod* 21, 7 (April 1909): 6.
9. TM 135 (12 June 1878).
10. *The Tripod* 22, 2 (November 1909) contains obituaries of Daniell, who left R.L. for financial reasons in 1884 to become principal of Chauncy Hall. See also the *Record of the Class of 1863 (Fiftieth Anniversary), Harvard College,* 39–41.
11. "Crossing the Street," in *The Tripod* 38, 1 (October 1925): 5.
12. TM 165–66 (10 September 1879).
13. Drake, *The Town of Roxbury,* 264.
14. *The Tripod* 24, 5 (February 1912): 7.
15. On cricket and sport in general, see C. Frank Allen, "The School in the Civil War" in Francis Russell, *Forty Years On* (West Roxbury: The Roxbury Latin School,

1970), 22–23. For the quotation, see Walter Eliot Thwing '68 in *The Tripod* 24, 5 (February 1912): 7.

16. Charles S. Hamlin in the *Roxbury Latin School Alumni Bulletin*, May 1931, 1. Allen, "The School in the Civil War," says Miller's Field was "perhaps half a mile away"!

17. TM 232 (19 September 1883).

18. TM 297 (14 September 1886) and 301 (December 8, 1886).

19. *The Tripod* 5, 1 (October 1892): 9.

20. RSG-Secretary's Record, 1843–1870, 85, 90 (14 March 1848, 25 April 1848).

21. RGS-Secretary's Record, 1843–1870, 314 (11 December 1866).

22. *Roxbury Latin School Alumni Bulletin*, January 1931, 1, says it was founded 26 May 1881, and that Gardiner '72, Rousmaniere '79, and Grant '79 wrote its constitution.

23. *Roxbury Latin School Alumni Bulletin*, June 1961, quoting a clipping from the *Boston Home Journal* of 1881.

24. John Roach, *A History of Secondary Education in England, 1800–1870* (London: Longman, 1986), 8–12.

25. Oscar Handlin, *John Dewey's Challenge to Education* (New York: Harper, 1959), 20.

26. TM 125 (12 September 1877).

27. TM 138 (12 December 1877).

28. TM 143 (11 September 1878).

29. TM 147–8 (11 December 1878).

30. H. C. Bernard, *A History of English Education from 1760*, 2d ed. (London: U. of London Press, 1961), 16.

31. Henry W. Putnam, "Oration Delivered Before the City Council and Citizens of Boston . . . 4 July 1893" (Boston 1893). Putnam speaks of "that great human stream of unity and progress which the English speaking races are pouring out . . . wherever the American or British flag is carried"(p. 9). "It cannot be wholly the bias in the blood which pronounces the stately march of the [English-speaking] race to universal freedom and almost boundless empire, to be the foremost movement in human history. . . . [T]his grand thought is at once the comfort and the inspiration of the English-speaking millions and of their *adopted* [emphasis added] fellow citizens. . . . (p. 10)." He then works up a lather over all the evils of American society: "great cities sinking in the mire of corruption as they grow larger and more heterogeneous in their population . . . alien races, seemingly almost incapable of assimilation with our political and social systems, seeking in unlimited numbers the untrammelled and irresponsible enjoyment of both. . . . "(pp. 11–12). "The grave difficulties thrown around the problem of municipal government, and, indirectly, of all government, by our inpouring foreign population" are next addressed (pp. 35–36). "What the Persian hosts were to Greece . . . what the Moors were to Spain . . . that the Chinese are, or seem, to our friends in California . . . whether the Oriental comes with sword and spear or with flatiron and pick it is himself, his habits, his religion, and his social order that have ever been the stumbling block. . . . " (38–39). "The question must be, at any given moment, Have we so digested and

assimilated what we have got that we can receive more without imperilling the results which it is the mission of the Anglo-Saxon race to accomplish?"(41) . . . [W]e have decidedly less restraint than is desirable upon immigration from Europe . . . we have been too hospitable to the anarchist, the nihilist, the socialist, the dynamiter. We gamble with our birthright"(42).

32. See Alexander von Hoffman, *Local Attachments* (Baltimore: Johns Hopkins U. Press, 1994), 169ff. The town of West Roxbury voted 720 to 613 in favor of annexation to Boston in 1873 and was annexed in 1874.

33. Turning back to the discussion in Part II of the term "free school," the reader will note that A. W. Parry and others clearly demonstrate, in fact, that the term "free school" (the term Bell himself and the feoffees used) means open to all, not limited to inhabitants of a certain geographical area. Parry asserts, *Education in England in the Middle Ages* (London: University Tutorial Press, 1920), 67–71, that "We may consequently regard the institution of 'free' grammar schools as marking a stage in the policy of breaking down the barriers which separated parish from parish, and township from township." See also George H. Kidder, "Report to the Trustees of Roxbury Latin School" (Boston 1981), 10–13, with numerous citations of legal cases.

34. This report of J. G. Fitch, Esq. is typical of what the commissioners heard and concluded. See *Schools Inquiry Commission*, IX, 152–53. See also A. H. D. Acland and H. L. Smith, *Studies in Secondary Education* (New York: Macmillan, 1892), 18, 41–42.

35. TM 208 (14 June 1882). For years following there were heated discussions about the boundaries of "Old Roxbury." See TM 227–229 (9 June 1909); TM 234–35 (22 September 1909) when a lawsuit was threatened; TM 243 (8 June 1910) when a fee was remitted; TM 278–79 (18 December 1912) where the territory is defined; TM 344 (15 December 1915): "Voted, that the secretary be authorized to obtain a map or maps showing as nearly as may be the limits of the Town of Roxbury in 1672"; TM 354 (14 March 1916) when it was voted to have the city engineer prepare a map; TM 381 (21 March 1917) where a circular was to be prepared which included a map of the "free district." Disputes continued unabated until the geographical discrimination ceased in 1960.

36. Oscar Handlin, *Boston's Immigrants*, rev.ed., (New York: Atheneum, 1959), 15.

37. Oscar Handlin, *Boston's Immigrants*, 99. Sam Bass Warner, Jr., *Streetcar Suburbs*, 2d ed. (Cambridge: Harvard U. Press, 1978), 84 and 109, describes how, for a time, the School "delayed class movement" in the area. Henry C. Binford, *The First Suburbs* (Chicago: U. of Chicago Press, 1985), p. 88, says coaches to Boston every other hour were instituted in Roxbury in the mid-1820s. See also p. 12 on population. See R. W. Hale, Jr., *Tercentenary History* (Cambridge: Riverside Press, 1946), 141, on the homogeneity of the School's population in the mid- and late-ninteenth century.

38. *Tercentenary Celebration of the First Church in Roxbury*, Roxbury 1930.

39. James DeNormandie, "The Ancient Landmark: A Sermon, 4 May 1902" (Boston: South End Industrial School, 1902), 12–13.

40. Roger Ernst letter to Arthur Perry, 10 June 1946. The results in the School's 1920 mock presidential election show that the parents (whose influence is presumably reflected in the results) were still staunchly conservative. The Republican candidates (Harding and Coolidge) won 115–20.

41. *The Tripod* 60, 2 (January 1948): 5.

42. *The Tripod* 12, 2 (November 1899): 5.

43. *The Tripod* 1, 4 (June 1889): 6. The column concludes on a "Who-wants-a-brick-building?" note, further illustrating the author's defensiveness.

44. *The Tripod* 2, 6 (March 1890): 4.

45. *The Tripod* 4, 3 (December 1891): 4.

46. TM 369 (11 March 1891).

47. Two of the seven trustees asked that their declination to vote be recorded. See TM 380–81 (9 December 1891).

48. *The Tripod* 7, 6 (March 1895): 4. See also 9, 2 (November 1896). The need for "a hot, palatable lunch" and a gymnasium had been discussed as early as 1889 in *The Tripod* 2, 2 (October 1889): 3.

49. *The Tripod* 15, 5 (February 1903): 5.

50. *The Tripod* 16, 8 (May 1904): 7.

51. *The Tripod* 66, 4 (June 1954): 6. For an account of the graveyard, see also Lindsay Swift '74 in *The Tripod* 29, 1 (October 1916): 6–7.

52. TM 359 (11 June 1890). The First Church first deeded the cemetery to the School, but the City of Boston successfully exerted its claim to ownership of the graveyard, as inheritor of the properties of the former town of Roxbury.

53. *The Tripod* 1, 1 (March 1889): 5. Collar is credited on this page with inspiring the founding of this publication. Its first Board is noteworthy: David Taggart Clark '89 was editor, A. H. Thorndike '89 associate editor, and Frederick Law Olmsted, Jr. '90 business manager!

54. *The Tripod* 3, 10 (July 1891): 4.

55. *The Tripod* 4, 10 (July 1892): 4. See also TM 371 (10 June 1891).

56. TM 389 (8 June 1892). See also *The Tripod* 5, 7 (April 1893): 9.

57. *The Tripod* 5, 8 (May 1893): 7.

58. *The Tripod* 15, 1 (October 1902).

59. *The Tripod* 8, 8 (May 1896): 6.

60. TM 35 (21 December 1898).

61. *The Tripod* 11, 4 (January 1899): 7.

62. Russell, *Forty Years On*, 29.

63. Russell, "The Pattern of a City," in *Forty Years On*, 45.

64. *The Tripod* 1, 2 (April 1889): 7.

65. *The Tripod* 2, 1 (October 1889): 4–5. See also, 4, 1 and 5, 1, *et seq.*

66. *The Tripod* 5, 1 (October 1892): 5.

67. *The Tripod* 5, 8 (May 1893): 4.

68. TM 372 (10 June 1891). Hale, *Tercentenary History*, 137, asserts that "Mr. Collar's

interests were in physical training rather than competitive sports. He would have preferred a gymnasium to military drill . . ., and when military drill was discontinued he instituted fencing in the basement, which was later partly fitted up as a gymnasium."

69. *The Tripod* 6, 1 (October 1893): 6.

70. TM 425 (13 June 1894).

71. TM (9 June 1897): 16–17.

72. *The Tripod* 6, 4 (January 1894): 3–5. See also 5, 2 (November 1892): 9. 6, 9 (June 1894): 2 has a wrap-up of the season: "Our success was not great. Still we managed to beat Hoppy and keep out of last place—two laudable attainments."

73. *The Tripod* 7, 3 (December 1894): 14.

74. *The Tripod* 6, 1 (October 1893): 5–6; TM 412 (27 September 1893).

75. *The Tripod* 6, 4 (January 1894): 5.

76. Ibid.

77. TM 448 (25 September 1895).

78. *The Tripod* 8, 1 (October 1895): 5.

79. *The Tripod* 8, 3 (December 1895): 5, 12.

80. *The Tripod* 9, 2 (November 1896): 7.

81. *The Tripod* 10, 1 (October 1897): 5.

82. *The Tripod* 11, 2 (November 1898): 4.

83. *The Tripod* 11, 4 (January 1899): 11.

84. *The Tripod* 11, 7 (April 1899): 5.

85. *The Tripod* 66, 2 (January 1954): 4.

86. See Ellery Clark, "The School's First Olympian," in *The Roxbury Latin Newsletter*, 57, 3 (April 1984): 11.

87. *The Tripod* 6, 6 (March 1894): 4. For a lengthy review, see 6, 7 (April 1894): 6–7. Hale, *Tercentenary History*, 140, says the orchestra originated in 1889.

88. *The Tripod* 6, 7 (April 1894): 4.

89. Hale, *Tercentenary History*, 140, gives a detailed account of the venue of the plays between 1894 and 1945.

90. DeNormandie, "The Ancient Landmark: A Sermon," 9–12.

91. See TM 35 (21 December 1898). Azariah Smith tendered his resignation as a trustee. The trustees did not accept it and voted "that in the opinion of the Board Mr. Smith's removal from Roxbury did not necessitate his resignation. . . . " He withdrew his resignation. If this "removal" was permanent and not temporary, his remaining in office was a clear violation of the Charter of 1789.

92. *The Tripod* 14, 7 (April 1902): 2.

93. TM 446 (25 September 1895).

94. TM 455–56 (11 March 1896).

95. TM 8 (23 September 1896).

96. TM 11 (9 December 1896).

97. *The Tripod* 13, 1 (October 1999): 4.

98. TM 36 (6 February 1899) and 38 (15 March 1899).

99. TM 34 (21 December 1898). See also TM 41 (15 March 1899).

100. See TM 46 (27 September 1898), 45 (28 September 1900), 78 (18 December 1901); and *The Tripod* 11, 6 (March 1899): 5, and 13, 3 (December 1900): 2.

101. *The Tripod* 14, 7 (April 1902): 2.

102. TM 81 (19 March 1902).

103. TM 87 (11 June 1902). See also, slightly earlier, Putnam's rejection of a fee for Roxbury boys who wanted to fence: TM 76 (18 December 1901).

104. N. Henry Black, "Science Teaching at the Roxbury Latin School," undated, unpublished MS.

105. *The Tripod* 37, 2 (November 1924): 9.

106. *The Tripod* 30, 2 (November 1917): 5.

107. *The Tripod* 59, 3 (May 1947). See also *The Tripod* 30, 2 (November 1917): 4; 23, 9 (June 1911): 7–8; and 30, 6 (March 1918): 3–5.

108. TM 96–97 (18 March 1903).

109. TM 110 (16 March 1904).

110. Unpublished MS, 65; TM 141 (14 June 1905).

111. TM 151 (21 March 1906).

112. *The Tripod* 20, 9 (June 1908): 19.

113. *The Tripod* 18, 6 (March 1906): 4–6.

114. Letter to William A. Gaston, 22 June 1903.

115. Letter to William A. Gaston, 30 June 1903.

116. Letter to Robert H. Gardiner, 27 June 1903.

117. Letter to Robert H. Gardiner, 1 July 1903.

118. TM 112 (21 May 1904).

119. TM 112–113 (21 May 1904).

120. TM 113 (21 May 1904).

121. Ibid.

122. TM 128 (21 December 1904).

123. *The Tripod* 17, 6 (March 1905): 5.

124. TM 131 (15 March 1905).

125. TM 136–141 (14 June 1905).

126. TM 153 (21 March 1906). The Act is officially Chapter 113 of the Acts of Legislature of 1906: "An Act Relative to the membership of the Board of Trustees of the Roxbury Latin School." See the letters of Putnam to Gardiner of 20 March, 22 March, and 13 April 1905 in which Putnam tries to head Gardiner off on the Charter change.

127. TM 144 (27 September 1905).

128. TM 147 (20 December 1905).

129. TM 160 (26 September 1906) and 187 (24 September 1907).

130. *The Tripod* 18, 6 (March 1906): 4–6.

131. TM 161 (5 November 1906).

132. TM 162 (5 November 1906). The alumni meeting was held on 2 November 1906.
133. TM 162–63 (5 November 1906).
134. Letter to Philip Cabot, 6 November 1906.
135. TM 164–65 (16 December 1906).
136. The Alumni Association had been formed in 1881. It met annually until 1889 and then lapsed. It then met again for the 250th anniversary and by the 1906 Act became the vehicle by which the alumni nominated their representatives to the Board of Trustees.
137. TM 170–71. The meeting was held 8 March 1907 at the Exchange Building, 53 State Street.
138. See *The Tripod* 29, 7 (April 1917): 3–4; TM 173 (8 March 1907) and 179 (20 March 1907).
139. TM 185 (12 June 1907).
140. "Revised Proposal for the Benefit of the Roxbury Latin School." Undated, it refers to the 261st school year (i.e., 1905–06), but it was probably issued in the summer of 1907. See TM 181–82 (1 May 1907) and TM 184–85 (12 June 1907).
141. Letter in the *Boston Evening Transcript*, 21 June 1907. The trustee minutes do not record Putnam's negative vote, but he says in his letter that he voted against the proposal.
142. T. H. Palmer in his introduction to Williams' *Georgics and Eclogues of Vergil*, quoted by Walter H. Marx in "Theodore Chickering Williams, Class of 1872" in *The Roxbury Latin School Newsletter*, 58, 2 (January 1985): 10.
143. *In Memoriam, William Coe Collar*, printed for the Friday Evening Club (Boston: Ginn & Co., 1916), 19–20.
144. Letter of W. C. Collar to D. O. S. Lowell, 25 June 1907. And TM 204 (10 June 1908).
145. TM 216 (22 December 1908).
146. TM 217 (23 December 1908).
147. TM 223–24 (17 March 1909).
148. *The Tripod* 21, 5 (February 1909): 8; 21, 6 (March 1909): 4; and TM 222 (17 March 1909). *The Tripod* 27, 8 (May 1915) contains his obituary.
149. This is a conflation of *The Tripod* 21, 6 (March 1909): 4–6; 33, 9 (June 1921): 7–8; and 40, 7 (April 1928): 7–17. Lowell's *A Munsey-Hopkins Genealogy* was published in 1920.
150. TM 252 (20 December 1911). See also TM 328 (22 December 1914), an example of the ongoing discussion of this and related topics.
151. *The Tripod* 64, 2 (February 1952): 5–6. See also Thomas Goethals's tribute in the *Roxbury Latin School Alumni Bulletin* (March 1952).
152. *The Tripod* 24, 7 (April 1912): 5.
153. *The Tripod* 62, 3 (March 1950): 11.
154. *The Tripod* 62, 1 (November 1949).
155. *The Tripod* 24, 7 (April 1912): 5.
156. See the obituary in *The Tripod* 24, 9 (June 1912) and the letter of Charles W. Eliot

to William B. Wheelwright, 4 June 1923. See also letter of William Coe Collar to W. Dudley Cotton, 26 December 1911, commenting on plans for building a new school: "But what a wall of resistance you are going to encounter in the Board itself! . . . The same man [H. W. Putnam] who thwarted, in my opinion, the recent effort to raise a large sum, will oppose this change to the bitter end. If you can carry this scheme through, you will be the School's greatest benefactor."

157. TM 267 (30 July 1912).

158. TM 284 (19 March 1913). The official title was "An Act Relative to Membership on the Board of Trustees of the Roxbury Latin School", Chapter 129 of the Acts of 1913.

159. See Richard T. Flood, *The Story of Noble and Greenough School, 1866–1966* (Dedham: Nobles, 1966). Noble's Classical School was founded in 1866. Mr. Noble brought in his son-in-law, James J. Greenough, in 1892, and the school became Noble and Greenough. Arthur L. K. Volkmann had emigrated from Germany in 1872 at age fourteen. A graduate of Cornell, he came to Boston to teach at Hopkinson's School. In 1895, he founded his own school, the Volkmann School. In 1897 Mr. Hopkinson closed his school, the pupils going mostly to Noble and Greenough. Mr. Greenough died in 1913, and the school was incorporated that year as a non-profit institution. In 1917 Mr. Volkmann's School, suffering from the anti-German hysteria of the Great War of 1914–18, was merged into Noble and Greenough. Charles Wiggins II was chosen as headmaster following Mr. Noble's death in 1919, and his ardent championing of the "country day concept" underlay Nobles' move to Dedham.

160. A similar movement was underway in England. Most of the great London schools (Westminster being the notable exception) moved to the edges of the city (as St.Paul's from the Cathedral to Hammersmith in 1890) or to country towns (as Charterhouse to Godalming in 1872, and Christ's Hospital to Horsham in 1902).

161. TM 281 (8 January 1913) and 284 (19 March 1913). See also the lengthy rationale of W. Dudley Cotton, Jr., secretary of the board, 8 January 1913.

162. TM 285–86 (25 March 1913).

163. *The Tripod* 26, 1 (October 1913): 34.

164. Sturges's plans were approved in June 1913. A year later—see TM 307 (4 April 1914)—the trustees decided to add seven thousand square feet of adjoining land in order to have a proper football field. Olmsted donated his work on the new lot as his contribution to the appeal—see TM 353 (15 March 1916). Hale, *Tercentenary History*, 145, says the Seaver Street site was the only undeveloped plot of land of sufficient size remaining in the "easterly part of Roxbury."

165. Letter of Collar to Cotton, 12 January 1913.

166. *The Tripod* 26, 5 (February 1914): 10; 26 (March 1914): 11; 27 (November 1914): 4.

167. *The Tripod* 32, 5 (February 1920): 9.

168. In the summer of 1917 (the year of America's entry into the war), the School established an "agricultural camp" in Dover. Sixteen R.L. boys lived there in tents and helped grow 800 bushels of onions and 250 bushels of carrots for the war effort.

169. See 3 February 1917 letter of James A. Tobey '11 to W. Dudley Cotton.
170. *The Tripod* 30, 4 (January 1918): 11.
171. TM 369 (20 December 1916).
172. TM 370 (20 December 1916).
173. TM 381 (21 March 1917).
174. TM 392 (13 June 1917), 412 (12 June 1918), and 420 (25 September 1918).
175. Statistics furnished by Lowell to Stanwood G. Wellington as recorded by him in a letter to Dr. Hilbert F. Day, 18 March 1918. See addendum to Lowell's report to the trustees of 18 December 1918 for the 1918 figure.
176. TM 333 (18 March 1915).
177. TM 369 (20 December 1916), 407 (20 March 1918).
178. *The Tripod* 29, 5 (February 1917): 5–7; see also TM 421 (18 December 1918) which sets forth Prof. Grandgent's statistical standing of R.L. boys in comparison to boys of certain other schools. "This showed that our boys had on the whole done better than boys from the schools selected for comparison, especially in science."
179. TM 401 (7 August 1917).
180. TM 413 (12 June 1918). See also *The Tripod* 31, 1 (October 1918): 5.
181. See *The Tripod* 33, 1 (October 1920): 8; and 60, 1 (November 1950): 6; 67, 2 (February 1955): 20. See also *Roxbury Latin School Alumni Bulletin* (June 1961) and *The Roxbury Latin School Newsletter* (January 1974).
182. See Neil J. Savage, "How the School Acquired its Present Property," *The Roxbury Latin School Newsletter* 58, 1 (October 1984): 7.
183. TM 2 (11 June 1919).
184. See O. M. Farnham's 20 March 1920 letter to Lowell, attached to Lowell's report to the trustees.
185. Letter of Theodore D. Hersey '20 to Roger Ernst, 18 September 1920. See also the letter of Trustee W. Dudley Cotton to Robert S. Hale, 6 December 1917: "Dr. Lowell is a pedagogue and a successful one, but his influence on the school and the teachers is necessarily reactionary. . . . If it were possible to persuade some man of position, means and a fit for leadership to take command, I believe all our discouragements would cease." Lowell, in his report to the trustees of 11 June 1919, expresses the desire to remain until 1924 (his fortieth year), but acquiesces to the board's new policy requiring retirement by seventy—which would for him mean 1921 or 1922.
186. See Lowell's report to the trustees, 26 September 1917: "A 'country day school' seems to mean *a day school in the country*. We are not in the country, neither is the new schoolhouse lot. Ideal conditions seem to demand a lot of ten to twenty acres, in the *Westerly* Part of the Town of Roxbury, near a lake, either natural or artificial, with two or three football fields, four or five baseball fields, six or eight tennis courts, a running track, an athletic building . . ."
187. See Lowell's report to the trustees, 16 December 1919.

Part Five

It will be the duty of the lower school, who will have seen both the old and the new, to make sure that Roxbury Latin, though dressed in more modern apparel, is the same underneath and still represents the same aristocracy of learning and democracy of spirit which it has in the past.

—EDITORIAL IN The Tripod, JUNE 1926

Roxbury Latin School: In an anti-classical age, a small rock.

—CAPTION IN Time, JUNE 4, 1945

Part Five

West Roxbury
The 1920s to the Present

⟶ ⟨▨▨▨▨▨▨▨▨▨▨▨▨▨▨▨▨▨▨▨▨⟩ ◦

W HEN THE Reverend James DeNormandie resigned the pastorate of Roxbury's First Church and the presidency of the School's trustees in 1917—the year of America's entry into World War I—the trustees had forthwith elected Robert Hallowell Gardiner '72 to succeed him. As we have seen, Gardiner had spearheaded the alumni revolt against the old guard trustees. Year by year, the board was now being invigorated with new blood: in 1906 there had been only two alumni on the thirteen-member board; by 1920 the entire board, except the church's three representatives, were graduates.

The new trustees realized the magnitude of the difficulties facing the School. Trustee Robert Sever Hale '87 perhaps best summarized the way they viewed the School when he wrote Gardiner on August 21, 1917:

> Roxbury Latin School thirty years ago stood well up in the list of schools which taught straight writing and straight thinking. Since that time education, like all other branches of learning, has made many steps ahead. Our school has practically stood still, and to my mind is in the condition of an old firm whose past reputation is high, but which has kept its books by single entry, and has never taken account of stock. Such a firm cannot get new money for extension . . . unless its management shows a desire to adopt the most efficient methods whenever they are different from the old ones.

As the war ended, the trustees turned their attention first to finding a dynamic headmaster who could galvanize alumni, parents, and boys for the all-out effort that would be required to move and re-endow the

FIG. 1. Robert Hallowell Gardiner
'72, president of the trustees
1917–1924, the savior of the School.

school. In September 1919 they offered the post to the Reverend Remsen B. Ogilby '98, an Episcopal priest who later became president of Trinity College in Hartford.[1] His refusal was a sobering confirmation that the School's reputation had fallen.

Meanwhile, the R.L. community wondered why no appeal for funds was being mounted. Clarence Gleason spoke for many when he "went public" in *The Tripod*:

> Other institutions which needed new buildings and increased endowments have shown a great activity, some of them starting [campaigns] even before the war ended. Our own objective seems very modest in comparison with the millions raised and being raised by other schools and colleges. For example, Andover aims at a million and half, and will likely reach two millions and a half. . . . Will the alumni let this 275th anniversary of our founding pass without at least an effort to finish the work begun in 1913?[2]

At their May 1920 meeting the trustees concluded "that there was no immediate prospect of raising the money needed for building and that conditions might alter materially before that time came." The 2.73–acre Seaver Street lot, purchased in 1913, still had a sign on it reading "Future Site of the Roxbury Latin School." In just seven years, however, the Seaver Street neighborhood—which was not very far from Kearsarge Avenue—had declined perceptibly. In October 1920, the trustees "asked the [Alumni] Council's opinion as to the advisability of further developing the new school grounds on Seaver Street in case funds should be available. It was the [Council's] unanimous opinion . . . that it would not be advisable to make further developments on the Seaver Street lot on account of changed conditions during the past few years."[3] John Eliot would doubtless have proclaimed that "God's wondrous Providence" had intervened—by the aborted 1914 campaign and the intervening Great War—to prevent the trustees from creating a new campus on the Seaver Street lot, which was inadequate in size and now poorly located. But without a suitable site for the School, the trustees were in no position to raise money for a building. Even so, an endowment drive for $100,000 for teachers' salaries was undertaken for the 275th anniversary and more than $50,000 was raised by the time of the celebrations in June 1920.[4]

In January 1921 the trustees suffered a second humiliation when R. J. Shortlidge rejected their offer of the headmastership, and a third in February when W. D. Head said the salary offered was too low.[5] Their fourth choice, Daniel Varney Thompson, accepted election in April.[6] Thompson had grown up in Augusta, Maine, and had graduated from the high school there. His father, a country doctor, kept five horses to make his rounds, and his son relished taking care of them; "I lived in the saddle," he wrote. He also enjoyed other advantages of rural life:

> While I was still sixteen, I was given one of the most precious chances of my life. I taught in a country school of twenty children in a little white schoolhouse, set in aged trees at the foot of a long steep hill. The "children" ranged from six to twenty-one and were a fine lot. . . .
>
> Life in a remote section of Maine was very simple in those days.

> There was no organization of school activities. We played football
> without sides of a limited number, or any rule whatever except to
> advance the ball. . . . [In those days] we had more work to do for
> others, but we had more ideas of our own; we missed the movies,
> but we entertained ourselves; our games were disorganized but
> they were played in the spirit of pure enjoyment.[7]

He received his bachelor of arts degree from Amherst in 1889 and immediately returned to teaching—at the Newark Academy. He then
headed the English department at Sachs School in New York City
(1896–1903), and ran the lower school at Hackley for a year while
Theodore C. Williams '72 was headmaster there. Since 1904 he had
been at Lawrenceville School where he was a housemaster and head of
the English department. "Mr. Thompson," wrote *The Tripod*, "is not an
athlete, but [he is] fond of out-door life, especially riding on horseback,
boating and cruising, camping and golf. He is a lover of all the arts,
especially music."[8] This latter passion he shared with his son, the well-
known composer Randall Thompson who taught at Harvard from 1948
to 1965.

1. *The Move to West Roxbury*

Thompson's arrival and the promise of new leadership brought forth an
outburst of optimism. In December 1921, a "self-appointed" Volunteer
Committee of Parents of former students sent out a request for funds to
parents of alumni. After reminding their fellow parents that their sons'
education came as a "splendid free service that the institution has always rendered to the community," they wrote that "the need for money
has become extremely acute." Putnam's influence remained strong: the
letter went on to state that the parents had voluntarily organized themselves to solicit gifts "because the charter prohibits the collection of a
tuition fee."[9] The solicitation set a goal of $12,000 from former parents
to cover the School's projected deficit for two years, by which time "it is
reasonably hoped that the Alumni Endowment Fund will have been
completed."

FIG. 2. The faculty circa 1922–24 in the hall at Kearsarge Avenue. *From left:* O. M. Farnham, Joseph H. Sasserno, Howard A. Wiggin, J. Leo Foley, Headmaster D. V. Thompson, N. Henry Black, Earl W. Taylor, Clarence Gleason, William P. Dickey, D. O. S. Lowell.

Realizing that raising money to build and endow a new school would be possible only if there were actual property and plans to rally around, the trustees turned their energies to finding a site for the School's future. On Saturday, June 10, 1922, five trustees—including Gardiner and Charles Sumner Pierce—spent the day exploring possibilities in the western part of the original town of Roxbury. In Jamaica Plain, they visited the Slocum property on Moss Hill and the Curtis property on Centre Street. They then ventured to West Roxbury to look at two sites: the abandoned Brook Farm and the Weld farm. Discouraged by the inadequacy of each of these sites, they chanced to notice a For Sale sign as they motored back along Centre Street. The trolley had recently been extended along Centre Street, and Richard Codman had determined that his fifty-acre estate was ripe for development. For the five trustees, the property was "love at first sight," the ideal location for the School's future. Mr. Codman informed them that his nephew John S. Codman, who lived nearby at 57 Quail Street (the present headmaster's

FIG. 3. The Richard Codman estate on Centre Street in West Roxbury. Cottage Avenue, the lane that was later widened and renamed St. Theresa Avenue, is along the stone wall at the left. Note the double streetcar tracks along Centre Street, circa 1924.

house), was handling the sale. Pierce called the younger Codman on Monday. Codman said he was offering an option on the fifteen acres along Centre Street to a real estate development syndicate for $30,000 unless the School could immediately come up with $50,000 for the entire fifty acres. Quickly the trustees consulted Frederick Law Olmsted, Jr., '90, who pronounced the property suitable for a school, and a real estate expert who said the price was reasonable. The headmaster was directed to consult with Mrs. Davol, H. W. Putnam's daughter and a prominent and active parent (living in Brookline), who said the parents would be pleased.

However, Codman was not about to give the School the thirty days it requested and abruptly sold the option on the front fifteen acres. Fortunately, the developers—who were poised to begin building residences—agreed to give up their option for a quick profit of $5,000. Codman now said he would sell the remaining thirty-five acres for $20,000, but subject to two new conditions: that his uncle be allowed to

FIG. 4. The Richard Codman estate, circa 1924, looking from the present varsity football field down toward Centre Street (note the streetcar passing at the left). Cottage Avenue (later renamed St. Theresa Avenue) is on the right. St. Theresa's Church had not yet been built.

FIG. 5. The Richard Codman estate, circa 1925, looking across the present varsity soccer field (end to end) toward buildings that stand on the site of the present St. Theresa's School and Church. The field had just been cleared and leveled.

FIG. 6. The Richard Codman estate, circa 1924, looking from the far end of the present varsity football field toward the estate house (torn down in 1965) that stood in front of the site of the present Robert P. Smith Arts Center.

FIG. 7. The Richard Codman estate house (torn down to make room for the Ernst Wing in 1965) is on the right. On the left are the stables that stood on what is now "Flea Patch" field; they burned to the ground in 1932.

live out his life in the estate house (or in one provided by the School elsewhere at a cost of not more than $10,000), and that his own unmarried daughter Margaret be permitted to build a house (for life occupancy) on four-fifths of an acre, if she chose to do so, after his death. But when the trustees voted to agree to his terms, Codman upped the price another $5000. Since that was in excess of the $55,300 previously authorized, the trustees had to convene another meeting. The more adventurous members of the board prevailed, and the School acquired the property on August 15, 1922, for $60,000.[10] The immediate sale of half the Seaver Street property for $36,000 plus the eventual sale of the Kearsarge Avenue site to the city for $30,500 more than covered the cost of the new property.[11] The trustees authorized funds to grade and seed the pasture along Centre Street, and it was first used for football practice in the fall of 1923.[12] By that fall, eighty-seven of the School's 136 boys were living in West Roxbury, Roslindale, and Jamaica Plain; only twenty-six still dwelt in Roxbury.[13]

Meanwhile, the trustees began to gear up for a campaign to raise the necessary money to erect and endow a new school. They were shocked to discover in June 1923 that the building of a schoolhouse for 180 boys and the minimal development of two athletic fields would cost $390,000—a figure they felt was "inexpedient" to reveal![14] On January 4, 1924, the trustees unveiled to 150 selected alumni the plans for the new school rendered by the eminent architect William Perry of Perry, Shaw & Hepburn (the firm which would later—on the basis, in part, of their success at Roxbury Latin—be entrusted with the restoration of Colonial Williamsburg). President Lowell and Professor Grandgent of Harvard, Dr. Drury of St. Paul's School, Treasurer Charles J. Nichols representing the people of West Roxbury, as well as Gardiner and the headmaster, all addressed the dinner gathering which opened the campaign.[15] On January 10, 1924, the trustees wrote all the alumni announcing that pledges of $100,000 were already in hand. Included in the mailing was a handsome and illustrated booklet: "Roxbury Latin School—Past, Present, and Future," showing pictures of the new site and the

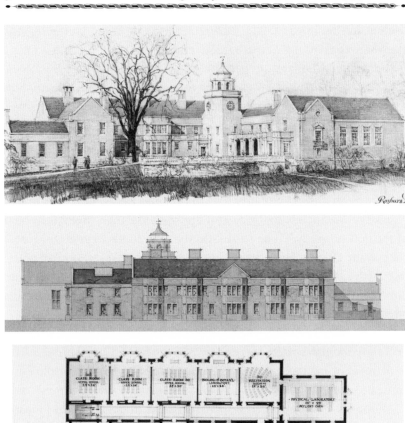

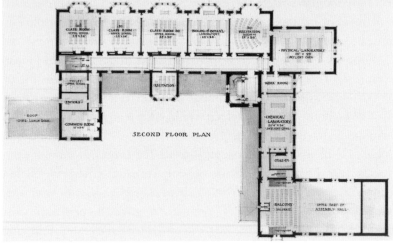

FIG. 8. William Perry, of the architectural firm of Perry, Shaw & Hepburn, was commissioned in 1923 to design the new schoolhouse. His plans were presented in the 1924 campaign brochure.

proposed building and explaining the projected cost of moving the School. Also enclosed were two short flyers, "Refounding the Roxbury Latin School" and "About Roxbury Latin—A Short Catechism."

In his foreword to the campaign booklet, Charles William Eliot, President Emeritus of Harvard, articulated why the School had to change in order to remain the same:

> The Roxbury Latin School . . . can no longer be carried on at its present site. The extensive changes in the programmes and functions of schools preparatory to college make it necessary to convert the School into a country day school, in order fully to maintain its honorable traditions, and continue for coming generations the high level of services to the earlier.[16]

Despite these efforts, the campaign stalled. On February 18, 1924, trustee Roger Ernst wrote in despair to Gardiner of "an apathy and an indifference on the part of the alumni body so complete that it looks as if the campaign [will] fail unless we adopt some drastic change in tactics." In desperation, the trustees in March contracted with Tamblyn and Brown of New York—for a $13,000 fee plus $13,000 for publicity and other expenses—to conduct a campaign for the remaining $300,000 needed to relocate the School.[17]

Then, on June 10, 1924, the campaign was dealt another blow: Robert Hallowell Gardiner, the principal architect of the School's future, suddenly died. Although he had led the children of Roxbury across the Red Sea, like Moses he himself would not see the promised land: a new school built and paid for. Because of Gardiner's reforms, however, the School's leadership had been renewed; the cause for which he had fought so hard therefore did not perish when he died.

The official campaign was finally kicked off in January 1925. A member of the First Class (1925) was asked to reflect on the condition of the school:

> The campus of the present building on Kearsarge Avenue is a disgrace. . . . It has been utterly impossible to use the campus either for football or baseball. . . . The conditions inside the school are

FIG. 9. The Kearsarge Avenue campus in the final days. The schoolhouse is on the right out of the photograph.

even worse. There are but two rooms in the whole school that are sufficiently lighted, and these only on bright days. The rest of the rooms, poorly lighted only on one side or shadowed by tenements, provide insufficient illumination for study. . . . In the past three years a few electric lights, class gifts, have been installed in several rooms. . . . In the chemistry laboratory, the lighting over the benches is gas. . . . The basement is badly lighted, cold, low-ceilinged, and cramped. The lunchcounter therein is small and has very meagre facilities. The students eat standing at shelves along the walls, unless lucky enough to obtain seats on the sole bench in the basement. The two [coal] furnaces are at opposite ends of the basement and are not even shut off from the so-called lunch-room. . . . The present building . . . requires superhuman efforts on the part of the janitor to keep the rooms at a temperature above fifty degrees on a cold day. . . . Often during an ordinary winter, there are no chapel exercises for days at a time, as the heat required to warm the frigid hall is needed to keep the remainder of the building at a habitable temperature.[18]

William P. Dickey, a master since 1912, then put the case succinctly: "Roxbury Latin School has reached a critical stage; its modern spirit must have a modern body."[19] It also needed to be accessible to its students—only 25 percent of whom still lived in the vicinity of the School and some 65 percent of whom lived in West Roxbury, Jamaica Plain, and Roslindale.[20] The campaign's minimum goal of $400,000—$237,000 in addition to the $163,000 already pledged—was officially announced: $250,000 for the new building, $20,000 for fields and for converting the barn to a temporary gymnasium, and $130,000 to endow teacher salaries.[21]

The Tripod gives this exciting account of the herculean effort that ensued:

> Throughout the three weeks of intensive campaign, luncheons were held for the report of progress every Tuesday and Friday, but the beginning and end were marked by sumptuous banquets, the first at the Hotel Somerset, the last at the City Club.
>
> At the Somerset about 250 were present . . . [Roger Ernst] explained the "181" slogan of the drive. The figure represents $181, the average cost of educating a boy for one year at Roxbury Latin. In consideration that most all of the alumni spent *five* or *six* years at the school, it did not seem unreasonable to ask each to 'get or give' this amount before the end of the campaign. [He then announced that $163,500 had already been pledged.]
>
> At this point Mr. [Philip Melancthon] Tucker of '95 was introduced and the second big event of the evening ensued; the success of the campaign seemed assured. He announced that, provided the rest of the bunch raise three-quarters of the money needed, his class alone would furnish the remaining quarter. Amidst wild applause he sat down. . . .
>
> [But by] January 23 . . . , the scheduled date for the end of the campaign, the fund was still $25,000 short including the contingent gifts. It seemed as if defeat faced the campaign, but the classes of '95 and '98 lengthened the period of contingency to January 31st, and the campaign was prolonged till a final meeting on January 29th.
>
> Over 100 alumni were present at the City Club on that date and heard the announcement that the campaign had reached its objec-

tive, done better than that, had gone to $415,315. Pandemonium reigned.[22]

After the euphoria, the trustees sat down to a more complicated reality. Much of the $415,000 raised was in pledges payable until 1929. Gardiner's successor as president, Professor Grandgent of Harvard, spelled out the reasons why the trustees, in May 1925, postponed the building for a year:

> The amount now in hand . . . is disconcertingly small; should we then proceed at once to erect the beautiful structure our architects have planned, we should have to procure by loan a large share of the necessary cash.
>
> But that is not the whole story. Those of you who have built houses know what a hiatus there is between the original estimate and the final bill.[23]

By December the trustees decided to begin construction as soon as another $75,000 was added to the $275,000 already available.[24] By June 1926 they had accepted the lowest bid for the new building, that of the Leighton Mitchell Company, which totaled $191,635 without the hall.[25] Building was begun at once. By the middle of the fall, Mrs. Edmund Swett Rousmaniere gave the $35,500 (which she later increased to $50,000) necessary to add an assembly hall, in memory of her late husband, the dean of St. Paul's Cathedral, Boston, a member of the Class of 1879.[26]

The School was about to move, but the question remained as to the extent to which the benefits of the School should be confined—if at all—to those boys who lived within the borders of the original town of Roxbury (the so-called "Old Roxbury District"). In December 1921, Roger Ernst—along with W. Dudley Cotton, C. S. Pierce, and Andrew Marshall—had been appointed as a special committee to determine "the extent to which the Trustees may admit applicants from outside the Free District, and to what extent there may be expended upon their education the present or any future trust funds of the School." Relying

FIG. 10, *left.* Philip Melancthon Tucker '95, whose gift of $80,000 ensured the success of the campaign to build the new school. (Harvard University Archives Collection)

FIG. 11, *right.* The Very Reverend Edmund Swett Rousmaniere '79, dean of St. Paul's Cathedral, Boston, in whose memory the hall was given by his wife.

on Putnam's 1882 and 1902 Reports as authoritative and undertaking no new research on the subject, the committee concluded that the School's 1789 Charter needed to be amended by the Legislature "to permit the Trustees to receive donations, either unrestricted or with express power to use them for the education of boys outside as well as inside the Free District."[27]

When soliciting gifts and pledges in the 1920s for the new building and new endowment, the trustees therefore exercised extreme legal caution. Each donor to the building fund signed a statement which acknowledged the purpose of the solicitation:

> To enable the Trustees of the Roxbury Latin School, in reliance on this and other Subscriptions, to construct a new building, to increase the salaries of the faculty of the School, or generally to carry out the objects and exercise the powers which are now *or hereafter* contained in the charter of the School. [Emphasis added.]

As prudent stewards, the trustees in December 1925 followed the recommendation of the 1922 special committee and voted to petition the
Legislature to amend the charter so as "to remove all question" as to
their right to educate students regardless of their place of residence and
to charge them tuition or not as they deemed appropriate.[28] No sooner
had the trustees voted to go to the Legislature than an internal debate
erupted over whether this was the best way to secure their rights. Writing to fellow trustee W. Dudley Cotton in January 1926, Andrew Marshall—who had been a member of the special committee—expressed
the sentiments of most alumni who had recently given to the campaign.
They had not contributed in order to preserve the School as a right for
Roxbury boys but, rather, in order to preserve the School's traditional
classical tone and character:

> Very much more money was subscribed by those eager to retain
> the traditional tone [of Classical education] of the School through
> admitting a reasonable number of boys living outside of Roxbury
> than by those people who were interested purely in keeping the
> school exclusively for Roxbury boys.

Marshall reminded Cotton that alumni had been assured by the
trustees that the creation of a separate trust to support non-Roxbury
boys was unnecessary and that they had made their gifts under that
assumption. Now that the gifts had been made, the trustees could not
renege on the assurance they had given. It was now too late to create a
separate foundation for non-Roxbury boys. The trustees were in good
faith obliged, therefore, to secure their right to use the newly-raised
funds in accordance with the donors' intentions.

As to *how* the trustees should secure their right, Marshall was more
open-minded. He expressed considerable doubt, in fact, about whether
the trustees should go to the Legislature, as they had in 1906 and 1913,
for authorization by means of an amendment to the charter. Instead,
Marshall suggested going the judicial route: "It is the court of equity
which has the real jurisdiction over us as Trustees, and it is very easy to

FIG. 12. Charles Hall Grandgent '79, professor of French at Harvard, president of the trustees 1924–1935.

lull oneself into a false sense of security by merely getting a legislative act purporting to authorize what we wish to do."[29]

Responding to this letter, which had been forwarded to him, President Grandgent seemed to side with Marshall. Regarding the question of whether the School was primarily a classical school with high standards or primarily a high school for Roxbury residents, Grandgent articulated the dilemma with pungent clarity:

> The advantage of increased freedom on our part [to charge tuition], however it be obtained, would be greater probability of continuing the scholastic tradition of our institution by gathering in the sons of graduates and others of the same type who may not be residents of the old district.
>
> The danger of the projected amendment lies in the possibility that it may change a free school with a few paying pupils into a paying school with a few free pupils.[30]

The minutes of the March 1926 meeting record only that "The sentiment of the Trustees was unanimously in favor of adopting measures of some kind to remove all question as to their rights to educate some boys from outside the limits of old Roxbury."[31] By September, they had settled their differences and—for reasons undisclosed—had decided to go the legislative route.[32] The result was "An Act to enlarge the authority of the Trustees" (Chapter 214 of the Acts of 1927).[33] Section 1 deals with the tuition issue:

> The Trustees . . . are hereby given full power and authority to provide for the education of youth, with or without regard to the place of residence or to the financial ability of them or their parents, and with or without charging tuition therefor.[34]

As regards the building of the new school and the receiving of new endowments for faculty salaries, the trustees are given full power "to receive, hold and administer real and personal property given, conveyed, transferred, devised or bequeathed to said corporation for its purposes."

Section 2 of the Act concerns previous gifts to the School and makes clear that such property is "subject to the specific trusts upon which said property had been received by said corporation." [35]

In the School's first year in West Roxbury, its enrollment increased to 157. More than two-thirds of these boys lived in West Roxbury, Roslindale, and Jamaica Plain, while only thirteen were residents of Roxbury. Since thirty of the 157 came from outside the "Old Roxbury District," $7500 in fees could be collected—a big boost for the annual budget. The first "morning chapel exercises" were held September 23, 1927, in Rousmaniere Hall, and *The Tripod* commented ecstatically, "Through the windows of the old building one could see only the uninspiring backs of tenement houses. In our new site it is hard to realize that a great city is within a few miles. Everything about this new home of ours is a joy to the eye."[36]

The campus had already received the devoted attention of Charles James Nichols, West Roxbury resident and R.L. father. He had the lower field along Centre Street graded and drained, and he arranged for and supervised the building of tennis courts. He organized work parties of boys to pick up stones, and he planted a large number of trees to "screen" the campus.

The new building was dedicated on October 28, 1927, following the Browne & Nichols football game and supper in the new "lunch room." Announcement was made for the first time that Mrs. Rousmaniere had donated the hall. Dean Rousmaniere's classmate, the Reverend Augustus M. Lord, gave a touching address about his lifelong friend,[37] and President Grandgent averred that "certainly no one ever won better right to such a memorial than our beloved Ned Rousmaniere. . . . Even as his life was devoted to the enrichment of other men's lives, so shall his spirit forever preside within these walls, enriching the souls of the young indwellers."[38] The principal speaker was President A. Lawrence Lowell of Harvard:

> You remember Ponce de Leon searched in Florida for the fountain of perpetual youth. He did exactly the wrong thing, as most people do whose aspirations are greater than their common sense, and who expect to get gold by a philosopher's stone. You cannot find the fountain of perpetual youth by seeking it. You can plant it, and the men who came to New England, John Eliot and others, planted it. They planted a fountain of perpetual youth, and it is flowing today, flowing stronger than it has ever flowed before,— and the fountain is the Roxbury Latin School. It is because they planted it that it is here. Those of you who have been here know that a school, or any institution for young men, is a fountain of perpetual youth, and never grows old. It keeps on through the ages, always young, always living, always throwing its waters up higher and higher.[39]

Geoffrey Lewis '28 was a member of the first class to graduate from the new school. Later in life he would go on to serve as headmaster of Browne & Nichols School and as ambassador to several countries. While he was in college, he returned to his old school to coach. His 1931 description of a typical school day of this era captures some of the excitement of the School's rebirth:

It is twenty minutes of nine on a spring morning. Boys are hur-
rying through the corridors to their class-rooms, laughing and
talking. Some, who make it a point to take no chances of breaking
the commendable School rule that 'no one shall be admitted to the
building before half-past seven in the morning,' have just panted
into the building and are hanging up their hats, while outside the
radiators of the automobiles belonging to a privileged few (or to
their fond parents), are still hot after the run out from Jamaica
Plain or Roslindale. Mr. Farnham, by banging on his little bell, is
gradually reducing the imps that make up the Sixth class to a state
of reasonable quiet, while upstairs the older boys are beginning to
take their proper seats.

A bell rings. It is the signal to form by classes to march into the
spacious auditorium for morning assembly. The piano, accompanied perhaps by a violin, strikes up a march, and the School files in,
the youngest boys first, the oldest bringing up the rear. Only a few
of them remember the old building on Kearsarge Avenue, with its
gloomy corridors and low-ceilinged, ill-shaped assembly-hall, furnished with long settees painted a bilious yellow. But to these few,
the splendid auditorium, with its handsome wooden panels, its
plush curtains, and its comfortable chairs seems all the more wonderful. They alone of the School body can fully appreciate what the
new building has meant to Roxbury Latin.

But the masters have all seated themselves on the stage in the
familiar straight-backed chairs, each given by some class long-
since graduated. Mr. Taylor rises, announces the hymn for the
morning, and signals to the pianist for the pitch. There rises a low
murmur from the boys while they are finding their places — of
appreciation if the hymn is well known, and of disappointment if
it is new. Through two or three verses Mr. Taylor leads, the School
following him well or ill according to their familiarity with the
tune. On the last note of the "Amen" Dr. Thompson rises behind
the solid reading-desk with the head of Homer carved on its front,
and slowly begins the "Pater Noster," the majestic lines of the old
prayer rolling up to him from the boys in the seats below. Everyone, from the youngest member of the Sixth class up, knows the
words, and the murmur goes steadily on with no faltering at the

FIG. 13. Geoffrey Whitney Lewis '28, member of the first class to graduate from the West Roxbury school, who returned to coach during his college years. He later served as headmaster of Browne & Nichols School and as an ambassador.

difficult passages. The prayer completed, the headmaster reads from the huge Bible some selection that he has chosen as being particularly appropriate. After the reading he speaks very briefly, sometimes on some item of purely School interest, such as the frequency and speed with which baseballs seem to be entering the class-rooms through window-panes, or on some slightly larger and less personal topic, such as the Spanish Revolution, or the earthquake in Nicaragua. When he has finished he motions to Mr. Dickey, who announces that in the afternoon of the next day there will be a game with Country Day on the lower field. Then the piano again strikes up a march and each class files to its own room to begin the real work of the day.

The School day is divided into six periods. The first four are each forty-five minutes long, with a five-minute recess between the first two and the last two. Then comes a lunch-hour lasting about thirty minutes, ample time to devour the hot luncheon served in the sunny lunch-room—a very different place from the dark and uninviting counter in the basement of the old School. For those who bring most of their lunch from home and want only to supplement it with a bowl of hot soup or a dish of ice cream there is another room where such food may be procured without crowd-

FIGS. 14–16, *left.* The exterior of Perry's West Roxbury schoolhouse in 1927.
FIG. 17. The loggia of Perry's building modelled after the loggia of the Convent of St. Mark in Florence. The present windows were originally doors .

ing the lunch-room. But many seem to eat no lunch at all, for as soon as the bell rings there are yells and laughter from the playing-field, and the crack of bat against ball—but these only from "beyond the flagpole," for it is a fixed rule that no playing shall go on between the flagpole and the building, thus decreasing some-what the number of casualties among the window-panes.

Recess over, the boys troop back to their desks for two more periods, each forty minutes long, with the exception of the Sixth class which has a compulsory "gym period" every day during the last forty minutes. After the end of the session, at quarter of two, there may be class meetings, held with no master present and with the class-officers in charge of affairs. Matters of class interest are discussed, such as the annual class gift to the School, usually of some small article for the class-room, such as a picture, or some books, or a fire-set. Or class morale is stiffened through talks by the officers if such a step seems necessary. Often some good sug-gestions as to the better conduct of School affairs are evolved in

FIG. 18. Rousmaniere Hall in Perry's building in 1927.

FIG. 19. The lunchroom in Perry's building in 1927.

such meetings and are passed on to Dr. Thompson. But this function is usually reserved for the Student Council, a purely voluntary body completely in the hands of the students, with a Chairman from the First class, a Secretary from the Second, three additional members from the First class, two besides the Secretary from the Second, and delegates from the lower classes who may discuss but not vote. Its meetings, also are held just after School.

FIG. 20. The physics laboratory in Perry's building in 1927.

But the major part of the School is not involved in these meetings, and for them there are many things to do. Occasional minor explosions and horrid smells emanating from the Chemistry laboratory tell the world that the long-suffering Mr. Houser is being forced to supervise some impromptu experiment! Doleful sounds (they are becoming less so) from the auditorium inform the initiated that the Orchestra or Glee Club is practising. From the tennis courts comes the ping of tennis rackets and the helpful "razzing" of impatient spectators waiting their turn. On the upper field the three junior teams are practising or playing an informal game, shepherded by two young men specially imported from Harvard, and on the lower field Mr. Foley and his varsity team are working. Over in a corner certain young gentlemen are rapidly becoming expert at pole-vaulting, while up in the woods Mr. Dickey is endeavoring to prevent earnest but awkward youths from chopping their own shins instead of tree trunks.

At ten minutes of four comes the warning-bell. All coats and books must be extracted from the two upper stories before four o'clock. This time officially marks the end of the school day. After quarter of two, however, the boys are free to stay or go home as they please, unless, of course, punishment is in order. There is no form of compulsory play except for the forty minutes demanded of the Sixth class, and for this reason there is little grouchiness or ill-temper displayed on the playing-field. On the other hand, there are always some who go home and who need the exercise badly but who cannot be persuaded to stay even by the force of public opinion. [In 1929 Headmaster Thompson estimated that only one-third of the boys stayed at school regularly after classes and that one-fifth never did.]

This is a picture of the school day of today. It probably does not differ in its essentials from that of forty or fifty years ago, but the atmosphere has changed. There is an air of freshness and alertness given by the new plant that was not found in the old building. But at the same time, the traditions of Old Roxbury are still being carried on. The boys are as proud of the age and standards of their School as they were in the old building, and Mr. Farnham, Mr. Gleason, and the other masters continue to instill into them the same old spirit.[40]

Farnham and Gleason were the faculty's eminent ancients. Since 1893 O. M. (known to all as "Old Man") Farnham had been master of the Sixth Class. Both Francis Russell '28 and David Mittell '35 have immortalized him in print,[41] and the library of the 1927 building was transformed into a history classroom-debate center in his memory in 1989. He loved "the Hub of the universe" and imbued his young pupils with the history, architecture, and poetry of New England. Sixty years after his retirement in 1934, older alumni recall as yesterday his famous word use (e.g., lie and lay) and spelling tests, as well as the two-minute talks they had to give (by which he introduced them to public speaking). Clarence W. Gleason came to the School even earlier—in 1889—and, save for a brief sojourn at Volkmann's School from 1905 to 1912, he served the School even longer—until 1939. A brilliant teacher of Greek, whose textbooks became as famous as Collar's, he bequeathed to the School two of its enduring traditions. He originated Exelauno Day,

FIG. 21. David Taggart Clark '89, professor of economics at Williams College, who endowed the Exelauno Day Greek and Latin declamations in 1957.

whose name derives from the recurring verb, "march forth," in Xeno-phon's *Anabasis*. On March fourth every year, he decreed that there be no homework for students of Greek and established it as the annual Greek and Latin declamation day. David Taggart Clark '89, professor of economics at Williams, endowed declamation prizes which students have eagerly competed for on March fourth since 1957. Gleason's other legacy was "The Founder's Song," which he wrote to the tune of "Lord Jeffrey Amherst."[42]

When Daniel V. Thompson was elected in 1921, he was the first headmaster new to the School since Collar's predecessor in 1853. Both Gleason and Farnham had been hired by Collar, whose headmastership they always referred to as "the golden age of Collar," and both had also worked under D. O. S. Lowell. Though the School—by nearly uni-versal consent—needed fresh air, both these grand old men bitterly resented Thompson. Gleason seems to have taken the lead in under-mining the headmaster. The tension and acrimony between the faculty and Thompson became so intolerable that trustee president Professor Grandgent finally took action. He wrote Thompson as follows on December 22, 1928:

> It is no news that there is, and has been for years, among the mas-ters an evident dissension which has worked to the detriment of

FIG. 22. Daniel Varney Thompson, headmaster 1921–1933.

discipline and loyalty. Palliatives have been tried in vain. The time has come for a major operation. Convinced as they are that the trouble centres in one master, the Trustees, with exceeding reluctance and after exhaustive study, have reached the conclusion that this man, the principal source of disaffection, must go, in spite of his long and distinguished service, and in spite of the affection in which he is held. The irreconcilable, as you know, is Mr. Gleason. Our evidence comes entirely from parents and from past and present pupils. We have been careful not to draw you and the rest of the Faculty into the camp. Mr. Farnham is somewhat inculpated also, and perhaps cherishes as much animosity; but he at least has tried to conceal it. The Trustees finally voted that 'they do not intend to reappoint Mr. Gleason for the coming year, because of his attitude toward the Administration.' . . . The Board was nearly unanimous. I have notified Mr. Gleason in writing, and have made it clear to him that you had nothing whatever to do with our action.[43]

Upon receiving Grandgent's letter, Gleason agreed to change his ways and to support Thompson. The headmaster was a kindly man and persuaded the trustees to reappoint him. Open hostility ceased from this time on, and Thompson in future correspondence was always cordial to Gleason.

From Thompson's viewpoint, the faculty—or a large part of it—was too rigid and unbending in its standards. The high "mortality rate" of students is a recurring lament in his reports to the trustees in his early years. In March 1922 he asked trustee support for his efforts to create a more supportive environment:

> There is still a disastrously large number [of boys] near to failure. . . . I feel that there is a measurable increase in the sympathy of the masters with such boys and in the efforts tactfully put forth for their encouragement and stimulation. May I suggest that visiting Trustees, if they approve, bear in mind this tendency and encourage it as opportunity offers. . . . [T]he best citizens are not infrequently made of boys slow in development, and in the process such boys compose an important element in the life of the school. Amputation is sometimes necessary, but it should be the last resort of the school surgeon.

The following September, discouraged by the loss of seventeen boys whose summer work did not qualify them to return, Thompson suggested the division his efforts were causing in the faculty:

> Many of these 17 I had hoped to save to the school, and certain masters earnestly co-operated to that end. Others did not readily take the time, pains, and sympathy requisite for such a special service. Perhaps there is a feeling that the routine, if efficient, should satisfy all needs. This is not my view, and I shall not be satisfied till we can greatly reduce the 'mortality' of our classes without surrendering standards.

Thompson suffered not only the enmity of Farnham and Gleason, but the general recalcitrance of a number of established faculty who had begun their teaching in an era in which "sympathy" and "understanding" were not part of the job description.

Thompson had been a very successful master at Lawrenceville, but he was not well suited to the role of headmaster. His was not a forceful personality and he was reluctant to "take command" of the School. The faculty minutes of his era reveal a lack of leadership on his part and a tendency to acquiesce to the faculty in the face of disagreement and unpleasantness. Roger Ernst summarized Thompson's regime in a letter to Harvard's President Conant in 1947:

> Remembering the sad experience that we had with Thompson, who came from Lawrenceville highly recommended as a master, but who entirely lacked leadership, I want to be satisfied that we would not [in choosing a new headmaster in 1947] be stepping into a repetition of that experience.[44]

Even if they did not have the ideal leader in Thompson, the trustees did have a schoolhouse and campus which fulfilled the hopes expressed in their fund-raising brochure:

> Ample and beautiful surroundings, while our present are cramped and ugly. Varied winter sports, indoor and outdoor, for which we now have no opportunity. A reading-room in connection with our Library, to which boys will be tempted for browsing and research. Adequate facilities for music and dramatics. . . . And a chance which we have never had to invite our rivals in sport to our home-grounds for interscholastic games.[45]

Now that this dream had become a reality, the trustees had to find a way to finance the School without closing it to all but the affluent. The School had been reborn in West Roxbury in 1927, at a time of national prosperity and optimism. But as the trustees turned their attention to the School's finances, they were almost immediately dealt a crippling blow by the Wall Street Crash of October 1929 and the decade-long Great Depression that followed.

Early in 1930, before they realized how severe and protracted the Depression was going to be, they had determined for the first time to provide the faculty with pensions. They voted to contribute $180 a year for each teacher to TIAA-CREF (Teachers Insurance and Annuity Association and the College Retirement Equities Fund, the national retirement program for teachers at private schools and colleges), in addition to the contribution (5 percent of salary) which each faculty member was required to make.[46] The trustees were confident that they could raise the necessary funds to back this investment in the School's greatest asset, its faculty.

By March 1932 that confidence had evaporated, and it was necessary to reduce faculty salaries. "It was a matter of deep regret that the existing financial emergency was so urgent that decreases in salaries could not be avoided."[47] In August of the same year, the School was dealt another blow by the sudden death of headmaster Daniel V. Thompson. Ironically, the trustees appointed as his temporary successor the man who had shown such hostility towards him: Clarence Gleason, at age sixty-six the oldest of the masters. As it turned out, the interim year was an especially happy one, thanks, it would seem, to Gleason's tactful leadership.[48] Because Thompson was sixty-five and ready to retire, the trustees had appointed a committee to select a new headmaster several months before he died. They had therefore already begun to compile a list of potential candidates at the time of his death.[49]

2. The Northrop Era

On May 8, 1933, the very day that the trustees elected George Norton Northrop headmaster,[50] the Harvard Corporation nominated James Bryant Conant '10 as president of the university. This coincidence, added to the fact that Conant's selection was not anticipated, perhaps accounts for the apocryphal story, still widely circulated. The story goes that the School's trustees had not considered Conant for the headmastership, because he was so young and obscure that they didn't know of him. When *The Christian Science Monitor* recirculated this tale again in 1953, trustee president Roger Ernst set the record straight:

> When this story was first coined and published in *Time* Magazine in 1933, our trustees decided not to spoil a story too good not to be true by stating the actual facts. . . . I happen to have been a trustee in 1933, and chairman of the committee to choose a new head. . . . The real reason that Mr. Conant was not considered seriously as a candidate for headmaster is just the opposite of the one [New

Hampshire U.S.] Senator Tobey [R.L. Class of 1897] gives—
namely, he had already attained such eminence as a Professor of
Chemistry at Harvard as to make it certain he would not consider
an offer to become headmaster of a comparatively small boys
school. That Mr. Conant was not unknown to our trustees at that
time is proved by the fact that one year earlier I, personally, as acting president of our board, had invited him to give the principal
address at the School's graduation exercises, and had introduced
him when he did so.[51]

Northrop, fifty-two, was headmaster of the Chicago Latin School,
and *The Tripod* introduced him in this way:

> Breaking tradition, the trustees have named a westerner for the
> position which has, since 1645, been held by New Englanders. . . .
>   Mr. Northrop was born in Platteville, Wis., in 1880. He studied
> at the University of Wisconsin for a year and then transferred to
> the University of Minnesota where he received his Master of Arts
> degree in 1902. Later he studied for two years at Magdalen Col-
> lege, Oxford, England. From 1909 to 1920 he taught English at the
> University of Minnesota, becoming an assistant professor. In 1920
> he became headmaster of Brearley School, New York. Six years
> later he resigned his position to become headmaster of the Chi-
> cago Latin School. During the war he was, successively, lieutenant,
> captain, major.[52]

The trustee minutes disclose that Northrop "is leaving [Chicago
Latin] due primarily to the financial difficulties of the School."[53] If so,
Northrop's move to Roxbury Latin can best be described as "out of the
fire into the frying pan." Northrop arrived as both the market value of
the School's endowments and the income from its investments plummeted.

Since there was no possibility of raising new endowments in such a
climate, the trustees turned to the only other possible source of income:
tuition. Whether or not a boy lived within the "Old Roxbury District"
(i.e., Roxbury as it was in 1671) was still officially the determining factor
in the charging of tuition. The year the School moved, the trustees

FIG. 23. George Norton
Northrop, headmaster
1933–47.

raised the tuition for boys living outside the district to $250; district boys still paid nothing. By 1932–33, the trustees took steps to protect and enhance the number of tuition-paying students. They told Acting Headmaster Gleason informally to limit the number of free students admitted for 1933–34 to two-thirds of the total: "In other words, we aim at limiting the number of boys admitted free approximately to the proportion of income which came from restricted funds. Two-thirds is probably in excess of the actual proportion, but we decided to go slowly."[54] In 1933–34, thirty-two out of 170 (18 percent) paid tuition. Official limitations were placed on the number of free students for 1934–35:

> Beginning with the School year next fall, only twenty free scholars will be admitted to the Sixth Class, and . . . all others admitted whether within or without the free district should pay the $300 tuition, and . . . the status of boys so admitted should continue throughout the entire period they stayed in the School.

Little noticed at the time was the rebirth of an important principle of the School's early days when poor boys were admitted *gratis*: the principle of need-based tuition reduction. Both Eliot and Bell had been specially interested in "poor mens children," not in providing a benefit to the affluent who happened to live in a particular location. In announcing the new tuition policy, the trustees expressed their concern about benefitting boys who could not afford to pay tuition, stating:

> The Board might consider setting aside some special fund which could be used in the discretion of the board in very special cases to reduce or eliminate the tuition paid by some boy in the free district who had been admitted as a paying scholar but whose scholastic record later in the school and whose financial condition would justify making him the recipient of financial aid from that fund.[55]

The following year, as conditions worsened, the trustees were forced for the first time to levy a tuition charge—set at $100—on all boys living *within* the "Old Roxbury District."[56] In doing so, however, they reiterated the principle of need-based tuition reduction: "the power to remit tuition fees in special cases, conferred upon the Committee on examinations by vote of September 26, 1934, to remain in full force and effect."[57] In September 1935, when the new policy went into effect, the headmaster presented to the trustees

> the names of the boys for whom reductions in the amount of tuition payable by them had been made on account of the special exigencies of each case, and such reductions as recommended by the headmaster were approved, accompanied by the expression of the sentiment that during the present financial emergency of the School such reductions should be granted only in cases of strict necessity.[58]

The account the trustees presented to the alumni is an excellent summary of the School's financial trials:

> A year ago the Trustees laid before you the serious position of the School's budget and appealed to you for contributions toward the annual income. You responded with a total contribution of $2,000.

Even with that the deficit for the fiscal year ending August 31, 1934 was $13,000. The total deficit for the past five years, including the estimated deficit for the current year, is about $50,000, or about 10% of the present market value of the School's invested funds.

This deficit is due primarily to shrinkage in the annual income from investments, which in 1930 was $40,460, and last year was $27,553. To offset this, expenses have been reduced as much as possible and the already meagrely paid teachers have for the past three years been cheerfully accepting a 10% reduction in their salaries. To maintain the School's past educational standards and attain the higher one to which we all aspire, we must place the School in a financial position to pay salaries which will attract and hold the highest type of teacher. The Trustees are convinced that this is a fundamentally vital policy if the School is to live and thrive.

All practical sources for an immediate increase in the endowment fund, except a general appeal to Alumni, which is not now feasible, have been explored without success. The only two sources of increase of the annual income are to increase tuition charges and ask for your contributions. The Trustees have decided to do both— to divide the burden between the parents and the Alumni. Beginning next autumn, all boys in the School coming from the so-called "free district" (about 130) will pay $100 per year tuition. The boys from outside the district (about 30) now pay and will continue to pay $300. In both cases the amount charged is substantially below the cost of educating each boy, so that the essentially charitable character of the School is preserved. The announcement was made to the parents nearly two months ago and the response has been most favorable—an indication of the value of the education which the School is giving.[59]

Since the onset of the Depression, the numbers in the School had been slowly declining. Interestingly, the new tuition policy—whereby previously "free" boys now paid $100—had no noticeable effect on numbers; the size of the school remained steadily between 147 and 149 in the last four years of the 1930s. That is a drop from the 175 early in the decade, but nothing like the decline many other schools were experiencing.

Despite the new tuition charges, deficits still remained and the School was hard pressed. Everyone agreed that this was no time to raise capital. Like the school, individuals had watched their capital disappear as the stock market fell to 10 percent of its 1929 level and as property values collapsed. In 1937, therefore, the trustees returned to a form of fund-raising remarkably close to that of the School's founders: they decided to seek pledges and gifts *on an annual basis* from donors — alumni, parents, and friends.[60] Thus was established what came to be known as the Annual Fund, which today provides 18 percent of the School's operating budget.

Surprisingly, despite the Depression, the 1930s were a golden age in the life of the School. Much of the credit for the School's high morale in this time of national malaise must go to the new headmaster. Some regarded Northrop as "affected" — he called the alumni "old boys," for example, and his speech retained a certain British clip from his Oxford days. But boys like eccentricity, and they took to him immediately. From the first impression on, he was a memorable character, as James Ryan '45 notes:

> He was a big man, more than six feet tall and broad in his shoulders. He was homely, but formidable and impressive in appearance. His almost complete lack of hair caused him naturally enough, to be known as "Baldy". . . . If you met him on Mars, you would know his occupation. With his elegant tweed sports jacket [and checked waistcoat] and pipe you would be sure he had been sent over by central casting to play the role of a headmaster . . . of a small school. A boys' school. A private school.[61]

To Joseph Garland '40 he was a man for all seasons: "G.N.N. had the vitality of the Midwesterner, the native wit of the Yankee, the savoir faire of the New Yorker, the grace and accent of the Oxonian and the didactic style of Socrates."[62] Eric Solomon describes him as a figure to be reckoned with:

> As leader of the school he displayed a truly Olympian presence. From the terrifying moments of our first interviews, when he

tested our scholarly potential by delightedly discovering that we couldn't spell "raspberry," through our brief sights of the stern master who could quell every sound in a riotous classroom with one hawk-like glance, we learned that he was a headmaster with authority. And George Northrop practiced this authority with complete ease and confidence, whether in the amused and probing comments with which he would shock us . . . each morning in hall, or in those occasional utterly individual interviews where he could pack into a phrase or two a remarkable measure of disgust for our antisocial behavior.

Edward Merrill '41 recalls such an interview one day while he was an underclassman:

> I appeared at his office with a vest on but no coat. He sent me back for the coat. He would absolutely not accept sloppiness. He insisted on proper standards of conduct and appearance. . . .
>
> Mr. Northrop led us in many ways to understand the differences between excellence and mediocrity. He discussed mediocrity in a much wider sense, in terms of art, literature, and human effort in general, and in so doing defined excellence and inspired us to strive for it.

Perhaps because both he and they were secure and clear about who he was, boys could "relate" (as we now say) to Northrop as a friend. He and Mrs. Northrop invited boys to their campus home for tea in small groups. Northrop enjoyed playing tennis with boys at school, and he invited older boys off the campus for golf. He said when he came that he wanted his office to be their home at school and it quickly became that, according to *The Tripod*:

> The headmaster's study has become what he desired—our school home. Every lunch period a crowd of boys may be seen there, discussing with Mr. Northrop the latest 'picture of the week,' or having him demonstrate the use of the efficient-looking spear-head, which rests on the mantle, or even making dates to pitch horseshoes with him. Already he has shown that he wants to be regarded

as our friend rather than as our boss; and by doing this has increased the respect due him as our headmaster.[63]

He taught English to Class I, and his greatness as a teacher was twofold. First, as Solomon notes, he conveyed his love for the subject:

> George Northrop was the finest teacher most of us ever encountered. . . . He merely had the ability, so rare, to communicate his own sense of delight in the authors he loved, in Chaucer and Shakespeare, in Milton and Johnson, in Byron and Shaw. . . . The atmosphere in his office, packed with paintings and books, a fire roaring, students relaxing in overstuffed chairs while Mr. Northrop joyously chanted lines from *Beowulf* or *Hamlet* made literature—really, the life of the mind—seem worthwhile.
>
> I like to consider those senior English classes as somehow symbolic of George Norton Northrop: his mind was as full of art treasures as his office walls; his interest in the lyric beauty of poetry and the intellectual toughness of ideas was as intense as his fire; and his belief in education was as active as the responses his Socratic wit could draw from the students surrounding him.[64]

Secondly, Northrop's Voltairian philosophical skepticism and his Socratic methodology not only made an indelible impression on his students, but pushed them beyond the technical aspects of literature to consider the great issues of life. Merrill asks,

> Can any among us who had the good fortune to be his students forget the picture of him, head thrown back and eyes closed, tossing with such apparent innocence from the great wide mouth some bone of iconoclasm for the flexing young minds to ruminate on and contend over? What a devil's advocate he was! And how he would sit back and roar with laughter at our discomfiture!

Merrill adds, from a perspective of twenty-five years:

> It occurs to me that Mr. Northrop, under the guise of teaching English, taught us many things about life far more valuable than English literature. . . . In the middle of our study of "Hamlet," I remember one day taking notes on the digressions that Mr.

FIG. 24. George Norton Northrop, teaching English to Class I, in the headmaster's study (filled with his objets d'art), photographed by *Life* magazine in 1945.

Northrop had made in the course of a single class meeting and reading it to my parents that night. I believe the total number of digressions that day was fifteen, and they encompassed ethics, morals, religion, manners, law, the structure of society, and art.[65]

A man of culture and erudition, he had acquired handsome furnishings, paintings, and objets d'art from Britain and Europe with which he adorned and beautified both his own home and the new schoolhouse.[66] His study at school was filled with treasures. Each week he placed a different art object in the glass case in his study, and boys were bidden to come in and view it (and certain students were required to write brief comments). Northrop, in short, was no humdrum schoolmaster, but a sophisticated man of the world. Comfortable in "society" (he was a member of The Country Club), witty and urbane, he brought to the School "a touch of class."[67]

Northrop was the first headmaster to attend trustee meetings;[68] his predecessors had sent a written report and were told the next day what happened at the meeting. Working closely with the trustees, Northrop

FIG. 25. The May 1952 *Tripod* aerial view, drawn by Edward P. Williams '52, shows the track's location, as well as the Richard Codman estate house in which the headmaster lived.

FIG. 26. The running track built in 1934 at Northrop's initiative.

forcefully led the School to a fuller implementation of the "country day school concept" that underlay its move to West Roxbury. That implementation boiled down to the development of a required program of afternoon athletic activity. Since Northrop himself enjoyed sport, he enthusiastically fulfilled the trustees' mandate "that the country day school program be further developed at the school."[69] Within two years of taking office, he had arranged for a new outdoor track (with nearby pits for pole vaulting and broadjumping), handball courts, and a hockey rink, and had introduced crew and boxing.[70] In the fall of 1935, he changed the closing time from 1:45 to 4:00 P.M. and required that "every boy must stay on the grounds and take part in some sort of exercise" except on Fridays.[71] Picking up the catch phrase from President Roosevelt's first term, *The Tripod* described these innovations as the "New Deal." One of the new exercise options was Mr. Dickey's woodchopping corps that provided wood for the School's fireplaces. *The Tripod* for November 1935 notes that "Four (count 'em) of Mr. Dickey's stalwarts have been hacked and whittled by whizzing axes."[72]

It was therefore no accident that the fall of 1935 brought the first undefeated and untied football team in the School's history.[73] This unbeaten streak continued through 1936 and 1937. The architect of these triumphs was J. Leo Foley. Long the *vox clamantis in deserto* of R.L. athletics, he was no longer alone. Northrop seized every opportunity to appoint younger men—committed to a "full day" experience with boys within and beyond the classroom—to the faculty. Will Cloney, sports writer for *The Boston Herald*, was brought in as apprentice master and assistant football coach; in his second year he was asked to be hockey coach. Lynwood Bryant and Philip Wadsworth taught younger boys soccer; Dick Whitney, softball.[74] Albert Kelsey was both typical and the best of the type: in 1937 he introduced the sport which became R.L.'s perennially most successful—wrestling.[75] The following year, he reintroduced debate to the School, and on March 11, 1938, R.L. won its first debate—taking the affirmative against Noble and Greenough: "Resolved: It would be better for England to follow Neville Chamber-

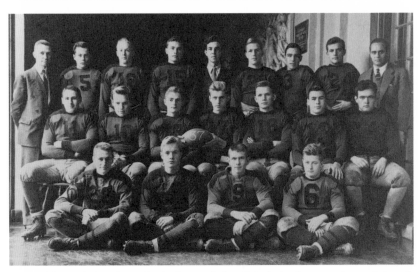

FIG. 27. The undefeated 1937 football team, J. Leo Foley's third consecutive undefeated team. The fourth person from the left in the middle row is Charles T. Bauer '38, captain, presently a trustee of the School.

FIG. 28. The private school championship 1939 track team, with coach J. Leo Foley standing on the far left.

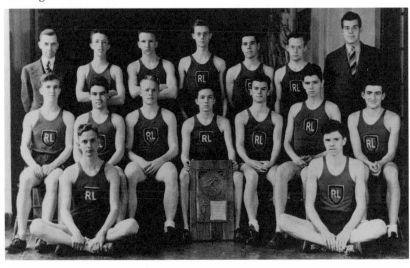

lain's foreign policy rather than Anthony Eden's."[76] The next fall brought a Glee Club "springing up under the auspices of Mr. Northrop and the musical direction of Mr. Fine."[77] In 1939 Northrop submitted detailed plans for a gymnasium,[78] and by 1941 nearly $15,000 of the necessary $22,000 had been raised to build it.[79]

Gone were *The Tripod's* lamentations of earlier decades regarding poor school spirit. Examining committees regularly exuded praise for the quality of the teaching, and boys perennially did well on examinations. Despite the Depression, Northrop had somehow managed to usher in the halcyon era all had hoped for in the Arcady of West Roxbury.

The principal factor in this remarkable turnaround in morale was Northrop's vision of the new role of faculty and parents in the country day school. Some of the School's veteran masters must have squirmed when they heard their relatively new headmaster paint this picture of the faculty of the future:

> Older teachers who operated in the old day-school free from the responsibilities of a programme of supervised play in the afternoon, are naturally loth to adapt themselves to the new system which calls for sacrifices of time and freedom.[80]
>
> So it becomes advisable in filling vacancies in the staff to choose younger men who exemplify that not-impossible combination of physical prowess with intellectual acumen and scholarly interests. Was not Odysseus a good oar as well as an intellectual? Such a policy is now operative in the selection of new members of the staff.[81]

When Farnham passed his sixty-fifth birthday at the end of Northrop's first year, Northrop quietly insisted on his retirement. Two years later he engineered the departure of Howard Wiggin, who had taught at the School since 1912 and who had not reached retirement age.

The masters he hired became R.L. legends in the next generation. M. Philbrick Bridgess and Richard M. Whitney both came to R.L. in 1936. Bridgess was a Phi Beta Kappa graduate of Tufts (1928) who had taught at Colby College and several other schools. An intrepid punster,

FIG. 29. The Northrop faculty, taken in 1945 or 1946 after Mr. Bridgess returned from World War II. *From left:* Ralph H. Houser, Earl W. Taylor, Headmaster G. N. Northrop, Joseph H. Sasserno, M. Philbrick Bridgess, VanCourtlandt Elliott, Richard M. Whitney, Albert W. Kelsey, J. Leo Foley, Richard W. Hale, Jr.

he once told a gathering of Sixth Class parents: "My job is to make sure that your little live wires are well grounded." After taking a leave of absence to serve during World War II as a lieutenant in the Navy, he returned in 1945 and was made master of the First Class and, soon, business manager. But he is best remembered as a brilliant teacher of mathematics at every level. His arithmetic book is still used today in the Sixth Class. As one student remarked:

> Few will forget the dreaded moments when he called you to the blackboard to explain a problem. Invariably your solution was wrong, but the intense Socratic dialogue which followed always illuminated the error. Never did you sit down knowing less than when you began.

The ultimate practitioner of the Socratic method, however, was Richard M. Whitney. At one point or another Whitney taught every subject in the curriculum, but ultimately he settled on science. Not only did he teach biology, physics, and chemistry, but he helped write textbooks in all three areas. His questions were a terror even to the brightest students, and it was not unusual for a boy to get a C in physics and an 800 on the College Board. He and his wife and five children lived in the old gate house at the School's entrance. A great bibliophile, he filled every corner of that tiny house with books. Here on Saturday mornings he would read *Dracula* to the Sixth Class, of which he was master. Bridgess and Whitney both ended their respective thirty-six and forty-three-year careers as senior master.[82]

Northrop's next addition to the faculty came the following year (1937): Albert W. Kelsey, a Princeton graduate, who taught English. Kelsey is best remembered as the originator and twenty-nine-year coach of debate and wrestling at R.L. Jared Diamond '54 comments: "When I compare Roxbury Latin debating under Mr. Kelsey with my subsequent intercollegiate experience at Harvard, the former stands out in my mind as even more stimulating, more enjoyable, and more profound." Kelsey's wrestlers became the School's perennially most successful teams, and the Independent School League tournament still today bears his name. He was, as Eric Solomon '45 notes, an ideal role model:

> It was his persona, his quite clear and confident role as a robust, masculine—athlete, if you will—that made such suspect activities (in a time of adolescent doubt) as debating and English literature respectable. That Bert coached both wrestling and debating is terribly important, I think. His joining of the sports of body and mind made feasible in a certain way some of the old Greek concept of the academy that remains my most treasured memory of Roxbury Latin School.[83]

Northrop's fourth memorable appointment was that of Van Courtlandt Elliott, a true classical scholar and worthy successor of the great Clarence Gleason, whose shrine—the Classical Study—he was to occupy for twenty-five years. "Doc" taught both Latin and Greek, demanding from his students meticulous precision and elegant simplicity in translation. He instilled in many boys a lifelong love of the Classics. He was also the Class III master and advisor to *The Tripod*. At exactly 1:30 each afternoon he could be seen walking briskly down St. Theresa Avenue to catch the bus back to Cambridge—where he was associate editor (and later executive secretary) of the Mediaeval Academy of America.[84]

From the moment he arrived, Northrop brought in professional men to speak to the students in "hall" on their various vocations. He also ruffled the feathers of the old guard by asserting the importance of aesthetics in an R.L. education: "We ought to have a full time teacher of music and the fine arts to instill in the younger boys standards of taste." By 1936 he had turned the Green Room adjoining the stage in Rousmaniere Hall into a music listening room equipped with a victrola and a library of classical music.[85]

Another aspect of the country day philosophy that Northrop developed was the involvement of parents. At the old school, parents had virtually never entered the campus: no games were played or concerts or plays given there. Although the Parents' Auxiliary was established in embryo in 1929–1930, two years after the School came to West Roxbury,[86] it was Northrop who developed and encouraged its activities. At first the auxiliary confined itself to raising money for items that would enrich the School's life: uniforms, movie projectors, victrolas, the two-inch pipe for the 1934 hockey rink, and the like. Northrop encouraged parents to come to the campus, and gradually the auxiliary took charge of receptions for special events such as debates. The auxiliary's role today—its special events such as the Giant Yard Sale and the Auction, as well as the hundreds of receptions it hosts for athletic and cultural events—is the outgrowth of Northrop's vision of the place of parents in the country day school.

Northrop delighted in the diversity of the parents and students. He records, in his September 1941 report to the trustees, the first known religious census of the student body:

FIGS. 30—31. The courtyard (*above*) and library (*below*) in about 1940.

> It may be of interest to the Trustees to know something of the woof and the warp that make up the religious fabric of the school. We have [out of 141 students] 81 Protestants [here he included anyone who was not Roman Catholic or Jewish], 48 Roman Catholics, and 12 Jews. . . . The social background could hardly be more representative of the democracy we profess. . . . Of the fathers of our pupils, 16 are manufacturers, 13 salesmen, 11 doctors, 8 teachers, 7 lawyers, 6 engineers, 5 insurance salesmen, 4 in government service, 4 purchasing agents, 4 contractors, 3 bankers, 3 clergy, 2 judges, 2 architects, 2 distributors, 2 wool brokers, 2 importers. . . . We have an optometrist, a steamfitter, a botanist, an army officer, a radio announcer, an author, and finally an undertaker. Surely the school represents as typical a cross-section of our American middle-class life as can be found anywhere.

Roxbury Latin was unique in being so thoroughly "middle class" in its clientele. Its rival independent schools were much more the denizens of the well-to-do, as were the private colleges (including Harvard). It is unfair, perhaps, from our perspective over a half-century later to note that the idea of "diversity" did not extend to finding and including sons of "blue collar" fathers. Even stranger to us, perhaps, is the fact that no mention is made of "working" mothers or of members of racial and ethnic minorities.

Northrop had steered the School through the nation's worst-ever depression and somehow contrived to make it a golden age. But just as better times—and the hope of realizing his vision fully—appeared to be around the corner, the nation was plunged into World War II by the Japanese bombing of Pearl Harbor on December 7, 1941. The headmaster reported that month that

> Like other schools, we are preparing for possible air raids. We have pails of sand on all floors, and large containers of sand in the attic and outside the doors on the ground floor. The boys are to have the appropriate drills. The large corridor in the basement makes an excellent and roomy air raid shelter, since it has no windows, has five exits, brick walls, and is below concrete floors.[87]

The war quickly took its toll on the School, disrupting almost every aspect of its life.[88] Since oil was virtually unobtainable, one of the boilers was converted to burn coal, and a fireman had to be hired to stoke and tend it.[89] When oil was finally received in 1944, it was too thick to burn, and the insurance company refused to let the School warm it to make it usable.[90] Lack of fuel resulted in the sealing off of Rousmaniere Hall during the winters of 1942–43 and 1943–44.[91] A power saw was purchased to increase the amount of wood that could be cut on campus for classroom fireplaces—in order to maintain a reasonable level of warmth.[92] Gas rationing made transportation to away games difficult, and much of the energy normally channeled into sport was now concentrated on the new obstacle course set up on the grounds.[93] While this "commando course," as the boys called it, was not as much fun as sports, boys admitted that it "kept us physically fit and prepared us for whatever the armed services may demand of us." The same was true of the "self-defense" course offered by Mr. Whitney and Mr. Hale during the winter.[94] Last but not least, the manufacture of knickers ceased as industry was pressed more and more onto a war basis, and the Sixth Class was no longer able to wear its traditional garb.[95]

Extensive curricular changes were introduced in order to prepare boys for the armed services. Trigonometry was made compulsory, geography was revised to include extensive work in map-reading, a class in navigation was instituted,[96] and Sixies were taught the Morse code.[97] The program was accelerated starting in Class III, and a summer school was established so that boys could receive their "war diplomas" early and go into the service.[98] Even so, quite a number of boys left before graduating to attend cram schools to prepare for quicker entry into the armed forces.

Because older boys were leaving early, the numbers in the upper classes were decimated. In 1943 and 1944, the play was abandoned. By the fall of 1943 there were not enough older boys to constitute a football team, and the schedule was dropped.[99] Hockey and crew were also abandoned and other "schedules" drastically curtailed.[100] Gasoline rationing added to the School's enrollment problems by making it difficult for boys to drive in from the suburbs. As a result, School opened in 1942 with only 136 boys, and in 1943 with a mere 128, nearly fifty fewer than a decade earlier.[101]

The high "school spirit" of the 1930s naturally plummeted under such conditions. The popular young math teacher, M. Philbrick Bridgess, was called into the Navy in the fall of 1942. Diminished numbers, frequent student departures during the school year, the cancelling or curtailing of sports, drama, and other activities all took their toll on student morale. In November 1944, *The Tripod* noted, "We are very sorry to announce that during the past few years school spirit has reached an unparalleled low."[102] The strain of coping with endless crises exhausted the headmaster—who was hospitalized for a protracted period in 1943–44. Extra responsibilities also burdened an already overworked faculty. A joint meeting of the trustees and Alumni Council in February 1944 showed how the general war-weariness had tested the patience of all; there was much talk about revitalizing the School under new leadership.[103] Northrop, however, remained much beloved by the boys. The Class of 1945—twelve in all!—not only gave, as their class gift, money for a portrait of the headmaster, but also dedicated their yearbook to him: "We have been honored indeed to enjoy your kindly ministrations and heartfelt understanding. Your ready wit and zeal for the beauties of English literature have made your classes a delightful experience."[104]

The School's tercentenary came in 1945 midst all the dislocations of war. To celebrate, Van Courtlandt Elliott and Richard M. Whitney directed the first school play in three years: a production of Aristophanes' *The Clouds* in English (with prologue in Greek) on June 1 in the Hall. The alumni did their part by raising a record $11,299 for the annual fund from 578 donors. *Life* magazine commemorated the tercentenary with a picture essay on the School. And the trustees commissioned the School's young history master (later Archivist of the Commonwealth), Richard Walden Hale, Jr., to write a history of Roxbury Latin.

Because so many alumni were still in the armed services and since gasoline rationing and war restrictions on other forms of transportation were still in effect, the principal celebration of the 300th anniversary was postponed to the weekend of May 16–18 in 1946. The festivities began with Mr. Whitney's Thursday evening production of Ben Jonson's *The Alchemist* in Rousmaniere Hall with all roles taken by boys. On Friday, alumni and their wives were invited to the baseball game at 4:00 P.M. (in which R.L. defeated Rivers), then to a buffet supper and dance sponsored by the Alumni Association. On Saturday, alumni could choose between a golf tournament and an all-day educational symposium. In the morning Harvard President James Bryant Conant '10 and Columbia psychologist Edward Lee Thorndike '91 addressed the topic "Selection and Guidance in Secondary Education," and Lewis Perry of Phillips Exeter Academy presided over the ensuing discussion that involved a number of guests from other schools. The afternoon session, featuring Headmasters Fuess of Andover and Eames of Governor Dummer along with New York State Commissioner of Education George D. Stoddard, addressed the issue of what schools should teach; Headmaster Northrop led the discussion that followed. The Tercentenary Dinner—for alumni only—was held that night at the Harvard Club; President Conant was the principal speaker.

Ironically, the war era had somewhat eased the School's financial situation. Throughout the 1940s, the budget was usually balanced and faculty salaries were increased. When the six-acre John S. Codman property at 57 Quail Street (the present headmaster's house and part of "Bogandale Field") came on the market in 1935, Trustee President Roger Ernst had written, "Of course there cannot be any question that we are in no position to make such a purchase." But by 1945, confidence had returned and the trustees snapped up the property when it was offered again for $17,000.[105] Work was begun on the "Codman Meadow" (today's "Bogandale Field") in the summer to clear a small space for younger boys.[106] At her death in the tercentenary year, Dean Rousmaniere's widow—who had given the Hall—left the School $50,000.[107]

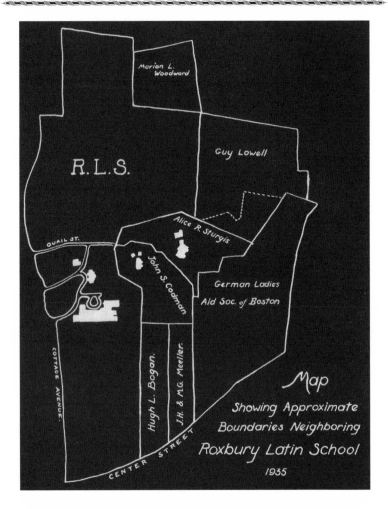

FIG. 32. Rough blueprint, 1935, showing the School's property, that is, the original Richard Codman Estate (from Centre Street [here misspelled] up Cottage Avenue [later renamed St. Theresa Avenue] and beyond). The John S. Codman estate was purchased by the School in 1945. The estate house is the present headmaster's house; the property is the present "Bogandale" field. The Alice R. Sturgis estate was in the possession of Jerome L. Rappaport when it was purchased in 1980 by the School. The Sturgis estate house was torn down in the mid-1980s when the upper fields (completed in 1990) were developed. The Hugh Bogan property was developed as present Bogandale Road.

Though Roxbury Latin's invested funds had risen in value to nearly $800,000 by the war's end,[108] the trustees realized that much more would be needed to keep the School strong in the future. As they set to work raising money, however, they went out of their way to state in strong terms that they did not wish Roxbury Latin to become a private school that catered to the aristocratic or plutocratic classes. In his address at the 300th celebration, President Roger Ernst stated that since there were plenty of private schools "fully taking care of the more favored economic strata—there is no need for another such school."[109] Roxbury Latin's mission was different. Its destiny was to be "an endowed school with a democratic background in an urban area . . . , composed of boys of special ability and promise, open to any boy of high character and outstanding ability, whatever his means."[110] To maintain such a school, the trustees concluded that the School needed at least $1 million in new funds. They therefore launched an appeal in 1946 to enable the School to double its annual expenses, "which is more than necessary to enable it to compete in teachers' salaries and the appropriate number of teachers."[111] Their immediate effort to raise $100,000 toward the goal from ten wealthy alumni, alas, succeeded in securing only $55,941.[112] And only $17,500 was in hand toward the goal of erecting the long-desired gymnasium (estimated in 1946 to have risen in cost to between $80,000 and $90,000).

Following the war's end, the easing of gasoline rationing brought an increase in applications, so that in Northrop's final year the twenty-nine members of Class VI were chosen from seventy-five applications.[113] With ranks swelled by several war veterans returning for a refresher course, the total student population jumped to 165. The Class of 1947 tied with one other school for the highest number of students admitted to Harvard in proportion to the size of the senior class. The School's sporting fortunes—and therefore its morale—also bounced back with the end of the war. The 1946 varsity football team was undefeated, and the 1947 baseball team had only one loss.

In conjunction with the 300th anniversary, the trustees tried to put

FIG. 33. The undefeated 1946 football team, with J. Leo Foley standing far left and Albert Kelsey far right.

their house in order. They went again to the Legislature to secure changes in the School's 1789 Charter. Chapter 345 of the Massachusetts Acts of 1947[114] made *de jure* what had long been *de facto* by changing the School's official name from "The Trustees of the Grammar School in the Easterly Part of the Town of Roxbury" to "The Trustees of the Roxbury Latin School." It also recognized the decline of the First Church by reducing its representation from three trustees to one. At this same time, it increased the maximum number of trustees from thirteen to fifteen: one ex-officio trustee from the church, five alumni trustees, and up to nine life trustees.[115]

Northrop was now over sixty-five and tired from the strain of depression and war. It was time to pass the baton. Nothing better exemplifies his breadth of vision than his swan song to the Parents' Auxiliary in his final year. Although the old New England Protestant families had by now largely deserted the School, middle class Protestant families dominated in the 1920s and 1930s. In the 1920 mock presidential election, the Republican candidates (Harding and Coolidge) won the School 115–20; in the 1934 Massachusetts gubernatorial election, the School voted 129 for the Republican Bacon and twenty-three for Curley—though Curley won the real election; and in the 1936 presidential election, in which Roosevelt carried all but two states, boys voted for Alf Landon 3–1! But by the 1930s, and especially by the 1940s, the student body was becoming more local and more Catholic. By 1944–45, only 38 percent of the student body was Protestant, while 38 percent was Catholic and 14 percent Jewish.[116] Northrop confided his concern privately to a trustee when—as he saw it—the Catholics on the Parents' Auxiliary deliberately connived to take control of that organization. He said nothing in public, but in his final—amazingly "modern"—word to the parents he warned against narrowing the School's openness to boys of all backgrounds:

> Nothing could be more unfortunate than for this school to turn into a local institution. . . . We did not come here for that purpose. To live up to our tradition, we must minister to the wide area we were incorporated to serve and welcome all corners of greater Boston boys . . . to enable them to take their place to serve the commonwealth. I only wish we had able representatives of the black race, sons of Asiatics and of South Americans to give us an even more cosmopolitan flavour than we have and to present to the world a living laboratory of the United Nations in a coöperative enterprise.

3. *Weed—Years of Rigor*

Frederick Redfield Weed succeeded Northrop as headmaster in June 1947. Born in Brookline in 1906, he attended Country Day School and graduated from St. Mark's School (1924) and Harvard College (1928). After travelling around the world, he settled down to a career in banking, but found it monotonous and unfulfilling. Shortly after marrying Margaret Jarvis in 1930, he returned to Harvard to obtain a master's degree in English and then went back to his alma mater, St. Mark's, to

FIG. 34. Frederick Redfield Weed, headmaster 1947–1965, here pictured in his early years.

teach. At St. Mark's he headed the English department and served as assistant headmaster and acting headmaster.

Weed was only forty, and he seemed to offer the rejuvenating leadership which the School needed to renew itself after the decimating years of the Great Depression and World War II. Roxbury Latin was by no means ideally positioned to face the new challenges of the post-war era. The School had a tiny faculty. Nine full-time masters (including the headmaster), two part-time masters, and an athletic director were teaching a curriculum almost devoid of choice to 159 boys. There was no gymnasium and very limited field space for outdoor sports. Admission was almost completely limited to Class VI because boys began Latin then, and boys could enter the School in later classes only if they had taken the equivalent Latin at another school. These realities—not to mention the competition of other, better-positioned private and public schools—made Weed's task a difficult one.

He immediately focused on broadening and enriching Roxbury Latin's academic and extracurricular life. By his second year, for instance, he had freed up Ralph Houser to offer the School's first-ever course in biology. That same year Weed enlisted Gerhard Rehder (history master, 1947–1975) to produce the first "junior play" (for boys in Classes VI, V, and IV), a tradition that has been maintained every year since May 1949. That year also saw the appearance of the first "free-standing" yearbook (which, until then, had been the final issue of *The Tripod*).

Despite Northrop's valiant efforts in the 1930s, the School did not yet have a country day school program. Mark Granofsky '51 recalls that few masters coached or helped with extracurricular activities: "I came back as a college student to coach at R.L. and the students were still doing then just what we had done at their age: joke about which master would be the first one down St. Theresa Avenue after school on a given day—whether by foot or by car." When the German teacher was unable to continue at R.L. at the end of Weed's first year, Weed proposed that German be "temporarily" dropped[117] and that a new faculty member be hired to help Mr. Kelsey—whose eyesight was failing—with English. Weed offered this position to fellow St. Mark's graduate Cary Potter. Weed's most enduring legacy to Roxbury Latin was the appointment of excellent all-around "country day school types" like Potter to the faculty.

In addition to helping with English, Potter offered a "modern" elective in contemporary history. At Weed's request he also revived hockey. Hockey had continued strong (on the 1934–35 homemade rink) through the 1930s but died during the war. Weed asked Potter to revive it: "There was no sign of the 1930s rink when I arrived. We practiced off campus on Turtle Pond, in Westwood, and anyplace else we could find ice. We competed at the varsity level only with the smallest schools—Brooks and Rivers. Otherwise our opponents were all j.v. teams. It was a huge expenditure of time and effort for a few boys and we soon gave it up."[118] Potter also reintroduced soccer as a recreational activity between the fall and winter seasons. It quickly became popular, and by 1952 Potter was coaching a varsity soccer team at the other end of the varsity football field. By 1953 Weed had made him assistant headmaster, a position he held for four years before going on to an illustrious career as head of

FIG. 35. Cary Potter pictured with the School's first soccer team in 1952.

what is now the National Association of Independent Schools. He later returned to serve as a trustee from 1961 to 1973.

One of the first problems Weed faced was that of admissions. Right after the war ended, there had been an initial bump up in numbers. Unfortunately it was not sustained. The ten years following World War II were the heyday of American public education. In 1952, Weed reported to the trustees on an address by Harvard's President Conant. The fact that Conant was an R.L. graduate and trustee made his warning all the more alarming: "[In] President Conant's unofficial talk to the National Council of Independent Schools, [he] visualized a situation in fifty or more years when public schools would be sufficient for the education of American youth."[119]

Roxbury Latin did not have to wait fifty years; it was only too aware of the keen competition provided by Boston Latin and by nationally-renowned public school systems such as Newton, Brookline, and

Wellesley. By 1949 applications had dropped to sixty, of whom thirty-three were accepted. There were therefore no longer enough incoming students to balance those who left each year by attrition, and by 1951 the number of boys in the School had slumped to 144—down twenty-one from 1947.[120] Some of the younger alumni sought to help recruit potential students for the School and to make it better known in greater Boston.[121] They discovered that suburban Protestant families regarded Irish Catholic West Roxbury as an alien world, far removed from their own. The alumni recruiters therefore contacted suburban Protestant clergy in order to tell them about Roxbury Latin. The School also advertised in the Symphony's programs, *The Harvard Alumni Magazine*, and *The Christian Science Monitor*.[122] Trustees Dennis, Mittell, and others arranged Sunday afternoon "teas" in towns such as Wellesley and Needham for parents of potential students.[123]

Another detriment to the School's recruiting effort was its limited physical plant. While older alumni regarded the "new school" as a veritable palace, Roxbury Latin was competing with surrounding public and private high schools that had far more lavish buildings and grounds. Roxbury Latin called itself a country day school, but it had neither the facilities nor the program to back that claim. There was only one standard-sized field: the present varsity soccer field along Centre Street (then used for football, soccer, and baseball). Today's varsity football field (paralleling St. Theresa Avenue) sloped heavily at the schoolhouse end and was barely adequate for the junior teams to practice and play on. The School still had no gymnasium and therefore no basketball program. Hockey had died in 1953 after Potter's brief revival. That left two winter sports: wrestling (which attracted nearly forty boys) and track on Leo Foley's wooden track set up over the swamp (where the practice field adjoining the varsity football field is now located). After 1958, however, track also died, leaving wrestling the School's sole winter sport.

The boys of R.L. had been clamoring for a gymnasium since the 1880s, and the construction of such a facility had been "just around the

FIG. 36. The foundations of the Albert H. Gordon Field House being laid in 1956–57.

corner" through most of the intervening years. Finally in 1954, realizing that without a gymnasium the School could not compete successfully for the best students, the trustees—with Weed's urging—hired Hugh Stubbins and Associates to design a field house and launched a campaign to raise $190,000 to build it. Opened in 1957—at an eventual cost of $278,000—it contained a gymnasium, wrestling room, squash court, and locker room. Its graceless exterior—happily long since surrounded by plantings—is redeemed by its enduring interior functionality. The Albert H. Gordon Field House was named for the moving spirit behind the whole venture: "It was his enthusiasm that persuaded even the hesitant trustees that the project was feasible, and that the time was fitting; it was his generosity which allowed the building to be ample, rather than merely adequate."[124]

Weed had long desired to offer woodworking as a curricular and extracurricular activity. When the old wrestling room was vacated in 1957, it was transformed into a woodworking shop by a new teacher who had recently been discharged from the Marines: Robert S. Jorgensen, who is today—thirty-eight years later—senior master. When shop was abandoned in 1988, the room became the art studio. When art moved to the new Arts Center in 1993, the room reverted to its earlier use and became the junior wrestling area.

The trustees next turned their attention to finding adequate field space. Between 1960 and 1962 they authorized funds for three major projects. First, they developed the "Quail Street Field" at the corner of St. Theresa Avenue and Quail Street, along with the adjoining practice area (called "Potter's Field" then and "Flea Patch" now) at a cost of $35,000. Then they enlarged the play area that had been cleared in 1947 at the end of Bogandale Road, blasting and bulldozing a soccer field and baseball diamond at a cost of $37,500. These three new fields—Quail Street, Flea Patch, and Bogandale—were not regulation size, but they were extremely useful spaces for younger boys. Finally, in the fall of 1962, the trustees authorized $52,400 to level the present varsity football field next to the School and to build a practice field next to it on the site of the old board track (which had been torn down in 1958). When the new field had been leveled, the varsity football team moved "up" to it. The soccer team then had the Centre Street field to itself; previously, it had practiced at the other end of the field from the football team and played almost all its games "away."[125] With increased field space, "lower" teams proliferated and all boys could now be accommodated in fall and spring. By 1960 Warden Dilworth (master, 1956–1972) had won approval to launch lacrosse as a spring sport.

Such facilities doubtless helped to make the School more attractive to the discerning parent, but, while the field house and new fields were still aborning, the School's numbers rose—along with those of other schools—largely because of the "baby boom." In 1952 the School numbered 157; by 1956, 183; by 1960, 200. In 1952 the School admitted forty-three of the fifty-eight applicants; in 1958 fifty-one out of 122.

With the numbers and facilities crises ameliorated, the trustees in 1960 could at last focus on the most important question: the School's identity. Two earlier reports had addressed the identity issue: the 1931 Ernst-Donald Report, made two years before Northrop was elected headmaster, and the 1945 Holmes Report, made two years before Weed took the helm.

The 1931 Report of trustees Roger Ernst and Malcolm Donald is poignant and nostalgic in tone. Reviewing the rise of eminent New England boarding schools and strong Boston area private day schools, they conclude:

> These schools draw many boys of the type which thirty to fifty years ago would have entered Roxbury Latin School. They are active competitors and they are growing. . . .
>
> One other factor must be taken into account. The boarding schools and certain of the metropolitan day schools have acquired *social standing* which, rightly or wrongly, is an important consideration in the minds of most parents choosing a school for boys. *It is doubtful if the Roxbury Latin School can ever hope to compete in this respect,* even if it should wish to do so.
>
> During this period the Roxbury Latin School has constructed an attractive, new schoolhouse and enlarged its endowment, but, comparatively speaking, *it has fallen seriously behind in financial strength and in prestige and popularity,* not due to its being a less effective school, but due to the rise and development of these other schools. [Emphasis added.]

Years of procrastination—1890 to 1926—had cost the School dearly: as Roxbury Latin dithered about its future, its traditional clientele vanished to new schools which quickly outstripped the old school in campus, facilities, program, and social prestige. What then, was to be Roxbury Latin's future "place"? Ernst and Donald's answer was to locate the School's identity in *academic rigor*:

> The School [should] select boys of real intellectual promise and maintain a really high standard of scholarship. No boy who did not measure up to the standard would be admitted or retained. . . . There is no school at present which devotes itself to the intellectual training of a group of selected boys of unusual intellectual capacity. . . . The purpose of the trustees would be to have the School devote itself to the most useful function that it can perform. To

FIGS. 37–38. Malcolm Donald '95, trustee 1924–1949 (vice president 1942–46), *left* (Harvard Archives Collection); Roger Ernst '98, trustee 1919–1955 (president 1935–1955), *right.*

attempt to make the school compete with other schools in a field in which they probably have an advantage [i.e., socially] is likely only to destroy the prestige of the school and serve no useful purpose.[126]

The 1945 Report of Henry W. Holmes, former dean of the Harvard School of Education—written near the end of the Northrop years—was a reiteration of the 1931 Ernst-Donald Report. This is hardly surprising since Roger Ernst (trustee, 1919–1955) was president of the trustees from 1935 to 1955, and Malcolm Donald (trustee, 1924–1949) vice president from 1942 to 1949. The School's "niche," Holmes said, was to be a place for the academically gifted:

> In the public schools it is especially difficult to use the knowledge now available for guidance, because the public schools have to deal with large numbers and are forced to spend much effort on the maladjustments due to various types of disability. . . . The delicate processes by which special talents [of the gifted] may be detected and fostered at critical junctures are hard to initiate in public-school systems. . . . In practice, the special treatment of the gifted is resented. Public schools, moreover, find it hard to arrange

programs, assign teachers, and make other necessary adjustments which special provision for pupils of high ability requires.

The Roxbury Latin School is committed by its charter and tradition to the selection of gifted youth. It is committed to giving them an education suited to their abilities without let or hindrance due to poverty.... Here is a type and field of educational endeavor clearly related to the basic purposes of public education in America. Here the Trustees of the School believe they can 'raise a standard to which the wise and honest may repair.'[127]

In 1954, the year before he died, Ernst was still mourning the loss of the "socialite" (i.e., old Protestant, Yankee) element in the School's population and still reiterating his pessimism about attracting it back to the School:

> I still feel . . . that we should still endeavor to persuade boys of the group which Mr. Farnham describes as "socialites" to enter the School, simply because they are part of the community and we should like to have an element of them, even though it is a small element, still in the School. As a practical matter, however, it is becoming much more difficult to persuade the parents of such boys to enter them as applicants, simply because they want their boys to be in a school that is more predominantly of the same social group. . . . I am quite reconciled to the practical probability that the School from now on will find its function to be to give superior preparation for college to boys of better than average intelligence and character in the non-socialite element of the Greater Boston community. . . . I am somewhat concerned with the failure of the School to attract . . . a sufficient number of boys of the non-socialite group who are definitely above [average intelligence].[128]

Weed accepted the mandate of these two reports, and pursued a policy of seeking out boys of high intellectual capability for a School which, throughout his years, increasingly became known as a "grind" school in which the prevailing atmosphere was "sink or swim." Weed himself admitted in 1952 that "our reputation for having a high rate of mortality is already considerable."[129] Midway through Weed's headmastership, however, President Ernst and Vice President Donald both died in office, in 1955 and 1949 respectively. By that time a reaction had set in against their policy.

With the ascension of Arthur Perry '02 to the presidency in 1955, the winds of change began to blow. In an effort to open the windows on the board, Perry appointed a committee to consider ways in which fresh voices—including non-alumni voices—could be heard. By 1960 the trustees had asked for and received from the Legislature an Act (Chapter 143) which provided for the election of five trustees-at-large for three-year terms.[130]

The new president also appointed a long-range planning committee whose principal moving force was David A. Mittell '35. This committee met at great length to consider every aspect of school life. Its 1961 Report made thirteen major recommendations for change, and in essence redefined the School's identity—away from the 1931 and 1945 Reports—by the manner in which it addressed the three most critical issues:

1. THE PROBLEM OF ATTRITION. The School admitted boys almost entirely on the basis of intellectual ability. Its academic rigor had become more and more notorious. Of the 192 boys in School in 1957–58, for instance, twenty-one were dismissed for academic reasons, and a further ten withdrew. Of the forty boys admitted to the Class of 1960, only sixteen survived until their Class I year, and *The Tripod*'s editors asked, "Isn't 40% a poor batting average?" The public perceived that Roxbury Latin cared little about anything except academic achievement. The committee recommended that the School "Maintain our academic standards at the highest level *commensurate with the non-academic ends we seek to attain.*"

The committee firmly reasserted the priority which the Founder had placed on *character*: "Each student should be made to realize that it is the School's hope to give the best education it can for an individual's eventual service to his fellow-man, and not for self-aggrandizement."[131]

The faculty needed to care more about the totality of the individual boy, and not just about his academic attributes: "With an honest, willing boy the School should work with understanding and patience even if he is marginal academically by school standards."

Since 1957, three and a half positions had been added to the faculty (which made a net of six added since 1947) in order to reduce the faculty-student ratio to twelve to one.[132] The committee recommended that two more masters, at (a for-the-time generous) $5000 each, be added as well as "more classroom space." They hoped that these measures would enable the faculty to provide more individual attention. What they desired was a faculty less concerned with judging students and more committed to supporting them, less concerned with "weeding them out" and more committed to "keeping them in."

2. THE PROBLEM OF DIVERSITY. Though the School failed to lure back "socialite" old Protestant families, by 1960 it had attracted a large number of boys from affluent suburban families. By 1960 there were only thirty-six students from the "Old Roxbury District," and thirty-one of these boys lived in the comparative affluence of West Roxbury and Jamaica Plain. There were very few boys from "blue collar" families, very few city boys from poor neighborhoods, and (except for one boy for two months) no blacks, Hispanics, or Asians.

The committee felt the School's definition of an "able boy" was too narrowly academic. (In 1959 Phillips Exeter Academy bragged about the giant leap its median SAT scores had taken: 640 verbal and 693 mathematical; Roxbury Latin's scores that year were 682 and 710.) In seeking candidates for admission, the committee recommended that the School seek out a more diverse group of students in *talent* (strong musicians and athletes, for example) and in social and in economic *background*: "We urge that our recruiting program strengthen its efforts to attract a larger percentage of able poor boys than at present"—ideally with a third of the students on full scholarships. Until 1960, the headmaster interviewed almost all applicants himself, and after reviewing their school records, determined who would or would not be taken. In 1960, in response to the committee's efforts, the first director of admissions was appointed. One problem identified early on was "a lack of interest in our school on the part of the Protestant Christian community."[133] Another affirmative action effort was undertaken to contact Protestant clergy in greater Boston. In 1964 Weed noted that "a considerable amount of time and effort was devoted to securing negro boys for the entering sixth class." The first black boy entered the School in the fall of 1960, but left after less than two months. Three black boys from Roxbury entered in 1964 as the result of the School's recruiting efforts. Students in the upper three classes were also actively engaged in tutoring inner-city children at St. James' Church in Roxbury that fall.

To attract a diverse student body, the committee recommended that the School should "Maintain a somewhat *lower tuition rate* than the other independent day schools, with an *adequate scholarship program* to permit our selection of students we would like to attract regardless of their ability to pay."

3. THE PROBLEM OF THE QUALITY OF THE SCHOOL'S LIFE BEYOND THE CLASSROOM. Although the Gordon Field House had been in use since 1957, there was still no basketball program. The committee recommended that the School broaden its athletic offerings to include such sports as basketball and hockey. (R.L.'s first interscholastic basketball season came, as a result, in 1962–63.)[134] There was also concern that many of the School's athletic teams were perennial losers. Extracurricular activities also "should be various and numerous." Underlying this recommendation was a worry which could not be publicly expressed: that the ambience of the School had become joyless and stressful because the academic pressures were unrelieved by balancing outlets beyond the classroom or by affectionate support from the faculty.

After the trustees considered all the committee's recommendations, they forthwith implemented several. To accommodate a larger number of faculty teaching boys in smaller groups, for example, they could and did provide the necessary physical facilities. Perry's 1927 building had been designed for 180 boys in six individual classes of thirty. By 1963, there were 216 boys in the school plus additional faculty to teach them

FIG. 39. Aerial view of the School taken April 4, 1962. The gymnasium had been added in 1957, but the Ernst Wing was not yet built.

in reduced sections. The trustees therefore asked architect William Halsey to design a classroom and office addition. Rejecting his first efforts—a semi-detached building in a style incongruent with Perry's 1927 building—the trustees insisted on a Perryesque addition which was opened, at a total cost of $483,000, in 1966. It was dedicated to Roger Ernst, trustee president 1935–1955.

The trustees addressed the issue of diversity by coming to grips with the last vestiges of the Putnam legacy: the fact that tuition reduction was still based neither on need (with rare exceptions) nor on merit but on place of residence. At the start of the Weed regime in 1947, families living in the "Old Roxbury District" paid $100 a year, while families living outside paid $300. That year 78 boys came from within the district and 77 from outside.[135] The comfortably middle class families who lived within the district, mostly in West Roxbury and Jamaica Plain, there-

FIG. 40. The foundations of the Ernst Wing being laid in 1964.

fore paid only a third of what a poor family from Dorchester (for instance) was asked to pay.

Making geography, rather than need or merit, the basis of reduced tuition had often been questioned over the years.[136] Prominent alumnus Stanwood G. Wellington '96 wrote in 1918: "It does seem rather foolish that a boy who, for example, lives on Commonwealth Avenue or Berkeley Street in the Back Bay can attend the School free of charge, while if he lives on Beacon Street or Arlington Street he will have to pay tuition."[137] When Arthur Vining Davis '84—the aluminum magnate— was asked for a major donation in 1948, he objected to geography still being the basis of reduced tuition.[138] Their doubts ever-increasing, the trustees left the outside tuition at $300, but raised the district tuition first to $150 in 1948–49 and then to $200 in 1951–52.

Trustee President Roger Ernst expressed the prevailing feeling that "there no longer exists the marked difference between the old free district and the broader area of metropolitan Boston." Obviously, modern modes of transportation had made the School more easily accessible to greater Boston in the twentieth century than it was to much of Old Roxbury in the seventeenth. The School's availability to boys who lived near enough to attend it, "when circumstances might otherwise keep them from getting an education of the caliber offered by the better independent schools" was, in his view, "the general objective of the School."[139] Over time the trustees came to realize that, if anything remained of his bequest, Bell would have wanted it to be distributed not on the basis of where a boy lived but on the basis of a boy's need. Bell's desired beneficiary, as we have seen, was "poore mens children."[140]

In June 1960 the trustees finally put an end to geographical discrimination.[141] Starting in the school year 1961–62, tuition would be uniform for all. Since the School's objective was to admit a diverse and able student body without regard to a student's ability to pay, in the future tuition reduction would be made only on the basis of need. The trustees had been giving such reductions ("scholarships") since they raised the district tuition in 1951. Tuition reductions that year totaled $1,840. By 1954, 13 out of 163 boys were receiving scholarships totaling $2600. In 1960, when a uniform tuition of $550 was voted, the trustees simultaneously announced a liberalized scholarship program. Three years later, 53 boys were receiving $26,400. At last the School had unshackled itself from the remaining fetters of Putnam's legacy. At last the School would be free (i.e., accessible) to all, from the richest to the poorest. At last the School would be operating in conformity with the spirit of Eliot's and Bell's intentions.

This policy had the intended effect of enhancing the diversity of the student body by increasing the number of boys from less affluent families — and in particular by enlarging the number of boys from the School's historic catchment area — the "Old Roxbury District" and the City of Boston. In 1960–61, in the last year of the tuition differential, 38 boys out of 200 (19 percent) lived in the City of Boston. In 1994–95, 78 boys out of 275 (28.4 percent) live in the City of Boston, even though, in that period, the number of school-aged children in the City has *decreased* dramatically. In 1960–61 there was one boy from Roxbury and none from Dorchester. In 1994–95 there are 7 boys from Roxbury and 16 from Dorchester. In 1960–61 there were (with one brief exception) no blacks, Hispanics, or Asians in the School. In 1994–95 72 out of 275 students (26.2 percent) are "minority" students, including 39 blacks (14.2 percent). In 1961–62, 7 percent of the student body received $5,625 in scholarship aid; in 1994–95, 32 percent received $616,725.

All the recommendations in the 1961 Report—increased faculty, better facilities, an equitable tuition and scholarship program that encouraged diversity—could be and were addressed by the trustees on their own. And they did so without opposition from the headmaster. But on the all-important issue of the School's "atmosphere"—which the attrition rate came to symbolize—the trustees could not effect the change they wanted.

As to the problem of attrition, Weed could point out that he had appointed well-rounded schoolmen who realized that teaching was not limited to the classroom: Cary Potter and Warden Dilworth, mentioned above; Ted Sizer (on his way to becoming Harvard Education School dean and innovator); John Ambrose (future Bowdoin College classics professor); and Hugh Campbell (who, on his way to a headmastership, put the School on the "cutting edge" in modern language instruction by lobbying for and obtaining for R.L. a "language laboratory" in late 1963). While these men went on to great accomplishments elsewhere, others chose to stay for most of their lives, to labor, with great accomplishment, in the R.L. vineyard: E. Robert M. Yerburgh, classics master and drama director, for twenty-four years; Kay Hubbard, School secretary, college guidance director, and assistant to the headmaster, for twenty-six years; and Gerhard Rehder, history department chairman and alumni secretary, for twenty-eight years. And three of Weed's appointments are still going strong after thirty-five years or more: Robert S. Jorgensen, the senior master, who led the School into the age of computers and who served as "clerk of the works" in the transformation of the campus; William E. Chauncey, assistant head-

FIG. 41. The Weed faculty, 1962–63. *Seated from left:* Gerhard Rehder, Albert Kelsey, M. Philbrick Bridgess, Headmaster F. R. Weed, Richard M. Whitney, Van Courtlandt Elliott, E. Wesley O'Neill. *Standing:* Robert W. Siemens, Warden Dilworth, Edward F. Galvin, Jr., Hugh D. Campbell, Robert S. Jorgensen, E. Robert M. Yerburgh, William E. Chauncey, J. F. Maguire, Desmond C. B. O'Grady, John A. Davey.

master, varsity baseball coach for twenty-seven years, director of admissions, sometime Sixth Class master and coach of sixie football; and John A. Davey, Arthur Vining Davis Professor of Greek and Latin and sometime chairman of that department, photographer, archivist, and librarian. Nothing speaks more highly of Weed than this living legacy to Roxbury Latin!

The men Weed appointed in their twenties all mention his interest in them and his kindness towards them. Bill Chauncey notes:

> Fred was beloved by the young faculty and their wives. He backed us to the hilt and I think many times he took flak without embarrassing the faculty member who caused it. In my early days as varsity baseball coach, when R.L.'s baseball fortunes were not what they are today, Fred would frequently stop me in the hallway and, always with a smile and kindly twinkle in his eye, say, 'Bill, tell me about your game yesterday.' (He would never ask, 'Did you win or

lose?' His approach was always one of interest in how things had gone.) Successes—large and small—or personal milestones such as the birth of a child would be followed by a congratulatory note from Fred. He would sometimes call me into his office and ask, 'Bill, what do you think about such and such?' As a young master I often had no knowledge about the issue, but I was flattered that he asked my opinion. I recall a cookout at the Weeds' house and a golf game at The Country Club. He always seemed affectionately interested in our lives.[142]

Those who knew Weed well unanimously describe him as a modest, kind, and gentle man, but to most of the boys he remained a detached and distant figure. "He was not a forceful public personality. He was not a tone setter," says Cary Potter. "His style was to lead by example, quietly." One alumnus who bridged the Northrop-Weed eras comments that "The contrast between Mr. Northrop's witty and sparkling words in 'hall' or in personal encounters and Mr. Weed's seemingly dry and perfunctory demeanor was striking. He never seemed very relaxed with us. It was as if he wanted to relate, but he just lacked the 'feel'." Later alumni, who knew no other headmaster, concurred. One remarks, "Mr. Weed looked right through me for six years, as if I didn't exist; I remember no expression of interest whatsoever. He was removed and aloof." Another recalls, "I do not remember being personally addressed by him from the day I arrived to the day I left."

Michael Hager '56 speaks of how much he enjoyed Class I English with Weed: "The class was conducted with such spark and good humor that we learned well without realizing we were learning at all. Chaucer, Shakespeare, Shaw, Benet, and others competed with our fascination with the teacher."[143] But Hager adds, "I am aware, however, that many of my classmates did not share this view."

Michael Lydon '61 offers this somewhat hyperbolic but poignant description of the "feel" of the School:

A dour spirit of 'do it our way or goodbye' dampened risk and creativity in those days. Latin-History-English-Greek-Latin-

History-English-Greek; that plus football and soccer in the fall, baseball and tennis in the spring, was Roxbury Latin, year in, year out. Kids who fell in step were rewarded, those who didn't left. Routine was enforced by instant discipline—"triangles" marked on a clipboard hung in the front of the class—that saw the *fact* of unruly behavior, not *why* a boy was acting up. Counseling, talking over a tangled situation, didn't exist. No one considered that flunking out could be an enormous blow for a teenager, as it was for my brother John, who was cut after five years. . . . I remember anxious, competitive times, and the mean spirit they bred. I and other boys developed caustic tongues at Roxbury Latin, priding ourselves at our skill at wounding with words.[144]

Another alumnus speaks of "the feeling of opposition between faculty and students. What camaraderie existed among the students was based mostly on being shelled in the same foxhole." A sample 1959 *Tripod* editorial—written in an era notable for its complacency and lack of rebellion—also captures the mood:

No one can define school spirit. . . . There are, however, broad areas of agreement on related subjects. It is almost universally accepted that the marking system is obsolete, the athletic program a total disgrace, student activities are dead for lack of interest, the faculty's conservatism is pervading the whole mess with an air of stiffly Victorian decadence.[145]

"I suppose it is fair to say that Roxbury Latin was to some degree a cold place," says Cary Potter. "But I have trouble blaming Fred Weed for that. He was basically a kind and sympathetic person. His reserved bearing and manner unfortunately, I fear, were often interpreted by boys as coldness. Some of the older masters were definitely of the 'throw-'em-out' mentality. Fred often talked about his own academic career as modest. Whenever Fred advocated holding onto a boy with poor grades, the old guard would immediately start in on how standards were being lowered. Such faculty meetings could be bitter. Fred usually gave in: he was not a driving kind of person, not one to come on strong."

FIG. 42. Frederick R. Weed in the later years of his headmastership.

Weed was caught in the middle. On the one hand, the older faculty looked upon him with suspicion. They worried that he was soft, and they pushed him relentlessly not to lower the academic standards an iota. On the other hand, the trustees were up in arms about the ludicrous (in their view) standards to which the boys were being held, the lack of support they were given by the faculty, and the resultant bleak and competitive atmosphere. When Weed tried to explain the trustees' position to the faculty, they charged him with pandering to mediocrity. When Weed tried to explain the faculty's position to the trustees, they concluded that he was not going to do anything to reduce the attrition rate or to change the "feel" of the school.

Caught in this withering crossfire, Weed had to opt for one side or the other. In his December 1962 statement to the trustees, he sided with the faculty to resist changing the School's methods and emphases. He even rejected character development as the School's primary aim:

> I believe that the academic field should be the school's principal aim, and we should not be diverted from this by phrases, idealistic and appealing as they may be, but ones to which a school can only be a contributing factor, rather than a controlling force. The devel-

opment of character, the development of personal integrity, the development of physical and temperamental strength, the development of interests beyond the formal curriculum [i.e., in extracurricular activities] are of course important, and we all recognize as a desirable end the "all-round" citizen, much as many of us dislike the term itself. Yet these things, valuable as they are, cannot be taught directly, and we like to think of them as by-products of a boy's total experience. His book-learning, however, comes directly from the School and I should like to emphasize our point of view in regard to the academic approach, possibly to some over-academic, but nonetheless a thing which a good school can do and should know how to do, and I feel that Roxbury Latin over the years has not made a mistake in its concentration on the academic.

He then lays down the gauntlet to the board, labeling any reduction of rigor as a sign of mediocrity:

I feel that there are those, even on our Board of Trustees, who would like to liberalize somewhat our demands upon the students at Roxbury Latin. The faculty, however, would like to maintain the standards where they are and where we believe they have been. As we all know there are forces constantly working for mediocrity. Many of our parents feel that their boys have too much work to do at too advanced a level and yet the faculty is of the opinion that with capable boys their mental ability should be exercised and stretched, and their courses should not be watered down to make it happier or easier for the less apt student.

I can only feel that it would be a great mistake to water down or reduce our requirements even if this approach should somewhat minimize the adverse criticism against the School. Our reputation in circles where it seems to count, in the minds of many college admissions men, college teachers and people familiar with other schools, seems to be an enviable one. . . . I feel that the complaints come from the less knowing and are the result of gossip and of hearsay.

Weed's citing of the School's reputation among "many college admissions men" is instructive: his years as headmaster coincided with

FIG. 43. The trustees in June 1961. *Seated, from left:* Headmaster Weed, Albert H. Gordon, Samuel H. Wolcott, Arthur Perry, Albert P. Evarts. *Standing:* David A. Mittell, Wilbur Bender, David W. Lewis, Samuel S. Dennis 3d, Eliot T. Putnam, Hollis P. Nichols, Leslie Soule, Richard B. Fowler, Leonard F. Holmes.

the tremendous heightening of competition for college entrance. Though the college admission record of his time is excellent, Weed's annual reports reveal an extreme sensitivity to the criticisms he received from disgruntled parents unwilling to adjust to new conditions: "I sent him to R.L. so he'd get into Harvard." Weed knew that high SATs (Scholastic Aptitude Tests) and College Board achievement tests were important for admission, even though some colleges noted that R.L. boys tended to be one-dimensionally academic. But perhaps he and the faculty did not understand that non-academic achievements (beyond the classroom) were becoming increasingly important as colleges grew ever more selective. Nor did they seem to understand that the School's growing notoriety for rigor and stress was deterring many desirable boys from applying.[146]

To the trustees, Weed's December 1962 statement was the final proof that he and the faculty just did not "get it." As a result, Weed's statement, in effect, sealed his fate; the key trustees now lost confidence in his leadership. Frustrated, the trustees accepted the suggestion of Harvard Admissions Dean Wilbur Bender, and in June 1963 appointed a blue ribbon committee of outside educators to evaluate the School: Wilson Parkhill, former head of Collegiate School in New York City; Alan R. Blackmer, dean of the faculty at Andover; and Richard W. Mechem, principal of Newton High School. The Parkhill Report (as it became known), was presented at the December 1963 trustees meeting (the headmaster having been asked to withdraw). It was basically an affirmation of the trustees' own 1961 Report. No copy of the Parkhill Report to the trustees remains, if in fact there was a written report. The faculty objected to the fact that separate and different reports were made to the trustees and faculty, and in May 1964 they fired back at Parkhill on almost every key issue: no changes were desirable in the extracurricular programs or in the School's demanding academic program. They rejected altering the requirement of two languages, the adding of senior electives such as cultural anthropology, the enlargement of the school to 250, and the reduction in size of the Sixth Class. In summary, "The faculty did not agree that the complexities of modern life have 'moved beyond the limits of the methods previously used by the Roxbury Latin School in developing and defining its program.'"

The tension of being "caught in the middle" wore Weed down. Health problems exacerbated the weariness of the struggle: he suffered from a blood problem which made him itch perpetually. Just before he withdrew from the December 1963 meeting at which Parkhill made his report to the trustees, Weed tendered his resignation, effective June 1965.[147] After leaving the School, he was alienated from it until the present headmaster invited him to give the Commencement Address his first year, 1975. The Weeds and the School were thereafter happily reconciled. Some months after his death in 1980, his ashes were placed at the far end of the football field and his favorite tree—a copper beech— was planted to mark his final resting place at the School he loved and served for eighteen years.

FIG. 44. Richmond Mayo-Smith, head-master 1965–1973.

4. *Mayo-Smith—Years of Change*

In March 1964, three months after Weed tendered his resignation, Richmond Mayo-Smith, Jr., aged forty-one, was elected headmaster. According to Mayo-Smith, "Hollis Nichols was the key trustee, and when I was home on leave in the summer of 1963, he and some of the other trustees talked with me about education and Roxbury Latin."[148] Nichols knew of Mayo-Smith through his wife's sister who was married to a faculty member who taught with Mayo-Smith at Phillips Exeter Academy.

Mayo-Smith had grown up in Dedham, graduating from Noble and Greenough School in 1940. He received his bachelor's degree summa cum laude from Amherst College with the Class of 1944 and served in Europe in World War II. He then went to Exeter as a science teacher. He had taken leaves from Exeter to obtain his master of arts in teaching from Harvard and to go to England as a Fulbright Scholar. In the early 1960s he and his family were living in India where he first helped educators develop a science curriculum for the State of Punjab and later served as acting director of Literacy House at Lucknow. In early 1964, when Nichols learned that Mayo-Smith had been offered the headship of the American School in Delhi, he arranged for Mayo-Smith to fly to Boston for an interview, and pushed the search committee to abort the process and choose him. He was duly elected by the trustees at their March 1964 meeting.

At the same meeting, the trustees also approved the building of the Ernst Wing (described above). This addition would necessitate the tearing down of the headmaster's house since it was located immediately adjacent to the site. On July 31, Headmaster Emeritus Northrop died, thereby freeing the John S. Codman House for use by the new headmaster, his wife (Nancy Fox, whose father was an R.L. alumnus), and three children when he "came into office" in the summer of 1965.

The tone of the country had changed dramatically in the months that followed the November 1963 assassination of President Kennedy, and Mayo-Smith's time at Roxbury Latin must be viewed in the context of the concurrent national unrest: the assassinations of Martin Luther King, Jr., and Senator Robert Kennedy, the civil rights movement, the Vietnam War, and the emergence of marijuana and other drugs as a fact of life among adolescents. These events polarized the nation: "progressive" voices demanded social and political reforms in order to transform the nation, and inevitably voices of reaction were raised expressing the fear that fundamental values were being undermined and venerable traditions flouted.

Schools and colleges quickly became the major battlegrounds on which these opposing viewpoints clashed. It was the most difficult of times to head an educational institution; presidents and headmasters dropped like flies. Roxbury Latin was inevitably caught up in these divisive national confrontations. The central cadre of life trustees were conservative, especially as regards educational philosophy. Mayo-Smith was a liberal in educational philosophy and on most political and social issues. He would later reflect, "I was a curious fit with the board that elected me. But, given all that was happening on college and school campuses, I think Roxbury Latin's trustees had a relatively easy time of it. I think the School came through these tumultuous times pretty well."

The trustees hired Mayo-Smith—following the Reports of 1961 and 1963—to make the School a happier place: to reduce the high attrition rate, to be more nurturing of it students, to stress character development as well as academic rigor, to open the windows and let in fresh air. At Exeter, Mayo-Smith had chaired the counseling committee at one point and had also headed a committee looking into the various educative forces at work beyond as well as within the classroom. He was— and remained—extremely well-read in the area of educational philosophy. The Roxbury Latin faculty soon got used to hearing him talk about McLuhan, Kozol, Postman, Rogers, et al. He was perhaps more comfortable with theory than with practice: he was genuinely concerned about the individual student, but many boys and faculty felt that a certain shyness sometimes inhibited him from expressing that concern with warmth and ease.

The trustees were quite pleased by his early "moves" at R.L. In his first fall, Mayo-Smith replaced competitive interscholastic sports in Class VI with a program of physical fitness that introduced boys to a variety of athletic activities.[149] In 1966 he appointed William Graf to be full-time "director of study counsel" in an effort to help boys in academic and other kinds of trouble, and thereby to reduce the attrition rate. His first interview with *The Tripod* promised further changes resulting from his individual-centered educational philosophy:

> When *The Tripod* asked Mr. Mayo-Smith about his plans for the School, he gave the following 'wishes for a graduating senior':
> —that he will have developed skills in using his mind,
> —that he will have the satisfaction of reaching goals he has set for himself,
> —that he will have had the courage to try different ways of doing things in studies and in other activities to discover which ways fit *him* best.

> Inherent in these wishes [commented *The Tripod*] are, if not a mass
> of innovations, at least a number of fresh, lively views. . . . It is even
> now clear to the First Class that under the 'new freedom' their
> standards and responsibilities are much different from those of the
> lower school.[150]

Bit by bit it became clearer what "the different ways of doing things" were going to be. In 1965–66 the English department dropped its required Class I course in favor of a range of electives; this change was soon extended to Class II. In 1968–69 the Class I required course load was reduced from five to four. And the same year the middle six weeks of the school year (early January to mid-February) were set aside so that each senior could work on an individual project of interest to himself; regular senior course work was suspended during this period. In response to a Class I petition, the faculty voted to leave it to individual teachers whether or not their senior course had a final examination. In April 1969, Class I boys were given permission to walk off campus to Centre Street during the school day. (This was a small step towards the full-fledged "open campus" privileges granted in 1972.) The April 8, 1969, faculty minutes note: "Once more the vote was very close, indeed questioned, but the headmaster ruled the matter closed and accepted the motion as passed."

These changes caused a certain amount of unease among the trustees for two reasons: first, the headmaster seemed to defer to the faculty rather than to lead it; and secondly, the trustees wanted the headmaster to consult with them rather than to inform them about such decisions. Mayo-Smith reflects: "Because I believe students should have some autonomy in *their* school lives, I was operating on the principle that a faculty should have decision-making powers in matters such as these."

In his December 12, 1968, report to the trustees, however, Mayo-Smith asked for and received trustee approval in concept of a coeducational experience with Beaver Country Day School (then a girls' school). He stated, "We believe it would be of great value for our boys to be able to share intellectual and emotional experiences with girls in a

FIG. 45. Aerial view of the School in the 1970s.

serious setting, to open up to them the opportunities to know girls as individual human beings with unique thoughts and feelings." By the fall of 1969, this "opportunity for student initiative" had been established in the form of weekly coeducational seminars which took up all Wednesday morning for boys in Classes I and II. Much attention was given to "group dynamics," and each group chose its own discussion topics. The occult, violence and revolution, cinema, art, problems in education, current events, and various aspects of psychology were chosen for discussion. Gerhard Rehder, history master 1947–1975, comments, "The program was not a successful educational experience. It had a circus atmosphere about it and soon collapsed."

Like many other schools, Roxbury Latin had its own student protest paper, *Orexis*. The March 27, 1969, issue tackled, among other things, the dress code: "In a free society, one has the right (not the goddam privilege) of wearing what he damn well pleases." In December 1969 the faculty abolished the coat-and-tie dress code; unable to agree on a new code, they simply counseled "good judgment." In his letter to the parents that month, Mayo-Smith wrote: "We are not replacing this code with another specific code. . . . It now seems inappropriate to us to select this particular facet of an individual's behaviour for a restrictive code, thereby giving dress a greater emphasis than it deserves." Asked by *Orexis* to elaborate his position on the abolishing of the dress code, he replied (in the February 26, 1970, issue):

> One reason, I think an important one, is that it would increase the feeling of a student controlling his own life. The feeling of autonomy, of being looked at like a human being. . . . After a meeting we had with students and the Educational Policy Committee of the faculty, one thing that impressed me very much was the extent to which students see teachers as teachers and not as people and also the extent to which teachers see them as students and not as people. That's what I mean by increasing the feeling that I'm a person with a certain freedom, such as I don't have to go there with a coat and tie.

The Parents' Auxiliary president expressed his unhappiness at the dress code change, as did a number of the trustees—who had not been consulted in the process.

There were other symbolic changes. Mayo-Smith recalls that "all the hallways were painted a gloomy pea green. I had the walls painted off-white and put up display boards for student art." Some viewed Mayo-Smith as iconoclastic. The oil portraits of past worthies were removed to the attic—where several were damaged or destroyed. The hallways were stripped of many of the handsome furnishings which Northrop had given and placed there. The elegant brass table lamps in the paneled library were replaced by overhead fluorescent lights. Plastic chairs and modern tables were placed in the Hall which was now used throughout the day as a study hall—and overhead fluorescent lights were added there as well.

To some, Mayo-Smith's statement in the *Alumni Bulletin* in the winter of 1970 typified an attitude of professional superiority which

showed too little respect for the achievements of the past and too un-
critical an exaltation of contemporary ideas:

> From time to time I pass the portrait of William Coe Collar,
> Headmaster 1867–1907, and the thought crosses my mind that the
> changes which have taken place in the school in the past four years
> are greater than the changes which occurred during his forty years
> in office.[151]

Although this statement is wide of the mark as history, one must bear in
mind that 1970 was a heady time in which many educators believed
their reforms were going to usher in a brave new world.

At the 325th anniversary celebration Mayo-Smith insisted on reading a statement, signed by students and faculty, condemning the bombing of Cambodia, and he also quite consciously eschewed the commemorative—backward-looking—nature of the occasion. He chose,
instead, to use it to share his vision of the future for Roxbury Latin:

> Much of what we have done to celebrate our 325th Anniversary has
> paid honor to the past. I wish to spend a few minutes looking to
> the future.
>   *The teaching and learning of skills will become more individu-
> alized. Students will be given challenges they can meet and not
> be assigned to failure. The phrase 'assigned to failure' may seem
> too harsh, but our system of trying to move whole groups along at
> a set pace leads to highly inefficient learning. By failure I do not
> mean failure in terms of grades, but failure in terms of unrealized
> potential.
>   *Students and teachers will relate to one another differently; stu-
> dents will have more autonomy. They will share initiative for plan-
> ning learning activities more fully with faculty than they do now.
>   *Students will spend less time in class being taught by teachers;
> more time in conferences with teachers and students, in individual
> research and in learning situations sponsored by the school, but
> outside the school. We will begin to act on this advice from *Teach-
> ing as a Subversive Activity,* namely, "the critical content of any
> learning experience is the method or process through which the

learning occurs. . . . It is not what you say to people that counts; it is what you have them do." [Mayo-Smith gave copies of this book to all the faculty and some trustees during 1970.]

*The faculty will be different. They will help students learn skills, but they will spend less time in class and more time being accessible to students as resource people and colleagues.

*Roxbury Latin will make an increasing commitment to co-education. The most interesting students will be choosing co-educational schools because they value the increased intellectual and social variety co-education will provide.

*Students and teachers will be learning and experiencing ideas in a variety of media. Let me quote a statement from the *Quality of Life* by James A. Michener. 'We will soon start producing well-educated men and women to whom the book will be a minor aspect of culture. They will be visually oriented and will be just as alert as their book-oriented fellows, but they will learn intuitively rather than solidly . . . and in time they will rule the nation.'

*Our curriculum will become increasingly flexible. . . .

*Roxbury Latin will offer a wider variety of opportunities for physical education. . . .

*Roxbury Latin will become somewhat larger.[152]

The 325th anniversary celebration marked the watershed of the Mayo-Smith years. The key life trustees now turned against him. Their disenchantment was further enhanced when the 1970 yearbook appeared. The departing photography teacher had used the money available to produce a one-man show of his own photographs. Many of the photographs had nothing to do with the School; those that did were largely unflattering or worse. The book had no written text. Mayo-Smith notes, "My son was in this class and I liked the creative idea behind the yearbook, though I regretted some of the pictures when I saw it." At the trustees' insistence, most copies of the book were confiscated before being distributed.

By this time, part-time faculty such as the photography teacher had become a bone of contention. Mayo-Smith saw them as a means by which—for relatively little cost—the faculty could be enriched. "I wanted

a variety of role models for our students. One of my biggest disappointments was that many of the faculty found it difficult to accept these
part-timers." Many of the full-time masters saw these part-time teachers as favorites of the headmaster who could come and go as they wished
and live by their own rules, while the full-time faculty were left holding
the bag with the onerous duties of school life. Many of these same full-
time masters, moreover, were even more fundamentally upset by what
they regarded as Mayo-Smith's poor judgment in hiring new faculty—
whether full-time or part-time. There was a growing perception in
other quarters, as well, that the quality of the faculty was in decline.

The faculty minutes of September 16, 1970, record the headmaster's
observation that

> there were forces of reaction to some changes in school building up
> among trustees and families especially on such issues as the dress
> code and Independent Study Project (adding that the 'flack' on
> these two had been considerable). . . . As a minor concession he felt
> that members of the faculty should appear in coat and tie. He
> agreed that he himself would welcome a relaxation in this area but
> that this was just not the time for it. Mr. Schlosser felt that in this
> way the faculty are being treated less liberally than the students.

When this issue arose again at the opening faculty meeting in 1971,
Mayo-Smith said he was willing to have the faculty members dress as
they liked—though he preferred coat and tie.

The minutes of the September 1970 meeting reveal that "forces of
reaction" were building *within* the faculty as well as outside:

> Mr. Farris asked whether faculty could do something about the
> objectionable dress in their classes to which the headmaster replied
> that he felt masters did have the right when it affected their class.
>   [Mr. Bridgess asked—in reference to the practice of certain
> teachers—] whether a master could meet a class for ten minutes
> and then dismiss them for half an hour. The headmaster felt this
> was a matter of judgment for the master to decide; he did feel that
> a certain flexibility was desirable.

These "forces of reaction" were further disillusioned when, in May 1971, final examinations were made optional.

Far more dangerous to Mayo-Smith, "forces of reaction" were growing on the board of trustees. The immediate casualty of this discontent was a project dear to the headmaster's heart: the library-media-arts center, which had been a million-dollar component of the 1970 325th Anniversary Campaign. Architects had been hired to design a free standing library-media-arts center (to be located some two hundred feet behind the headmaster's office) with copious space for "individual study" and "independent work." It was a bricks-and-mortar expression of Mayo-Smith's philosophy of education. But in the months following the 325th anniversary, as trustee discontent mounted, the $2,250,000 capital campaign was aborted on the grounds that the time was not ripe for raising money.

Unfortunately, the troubles on the "inside" were not compensated for by gains on the "outside." Total admissions interviews for Class VI during the 1970–71 school year fell from 132 (the previous year) to 117, and the "yield" of those choosing to attend fell from 39 out of 49 (the previous year) to 35 out of 55 admitted. In 1971–72, interviews for Class VI fell to 116 — of whom 65 were accepted for a yield of 44.[153]

But Mayo-Smith pressed on. In March 1971 he appointed, under his own permanent chairmanship, a new faculty committee — significantly named the Educational Change Committee — which was to be the principal engine for reform. One of the first issues to come before this group was tracking (separating students in some courses according to their ability). John Mergendoller, one of the four members, stated passionately that "the damage [tracking] does to the self-image of students in the slower sections outweighs any academic gains to students in the faster sections." By early 1973, Mayo-Smith's grading task force agreed that "any indication on transcripts that a student has failed a course or has not qualified for credit is superfluous and punitive." It called for a de-emphasis on the reward/punishment aspects of grading, and urged the abolition of the Cum Laude Society as "an anachronism." But the committee's hot issue was coeducation. The headmaster reported to the trustees that faculty sentiment was now strongly in favor of it, and in January 1972 he called for a joint meeting of the Educational Change Committee and the Executive Committee of the trustees to discuss how to implement "a coeducational experience for R.L. students." His former Exeter colleague—by then a trustee—Henry Bragdon urged Mayo-Smith, in a letter of February 12, 1972, to push for something short of coeducation. But coeducation was in the air.[154] His old school, Noble and Greenough, was deeply immersed in talks with Winsor regarding a merger of the schools to achieve coeducation. When these talks collapsed in November 1972, Nobles' trustees voted to admit girls.

Sensing that the key life trustees—the old guard—were opposed to reforms he regarded as important, Mayo-Smith sought to dilute their influence by adding progressive voices to the board.[155] He and Albert R. Smith (who had been appointed "executive vice president" for administration in 1969 when the trustees perceived that Mayo-Smith could use support in this area) pressed the 1972 trustee nominating committee to appoint more parents to the board, and noted that "to go from a trustee meeting to a parent meeting is at times like going from night to day."[156]

That same month, on March 6, 1972, the faculty approved and adopted "open campus" privileges for members of Classes I and II whereby they could leave the school grounds by car or foot whenever they had no obligations. This decision had not been referred to or discussed by the trustees, and the March 23, 1972, trustee minutes state:

> Both the Chairman of the Educational Policy Committee [Cary Potter, who was now a trustee] and the President of the Board had expressed concern to [Mayo-Smith] that the Trustees had not had the opportunity to react to these contemplated changes prior to their adoption. [Mayo-Smith] declared that in not providing an opportunity for trustee or committee involvement he had neglected an important and necessary step in the decision process which he felt would be corrected in the future.... In the discussion which

followed, questions were raised about the appropriate procedure for communication with and involvement of Trustees in decision or change.[157]

At the same meeting, Mayo-Smith announced that assistant head-master (and college guidance director) Warden Dilworth, one of the faculty's leading lights, had decided to leave Roxbury Latin after sixteen years to teach at Groton.

These two events were catalytic in bringing a number of middle-of-the-road trustees over to the side of the key old guard trustees who thought Mayo-Smith should go. The unilateral enactment of "open campus" was regarded as high-handed—a failure of communication and of appropriate procedure—and Dilworth's departure (rightly or wrongly) confirmed a growing perception that the quality of the School's faculty was declining.

A dispute over the place of hockey in the athletic program further fueled the controversy. Since the special trustee committee on athletics in 1968, a number of trustees had continued to push for the addition of hockey, and there was on-going discussion about building a rink on campus. Mayo-Smith strongly resisted several efforts to include a rink in the 1970 325th anniversary capital campaign. When—in the spring of 1972—Dexter School was short of money to build a hockey rink on its property, this situation seemed to three key life trustees a golden opportunity to share in the cost and therefore in the benefits of Dexter's rink—only ten minutes drive from Roxbury Latin. When it was announced that these three had contributed $150,000 towards the rink and that the School had use of it for two hours every afternoon, many teachers were furious. The faculty eventually passed a formal resolution, in fact: "that the faculty does not feel a full-blown hockey program is in the best interests of education at the Roxbury Latin School."[158]This attitude further antagonized the "old guard" trustees, as did the fact that by the fall no 1972 yearbook had appeared (which inflamed again their lingering outrage concerning the 1970 book).

Milton Roye's January 19, 1973, article in *Juba*, the weekly mimeographed school newspaper of the era, offers some insight into the feeling of a growing number that the pendulum had swung too far in the direction of individual (as opposed to community) interest:

> Many changes have taken place in RL during the four and a half years that I have been here. Alot [*sic*] of them have been for the better, but one area of the school has suffered: school spirit. There is no unity in the school now; people just don't give a damn. They would rather the school fall apart or destroy it themselves, than lift a finger to help it. People have no respect for other peoples' rights. Books, jackets, papers, and money are stolen by students from their classmates; food is stolen from the lunchroom; basketballs and tape recorders and books are stolen from the school. People just don't care who their deed may affect; they themselves are all-important. Their motto: ME FIRST, THEM SECOND. . . . The students in the school have become so self-centered, that the school community has been destroyed, and the school as an institution is slowly but surely being destroyed.

After serving for only one year, Hollis Nichols resigned the presidency in June 1972, and his fellow life trustee Samuel S. Dennis 3d was chosen to replace him. Dennis believes he was chosen because he had been only modestly active on the board and was regarded as being non-controversial. Yet he harbored grave doubts about Mayo-Smith's leadership, and upon assuming the presidency requested from him a considerable body of factual information about all aspects of the School's operations. The president and the headmaster were soon immersed, as well, in written and spoken discussions of educational philosophy. By the end of the fall, Dennis felt his doubts had been confirmed and, at a closed meeting of the trustees on January 30, 1973, he expressed his loss of confidence in Mayo-Smith's leadership and, along with several others, raised the question of his continuance as headmaster.

The following day, Henry Bragdon—Mayo-Smith's Exeter colleague who had been placed on the board at Mayo-Smith's request—replied in writing to Dennis's request "for an expression of opinion as to whether Mayo-Smith should be retained or asked to resign":

I have reluctantly come to the conclusion that he must be encouraged to resign. This is a conclusion that pains me profoundly, not only because he is my friend, but because Roxbury Latin will lose a headmaster of great humanity, imagination and integrity.

I reach my decision less because of the facts of the situation—many of which are not clear—but because Dick has obviously lost irrevocably the confidence of the three key figures on the Board of Trustees—Hollis Nichols, Al Gordon, and you. You all made this so perfectly clear last night that it is obvious the point of no return has been passed.

After expressing his philosophical disagreements with Dennis and Nichols, Bragdon then adverted to one of the principal criticisms leveled at Mayo-Smith: his alleged poor judgment in recruiting and choosing new faculty, his excessive use of part-time teachers, and the rapid turnover of faculty (six new faculty out of twenty-five in 1969–1970, eight out of twenty-six in 1970–71, seven out of twenty-five in 1971–72):

I unhappily accept George Goethals' judgment that [Mayo-Smith] has failed in what is to my mind a headmaster's most important task—enlisting and keeping a cadre of able and devoted teachers. In other ways he has apparently proven to be less than an able administrator. These seem to me the only clearcut reasons for asking him to go.[159]

Dennis now invited Mayo-Smith to present his case to the trustees at a special meeting on February 20, after which "by an overwhelming majority"[160] they asked for his resignation. The president invited him to remain for the rest of the school year and hoped for an amicable separation. Mayo-Smith reflects, "They were disappointed that I wouldn't 'play the game' by sending out the usual letter saying I had decided to resign. But such a process seemed to me hypocritical." When Mayo-Smith told Dennis he would fight the decision—which he did in a letter to the parents—he was required to leave at once.

A storm of outrage and dismay greeted the announcement of Mayo-Smith's dismissal. Faculty, students, and parents had no previous

FIG. 46. Assistant Headmaster William E. Chauncey with the Class of 1980 as sixies at Beaver Brook.

inkling that the trustees were at odds with the headmaster, and there was much criticism of the trustees. Acrimonious public meetings ensued, and *The Boston Globe* did two extensive stories on the School in turmoil.

The trustees named William E. Chauncey acting headmaster. Chauncey was one of Weed's great appointments and had taught at the School—and served in a variety of administrative capacities—since 1959. The personification of integrity and stability, Chauncey held the School together for a year and a half, calming the crisis and preparing the way for a new headmaster. Three of Chauncey's appointments—Edward S. Ligon, Classics department chairman; Clayton H. Conn, French department chairman, and Bradford C. Perham, athletic director—have served Roxbury Latin for more than twenty years and taken their place among the all-time faculty greats.

It is certainly too early to give an objective assessment of the Mayo-Smith years. But it is fair to say that he made the School a more supportive place for boys and that he "opened the windows" and let in the fresh air of new ideas. A number of his reforms—open campus, senior independent study, an informal dress code, for instance—remain, albeit in modified form. Perhaps his most enduring legacy was his vision of the importance of the arts, which had been largely neglected throughout most of the School's history. Northrop—the most aesthetically aware of all the School's headmasters—found resources, during depression and war, only to appoint apprentice masters who could offer art to younger boys on a part-time basis from 1935 to 1941. From 1941 to 1960, music—also on a part-time basis—replaced art. By 1960, an art master came twice a week. Among Mayo-Smith's first appointments was Roderick M. MacKillop, who within a few years was teaching art full time to both older and younger boys. Fortunately, a room with a double exposure of light had been built as an art studio in the 1965 Ernst Wing. As a result of MacKillop's charisma, art quickly became an important element of the R.L. curriculum—and has since remained so. By 1969 a photography lab had been added in the attic and a part-time instructor hired. It is interesting to note that twenty-five years after Mayo-Smith opposed putting a hockey rink in the "package" for the 325th anniversary capital campaign, the School has no hockey rink on its campus. And the Robert P. Smith Arts Center—the 350th anniversary building—fulfills hopes which Mayo-Smith articulated in the mid-1960s.

5. *The Present Age*

The "voice" of this chapter now changes from the objective to the personal. Modern historiography, of course, teaches us that there is no such thing as historical objectivity, and what I have "selected" in the chapters above reveals my own prejudices. What I mean to say, then, is that I have *tried* to be objective—evenhanded, seeing the flaws as well as the virtues—in what I have written so far. In what follows I can only be subjective. I shall not attempt a chronicle of the past twenty years; I have tried to provide that in the eighty-four quarterly reports I have written in the *Newsletter*.

In my first few months as headmaster, I was repeatedly warned by several trustees and by many faculty that Roxbury Latin would not survive unless it changed dramatically: it had to go coeducational ("In five years no one will consider attending a boys' school"), it had to stop requiring Latin ("The School's archaic curriculum—still forcing students to study Latin—may, for a time, have had a certain charm; now it is a fossil"), it had to increase in size ("You'll never compete athletically" and "You can't offer enough elective courses"), and it had to move to individualized learning ("Classroom teaching is a thing of the past"). I was also told emphatically that "the era in which a headmaster can give speeches to a student body is long gone; they simply won't listen—or worse."

All this advice I eschewed—as only a brash and naive thirty-four-year-old can do. My strong feeling was that Roxbury Latin should be Roxbury Latin. My first summer we rewrote the catalogue and proclaimed from the rooftops that Roxbury Latin was a small classical school for boys. One trustee graciously told me later, "I was sure it was the end of R.L." In fact—whether *despite* the catalogue and what it proclaimed, or *because* of it—applications for admission soared 70 percent in a single year. As one wise man observed to me at the time: "I don't know whether they *like* the philosophy your new catalogue proclaims, or whether they're just relieved that *someone* believes in something so solid sounding."

I spent much of my first summer scheduling the School myself, introducing a more flexible modular schedule. That same summer—in a step regarded as contradictory—I put all the portraits that had not been destroyed back on the walls and brought banished objets d'art down from the attic; I also removed all the plastic chairs and metal tables from Rousmaniere Hall.

A school is defined and judged by its faculty. My first two appointments were David S. Rea, popular teacher of economics and math and coach of football and lacrosse, and Philip H. Hansen, history department chairman and guru of debate and Model United Nations. In my

FIG. 47. The 1983–84 faculty. *Seated, from left:* Bradford C. Perham, William E. Tally, John A. Davey, William E. Chauncey, F. Washington Jarvis, Robert S. Jorgensen, Kay Hubbard, Edward S. Ligon, Clayton H. Conn. *Middle row:* Steven E. Ward, Maurice A Randall II, David S. Rea, Karl Tabery, Philip H. Hansen, Joseph R. Kerner, Jr., Richard J. Russell, Kerry P. Brennan, David W. Frank, John P. Brennan. *Top row:* James L. Jordy, William M. Blood, Paul E. Sugg, Jr., John A. Marrella, Hunter M. White, Michael T. Pojman, Thomas A. Knowlton, James E. Thompson, Richard G. Dower.

second year, when my leadership was denounced by a group of younger faculty, I had the opportunity to replace eight of the twenty-five masters. Included among these eight new appointments were Joseph R. Kerner, Jr., English department chairman; Maurice A Randall II, master of Latin and English and varsity hockey coach; and Steven E. Ward, history master, varsity wrestling coach, and dean of students. All three are now in their twentieth year at R.L. These new men of character and scholarship plus the devoted old guard faculty provided the foundation upon which to build Roxbury Latin as it had now been defined.

Even today people who do not particularly *like* that definition admire the School and send their sons here because "You people know exactly who you are and what you're trying to do."

Since I have fought hard to maintain and enhance the School's classical curriculum, I am, I suppose, regarded as a "traditionalist" in curriculum. Roxbury Latin was founded as a classical school and it has, in all the best eras of its history, adhered to a classical curriculum. I believe that no curriculum is divinely ordained, but it seemed to me in 1974—and it seems to me now—that our School should go with its traditional strengths. The classical curriculum has shown itself remarkably open to innovation and modification. The reforms of the Collar era, for example, are a testimony to its flexibility. Our departments today are hardly polishing tombstones. Each is always searching for better ways of "doing its thing"—and change is constant. We are rather like the owners of one of those temperamental British sports cars: we like the basic engine, but it needs constant and sensitive retuning. I believe that the basic engine of the classical curriculum—when finely tuned—is the best vehicle ever designed to teach a boy how to sort out information, how to read (in the broadest sense) with understanding, how to think with lucidity, and how to express himself with clarity.

While the development of the mind is important, in my view it is nothing like as important as the development of character. We say in our catalogue—and every master means it and every boy understands it—that "we care most of all what kind of *person* a boy is." I have aspired to make this era in the School's history one in which "every individual boy is known and loved." By "loved" I do not mean coddled or indulged. If you love a student you hold up high aspirations for him—most of all in the area of character—and you encourage and rebuke him, as needed, to be his best self. I believe that loving boys also means urging them to "do something great with their lives" (and greatness is not defined only by power or wealth or fame).

For this reason I regard the School's relative smallness as its most valuable characteristic. Boys here rarely fall between the cracks. I often tell parents that I promise them nothing except that we shall know and love their sons. That is possible because of our size.

The School's second most important characteristic, in my view, is the diversity of its student body. While it is true that the School was founded by the prosperous planters of Roxbury for their sons, there

FIG. 48. The trustees in June 1981. *Front row, from left:* David A. Mittell, William A. Oates, Jr., David W. Lewis, Albert H. Gordon, Samuel S. Dennis 3d, Richard B. Fowler, John Wallace, Paul A. Powell. *Back row:* Nathan H. Garrick, Jr., Nathaniel J. Young, Jr., Harry R. Lewis, Virginia Wing, Robert E. Gibbons, Thomas E. Payne, James H. Rosenfield. Miss Wing was the School's first female trustee.

FIG. 49, *left.* Samuel S. Dennis 3d '28, left, at the Closing Exercises 1984. Having served as president 1972–1984, he delivered the commencement address at the conclusion of his term. He has been a life trustee since 1951. Standing at the center is David W. Lewis '31, president 1984–1991. On the right is Mrs. Lewis, whose father, Arthur Perry '02, was president 1955–1960.

were, as we have seen, boys admitted *gratis* almost from the start. The clear intent of Bell's bequest in 1671 was to help "poore mens children."

Towards the end of Weed's headmastership the School created the Joseph Warren scholarships as a sign of its recommitment to the city. Today city boys represent 28 percent of the School—the remainder hailing from forty different suburban towns. Today the School is racially highly diverse as a result of strong "affirmative action" in admissions recruitment. I shall not cite statistics on the racial, religious, or economic diversity of our student body, because I think the School is so truly democratic that boys and masters no longer think in these categories. I am proud when I hear—as I do often—that "Roxbury Latin has the kind of student body that public schools are supposed to have." We are, thanks to the commitment of our trustees and the generosity of our school family, the only independent school in greater Boston which admits students without regard to their parents' ability to pay.

Ancient charters, with the language and assumptions of another age, have provided many a troublemaker ample opportunity to harass the institutions established by such charters. In 1990 it seemed prudent to the trustees that they should protect themselves and their successors from such predators by seeking court approval of their exercise of fiduciary responsibility. In particular they wished to establish that no discrimination should be made for or against an applicant on the basis of geography. Boys should be admitted on merit—not on the accident of their parents' place of residence. Going with the attorney general to the Superior Court, the trustees received confirmation on March 9, 1990, that they were acting in conformity with the School's charter and all its other early documents. As a sign of the School's commitment to the "Old Roxbury District"—where it has been located for 350 years— the trustees that year formally set aside $1.5 million in unrestricted funds as an endowment for the exclusive benefit of Boston boys (the "Old Roxbury District" having been subsumed in the city since 1868). In actuality, the School in 1994–95 is paying $756,906 from its own resources (*after* all the Boston boys' tuitions have been received) to educate city boys. That figure, of course, vastly exceeds the income from the $1.5 million endowment set aside for city boys in 1990.

In the past twenty years the trustees have, in essence, reendowed the School. In 1974 the endowment stood at $3,502,351. At the close of fiscal 1995 it stood at more than $42 million. Just as impressive is the fact that the 1995 annual fund covered 18 percent of the School's operating expenses.

The last twenty years have witnessed a great expansion and improvement of the School's buildings and grounds, and I am all too keenly aware that my headmastership will be recalled as an era of buildings and grounds expansion, comparative financial prosperity, and athletic success. These achievements — if such they be — are not, as is so often the case, the things for which I would choose to be remembered. My highest aspirations have been two-fold: First, to establish a "tone" or "ambience" in which all members of the School, whether adult or adolescent, treat each other with respect, affection, and good humor. (Shortly after I accepted the School's headmastership, a college admissions director said to me: "R.L. has lots of head but very little heart." I can imagine no more scathing indictment of a school.) And second, to appoint outstanding men and women to the faculty — for it is the masters far more than the headmaster who create the sort of tone and ambience I have described above. It is the masters more than the headmaster who create a great school in which each student is known and loved.

I believe that we have the finest faculty of any school in the world, including a number of younger teachers who are eminently worthy of their predecessors. I also believe that the same high quality, in character just as much as in scholarship, distinguishes our student body. However, I realize that I must leave the evaluation of both our faculty and our student body (and far more, our present headmaster) to later and more objective observers.

As regards the School's trustees I feel no such reticence in "passing judgment." In 1990, Albert H. Gordon — the greatest benefactor in the School's history — tied the previous service record of Governor Joseph

FIG. 50. Elizabeth Mary Gordon and Mary Elizabeth Gordon, "the Gordon Twins," who—with their brother Albert—gave the Mary Rousmaniere Gordon Building in 1987: refectory, library, and great hall.

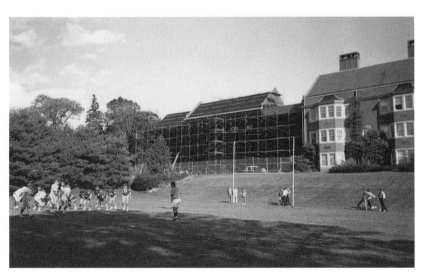

FIG. 51. The steel skeleton of the Mary Rousmaniere Gordon Building in the fall of 1987.

FIG. 52–53, The Robert P. Smith Arts Center was launched by an address by Poppy Anderson in the spring of 1992. *Above, left to right:* Dr. Eric Anderson, headmaster of Eton College; Architect William D. Buckingham; Poppy Anderson; Robert P. and Salua J. A. Smith, donors. *Below:* the site of the Arts Center before the land was cleared.

FIG. 54, *left.* The closing exercises 1991. *Left:* William A. Oates, Jr., treasurer since 1975 and life trustee. *Center:* Albert H. Gordon '19, chairman of the trustees and a trustee since 1940. *Right:* Professor Harry R. Lewis '65, life trustee, who became president in 1991.

Dudley (1670–1720) by serving as trustee for fifty years. And he has now gone way beyond him. In the 1950s and 1960s almost all schools placed term limits on all their trustees; trustees were to hold office for a specified period and then rotate off the board. While Roxbury Latin expanded its board in 1906 with alumni trustees (specified in 1913 to be five for five years each, in staggered terms) and in 1960 with trustees-at-large each for three-year terms, it nonetheless retained nine trustees-for-life. From this category—in addition to Mr. Gordon—have sprung men of extraordinary generosity and devotion: Samuel S. Dennis 3d, John Wallace, David A. Mittell, David W. Lewis, and Richard B. Fowler, to name but a few of "the old guard." A school must have a soul: it must know who it is and what it wants to accomplish. And it must have a heart: its faculty must enjoy and nourish its students. But soul and heart, while primary and critical, alone are not enough. A great school needs the financial wherewithal to achieve its objectives. The life trustees have been faithful guardians of the School's mission; in most generations they have kept it from straying from its essential objectives. This generation of trustees has surpassed its predecessors in attending to the School's spiritual health and financial well-being. As Roxbury Latin faces the future, it must hope that the trustees of the future will be the equal in devotion, strength, and energy to those who have gone before them.

And so our story ends, although, of course, it does *not* end. John Eliot and the other exiled fathers who crossed the seas came to New England to establish the City of God—a city set upon a hill. In 1645, "out of their relligious care of posteritie," they founded in the wilderness of Roxbury a School whose mission was to "fit students for public service both in church and commonwealth." When it has been faithful to its heritage and mission, Roxbury Latin has truly been Mather's *Schola Illustris*. The School's story does not end because, as President Lowell of Harvard observed at the dedication of the new school in 1927, Roxbury Latin is a "fountain of perpetual youth, and it is flowing today, flowing stronger than it ever flowed before." It must be our hope—our prayer—that this "fountain of perpetual youth will keep on through the ages, always young, always living, always throwing its waters up higher and higher." That hope—that prayer—is perhaps best expressed in the familiar words of the Founder's Song: "May the lustre of thy glory through thy children ever brighter grow."

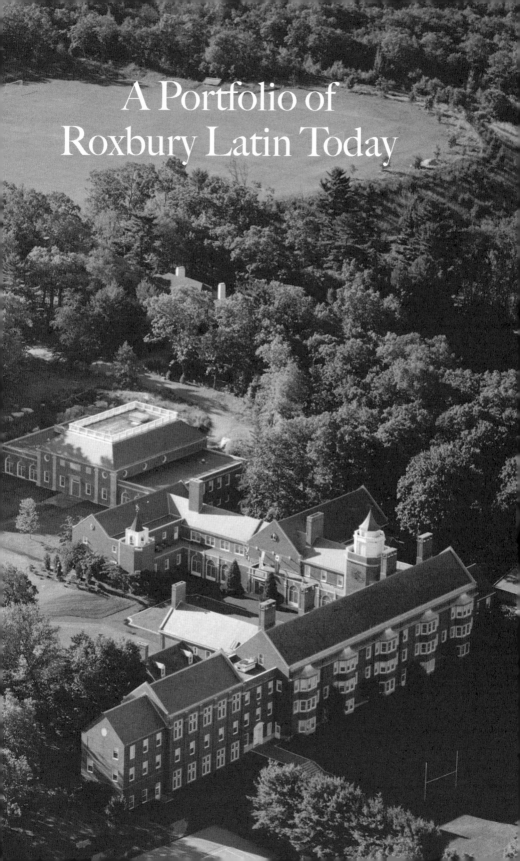

A Portfolio of
Roxbury Latin Today

The Faculty, 1994–95. *Left to right, seated:* Philip H. Hansen, Clayton H. Conn, Edward S. Ligon, William E. Chauncey, F. Washington Jarvis, Robert S. Jorgensen, John A. Davey, Bradford C. Perham, David S. Rea. *Second row:* David B. Smoyer, Livingston Carroll, Michael T. Pojman, Richard G. Dower, Richard J. Russell, Steven E. Ward, Maurice A Randall II, Joseph R. Kerner, Jr., David W. Frank, John P. Brennan, Paul E. Sugg, Jr. *Third row:* Marjorie S. Bullitt, Eileen M. Urtz, C. LaRoy Brantley, Michael C. Obel-Omia, Brian B. Buckley, Barbara G. Melvoin, Frank F. Guerra, Michael J. Earley, Ethan L. Sperry, Jonathan McK. Kaufmann, Ousmane Diop.

The Trustees, June 1995. *Left to right, seated:* William B. O'Keeffe, David A. Mittell, Samuel S. Dennis 3d, Harry R. Lewis, Albert H. Gordon, William A. Oates, Jr., Stanley J. Bernstein. *Standing:* Mary G. Roberts, William P. Collatos, John J. Regan, Charles T. Bauer, Rhoda Fischer, Robert P. Smith, Christopher R. Walsh, Carolyn McClintock Peter, William E. Fruhan, Jr., Michael J. Giarla. *Missing:* Peter J. Gomes, John M. Hennessy.

Above: The visit of President George Bush, May 1995. President Harry R. Lewis, center; the headmaster on the right. *Below:* The President addresses the trustees, masters, boys, and guests in Rousmaniere Hall. The occasion marked the first use, for congregational singing, of the new organ designed and built by Jeremy Adams '58.

Notes to Part Five

1. Trustee Minutes (hereafter TM) 5 (24 September 1919).
2. *The Tripod* 32, 5 (February 1920): 9f.
3. *The Tripod* 33, 1 (October 1920). See also TM 12 (9 June 1920).
4. See *The Tripod* 33, 3 (December 1920).
5. TM (21 January 1921) and W. D. Head's letter to Roger Ernst, 3 February 1921.
6. TM (16 April 1921).
7. *The Tripod* 34, 1 (October 1921): 8f.
8. *The Tripod* 33, 8 (May 1921): 9.
9. Roxbury Latin School Volunteer Committee of Parents' four-page brochure dated 1 December 1921.
10. TM (27 June 1922), (10 July 1922), and (28 July 1922). Actually, $65,000 was authorized. See also Neil J. Savage, "How the School Acquired its Present Property," *Newsletter* 58, 1 (October 1984), 7–10. Richard Codman died in the late fall of 1928. From 1929 until it was torn down to make way for the Ernst Wing in 1965, his home served as the headmaster's house. The trustees had a low opinion of Richard's nephew John Codman, who was Richard's agent for the sale. See Roger Ernst's memo of 31 May 1944 in the archives. See also his 3 October 1944 letter to Northrop: "John Codman proved to be a very hard bargainer when we bought the original land from them in 1922, as, because of our inability to get a quorum of the Trustees before a certain deadline, he 'had' us. He was quite forgetful of the fact that various members of the Codman family had had the benefit of a free education in the School, and traded for every dollar there was in it. I am afraid he will do the same thing now if he finds we appear at all eager to buy his land." In fact, Codman did worse, but in 1945 the trustees were not to be "had." See below.
11. TM (20 December 1922) and (16 March 1927).
12. TM (1 October 1923). See *The Tripod* 35, 9 (June 1923): 5; and 36, 1 (October 1923): 8.
13. Roger Ernst letter to D.V. Thompson, 27 October 1923, has the 87 right, but the School (according to the Catalogue) had 136 boys, and according to the headmaster's report, 135.
14. TM (13 June 1923).
15. For a full account, see *The Tripod* 36, 5 (February 1924): 3.
16. "Roxbury Latin School—Past, Present, and Future," 5.
17. TM (27 March 1924).
18. *The Tripod* 37, 4 (January 1925): 4f. See D.V. Thompson's report to the trustees for 16 December 1925 regarding a major break-in at the School (the latest of many). He also expresses a fear that the building will be burned down. The neighborhood was becoming less and less safe.
19. *The Tripod* 37, 4 (January 1925): 5.

20. Ibid., 11–13.
21. *The Tripod* 37, 5 (February 1925): 5.
22. Ibid., 3–5. Two accounts are here conflated. See Roger Ernst's letter to Weed, 30 January 1950: "I presume you know that Tucker pledged, and eventually paid, about $80,000 toward the $100,000 total which the class of 1895 gave toward the Fund for the new school in 1925." Tucker committed suicide—having lost everything following the 1929 Crash.
23. *The Tripod* 38, 1 (October 1925): 8.
24. *The Tripod* 38, 3 (December 1925): 4.
25. TM (9 June 1926).
26. TM (16 November 1926).
27. Report of the Special Committee, 15 March 1922, 2.
28. TM (16 December 1925).
29. Letter of Andrew Marshall to W. Dudley Cotton, Esq., 23 January 1926.
30. Letter of C. H. Grandgent to Deacon Walter Eliot Thwing, 29 January 1926. Duplicate to W. Dudley Cotton, Esq.
31. TM (17 March 1926).
32. TM (22 September 1926).
33. Approved and adopted by the Trustees. TM (16 June 1927).
34. TM (16 December 1925).
35. Because all the School's assets were commingled by the 1789 Charter, it is impossible to ascertain what portion remained—if any—of Bell's bequest for the one-room school of 1671. If any portion remained (which is doubtful), it would have had to be contained within the general endowment fund at the time of the 1927 Act. This endowment totaled $665,614, not including separately accounted funds that had just been raised for building the new school.
36. *The Tripod* 40, 1 (October 1927): 8.
37. *Roxbury Latin School Alumni Bulletin*, February 1928, 7–8.
38. Ibid., 4.
39. Ibid.
40. *Roxbury Latin School Alumni Bulletin*, May 1931, 2–4.
41. See Francis Russell, *Forty Years On* (West Roxbury: The Roxbury Latin School, 1970), especially 47–55 and 58–67. See also "Old Man Farnham" by Russell in *The Roxbury Latin School Newsletter*, 62, 1, (October 1988), 12–14. David Mittell's Address at the Farnham Room dedication is in *The Roxbury Latin School Newsletter*, 62, 3 (April 1989), 8–10.
42. See Russell sketch in *Forty Years On*, 67–77. *The Tripod* 25, 3 (December 1912): 6, contains the first mention of the Founder's Song.
43. Letter of C. H. Grandgent to D. V. Thompson, 22 December 1928, following trustee meeting and vote (TM 19 December 1928). Thompson replied 2 January 1929. In his letter of 3 January 1929, Grandgent expressed his delight that things might work out. The trustees later rescinded their dismissal. See also the unpub-

lished signed statement by Roger Ernst dated 3 January 1954, who gives a slightly sanitized—but corroborative—version. See also W. Dudley Cotton's letter to R. H. Gardiner, 23 January 1924: "At the last trustee meeting there was considerable discussion of the unsatisfactory relation that appeared to exist between Mr. Thompson and the teachers."

44. Roger Ernst letter to James Bryant Conant, 8 April 1947.
45. "About Roxbury Latin—A Short Catechism."
46. TM (4 June 1930). Not until 1948 was the School's fixed amount—$180—changed to 5 percent of the teacher's salary. See TM (23 September 1948).
47. TM (16 March 1932).
48. TM (7 June 1933). See the faculty's resolution.
49. TM (16 March 1932) and (8 June 1932).
50. TM (8 May 1933). A very complete file on the headmaster search reveals that no consideration was given to Conant. Northrop was the trustees' second choice, their first choice—Henry C. Kittredge (later first lay rector of St. Paul's School, Concord, N.H.)—having turned them down on 13 June 1932, in part for financial reasons. He was the son of Prof. G. L. Kittredge, Class of 1878.
51. Roger Ernst letter to E. D. Canham, editor, 16 January 1953. The *Monitor* published the letter a few days later. James G. Hershberg, *James B. Conant* (New York: Knopf, 1993), 69, relies on the apocryphal tale passed on to him by John Davey (see his footnote, 792), an unreliable part of the R.L. oral tradition widely in circulation at the time of the interview.
52. *The Tripod* 14, 6 (June 1933): 32f.
53. TM (8 May 1933).
54. Roger Ernst letter to G. N. Northrop, 8 June 1933.
55. TM (21 March 1934).
56. See 25 June 1941 letter of Roger Ernst to Charles S. Pierce. Interestingly, no one from 1935 to 1941 questioned the legality of this tuition charge. Ernst says that the Committee that recommended the tuition charge "felt that . . . we could very well claim that so much more is being given nowadays in the way of instruction in our School than it was contemplated should be given in the seventeenth century when the school was started as a 'free grammar school', that we could amply justify a charge of $100 for the instruction in those additional subjects." Also, "because it was absolutely necessary to charge the tuition . . . [any] court would either hold, for the reason above stated, that they had the right to make the amount of charge, or, on the doctrine of *cy pres*, would, in view of the altered financial situation of the School, allow a charge to be made." See also Ernst's letter of 9 January 1934 to Malcolm Donald in which he discusses the case of *Attorney General v. Bishop of Worcester*.
57. TM (22 April 1935).
58. TM (24 September 1935).
59. Letter to the Alumni from the Board of Trustees, June 1935. See *The Tripod* 47, 5

(March 1935) for the announcement at School.

60. TM (4 May 1937) and (15 December 1937).

61. "Memories of George Norton Northrop" in *The Roxbury Latin School Newsletter*, 60, 3 (April 1987): 12.

62. *Roxbury Latin School Alumni Bulletin*, Fall 1964, unpaginated. The two quotations which follow are also from this source.

63. *The Tripod* 46, 2 (December 1933): 19–20.

64. *Roxbury Latin School Alumni Bulletin*, Fall 1964, unpaginated.

65. Ibid.

66. He also arranged for the School's portrait of John Eliot. The original (and only) portrait of John Eliot hangs in the Huntington Library in Pasadena, California. The artist is unknown. Thomas Slocum '86, trustee, gave the $500 necessary to copy the original for the School. See TM (25 September 1935). At first it hung briefly over the mantle in the library, but by 1936 it was placed on a side wall in the Hall. It was made the centerpiece of the Hall's renovation in 1994. See also TM (23 September 1936) for the trustees' gratitude for what Northrop had done to "make the appearance and atmosphere delightful."

67. A small group of alumni were threatened by Northrop's social position and in the mid-1940s spoke of him (behind his back) as "an aristocrat." See, for example, the letter of Scott Foster '29 to Roger Ernst, 12 July 1944, that refers disparagingly to Northrop's membership in The Country Club "which in West Roxbury is considered the tops in snobbishness. . . ."

68. See Roger Ernst letter to S. H. Wolcott, 18 August 1943.

69. TM (19 December 1934).

70. *The Tripod* 47, 2 (December 1934): 14, and 49, 1 (November 1936): 21. The track was at the far end (toward Centre Street) of the present varsity football practice field. The hockey rink was at the near end (toward the Schoolhouse) of the same practice field, about fifteen feet inside the Bogandale Road fence, and exactly parallel to Bogandale Road. It was fed by an above ground stream that was put underground when the present practice field was developed.

71. *The Tripod* 48, 1 (November 1935): 9. See the description of a typical day in 1931 by Geoffrey W. Lewis '28 in the *Roxbury Latin School Alumni Bulletin*, May 1931. Boys started school at 8:45 a.m. and most went home at 1:45 p.m.

72. *The Tripod* 48, 1 (November 1935): 9.

73. *The Tripod* 48, 2 (December 1935): 9.

74. *The Tripod* 49, 1 (November 1936): 21ff.

75. *The Tripod* 50, 2 (December 1937): 5.

76. *The Tripod* 50, 4 (March 1938): 5. *The Tripod* 1, 1 (March 1889): 9 says that Frederick Law Olmsted, Jr., '90 organized a Debating Club in November 1887, but it receives little notice in future issues.

77. *The Tripod* 51, 1 (November 1938): 6.

78. TM (20 December 1939). See also *The Tripod* 53, 4 (May 1941): 3.

79. TM (19 March 1941).
80. *Roxbury Latin School Alumni Bulletin*, June 1940.
81. *Roxbury Latin School Alumni Bulletin*, May 1936.
82. On Bridgess, see *The Tripod* 64, 1 (November 1951); *Roxbury Latin School Bulletin*, Summer 1971; and *The Roxbury Latin School Newsletter*, 68, 4 (July 1995). On Whitney, see *The Tripod*, 64, 3 (May 1952); *The Roxbury Latin School Newsletter* (July 1979) and 68, 2 (January 1995).
83. See *Roxbury Latin School Alumni Bulletin* Spring and Summer 1966, and *Roxbury Latin School Bulletin*, July 1973.
84. See *Roxbury Latin School Alumni Bulletin*, Fall 1964; *Roxbury Latin School Bulletin*, Summer 1971; and *The Roxbury Latin School Newsletter* 60, 3 (April 1987).
85. *Roxbury Latin School Alumni Bulletin*, June 1940. *The Tripod* 48, 5 (May 1936).
86. *Roxbury Latin School Alumni Bulletin*, May 1930.
87. Northrop's report to the trustees, 17 December 1941.
88. By June 1942, for example, the treasurer was authorized to insure the School against war damages: TM (11 June 1942).
89. TM (16 December 1942).
90. TM (16 March 1944).
91. *The Tripod* 56, 2 (April 1944).
92. TM (16 March 1944).
93. *The Tripod* 55, 1 (December 1942): 7.
94. *The Tripod* 57, 2 (March 1945): 1.
95. *The Tripod* 57, 1 (November 1944): 2.
96. TM (18 March 1942).
97. TM (23 September 1942).
98. Ibid. See also TM (16 March 1944), (8 June 1944), and (15 March 1945).
99. *The Tripod* 56, 1 (November 1943): 7.
100. TM (18 March 1943) and *The Tripod* 55, 2 (April 1943): 3.
101. TM (23 September 1942); *Roxbury Latin School Alumni Bulletin*, August 1944.
102. *The Tripod* 57, 1 (November 1944): 3.
103. TM (16 February 1944).
104. *The Tripod* 57, 4 (June 1945).
105. See Roger Ernst letter to W. Dudley Cotton, 1 February 1935. The trustees worried about this piece of property—which jutted into the School's property—falling into the hands of a developer (see TM 22 September 1937) and they made discreet inquiries in 1945 about acquiring it. TM (7 November 1945) records that they came to terms with John S. Codman. Upon discovering that the offer he claimed to have been made by a rival bidder was not bona fide, the trustees insisted on renegotiating the deal: TM (29 November 1945). The house was in poor condition—See TM (16 December 1946). The trustees had to spend $10,000— TM (25 September 1947)—to get it ready for Northrop to move into in his retirement. See also Northrop's letter to Ernst, 20 March 1945. Codman tried to intim-

idate the School by threatening to sell the property to "a Jewish gentleman." See also Roger W. Ernst's letter to Edward W. Grew of 15 June 1942, in which he said the School did not have the resources to purchase the Rock (later Rappaport) property of eight and one-half acres adjoining the School. Again in 1953, the Rocks offered this property to the School for $15,000. Again the School couldn't afford to purchase it.

106. TM (20 March 1947).

107. TM (20 December 1945).

108. "Roxbury Latin, Its Purposes and Its Needs," 1946, 12.

109. Unpublished manuscript, "Roger Ernst's Address at the Tercentenary Dinner," 8 May 1946, 2.

110. "Roxbury Latin, Its Purposes and Its Needs," 1946, 11.

111. "Roxbury Latin, Its Purposes and Its Needs," 1946, 9.

112. TM (3 December 1946).

113. TM (12 June 1947). Numbers soon dropped down to the pre-war 150 level where they settled for the rest of the decade.

114. TM (12 June 1947).

115. TM (3 December 1946). See also the 16 November 1945 letter of Roger Ernst to Judge Albert F. Hayden outlining how the connection of parish and School had all but lapsed.

116. Northrop's report to the trustees, 26 September 1944.

117. TM (25 March 1948). Though the trustees voted "that German should not be permanently dropped from the curriculum," it has never been restored.

118. This and all subsequent quotations from Cary Potter are taken from the author's interviews with him in 1994.

119. TM (12 September 1952).

120. TM (15 June 1949) and (27 September 1951).

121. TM (16 March 1950) and (8 June 1950).

122. See TM (7 June 1951).

123. See TM (15 June 1949).

124. *Roxbury Latin School Alumni Bulletin*, April 1957, 3.

125. In the fall of both 1959 and 1960, for example, the varsity soccer team's only home game was its last, against Boston Latin, after the football season.

126. Ernst and Donald pushed these ideas on Gleason, Taylor, and Sasserno, as Ernst's memorandum of 26 May 1931 shows. When Northrop came they pushed their ideas on him as well. He seems to have held out, however. His letter of 27 May 1941 shows that Ernst could upset him by needling away at the success—or lack of it— of R.L. boys at Harvard. Ernst's 12 June 1941 letter to Delmar Leighton, dean of freshmen at Harvard, betrays the trust implicit in Northrop's letter.

127. This view was reflected in the 1946 Capital Campaign brochure ("Roxbury Latin School—Its Purposes and Its Needs"), 7. Neither the Agreement of 1645 nor the 1789 Charter contains any mention of the "selection of gifted youth."

128. Roger Ernst letter to D. A. Mittell, 21 June 1954.
129. Headmaster's report to the trustees, 25 September 1952.
130. TM (17 March 1960).
131. Even Roger Ernst, in his 24 January 1951 letter to Weed, stresses the primacy of character over raw tested ability in admission.
132. TM (14 December 1961): 8.
133. "Public Relations Report" of Robert W. Siemens, included with headmaster's report to the trustees, 13 December 1962.
134. TM (6 March 1963). Bill Chauncey comments: "Basketball hadn't started up until then because Leo Foley wasn't very interested in basketball, nor was there anyone else who had an interest in it or who could coach it."
135. The figures remained roughly the same until the end of the decade: 78/66 in 1948–49 and 79/77 in 1949–50. See TM (15 June 1949).
136. On a par, perhaps, with geography as a basis of tuition reduction is the Alumni Council's request to the trustees in 1942 that the sons of alumni should be given a preferential rate! TM (11 June 1942). See also TM (12 December 1957).
137. Letter of Stanwood G. Wellington to Dr. Hilbert F. Day, 18 March 1918.
138. TM (25 March 1948). See also the letter of Roger Ernst to James B. Conant, 6 January 1948.
139. TM (21 December 1950).
140. See TM (12 December 1957) for the 1957 discussion, for example.
141. TM (9 June 1960).
142. See also Cary Potter's memorial to Weed in *The Roxbury Latin School Newsletter*, July 1980, 6–7. Alumni of the time take issue with its accuracy regarding students, but not with its insights into Weed as colleague.
143. *Roxbury Latin School Alumni Bulletin*, Fall 1965, unpaginated. This brief quotation comes from a lengthy panegyric by him at the time of Weed's retirement.
144. *The Tripod* 100, 1 (2 September 1994), 6.
145. *The Tripod* 71, 3 (Summer 1959): 3; see also 71, 4 (Fall 1959): 2; 71, 1 (January 1958): 2; 71, 2 (May 1959): 3; 72, 1 (Winter 1959): 2, 16.
146. The School's decennial evaluation by the New England Association in 1967 corroborated the general feeling, as well, that the faculty was not open to innovation (3): "a fair part of the curriculum [is] unduly restrictive and unimaginative. . . . There [are] many areas of the curriculum where too little [attention] is being paid to well-proved innovations in education."
147. TM (12 December 1963), 6–7. Bill Chauncey and many others note that Weed was afflicted by a terrible itch, about which he never complained, but which caused great discomfort: "Fred had not been well."
148. This and all subsequent quotations from Richmond Mayo-Smith (unless otherwise attributed) are taken from the author's interviews with him in 1994.
149. TM (7 October 1965), 6; Headmaster's report, 7 October 1965, 5.
150. *The Tripod*, 1 November 1965.

151. *Roxbury Latin School Bulletin*, Winter 1970.

152. *Roxbury Latin School Bulletin*, Spring 1970.

153. Headmaster's reports to the trustees, 12 June 1971 and 9 June 1972.

154. As we have seen above, Mayo-Smith declared at the 325th anniversary that "Roxbury Latin will make an increasing commitment to co-education. The most interesting students will be choosing co-educational schools." In 1967, he had commissioned Richard A. Siegel '63 and Joel Martin '61 to study the School and to offer their observations and recommendations. Siegel declared flatly that "the days of the all-male or all-female school are, and should be numbered. . . . The segregated atmosphere is unreal." Martin asked: "Is there a reason why the school should not be co-ed?" and offers no answer. In his 29 October 1971 report to the trustees Mayo-Smith reported that, of the seventeen faculty who had responded on the subject of coeducation, ten strongly favored coeducation, four more were somewhat in favor, two felt the School should go slow if at all, and one was opposed. Mayo-Smith, however, admitted that at a recent parent meeting "more than a third voted against coeducation and less than a third in favor."

155. Starting in March 1970, Mayo-Smith took an increasingly reformist stand regarding the organization of the board. In his report to the trustees of 18 November 1970, he discussed new patterns by which the trustees could function more effectively.

156. Joint letter of Richmond Mayo-Smith and Albert R. Smith to the president, Samuel S. Dennis 3d, 10 November 1972. See also Albert R. Smith's letters to David Mittell, 7 and 8 March 1972.

157. TM (23 March 1972): 4; see also Headmaster's Report of the same date.

158. See Faculty Minutes of 13 September 1972 and 12 November 1973. For trustee vote of approval, see TM (14 June 1972) and (26 September 1972).

159. Henry W. Bragdon letter to Samuel S. Dennis 3d, dated 31 January 1972, but actually (from Dennis' response) written on 31 January 1973.

160. TM (20 February 1973): 2.

Memoir

Memoir

Seven Decades of Roxbury Latin

by David A. Mittell '35

❖ ⸻⸻⸻⸻⸻ ❖

E
VEN WHEN I WAS A VERY SMALL CHILD, I was conscious of the existence of The Roxbury Latin School. My older brother, Kenneth '30, entered the School when I was only five and a half. Dr. Arthur N. Broughton '89, longtime trustee of the School, delivered both Kenneth and me at the Faulkner Hospital in Jamaica Plain. We lived next door to him when Kenneth was born, and in another house—still a hundred yards away from his—when he picked up mother (and me!) in his sleigh to take us from Eliot Street to the Faulkner when I was born in 1918. Dr. Broughton was a big man, ruddy-faced with bright blue eyes. He had a white mane of hair and a white mustache. He drove fast in Buick coupes with "Mass. 2002" on them. (In fact, he drove his Buicks in low gear and reverse so hard that the resulting whine made me ask my parents if he bought his cars at the *Noise* [really Noyes] Buick Company, rather than at Boston Buick where Father got his.) He was the personification of "the cool hand on the fevered forehead." At his appearance when one of us was sick, the world immediately got better. He was pediatrician, minor surgeon, obstetrician, gynecologist, general practitioner, and, when necessary, psychiatrist all wrapped up in one.

My memory tells me that I can remember Dr. Broughton saying it in person, but, of course, that memory could be fooling me and maybe I only heard my parents repeat it, but the message was clear: "Edythe, you must send those two boys of yours to The Roxbury Latin School. It is neither public nor private, but a different kind of school called 'endowed'. Because it is endowed it can pick and choose just the bright boys it wants. Since the 1600s, its endowment has enabled it to be an independent and therefore democratic place. It offers a wonderful education."

The Mittell family lived on a cul-de-sac off Eliot Street in Jamaica Plain. Eliot Street is the site of the Eliot School, founded in 1680 and endowed with seventy-five acres by John Eliot as "the Grammar School for the Westerly Part of Roxbury." (Still in operation there today, it devotes itself to after-school programs in the "useful" arts.) My brother Kenneth went to Miss Seeger's School, also on Eliot Street, which prepared boys—though not exclusively—for Roxbury Latin. Although my parents went to the Episcopal church, they sent Kenneth to the Unitarian Sunday School at the Third Church in Roxbury (now called the First Church of Jamaica Plain) at the end of Eliot Street. Its minister was the Reverend Charles F. Dole, then a life trustee of Roxbury Latin and father of James Drummond Dole '95 who brought pineapples to the Hawaiian Islands. As a result, my brother's world was circumscribed by that short length of Eliot Street.

My properly protective parents questioned whether this small boy, barely eleven years old, should be allowed to take the streetcar to Roxbury Latin "way over there into Dudley Street" in "the easterly part of Roxbury"—an area that had been gently declining for twenty-five years. However, good sense prevailed and so Ken set off in September 1923 to join the Class of 1929 at the wood-frame school on Kearsarge Avenue. (A bout with infectious diseases in the winter of 1924 caused him to miss so much school that he joined the Class of 1930 in the fall of 1924.)

The faculty that greeted Kenneth in 1923 was exactly the same group of gentlemen who greeted me six years later in 1929, with one exception. N. Henry Black, who had been at the School since 1900, left in 1924 to join his former student—now collaborator and colleague—Dr. James Bryant Conant '10 as a teacher of chemistry at Harvard. Stories about

Black still abounded in my time. He had taught geography to Class V, and one year at the end of the first marking period had failed all but four or five boys. Shocked parents launched a campaign of letters to Dr. Thompson, the headmaster, and the trustees; my father, I know, spoke to Dr. Broughton. Black was succeeded by a much beloved man, A. John Holden, who unfortunately stayed at the School only four years. He also went on to higher education and retired as Commissioner of Education for the State of Vermont. Ralph H. Houser, then a master at Noble and Greenough School and a former Oberlin star football player, succeeded him in 1928 and stayed until his retirement in 1955. So, with the exception of the science masters, the faculty in the 1920s was remarkably stable: Clarence Gleason, master of Greek and Latin, served the School for forty-three years; Sixth Class Master O. M. Farnham, Latin master Earl Taylor, and Athletic Director J. Leo Foley all for forty-one; French master Joseph Sasserno for thirty-nine; and mathematics master Howard Wiggin for twenty-four years.

Kenneth's years at School were split almost exactly between the old and new campuses. The old Kearsarge Avenue campus near the former Dudley Street Elevated Railway Station was so conveniently located that most boys came to it by elevated train or streetcar. Since the School's only "grounds" were a small sloping abandoned graveyard, all games had to be played "away." By the time I was ready for Roxbury Latin in 1929, the School had moved to West Roxbury and was in process of becoming a "country day school." William Perry's award-winning schoolhouse had opened in 1927 on the fifty-acre Richard Codman "country" estate in West Roxbury where it could have fields, tennis courts, a track, a skating pond, and later a makeshift hockey rink. Some older Roxbury Latin alumni resent the term "country day school," thinking that it evokes a sense of social elitism. But the School probably would not have survived had it not moved from its dilapidated quarters and constricted campus in Roxbury.

Roxbury Latin was unique among the Boston day schools in being an "endowed" not-for-profit school. Most of the Boston day schools were originally proprietary—owned by their founder and run for a profit. These schools—such as Mr. Dixwell's, Mr. Hopkinson's, Mr. Stone's, Mr. Noble's, Mr. Browne's, and Mr. Volkmann's—were established to prepare boys (whose parents could afford to pay) for college. They had many "cram school" characteristics. Only gradually, in response to growing parental demand, did these schools offer any sort of athletic programs. As parents began to be attracted to the newly established boarding schools away from the city, these proprietary schools had to respond. Mr. Noble's school, by then Noble and Greenough, acquired sports facilities off St. Paul Street in Brookline; boys travelled there each afternoon by streetcar. Mr. Browne's school sent its boys from Harvard Square for sports at Gerry's Landing (where the Buckingham Browne & Nichols upper school is now located). Together these schools formed a private school league which included Roxbury Latin.

Though the "country day school" concept was sweeping the country by the 1890s, Boston had no bona fide "country day school" until 1906 when Shirley K. Kerns founded what was appropriately called "Country Day." Its official name became "The Country Day School for Boys of Greater Boston"; naturally, it was known among its boys as "The Country Day School for Greater Boys of Boston." The school was located on Nonantum Hill on the Newton-Brighton line. Its varsity field and hockey rink were at a much lower level where an ancient glacier had left a pond and a broad meadow. It was on the bluff overlooking this meadow that John Eliot preached to the local Indians in 1646. Robert W. Rivers started his proprietary school in 1915 at Dean Road and Eliot Street, Brookline. It was "open air" all year in keeping with the disease-prevention theories of leading Boston physicians of that era. Country Day flourished until 1940 when Mr. Kerns's successor, Linwood Chase, retired and it merged with Rivers. (William Cardinal O'Connell purchased the Country Day campus and established St. Sebastian's Country Day School there in 1941. It moved to Needham in 1982.)

As the proprietary school founders began to grow old, they either sold off to other schools or converted to public charities under boards of trustees. Mr. Volkmann's School was merged with Noble and Greenough during the anti-German hysteria of World War I, and the enlarged school became non-proprietary and moved to the Nickerson estate in Dedham. Belmont Hill was founded at Belmont in 1923. Roxbury Latin, with its ramshackle building, without a real field, midst the tenements of Roxbury, was being left behind. The trustees and faculty watched with dismay as potential students melted away to these country day schools that offered a fuller program in attractive and healthy surroundings. As more and more American families acquired automobiles in the post-World War I years, "country" campuses became easily accessible—and desirable. Roxbury Latin's location on the existing public transportation system was no longer an advantage.

Throughout the first two decades of this century, Roxbury Latin's trustees and alumni debated how best to secure the School's future; by 1927 they engineered the School's move to the "country." Roxbury Latin's Charter established a school governed by trustees who served without limit of time. The School today is almost unique in preserving nine life trustees on its governing board. As I have watched the tides flow and ebb at surrounding schools and other charitable institutions, I have come to the strong conviction that the successful "eternal" institutions are those that have a small group of people who make a lifetime commitment to them. I believe Dr. Broughton was right when he repeated over and over to my parents that Roxbury Latin was unique. Its governance by a small and dedicated corps of trustees has enabled it to preserve its independence and vitality through the centuries.

The New School in West Roxbury

I only experienced the move to Cottage Avenue (now called St. Theresa Avenue) vicariously through Kenneth's daily reports. The whole School reported back in September 1927 one week early and helped load and unload the books, statues, pictures, and furniture for the big move.

By the time we entered the Sixth Class in 1929, the School was beginning to develop a full country day school program. West Roxbury parent Charles Nichols had provided for the leveling of the field along Centre Street and had built a small green wooden shed that served as a storage place for equipment and as a dressing room before the new building was finished. I remember seeing baseball and football games there in the mid-1920s.

Though I was only nine, I vividly recall Stacy Holmes '27, later a trustee, leading the cheers at games that season. Stacy, a brilliant amateur musician, wrote me in 1986:

> Your idea for a piece on those great R.L.S. jazz artists Newell Chase and Charlie Henderson is a good one. . . . Perhaps the article would have broader nostalgic appeal under a title like "R.L.S. grace notes in the jazz age." . . . The subsequent Hollywood careers of Newell and Charlie would come as the climax or coda. Here are some sharps and flats from my libretto of memories.
>
> Newell Chase was in the First Class when I was in the Sixth Class, so my admiration and reverence for him was as that of the tadpole to the bullfrog. Charles Henderson was something else again. He was at R.L.S. during most of my formative musical years. He accompanied the hymns and songs ("Nicodemus", "Forty Years On", the Founder's Song) led by Mr. Taylor in the hall. He also accompanied or starred in other musical diversions on the special "hall days."
>
> One of these was my first public performance as a vocal soloist. Before my voice changed I had the lark falsetto of a Vienna Choir Boy and was the target of fiercely competitive recruiting by the choirmasters of Trinity Church, West Roxbury Congregational, and new Old South. Charlie coached and accompanied me in singing "Mandalay" one hall day. I must have sounded more like a "waitin'" Burma girl than a soldier who had raised a thirst, but the performance, thanks to Charlie's Bravura background, was considered a success.
>
> Charlie also did a hilarious specialty as the pianist providing color to the Pathé or Movietone News of the day. This was the era of silent film, remember, pre-television and even pre-radio until the late twenties. Every movie theatre had a piano player with a full repertoire of passages suitable for fires, parades, political gath-

erings or balloon ascensions. As there was no movie screen in the hall, Charlie spoke the film captions aloud and the audience imagined the scene painted by his fingertips. I remember the sequence that started: "Five hundred tots in kiddiekar race in West Palm Beach" followed by frantic race music. Then "Long speech by President Coolidge." Two quick chords. "Prince of Wales has spill at fox hunt." You can imagine; Reynard the Fox, thundering hooves, the crash, gypsy violins as the body is carried off on a stretcher.

Your recollection of me as cheerleader is correct. But the saxophone hung from the neck of Gordon Mills, '27, the R.L.S. marching band. We had three cheers: the long "R-O-X-B-U-R-Y" followed by nine "rahs," the short "Roxbury, rah!" and "Alpha, Beta, Gamma, Hammer, Roxbury, Hammer. Do 'Em Up and Win the Cup, Hammer, Roxbury, Hammer." This last was written by Mr. Gleason, the Greek and Latin master.

Charles Henderson's musical career took him to Hollywood, where he wrote and scored music for many moving pictures. In the early 1930s, he wrote two ballads, still played today, collaborating with Rudy Vallee, the popular radio "crooner." These songs were "So Beats My Heart for You" and "Deep Night."

In the first two decades of this century, the number of students from the old easterly part of Roxbury diminished as the neighborhoods there changed. Jamaica Plain and Brookline remained well represented, but by the time the new building was opened in 1927 nearly a third of the student body lived in West Roxbury, the middle-class neighborhood in which the school was now located, and a further third in Roslindale and Jamaica Plain. At one celebration, Professor Grandgent, later trustee president, gave a toast to Roxbury Latin's philosophy: "Well have the descendants preserved the sturdy, wholesome democracy of the Founders, and well may they keep it." They have.

My parents sent me to the public school, Agassiz School on Burroughs Street, Jamaica Plain, though many of my friends went to private schools (such as Miss Bertha Hewins' School on Emmonsdale

Road, which later moved to Dedham and eventually became the present Dedham Country Day School). From the time I was five until I went to Roxbury Latin at age eleven and a half, my three closest friends were "Boy," "Buster," and "Bubby." "Boy" was James E. McLaughlin II, named for his eminent architect uncle who designed Boston Latin School. Boy and I trudged to the Agassiz School and back together each day. "Buster" was Milton John English. His family's chauffeur, "Dinny" McNamara, drove him in a Packard to the Longwood Day School, no longer in existence but then a leading private elementary school. It was located off St. Paul Street on Browne Street in Brookline. "Bubby" was Calvin Barstow Faunce, Jr., whose doctor father drove him every day to Noble's Lower School on Freeman Street (which became Dexter School in 1926), at the other end of the park from the Longwood Day School.

One of my brother's classmates at Miss Seeger's was picked up each day in a horse and buggy by Malone & Keene who had their stable on South Street, Jamaica Plain. Later he transferred to Mr. Rivers's Open Air School in the country part of Brookline. I remember watching the Rivers bus pick up boys on our street. The bus had the same color combination as their sports jerseys, brown with red stripes.

Finally, in 1929, it became my turn to experience the School first hand. Each morning my Jamaica Plain schoolmates and I would first take the bus to the corner of Belgrade Avenue and Centre Street. From there we would either walk to school or get a transfer and take the Centre Street streetcar to the corner of Spring Street. If we walked, we were often picked up by Mr. Taylor, Mr. Houser, or Mr. Wiggin along the way. Or we might hitch a ride from the Reverend Henry Ogilby '03, Rector of All Saints' Church in Brookline, who drove John '34 from there each day, or from Dr. Frederick W. Stetson who brought his sons over from Brattle Street, Cambridge.

West Roxbury boys walked or bicycled (parking in the bicycle room). The Needham boys took the New York, New Haven, & Hartford Railroad's commuter train from Bird's Hill (modern-day Hersey) or one of the other Needham stations to the West Roxbury station on LaGrange Street. Others took the train from Dedham, which joined the Needham line just before reaching West Roxbury. Judge Grover drove Tom '37 and his younger brother, Bill '40, each day from Canton. At least two of my contemporaries had "family drivers" or chauffeurs.

School started with the 8:45 bell. That was the signal for classes to march into Rousmaniere Hall, the Sixth first with the other classes following, so that the big boys ended up in the back rows. When we were settled, the Headmaster would read from the Bible, and then Mr. Taylor would come to the edge of the stage and announce a hymn. This was accompanied by a piano or reed organ. Several boys were musicians. J. Minot Fowler '33 played the piano in "hall," as did A. Ross Borden '35. They were sometimes accompanied by Austin Ivory '30 on the violin or Robert Adams '33 and Gordon Hughes '33 on the alto saxophone. After the hymn, the headmaster would make announcements. On the day of a big game there might be a cheer for the team and sometimes its captain. Occasionally there were outside speakers, some of whom used Latin quotations. We small boys squirmed when an orator stretched into his second hour. Some speakers were stimulating: I remember in particular Malcolm Farmer '01, athletic director at Yale. By about 9:00 we were off to class, though sometimes "hall" impinged on the first period. At 10:25 there was a ten-minute recess, after which classes continued until lunch at 11:55.

In most schools, students move from class to class. At R.L., however, the masters came to us while we stayed put in our own homeroom. There were exceptions: in Class V when we studied elementary science with Mr. Houser, we went to the science demonstration room. In Class III we had to choose between Greek and German. The "Germans" met in what we called "The Trophy Room," the room in the middle of the building behind the bookstore. The "Greeks" met upstairs in Mr. Gleason's classical study.

Lunch was a variable affair. Mr. and Mrs. Small, who lived in the tiny Codman Gate House at 111 St. Theresa Avenue (later occupied for years by the Richard Whitney family and razed in 1993), had the concession for serving meals in the lunchroom. They also ran the little store next to Mr. Foley's and Dr. Howell's office in the middle of the long first floor corridor, where we could buy a sandwich, candy bar, or milk. In the Sixth Class most of us brought a sandwich from home and purchased milk. Some of us continued to eat in our homerooms throughout our six years; others partook of Mrs. Small's fare, which was more often chop suey than anything else, in the lunchroom (located in what is now the Malcolm Donald Room in the admissions suite). The masters sat by themselves — away from the students — at a round table in the far right-hand corner.

School ended at 1:45. What we did then varied from class to class. Students were not required to do sports. If you chose not to participate, you could leave at the end of classes, and many did. None of the faculty except J. Leo Foley, the athletic director and coach of all three sports (football, track, and baseball), assisted in the sports program. Could this failure to associate and communicate with students outside of the classroom be a clue to the School's high attrition rate? In the 1920s only 45 percent of those admitted graduated. All the coaching — except by Mr. Foley — was done by alumni in college. Geoffrey W. Lewis '28, Charles A. Keene, Jr. '27, and Robert A. Gilman '27 taught the little boys football and baseball, often recruiting their college friends to help out. Once, Geoffrey Lewis, soon to be a dean at Harvard and (before he was thirty) headmaster of Browne & Nichols School, drove the whole junior baseball team to Rivers School in Brookline in his Model T Ford touring car with the top down! It was well we were little.

The Sixth Class with Mr. Farnham

On our arrival as Sixies we first encountered Dr. Thompson, headmaster, and Onsville M. Farnham, Sixth Class master, who had administered our entrance exam. The exam was an awesome experience since we were in a strange place, dealing for the first time with a male teacher, and we knew we were competing for one of the thirty places. Francis

Russell in *Forty Years On* has so graphically described Mr. Farnham's examination that detail is not necessary here, except to say that his kindness and warmth turned that challenge from something terrifying into something bearable.

Daniel Varney Thompson had come as headmaster in 1921. He was a distinguished Shakespearean scholar and had been head of the English department at Lawrenceville School. His scholarly attainments were recognized by the honorary L.H.D. which his alma mater, Amherst College, bestowed on him in 1924. I found him kind, pleasant, soft-spoken, but firm. I only heard him raise his voice once, and that was when some of the older boys were not settling down at the time the quinquennial picture of the whole school was being taken in the courtyard. His loud "Boys! Boys! *Be quiet!*" brought order out of chaos. However, on the firm side I have found notes to my parents and me of this sort:

> January 22, 1932
> Mr. Carl L. Mittell,
> 35 Prince Street,
> Jamaica Plain, Mass.
>
> Dear Mr. Mittell:
>
> I wish before long I could have a talk with you, or Mrs. Mittell, about David. We ought to unite our wisdom and efforts before it is too late.
>
> > Faithfully yours,
> > (signed) D. V. Thompson

> February 19, 1932
>
> Dear David:
>
> Please call to see me tomorrow morning (Saturday) between ten and eleven.
>
> > Faithfully yours,
> > (signed) D. V. Thompson

FIG. 1. The Class of 1935 as the Sixth Class in 1929–1930. *Back row, from left:* Ernst, Balboni, Meskill, Culley, Goggin, Reed, Steeves, Osgood, True. *Third row:* Hanlon, MacFarlane, Lacouture, Clarke. *Second row:* McMorrow, Vandersall, Sax, Myers, Barker, Moore, Kettendorf, Casassa. *Front row:* Bunker, Tyler, McNulty, Nolan, Pamp, Borden, Fisher. *In front:* Niles, Mittell.

Dr. and Mrs. Thompson lived at "The Warren" on Warren Street in Roxbury until Richard Codman died and they could move into the Victorian mansion (razed in 1965) adjoining the new schoolhouse in West Roxbury. Mr. Codman had been granted lifelong use of the house when he sold his estate to the School. Dr. Thompson led the School during its transition from a city school to a country school. Though he inherited a stable faculty, he did recruit Lynwood S. Bryant in 1931, a young history and English teacher, who was the first master—in addition to Mr. Foley—to assist with sports in the afternoon.

The trustees still functioned as they had in earlier centuries—involving themselves in the detailed decisions of school life. Treasurer Sam Wolcott '99 told me that in the 1920s, Headmaster Thompson sat outside the trustees' Harvard Club meeting room under the portrait of a World War I French general, so he could be summoned if necessary. I am told that when Roger Ernst was president of the board (1935–1955), he conferred with the headmaster, approving or disapproving every admission decision. Today the complexities of admission are wisely handled by a sensitive and conscientious faculty committee that anguishes to the small hours over each decision.

I was prepared to love and respect the Sixth Class master Onsville M. Farnham when I came to the School in 1929, for he had made a great impact on my older brother and, indeed, on my parents. We had visited him at his eastern-most house in Orleans, Cape Cod, and we sometimes met him in the Arnold Arboretum when he walked there on Sunday after church.

When the Class of 1935 entered Mr. Farnham's custody in September 1929, we were dressed in the fashion expected of the littlest boys: in knickers (no long pants), shirts, ties, a figured, argyle, or plain woolen sweater, plaid cotton knee socks, and leather shoes. The first thing Mr. Farnham did was to seat us alphabetically. Then he went around the class beginning with Albert Balboni, who was in the first row to his left, and gave each boy a nickname. Some were obvious. Balboni being "Albert" was nicknamed "Al." Behind him was Borden who was called by his middle name "Ross." Meskill, who sat in front of me, had the same first name I had. Mr. Farnham give him the first half of the name ("Dave") and I received the second half ("Vid"). This nicknaming gave all of us an immediate sense of belonging and intimacy. We quickly picked up calling each other by the nicknames Mr. Farnham had given us. He himself always used these nicknames even in his most unsmiling, explosive disciplinary rebukes.

Mr. Farnham was a firm disciplinarian. My classmate Father Joe McNulty recalls vividly the scolding that Mr. Farnham gave Karl Sax for looking out the window on our first day in Class VI. Within the first few days, Mr. Farnham had given us our basic training, the ground rules for survival at Roxbury Latin, what was approved and what was forbidden. The much-feared "censure card," he explained, would be sent home for poor academic results or for serious disciplinary infractions. Two E's in any subject or a major infraction of the rules resulted in a censure card. Two censure cards and you were out. The disciplinary system was meticulously worked out. If one of us did something wrong, he would receive a "bullet." Mr. Farnham might bellow, "Vid, come up here; that will be a 'bullet' for you." A bullet was a dot placed as the start of a triangle (the Greek letter delta—a "D" for Deportment). Three bullets equaled a triangle, three triangles automatically resulted in a D (then, as now, a failure), while four brought an "E" in deportment. A neatness deficiency was "N," fidelity "F," attention "A." All these marks were recorded on a clipboard and were reviewed each month. It sounds complicated, but we understood it; it worked and kept us in line.

Mr. Farnham showed us how to make out our own bill and buy our books and supplies (including the various sizes of block paper) from Mr. Taylor. In a few days we felt "part of the team." He soon introduced us to his "double words" in spelling. Get one of these difficult words like "parallel" wrong and it counted two wrong, and two wrong was an automatic C. We then moved on to learning how to do his famous two-minute talks, which prepared us superbly for the public speaking we would all be required to do in later life.

Early in Class VI we were summoned individually from our morning classes to Mr. Foley's office for our physical examinations. There kindly, smiling Dr. William W. Howell listened to our hearts and lungs, made us jump up and down some fifty times, and listened again. He then tested us for rupture and made a record of our childhood diseases. He diagnosed a minor heart murmur in one of my classmates that kept him out of football for a year or two.

Mr. Farnham took us Sixies to the Paul Revere House, the Shirley-Eustis House, the Athenæum, the Museum of Fine Arts, and even to the L Street Bathhouse in South Boston, where the "L Street Brownies" swim every day of the year, even in winter. Our pilgrimage to see the Abbey paintings at the Public Library interested many of my classmates, but I was too immature to appreciate this introduction to art history.

I could go on for many pages about Mr. Farnham. To many of my contemporaries and to those who had come before us, he was the greatest teacher; he incarnated Roxbury Latin. There were other favorites: classicists took to Mr. Gleason; literature and English enthusiasts to Dr. Thompson or his successor, Mr. Northrop; boys destined for M.I.T. for scientific or engineering careers enjoyed Mr. Houser. But everyone revered Mr. Farnham.

I have tried to analyze what it was about Mr. Farnham, this firm, disciplined, exacting master, that made generations of boys venerate him. The answer lies, I think, partly in his basic trust in small boys (he would allow us to go to the attic to study French or to practice reciting a poem) and partly in his enthusiasm for his own life (his family, his summers on Cape Cod, his profession). But most of all we venerated him because we knew he loved us all—tall or short, introvert or extrovert, bright or not so bright, bad or good. There is something magic in a great teacher that transcends logical explanation; something "chemical" happens when you put together—in just the right combination—affection, respect, understanding, and firmness. Little boys cannot be fooled; we knew Mr. Farnham was on our side. The plaque in his honor in the Farnham Room comes close to describing him: "Excellence was all his aim, and every boy was his concern." He was a great teacher because he loved us.

We naturally got a full dose of Mr. Farnham's beloved New England poets. He believed that New England in the 1800s was the Mecca of culture, education, literature, and civilization. Stacy Holmes wrote me in 1989, after we had dedicated the former library as the Onsville M. Farnham Room:

> The dedication of the Farnham Room . . . reminded me of many of the things that O.M.F. taught me that I had not thought of in years: how to make a polychosohedron, how to fill a mechanical drawing pen with India ink, how to design a log cabin, how to make a card catalogue, to say 'Massachusetts Avenue,' not 'Mass. Ave.,' how to develop penmanship as an alternative to the push-pull of the Palmer method, how to make an imitation stained glass

window out of colored transparent paper, and more and more and more. What a man.

Mr. Farnham presided over our lunch hours in his "drawing room" (literally the room in which he taught drawing, the present "English Room" or Room 14). As we ate our mothers' sandwiches and he drank his tea, he might auction off lost items which he had found lying around—pencils, erasers, triangles, compasses.

The year-end class picnic at Walden Pond was a trip to the shrine of one of Mr. Farnham's heroes—Thoreau. Having just learned to drive a year or so before, when the School gave him a Model A Ford, he motored out Massachusetts Avenue from Cambridge to Lexington in second gear the entire way. Ross Borden tells me that Gus Casassa could not swim, that John Lacouture and others tied a rope and life preserver to him and towed him to the dock, the distance Mr. Farnham required that we swim for admission to the Fifth Class. Sixty-year hindsight suggests to Ross that Mr. Farnham let it happen and pretended not to see the charade. That class picnic capped a happy year of adjustment to male teachers, homework, and contact sports.

Sports and Extracurriculars in Class VI

On our first day in Class VI, the thirty of us went to Mr. Foley's little closet-shop in the basement and bought our first football shoulder pads, helmet, and pants. (Though the School's prices were low, some went to Raymond's or M. S. Rosenbaum's stores in Boston to get their equipment for even less.) Thus began, for many of us, a commitment to sports that was to last throughout our six years, and for some of us throughout our lifetimes.

Fred Pamp and I, the smallest in the class, weighed sixty-five pounds and were four feet three inches tall when we were fitted out for those uniforms that fall, whereas Ben Goggin had virtually all of his growth and immediately played, I believe, on the senior team. R.L. was a member of the loosely organized Private School League that had established a coefficient system. They added up age, height, and weight and divided it by a factor, and came up with a coefficient that theoretically insured that boys competed with boys of similar size.

At the first game in which I played, our opponent lacked sufficient small boys to make up a full eleven. They therefore put in a fourteen-year-old, who measured about five feet six, one hundred pounds, who could run like a deer, and balanced him with two nine-year-olds on the weak side of the line who might have weighed fifty pounds, even less than Pamp and I. The older, bigger boy, however, made the game one-sided. We not only lost, but our best player, George MacFarlane, was carried off the field with a concussion about the twelfth time he tackled the big halfback. (MacFarlane came from a family of strong athletes. His brother, Tom '33, was football captain and later played at Harvard. The brothers had practiced blocking and tackling each other.)

That day made a great impression on me, for we rode to the game with Al Balboni's mother, a most attractive and charming lady, and my parents came down to watch me do a little bumping and to bring me home. We also brought home our hero, who had received the concussion. We quickly lost our fear of physical contact, and before long even the smallest and most timid were enjoying tackling and blocking.

At the end of the football season, after the last varsity game, the schools in the Private School League competed against one another at all levels in an event called "The Private School Meet." I have a 1927 clipping that tells of Browne & Nichols winning the meet that year. Boys competed in punting, drop-kicking, passing, and centering. The events were carefully supervised. Those competing in centering, for example, got to attempt ten centers from an appropriate distance: each center that went through the square wooden frame was awarded a point. In punting and passing, points were awarded for distance, and in drop-kicking, for accuracy. All the classes were involved together and, like the Harvard-sponsored Private School Track Meet, which concluded the winter season, it was a friendly competition characterized by good sportsmanship.

When the fall season was over, we Sixies suddenly had time on our hands. We put our newfound freedom to interesting use. Some of us, for example, explored the various routes of the (now razed) Boston Elevated Railway. At least once a week we caught a streetcar at Spring Street, changed at Forest Hills, and went into the retail district to ogle electric trains at Jordan Marsh or sporting goods at Raymond's. If we did not go in town, we often crossed Centre Street at the Belgrade Avenue stop for a hot fudge, marshmallow, walnut sundae with chocolate ice cream for fifteen cents, a hearty supplement for a thin sandwich lunch.

About that time of year, dancing schools began their "season." Those of us in Jamaica Plain were invited, if we were lucky, to Miss Marguerite Souther's Eliot Hall Dancing School. Her brothers were R.L. alumni: Channing '02, Dana '02, and Glendon '04. My brother Kenneth joined the dancing school when he was five or six; I started at nine. In West Roxbury there was Miss Widmer's Dancing School at the old Highland Men's Club on the corner of Corey and Centre Streets that has since been razed. The "Lord Byrons" were held in West Roxbury at the American Legion Hall. There were the Beaconsfields in Brookline and the Buckinghams in Cambridge. As we got a bit older—and girls became of more interest to us—we moved to dancing "assemblies." Three of my classmates married their childhood sweethearts: Dave Meskill married Adelaide Hogan, Al Hanlon married Barbara Foster (sister of Scott Foster '27, trustee and secretary), and "Red" Culley married Catherine Patterson.

Track had been a strong sport at Roxbury Latin since the 1880s. Before Mr. Foley's arrival, Jack Ryder, the famous Boston Athletic Association's coach, instructed boys at the old school. Now in his winter capacity as track coach, Mr. Foley encouraged us little boys to participate in that sport after the fall season ended and the track was set up on the far end of the present varsity football practice field. He often drafted us for the chore of shovelling the track so that the older boys could enjoy it. Mr. Foley would allow us to undress to our underwear in the nine-foot high basement room (now the junior wrestling room, formerly the shop, then the art room) which was then all the gymnasium we had. He would teach us how to high jump, a sport which I enjoyed much more than the foot races on the square track with the straight-away for dashes, which left some of us nauseated.

During this winter we got to know our classmates better. Because we knew how to take public transportation, we felt independent and self-confident. We could go home with a friend and visit for an afternoon, engaging in activities as serious as running an electric train or turning the garden hose on a younger sister. (Both things happened! That particular younger sister grew up to be a raving beauty, and while no duels were fought over her, several of my contemporaries were smitten by her.)

In the spring we all played baseball. Our coaches, Roxbury Latin alumni in college, provided fine role-models. Baseball was an easier game to adapt to than football, since all of us had thrown and caught a ball. The three tennis courts near the School, given by Charles Nichols and built on fill supplied from the excavation of the old boiler room (now a student lounge for Classes I, II, and III), had already been completed, but they were dominated by upperclassmen; so some of us from Jamaica Plain would retreat to the Loring Greenough House tennis court behind Curtis Hall.

This description of after-school activities has failed to emphasize that we were left alone, unsupervised, to explore virtually all fifty acres of the campus plus the woods across Quail Street—including the brook, the ledges up toward Welch's Pond, and the carriage house which burned down in 1932. No accidents or harm came out of these leisurely pursuits. This absence of supervised after-school activity contrasts greatly with the organized and monitored sports and extracurricular programs which vie for students' attention today.

My Sixth Class year ended on a high note: my brother's graduation. We then left for the summer, cajoled by Mr. Farnham to read Sir Walter Scott's *Ivanhoe* and by Mr. Sasserno to read *Le Voyage de Monsieur Perrichon*. Most of us did so, but not until the week before school opened in the fall.

A look at how and where my entering classmates spent their sum-mers gives, perhaps, a hint at what sort of "mix" we were socially and economically. Five of us summered on Cape Cod—at Harwichport, Truro, Cataumet, South Hyannis, and North Chatham. The others spread out to places such as Rutland, Ferry Hill and Ocean Bluff in Marshfield, Sagamore Beach, and Sand Hills in Scituate. One sum-mered in New Hampshire. Twelve classmates stayed home in the Boston area. Many of these boys had part- or full-time jobs to help with the family finances. While the "mix" was nothing like as broad as it is today, there were some moderately well-to-do (though no "old") fami-lies represented in our class as well as some quite poor boys. There was also a pretty good religious mix. By the standards of the time the School was very democratic.

On to the "Little Captain's" Domain

The Fifth Class was quite different from the Sixth. The classmaster, Joseph Sasserno, was nothing like Mr. Farnham in personality or style. Mr. Sasserno was short. He had been an officer in France during World War I. He came to us from Norwich University, a military school, and his approach and bearing were military. He was extremely proud, proud of his Italian ancestry, proud of his Harvard degree. He would not tolerate any breaches of good conduct and had little or no trouble with discipline. Instead of being called by nicknames, we were called by our surnames. This had the somewhat beneficial effect of making us feel more grown-up. Indeed, we were more grown-up, for we had been through the mill once, and the Class of 1936 were now the neophytes. They were learning that, if they wore long pants, we Fifth Classmen would discipline them, according to the tradition, by removing their trousers and hoisting them up the Hugh Nawn '07 flagpole.

If a good teacher is one who is able to make his or her pupils assimi-late knowledge without much pain and without their realizing how much they are learning, Mr. Sasserno was a good teacher. When we took our CP-2 (two-year) French examination at the end of our Third

FIG. 2. The Class of 1935 as the Fifth Class in 1930–31. *Back row, from left:* Hoague, Culley, Osgood, Reed, True. *Third row:* Balboni, Poland, Meskill, Goggin, Towns, MacFarlane, McNulty, Fisher, Borden. *Second row:* Ernst, Clarke, Vandersall, Lacouture, Hanlon, Kettendorf, Moore, Casassa. *Front row:* Nolan, Bunker, Pamp, Niles, Mittell, Myers, Regan.

Class year (we had studied French for four years), we all got honors marks of 80 or higher. This sort of achievement was a typical "harvest" of the R.L. faculty's excellent instruction. It was often said that, if one graduated from Roxbury Latin, freshman year at any college was easy.

By this time Mr. Sasserno had succeeded Mr. Gleason in directing the school play. In earlier years the annual play had been presented in Eliot Hall on Eliot Street, Jamaica Plain, then in the 1920s in Whitney Hall, Coolidge Corner, Brookline, and finally, after the move to West Roxbury, in Rousmaniere Hall. A dance followed the play, and this event was the social highlight of the year along with the junior and senior proms. Mr. Sasserno also organized the R.L. Night at the Pops at Symphony Hall each year. He insisted on the playing of Tchaikovsky's "1812 Overture" at the end, and his former students still claim that he is responsible for originating the tradition that prevails today: the "1812" is always the finale of the Fourth of July esplanade pops concert.

Mr. Sasserno was not exempted, however, from some of the chicaneries boys can conjure up. My brother's class alleges that they put a whole envelope-size blotter full of thumbtacks on his chair before he arrived for a French class and that he sat on the thumbtacks for the entire period. Either he had lost feeling in his posterior or he was too proud to acknowledge the pain.

Mr. Sasserno smoked cigars. As a result, the second floor corridor beyond the chemistry laboratory always smelled of a combination of "Josie's" cigar smoke and Mr. Houser's chemicals. One day, as Mr. Sasserno was preparing a class in the faculty study, he tossed his lighted cigar into the fireplace. Meanwhile, he carried on reading without realizing that, though the damper was closed because it was not yet winter, the fireplace had been set with kindling and wood. Suddenly he was seen running down the second floor corridor, soaked from head to foot; his cigar had lit the fire in the fireplace which in turn had set off the automatic sprinkler giving him an unexpected shower.

He jocularly pressured us into higher achievement in the classroom by making allusions to the fact we were performing on about the same level as "the girls at Chelsea High." One of the wags in my class therefore wrote a short cheer for Mr. Sasserno:

> *Oh! Me! Oh! My! Oh! Mother!*
> *Oh! Mother! Oh! Me! Oh! My!*
> *Three cheers for "Little Josie"*
> *And the girls of Chelsea High!*

Although two or three of our original classmates had fallen by the wayside, our Fifth Class year was a happy one. The excitable Mr. Houser tried with mixed success to teach us geography. Snooping around Mr. Houser's science lab after school that year we discovered that he had stored in his private closet off the chemistry laboratory some five or six fetuses, in various stages of development, preserved in formaldehyde. We, of course, were fascinated. Unhappily, the discovery led one boy's mother, shocked that the School could allow a teacher freedom for such irreverence, to remove her son immediately from the School.

Academically the Fifth Class was an extension of the Sixth. But socially and athletically it was a quantum leap: we were now confident veterans. In the first place, we knew what we were doing on the football field. We knew how to hold the ball, how to pass it. We had been taught how to throw an "Indianizing" block—leaving our feet and throwing our bodies across the knees of our opponents. It was outlawed, along with the flying tackle, after Richard Brinsley Sheridan, a West Point end, was killed in an Army-Yale game in the 1930s.

We played Fay School, Browne & Nichols, and Belmont Hill on their turf. Some of us were awed that there was a nurse in uniform at both Fessenden and Belmont Hill. We figured they were going to give us a pretty rough time if they had to have a nurse there anticipating the injuries that might occur. I felt sorry for the little boys boarding in their wooden cubicles at Fay School on a cold November Day. While I nearly froze riding home in the back seat of Professor Sax's 1929 Model A Ford touring car, I knew at least that when I got home there would be an open fire in the fireplace and parents to greet me. My abiding belief in the country day school was enhanced by that experience.

One event that occurred the fall of the Fifth Class year illustrates how little supervision there was in the afternoons. I was carrying the ball around right end, and Fred Myers, my good friend, tripped over his own feet trying to tackle me and landed on his left arm. We took one look at the bend of his forearm and realized it was broken. I assured the coach not to worry, that I would take Fred to the Faulkner Hospital and get him fixed up. My mother had spent three weeks at the Faulkner in 1929 after an automobile accident. I visited her most days for several hours, so I got to know Miss Ladd, who was the general superintendent. I also knew Dr. Morrison, who, like his brother on Beacon Street who had x-rayed me, was a distinguished radiologist, then called a roentgenologist.

So we dressed Fred and walked to Centre Street, took the streetcar to Belgrade Avenue and the bus to the foot of the Faulkner Hospital, and walked up the hill. I asked for Miss Ladd, who took one look at Fred and said, "Yes, Dr. Morrison is in." Dr. Morrison took an x-ray. They notified Mrs. Myers and she came and picked up Fred after his arm had been set in a plaster cast. He was back in school the next day. A month later, Fred slipped in mud season kicking a football and landed on his bad arm (still in a sling), and once again I had to take him to the hospital.

Our excursions to Boston and visits to other boys' homes in different neighborhoods expanded during our Fifth Class year. We were allowed to do winter track, but many of us preferred to go home, pick up skates and sticks, and go skating on Jamaica Pond, Slocum's Pond (on the estate of Trustee Thomas Slocum '86) at the end of Louder's Lane near the Arboretum (now filled in), or wherever there was ice, including our Centre Street field which Charles Nichols arranged to have the Fire Department flood just for that purpose.

When spring came, and the freshets from the ledges on the campus came down the brook (now long-since encased in a large pipe under the Ernst Wing and Gordon Field House), someone suggested that there was gold in the stream. So we all made sluices and spent many an afternoon out there hoping to discover a piece of gold. Someone went to a hardware store, bought several brass curtain rods, and cut them up in little pieces, which for a time fooled us into thinking we had actually found gold. This stream went into a freshwater swale that formed a pond at this time of year. We used the boards from the track of the old school as rafts, and we played pirates raiding each other, steering our ships with poles. Of course, we fell in and got wet and cold. Ross Borden, my classmate, remembers having to dry his clothes in the boiler room, courtesy of Louis Nickerson, the School's jack-of-all-trades one-man maintenance staff. But nobody drowned.

On April 2, 1931—"a date that will live in infamy"—Myers, someone else (several claim the fame), and I snuck up, through the ledges, to

Welch's Pond, now a hundred feet deep as the result of sixty years of quarrying. Spring had come early and the temperature was close to eighty degrees. We went to Tom's Rock, which was on the deep (northern) end of Welch's Pond, stripped, and dove in. We told nobody about this episode, fearing that it might get us in trouble, but unfortunately Fred Myers came down with a case of poison ivy and had to acknowledge that he had gotten it on our skinny-dipping escapade.

We Are Almost Big Boys

The Fourth Class brought another transition: the more physically mature boys were beginning to try out for the varsity teams, starting to shave, and one of them even had a license to drive a car. The smaller of us were still playing on the junior or intermediate teams.

That fall of 1931 we moved way down to the north end of the first floor into Mr. Howard A. Wiggin's room. Mr. Wiggin was a widower; his wife had died of puerperal fever shortly after their last child was born in the early 1920s. He lived in a lovely large Victorian house on Fairmont Avenue in Hyde Park, a fine place to raise his large family. He had a daughter, who saw the family through until he remarried in 1932, and he seemed to have made peace with his lot in life. The School and his family were his whole life.

Unlike either Mr. Farnham or Mr. Sasserno, Mr. Wiggin called us by our real first names. He was a kind and mild State of Mainer. He spoke with a Maine twang and had a Maine sense of humor: he was an inveterate punster. He was invariably fair in his relationships with all of us and had few disciplinary problems. I think the students rather took to him and saw no reason to make cutting remarks about him or to do the other things which boys can do to make life difficult for a teacher. Andy Marshall, Jr., '30 and my classmate Ben Goggin both remember his favorite saying: "That answer is numb, dumb, glum, and then some." Whether he was a good mathematics teacher I would not try to judge, but a new headmaster, Mr. Northrop, would later conclude that he was not. As a result, he was retired in 1936.

FIG. 3. The Class of 1935 as the Fourth Class in 1931–32. *Back row, from left:* Balboni, Meskill, Goggin, Culley, Osgood, Reed, Ernst, True. *Third row:* Borden, MacFarlane, Lacouture, Vandersall, Poland, Barker, Casassa. *Second row:* Nolan, Hanlon, Sax, Kettendorf, Regan. *First row:* McNulty, Niles, Bunker, Myers, Clarke, Mittell, Pamp, Fisher, Moore.

Mr. Wiggin saw me and another classmate comparing answers on an algebra test. He said nothing about it for two or three weeks until I went up to ask him a question during a study period. After he patiently and politely answered my question, he looked at me and said, "David, I have pretty good reason to believe that you and your friend were comparing notes during a test two or three weeks ago. *If it is true, don't ever do it again.* If it is not true, please forgive me for bringing the subject up." This was a great lesson to me, and it was a wonderful way of handling the problem.

After Mr. Wiggin left the School he went to work for the New England Mutual Life Insurance Company. Of course, he had a customer list of everybody in the Roxbury Latin Quinquennial Catalogue, and many of us bought insurance from him. He moved to a smaller house in

Newton and lived there for a long time until, as a widower again, he retired to Rogerson House on the Jamaicaway in Jamaica Plain. I called on him there when he was in his late eighties. As I sat in his overheated room, he detailed to me the terror he experienced when his first wife died at the Forest Hills Hospital (no longer in existence). In talking about the various boys in my class, he pinpointed one in particular who always had an unusual interest in pretty young females. Thirty years later (on the occasion of my visit), he said, "He had to have a girl at all times, didn't he? And he still does." We didn't realize at the time how well he and the other masters knew us.

Bob Adams '33, for a time two years ahead of us, had died in January from meningitis, supposedly because he blew his saxophone too hard and caused the infection to spread through his Eustachian tube into his inner ear and finally to his brain. His was the first dead body I had ever seen.

In March I came down with a severe streptococcus inner ear infection—of exactly the sort that killed Adams, perhaps from blowing my E Flat alto saxophone too hard. (We had a Fourth Class orchestra that practiced regularly at the Goggins' house, 3 Storey Place, Jamaica Plain across from the fence from the Loring-Greenough tennis court. It consisted of Ross Borden, piano; Ben Goggin, banjo; Fred Myers, clarinet, and myself on sax. We bought standard arrangements of "Sweet and Lovely," "Three Little Words," "Mood Indigo," or "I'm Through with Love." We never had a concert.) I have never been as sick in my life. I ran a high fever for ten days, and Dr. Broughton visited the house at least once every day to monitor the infection's progress, lest it become a "mastoid." He would come in and press my mastoid bone and ask if it hurt more or less. Finally, he got Dr. Harold Tobey, who lived in one of the remodelled farm houses on the Souther estate on Allandale Street across from the Faulkner Hospital, and father of Grant Tobey '41, to lance my eardrum. I was watched for four or five days, but I insisted on going back to school a week earlier than the doctors wanted me to. The minute I walked shakily into Mr. Houser's room that Monday morning, he called on me to come up and do the experiment. I had no idea what he was talking about and apologized that I could not do it because I had not done any work on it. I have never keeled over in my life, but the closest I ever came to it was that morning when he said, "Mittell, what is the matter with you? What have you been doing, just sitting at home playing the last three weeks?"

There are two episodes involving Mr. Houser that I do not think are apocryphal and that allegedly occurred shortly after our class left the school. On one of the coldest days of winter, Mr. Houser, the scientist, decided to pour some alcohol or gasoline into a pan and put it under the engine of his car to warm it up to make it easier to start. He had a large gray six-cylinder car—a Peerless, I think. He lit the liquid in the pan and waited for it to warm the engine up. Unfortunately, it set the engine on fire and the Fire Department had to come and put out the flames. The second story also involves this car. In the 1930s you could buy a smoke bomb that was simple to install in a car by disconnecting the spark plug wire and connecting one wire from the bomb to the spark plug wire and the other wire to a head-bolt. Of course, when the engine was turned over, the electricity would ignite the smoke bomb. My brother and I put one on my father's car, and, I can tell you, he was not amused. Neither was Mr. Houser. As the story goes, he went out and started his car to go home and headed down the old driveway toward the tennis courts. First, there was an ominous whistle sound, then an explosive "boom," and finally a great cloud of smoke, while the boys watched from behind the ancient Codman rhododendrons. Mr. Houser reported the incident to Mr. Northrop, who threatened to censure the whole class if the perpetrators did not own up, which they finally did.

During the Fourth Class most of us began to be conscious of the other sex. This consciousness brought some changes in the way we spent our afternoons. We often went coasting or skating—or engaged in some equally innocent activity—with girls our age. I emphasize this because some people have criticized the single sex school as damaging the ability of the young male to associate with the young female. Our class did not have that trouble.

Transitions

The summer between Classes IV and III was not unlike others: an English novel to read, something French to struggle through. (*L'Avare* and *Tartuffe* are two I remember.)

In July 1932, Kenneth and I picked up the *Herald* on the way to tennis in Chatham and read on the front page of the sudden death of our headmaster, Dr. Thompson, from a heart attack. I therefore had my second experience of death at his funeral in the drawing room of the Codman mansion. The picture of his three sons standing by the casket as it was closed remains in my memory. The headmaster's house was filled with mourners.

Mr. Gleason was appointed acting headmaster, and, to me and my friends, the 1932–33 school year was one of the calmest, most pleasant, and most positive years in our time at School. Great credit should to go Mr. Gleason, although Dr. Thompson's death brought out the best in everyone. All of us had gotten to know Mr. Gleason when he taught us beginning Latin in the Fifth Class, and we all liked him. He was exacting of the brightest boys, but quite understanding of those who had to struggle. His sense of humor made his class a happy time. In describing Mr. Gleason's affability, wit, and patience, it is too easy to overlook the fact that he probably was the faculty's greatest scholar. He picked up where Dr. Collar had left off and wrote Greek and Latin textbooks that we and many other schools used. He both set and corrected the College Board examinations. Dedicating his life to the classics, he inspired quite a few of his pupils—especially his Greek students—to a lifelong devotion to that field of study. He would liven up classroom recitations by calling on a certain boy "*in angulo.*" He would call on me as "David Minor" and on David Meskill as "David Major." Mr. Gleason was loved and respected in the same way Mr. Farnham was, and his service, except for a short hiatus in the early 1900s, lasted from 1889 to 1939.

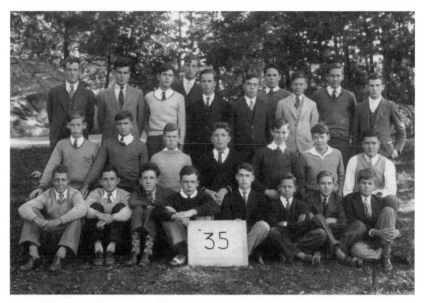

FIG. 4. The Class of 1935 as the Third Class in 1932–33. *Back row, from left:* Ernst, Meskill, Borden, Culley, Fisher, Poland, Myers, Cohen, Balboni. *Second row:* Nolan, Niles, Moore, Kettendorf, McNulty, Merritt, True. *First row:* Lacouture, Regan, Vandersall, Hanlon, Clarke, Pamp, Mittell, Bunker.

Mr. Taylor, master of the Third Class, was all business. He ran our homeroom in the same surgical, clean, and efficient manner in which he ran the bookstore. He disliked small talk and brooked no breaches of discipline. He reacted quickly and firmly when anything out of order occurred. He was, however, scrupulously fair. He treated all boys the same whether they were at the top or bottom of the class. He expected perfection in translation but did not always get it, and those of us who failed to perform to his standard were duly marked down. But we learned a lot. Mr. Taylor retired in 1952 to receive the honor of becoming Grand Secretary of the Grand Lodge of Massachusetts of the Scottish Rite Masons. He was a vigorous outdoorsman, active with Mr. Dickey in the Appalachian Mountain Club. He also had a pretty daughter, who unfortunately was older than I.

By this time many of my classmates had licenses, and they could drive us places. Fred Myers and I went to La Flamme's Barber Shop in Cambridge and got the shortest "crew cuts" one could get. We did this without parental knowledge or permission, and I think it was the only thing that my father ever forbade me to do again. The next day at School neither Myers nor I could translate our Latin assignment. We had expended all our energy getting crew cuts. Mr. Taylor, who had a fine sense of humor, realized what we had done and, of course, he called on both of us first. When neither of us could function, he gave a long sermon on the Biblical story of Samson.

He had a keen sense of humor. Once on an English-to-Latin test, he asked us to translate, "The Beautiful Babe Walked Down Broadway." He thoroughly enjoyed watching us struggle, and he was much amused by our attempts to translate "Broadway"—*Lata via*—such as "Broadwayam," and "Broadvium." Sometime later we were translating Cicero, who calls Cataline the "bilge water of the State." One of my unnautical classmates, never having spoken the word "bilge," translated correctly except that he pronounced bilge "*blige.*"

The Impact of the Great Depression

It is not possible to tell the 1930s story of Roxbury Latin without looking at what was going on in the world at large. The year 1933 brought immense change not just to Roxbury Latin with the coming of a new headmaster, but to the whole country with the inauguration of President Roosevelt. The real estate boom that had crashed in Florida and Cape Cod in 1928 and later throughout the country (I remember several uncompleted houses on the old Weld estate at Centre and South Streets by the Monument in Jamaica Plain and also on Cape Cod) was followed by the stock market crash during our second month in the Sixth Class. By Class IV we were in the throes of the worst depression the modern world has known.

At Thanksgiving 1932 my parents asked the Reverend Thomas Campbell, rector of our St. John's Church in Jamaica Plain, who the poorest family in our parish was. We then made up a large basketful of dolls, toys, clothes, and, of course, the traditional turkey dinner. We parked in front of the house and climbed past two unoccupied floors to the flat on the third floor. The tenement smelled of poverty—dirt, dust, plaster, mildew. When we got to the top flat, there was a pale, drawn woman perhaps forty with three sniveling little girls behind her. Her husband, a World War veteran, was in the sanatorium at Rutland with tuberculosis. That was *poverty.*

In spite of this experience, somehow I little noticed that the Depression was affecting the School and my classmates. One went to work in a creamery on Saturdays and Sundays to help augment the family income. Another later told me that his father lost not only his business but his house, and that his family had to move into his grandparents' floor of a two-decker. A third, whose father my father knew as an architect in one of the large engineering firms, had to move out of his rented apartment in West Roxbury and hole up in a small summer camp in southern New Hampshire. This classmate in our First Class year secretly slept each night in the *Tripod* room until Mr. Northrop found out and invited him to sleep in one of the maid's rooms on the top floor of the headmaster's house and to partake dinner with him and his wife in return for small chores. But in our youthful way we were largely insensitive to the times and preoccupied with the little world of school.

However, our parents were terrified: as they watched their friends get wiped out, they developed a gnawing fear of being wiped out themselves. My classmate Ben Goggin recalls that Saturday in March 1933 when President Roosevelt ordered all banks closed. That evening, Ben was taking one of the handsome Hill twins to a school dance. They were daughters of Dr. Lewis Webb Hill '06, distinguished pediatrician at Children's Hospital. When Ben arrived at the Hill family's lovely home on St. John Street, Jamaica Plain (their grandmother had given the land for the first St. John's Church on that street), Dr. Hill asked Ben if he had any money. "Of course I do," he replied. "My father always gives me mad money when I go out." Ben showed Dr. Hill the money in his wallet, and Dr. Hill took it. The Hill family was caught with no money in the house; Ben's loan tided them over until the banks opened four or five days later. My brother, then at Harvard, phoned home in a panic to tell Mother the banks were closed. My mother had a little money, but she walked to Robert Seaver & Sons (founded 1796) on Centre Street, Jamaica Plain. After twenty years of trade, Mr. Daly, the proprietor, was happy to cash mother's $10 check. The banks reopened in less than a week, but for a few days no one knew whether the reopening would take days, weeks, or months. The gnawing fear to which President Roosevelt referred was real.

While Franklin D. Roosevelt was opposing Herbert Hoover in 1932, Mr. Sasserno's brother Henry, later a successful stockbroker, was running for School Committee, and many of us at the School got excited about this race and helped him. We passed out cards and put stickers on cars and in windows wherever allowed. Henry Sasserno did not win, but politics had been such fun that we decided, facetiously, to organize a campaign for Mr. Lynwood S. Bryant, who had joined the faculty in 1931 after his graduation from Harvard. He survived the inevitable student ragging of a new teacher with good-humored patience, low-key firmness, and an occasional slightly sarcastic remark and was a fine English and history teacher. One of my classmates pinned on him the nickname "Bat." The next thing we knew, there were signs all over West Roxbury: "Bat Bryant for President." He didn't win, either, but the nickname stuck.

Roosevelt's "New Deal" programs brought no dramatic change to the economy. My father's skylight and sheet metal business suffered a 92 percent drop in annual sales in 1933. The future seemed grim, if one projected the trends since 1929, and the lives of all the School's families were now being impacted. Older brothers, like mine, soon to graduate from college, could not find jobs.

But our schoolboy minds were focused on other concerns that spring. Tennis had begun to come into its own and was officially accepted by the athletic association as a regular sport. The two Davis brothers,

Wilbur '32 and Alanson '33, sons of a regular army officer stationed in Boston, were excellent tennis players and raised the quality of the game at the School. Soon outside matches were arranged. That spring I tried hard to become a varsity baseball player and thought I was doing quite well getting four hits one day off a varsity pitcher. I therefore went to Mr. Foley and said, "Mr. Foley, my father played on a championship baseball team, 'The Eliots,' in the 1890s and is interested in baseball and I am trying hard to be a baseball player. I had four hits yesterday and handled the ball several times. Do you think I should go out for the varsity or do you have the team pretty well already picked, in which case I will play tennis?" He replied, "I have my team pretty well picked: I think you should play tennis." Hurt as I was, I guess Mr. Foley did me a great favor; I made the tennis varsity at R.L. and tennis has remained a life-long interest. But I have always felt that he should have encouraged me to give baseball a try.

In tennis we were not as good as some of the other schools. Rivers, for example, had a junior state champion, Walter Muther; in Class II, I tried to stay on the court with him but could not. The tennis article in the June 1935 *Tripod* notes with youthful if unfounded optimism: "With such improvement within the School, the tennis team looked forward to a season full of excitement and interest. . . . Browne & Nichols swept every match to defeat us 5 to 0, and only Bill Merritt's win prevented a similar loss to Rivers." I am still playing tennis with the Browne & Nichols team captain who beat me badly in a match we played more than sixty years ago—a match we played right through a strong gale on the gravel (quick-drying) courts at the Oakley Country Club in Watertown.

As boys in the lower school, we did not see much of Mr. Foley, for he was concentrating on his varsity teams. He gave us a course in anatomy, which seemed to embarrass him even more than us. He did encourage any and all to come out for track. My father, who, as I said, did know baseball, did not think Mr. Foley was as strong a baseball coach as he was a football coach.

But he certainly was a strong and imaginative football coach: the teams of 1935 through 1938 were undefeated Private School League champions, as was his 1946 team. In brother Ken's First Class year, his team lost the Private School championship to Country Day, 12–7. Late in the fourth quarter, the diminutive Lionel O'Keeffe, who was a tough and talented quarterback at five feet three and 130 pounds, got pretty well banged up. Roxbury Latin had the ball on the Country Day twelve-yard line, fourth down and about two. Kenneth was sent in to substitute for O'Keeffe with a specific play. However, Mr. Foley's substitution turned out to be an illegal one, and there was a five-yard penalty, so Kenneth changed the play and called for a pass which failed. He always felt that Mr. Foley blamed him for losing the Private School championship.

The week before that 1929 Country Day game, in the fourth period at Rivers, we were ahead 27–0, and some of us knew what was going to happen for the twenty-eighth point: Charley Denny '30, who was well over six feet and a tackle, swapped position with the end on his side making Denny a legal receiver. Lionel O'Keeffe lined up directly in back of him. The ball was snapped to Pinkul, a fine pitcher in baseball and passer in football. O'Keeffe climbed Denny's back and got on his shoulders. Denny took two steps into the end zone. Lionel O'Keeffe could catch anything which came within three feet of him, and Pinkul hit him right on the fingers for Roxbury Latin's twenty-eighth point.

Over the years my friends from other schools have chided me about some of Mr. Foley's imaginative plays. "Foxey" Foley's creativity was generally admired, although Eliot Putnam of Nobles—a great sportsman—"was not amused" when his teams went down to defeat because of trick plays he felt went too far. Here are two sample plays Mr. Foley used: On kickoff Mr. Foley would line up his fastest back just inside the sideline so that he faded into all the substitutes' same colored jerseys just outside the sideline. He would put a passer in the center receiving position. On the kickoff, the ball would go to our passer who would run to the left. Our team would form a wall between the left and right side of the field, and our passer would throw a lateral pass virtually across the field to the player on the sideline who would have an open course toward the end zone. Lining up players in front of substitutes has since been outlawed. Mr. Foley also used a spread formation that was successful because it would take the other team by surprise; their players couldn't figure out who their man was.

Trick plays were probably an inheritance from the time when Roxbury Latin was the smallest school, without a field; from the earliest days of football, R.L. teams had had to rely largely on their wits. Mr. Foley was a fine gentleman, and I am convinced would never had done anything unsportsmanlike. However, he had a wicked twinkle in his eye when one of his trick plays worked. I am told reliably by football players from the 1940s and 1950s that, when that majestic hymn "Holy, Holy, Holy" was sung by the School in Rousmaniere Hall, they paraphrased it "Holy, Holy, Holy, Here comes Foxy Foley." When Mr. Foley died in 1974, James Arnold Lowell, nicknamed "Domey," a former Noble and Greenough teacher and later headmaster of Park School, Brookline, wrote our chairman, Albert H. Gordon: "I have never faced a keener competitor or better sportsman. He showed us, and everyone else, how much sports can do toward developing fine people."

The big news of the 1932–33 school year was the appointment of George Norton Northrop as our new headmaster. There had been a lot of speculation about who would succeed Dr. Thompson. The word around the School and from parents and friends was that it would be either Mr. Farnham or Mr. Gleason. We heard nothing at the time about the later apocryphal tale that James Bryant Conant '10 was a candidate. Conant was a little-known professor of chemistry at Harvard and *Time* magazine invented the story that, just prior to his being appointed president of Harvard in 1933, Conant was interviewed by the R.L. trustees and rejected because he was "too young." The story gained a wide circulation; Andrew Marshall, Jr. '30 even told me that he recalls being home from Harvard one evening in 1933 when his father, a Roxbury Latin trustee, announced that they had interviewed, but decided

FIG. 5. Members of the Class of 1935 at Sagamore Beach in June 1933, following the Third Class. *Top:* Pamp, left, and Nolan. *Middle:* Mittell, Ernst, Moore. *Bottom:* Hanlon, Lacouture, Meskill, Goggin.

not to offer the headmastership to, Dr. Conant. The story is almost too good not to be true, but the trustees never considered him—not because of his youth, but because of his eminence as a scholar of chemistry; he was never interviewed. Shortly after becoming president he accepted election as a life trustee of the School.

The trustees went "outside" in choosing Mr. Northrop, a native of Minnesota and headmaster of the Chicago Latin School. We did not know what to expect from the new headmaster, and some of us were surprised and pleased when Mr. Northrop, who to us was old (age fifty-three), appeared on the tennis court right away in his first fall and played a lively, if unorthodox, game. In spite of his midwestern background, his accent was clearly influenced by his years of study at Oxford. He (and his wife Catharine Clerihew Northrop) started off on the right foot by inviting all the members of the upper two classes to dinner in small groups at the headmaster's mansion. These were formal evenings, and began with a Martini or two for Mr. Northrop. Dinner was served graciously by a maid. I still recall with pleasure the great warmth of this couple to me and my classmate, Fred Myers, that pleasant evening in their library and dining room.

There was talk both at the School and at home, the latter I suppose drifting down from trustees, that both Mr. Farnham and Mr. Gleason were disappointed that one of them had not been selected as headmaster after their long, successful, and dedicated service to the School. Both of them, it was said, had given Dr. Thompson a difficult time. Perhaps that is why Mr. Farnham was retired at the end of Mr. Northrop's first year in June 1934. Naturally, those of us who knew, loved, and admired Mr. Farnham felt this was a mistake.

Mr. Northrop's arrival brought change. He redecorated the lunch room with handsome framed British railway posters, and placed over the fireplace "The Siege of the Island of Rhé." Objects of art and handsome furnishings began to appear in and around the schoolhouse, to me a smart way to inoculate boys with culture without their realizing it.

Mr. Northrop would often look up at the ceiling, squint his eyes, peek over his glasses, force a wide smile on his lips, and in his best British accent say, "It's getting late, boys. It's getting late." He could apply this statement to almost any situation in our adolescent lives—homework not done or carelessly done, or impending college boards.

A Chicago Latin friend remembers Mr. Northrop addressing his class, asking, "You boys do know how to make babies, don't you?" His openness about the previously taboo subject of sex was a sign of Mr. Northrop's enlightenment, but also of his enjoyment in shocking people. Some of the conservative and proper parents who typified Roxbury Latin disapproved of his inclusion of Walt Whitman in his English class. One loyal alumnus, father of two Roxbury Latin boys, considered removing his sons and spread the word to parents and alumni that he was not sure Mr. Northrop was good for the School. I think Mr. Northrop was good for Roxbury Latin. Cultured, urbane, and enlightened, he showed respect for the past but was not confined by it.

College Boards and Class II

At the end of Class III we had all gone into Wentworth Institute to take our first College Board examinations in French and algebra; all of us got honors in French, to Mr. Sasserno's joy, and quite a few did well in algebra. We were, therefore, ready to enter Class II. We expected to be under Clarence W. Gleason, since, with Mr. Northrop's appointment, he was no longer acting headmaster. Instead, we got Mr. Taylor for a second year. By Class II, all of us wore long pants, and most of us a shirt and tie. All but a few of us by now had licenses to drive, and those who did not would soon get them. Many of us had inexpensive ($50.00) cars or access to cars, so our mobility was substantially increased.

In 1934, the new headmaster appointed William T. Cloney as an apprentice master. He supervised the library, sitting in the small office at the end of what is now the Farnham Room. He had just put himself through Harvard as *The Boston Herald*'s college reporter. Until Mr.

FIG. 6. The Class of 1935 as the Second Class in 1933–34. *Back row, from left:* Moore, Meskill, Balboni, Borden, Poland, Ernst, True, Culley. *Second row:* Fisher, Stone, Vandersall, Merritt, Niles, Clarke, Mittell. *First row:* Nolan, Butler, Pamp, Bunker, Hanlon, Lacouture, McNulty, Myers, Regan.

Cloney's arrival Mr. Foley had coached varsity football without assistance. Mr. Cloney now became line coach, teaching the linemen techniques of blocking and tackling which raised the quality of their performance substantially. With 135–pound guards and 150–pound tackles, technique was critical. In the winter of 1935 he also became our hockey coach. He was beloved by all of us. Mr. Cloney continued simultaneously to write schoolboy sports for the *Herald* under his own by-line. As a result, school sports received more coverage; he was eminently fair in giving the other schools their share of publicity.

Mr. Cloney drove what they used to call "a pregnant Buick." It was a coupé, a one-seater, maroon in color. It was called "pregnant" because General Motors built a bulge in its 1929 Buick that it eliminated the next year. Perhaps the most serious misdemeanor of Will Cloney's life was picking up about seven of us walking along Centre Street and driving us to the School. A well-known motorcycle policeman in West Roxbury nabbed him mid-journey. After leaving Roxbury Latin in 1936, he became sports editor of *The Boston Post* until it closed, and then professor of journalism at Northeastern University. He ended his career as a public relations executive for one of the investment management firms in Boston. For several decades he also headed the committee that supervised—and saved for perpetuity—the Boston Marathon.

By our Class II year, we had become the mainstays of the varsity teams. We had an exciting, if losing, hockey game with Tabor Academy with boards set up on black ice on a Marion cranberry bog to which we drove in Alex Stohn's open 1929 Ford touring car. We also lost to Country Day School in hockey on their tiny junior rink on a water-covered football field.

Sam McDonald '34 was hockey captain that year, and he and (later life trustee) Richard Fowler '34, the manager, badgered our counterparts for hockey game dates. They were so successful that—aided by the coldest winter in this century—we played many more games than ever. Sam was also well known to the captain and members of the May School field hockey team. May School, part of what now is Brimmer and May, was located then on the Charles River side of Beacon Street, but they played their sports on a field on Dummer Street, Brookline. Sam quietly arranged for our team to play the May team on a beautiful spring Sunday afternoon. There was to be no contact, of course, and we found it hard not to lift the field hockey stick above the allowed level, a rule designed to prevent facial injuries. We had been told to show up in tennis "whites." This we did, and Sam—all six feet plus of him—looked resplendent in his white flannels and white shirt. It was indeed a warm day, but I am sure what followed was carefully preplanned. Halfway through the second period Sam stopped in the middle of the field and took his pants down! There were a few shrieks and shy looks in other directions, but Sam, gentleman that he was and is, had a neat pair of white tennis shorts underneath! May failed to score and Roxbury won by two or three goals, and we all—boys and girls—rolled off the field in laughter. The score was duly phoned to the Boston papers where it appeared in the Monday editions.

Several of our classmates had parts in the school play, and several of us took girls to watch it and to enjoy the dance that always followed the performance. Then, of course, there was the junior prom. Our increased mobility enabled us to search for girls on a larger geographical scale. The "assemblies," always properly chaperoned and supervised, continued to be an excellent mixing place. We were no longer confined to the local Miss Widmer's or the Eliot Halls. Some of us were invited to Cambridge to the "Bucks," held at Buckingham School that attracted young women from Cambridge and Belmont, many of them Harvard faculty daughters. After a few years we graduated from the "Bucks" into the "Brats," held in Brattle Hall, Cambridge.

Only two schoolroom memories of the Class II year remain, both involving Mr. Houser. In the physics laboratory one day he angrily commanded John Lacouture, after some misdemeanor, to come to the front of the room. Brave fellow that he was, John did so by circling all the way around the room the wrong way to get to the front. We thought Mr. Houser was going to explode, but it actually had the effect of cooling him down. At examination time in June 1934 Sam McDonald was on the borderline of failing chemistry, a course he had to pass for admission to college. Dr. McDonald, his father, sensing the crisis, arranged for him to attend Manter Hall, the tutoring school in Cambridge, which catered to just such situations. Two days before the Roxbury Latin final, Manter Hall administered an old College Board chemistry examination, corrected it, and explained all the complicated formulae and questions involved. Quite by chance Mr. Houser chose the same examination for his final at Roxbury Latin two days later. Sam, of course, got the highest mark in the class, in the high 90s. When he jubilantly met Mr. Houser in the corridor and asked him his course grade, Mr. Houser informed him he had failed. "But, sir, what was my exam score?" "Ninety-seven, but you couldn't get that high a mark. You had to have cheated." "But, sir, my father sent me to tutoring school and I really know the subject." "I don't care. You are not bright enough to get a mark that high. You had to have cheated. The failing grade stands." And it did!

Now that we could drive, summer was more fun. The vacation weeks I spent in Boston were passed largely on the school tennis courts with schoolmates or friends, going swimming at Wollaston Beach, and once providing valet parking for the Northrops' guests the day their daughter was married in Rousmaniere Hall.

Finally: Kings of the Mountain

At last we entered the First Class under Mr. William Dickey. We had arrived. Our classmates were editors of *The Tripod*, grandees of the Student Council, captains of the five varsity teams. (Hockey and tennis had been formally added to the ancient three.)

Mr. Dickey was a southern gentleman, ruddy-cheeked, low-key, smiling, calm. His rendition of "Br'er Rabbit," in his Southern drawl, was a highlight of the year. Some of our classmates had worked on his wood-chopping crew, providing wood from the campus for the fireplaces then often used to heat the classrooms. As I have said, both Mr.

Dickey and Mr. Taylor were active outdoorsmen, long-term members of the Appalachian Mountain Club. Francis Russell '28 has written about "Mutter Dickey" taking *Die Harzreise*, a walking tour through the Harz Mountains in Germany, at the outbreak of World War I and nearly being detained in Germany for the duration of the war. Those of us who had taken German had already had him in class. But in the First Class he taught all of us American history.

When I first knew him, Mr. Dickey lived in bachelor digs at the Technology Chambers on Irvington Street, behind the Trinity Place Station of the Boston & Albany Railroad. (Both the street and station have now been obliterated by the Westin and Marriott Hotels.) We visited him there one Sunday. By the time we were in the First Class, however, he had moved over to a top floor room on the west side of the Hotel Lenox overlooking the Boston & Albany railroad yards which have now become the Prudential Center. He remained there until his first stroke a couple of decades later. He served as secretary of the Alumni Association, advising the officers on policy and personnel, for he knew the alumni body well. In Class I, I was lucky enough to be given the chore of being alumni editor of *The Tripod*, and Mr. Dickey was an immense help to me in pointing out interesting alumni items.

I shall never forget the thrill of being a First Classman. Athletically we had our successes. Those who didn't play on the football team watched the team compile a 4–2 record on six successive Friday afternoons.

Much can be said about what George Norton Northrop did for Roxbury Latin in his astute fourteen-year administration of the School, but an incident that occurred in the fall of our final year revealed his commitment to a full country day school program for R.L. I was studying in a classroom when a Third Classman came up and told me that Mr. Northrop wanted to see me. When I went to see him, he questioned me on how the fall tennis tournament was going. I told him that it had reached the finals and that the finalists were Eckman and Faden of the Third Class. He chided me, as tennis captain, for not informing him

FIG. 7. The Class of 1935 as the First Class in 1934–35. *Back row, from left:* Meskill, Culley, Poland, Hanlon, Borden, Green, Ernst, Myers, Moore, Butler, Stone. *Second row:* Fisher, Balboni, Regan, McNulty, True, Nolan, Niles, Stedman. *First row:* Bunker, Lacouture, Pamp, Clarke, Merritt, Goggin, Mittell.

that one of them had beaten me. I responded that I thought that it was the manager's job to report wins and losses and not the captain's. As I was about to leave the room, he said, "David, stay here a minute. You do want a hockey rink, don't you?" "Yes, sir," I replied. "Well you are going to have one," he said. "The Parents' Auxiliary will give you a two-inch pipe. Louis Nickerson will dig the posts in the ground for the boards. We will use the old track for the boards, and if your squad will go down and help dig the corners and the post holes, you will have a hockey rink this winter."

All of us interested in hockey were exhilarated. We had a working crew of Roxbury Latin boys all the way down to the Fifth Class. We learned how to use grub hoes, pickaxes, and post-hole scoops. I've never seen anyone work as hard as Louis Nickerson. He, Mr. Tuttle, the painter, and Mr. Berdeen, the head custodian who lived in the apartment on the ground floor, maintained the whole school, inside and outside. The March 1934 *Tripod* is dedicated to these three men: "It sometimes happens that the men who make the smallest noise live the most useful lives. Louis, Tuttle, and Berdeen deserve special tribute for keeping our grounds and building in good shape."

In the winter, Louis shovelled all the sidewalks and boardwalks to the School which extended all the way from the St. Theresa gate by the baseball backstop to the basement door next to the Berdeen apartment. In the summer, Louis rode the old Ford tractor mowing the grass. He did the heavy carpentry work necessary to complete the rink that fall. We would go down there after school and work until 4:30 or 5:00. At about 4:00 the football squad would come by after their practice. They would grab a shovel or a post-hole scoop and pitch in. With our eyes on the prize, building the rink in jolly company was a sheer joy.

We went to Boston and bought fish-netting. My father had the goals built in the metal-working plant in Roxbury as a gift to the School. We acquired hoses. The freshet trickled down the brook when frost came and filled the pond, the same one where we had played "pirates." As was the practice, we used regular laundry bluing to make blue lines on the ice. I still have a letter from Sam MacDonald who, as captain the previous year, had really resuscitated hockey. He was now a freshman at college and wrote me that he did not know how I had achieved the rink. But I had not done it; Mr. Northrop had.

Mr. Northrop had begun by placing paintings and objets d'art in the School. Now he was engendering hockey. He would soon have crew. The School was becoming a broader place. Shortly after Mr. Northrop's arrival, the attrition rate noticeably declined. Attractive, well-rounded boys who might be having academic difficulties were encouraged to repeat a year and stay in the school. At least five members of the Class of 1936 stayed back to enhance the Class of 1937. All graduated successfully and have led useful lives.

With winter came a spirited rivalry between track and hockey. We had an outstanding track team with a fine captain, my classmate Alfred

FIG. 8, *left*. David Mittell at the goal on the School's hockey rink—on the site of the present practice field.

FIG. 9, *above*. The 1935 Hockey Team, the first to play on the new rink. *Back row, from left:* William T. Cloney, coach, Young '37, Sullivan '36, Culley '35, Myers '35,Regan '35, Meskill '35, manager. *Front row:* Stohn '37, Murphy '37, Mittell '35 captain, Balboni '35, Eckman '37.

Hanlon, who won the 600-yard dash in the Boston Athletic Association meet in 1935 against all runners. We hockey players lost an early season game to Beacon School in Wellesley Hills, which, like Country Day, ceased to exist in the early 1940s. It was a day cold enough to be memorable. Route 9, the Worcester Turnpike, was covered with ice—matted, unplowed frozen snow. Upon arriving, we changed in the turn-of-the-century mansion that housed the school. We had to walk and carry our gear through a wooded trail perhaps a short half-mile to Rock Ridge Pond, then still in the wilderness. Boards had been set up on the pond. The ice was good, but not as black as the cranberry bog ice at Marion the year before. We had cocoa after the game in a room nicely warm but smelling of coal gas. Soon after this time, this part of Wellesley developed into one of Greater Boston's most attractive and sought-after neighborhoods. On the Friday before the track team was to run against (and lose by a point to) its arch rival, Moses Brown in Providence, we played Belmont Hill in hockey on their rink in Belmont. Belmont Hill was one of the schools that dominated the Private School League in those years, and *mirabile dictu* we beat them 2–0. Hockey had again truly come of age at R.L.! The quality of R.L. hockey improved in the late 1930s and the School became a contender for the private school championship with players like the Kittredge brothers, '38 and '39, James Gormley '39, Hubert Murphy '37, Alex Stohn '37, Paul Lacouture '38, Richard Ohler '38, and others.

Our school play, "The Queen's Husband," by the famous playwright Robert Sherwood, was a huge success with Bob Bunker playing the king and Ross Borden the queen. Who there can forget John Lacouture '35 and Hubert Murphy '37 as six-foot properly falsified ladies-in-waiting?

The impending College Boards did not undermine the full enjoyment of our final R.L. spring. The baseball team had a large number of lower classmen, a harbinger of good times to come. My tennis team enjoyed its struggle—even though we did not have a winning season. Luxuriating in our mobility, we made weekend trips to the Lacoutures' place in South Hyannis and even helped the Barnstable Volunteer Fire

Department put out a brush fire on Route 132 where the Hyannis Mall now stands. John Lacouture and I once borrowed John Regan's 1927 Dodge sedan and packed a whole dinner party in Brookline into it before a costume ball at Eliot Hall, only to be scolded for being late. My parents censured me when, on a school night, Al Hanlon, John Lacouture, and I went to Nutting's-on-the-Charles in Waltham to hear the Casa Loma Orchestra, an early big band.

Then—suddenly—it all ended with graduation. During one of our final English classes, Mr. Northrop had said again, "It's getting late, boys. It's getting late." He then told us to look around at each other because never again would all of us get together as a class. We protested strongly, but, of course, history proved him right. We held a class dinner at the old Boston City Club on Ashburton Place that next December, but not until after World War II did we attempt another reunion. Never again were we all together.

The Alumnus Years

In my student years at Roxbury Latin, I always felt that my classmates, the other undergraduates, and I owned the School. After all, the masters were there for the exclusive purpose of teaching us, the coaches to coach us, and everyone else to help us. To be sure, there were trustees, but they only showed up at the closing exercises, or to orate somewhat long-windedly on some subject dear to them, so they seemed a great distance away. Then there were the parents. They tried to cajole us to better academic performances, and they attended games and plays, but their intimacy with the school was far less than that of the parents of today's students. Finally there were the alumni, but they were long gone and pursuing other interests.

Of course, once I graduated my view changed. I was a young alumnus in college and then a fledgling businessman who returned to School because of my friends and because my interest and belief in it continued. By the 1940s I was active in the Alumni Association, and by the 1950s I had become trustee. At each stage my perspective changed.

Upon graduation, we dispersed to college. Ten went to Harvard; two each to Amherst, Annapolis, and M.I.T.; and one each to Bentley, Boston College, Brown, Cornell, Dartmouth, Notre Dame, Tufts, Wesleyan, and Wooster. At least one of our classmates was unable to go directly to college because of the Depression. When I look at the thirty little boys in our Sixth Class picture, I still find it hard to believe that five of them went on to earn Ph.D.'s, two LL.B.'s, two M.B.A.'s, four M.A.'s or M.S.'s, and one who earned at least two M.S.'s in engineering and an M.Litt. Five became captains in the Navy, one an Air Force colonel, one a priest, one a founder of schools for the mentally retarded, and several went into business. I am not trying to establish 1935 as "the best damned class that ever graduated," as John Marquand's Harvard Class Secretary "Bojo" Brown expostulates in *The Late George Apley*. However, in retrospect it would appear that Dr. Thompson and Mr. Farnham had chosen wisely among the candidates for admission in 1929. I believe we made the contribution "to Church or Commonwealth" the School's Charter expects from its sons.

It was easy for me to stay close to the School after I graduated. I had many friends in the classes of 1936 to 1940. As an enthusiastic hockey player, I returned many times to practice hockey on the rink I had helped to build. I also continued to play often on the School's tennis courts throughout the late 1930s. Richard Ohler '38 and Alex Stohn '37 were ushers in my wedding in 1941, and I took my new bride to the Noble and Greenough football game that fall. I visited the old masters several times a year and attended all alumni affairs.

Returning to the School and listening to my younger friends there, I was conscious of the strides Mr. Northrop continued to make. I was aware that he had arranged the acquisition of a secondhand eight-oared shell, and that R. L. now had crew. I knew that Al McCoy, a professional boxer, had come to coach boxing and that there was a ski team. I applauded Mr. Northrop's adoption of some of the good things the other day schools were doing. The country day program that he was evolving broadened the School's attractiveness to potential students.

Finally, I knew that many of my younger friends were inspired by his culture and teaching to surprisingly high academic achievements. While a bit of a dilettante and sometime pompous, Mr. Northrop was a most likable, charming, witty, enlightened educator, who, in my opinion, moved the School ahead dramatically, only to have its momentum reversed by the travails of World War II.

If the trustees' most important duty is to pick a talented headmaster, the headmaster's most important duty is to select his fellow masters. I got to know the new masters as they came to the School. M. Philbrick Bridgess replaced Mr. Wiggin as head of the mathematics department in 1936. He impressed the boys by quickly appearing on the tennis courts. A genial punster (like his predecessor), he was nonetheless an exacting teacher and he raised the standard of mathematics. When he was senior master he was a member of the Long-Range Planning Committee that I chaired in the late 1950s; by then he had become one of the R.L. "greats." Richard M. Whitney also came in 1936. He ultimately succeeded Phil Bridgess as senior master in the 1970s. He was a jack-of-all-trades. He taught English, math, geography, and science. For many years he served as Sixth Class master and broke in the new boys, a latter-day Mr. Farnham. Later as chairman of the science department he taught all three advanced science courses, and his textbooks were used nationally, like those of Messrs. Collar, Daniell, Gleason, and Black. He was a rigorous and demanding teacher. Albert W. Kelsey came in 1937 as an English teacher. Though the School became more and more academically demanding in his later years, he managed to keep large numbers out for wrestling each winter. His teams were notably successful. The Graves-Kelsey Tournament of the Independent School League still honors this fine coach. Mr. Kelsey also established debate at R.L., and the Prize Day award in that activity commemorates his dedication.

In the late 1940s, I was elected to the Alumni Council, a group of loyal graduates who rekindled alumni interest after the hiatus of World War II. Some of the younger alumni joined with some of the older graduates (such as Jack Cram '98, Arthur Anderson and Collins Graham '07, "Bunny" Drisko '13, Mal Rees '14, Don Packard '11, Bill White '15, Stacy Holmes '27, and Leigh Fitzgerald '31) to reorganize the alumni annual fund, to put out a newsletter, and to reissue the School necktie which Collins Graham '07 had earlier designed.

During that period, I sometimes saw Mr. Northrop on visits to the School. He was always outgoing with a quip, story, or observation. After his retirement, I saw him often at The Country Club having a libation in the then Men's Grill or teeing off for nine holes with his cronies. He always greeted me warmly.

We saw a good deal of Fred and Peggy Weed after Fred became headmaster in 1947. I chaired the annual fund in Mr. Weed's early years. As one of the younger members of the Alumni Council, I was delegated to chair an alumni dinner meeting. In those days we shook up strong Martinis and Manhattans. Since Mr. Weed felt that the serving of alcoholic beverages in the schoolhouse was a mild sacrilege, he compromised by inviting us to his house for the cocktail portion of the evening. He preferred that we violate his privacy rather than the School's sanctity.

The Weeds had moved into the ancient Victorian Richard Codman mansion with some skepticism: it was high-studded, large, drafty. To me, however, it was a noble Victorian relic and I have always wondered whether it should have been razed (in the name of progress) in order to build the Ernst Wing. The Weeds survived in the mansion for eighteen years, always looking over their shoulders longingly at the John Codman house, now the headmaster's house, occupied all those years by the Northrops in their retirement.

I always sensed that Mr. Weed was disappointed not to get the headmastership at his alma mater, St. Mark's. I have several times been told Mr. Weed referred to Roxbury Latin as "the best of the low-price schools." However, he was young, idealistic, and energetic. He quickly hired fellow-St. Marker Cary Potter as Assistant Headmaster. Mr. Potter helped expand the country day program, initiating soccer at the School. One of the smaller fields for many decades was referred to as

"Potter's Field," where the little boys practiced. When he left, Mr. Potter succeeded Francis Parkman as head of what is now the National Association of Independent Schools.

Mr. Weed soon saw that without a gymnasium the School could not consummate Mr. Northrop's progress, slowed by World War II, toward a full country day school program. He therefore pushed for the design and construction of what we know as the Albert H. Gordon Field House, and he took a major part in the fund-raising for the first new building since 1927. Planned by the mature Mr. Foley, the building works well nearly forty years later, even though it was built for a school of only 180.

Attrition and Diversity

Ever since my brother had entered the School, I had been aware that, unlike other schools, Roxbury Latin dismissed, along the way, as many boys as it graduated. This high attrition rate seemed neither fair to the developing adolescent nor good for the School's reputation. While an occasional success resulted from the shock of being dismissed, more often bitterness was the result. And our non-graduate alumni over the last hundred years appear to have been as interesting and successful in later life as the graduates. Sadly, the departure of these non-graduates was the School's loss at least as much as the individual boy's.

The following table shows how effective Mr. Northrop was in the 1930s — and in most of the war-affected 1940s — in lowering the earlier attrition rate by giving boys help and allowing them to repeat a year. Under Mr. Weed (1947–1965) the attrition rate rose again, starting to diminish only when Richmond Mayo-Smith became headmaster in 1965. In the last twenty years, the rate has dropped dramatically to all-time lows as the chart shows. Gerhard Rehder '27, history master (1947–1975) and longtime alumni secretary, has made a study in which he estimates that at least two-thirds of the boys who left did so by dismissal.

The trustees alone did not originate the stringent academic environment that characterized the high-attrition years before and after Mr.

Graduation/Attrition Rates at Roxbury Latin

	TOTAL ADMITTED	GRADUATED		LEFT BEFORE GRADUATION	
1890s	434	204	(47%)	230	(53%)
1900s	393	173	(44%)	220	(56%)
1910s	374	183	(49%)	191	(51%)
1920s	388	176	(45%)	212	(55%)
1930s	414	257	(62%)	157	(38%)
1940s	364	200	(55%)	164	(45%)
1950s	377	203	(54%)	174	(46%)
1960s	484	282	(58%)	202	(42%)
1970s	515	382	(74%)	133	(26%)
1980s	438	373	(85%)	65	(15%)

Northrop's headmastership. As Dr. Thompson's and Mr. Northrop's great faculty aged, I think some of them lost patience with and understanding for young boys; they set standards that only some boys could meet—and then only with the utmost difficulty. Masters showed little inclination to assist boys or to encourage them. They had difficulty in relating to the adolescent boy. In fairness to the teachers, possibly they had been over-imbued with the unpublished 1931 study of the School made by Roger Ernst, Malcolm Donald, and Professor Charles Grandgent that emphasized the quintessential importance of academic performance at R.L. One of the newer masters told me that Mr. Taylor, rigorous and decisive as he was, trained the newer men not to have patience with anything but excellent work.

I never believed in what I have sometimes called "the Darwinian theory of education"—namely, the survival only of the brightest students. A boy's worth is difficult to determine at age twelve, thirteen, or fourteen. Mr. Weed used to tell me this as he anguished over admissions. Great teachers search for and find in a boy some appealing aspect of his total being to bring out, some small success to build on in academics, sports, or drama. Great teachers start with this tiny seed and try to nourish it to grow into a great plant.

Happily, the School today has a faculty that is determined, in the words of our present headmaster, "to know and love each boy." This they really do, and, in my opinion, the excellent achievement of our boys in college admissions, board scores, and activities—athletic or cultural—comes from the devotion of this fine faculty as much as it does from inherent ability.

Before we became trustees, Samuel S. Dennis 3d '28 and I, with our wives, sponsored admissions teas at our homes in Wellesley in 1949 and 1950. We invited parents and boys in the ten to twelve age groups to meet Mr. and Mrs. Weed, who were most attractive and who made fine impressions. These receptions, enthusiastically endorsed by Board President Ernst, attempted to broaden the School's diversity by attracting Wellesley and Needham boys, something Mr. Northrop had begun to do when World War II intervened and undermined his efforts to attract boys from the whole metropolitan area.

Until the early-1950s, the admissions policy at good colleges was largely a function of test scores, rank in class, and school record. As an active Harvard alumnus I was close to the college admissions office, and particularly to Dean Wilbur J. Bender, later a trustee-at-large of Roxbury Latin. From my work with Harvard admissions, I learned that Harvard and other colleges were placing increasing emphasis on personality, leadership, special talent, and diversity of background. I realized that, if Roxbury Latin continued its almost exclusive emphasis on academic ability as reflected in test scores, it would lose out in future college placement.

When we trustees called for a greater "diversity" of students in the 1950s and 1960s we had in mind a diversity of talents and interests—in academics, extracurriculars, and personality. In the last thirty years, schools and colleges have looked for diversity in another dimension as well, seeking students from an array of socio-economic, racial, ethnic, and religious groups. Historically Roxbury Latin has always prided itself on its democratic heritage; however, the school is now many times more diverse socially, economically, racially, and religiously, than in the

1930s when I was there (even though it led the field then). Because we are one of the few private schools that can maintain "need blind" admissions, we are able to bring together blacks, whites, Asians, Hispanics, Protestants, Catholics, Jews, rich and poor, in a community that is perceived to be more than the sum of its parts. What may be equally important, we are achieving this mix while simultaneously setting records in academic and extracurricular achievement.

I have been asked over the years why I did not send my three sons to Roxbury Latin when they reached age twelve in the 1950s and 1960s during Fred Weed's administration. This is not an easy question to answer for those of us who love the School and believe in its "eternal" verities.

I observed when still in college that some of the other schools were placing a greater emphasis on leadership and character, in a supportive and nourishing atmosphere, while offering an academic education nearly as strong as R.L.'s. Quite simply I felt that R.L.'s academic demands were too rigorous—and the atmosphere too bleak—for a normal developing boy. Further, no one at the School gave me the feeling that family continuity over the generations was valued at R.L. I was not alone: trustees David Lewis, Stacy Holmes, and Michael Harrington, and innumerable alumni sent their sons elsewhere, as our seniors on the board had often done before us. David Lewis, who gave four decades of loyal leadership to the School stated openly that he never gave a thought to sending his sons to R.L., for no one at the School ever gave him any inkling that his sons were welcome, in spite of the fact that they were double legacies as grandsons of Arthur Perry '02, board president 1955–1960. As the result of this attitude, his boys went to Milton. I doubt if any of us would make the same decisions today.

Trustee Involvement Since 1954

In 1959, Trustee President Arthur Perry '02 asked me to chair a long-range planning committee. This committee consisted of Headmaster Frederick R. Weed, Senior Master M. Philbrick Bridgess, and six trustees: David W. Lewis '31; Stacy Holmes '27; Dean Wilbur J. Bender of Harvard; Leonard Holmes '20; Eliot T. Putnam, headmaster of Noble and Greenough; and Hollis P. Nichols '27. We met for lunch every third Wednesday for two years, the only time I could find that this group from diverse occupations could gather. The committee made many recommendations, not the least of which was raising faculty salaries, something dear to Mr. Weed's heart. We recommended the full implementation of a country day program; even after thirty years on the new campus all boys were not involved in sports. We urged more emphasis on music, art, and drama. We recommended that the School reverse its policy of having a huge Sixth Class and a tiny First Class. We proposed easing the Latin and French requirements in order to be able to admit boys to the School after Class VI. We realized that our proposals would involve sectioning of classes and a larger faculty. We urged the School to recruit students who were more diverse in geography, talent, and background, and we sought to discover ways of making the School better known through dignified publicity. Though we advocated an increase in tuition, we felt that Roxbury Latin should maintain its middle class family base by continuing to keep its tuition lower than that at competing independent schools. Three recommendations deserve to be quoted in full because they underscore our emphasis on character rather than academics as the School's principal aim:

> That we should emphasize the importance of diversity in seeking the "able boy." Our student body should be composed of boys from varied social and economic backgrounds, as well as of diversified talents, interest, and special abilities in various fields: scholastic, of course, but also musical, artistic, athletic and others.
>
> That each student must be made to realize that the school's primary concern with the individual, given the necessary academic intelligence, is in regard to his character and his integrity, and secondly with his willingness to work. With an honest, willing boy, the school should work with understanding and patience even if he is marginal academically by school standards.
>
> That each student should be made to realize that it is the school's hope to give the best education it can for an individual's

eventual service to his fellow-man, and not for self-aggrandize-ment.

The trustees adopted these recommendations at their June 1961 meeting. When the implementation of the recommendations seemed to be making little progress two years later, Wilbur Bender urged the trustees to retain three educational consultants: Wilson Parkhill, retired headmaster of Collegiate School in New York City; Richard Mechem, then headmaster of Newton High School; and Alan Blackmer, dean of the faculty at Andover. They confirmed to the faculty the timeliness and appropriateness of the planning committee's recommendations. Mr. Weed was about to retire, however, and some of our proposals did not gain momentum until Richmond Mayo-Smith came as headmaster in 1965.

I was honored to be on the search committee which selected Richmond Mayo-Smith and recommended him to the board. When it became known early that Mr. Weed would retire in 1965, Mr. Mayo-Smith was on leave from Phillips Exeter Academy with his family in India and Tibet. Hollis Nichols '27, then treasurer and vice president of the board, pressed for Mr. Mayo-Smith's selection. The husband of Mrs. Nichols' sister was a faculty member at Exeter and spoke highly of him. The trustees flew the Mayo-Smiths to Boston for an early inter-view before we set up our national search. Dick Mayo-Smith seemed to have everything in his favor. He was familiar with the Boston indepen-dent school scene as a graduate of Noble and Greenough. Nancy Mayo-Smith was the daughter of an R.L. alumnus. There was a feeling that Roxbury Latin was closer in feel to Exeter—with its similar ancient emphasis on democratic diversity—than to many other schools, and so the Exeter connection helped. We did not get far in our national search (though we reviewed several curricula vitae and interviewed a couple of other candidates), before we shortened the process, believing that we would find no better "fit" than Mr. Mayo-Smith. So it was that the Mayo-Smiths—and Kuncho Palsang, their houseman from Tibet, who is still with us—came to Roxbury Latin.

My wife and I saw a lot of Nancy and Dick Mayo-Smith. They lived in our house in Brookline the summer they came, while the present headmaster's house was being remodeled. We went to dinner at the Quail Street house early and often. Nancy Mayo-Smith was a Smith classmate of two intimate friends of ours.

Why the relationship between Mr. Mayo-Smith and the trustees failed to work out is hard to say, but it began to appear that the the trustees' and the headmaster's views and instincts—while sincere and humane on both sides—were unalterably divergent.

The late 1960s and early 1970s were most difficult years for all schools, particularly on headmasters and faculties. Independent schools were not exempted from the turbulence. Student unrest and rebellion, the advent of marijuana and other drugs, the upheaval over civil rights and the Vietnam War occasioned the breakdown of accepted standards in schools and colleges across the nation. By happenstance, Roxbury Latin celebrated its 325th anniversary in 1970 on the very day of the Kent State "massacre." The headmaster read a statement of protest by our students as we gathered to rededicate the statue of General Joseph Warren, R.L. 1755, perhaps our most famous graduate. The trustees had rescued this statue, lying on its back abandoned in a warehouse, from almost certain destruction after it had been removed by local request from its perch in Warren Square, Roxbury.

Mr. Mayo-Smith in "breaking the lock-step," as one trustee put it, wanted to go further down the path of change than the trustees did; his vision of the future for R.L. was more permissive than that of the trustees. By January 1973 he and the trustees had come to a parting of the ways. Mr. Mayo-Smith's legacy lies—among other things—in his success in beginning to lower the attrition rate and establishing a flourishing arts program.

In the winter of 1973 I was asked to chair the search committee which resulted in the Reverend F. Washington Jarvis's appointment as headmaster in January 1974. Four representatives from each of five constituencies (students, parents, masters, alumni, and trustees) constituted the unusual twenty-member committee. I quickly came to realize that each constituency felt the same sort of "ownership" of the School that I felt; each loved the School in its own way. We met for the better part of a year in the headmaster's office, modestly turned over to us by our distinguished, dignified, and sensitive acting headmaster, William E. Chauncey. The task at hand was a big one—bigger than anything any of us had probably ever tackled. Our love of the School and our recognition of its unique character enabled us to pull together and function as a responsible group. I knew we had overcome our initial antagonisms when one of the younger students on the committee piped to an upperclassman on the committee, "You are wrong. You have to put the School first and your own ideas second."

So it was on July 1, 1974, that Mr. Jarvis took over the headmastership of Roxbury Latin. He had been the first candidate to call me, having heard of the vacancy from Francis Caswell, retired headmaster of Dexter School.

It is, of course, impossible to evaluate any situation while we are living through it. Objective assessment requires the passage of generations and the benefit of 20/20 hindsight. Nevertheless, it would be a serious omission not to list some of the accomplishments and developments I have witnessed during Mr. Jarvis's tenure.

Proof of a school's success cannot be established on the basis of high board scores, strong college admissions, winning sports teams, or successful theatrical and other artistic endeavors, all of which we now have. Rather one requires the benefit of the long view: contributing and successful alumni such as those who graduated under headmaster William Coe Collar. I hope we are turning out graduates who will become eminent educators such as the Reverend Samuel S. Drury '97, rector of St. Paul's School; or James Bryant Conant '10, Harvard president, scientist, commissioner of postwar Germany; or our incumbent president, Professor Harry R. Lewis '65, dean of Harvard College; or perhaps great scientists such as our Nobel prize winner James B. Sumner '06; or trustee Christopher Walsh '61, current director of Dana Farber Cancer

Research Institute; or fine lawyers such as Malcolm Donald '95, Roger Ernst '98, or Samuel S. Dennis 3d '28, all with eminent Boston law firms; or business geniuses such as Arthur Vining Davis, '84, founder of Aluminum Corp. of America; or James Drummond Dole '95, who brought pineapples to Hawaii; or Henry S. Dennison '95, who started Dennison Manufacturing Company; Charles R. Blyth '01, investment banker, of Blyth & Company; or our incumbent Chairman Albert H. Gordon '19 of Kidder, Peabody; or clergymen such as the Reverend R. B. Ogilby '98, president of Trinity College, Hartford; Rabbi Abram V. Goodman '19 of Temple Sinai of Long Island; or the Reverend Corby Walsh '56, Jesuit missionary. It is from lifetimes of contributing to the world that we can evaluate the quality of the School by the standard set by the Founder himself: service to Church and Commonwealth.

So, with that caveat in mind, and recognizing our own myopia, let me speak of the present. Perhaps Mr. Jarvis's most important achievement is the recruiting of a diverse, talented, committed faculty. These people are "role models" who by their lives, their words, and their actions set high standards of morality, commitment, and achievement. Because the faculty really do, in the headmaster's words, "know and love each student," the attrition rate is very low. The Class of 1986, for example, did not lose a single boy along the way to graduation.

Physically, all the buildings have been brought into excellent condition. The Mary Rousmaniere Gordon Wing, added in 1987, provides the School with a more adequate library—one which, while far larger, has the same "feel" as the 1927 library (modelled on that of Magdalen College, Oxford). In addition, it houses a refectory large enough for the School's 276 students and a Great Hall for exhibitions and formal gatherings. The Robert P. Smith Arts Center opened in 1993 to rave reviews. It contains a raked theater seating three hundred, as well as large spaces for art and music and a capacious area for scenery construction. Plays have become a far more important part of student life in the last two decades. I recently witnessed my favorite Gilbert & Sullivan operetta, "Patience," performed by R.L. and Winsor students, and as well as I know it, I could not find a missed cadence or emphasis. Two full-size new fields and a varsity baseball diamond have been added on the other side of Quail Street on the eight-and-one-half acre property (purchased by the School in 1980), once owned by the Rock and Rappaport families. The Malcolm Donald Room, the original dining room and the kitchen, has been remodeled into a comfortable admissions suite. An entirely renovated Rousmaniere Hall was ready for the closing exercises last year.

Mr. Jarvis importuned Mr. Chauncey to invigorate our admissions process. The School is overwhelmed with strong applicants. It has not only retained and enhanced its representation from the city (nearly a third of our students live in Boston), but attracted strong contingents from the surrounding suburban communities. This has come about through a dignified recruiting effort that includes faculty, parents, trustees, and friends. The result is the most diverse and able student body the School has ever had.

Outsiders tell me our *Newsletter* is the best one they receive. It not only contains the usual undergraduate and graduate news and other feature articles, but also carries Mr. Jarvis's messages to the students. These carefully crafted reflections are sufficiently wise and potent that friends of mine send them to children, grandchildren, and friends.

The School's *traditions* have been revived. Exelauno Day is celebrated with a flourish unknown even in Clarence Gleason's time. Founder's Day has been restored, and the entire school often makes a pilgrimage to an appropriate historical or other-

FIG. 10. David A. Mittell '35, trustee since 1954, vice-chairman.

wise significant spot. Fragments of the fabric of institutions that influenced the life of the Founder have been permanently affixed in the Ernst Wing loggia wall. Additional historical items concerning John Eliot and General Joseph Warren have been permanently displayed in the vestibule outside the Great Hall. And the headmaster's collection of Old Roxbury prints can be seen at the entrance to the library.

Extracurricular activities have been established in the full country day fashion. Our football team has won the league championship three times in the last decade. Our wrestling team has honored the memory of Bert Kelsey by winning the Graves-Kelsey tournament five years in a row. Our cross country team won the Class B New England tournament in 1993 and 1994, and our baseball and soccer teams were league champions in 1994. Our Glee Club recently travelled to England and Jamaica. The debating and Model United Nations teams excel year after year and win awards across the nation against all comers. Students each participate in a gamut of activities. The captain of the baseball team doubled as the Major General in the production of "Patience" I referred to—during the baseball season!

I find everyone at School—faculty, staff, and students—happy, courteous, thoughtful, and considerate whenever I visit, which is often. Boys and teachers alike greet each other and visitors with the caring which their headmaster unfailingly models in each interaction with students and colleagues. Respect, love, and idealism seem to abound.

So, the interim balance sheet looks strong. It is my increasing conviction that history will bear out the fact that this is a halcyon period for Roxbury Latin quite like that of the golden age of William Coe Collar in the last century. In his two decades at the School, I believe (and my colleagues agree) that Mr. Jarvis has become one of the giants of secondary education like our own Dr. Collar and Dr. Drury at St. Paul's School or Endicott Peabody at Groton. His presence among us has lifted the lives of all he has touched—students, faculty, staff, trustees, parents, alumni, and education at large.

Truly our cup runneth over.

Gaudeamus

At the closing exercises in 1961, just after the trustees approved the long-range report, I was standing in the courtyard with three young masters—Bill Chauncey, Bob Jorgensen, and Warden Dilworth. Mr. Weed had an uncanny ability to identify character and teaching ability in the faculty he recruited, and these three are good examples of his wisdom. One of them said to me, somewhat despairingly, "What's going to happen with Roxbury Latin?" "Just stay around," I replied, "This is going to be the most exciting place to teach in the whole country."

I did not foresee the turbulence that was shortly to hit our society and its schools when I said that. However, at this point in the 1990s, as these words are written, it seems to me that all the good created by the many devoted persons who have served the School over the past seven decades has come together in a whole beyond the fondest dreams of the most optimistic among us in 1961. The School, always a "good school," sometimes an "excellent school," is now, indeed, the "schola illustris" Cotton Mather described.

The last seventy years at Roxbury Latin are like the 280 years that preceded them. Roxbury Latin has had golden times and it has had difficult times. In no way would I declare that the past seventy years have witnessed a steady progression of improvement. I would, however, suggest that the median line running through the last seventy years has been upward. I therefore say, in the words I sang so often in Hall as a boy, "*Gaudeamus igitur.*" And as we rejoice, let us join our lips to the words that come later in that same song—our hope, our prayer for the future: "*Vivat academia! Vivant professores!*"

Appendix One

The School's Locations and Buildings

Year is that in which the facility was first used.

1. 1645. A rented room in the house of a "Father Stowe" ("Father" denoting not a clergyman but father of a son).
2. 1652. A one-room schoolhouse was erected for £34–0–11 in "the town street" on the ground now occupied by Guild Row in present-day Dudley Square, Roxbury, on land given, in all likelihood, by Thomas Dudley. One schoolmaster, Thomas Bernard (1679–1683), referred to it as a "hog stie."
3. 1742. A one-room schoolhouse erected on the same site, to which Paul Dudley gave a bell.
4. 1789. "The Brick Schoolhouse" erected on the same site, 40 x 26 feet, twelve-foot high walls, and a "hipp'd" roof. Total cost: £176 (or $589.50 in the currency about to be issued).

    1821. A second story was added to the schoolhouse.
5. 1835. A Greek-revival one-room (plus basement) schoolhouse costing $2500 was erected on Mount Vernon Place (later renamed Kearsarge Avenue) on part of the original Joseph Warren estate sold for $800 to the trustees. Money to purchase this land and to build this new structure came from the sale of the 1789 schoolhouse that was by then in the commercial district. This "Grecian temple" was "removed" for $100 in 1863.
6. 1860. The School moved to the building erected in 1853 on Kearsarge Avenue next to the 1835 building. The trustees had built this building for $4000 in 1853 to house seventy to eighty boys of the English high school which they had been contracted by the city to run. In 1860, when the City of Roxbury took over the English

high school and removed the boys of that school to another building, the trustees moved the Latin school boys into this building.
The building had two ground floor classrooms with an assembly
"hall" above.

1873. At Mr. Collar's request, the trustees erected a two-room addition to the rear of the building costing $5400.

1883. Two new classrooms, a small library, and headmaster's office
were added to the north side of the building at a cost of $7000.

1889. The School obtained the right to transform the adjoining city-
owned graveyard into a playground.

1892. Two classrooms, two "toilet rooms," a new teachers' room, and
a reception room were added to the south end of the building at a
cost of $18,370.

7. 1927. The School moved to its present location, in "the westerly part
of Roxbury," at the corner of Centre Street and Cottage Avenue
(renamed St. Theresa Avenue in 1932 in honor of the newly-built
church). On August 15, 1922, the trustees purchased the fifty-acre
estate of Richard Codman in West Roxbury for $60,000. (They
paid for it by the eventual sale of the Kearsarge Avenue property
for $30,500 and the Seaver Street property near Franklin Park for
$36,000.) The building was designed by William Perry of Perry,
Shaw & Hepburn (who soon went on to preside over the restoration of Colonial Williamsburg). It was built in 1926–27 for about
$200,000, and Rousmaniere Hall was added for an additional
$35,500 following a last-minute donation by Dean Rousmaniere's
wife.

1932. The large barn (which some had hoped could become the
School's gymnasium, with renovation), located, with stables, on
the present "Flea Patch" Field, burned to the ground destroying
two automobiles and a quantity of school furniture.

1945. The John S. Codman property of six acres (present Bogandale
Field) plus the 57 Quail Street house (present headmaster's home)
was purchased for $17,000.

1951. The house at 55 Quail Street was built for Miss Margaret Codman for $21,215. It reverted to the School on her death in 1970.

1957. The Albert H. Gordon Field House was added at cost of $278,700. Hugh Stubbins and Associates, Architects.

1963. Quail Street Field (at the corner of Quail Street and St. Theresa Avenue) and the adjoining "Flea Patch" (then called Potter's Field) were developed at a cost of $35,000. "Bogandale Field" was developed at a cost of $37,500.

1966. The Roger Ernst Wing was added at a cost of $483,000. William F. Halsey, architect.

1970. The statue of General Joseph Warren, Class of 1755, was dedicated on May 8, 1970, at the 325th Anniversary celebrations. The statue was commissioned from Paul Wayland Bartlett (1865–1925) in 1896 and was executed in Paris. It was erected in Warren Square on June 17, 1904. Dr. John T. Bowers '39 found it missing from its pedestal and traced it to a warehouse where it had been removed when street patterns were changed. There was no desire by the neighborhood for its return.

1980. The School purchased eight and one half acres of adjoining land with a house—at the end of Quail Street—from Jerome Rappaport for $340,000 on June 25, 1980. As early as 1953 the Rock family, the then owners, had offered the property to the School.

1988. The Mary Rousmaniere Gordon Building (refectory, library, and great hall) was added at a cost of $2,000,000. William D. Buckingham, architect.

1990. The Rappaport property was developed into two playing fields at a cost of $600,000.

1993. The Robert P. Smith Arts Center was added at a cost of $2,444,000. William D. Buckingham, architect.

1993. The campus entrance and courtyard were reconfigured, and new parking areas were added.

FIG. 1. Aerial view of the School in 1990.

Appendix Two

Major Legal Documents Since 1788

The School's early documents—from the Agreement of 1645 until the year of the Charter of 1789—are found in Richard Walden Hale, Jr.'s article "The First Independent School in America" in the Publications of The Colonial Society of Massachusetts 35 (1942-46), Boston 1951. Herewith follows the Charter of 1789 and succeeding revisions.

A. Acts of 1788, Chapter 34 [The Charter of 1789]

AN ACT FOR INCORPORATING CERTAIN PERSONS THEREIN NAMED, BY THE NAME OF THE TRUSTEES OF THE GRAMMAR SCHOOL, IN THE EASTERLY PART OF THE TOWN OF ROXBURY, AND FOR REPEALING ALL THE LAWS HERETOFORE MADE FOR THAT PURPOSE.

Whereas the education of youth, has always been considered by the wise & virtuous, as an object of the highest importance to the safety and happiness of a free people; and whereas Thomas Bell, late of London, by his last will & testament, bearing date the twenty ninth day of January, in the year of our Lord, one thousand six hundred and seventy one, gave certain lands and tenements therein mentioned, in the words following, that is to say, "I give unto Mr. John Eliot, minister of the Church of Christ, in Roxbury in New England, and captain Isaac Johnson, and to one such other like godly person, now bearing office in the said Church, and their successors, the minister and other such two head officers of the said Church of Roxbury, as the whole Church there, from time to time, shall best approve of successively from time to time forever, all my messuages or tenements, lands & hereditaments, with their and every of their appurtenances, situate, lying and being at Roxbury, in New England aforesaid, in parts beyond the seas, to have and to hold to the said minister and officers of the said Church of Roxbury, for the time being, and their successors from time to time forever, in trust only notwithstanding, to and for the maintainance of a School Master and free school, for the teaching and instructing of poor men's children at Roxbury aforesaid forever, and to be for no other use intent or purpose whatever." And whereas several other persons have heretofore bequeathed certain other lands and monies, to be applied to and for the purposes aforesaid, to be under the direction of certain feoffees to be duly chosen for those purposes; all which devises and donations have been ratified and confirmed by several acts of the Legislature of this (then Province) now Commonwealth of Massachusetts: And whereas the said acts are found to be inadequate to the regular carrying on of the affairs of the said school, and a number of the inhabitants of the said town of Roxbury have petitioned this Court, that an act of incorporation may be passed, to incorporate a competent number of persons for the purpose of carrying into effect the benevolent designs of the said Thomas Bell & others:

Be it therefore enacted by the Senate and House of Representatives in General Court assembled & by the authority of the same that all the laws heretofore made ratifying and confirming the doings relative to the free school in the easterly part of the town of Roxbury aforesaid, so far as the same are inconsistent with this act, be, and they are hereby repealed and rendered null and void.

Provided always, that the persons who act as trustees of the estate of the said Thomas Bell, & the persons who act as feoffees of said donations, shall have respectively full right in law to demand & receive all rents and incomes, or any arrearages thereof; or other sums of money, which, from any persons whatever, in consequence of any leases, contracts or bargains made with said trustees or feoffees, are or may become due; and provided also, that the said trustees and feoffees respectively, shall be held to liquidate and settle all their accounts with, and to pay over all monies which they have received or shall in their said capacities respectively receive, unto the trustees of said school appointed by this Act, or hereafter to be chosen in pursuance thereof.

Be it further enacted by the authority aforesaid, that honorable John Lowell esquire, Nehemiah Munroe, James Mears, reverend Eliphalet Porter, clerk, honorable Increase Sumner esquire, Samuel Sumner, Joseph Ruggles, esqr. Thomas Williams physician, and Joseph Williams gentlemen, be, and they are hereby nominated & appointed trustees of the grammar school in the easterly part of the town of Roxbury, and they are hereby incorporated into a body politick and corporate by that name; and the said trustees and their successors to be chosen and appointed in the manner herein after prescribed, shall be and continue a body politick and corporate by the same name forever.

Be it further enacted by the authority aforesaid, that all the lands, buildings and other property whatsoever, which have heretofore been given by the said Thomas Bell and others, to the said trustees and feoffees for the purpose of supporting the said free school, & all other estate, interest, claim or demand whatsoever, belonging to said school, or which are held in trust therefor, be and they are hereby confirmed to the said John Lowell, Nehemiah Munroe, James Mears, Eliphalet Porter, Increase Sumner, Samuel Sumner, Joseph Ruggles, Thomas Williams and Joseph Williams, & to their successors as trustees of the said school forever, for the uses, intents and purposes, and upon the trusts which in the said last will & testament of the said Thomas Bell, and in the donations aforesaid, are intended; and the trustees aforesaid, their successors, and the officers that may be appointed in pursuance of this act, are hereby required in conducting the concerns of the said school, and in all matters relating thereto, to regulate themselves conformably to the true design & intention of the said Thomas Bell & others.

Be it enacted by the authority aforesaid, that the said trustees and their successors, shall have one common seal, which they may make use of in any cause or business that relates to the said office of trustees of the said school, and they shall have power & authority, from time to time to change, alter or renew the same at pleasure; and they may sue and be sued in all actions, real, personal or mixed, and prosecute & defend the same to final judgment and execution, by the name of the trustees of the grammar school in the easterly part of the town of Roxbury as aforesaid.

Be it further enacted by the authority aforesaid, that the said trustees and their successors, shall be the true & sole visitors, trustees and governors of the said school, in perpetual succession forever, to be continued in the way and manner herein after pointed out, with full power and authority to elect by ballot, a president, secretary, treasurer and such other officers as they shall judge necessary & convenient, and to make & ordain such bye-laws, rules and orders, for the good order and government of the said school, from time to time, as to them the said trustees and their successors shall, according to the various occasions & circumstances thereof appear most fit & requisite, either with or without penalties, all which shall be observed by the officers, scholars and servants of the said school. Provided always, that the said bye-laws, rules & orders are not repugnant to the Constitution and laws of this Commonwealth.

Be it further enacted by the authority aforesaid, that the number of the said trustees shall not at any one time consist of more than thirteen nor less than nine, five of whom shall constitute a quorum for transacting business, and a major part of the members present at any stated meeting thereof shall decide all questions that may properly come before them. And to perpetuate the succession of the said trustees,

Be it further enacted by the authority aforesaid, that as often as one or more of the said trustees, shall die, resign, remove, or in the judgment of the major part of the said trustees for the time being, be rendered by age, infirmity or otherwise incapable of discharging the duties of his office, then and so often the remaining part of the trustees then surviving, or the major part of them, at some stated meeting, shall elect by ballot, one or more persons, being reputable freeholders in the town of Roxbury aforesaid, to supply such vacancy or vacancies: Provided always, that the minister and the two oldest deacons of the first Church of Christ in the said town of Roxbury, shall always, by virtue of their said offices, be members of the said corporation.

Be it further enacted by the authority aforesaid, that the trustees aforesaid, and their successors be and they are hereby rendered capable in law to take and receive by gift, grant, devise, bequest, or otherwise, any lands, tenements or other estate real or personal, provided, that the annual income of such real estate shall not exceed the sum of one hundred and fifty pounds, and the annual income of such personal estate shall not exceed the sum of one hundred and fifty pounds, (both sums to be estimated in silver at the rate of six shillings and eight pence by the ounce) to have and to hold the same to the said trustees, and to their successors in that office, on such terms and under such provisions and limitations as may be expressed in any deed or instrument of conveyance to them made; Provided always, that neither the said trustees nor their successors, shall ever hereafter receive any grant or donation the condition whereof shall require them or any others concerned to act, in any respect, contrary to the design expressed in the last will and testament of the said Thomas Bell, or any donation heretofore made. And all deeds & instruments which the said trustees may lawfully make, in their said capacity, as aforesaid, shall, when made in their name, signed & delivered by their treasurer, and sealed with their common seal, be binding on the said trustees, and their successors, and be valid in law.

Be it further enacted by the authority aforesaid, that there shall be held a meeting of the said trustees as soon as conveniently may be after the passing of this act, and afterwards once in every year at least, on some day to be stated by the said trustees, annually forever; at which meetings the major part of the said trustees present, shall proceed to elect a president, secretary, treasurer & such other officers as they shall deem meet, who shall continue in office for the term of one year, or until others shall be chosen in their room; and the said officers shall be under oath, faithfully and impartially to discharge all the duties of their said offices, during the time for which they shall be elected, and until others shall be chosen and sworn in their stead. And there shall be three quarterly meetings of the said trustees, besides the said annual meeting, to be held on such days as shall be prescribed by the regulations or orders of the said trustees, at either of which meetings any business relative to the government & well ordering of the affairs of the said school may be transacted, and vacancies filled up, if necessary: Provided however, that no vacancy in the office of trustee shall be filled up at any meeting of said trustees, unless previous notice shall have been given by the secretary to each of the trustees, that such vacancy exists, & is intended to be filled up at such meeting; which notice the said secretary is directed to give, at the application of either of the trustees. And that the state of the finances of said school may be known from time to time,

Be it further enacted by the authority aforesaid, that it shall and may be lawful for the inhabitants of the said town of Roxbury, at any legal meeting thereof, not exceeding once in any one year, to call on the said trustees for a state of their general accounts, at the then last audit thereof, and it shall be the duty of the trustees aforesaid, or some one of their officers, for the time being, to exhibit an attested copy of such statement accordingly.

Be it further enacted by the authority aforesaid, that Thomas Clarke, esquire be, and he is hereby authorized and directed to determine the time and place for holding the first meeting of the said trustees, & to certify them respectively thereof, ten days at the least previous to the holding the same.

January 21, 1789.

Approved January 23, 1789.

B. *Acts of 1870, Chapter 295*

AN ACT RELATING TO THE SALE OF REAL ESTATE BY THE TRUSTEES OF THE GRAMMAR SCHOOL IN THE EASTERLY PART OF ROXBURY.

Be it enacted, &c., as follows:

SECTION I. The trustees of the grammar school in the easterly part of Roxbury are hereby authorized to sell any real estate held by them in trust, and convey the same by deed duly executed: provided, the proceeds of such sales shall be held upon the same trusts as such real estate was held; and all sales and conveyances heretofore made by said trustees are hereby ratified and made legal and binding in law.

SECTION 2. This act shall take effect upon its passage.

Approved May 28, 1870.

C. *Acts of 1906, Chapter 113*

AN ACT RELATIVE TO THE MEMBERSHIP ON THE BOARD OF TRUSTEES OF THE ROXBURY LATIN SCHOOL.

Be it enacted, etc., as follows:

SECTION I. Chapter thirty-four of the acts of the year seventeen hundred and eighty-eight, being the act approved January 23d, 1789, entitled "An Act for incorporating certain persons therein named, by the name of the trustees of the grammar school, in the easterly part of the town of Roxbury, and for repealing all the laws heretofore made for that purpose", is hereby amended as follows:—

First. By striking out the words "not at any one time", "more than", and "nor less than nine", in the paragraph beginning with the words "That the number of", and ending with the words "come before them", so that the paragraph will read as follows:—That the number of the said trustees shall consist of thirteen, five of whom shall constitute a quorum for transacting business, and a major part of the members present at any stated meeting thereof shall decide all questions that may properly come before them.

Second. By striking out the words "And to perpetuate the succession of the said trustees, Be it further enacted by the authority aforesaid, that as often as one or more of the said trustees, shall die, resign, remove, or in the judgment of the major part of the said trustees for the time being, be rendered by age, infirmity or otherwise incapable of discharging the duties of his office, then and so often the remaining part of the trustees then surviving, or the major part of them, at some stated meeting, shall elect by ballot, one or more persons, being reputable freeholders in the town of Roxbury aforesaid, to supply such vacancy or vacancies: Provided always, that the minister and the two oldest deacons of the first Church of Christ in the said town of Roxbury, shall always, by virtue of their said offices, be members of the said corporation".

SECTION 2. The minister and the two oldest deacons in length of service of the first Church of Christ in that part of Boston formerly the said town of Roxbury, incorporated as the First Religious Society in Roxbury under chapter one hundred and thirty-three of the acts of the legislative year eighteen hundred and twenty-four, approved February 26, 1825, shall always by virtue of their said offices be members of the said corporation. Each of the other members of said corporation in office when this act takes effect shall remain such member until he shall die, resign, or in the judgment of the major part of the trustees for the time being be rendered by age, infirmity or otherwise, incapable of discharging the duties of his office. Any vacancies existing when this act takes effect, and any which may thereafter occur among the members then in office, other than the aforesaid minister and two deacons, shall be filled by the election by the board of members from nominations by the graduates of said school, as hereinafter provided, until five members have so been elected, and thereafter the said ten members other than the aforesaid minister and two deacons shall be elected by the board, five being elected from nominations by the graduates of said school and the other five members from the residents of the territory formerly constituting the town of Roxbury. The five members elected from nominations by the graduates of said school shall hold office for a term of five years, except as hereinafter provided, and the five other members shall hold office until they die or resign: provided, that, whenever in the judgment of the major part of the whole number of trustees for the time being any of said ten members shall be rendered by age, infirmity or otherwise, incapable of discharging the duties of his office, then and so often the remaining part of the trustees, or the major part of them, may declare his office vacant. All vacancies, from whatever cause arising, shall be filled in the manner provided for the election of the member whose office has become vacant.

The five members to be elected from nominations by the graduates of said school shall be elected as follows:—Within thirty days after the time when this act takes effect, if there then be any vacancy in said board of trustees, and thereafter whenever vacancies occur which are to be filled from nominations by the graduates, within thirty days after the occurrence of such vacancy, the secretary of the trustees shall call a meeting to be held in Boston not less than sixty or more than ninety days after the time when this act takes effect, or after the occurrence of such vacancy, as the case may be, of the graduates of said school of five or more years' standing. Notice of such meeting shall be given by mail to all of such graduates whose addresses are known to the secretary. At such meeting a chairman and secretary shall be chosen, and said secretary shall keep and transmit to the trustees a record of the proceedings of the meeting, attested by him, which the secretary of the trustees shall enter on his records. Such of said graduates as are present at the meeting shall select from the whole number of graduates of more than five years' standing, a committee of three, who shall nominate in writing to the trustees three times as many of the graduates of the school of more than five years' standing as there are vacancies to be filled from nominations by the graduates, and from such nominations the trustees shall elect one for every such vacancy. Each graduate so elected shall hold office for five years or until his successor shall be elected: provided, that the term of any graduate elected to fill an unexpired term shall be limited to that term. The election of trustees of either class shall be by ballot at some stated meeting.

Section 3. This act shall take effect when accepted by a majority of the trustees in office, on behalf of said corporation, at a meeting held within one year after its passage. The secretary of said corporation shall forthwith upon such acceptance record in the registry of deeds for the county of Suffolk a copy of the vote of acceptance, with a certificate of its adoption by the trustees as herein required, and the date of its adoption, duly verified by him.

Approved February 26, 1906.

Accepted March 21, 1906.

D. *Acts of 1913, Chapter 129*

AN ACT RELATIVE TO MEMBERSHIP ON THE BOARD OF TRUSTEES OF THE ROXBURY LATIN SCHOOL.

Be it enacted, etc., as follows:

Section 1. Chapter thirty-four of the acts of the year seventeen hundred and eighty-eight, as amended by chapter one hundred and thirteen of the acts of the year nineteen hundred and six, is hereby further amended by striking out section two of said chapter one hundred and thirteen, and inserting in place thereof the following:—Section 2. Said thirteen trustees shall be of three classes, denominated trustees ex officiis, trustees for life, and trustees for five years, respectively.

(1) The trustees ex officiis shall be the minister and two oldest deacons in length of service of the First Religious Society in Roxbury, incorporated under chapter one hundred and thirty-three of the acts of the year eighteen hundred and twenty-four, approved February twenty-sixth, eighteen hundred and twenty-five.

(2) The trustees for life shall be the five trustees who were members of said corporation on the first day of January, nineteen hundred and thirteen, by election prior to the twenty-sixth day of February, nineteen hundred and six, and their successors in office. Each of said trustees for life shall hold office until he dies, resigns or is declared by vote of the majority of the other members of said corporation to be, in their judgment, rendered by age, infirmity or otherwise incapable of discharging the duties of his office. Any vacancy in the class of trustees for life shall be filled by a majority vote of the remaining trustees of all classes.

(3) The trustees for five years shall be the five trustees who were members of said corporation on the first day of January, nineteen hundred and thirteen, by election subsequent to the twenty-sixth day of February, nineteen hundred and six, and their successors in office.

Said trustees for five years holding office on the first day of January, nineteen hundred and thirteen, shall continue in office until the thirtieth day of June next following the dates fixed at the time of their election for the expiration of the terms for which they were severally elected.

Before the expiration of the term of any trustee for five years, the trustees of all classes shall elect his successor, as hereinafter provided, who shall hold office for the term of five years from such expiration, except that the trustee to be elected in the year nineteen hundred and seventeen shall be elected for three years and the trustees to be elected in the year nineteen hundred and eighteen shall be elected one for three years and one for four years, from the thirtieth day of June in the said years nineteen hundred and seventeen and nineteen hundred and eighteen.

If any trustee for five years before the expiration of the term for which he was elected dies, resigns or is declared by vote of a majority of the other members of said corporation to be, in their judgment, rendered by age, infirmity or otherwise incapable of discharging the duties of his office, the trustees of all classes shall elect his successor, as hereinafter provided, who shall hold office for the unexpired term of his predecessor in office.

Notice of any vacancy in the class of trustees for five years through other cause than expiration of the term for which any such trustee was elected, shall be given forthwith in writing by the secretary of said corporation to at least two of the members of the nominating committee, hereinafter provided for.

(4) The trustees for five years shall be elected in the following manner:—

(a) A meeting of the alumni, who for the purpose of this act shall be taken to include every one who was for a least two years a member of a class which has been graduated from said school at least five years, shall be held in the building occupied by said school on such day not later than thirty days from the time when this act takes effect, as may be determined by the members of said corporation, and thereafter in each year on the day when diplomas are awarded to the graduating class, known as graduation day.

Notice of every such meeting shall be given by the secretary of said corporation by mail to all of the alumni whose addresses are known to him.

At every such meeting a chairman and secretary shall be chosen from the alumni present, and the secretary shall keep, attest and transmit a record of the proceedings of every such meeting to the secretary of the corporation, who shall enter the same upon the records of the corporation.

(b) The alumni present at such meeting shall choose for the whole number of alumni a nominating committee of seven members, who shall have power to fill its vacancies and shall hold office for one year, beginning with the first day of July next following its election, except that the nominating committee chosen at the first meeting, hereinbefore provided for, shall hold office from the time of its election until the first day of July, nineteen hundred and thirteen.

(c) Every such nominating committee shall nominate at least three times as many alumni as there are vacancies to be filled in the class of trustees for five years during the term of office of the nominating committee, and shall transmit such nominations to the secretary of said corporation not later than thirty nor more than sixty days before the occurrence of a vacancy by reason of the expiration of the term for which such trustee was elected, and forthwith upon the receipt of the notice from the secretary of the corporation, hereinbefore provided for, in case of a vacancy occurring through other cause.

(d) All vacancies in the class of trustees for five years shall be filled by a majority vote of the trustees of all classes from such nominations from the nominating committee, but if any such nominating committee shall fail to make and transmit nominations, as hereinbefore provided, the trustees for five years holding office at the time shall themselves make nominations which shall be voted upon by the trustees of all classes as if made by such nominating committee.

SECTION 2. This act shall take effect when accepted by a majority of the trustees in office, on behalf of said corporation, at a meeting held within thirty days after its passage. The secretary of said corporation shall forthwith upon such acceptance record in the registry of deeds for the county of Suffolk a copy of the vote of acceptance, with a certificate of its adoption by the trustees, as herein provided, and the date of its adoption verified by him.

Approved February 19, 1913.

E. *Acts of 1927, Chapter 214*

AN ACT TO ENLARGE THE AUTHORITY OF THE TRUSTEES OF THE GRAMMAR SCHOOL IN THE EASTERLY PART OF THE TOWN OF ROXBURY.

Be it enacted, etc., as follows:

SECTION 1. The Trustees of the Grammar School in the easterly part of the town of Roxbury, incorporated as a body politic and corporate under the provisions of an act approved January twenty-third, seventeen hundred and eighty-nine and entitled "An Act for incorporating certain persons therein named, by the name of the Trustees of the Grammar School, in the easterly part of the town of Roxbury, and for repealing all the Laws heretofore made for that purpose", are hereby given full power and authority to provide for the education of youth, with or without regard to the place of residence or to the financial ability of them or their parents, and with or without charging tuition therefor, and to receive, hold and administer real and personal property given, conveyed, transferred, devised or bequeathed to said corporation for its purposes.

SECTION 2. All real and personal property now held by said corporation is hereby confirmed to said corporation subject to the specific trusts upon which said property has been received by said corporation, and nothing in this act contained shall be construed as purporting to authorize any action by said trustees in contravention of the obligations of said specific trusts, or to impair the jurisdiction of any court now or hereafter of competent jurisdiction with respect to said trusts and the administration thereof by said trustees.

SECTION 3. This act shall take effect when accepted by a majority of the trustees in office, on behalf of said corporation, at a meeting held within one year after its passage. The secretary of said corporation shall forthwith upon such acceptance record in the registry of deeds for the county of Suffolk a copy of the vote of acceptance, with a certificate of its adoption by the trustees as herein provided and the date of its adoption duly verified by him.

Approved April 6, 1927.

F. *Acts of 1947, Chapter 345*

AN ACT CHANGING THE NAME OF THE TRUSTEES OF THE GRAMMAR SCHOOL IN THE EASTERLY PART OF THE TOWN OF ROXBURY, AND RELATIVE TO THE MEMBERSHIP OF SAID CORPORATION.

Be it enacted, etc., as follows:

SECTION 1. The name of the trustees of the grammar school in the easterly part of the town of Roxbury, incorporated by chapter thirty-four of the acts of seventeen hundred and eighty-eight, being an act approved January twenty-third, seventeen hundred and eighty-nine, entitled "An Act for incorporating certain persons therein named, by the name of the Trustees of the Grammar School, in the easterly part of the town of Roxbury, and for repealing all the laws heretofore made for that purpose", is hereby changed to the Trustees of the Roxbury Latin School.

Section 2. Said chapter 34 is hereby amended by striking out the provisions thereof which were amended by paragraph First of section 1 of chapter 113 of the acts of 1906 and inserting in place thereof the following provision:—That the number of the said trustees shall not at any one time consist of more than fifteen nor less than eleven, five of whom shall constitute a quorum for transacting business, and a major part of the members present at any stated meeting thereof shall decide all questions that may properly come before them.

Section 3. Section 2 of said chapter 113, as amended by section 1 of chapter 129 of the acts of 1913, is hereby further amended by striking out all of the words thereof down to and including the word "office" in line 15 and inserting in place thereof the following:— Said trustees shall be of three classes denominated a trustee ex officio, trustees for life, and trustees for five years, respectively.

(1) The trustee ex officio shall be that one of the minister and two oldest deacons in length of service of the First Religious Society in Roxbury, incorporated under chapter one hundred and thirty-three of the acts of the year eighteen hundred and twenty-four, as shall be selected from time to time by the standing committee of said society.

(2) The trustees for life shall be not less than five nor more than nine, as may be determined from time to time by a majority vote of the trustees of all classes, and shall include the five trustees for life who were members of said corporation on the first day of January of the year nineteen hundred and forty-seven, and not more than four others to be elected from time to time by a majority vote of the trustees of all classes.

Section 4. Said section 2 of said chapter 113, as so amended, is hereby further amended by striking out the paragraph marked (a) of subdivision (4) and inserting in place thereof the following paragraph:—

(a) A meeting of the alumni, who for the purpose of this act shall be taken to include every one who was for at least one academic year a member of a class which has been graduated from said school, shall be held in each year in such place within the city of Boston, Massachusetts, and on such day as may be determined by the members of said corporation from time to time.

Section 5. Said section 2 of said chapter 113, as so amended, is hereby further amended by striking out paragraph (b) of said subdivision (4) and inserting in place thereof the following paragraph:—

(b) the alumni present at such meeting shall choose from the whole number of alumni a nominating committee of not less than five nor more than seven members, who shall have power to fill its vacancies and shall hold office for one year from the time of their election or until their successors shall have been elected.

SECTION 6. Said section 2 of said chapter 113, as so amended, is hereby further amended by striking out paragraph (c) of said subdivision (4) and inserting in place thereof the following paragraph:—

(c) Every such nominating committee shall nominate from among those alumni whose class has been graduated for five years or more at least three times as many alumni as there are vacancies to be filled in the class of trustees for five years during the term of office of the nominating committee, and shall transmit such nominations to the secretary of said corporation not later than thirty nor more than sixty days before the occurrence of a vacancy by reason of the expiration of the term for which such trustee was elected, and not later than sixty days after the receipt of the notice from the secretary of the corporation, hereinbefore provided for, in case of a vacancy occurring through other cause.

SECTION 7. This act shall take full effect when accepted by a majority of the trustees in office, on behalf of said corporation. The secretary of said corporation shall forthwith upon such acceptance file in the office of the state secretary a copy of the vote of acceptance.

Approved May 6, 1947.

G. *Acts of 1960, Chapter 143*

AN ACT RELATIVE TO THE MEMBERSHIP OF THE BOARD OF TRUSTEES OF THE ROXBURY LATIN SCHOOL.

Be it enacted, etc., as follows:

SECTION 1. Chapter 34 of the acts of 1788 is hereby amended by striking out the sentence, as most recently amended by section 2 of chapter 345 of the acts of 1947, and inserting in place thereof the following sentence:—That the number of said trustees shall not at any time consist of more than twenty nor less than eleven, five of whom shall constitute a quorum for transacting business, and a major part of the members present at any stated meeting thereof shall decide all questions that may properly come before them.

SECTION 2. Chapter 113 of the acts of 1906 is hereby amended by striking out section 2, as most recently amended by sections 3 to 6, inclusive, of said chapter 345, and inserting in place thereof the following section:— Section 2. Said trustees shall be of four classes, denominated a trustee ex officio, trustees for life, trustees for five years, and trustees at large, respectively.

(1) The trustee ex officio shall be that one of the minister and two oldest deacons in length of service of the First Religious Society in Roxbury, incorporated under chapter one hundred and thirty-three of the acts of the year eighteen hundred and twenty-four, as shall be selected from time to time by the standing committee of said society.

(2) The trustees for life shall be not less than five nor more than nine, as may be determined from time to time by a majority vote of the trustees of all classes other than the trustees at large, and shall include the six trustees for life who were members of said corporation on the first day of January, nineteen hundred and fifty-eight, and not more than three trustees to be elected from time to time by a majority vote of the trustees of all classes other than the trustees at large.

(3) The trustees for five years shall be the five trustees who were members of said corporation on the first day of January, nineteen hundred and fifty-eight, and their successors in office.

Said trustees for five years holding office on the first day of January, nineteen hundred and fifty-eight, shall continue in office until the thirtieth day of June next following the dates fixed at the time of their election for the expiration of the term for which they were severally elected.

Before the expiration of the term of any trustee for five years, the trustees of all classes other than the trustees at large, shall elect his successor, as hereinafter provided, who shall hold office for the term of five years from such expiration.

If, before the expiration of the term for which any trustee for five years was elected, such trustee dies, resigns or is declared by a vote of a majority of the trustees of all classes other than the trustees at large to be, in their judgment, rendered by age, infirmity or otherwise incapable of discharging the duties of his office, the trustees of all classes other than the trustees at large shall elect his successor, as hereinafter provided, who shall hold office for the unexpired term of his predecessor in office.

Notice of any vacancy in the class of trustees for five years through any cause other than the expiration of the term for which any such trustee was elected shall be given forthwith in writing by the secretary of said corporation to at least two of the members of the nominating committee hereinafter provided for.

(4) The trustees for five years shall be elected in the following manner:—

(a) A meeting of the alumni, who for the purpose of this act shall be taken to include everyone who was for a least one academic year a member of a class which has been graduated from said school, shall be held in each year in such place within the city of Boston, Massachusetts, and on such day as may be determined by the members of said corporation from time to time.

(b) The alumni present at such meeting shall choose from the whole number of alumni a nominating committee of not less than five nor more than seven members, who shall have power to fill its vacancies and shall hold office for one year from the time of their election or until their successors shall have been elected.

(c) Every such nominating committee shall nominate from among those alumni whose class has been graduated for five years or more at least three times as many alumni as there are vacancies to be filled in the class of trustees for five years during the term of office of the nominating committee, and shall transmit such nominations to the secretary of said corporation not later than thirty nor more than sixty days before the occurrence of a vacancy by reason of the expiration of the term for which such trustee was elected, and not later than sixty days after the receipt of the notice from the secretary of the corporation, hereinbefore provided for, in case of a vacancy occurring through other cause.

(d) All vacancies in the class of trustees for five years shall be filled by a majority vote of the trustees of all classes other than the trustees at large from such nominations from the nominating committee, but if any such nominating committee shall fail to make and transmit nominations, as hereinbefore provided, the trustees for five years holding office at the time shall themselves make nominations which shall be voted upon by the trustees of all classes other than the trustees at large as if made by such nominating committee.

(5) The number of trustees at large who are to hold office at any time may be between one and five, but it shall not be required that there be any such trustee. No trustee at large need be an alumnus of said school. The number and composition of the class of trustees at large, and their nomination, election and powers shall be governed by the following provisions:—

(a) The number of trustees at large who are to be elected at any time shall be as determined from time to time by a majority vote of the trustees of all classes other than the trustees at large. At the last meeting of the board of trustees held before June thirtieth in each year, the trustees for life present at such meeting, by vote of at least a majority, shall nominate a slate of candidates numbering at least one and not more than three candidates for each trustee at large to be elected as so determined, and the trustees at large to be elected shall be elected from such slate by a majority vote of the trustees of all classes, other than the trustees at large, present at such meeting, or at a future meeting held during such year at which a quorum is present. Each trustee at large so elected shall serve for a period of three years from the time of his election.

(b) The trustees at large shall have all the rights and powers of the trustees of other classes except that they shall have no right to vote for the election of trustees of any class.

SECTION 3. This act shall take full effect when accepted by a majority of the trustees in office, on behalf of said corporation. The secretary of said corporation shall forthwith upon such acceptance file in the office of the state secretary a copy of the vote of acceptance.

Approved March 1, 1960.

H. *Suffolk County, SS. Trial Court, Superior Court Department, Civil No. 85541 (Equity)*

THE TRUSTEES OF THE ROXBURY LATIN SCHOOL, *Plaintiff v.* JAMES M. SHANNON, AS ATTORNEY GENERAL OF THE COMMONWEALTH OF MASSACHUSETTS, *Defendant*

Judgment entered on Docket March 9, 1990.

FINAL JUDGMENT

Pursuant to Mass. R. Civ. P. 58(a), the following Judgment is to be entered and docketed in this action in accordance with Mass. R. Civ. P. 79(a):

WHEREFORE:

A. The Trustees of the Roxbury Latin School (the "School") is a charitable corporation organized and operated for educational purposes under M.G.L. c. 180 and certain special laws of Massachusetts. The School is for boys in grades 7-12, and is located in West Roxbury, Suffolk County, Massachusetts;

B. James Shannon is the current attorney general of the Commonwealth of Massachusetts ("the Attorney General"). He is authorized by M.C.L. c. 12, 8 to enforce the due application of funds given or appropriated to public charities;

C. The Attorney General is a necessary and proper party to this action with exclusive standing, pursuant to M.G.L. c. 12, 8G and the cases decided thereunder, because the School seeks instructions, the application of the doctrines of equitable modification and/or deviation, and a declaratory judgment regarding the interpretation of the terms of an agreement of association, a will, a charitable trust, a corporate charter and amendments thereto, and the powers and duties of Trustees of the School;

D. This Court has jurisdiction of this action pursuant to M.G.L. c. 214, 1, c. 215 6, c. 212 3, and c. 231A, 1. Venue is proper in Suffolk County, pursuant to M.G.L. c. 214, 5, and c. 223 1, because both parties have their usual places of business in Suffolk County;

E. The School was founded as a private school in 1645 by The Rev. John Eliot, pursuant to a written Agreement of 64 subscribers known as "Donors." At that time, the School was governed as a private and independent charity by a board of seven "Feoffees" originally elected by the Donors. The School was in a locality in the Massachusetts Bay Colony called the "Towne of Roxburie," which has not existed as a legal or geographical entity for well over a century, and whose boundaries were continually disputed over time;

F. In addition to the property (or proceeds thereof) committed by the Donors to the School, further property (or proceeds thereof) was later held by Trustees under the Will of Thomas Bell of London, England, who died in 1672, *inter alia*, "... for ye Mainteynance of a schoolmaster and free schoole for ye teaching and instructing of poore mens children at Roxbury...";

G. By a Special Act in 1789, the Massachusetts General Court incorporated the School as a charitable corporation for educational purposes, and confirmed to the Trustees of the School lands, buildings and other property, including the property previously held by the Feoffees and by Bell's Trustees;

H. In 1927, upon the petition and with the consent of the Trustees of the School, Massachusetts General Court enacted Chapter 214 of the Acts of 1927, which confirmed to the School all real and personal property then existing and held by the charitable corporation, subject to the specific trusts upon which such property had been received by the corporation;

I. The Legislature further provided in Chapter 214 of the Acts of 1927 that the School's corporate charter was to be amended so as to make clear that the Trustees "are hereby given full power and authority to provide for the education of youth, with or without regard to the place of residence or to the financial ability of them or their parents, and with or without charging tuition therefor, and to receive, hold and administer real and personal property, given, conveyed, transferred, devised, or bequeathed to said corporation for its purposes";

J. The School's records indicate that, from the start, the School has been open to application from all who wished to attend it, "whether inhabitantes or strangers" (1680, after Bell's Bequest). Students from outside "Roxburie" have attended the School throughout its history. Beginning in the School's 238th year (1882), a fee was charged to non-resident students. The collection of this fee continued until 1934. From 1935 until 1962, all students were charged tuition, though at two different rates determined by geographical residence. Since 1962 the School has charged a single tuition, and provided scholarships (reduction of tuition and other fees) on the basis of financial need alone, without regard to students' geographical place of residence. The School conducts extensive outreach for Boston students who are financially unable to attend without financial assistance from the School;

K. The bulk of the School's current assets (including over 95% of the total value of its endowments) was received after the 1927 Amendment, and nearly all were received after the assets of the Bell Bequest were dissipated;

L. Questions have been raised with respect to the interpretation of Thomas Bell's will and trust, the 1789 Charter, and the 1927 Amendment thereto; whether students currently living outside what was once the ancient "Towne of Roxburie" should be treated differently in admission to the School because of their geographical residence; whether such students should be treated differently, because of their geographical residence, in their (or their parents') payment of fees to the School, including but not limited to tuition; and whether the portion of the actual cost of the education of students, over and above the amount of any tuition or other fees, should be charged to students depending on their financial status or geographical residence;

M. The School desires to continue to admit students of good character and demonstrated academic ability who, according to the School's best judgment, will best take advantage of the academic and other opportunities which the School offers and who will bring to the School a broad range of backgrounds, talents, and interests;

N. It is the School's strongly held view that none of the School's corporate or trust documents, including but not limited to the Agreement of 1645, Thomas Bell's Will and Trust of 1671-1672, the School's Charter of 1789, or the 1927 Amendment thereto, are to be interpreted as encouraging or requiring the imposition of any impediment or restriction on any applicant for admission or on any student on the basis of his or his parents' geographical place of residence. It is the School's strongly held view that none of the aforementioned corporate or trust documents are to be understood or interpreted as affording preferential treatment to any student or applicant for admission because of his or his parents' place of residence. It is also the School's view that, because of changed circumstances since Bell's Bequest and the Charter of 1789, it would be obstructive and inappropriate to the School's principal charitable purpose to treat students differently in admission or with respect to tuition or other financial charges on the basis of their geographical place of residence;

O. In order to remove any possible doubt about the School's policy of admitting students on the bases stated in Paragraph M above, and without regard to their geographical place of residence, race, color, creed, national or ethnic origin; and in order to remove any doubt about its policy of charging fees and of granting reductions from those fees on the basis of financial need alone, the School's Board of Trustees and the Attorney General desire to resolve by this Final Judgment the issues stated above and described in the Complaint;

P. In light of the School's location in the City of Boston, which now incorporates almost all of what until about 1868 was known as the "Towne of Roxburie," the School's Board of Trustees and the Attorney General seek the Court's approval to allow the Trustees to set aside and restrict a portion of the School's currently unrestricted assets, which are not believed to be subject to any specific trust, to benefit students with their principal place of residence in the City of Boston, who it determines are in financial need and who may otherwise be admitted solely on the basis of the School's evaluation of their merit;

Q. The Trustees and the Attorney General consent to the entry of this Final Judgment, and to an application of the doctrines of equitable modification and/or deviation, so as to allow a portion of the School's currently unrestricted assets to be set aside in a special, restricted endowment fund for a beneficial class of students, who the School determines are in financial need and who have their principal place of residence within the boundaries of the City of Boston, which includes almost all of the sometime "Towne of Roxburie," the School's historic location, which was incorporated into Boston in approximately 1868;

ACCORDINGLY, on the basis of the reasons stated above, the statements in the Complaint, the exhibits attached thereto, and the representations of counsel for the parties, and after a hearing regarding the same, it is hereby ORDERED and AD-JUDGED, in the exercise of this Court's equitable powers and pursuant to the common law and statutes of Massachusetts, that:

1. Students may continue to be admitted to the School, according to the School's best judgment, on the basis of their merits alone, no impediment or restriction in admission being made against applicants on the basis of geographical residence.

2. The Trustees of the School may continue to charge students attending the School fees, including but not limited to tuition. The Trustees may set such fees above or below the actual cost of students' education as they, the Trustees, shall in the circumstances deem appropriate. The Trustees may continue to reduce such fees, by scholarships or similar financial assistance, for those students who, in their judgment, are in need. No impediment or restriction shall be made against students, with respect to the payment or reduction of such fees, on the basis of their geographical residence, race, creed, color, or national or ethnic origin.

3. In light of the School's location within the City of Boston, which now incorporates almost all of what until about 1868 was known as the "Towne of Roxburie," the School, freely, willingly, and without any obligation to do so, shall set aside and restrict $1,500,000 of its currently unrestricted funds, which are not believed to be subject to any specific existing trust, for the benefit of students who have their principal place of residence in the City of Boston, as presently constituted, who may otherwise be admitted to the School. The School reaffirms that its commitment actively to recruit students from the City of Boston—who would be unable to attend the School without financial aid—is an essential element of its charitable purpose.

4. The $1,500,000 of unrestricted funds shall be transferred, within 60 days of the date of the entry of this Judgment, to a restricted endowment fund controlled solely by the School, and subject to M.G.L. c. 180A and successor provisions of law. The income on-

ly of such fund shall be used to benefit students from the City of Boston who may attend the School, by providing to them scholarships or similar financial assistance for reducing tuition or other fees in accordance with the School's criteria for determining their financial need, so as to support the attendance of students whose principal residence is the City of Boston, and who otherwise, in the School's judgment, shall be admitted to the School.

5. To the extent that income from such restricted endowment fund is not applied in any particular year for this beneficial class, the income shall be credited to an accumulated income account to be used as soon as possible in the next year or in future years for such purposes.

March 9, 1990.

I. *Articles of Amendment: General Laws, Chapter 180, Section 7* [*1991*]

We, Harry R. Lewis, President, and William B. O'Keeffe, Secretary, of The Trustees of the Roxbury Latin School located at 101 St. Theresa Avenue, West Roxbury, MA 02132 do hereby certify that the following amendment to the articles of organization of the corporation was duly adopted at meetings held on January 30, 1991 and April 10, 1991, by vote of all the trustees legally qualified to vote in meetings of the corporation:

The Charter of the Corporation, as amended, is to be further amended by deleting the sections of the Charter entitled (i) "Number of Trustees Limited," and (ii) Section 2 in its entirety, and inserting the following in lieu thereof:

"Be it further enacted by the authority aforesaid, that the number of said trustees shall not at any time consist of more than twenty nor less than eleven, eight of whom shall constitute a quorum for transacting business, and a major part of the members present at any stated meeting thereof shall decide all questions that may properly come before them.

The trustees shall be of three classes: trustees for life; alumni trustees; and trustees at large (collectively, "the trustees"). A nominating committee of trustees, appointed by the president of the Board of Trustees, shall nominate candidates for election to each class of trustees after seeking recommendations for such candidates, as provided in the School's by-laws.

(1) There shall be not less than five nor more than nine trustees for life, as determined from time to time by the trustees by majority vote. The trustees for life shall be those who were trustees for life on July 1, 1990, and their successors in office. Trustees for life shall be nominated and elected as provided in the School's by-laws.

(2) There shall be between one and five alumni trustees, as determined from time to time by the trustees by majority vote. The alumni trustees shall be those who were alumni trustees on July 1, 1990, and their successors in office. Alumni trustees shall be nominated and elected as provided in the School's by-laws.

(3) There shall be not less than one and not more than six trustees at large, as determined from time to time by the trustees by majority vote. No trustee at large need be an alumnus of the School. Trustees at large shall have all the rights and powers of the trustees of other classes. The trustees at large shall be those who were trustees at large on July 1, 1990, and their successors in office. Trustees at large shall be nominated and elected as provided in the School's by-laws."

J. *Articles of Amendment: General Laws, Chapter 180, Section 7* [*1995*]

We, Harry R. Lewis, President, and William B. O'Keeffe, Secretary, of The Trustees of the Roxbury Latin School located at 101 St. Theresa Avenue, West Roxbury, MA 02132 do hereby certify that these Articles of Amendment affecting Articles numbered: (2) of the Articles of Organization were duly adopted at meetings held on January 23, 1995 and April 10, 1995, by vote of all the trustees legally qualified to vote in meetings of the corporation: "There shall be five alumni trustees" to be inserted in place of "There shall be between one and five alumni trustees."

Appendix Three

The School Seal

The first reference to the School's Seal is in the Trustee Minutes of June 10, 1891: "*Voted* that Mr. [William Coe] Collar [Headmaster] be requested to submit to this Board an appropriate seal or emblem to be used in marking books that may be presented as prizes."

A year and a half later, the Trustee Minutes of December 14, 1892, record that: "The Committee on the Seal reported the design impressed upon the margin of the page, and the Board voted that the design be adopted as the Seal of the School for all purposes except those of a purely business character."

The Seal consists of the head of the blind Greek poet Homer from a bust of Homer in the National Museum in Naples. (Over the years, many have assumed the head to be that of the Founder, John Eliot.) Around the border is the School's name Latinized ("Schola Latina Roxburiensis"), the year of the School's founding in Roman numerals, and the Latin motto "Mortui vivos docent" ("the dead teach the living"). The motto is of unknown origin and had never been used before in connection with the School.

The Seal does not appear to have gained much favor at first. The April 1893 *Tripod* joked that the "inscription will not be regarded by anyone as a reflection upon the 'Faculty.'" Though it was used in connection with the 250th anniversary celebrations in 1895, it did not appear regularly in the annual school catalogues until the 1909–10 school year. *The Tripod* did not use the seal in any way for over forty years—until June 1933. It was not used on the School's stationery until 1965.

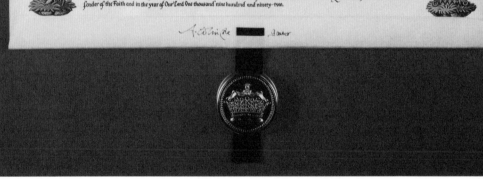

FIG. 1. The Letter Patent, signed by the Garter King of Arms, conveying the Honorary Grant of Arms by Her Majesty Queen Elizabeth II to the School on August 31, 1992.

Appendix Four

The School's Coat of Arms

Background: On August 31, 1992, the 347th anniversary—to the day—of the School's founding, the School received an Honorary Grant of Arms from Garter King of Arms. Since the fifteenth century, the Sovereign has delegated the granting of arms to Garter King of Arms and other members of the College of Arms in London. The School thereby became the first institution beyond Her Britannic Majesty's Realms ever to receive such a grant. The School's petition was endorsed by His Excellency William F. Weld, Governor of the Commonwealth. Since Roxbury Latin existed for its first 138 years under the Crown of England—longer than the total existence of many of its sister schools—the Earl Marshal of England determined that it should receive an Honorary Grant of Arms from Queen Elizabeth II in recognition of its 350th anniversary.

The Grant of Arms may come from old England, but it is redolent of New England:

At the center of the "Shield" is the pine tree. The pine tree was the earliest representation of Massachusetts. It appeared on the first coins (the "Pine Tree Shilling" and the "Pine Tree Sixpence") in 1652 with the legend "Masathusets in New England." The pine tree also appeared on the colonial flag in the 1760s (in the upper left corner of the English Cross of St. George). General Joseph Warren, Class of 1755, died at Bunker Hill under the "Pine Tree Flag" (a pine tree set against a white background in the upper left-hand quarter of a crimson flag) leading the Revolution against the British.

In the shield, the pine tree is rooted in John Eliot's Indian Bible, his translation of the Hebrew and Christian Scriptures into the Algonquian language. Published in 1663, this was the first Bible printed in North America. The open Bible bears an Alpha and an Omega, the first and last letters of the Greek alphabet, signifying the Puritan conviction that the Word of God "contains all things necessary to salvation."

The shield's three sections are in the School's traditional (since the 1880s) colors—crimson, black, and white; the three sections may be said to represent the three-fold direction the founders gave the Schoolmaster: "to instruct [students] in all scholastical, moral, and theological discipline."

At the top, in the "Crest," is a crowned gold lion "passant guardant." The Founder, arrived in New England on the good ship Lyon. Thomas Hooker's family crest has two lions passant guardant, and Thomas Dudley and Joseph Warren's families both feature

FIG. 2. The Somerset Herald (Thomas Woodcock) conveys the Letters Patent to Albert H. Gordon on Founder's Day 1993.

a lion rampant in their family arms. The lion is also a prominent feature of the shield of Cambridge University, where John Eliot was educated, and of the Royal Arms of England in Eliot's time and now. The crown on the lion's head is taken from the Arms of Jesus College, the college at Cambridge University of which the Founder was a member. The crown also appears on the shield of the English town of Boston and on the shield of Ely Cathedral where, it is thought, John Eliot was ordained. The crowned lion is holding a "Banner" which represents the School's shield in the form of a flag.

On either side of the shield are the "Supporters." On the left is John Eliot, the Founder, in the somber black garb of a Puritan divine, his face taken from the seventeenth century portrait of him at the Huntington Library in Pasadena, California, a copy of which hangs in Rousmaniere Hall at the School. The figure of Eliot reminds us that the School was founded by our Puritan forebears "out of their relligious care of posteritie." On the right is the Greek blind poet Homer, who appears on the School Seal. Homer is attired in Greek garb—crimson in color—of the ninth century B.C. The figure of Homer reminds us of the classical tradition of the School: it was founded to teach "Literature" (which meant Latin), and it has retained a strong commitment to both Latin and Greek through the centuries. At the bottom is found the motto from the School Seal: *Mortui vivos docent* (the dead teach the living).

The Letters Patent: The Coat of Arms was conveyed by Letters Patent from Garter King of Arms of the College of Arms in London. The border decorations of the Patent are of interest:

At the top in the center are the Royal Arms of Queen Elizabeth II within the circlet of the Order of the Garter. To the left of the Royal Arms are those of the Earl Marshal, the Duke of Norfolk, who is a Knight of the Garter. On the right of the Royal Arms are the Arms of the College of Arms, the recording authority. In the right-hand margin are, at the top, the Arms of the Office of Garter King of Arms, surmounted by a King of Arms' Crown. Below that are the Arms of the Office of Garter King of Arms impaled with the personal Arms of Sir Alexander Colin Cole, Garter King of Arms. At the foot of the Patent is the Badge (the crowned portcullis) of Office of the Somerset Herald, because Thomas Woodcock, Somerset Herald, was the agent for the Grant.

In the margins are various representations of Massachusetts: three ears of Indian corn in honor of the Native Americans to whom the "Apostle to the Indians," John Eliot, devoted so much attention and for whom he translated his Bible; the mayflower (the State flower); and two chickadees (the State bird). Also interwoven are the red and white roses of Lancaster and York from the English Royal heraldic badges.

The Seal at the foot of the Letters Patent has the Arms of the Office of Garter King of Arms impressed on it and outside the case is a representation of a King of Arms crown.

The Text of the Letters Patent: TO ALL AND SINGULAR to whom these Presents shall come Sir Alexander Colin Cole Knight Commander of the Royal Victorian Order upon whom has been conferred the Territorial Decoration Garter Principal King of Arms Sendeth Greeting. WHEREAS Albert Hamilton Gordon Gentleman Honorary Doctor of Laws of Harvard University in the Commonwealth of Massachusetts in the United States of America and only Honorary Member of the Wykehamist Society of Winchester College in the County of Hampshire in the United Kingdom of Great Britain and Northern Ireland Chairman of the Trustees of THE ROXBURY LATIN SCHOOL in the City of Boston and County of Suffolk in the aforesaid Commonwealth of Massachusetts hath represented unto The Most Noble Miles Francis Stapleton Duke of Norfolk Knight of the Most Noble Order of the Garter Knight Grand Cross of the Royal Victorian Order Companion of the Most Honourable Order of the Bath Commander of the Most Excellent Order of the British Empire upon whom has been conferred the Decoration of the Military Cross Earl Marshal and Hereditary Marshal of England that on the last day of August 1645 in the twenty-first year of the reign of His Majesty King Charles the First Thomas Dudley the Governor of the Colony of Massachusetts Bay did affix his signature first to the Agreement bringing into existence a school at Roxbury in New England which thereafter came to be known as THE ROXBURY LATIN SCHOOL and did make the first perpetual donation for himself and his heirs in support of the school THAT the Honourable General Court of the Colony did in 1670 Find that in the year 1645 there was an Agreement of many of the then Inhabitants of Roxbury for the laying of a foundation for a school for the instruction of youth in literature and that the school work carried on in that town hath been performed upon that Foundation . . . and did conceive that the Petitioners' desires should be granted in granting a confirmation of the school at Roxbury. . . . and that the present feoffees and their successors chosen as by that Agreement be confirmed and impowered as to collect former subscriptions so to take in others . . . That he Dr. Gordon with leave has quoted from the writings of Cotton Mather Doctor of Divinity of the University of Glasgow and Fellow of the Royal Society, who stated in Magnalia Christi Americana (1702) that 'One thing...has almost made me put the title Schola Illustris upon that little nursery; that is that Roxbury has afforded more scholars first for the College and then for the public than any Town of its bigness or if I mistake not of twice its bigness in all New England.' THAT Joseph Dudley son of the aforesaid Thomas Dudley served as the School's feoffee from 1670 to 1720 was appointed Governor of the Province of Massachusetts by Her Majesty Queen Anne in 1702 and held that Office until 1715. That THE ROXBURY LATIN SCHOOL flourished under the Crown of England for one hundred and thirty eight years until Great Britain signed the Treaty of Paris in 1783 recognizing the Independence of the United States of America: THAT the newly constituted Commonwealth of Massachusetts officially recognized the School by Charter in 1789 and by succeeding Acts: That THE ROXBURY LATIN SCHOOL is a registered charity recognized as exempt from taxation by the Internal Revenue Service of the United States of America and by the Attorney General of the Commonwealth of Massachusetts and claims the distinction of being the oldest school in continuous existence in North America: THAT the Trustees of THE ROXBURY LATIN SCHOOL with the consent of His Excellency William F. Weld Governor of the Commonwealth of Massachusetts are desirous of having Honorary Armorial Bearings established under lawful authority and he therefore as Chairman of The Trustees of THE ROXBURY LATIN SCHOOL and on behalf of the same hath requested the favour of His Grace's Warrant for my granting and assigning such Honorary Arms and Crest and in the same Patent such Honorary Supporters as are deemed fit and proper to be borne and used by The Trustees of THE ROXBURY LATIN SCHOOL as Honorary Armorial Ensigns according to the Laws of Arms And forasmuch as the said Earl Marshal did by Warrant under his hand and Seal bearing date the twenty-eighth day of February 1992 authorize and direct me to grant and assign such Honorary Arms and Crest and such Honorary Supporters accordingly Know Ye therefore that I the said Garter in pursuance of His Grace's Warrant and by virtue of the letters Patent of my

Office granted by The Queen's Most Excellent Majesty do by these Presents grant and assign unto THE ROXBURY LATIN SCHOOL the Honorary Arms following that is to say: Per pale Gules and Sable on a Pale Argent a Pine Tree Vert issuing from an open Book proper inscribed with the letters Alpha and Omega Sable and Gules And for the Honorary Crest upon a Helm with a Wreath Or Gules and Sable A lion passant guardant crowned Or supporting with the dexter paw a Flagstaff erect proper flying therefrom a banner of the Arms Mantled Gules and Sable Doubled Or And by the Authority aforesaid I the said Garter do by these Presents further grant and assign unto THE ROXBURY LATIN SCHOOL the Honorary Supporters following that is to say Dexter a Figure of John Eliot proper and wearing a gown Sable Sinister a Figure of Homer proper vested Gules as the same are all in the margin hereof more plainly depicted to be borne and used for ever hereafter by THE ROXBURY LATIN SCHOOL on its Seal or otherwise according to the Laws of Arms In witness whereof I the said Garter have to these Presents subscribed my name and affixed the Seal of my Office this thirty-first day of August in the forty-first year of the Reign of Our Sovereign Lady Elizabeth the Second by the Grace of God of the United Kingdom of Great Britain and Northern Ireland and of Her other Realms and Territories Queen Head of the Commonwealth Defender of the Faith and in the year of Our Lord One thousand nine hundred and ninety-two.

Appendix Five

The Founder's Song

The first mention of "The Founder's Song" appears in *The Tripod* 25, 3 (December 1912). Clarence W. Gleason (master 1889–1905, 1912–1939) wrote the words to the tune of "Lord Jeffrey Amherst," the Amherst College song. In 1992, the trustees altered Gleason's original words slightly after receiving a petition from the faculty to do so.

> *In the days when merry England was ablaze with civil war*
> *And the Cavaliers and Roundheads were at strife,*
> *In the wilderness of Roxbury lived a pious man of peace,*
> *Teaching men better ways of life.*
> *To the good Apostle Eliot it mattered little then*
> *Whether King or Parliament should rule;*
> *For he taught whites, blacks, and Indians to walk the narrow way,*[1]
> *And he founded this ancient Latin School.*
>
> REFRAIN
> *O Roxbury, Old Roxbury,*
> *Ever dear since the days of long ago.*
> *May the luster of thy glory*
> *Through thy children ever brighter grow.*
>
> *Oh, 'tis many, many years ago since Charles the First was king*
> *And the wilderness has mostly passed away;*[2]
> *But the good Apostle's work is going ever bravely on,*
> *Growing greater day by day.*
> *So give an Alpha, Beta, Gamma to the Founder of the School*
> *For he builded far better than he knew,*
> *And we'll celebrate his memory with a hearty song of praise,*
> *To his high ideals ever true.*

1. Gleason's original line read: *For he taught both whites and Indians to walk the narrow way*
2. Gleason's original line read: *And the Red Man has mostly passed away*

Author's Note

Sources and Bibliography

A *Quinquennial Catalogue*, the most recent in a long succession, has already been published this year. It contains the names of all the feoffees and trustees, masters, and alumni of the School back to 1645. It is an essential companion to this book.

Schola Illustris is the fourth published history of the School. The first, like this one, was written by the then-master of the School: R. G. Parker's *A Sketch of the History of the Grammar School in the Easterly Part of Roxbury*, published in 1826. The second was by a trustee (and former headmaster of Boston Latin School): Charles Knapp Dillaway's *A History of the Grammar School, or, "The Free Schoole of 1645 in Roxburie,"* published in 1860. The third was Richard Walden Hale, Jr.'s *Tercentenary History of the Roxbury Latin School*, published in 1946. Hale was the School's history master; he later became Archivist of the Commonwealth.

A collection of School documents and records of up to 1788 can be found in Hale's "The first Independent School in America" in *Publications of the Colonial Society of Massachusetts*, 35 (1942–46). Appendix 2 of this book picks up—as regards official documents—where Hale left off, starting with the Charter of 1789.

Other relevant published records include the *Report of the Record Commissioners containing the Roxbury Land and Church Records* (1881), Charles M. Ellis's *The History of Roxbury Town*, Francis S. Drake's *The Town of Roxbury*, and Walter Eliot Thwing's *History of the First Church in Roxbury*.

The School's most valuable possessions are the "Old School Book," the small mouse-eaten, jumbled record of the School from the Agreement of 1645 up to 1787, and the magnificently bound Indian Bible of John Eliot. Both are kept in the Houghton Library at Harvard.

The School vault contains many other documents, records, and manuscripts of note: the 1669 covenant with the schoolmaster, the feoffees' account book 1774–1851, John Bowles's personal account book, trustee minutes from 1789 to the present, financial records since 1789. Rufus Wyman's 101-page handwritten "Abstract of the Ancient Records and Papers of the Free-Schoole in Roxburie, 1645–1789," compiled in 1841–42, is also contained therein. (Dillaway's *History* is little more than a representation of Wyman's remarkable compilation.) The vault also contains all the School's catalogues, all issues of *The Tripod*, every yearbook, and all issues of *The Newsletter* (including the *Alumni Bulletin*, known by various names, which is its direct antecedent). Correspondence, photographs, playbills, and considerable miscellaneous memorabilia can also be found there.

I have tried to collect for the School all the books and articles that pertain to the School's history. The most valuable book in this collection is *New Englands First Fruits*, the 1643 account, published in London, of early colonial life and of Harvard's first commencement. This book was purchased from the personal collection of George T. Goodspeed '22. I have given the School the seventeen-volume *Sibley's Harvard Graduates* Mr. Goodspeed gave me when he closed his famous ground floor bookshop. The Colonial Society of Massachusetts and the Massachusetts Historical Society have most generously given the School nearly all the volumes of their published collections—including the "Indian Tracts" that recount the Founder's labors on behalf of the natives of North America.

I expended considerable time and energy chasing down the sources for statements made by previous historians of the School, none of whom documented their sources. In the process, some rather good "stories" had to be discarded when the facts simply did not corroborate their veracity. As a reassurance to the present reader and as a help to future scholars, I have documented Parts I, II, IV, and V extensively with the endnotes that follow. These notes contain considerable bibliographic information, and it has therefore seemed redundant and pretentious to publish a bibliography.

Index

𝕾𝖈𝖍𝖔𝖑𝖆 𝕴𝖑𝖑𝖚𝖘𝖙𝖗𝖎𝖘 was designed and composed by Scott-Martin Kosofsky at The Philidor Company in Boston. Steve Dyer assisted with the production. The typefaces are digital interpretations of English classics. The text was set in a modified version of Adobe Caslon, designed by Carol Twombly after the early 18th-century originals by William Caslon. The headings were set in two types: "Big Caslon," designed by Matthew Carter after the large types offered for sale by William Caslon (possibly of 17th-century origin), and Cloister Black, the standard English blackletter.

The book was
composed and assembled on
a Macintosh computer, in Quark XPress.
The pictures were scanned at Aurora Graphics,
Portsmouth, New Hampshire and at the Philidor
Company, and were digitally restored and enhanced by
Mr. Kosofsky in Adobe Photoshop.
The final film was produced at Aurora Graphics and the
book was printed by The Nimrod Press in Westwood,
Massachusetts on Glatfelter Text, an acid-free
paper. Acme Bookbinding Company, in
Charlestown, bound the book in
Holliston Roxite.